D0616755

VICTORIAN CONVENTIONS

Victorian Conventions

JOHN R. REED

OHIO UNIVERSITY PRESS

ACKNOWLEDGMENTS

I am grateful to the Simon Guggenheim Foundation for a Fellowship which in 1970-71, allowed me the necessary time to complete the basic research for this study. I am equally grateful to Wayne State University for providing generous research awards which have greatly facilitated the completion of this book, and although I am indebted to many colleagues and associates for their help, I particularly wish to thank Martin Stearns, Dean of the College of Liberal Arts.

Portions of my chapters on women and on memory appeared in different form in *Hartford Studies in Literature* (1970) and *English Literature in Transition: 1880-1920* (1971).

Contents

FOR RUTH

PREFACE

This study is not meant to be exhaustive. The reader can call to mind works that I have not included which clearly manifest one or another of the conventions that I have chosen to discuss. Likewise, many literary conventions not included here were evident in their time. For example, I might have treated the conventions of the shipwreck, the miser, the governess, or the pursuit, all of which occurred frequently in nineteenth-century literature. Some conventions I exclude because they have had sufficient treatment elsewhere. Those I deal with exhibit unique approaches, either in literary treatment or in the convention's relationship to a social condition. Conventional attitudes toward male or female types certainly extend beyond the few I have selected, yet my selection is intended to illustrate the typological nature of much characterization in nineteenth-century literature.

Literary conventions may involve character types, situations, sequences of actions or mental conditions. Our own century has developed certain conventions which writers exploit constantly—for example, the conscious exploitation of the Oedipal situation, which enables the modern writer to convey to an informed audience, by means of brief allusions or conventional clues, an entire psychological reticulation among his characters. A more superficial contemporary convention is that of the only survivor, or survivors, of a planetary holocaust.[1] With this device, a writer may reduce the moral terms of his narrative to an acute and immediate simplicity, while the implications of these moral terms remain complex in their associations for both reader and author, who comprehend the elaborate implications of how the holocaust would come about and what fundamental demands would instantly encumber any who survived. It may be easier to discern conventions of a previous century than those of our own, but doing so requires an examination of social attitudes, popular literary techniques and materials, and literary consciousness of its own methods. I have tried to include all of these approaches.

There is a certain degree of repetition in my discussion of literary conventions partly because I have tried to keep individual chapters self-contained and partly because I have sought to emphasize certain specific works, such as Dickens' *Our Mutual Friend,* or Thackeray's *The Newcomes,* which manifest more than one convention and represent masterful exploitations of these conventions. By having these and other works recur from one chapter to another, I hope to show that individual works employ not one convention, but a complex of conventional devices, which imply a larger moral arrangement or design.

Some readers may be disturbed that I treat minor, not to say utterly forgettable, writers equally with major literary figures. But, as Louis James suggests, it is probably wise to consider the minor literature of a period seriously if we are to understand satisfactorily the major writings which survive to our times.[2] Richard D. Altick, in an important article, "Victorian Readers and the Sense of the Present," emphasizes the need for modern readers to understand the immediacy of reference and the topicality of Victorian literature. Although he concedes that "a large margin of speculation and outright error always is involved," he contends that "the more energetically we put ourselves into the minds of the first readers, by steeping ourselves in their immediate, everyday knowledge and language, the more intelligible the author's intended message and the manner in which his readers would have responded to that message are bound to be."[3]

I do touch upon topical influences in some instances, but basically I try to show simple historical circumstances and the literary modifications of those circumstances as they relate to certain sharply defined literary conventions. Because they are the most obvious, I begin with character types, and move on to some conventions that were overwhelmingly evident in nineteenth-century literature, such as marriage, orphans, the return, and the inheritance. In some cases, I wish only to demonstrate how stylized conventions became, as, for example, with the Judith, the Griselda, the Magdalene, or later, the Prodigal. In other cases, I hope to indicate an ironic treatment of conventional clichés, as with the poor scholar, the Samaritan, or the return. Some conventions have little significance, and I thought that at least one example was required of this type. Other conventions were intimately related to social realities, as is true with the death bed, the orphan or the swindle. Yet other conventions departed markedly from actual conditions while revealing emotional predilections, as with the themes of duelling and gypsies.

Having demonstrated a variety of approaches, I conclude my study with more abstract and provocative conventions such as disguise, gypsies, memory and the occult, all of which imply profound assumptions about human identity and human existence. Very likely I have been tendentious in suggesting that the conventions I have selected reveal a growing dissatisfaction with nineteenth-century British culture and an increasing desire for some probable or improbable alternative.

I have presented a sufficient range of reference so that this study may be read both as a survey and as an interpretation; I have often quoted passages from obscure works and merely alluded to better-known compositions because I have presupposed a certain knowledge of major writings on the part of my audience, and my purpose has not been explication of major texts, but examination of cultural assumptions. My purpose is to reveal certain underlying assumptions about human existence and society, as well as certain literary strategies and techniques—conscious and unconscious—manifest in nineteenth-century literature, and therefore essential for a modern reader to be mindful of when approaching the writings of that time.

Errors or misconceptions which appear hereafter are solely my own responsibility. I appeal only to the compassion of students of nineteenth-century British literature, who know the wilderness I have traversed, and who therefore may appreciate any signposts, no matter how frail, that I have been able to erect.

VICTORIAN CONVENTIONS

CHAPTER ONE

INTRODUCTION

"No generation is free from the error of stylizing its scenes and its characters," W. L. Burn writes, forgetting perhaps for the moment that stylization need be no error.[1] In some cases it may be necessary for us, historically as well as esthetically, to assume an intellectual posture that comprehends the ensuing world in stylized terms.[2] It is not my intention to catalog the manner in which each period stylizes scenes and characters, but rather to suggest that in order to read the literature of the Victorian period accurately and rewardingly, it is necessary to acknowledge and recover the forms of stylization and convention with which Victorian authors and audiences were familiar.

REALISM AND IDEALISM

Victorian literature was not realistic in the same sense as that attributed to contemporary literature. In some ways it had as much in common with medieval literature as with twentieth-century writing, for behind much of Victorian literature were the now-explicit, now-implied conventional patterns and stylized characters or scenes that endowed it with a dimension which, accepted by readers of that

time, are no longer immediately evident to modern readers; in most
cases, those patterns and stylizations were moral. For us, circumstantial authenticity is a conclusive test of realism, but for Victorian
writers, fidelity to moral ideas was also important. Though that notorious realist, Anthony Trollope, defined his acknowledged mentor,
Thackeray, as a realist, he did so mainly in terms of style, while in-
sisting that "the realistic must not be true,—but just so far removed
from truth as to suit the erroneous idea of truth which the reader may
be supposed to entertain."[3] If, in saying this, Trollope was concerned
with naturalness rather than moral truth, in summarizing, his meaning was inescapably moral: "So much I have said of the manner in
which Thackeray did his work, endeavouring to represent human
nature as he saw it; so that his readers should learn to love what is
good, and to hate what is evil."[4] The rendering of the world as one
sees it is subordinate to the greater purpose of superintending readers' perceptions of good and evil, and counselling the proper preference. R. L. Stevenson, attempting to resolve the quarrel between realists and idealists, said that realism involved the technical method,
not the truth of a work of art.[5] By the end of the century, it is true,
some felt that the distinction was a false one. As Basil Hallward says
in Oscar Wilde's *The Picture of Dorian Gray* (1890), "We in our madness have separated the two [body and soul] and have invented a
realism that is vulgar, and an ideality that is void." (ch. 1) But throughout the century, there was a continuing belief that the ideal was
achievable through the real.

In Mrs. Humphry Ward's *Robert Elsmere* (1888), the preferred example of a noble life, Mr. Grey, is an idealist and Hegelian who "had
broken with the popular Christianity, but for him, God, Consciousness, duty, were the only realities." (ch. 5) These are, at least, the *essential* realities following a careful gradation from deity to duty. In
the specifically material world, there is another gradation of realities, indicated by Robert Elsmere's reaction to Catherine's *accouche-
ment*, which "went too deep; it brought him too poignantly near to
all that is most real and therefore most tragic in life." (ch. 19) The
"most real" aspects of this life are the immutable experiences we call
the verities—birth, suffering, death. They are "most tragic" because
they force us to acknowledge the distance between temporal circumstance and those essential realities which are abstractions—ideal and
separate from substantial life—and consequently not material for
tragedy, but signposts to joy.

Just as the realism of nineteenth-century literature was not a matter of journalistic precision, so character was not a simple matter of conscious psychological mimeticism. Victorians credited phrenology and, more seriously, physiognomy as explanations of character which made human nature accessible to straightforward, unbiassed, and unprofessional investigation because they conceived of human nature primarily in simple, objective terms.[6] In the twentieth century, we have substituted a more self-conscious "superstition" of character to satisfy the predilection we have acquired for a dynamic, internal concept of human nature, which, if it has no cranial excrescences or facial features to guide us, provides a hidden topography by which we construct modern conventions of character. Our stylizations are largely Freudian, as Victorians' were moral and physiognomical, and earlier centuries' were humorous or canonical. To understand each age, we must see it in terms of its own predilections and insights.

In Victorian literature, what we would call realistic motivation is often incorporate with type fulfillment. Characters do not act according to a system of humors or ruling passions, nor are they moved by the complexes and neuroses of the twentieth-century man; instead, they exhibit predictable combinations of attributes which result in conventional types. These types, moreover, often operate within equally conventional moral designs. In this way, Victorian writers could be faithful to the things of this world while employing a highly emblematic and occasionally symbolic manner of writing that modern criticism, for some obscure reason, tends to consider incompatible with their circumstantial realism.[7]

In his poetic drama, *The Saint's Tragedy* (1848), Charles Kingsley sought to convey a realistic picture of the Middle Ages, asserting that his character, St. Elizabeth, was believable in terms of the influences of her age, but this did not prevent him from asserting that Elizabeth was "a type of two great mental struggles of the Middle Ages." Stylization of this kind might easily resolve itself into melodrama, to which it is closely allied and for which Victorian audiences had a colossal appetite, but it is also characteristic, as F. D. Maurice indicates in a preface to Kingsley's play, of morality and mystery plays which seek the larger meanings of ordinary things.[8] Kingsley's play is a secularized and modernized morality play.

Maurice's view also recalls Puritan notions about existence. All experience, Puritans held, recapitulates eternal patterns of sin and redemption, suffering and salvation; written accounts should chronicle this essential reality. The strictness of this interpretive mode had, except in certain sects, disappeared by the nineteenth century, but a religious revival insured that the general tendency to read experience and the real world in terms of a greater moral reality would persist. The discovery of a superior morality in the doings of secular men is, after all, the object of much Victorian literature. Indications of belief in a universal design might vary considerably from one writer to the next. For Tennyson, all of existence might seem to be a "toil coöperant to an end," while later, less hopeful writers might view experience as a game played by vague Immortals or Indefinable Powers, as Hardy described them at different times. Nonetheless, throughout Victorian literature there runs a tradition of an assumed design of which individual lives are but a part. Realism, the faithful depiction of the details of life, therefore becomes compatible with idealism, which assumes a larger scheme to which those details are subordinate.

THE MORAL DESIGN

When, in Conrad's *Nostromo* (1904), Martin Decoud wishes to detach himself from what he considers a particularly English failing, he explains, "Life is not for me a moral romance derived from the tradition of a pretty fairy-tale." (Part 2, ch. 6) Later in the novel, an English chief-engineer seems to verify Decoud's judgment on the race by viewing Charles Gould's dilemma in terms of a fable, and at the same time suggests that fabulizing is a legitimate source of truth. "The tale of killing the goose with the golden eggs has not been evolved for nothing out of the wisdom of mankind," he says; and for him, the history of Costaguanian politics "sounds like a comic fairy-tale." (Part 3, ch. 1) For Gould, the events in Costaguana are not a comedy, but part of a "moral romance," while for Decoud, they resemble, after his Frenchified tastes, a "farce." The English may or may not have been, in the years of their international supremacy, a sentimental race inclined to view existence as a moral romance, but in their literature of the nineteenth century the tendency to conceive of existence in terms of moral structures with foundations of fairy-tale morality is evident.

Although I shall discuss moral design in Victorian literature, I do not wish to argue the case for reading Victorian literature as exclu-

sively moral, even in its form. It is perhaps sufficient indication that
Victorians themselves were aware of the relationship of morality and
esthetic form to recall Leslie Stephen's statement that "even a novel
should have a ruling thought, though it should not degenerate into a
tract; and the thought should be one which will help to purify and
sustain the mind by which it is assimilated."[9] Even R. S. Surtees,
whose tales can scarcely be considered ennobling, "acknowledged
the ascendancy of social morality" and sought to fortify that morality
in his own way in his fiction.[10]

Anthony Trollope averred that "the novelist, if he have a conscience, must preach his sermon with the same purpose as the clergyman, and must have his own system of ethics." (*Autobiography*, ch.
12) Moreover, for Trollope, as for many another Victorian writer, it
was the "system of ethics," not the narrative action, that determined
the form of the novel. Explaining that incidents and personages of
his novel, *Phineas Finn*, developed as they were written, Trollope
adds, "But the evil and good of my puppets, and how the evil would
always lead to evil, and the good produce good,—that was clear to me
as the stars on a summer night." (*Autobiography*, ch. 17)

It is a long step from Robert Plumer Ward's popular novel, *Tremaine, or The Man of Refinement* (1825), to Anne Brontë's *The Tenant
of Wildfell Hall* (1848), but the prefaces to both novels reveal a cardinal concern for morality informing fictional movement. Anticipating objections to the form of his story, Ward remarked simply that "it
was the dress in which the subjects were presented" to him; therefore he "was not willing to separate them from the narrative, from a
feeling that the lighter and more tender parts might enliven or interest the mind, while they would not derogate from the deeper points
brought forward for investigation." For Ward, fiction and its form
were derivative from moral purpose. Anne Brontë, with similar te-
nacity, maintained her need to convey not only amusement, but to
depict moral strength. For her, labor after " 'a perfect work of art' "
would be "Time and talents . . . wasted and misapplied." Instead, she
declared, "if I am able to amuse, I will try to benefit too; and when I
feel it my duty to speak an unpalatable truth, with the help of God,
I will speak it."[11] It may be true that *Tremaine* is little more than a tedious moral tract, and that *The Tenant of Wildfell Hall* is less
than a masterpiece, but finer works than these began with similar
moral assumptions, and writers of the stature of Dickens did not hes-

itate to defend their moral arguments. And even in autobiography, as in Borrow's unlikely accounts, readers would not have been offended, presumably, to have learned that certain facts had been altered to fit the more important moral structure of the accounts. But my purpose is not to examine the many ways in which morality and private systems of ethics affected the form of Victorian literature. By describing variations on one familiar moral design, I hope to show how, during the Victorian period, that design participates in the departure of morality from the traditionally religious to the morally secular by way of an esthetic perception of experience.

WELL-DEFINED EXAMPLES OF MORAL DESIGN

Elsewhere, I have stated the principal moral design operating in Tennyson's poetry.[12] It is a design familiar to poets, novelists, historians, and social commentators alike.[13] The movement is from an uninformed and sometimes pleasing condition, through redemptive struggle and suffering, to joy or resignation. For Tennyson, the movement was generally from pride, to suffering and humility, to redemption in selflessness. There are, however, other variations of the general scheme. This pervasive literary design applied not only to the individual, but could be historical, or, more significantly, metaphysical. Arthur Hugh Clough was not being revolutionary when he described human existence in terms of this pattern. Adam says to Eve that Cain "is born of us, and therefore like us," and consequently,

> bound to strive—
> Not doubtfully I augur from the past—
> Through the same straits of anguish and of doubt,
> 'Mid the same storms of terror and alarm,
> To the calm ocean which he yet shall reach,
> He or himself or in his sons hereafter,
> Of consummated consciousness of self.
>
> ("Fragments of the Mystery of the Fall")

Victorian readers, accustomed to consider earthly existence as probation for eternity, did not find affirmations of the redemptive effects of suffering unusual in their literature.[14] However, even without the prospect of eternity, suffering retained its therapeutic associations for a surprising number of writers and moralists largely because it acquired an esthetic and secular importance.[15]

George Alfred Lawrence's *Guy Livingstone, or "Thorough"* (1857) commends *The Heir of Redclyffe* (1853) and *The Newcomes* (1853-54) for their superb treatment of "simple and quiet sorrows" (Vol. 1, ch. 33). But these novels have more than "simple and quiet sorrows" in common in that they utilize the moral design that I have already described. In Thackeray's novel, several characters follow the necessary route from pride, through humility, to redemptive selflessness. Young Lord Kew's involvement in a duel is considered a punishment for an earlier life of "prodigality." Kew is wounded, but his injury occasions a salubrious illness which leads to reform by forcing him to make up "his account of the vain life" he has led. Kew's is a simple and sharply defined case. More subtly, Clive Newcome also moves from the pride of youth and love, through imprudence and idleness, to his necessary humbling, which consequently provides its reward. And even the excellent Colonel, Clive's father, moves from staunch pride in his goodness, to a selfless imprudence, which is corrected by a thorough humbling. Colonel Newcome's withdrawal to the Grey Friars almshouse is the outstanding example of worthwhile humility in the novel, concluding with an undeniable sign of salvation in the Colonel's dying answer of "Ad Sum" to the last heavenly call.

Ethel Newcome's case is more representative. She is beautiful and haughty, and her principal sins are vanity and pride, but "In after life, care and thought subdued her pride, and she learned to look at society more good naturedly." (Vol. 1, ch. 32) Ethel's sufferings come through family scandal and Clive's marriage to the innocent Rosa Mackenzie, who fails to make Clive genuinely happy. Humiliated by the prospect of a loveless marriage, Ethel's conscience revives, and thereafter vanity yields to humility. "She is very much changed since you knew her," Pendennis says to Colonel Newcome; "Very much changed and very much improved." (Vol. 2, ch. 27) Pendennis himself has been alerted to Ethel's transformation by his own faultless wife, who now sees the good in the once vain beauty. "Who would have thought this was the girl of your glaring London ballroom? If she has had grief to bear, how it has chastened and improved her." (vol. 2, ch. 24) Ethel devotes herself to good works and assistance to the poor; she no longer resembles Judith, Salome, and Diana, but assumes a saint-like aspect and is likened to the Good Samaritan. Accordingly, Ethel is rewarded by her union with Clive, which is implied at the novel's conclusion.

A similar pattern of pride, suffering, and redemption occurs in Charlotte Yonge's *The Heir of Redclyffe*. Like many another Victorian novel, this one overtly concerns itself with the nature of the hero. Although the reader quickly perceives that Philip Morville's besetting sin is conceit, for the most part he is regarded as a model hero not unlike Sir Charles Grandison. Set against Philip is Guy Morville. Inclined toward egoistic melancholy, and only with difficulty controlling his emotions, he is a familiar Romantic type. The expectation is that Guy will model himself upon the widely respected Philip, but Guy reluctantly acknowledges a dislike for Philip, whom he finds stuffy. Instead, it is Philip who must recognize Guy as the true model, a recognition that is anticipated throughout the novel. Guy's task is to subject his passionate nature to moral discipline. Suppressing his irritation at Philip's interference in his affairs, Guy forces himself to a genuine mood of forgiveness and calm by contemplating Christ's sufferings. Philip must rediscover "the great Example" through Guy's embodiment of His teachings.

Although it is Philip who fulfills the more familiar moral design, Guy enacts another design not uncommon in Victorian literature. Guy's favorite book is Fouqué's *Sintram*, and he himself resembles the Sir Galahad of that story. The pattern of Guy's life is foreshadowed in his summary of the book as "A strife with the powers of darkness; the victory, forgiveness, resignation, death." (Vol. 1, ch. 8) It is upon these moral designs that the structure of *The Heir of Redclyffe* depends; for the apex of Guy's design coincides with the nadir of Philip's. While travelling on the Continent, Philip stubbornly ignores warnings to avoid a village where fever is reported raging, whereas Guy and Amy prudently shun such dangerous exposure. As a consequence of his proud folly, Philip falls ill with the fever. Guy rushes to attend him, contracts the fever, and dies. But Philip's illness has its salubrious effect; he awakens to his own sin. When Guy arrives to nurse him he is able to confess this sin to one "over whom he had striven to assume superiority, and therefore before whom he could have least borne to humble himself—nay, whose own love he had lately traversed with an arrogance that was rendered positively absurd by this conduct of his own." (Vol. 2, ch. 10) And later, at Guy's deathbed, Philip sees "the glory of Guy's character and the part he had acted—the scales of self-admiration fell from his eyes, and he knew both himself and his cousin." (Vol. 2, ch. 14)

Although Philip has acknowledged his failing to himself and to Guy, he has not yet humbled himself before God; and therefore his symbolic illness returns. Philip's father had said to him when he was honored with scholastic prizes in childhood, "All this would I give, Philip, for one evidence of humility of mind." (Vol. 2, ch. 17) Ultimately Philip does achieve the crucial humility before God and, "if his father could have beheld him then, it would have been with rejoicing" that "the humble, penitent, obedient heart had been won at last." (Vol. 2, ch. 17) Philip makes his journey through the valley of the shadow of death and returns to the region of light, and therefore Charles, once a skeptic, now respects Philip. "Nay, I look up to him, I think him positively noble and grand, and when I see proofs of his being entirely repentant, I perceive he is a thorough great man." (Vol. 2, ch. 22) Still, Charles adds that he has known a superior model, and that was Guy. Guy's ordeal was the harnessing of passion to noble and selfless action; Philip's was the reducing of pride to useful and selfless nobility. For Charlotte Yonge, pride and passion are the cardinal dangers against which man contends; each must have its appropriate adversary. In Lawrence's *Guy Livingstone*, both of these weaknesses afflict a single man.

Guy Livingstone is one of the most conventional of nineteenth-century novels in that it employs a large number of literary conventions. Moreover, because of its popularity, it contributed to the solidifying of those conventions. Its titular hero, a proud, passionate, and physically imposing man, became so well known that Matthew Arnold, in his essay on Tolstoy, referred confidently to "the Guy Livingstone type."[16] This gifted, but self-indulgent hero falls in love with the virtuous Constance Brandon, while failing to reject altogether the fascinations of Flora Bellasys. As a result of momentary intoxication with the seductive Flora, Guy loses Constance, who gradually fails in health, until, on her deathbed, she calls her guilty lover to her. Though he has given himself up to dissipation, the vision of his saintly love, whose death is a "victory" of "loyalty and right," brings him back to his senses, and he promises to change his ways. Constance dead, Guy himself develops brain fever. His entire life has been a fever of pride, passion, and self-indulgence, obscuring the calm nobility of his soul. With his "brain fever," Guy's spiritual malady becomes a physical one. Like the hero of Tennyson's *Maud*, Guy sought to fix his love in a possessable form, and it was necessary that this form be removed in order that he might apprehend the true nature of the ideal. When Guy realizes the cost of his earthly indulgence, his earthly part is stricken. Guy's salubrious illness has a clear function, for, when he confronts his temptress Flora for the last time, she comments upon his altered state and he replies, "Yes, I have been very ill, and I am utterly changed." (ch. 30) Guy has undergone his necessary humbling and faces his future with hope. Frank Hammond, the narrator, confidently remarks, "The repentance that was begun by Constance's dying bed was completed, I am sure, on his own." (ch. 36)

These three novels exhibit the familiar moral design. They are by no means isolated examples. I have already suggested the consciousness of this design in Tennyson and Clough, but many another example might be cited. R. H. Horne's use of the design is secular in *Orion: An Epic Poem* (1843), where Orion "is meant to present a type of the struggle of man with himself, i.e. the contest between the intellect and the senses, when powerful energies are equally balanced."[17] The passionate and proud Orion is physically and spiritually humbled by a sequence of misfortunes, yet benefits follow from this suffering. His aspirations have "led to blindness and distress, / self-pride's abasement, more extensive truth, / A higher consciousness and efforts new."

Although Horne utilized this moral design largely in a secular fashion, other writers preferred more spiritual overtones. Faced with the obligation of making good an enormous and unexpected debt while facing poverty and suffering, Charles Aubrey in Samuel Warren's *Ten Thousand A-Year* (1841) indicates the sustaining pattern that strengthens him and which provides a moral structure for the novel as well. When his friend Lord De la Zouch demonstrates concern for Aubrey's melancholy state, the sober Charles replies:

> "My dear friend, I feel as if I were indeed entering a scene black as midnight—but what is it to the *valley of the shadow of death*, dear Lord De la Zouch, which is before all of us, and at but a little distance! I assure you I feel no vain-glorious confidence; yet I seem to be leaning on the arm of an unseen but all-powerful supporter!" (Vol. 2, ch. 1)

Charles Kingsley's character, Lancelot Smith, similarly discovers the importance of recognizing the Infinite plan in man's finite existence, after experiencing sorrow and suffering in a chapter entitled "The Valley of the Shadow of Death," in *Yeast* (1848-49). The chastened Rochester in *Jane Eyre* admits to Jane that he had resisted the divine dispensation that prevented him from marrying Jane when his mad wife still lived; "instead of bending to the decree," he says, "I defied it. Divine justice pursued its course; disasters came thick on me: I was forced to pass through the valley of the shadow of death. *His* chastisements are mighty; and one smote me which has humbled me for ever." (ch. 37)

Henry Kingsley's *Ravenshoe* (1861) is not remarkable for a keenly developed plot, and yet its numerous events are controlled by the novel's moral design. Murtagh Tiernay, after the death of Charles Ravenshoe's ostensible father, plays an organ composition emblematic of the good man's progress through life. So clear is the relationship of this composition to the design of the novel, that it is worth quoting in full.

> The music began with a movement soft, low, melodious, beyond expression, and yet strong, firm, and regular as of a thousand armed men marching to victory. It grew into volume and power till it was irresistible, yet still harmonious and perfect. Charles understood it. It was the life of a just man growing towards perfection and honour.
>
> It wavered and fluttered, and threw itself into sparkling sprays and eddies. It leapt and laughed with joy unutterable, yet still through all the solemn measure went on. Love had come to gladden the perfect life, and had adorned without disturbing it.
>
> Then began discords and wild sweeping storms of sound, harsh always, but never unmelodious: fainter and fainter grew the melody, till it was almost lost. Misfortunes had come upon the just man, and he was bending under them.
>
> No. More majestic, more grand, more solemn than ever the melody reasserted itself: and again, as though purified by a furnace, marched solemnly on with a clearness and sweetness greater than at first. The just man had emerged from his sea of troubles ennobled.[18] (ch. 24)

Assuredly this is not pride humbled to permit redemptive selflessness and love, but it is the germane design of goodness tested by suffering to emerge ennobled; it is the pattern not of a Philip, but of a Guy Morville. The former pattern appears in the case of Ellen Horton in *Ravenshoe*, who, having succumbed to temptations of the flesh, must undergo a humbling process that endures for the remainder of her life. Charles and Ellen, after a significant interview, were "not to meet till the valley of the shadow of death had been passed, and life was not so well worth having as it had been." (ch. 41) Accordingly, Charles does experience a severe illness, reviving in time to accept his proper inheritance and marry the charming and faithful Mary Corby. Even so, Charles has been altered by his sufferings, having become more resigned and more profound in his faith.

"The Valley of the Shadow of Death" is the title of a chapter in Charlotte Brontë's *Shirley* (1849), which describes Caroline Helstone's illness, caused by her unsatisfied craving for love. Caroline does not die, but learns through her illness to harness passions to moral purpose and is therefore prepared to attend Robert Moore in his subsequent illness and to recommend the lesson of her own suffering as a model. Accordingly, when Robert recovers, he is no longer the "proud angry, disappointed man" that he had been, and he and Caroline marry. (ch. 35) The quasi-illnesses of Louis and Shirley mirror Robert and Caroline's genuine movement through the valley of the shadow of death. In each case, passion is subdued and pride overcome. Each illness, no matter how slight, serves as a moral bloodletting that braces the spirit. The pattern is absolutely formulaic in Anne Thackeray Ritchie's *The Story of Elizabeth* (1867), where Elizabeth Gilmore falls ill from frustrated love, and is tended by Miss Dampier, a splendid moral model. Elizabeth recovers as the birds stir in the spring to their busy life. "Elizabeth's life too, began anew from this hour." Devoting herself to charitable activity, Elizabeth is rewarded by the return of her first love and marriage.

ILLNESS IN THE MORAL DESIGN

It is evident from the above discussion that illness frequently plays an important part in the completion of the moral design. And, most certainly, illness was a traditionally recommended occasion for meditation upon life's vanities, as Jeremy Taylor's *The Rule and Exercises of Holy Dying* (1651), a book read and valued well into the nineteenth century, indicates:

> Next to this, the soul, by the help of sickness, knocks off the fetters of pride and vainer complacencies. Then she draws the curtains, and stops the light from coming in, and takes the pictures down, those fantastic

images of self-love and gay remembrances of vain opinion and popular noises. Then the spirit stoops into the sobrieties of humble thoughts, and feels corruption chiding the forwardness of fancy, and allaying the vapours of conceit and factious opinions. For humility is the soul's grave, into which she enters, not to die, but to meditate and inter some of its troublesome appendages. (ch. 3, sec. 5.)

In Samuel Warren's cautionary tale, "Intriguing and Madness," a dissipated young man recovers from his illness disgusted with his past life and resolved on pursuing virtue. His doctor remarks that "these salutory thoughts led to a permanent reformation; his illness, in short, had produced its effect."[19] And Susan Ferrier makes the point more amply in *The Inheritance* (1824) when Gertrude St. Clair, who has been a good deal less than serious and wise, falls ill:

It was only then she was aware of the danger she had passed; she had walked unconsciously through the valley of the shadow of Death—the gates of eternity had been before her, but she had not descried them. It was then, while still hovering on the confines of this world, that she felt all the emptiness and the vanity of its pleasures; her dreams of greatness—her hopes of happiness—her gay-spent days—her festive nights, where were they now?—Gone—and where they had been, was marked but with shame—disappointment—remorse! All earthly distinctions had been hers—and what was the account which she had now to render to God for the use of these His gifts? On which of these was it that she would now build her hopes of acceptance with Him—miserable comforters were they all! (ch. 33)

Dickens employed the convention frequently in his novels. Martin Chuzzlewit discovers through physical illness and pride's abasement, the utter selfishness of his early life, and acquires the virtues of "humility and steadfastness." (ch. 33) Dick Swiveller undergoes a similar experience. Redemptive suffering in *Great Expectations* cleanses Pip of his selfishness and pride, opening for him a life of humility and steadfastness. In *Our Mutual Friend*, Dickens used the moral design in Eugene's salubrious illness and apparently redemptive recovery, but he also treated it ironically in the unredemptive recovery of Rogue Riderhood and the mimic baptism of Wegg in his own dust cart.

The device manifested itself in various ways. In Mrs. Gaskell's *Mary Barton*, Mary's illness obliterates her earlier vanity, and serves as a purification that makes her worthy of her steadfast lover, Jem.

Magdalene's proud and unwise ambitions are cured after her illness in Wilkie Collins' *No Name*. In Owen Meredith's "Euthanasia," in Part 6 of *The Wanderer*, the persona of the poem announces, after his severe illness, that his old passion is over and his fervor will be employed henceforth to higher ends.[20] Ernest Pontifex, in Butler's *The Way of All Flesh*, also experiences a certain regeneration after illness, though it is, as one might expect from Butler, not the ordinary recovery.[21]

Most illnesses in Victorian literature stay close to conventional moral sentiments, and echoes of the Bible, as has already been evident, strengthen the association. In Books 9 and 10 of Miss Braddon's *Charlotte's Inheritance* (1868), in which Charlotte Halliday is seriously ill and in danger of dying (as a result of poisoning, as it turns out), section headings give us a strong clue to the importance of the event. Book 9 is entitled "Through the Furnace," and Chapter 1 of Book 10 is called "Out of the Dark Valley." In this instance, however, illness operates on the witness, not the sufferer. When Charlotte recovers, Valentine Hawkeshurst, her lover, is relieved: "He had reason to rejoice; for he had passed through the valley of the shadow of death." (Book 10, ch. 1) He has faced the darkness, not of his own, but of Charlotte's possible death; now he ascends into the light with his beloved: "The struggle had been dire, the agony of suspense a supreme torture; but from the awful contest the man came forth a better and a wiser man. Whatever strength of principle had been wanting to complete the work of reformation inaugurated by love, had been gained by Valentine Hawkeshurst during the period of Charlotte's illness." (Book 10, ch. 1)

Examples of the convention of illness are endless, therefore it is probably just as well to indicate one novelist's conscious use of the convention. George Meredith's works serve the purpose. In *Rhoda Fleming* (1865), Robert Eccles is beaten and falls ill, but when he recovers, he changes his life and renounces his old self. This transformation is reflected later in Dahlia Fleming's career. After her sexual solecism, Dahlia suffers an illness which also proves to be improving for "her illness had pulled her down and made her humble." (ch. 29)[22] Later, after her recovery, Dahlia is ready to face her new beginning. It cannot be a new spring, but it is the next best thing: "Upon an autumn afternoon, Dahlia, looking like a pale spring flower, came down among them." (ch. 47) But the necessary humbling illness is

mere strengthening of character was required to justify suffering. "There is purpose in pain, / Otherwise it were devilish," says Lucile in Owen Meredith's *Lucile*. (Two. V, viii) Herself a model of noble suffering, Lucile can instruct her lover, Eugene, that "Vulgar natures alone suffer vainly." (Two. V, x) There is a greater harmony she says, of which human pain is only a note that may not seem correct until the whole music is known. And F. D. Maurice, also convinced of the value of sacrifice, renunciation and suffering, added the important caution that "Sacrifice cannot have this ennobling and mysterious power—it will be turned into self-glory, and lose its own nature and acquire a devil nature—if it is not contemplated as all flowing from the nature of God; if it is not referred to Him as its author as well as end."[25]

Not all writers and their readers would have agreed that suffering was necessarily a moral good. Wilkie Collins declared in *Armadale* that "Suffering can, and does, develop the latent evil that there is in humanity, as well as the latent good." (Book 3, ch. 1) And Miss Wade in *Little Dorrit* exhibits this sentiment in Dickens' novel, as do the suffering multitudes in *Barnaby Rudge* and *A Tale of Two Cities*. By 1884, Gissing could picture unfavorably the belief that life was meant to be a test and an ordeal in the fanatical Mrs. Bygrave in *The Unclassed*. Nor were those who wished to maintain a moral stability while refashioning man's mode of perceiving existence likely to agree with simple attitudes concerning the sanctification of suffering and renunciation. Pater's Marius reflects that there is "a certain grief in things as they are" that goes beyond the "griefs of circumstance which are in a measure removable. . . ." (*Marius the Epicurean*, Part 4, ch. 25) He wonders how man has endured this burden, "seeing how every step in the capacity of apprehension his labour has won for him, from age to age, must needs increase his dejection." He concludes that increased knowledge means increased hopelessness concerning the human condition. To counteract this waxing depression is "a certain permanent and general power of compassion—humanity's standing force of self-pity—as an elementary ingredient of our social atmosphere. . . ." It is this compassionateness that man must cultivate as a defense against despair.

Pater's putative solution to the growing pessimism of the late nineteenth century, which found an attractive creed in Schopenhauerian renunciation of the will to live, and despair for the domination of human suffering, was a modestly hopeful one. And yet it became more and more difficult for a culture deeply committed to material progress and comforts to excuse or explain pain. For some the justification itself became a weak consolation of an ambiguous evolution, expressed by H. G. Wells in *The Time Machine* in the epigrammatic phrase: "We are kept keen on the grindstone of pain and necessity. . . ." (ch. 4) From cleansing, redemptive fires to grim mechanical grindstones is a sad course, and yet the progress of metaphors indicates a genuine movement of thought in the age. The ecstatic imagery of flame argued an energy and passion equated with the natural exuberance of existence, while the passage through the Valley of the Shadow of Death, drawn from Scripture, captured the vitality of a genuine movement in space and time, through darkness to light. The man-made grindstone, on the other hand, implies nothing more than a fierce but passionless movement strictly confined in space, with one tedious and doubtful effect.

Early Victorian sentiments had assumed a human will driven by passions that must be restrained to harmonize with the divine plan like a supreme music. By the end of the century, the relentless wheel of circumstance and chance seemed to deprive man of the volition that made his part in a larger plan credible. If man was not on a journey, where he could take wrong turnings and be singed for them, but on a conveyor belt of history, then the grand moral design was not a model, but a mockery. Acknowledgment of this possibility bred an increased self-consciousness among Victorian writers about the stylizations of their time.

As the effectiveness of illness and suffering as part of a moral design began for many to appear doubtful, other purposes employing the same fundamental materials emerged. Works such as *Guy Livingstone*, *Maud* and *Orion* are mainly concerned with ideals, but in most of the works that I have mentioned, it is evident that the moral design is as much associated with physical rewards as it is with spiritual success. It is this physical aspect of the same design—now consciously contrived as a feature of esthetic order, relating not only to life and morality, but to the fictional structure of which it is a part—that I shall now examine.

CONVENTIONAL TYPES AND EMBLEMATIC FIGURES

There is a tradition of secularized and immediate typology in English literature which persists into the nineteenth century.[26] Consequently, it is not surprising to find Charles Dickens utilizing the model of *The Pilgrim's Progress* in *The Old Curiosity Shop*, or entitling his first novel *The Adventures of Oliver Twist: or, The Parish Boy's Progress*.[27] Nor is it remarkable when Thackeray entitles one of his novels *The Adventures of Philip on His Way Through the World Showing Who Robbed Him, Who Helped Him and Who Passed Him By*, and continues the Samaritan motif throughout the novel in allusion as well as illustration. Thackeray states his purpose early in the novel. Refusing to supply "pulmonary romance . . . melancholy, despair, and sardonic satire," he offers instead ordinary trials for his hero.

That he shall fall and trip in his course sometimes is pretty certain. Ah, who does not upon this life-journey of ours? Is not our want the occasion of our brother's charity, and thus does not good come out of that evil? When the traveller (of whom the Master spoke) fell among the thieves, his mishap was contrived to try many a heart beside his own—the Knave's who robbed him, the Levite's and Priest's who passed him by as he lay bleeding, the humble Samaritan's whose hand poured oil into his wound, and held out its pittance to relieve him. (ch. 2)

Scriptural allusions of this kind are predictably common in the literature of the time. Charles Aubrey, enduring his ordeal in *Ten Thousand A-Year*, is likened to Job in his suffering (see Vol. 2, ch. 7 and Vol. 3, ch. 5). The story of Jacob's experience with Leah and Rachel serves as a rough parallel to Stephen Blackpool's situation in *Hard Times* (see Vol. 1, ch. 13). He has married a wife who is no pleasure to him, while he dreams of the unattainable Rachel who is his true love. The friendship of John Halifax and Phineas Fletcher in Miss Mulock's *John Halifax, Gentleman* is sanctified by its resemblance to the scriptural model of Jonathan and David. These scriptural associations may be incidental or central to the stories concerned; they may be merely verbal or have a more stylized pictorial quality.[28] The illustrations to Dickens' novels show how much Dickens intended in his parallels—indicating, for example, Bradley Headstone's identification with Cain, David Copperfield's relationship to the Prodigal Son, Martha Endel's association with Mary Magdalen, and so forth.[29] Occasionally pictorial associations are forcefully suggested with or without the pictures, as, for example, in Thackeray's *The Adventures of Philip*.

'You remember that picture of Abraham and Isaac in the Doctor's Study in Old Parr Street?' he [Philip] would say. 'My patriarch has tied me up, and had the knife in me repeatedly. He does not sacrifice me at one operation; but there will be a final one some day, and I shall bleed no more.' (ch. 37)

And George Eliot, in describing Mrs. Poyser in *Adam Bede*, says that "The family likeness between her and her niece Dinah Morris, with the contrast between her keenness and Dinah's seraphic gentleness of expression, might have served a painter as an excellent suggestion for a Martha and Mary." (ch. 6)

Interpreting existence in emblematic terms was a customary approach for the nineteenth-century mind. Emphasizing the symbolic significance of man's achievements in his quest for freedom, Carlyle said: "Of this higher, heavenly freedom, which is 'man's reasonable service,' all his noble institutions, his faithful endeavours and loftiest attainments, are but the body, and more and more approximate emblem." (*Signs of the Times*)[30] George Borrow, declaring "I am no moralizer," added, "but the gay and rapid river and the dark and silent lake were, of a verity, no bad emblems of us two [he and his brother]." (*Lavengro*, ch. 1) Wordsworth used such emblems freely in his poetry to symbolize man's higher aims.[31] And the same notion appeared in Emerson's philosophy. But the attitude could also apply to more trivial perceptions. Thus Valentine Hawkeshurst, in Miss Braddon's *Birds of Prey*, exclaims to his private journal, "O paper, whose flat surface typifies the dull level of my life, your greasy unwillingness to receive the ink is emblematic of the soul's revolt against destiny." (Book 5, ch. 3)

The tradition of viewing existence emblematically was conditioned partly by works such as Francis Quarles' *Emblemes* (1635), which remained recommended reading for children into the nineteenth century,[32] and which were parodied in Robert L. Stevenson's collaboration with Lloyd Osbourne, *Moral Emblems: A Collection of Cuts and Verses*. But the tropes of these emblematic usages derived also from the familiar approach of the church sermon. It was, then, entirely characteristic to view fictions in emblematic terms. The very covers of monthly parts of novels suggested as much; for example, with Dickens' *Dombey and Son*, where Father Time and other typical figures foreshadow the story, or in Trollope's *The Way We Live Now*, where the cover illustration shows money bags surrounding a central scene in which Father Time sits upon a globe, holding one hand over his averted eyes, while the other hand is held up as though to ward off the sight of contemporary events. These illustrations were not anomalous, for Dickens viewed his characters as emblematic and so did his readers. One contemporary reviewer of *The Old Curiosity Shop* admired Nell as "an emblem and a portion of the Universal Beauty, an incarnation of gentlest heroism."[33]

Within novels, characters viewed their own lives as emblematic. Jane Eyre remarks of Adèle and Rochester that "She seemed the emblem of my past life; and he, I was now to array myself to meet, the dread, but adored type of my unknown future day." (*Jane Eyre*, ch. 25) Moreover, these characters often create actual pictorial emblems themselves. Thus Jane Eyre paints pictures of morally emblematic significance, and Lancelot Smith, in Kingsley's *Yeast*, produces a drawing entitled "The Triumph of Woman," which symbolically describes woman's ennobling purpose.[34]

Most emblematic suggestions in the literature of the time were incidental. Thus Miss Mulock could describe Muriel as "better than Joy—she was an embodied Peace," or say of Ursula that Phineas called her "The Mother" because she was "the truest type of motherhood" he ever knew. (*John Halifax*, ch. 22) But the habit of symbolic interpretation was too common to be overlooked by sophisticated writers who might wish to emphasize the convention. Hence, Oscar Wilde, in *The Picture of Dorian Gray*, quite openly creates a fable in which a picture itself becomes a symbol. "The picture, changed or unchanged, would be to [Dorian] the visible emblem of conscience." (ch. 7) But by this time the emblems are only ironically Christian, for, as Lord Henry observes, the basic experience of order is esthetic, "the mere shapes and patterns of things becoming, as it were, refined, and gaining a kind of symbolical value, as though they were themselves patterns of some other and more perfect form whose Shadow they made real." (ch. 3)

Whole novels might appear emblematic, or stylized to achieve the proper effects of poetic justice. In such stylized works characters assumed highly conventional roles. Both Dickens and Collins objected to conventionality of character in the writings of others,[35] but used the conventional types themselves. They were professionals and felt free to utilize the stylizations of their time, confident that they could transcend the banal. Dickens could work on three different kinds of fiction at the same time, just as Bulwer-Lytton could experiment simultaneously with sportive and sombre modes of fiction.

Bulwer-Lytton, like many of his contemporaries, was given to symbolic structures for his stories, and the extent to which he thought in typological terms is demonstrated in the modifications he recommended for his son's poem, *Lucile*.

> The young man ought to be a short and beautiful sketch—he has all the earnestness and purity which his father lacked—where he loves it is deep, silent, and for life. The girl might be a more joyous, vigorous, practical nature, but equally innocent—make a very innocent Poet and Virgin picture of their love which contrasts the worldlier and hardier loves of the preceding actors. . . . An idea! He might be a sort of type of the Poetical in Nature, she of the Healthful and Joyous in Nature. The existence of the one incomplete without the other. I think I see a beautiful close. These two young people kneeling near the old Gothic chapel. The open doors showing the ancestral tombs—the stained windows—the Duc blessing them—the setting sun on their locks.[36]

The tendency to view life in symbolic or emblematic terms, from Bulwer-Lytton's moral simplicities to Oscar Wilde's esthetic complexities, grew out of a notion that behind all of existence there was a pattern. Tennyson had asserted that behind the apparent chaos of existence, there was a design and that all "as in some piece of art / Is toil coöperant to an end." Although the nature of that design might not always be the same, there was a general agreement as to its basic character. As we have already seen, one fundamental pattern was that based on scriptural stories. But it was just as much the design as the morality that appealed to the consciousness of Victorian writers.

ESTHETIC DESIGN

In J. H. Shorthouse's *John Inglesant* (1881), Inglesant replies to Cardinal Rinuccini's observation that the myths of the world are slow to change, that the myth of Christ has persisted "because men found in it something that reminded them of their daily life. It speaks of suffering and of sin." What is more, "We must *suffer* with Christ whether we *believe* in Him or not. We must suffer for the sin of others as for our own; and in this suffering we find a healing and purifying power and element." The Christian pattern is largely involuntary, though faith may be chosen, and the pattern fashioned. The Cardinal, persuading Inglesant to leave his monastic refuge and resume the struggle of life, argues that "We did not make the world, and are not responsible for its state; but we can make life a fine art, and, taking things as we find them, like wise men, mould them as may best serve our own ends." (ch. 23) The moral design becomes a consciously controlled esthetic event, patterned upon, though not stipulated by, a sacred model. Art and morality are interfused in a Paterian blend of sanctity and beauty.

But years before Shorthouse's "romance" appeared, writers were conscious of the moral fable that operated behind much of Victorian literature.[37] Laurence Oliphant, in *Picadilly: A Fragment of Contemporary Biography* (1871), parodied conventional romance as well as morality. The first chapters of his tale read: I. Love; II. Madness; III. Suicide; thereby fulfilling a common melodramatic pattern. But in the first chapter, love is not what it seems, while selfishness and the lust for material goods· abound. In the second, no ordinary madness appears, though the nation as a whole is depicted as driving down an insane route, because England's "intellect can see truths which its heart will not embody." (ch. 2) In the third, there is no suicide, but Lord Frank Vanecourt has a vision of a fiery cross, a "supernatural indication of assistance," the lesson of which is not suicide, but "self-sacrifice." (ch. 3)

The next sequence of chapters mocks moral conventions, reading: IV. The World; V. The Flesh; VI. The "———." It is Oliphant's sermon against contemporary English society, and, in Frank Vanecourt's progress toward separation from all the vanities of existence, describes liberation from, not entrapment by, man's three great enemies. Frank's separation is realized when he leaves England with his "shadowy friend" to pursue a true course of faith, in which "a man's life is the result of his internal belief." Vanecourt—and Oliphant with him—sheds the romantic conventions and "theological dogmas" mocked by the form of his tale, in favor of the "divine conviction of truth imparted to the intellect through the heart." (ch. 6) For Oliphant, a personal moral design emerges antithetically by parodying the standard secular and moral literary patterns.

Oliphant's views resemble certain influential ideas of Matthew Arnold. Central to Arnold's concept of morality is the pursuit of "a best self" or "a whole self," and for him, the very idea of humanity and intelligence and of raising oneself out of the "flux of things" rests "upon the idea of steadying oneself, concentrating oneself, making order in the chaos of impressions, by attending to one impression

rather than another." (*Literature and Dogma*, ch. 1, sec. 2) This ordering of the self is achieved neither scientifically nor through metaphysics, but esthetically. Just as the "language of the Bible . . . is literary,
not scientific language; language *thrown out* at an object of consciousness not fully grasped, which inspires emotion," (ch. 1, sec. 4) so man's
life must also be an esthetic experiment, and hence Arnold's emphasis upon the experiential nature of faith. The Bible, for Arnold, becomes significant mainly as a model, not as stipulated truth. (ch. 1,
sec. 5) Christ, too, who "renewed righteousness and religion" with
"Self-examination, self-renouncement, and mildness," becomes a conscious model. (ch. 3, sec. 2)[38] Like Shorthouse's Cardinal, Arnold suggests that men, like Christ, can choose to make life a fine art.

Arnold recommends throughout his writings a conscious control of
one's own existence through the moral imagination. Christ becomes
the supreme poet whose method is a form of religious negative capability—the renunciation of self for the esthetic triumph of faith.
These Arnoldian views contributed to the fascination for esthetically
fashioned lives so evident in the works of Pater, Wilde, Baron Corvo
and other figures in the late nineteenth century. Arnold could quote
Goethe's remark, "Everything cries out to us that we must renounce,"
(ch. 7, sec. 4) but he would also have known the passage from Goethe's
"Confessions of a Fair Saint" in *Wilhelm Meister* where the Fair
Saint's uncle designates man's highest merit to be "as much as possible to rule external circumstances, and as little as possible to let himself be ruled by them." Describing life as a moral and esthetic endeavor wherein the individual, like an architect, fashions his nature from
the quarry of life lying before him, the wise uncle proceeds to show
the near relationship of the histories of art and moral culture, concluding with the advice that "those do not act well, who, in a solitary exclusive manner, follow moral cultivation by itself," for one must
also "improve his finer sentient powers." (Book 6) Life, then, is to
assume a moral, yet esthetically controlled shape. It will not be long
before Nietzsche exclaims, " 'Giving style' to one's character—a great
and rare art! It is exercised by those who see all the strengths and
weaknesses of their own nature and then comprehend them in an
artistic plan until everything appears as art and reason,"[39] or before
Oscar Wilde will remark, "there is no art where there is no style, and
no style where there is no unity, and unity is of the individual." (*The
Critic as Artist*) One example of this tendency to superimpose an

esthetic design upon a moral one in a thoroughly conscious way will serve to conclude my examination of moral patterns.

In a lay sermon, delivered early in Mrs. Humphry Ward's novel, *Robert Elsmere* (1888), the obviously ideal Mr. Grey provides the structural basis for the entire novel. His sermon is on St. Paul's line, " 'Death unto sin and a new birth unto righteousness.' " (ch. 5) Considering that this is a work by Matthew Arnold's niece, it is impossible to overlook the passage in *Culture and Anarchy* (1869) where Arnold, like Grey, concerns himself with St. Paul's notion of resurrection. For Arnold, St. Paul uses "resurrection"

> in the sense of a rising to a new life before the physical death of the body, and not after it. The idea on which we have already touched, the profound ideal of being baptized into the death of the great exemplar, his course of self-devotion and self-annulment, and of thus coming, within the limits of our present life, to a new life, in which, as in the death going before it, we are identified with our exemplar,—this is the fruitful and original conception of being *risen with Christ* which possesses the mind of St. Paul. (ch. 5)[40]

Robert Elsmere, troubled by new scientific and Germanic notions, experiences profound religious doubts. But Mrs. Ward asks, "Has not almost every Christian of illustrious excellence been tried and humbled by them?" (ch. 25) The usual design in which a simple physical collapse cures pride, passion, or selfishness does not operate here, for Elsmere suffers from none of these sins. He is seen, rather, as a modern Man of Feeling, already free from the burden of self. His curable infection is doubt, and after an important conversation with Henry Grey, Elsmere feels freed of his malady. "In that sense which attaches to every successive resurrection of our best life from the shades of despair or selfishness, he had that day, almost that hour, been born again. . . . The earth to him was once more full of God, existence full of value." (ch. 28) Grey tells Elsmere that there is nothing to dread in the collapse of old dogmas, and counsels him to seek God "not in any single event of past history, *but in your own soul*." He consoles Elsmere with the assurance that he will gradually discover a broader faith. "All things change,—creeds and philosophies and outward systems,—but God remains!" (ch. 28) And God is within.

For Robert Elsmere, ceremony and doctrine—the schematic beliefs of the past—have been replaced by a private design: the design of one's own life, of one's inward experience. Confused by doubt, Elsmere had compared the pattern of his life to Christian's in *The Pilgrim's Progress*; after his rebirth, Augustine's *Confessions* becomes one referent and parallel to Elsmere's career, along with the "great Example" of Christ. Unlike the "esoteric Buddhist" at Rose Leyburn's musical afternoon, Robert has freed himself from superstitious systems; and, unlike the esthete at the same event, "got up in the most correct professional costume," he has given his life a meaningful, instead of a merely pretty, style. Even Rose, who, as a talented musician, moves in the world of esthetic display, can see the common mistake men make. " 'How we all attitudinise to ourselves!' " she complains. " 'The whole of life often seems one long dramatic performance, in which one half of us is for ever posing to the other half.' " (ch. 39)

But Elsmere requires no false performances, for he has transformed his life to a modern saint's legend; and so, in her way, has his wife, Catherine. Indeed, her devoted life, aimed at respect for her saintly husband and concern for the poor and afflicted, resembles St. Elizabeth of Hungary's, with whom she is often identified.[41] But Catherine is no mere formal church-goer. "She had in fact undergone that dissociation of the moral judgment from a special series of religious formulae which is the crucial, the epoch-making fact of our day." (ch. 46) The moral judgment remains; the moral design remains; but the religious formulae are gone. Prescriptive moral design collapses and each life creates anew its own design, which, like a saint's life, in turn becomes a model, though no dogma. The lesson is no longer a dogmatic lesson, it is the esthetic lesson that Christ himself employed.

English literature, represented by *Robert Elsmere* and similar works of the time, self-consciously recognized what its moral design had become: an individual manifestation of a permanent pattern, having significance as an esthetic model, not as a religious stipulation. It was the attractiveness of the design as much as the message conveyed by that design that appealed to late nineteenth-century reading audiences. And there was good reason during the nineteenth century that esthetic modifications of Christian patterns of perception should occur. Formal Christianity came progressively under assault, and esthetic strategies like Arnold's often seemed useful in preserving Christian values without the Christian faith. Writers became increasingly aware that other fundamental designs might serve as well as familiar Christian ones.

FAIRY-TALE DESIGN

Christianity was in trouble, Arnold said, because men were dissatisfied with metaphysics. "Men will not admit assumptions, the popular legend [of Christ] they call a fairy-tale, the metaphysical demonstrations do not demonstrate, nothing but experimental proof will go down." (*Literature and Dogma*, ch. 12, sec. 3)[42] Arnold was anxious to replace the science and fairy-tale of religion with experiential models, and this is just what serious literature, with less self-consciousness, was doing.

K. M. Briggs, in *The Fairies in English Tradition and Literature*, indicates the manner in which nineteenth-century writers moralized by means of fairy tales—George Cruikshank going so far as to convert "*Hop o' my Thumb, Cinderella* and *Jack and the Beanstalk* into temperance tracts."[43] But, while fairy tales were becoming vehicles for morality, adult literature was developing the moral and esthetic use of fairy tales. For some time German writers had been making use of fairy tales, and fairy-tale elements, in their works. The writings of Tieck, Novalis, Hoffmann, Brentano and others demonstrate an acute consciousness of the esthetic value of this practice. But, in England, serious employment of fairy-tale devices served to unite esthetic and moral elements.

Charlotte Yonge's *The Heir of Redclyffe* is patterned on the Christian system of belief and emphasizes as its moral norm the example of Christ, but there is another less profound, though structurally intriguing device operating in the novel. After describing Philip as a model hero, the narrator explains that Guy "tried to esteem his cousin because he thought it a point of duty, just as children think it right to admire the good boy in a story-book." (Vol. 1, ch. 6) Charlotte Yonge, author of several children's books and fairy tales, was familiar with the good boys in storybooks, so it is not accidental that the morality of her children's world should be transferred to that of her fictional adults, and that childhood morality should arise to judge sinful adults. Of Philip, after his initial humbling, but before his final resignation, she says, "Sometimes in fairy tales, a naughty child, under the care of a fairy, is chained to an exaggeration of himself and his own faults,

and rendered a slave to his hateful self. The infliction he underwent
in his sister's house was somewhat analogous." (Vol. 2, ch. 16) By
uniting Christian fable and moral tale, Charlotte Yonge equates religion and ethics; faith and fairy tale are one, and it is experiential
model, not stipulated morality, that is of value.

Everyone is familiar with Dickens' use of fairy-tale materials in his
fiction.[44] In *David Copperfield* Dickens wrote that "At odd dull times,
nursery tales come up into the memory, unrecognized for what they
are." (ch. 22) But Dickens did recognize them and knew how to exploit them in his own fiction. In many cases, the fairy-tale passages
are, as John Harvey observes, openly pictorial, drawing upon the
images from children's books.[45]

Dickens' references to such moral children's tales as *Sandford and
Merton* indicate that, in his mind, there was no serious distinction
between adult and adolescent morality, and, like his acquaintance,
Hans Christian Andersen, he used one to reinforce the other. In
some instances, this reinforcement is peripheral, as in the use of the
Red Riding Hood tale in *Our Mutual Friend*; but at other times, the
fairy tale is of structural importance, as the Cinderella fable is for
Great Expectations. Pip starts his career in a low state before a forge
(if not a hearth), and, by the aid of a supposed fairy godmother,
achieves a high station. Because Dickens means to convert the fable
to Christian purpose, Pip must relinquish the glass slipper of pride
(a showy, but impractical item), and return to ordinary, but ennobled
circumstances, freed from the fairy-tale illusions that have so misled
him. It is worth noting that *Great Expectations* is also a Christian
tale, opening on Christmas eve, partly located in a manger-like forge,
and progressing to a symbolic crucifixion (Pip's wounded hands, symbolic illness, and resurrection). The child's fairy tale has been merged
with what Arnold described as the adult's fairy tale, and the models
of Cinderella and Christ confused, until Christ emerges as an exalted
Cinderella, with all the esthetic fascination of a storybook figure, but
also with the moral power of a divinity. Biblical parable and child's
tale become coequal in instructive power, though both are subordinate to the secular and esthetic purposes of the novel.

Similarly in Thackeray's novel, *The Newcomes*, for example, animal fable and Christian parable are interfused to convey the moral.
Allusions to Good Samaritans and Prodigal Sons occur throughout
the novel, but the story is bracketed by an Aesopian device. *The New-*

comes opens with an animal fable, and then anticipates a supposed critic's exclamation: " 'What a farrago of old fables is this! What a dressing up in old clothes! . . . That wolf in sheep's clothing?—do I not know him? That fox discoursing with the crow?—have I not previously heard of him?' " Thackeray goes on to admit the charge and then to add, "What stories are new? All types of all characters march through all fables. . . . So the tales were told ages before Aesop: and asses under lions' manes roared in Hebrew; and sly foxes flattered in Etruscan; and wolves in sheep's clothing gnashed their teeth in Sanscrit, no doubt." (Vol. 1, ch. 1)[46] His own, says Thackeray, will be another such tale. At the novel's finish, the author, unwilling to stipulate a conclusion, generously remarks to the reader:

> But for you, dear friend, it is as you like. You may settle your fable-land in your own fashion. Anything you like happens in fable-land. Wicked folks die à propos (for instance, that death of Lady Kew was most artful, for if she had not died, don't you see that Ethel would have married Lord Farintosh the next week?)—annoying folks are got out of the way; the poor are rewarded—the up-starts are set down in fable-land,—the frog bursts with wicked rage, the fox is caught in his trap, the lamb is rescued from the wolf and so forth, just in the nick of time. And the poet of fable-land rewards and punishes absolutely. (Vol. 2, ch. 42)

Not only are animal and Christian fable closely involved, both are assigned to the fable-land of the imagination where each reader may contrive his own design.

So closely had fairy tales and adult morality drawn together that in the May 1866, issue of *The Cornhill Magazine*, a series of everyday fairy tales began to appear. "The Sleeping Beauty in the Wood," was followed by "Cinderella," "Beauty and the Beast," "Little Red Riding Hood," and "Jack the Giant-Killer."[47] No unreal details appear beyond the titles, but each title sufficiently indicates the structural basis for its story, which is otherwise an example of ordinary Victorian fiction. Anne Ritchie's explanation for this device appears at the opening of her second tale of the series, "Cinderella."

> It is, happily, not only in fairy tales that things sometimes fall out as one could wish, that anxieties are allayed, mistakes explained away, friends reconciled; that people inherit large fortunes, or are found out in their nefarious schemes; that long-lost children are discovered dis-

guised in soot, that vessels come safely sailing into port after the storm; and that young folks who have been faithful to one another are married off at last.[48]

When Mrs. Ritchie goes on to explain that she was obliged to moralize because happiness does occur in this life and is worth noting, she implicitly defends the attitude so urbanely attacked by Martin Decoud in Conrad's *Nostromo*. A strong, though by no means exclusive, tendency in English literature of the nineteenth century was toward the interpretation of life as a moral romance derived from a pretty fairy tale. Not all writers saw the myth of Christ as a fairy tale, but most saw its fabular potential and attempted to provide for their time an experiential model of individual morality, which, while departing from traditional morality, yet sustained the moral hardihood of that tradition. Many achieved this aim by recognizing the importance of esthetic control over experience. Life, viewed as an imitation of Christ, an Aesop's tale, a Pilgrim's Progress, or a fairy tale, is still life shaped from the quarry of experience, still a "making order in the chaos of impressions," toward a moral end. It is still the fashioning of life into a fine art, in a manner resembling Pater's Marius, or Shorthouse's Inglesant. It is, in short, a moral romance—a union of secular fable and moral purpose; and, both when it is conscious and when it is unpremeditated, it indicates one forceful current of English literature, which may be seen in such different works as Oscar Wilde's sophisticated fairy tales in *The Happy Prince*, or his stylized dramas *Salomé* and *La Sainte Courtisane*; in Hardy's parable of a search for the ideal in *The Well-Beloved*; in D. H. Lawrence's "The Man Who Died," or in Joyce's *A Portrait of the Artist as a Young Man*, where a story that begins "Once upon a time," concludes with an artist-hero renouncing stipulative morality in favor of a priesthood of the imagination and the freedom to fashion not only his own, but his nation's consciousness.[49] Or it may be seen in Conrad's *Nostromo*, where the atheistic Decoud disappears into the void, while the English Monygham, having passed through his valley of the shadow of death, refashions his life into a moral romance, which, though secular, is governed by an esthetic ideal.

Victorian writers were highly conscious of the stylizations of their own time and a large number of them—among whom were the best writers the age produced—found it possible to adapt and alter those stylizations to their own ends. To understand the stylizations and then the changes played upon them by inventive artists is to gain a greater appreciation not only of what the Victorian age meant, but also of what it wished to say. Once we understand certain general assumptions of Victorian writers and their readers, it may become easier for us to appreciate the function of certain conventions that operated within the larger designs of Victorian literature.

CHAPTER TWO

WOMEN

WOMAN'S PLACE

Much has been written on the position of the woman in nineteenth-century England, and I do not propose to examine that subject in depth here. I am concerned mainly with stylizations of types of women in the literature of the period. Still, it is not possible to discuss literary types without considering some social conditions with which they were allied. Of course, there have always been stylized types for women in literature in any age. However, the change from the eighteenth to the nineteenth century in English literature was marked. The battle of the sexes was declared and fought in Restoration literature, and the social, if not the legal, position of women was somewhat freer than in later years. The late eighteenth century brought attacks upon learned ladies which persisted in the nineteenth-century aversion to "bluestockings."[1] Meanwhile, patriarchy established itself as the basic form of domestic rule, and progressively woman's sphere became more restricted.

Mary Wollstonecraft, in an attempt to correct the growing tendency to isolate women from any usefulness or intellectual development, argued in *A Vindication of the Rights of Woman* (1792) that women should be treated as human beings with the right to the development of their intellectual faculties and the pursuit of knowledge and virtue. Ignorance, false refinement and sham she denounced. But hers was an eccentric view that found little support even among women of the time.[2] Most respectable women were content to follow the prescriptions put forth by writers such as Mrs. John Sandford in *Woman in her Social and Domestic Character* (1831) and *Female Improvement* (1836), or Mrs. Sarah Stickney Ellis in volumes like *The Women of England* (1839), *The Daughters of England* (1842), and *The Wives of England* (1843). Although Mrs. Ellis stressed the influence woman could exert, she also readily acknowledged the superiority of men.[3] Mrs. Sandford asserted that nature had assigned woman "a subordinate place as well as subordinate powers; and it is far better that she should feel this, and should not arrogate the superiority of the other sex, whilst she claims the privilege [indulgence] of her own."[4]

There were, of course, numerous champions of women's rights at that time, among them such luminaries as Elizabeth Barrett Browning, Charlotte Brontë, Richard Monckton Milnes, Florence Nightingale, Mary Howitt, J. S. Mill, and Charles Kingsley; but in general women were oppressed legally and socially, and in most cases, they submitted to their oppression. And although they were "no longer reproached for the sin of Eve," as in medieval times,[5] "the example of Eve was constantly pointed to as a warning of their own weakness in the face of temptation of their own propensity to entice men."[6] Women were persuaded to view themselves as frail beings requiring the protection of virile males. As Katharine M. Rogers points out in *The Troublesome Helpmate*, "Insistence on women's weakness and the sweetness of submission was a gentle way of keeping them in subjection, and in subjection, of course, they were prevented from doing harm."[7]

Throughout the nineteenth century, the demand for a humane view of woman's place and a recognition of women's rights grew more and more pronounced. Women's rights movements, beginning in 1848 in America, soon took hold in England. Women's legal rights became a prominent issue. Women sought to correct inequitable divorce laws, to establish new laws governing financial arrangements in marriage, and above all to demand participation in the ballot. From Mrs. Hugo Reid's *A Plea for Women* (1843), to Miss Frances Swiney's shrill *Cos-*

mic Procession (1906), demands for equality became assertions of female superiority. As the issues for suffrage and legal rights grew in the late nineteenth century, men resisted more vigorously; newspapers, journals, and books issued from the press denouncing the movement as female madness. Such eager resistance may now appear strange, but to the Victorian mind, an independent woman challenged moral and social assumptions which Victorians considered essential to a stable society. Furthermore, such a woman promised to be dangerously uncontrollable. Coventry Patmore expressed the sentiments of his time when he asserted that women were meant to be controlled by their men. When a woman is in love, he wrote, she becomes childlike and dependent:

> There's nothing left of what she was;
> > Back to the babe the woman dies,
> And all the wisdom that she has
> > Is to love him for being wise.

> ("Espousals," canto 8)

No one who approved this view could accept a woman who challenged man's superior wisdom.

The new century did not bring widespread sympathy to the woman's movement. Samuel Hynes, in *The Edwardian Turn of Mind*, observes that Arthur Wing Pinero's easy assumption, in his problem play, *The Notorious Mrs. Ebbsmith* (1895), "that the desire for rights and freedom in a woman is a neurotic symptom is one that continued through the two decades that followed, and not only among writers of Pinero's conservative stand."[8] As late as 1908, Lucy Honeychurch, in E. M. Forster's *A Room with a View*, could wonder why women were not free like men, and express contempt for the "medieval" concept of women that the generality of men in her day entertained. In Ford Madox Ford's tetralogy, *Parade's End*, it was manifestly clear that emancipation would not be fully achieved even after the Great War, though laws would gradually begin to ameliorate women's circumstances. Meanwhile, as the issue of women's rights and the question of woman's place remained an important social question, in literature a unique mode of dealing with women developed.

The opposition of a proud, domineering woman to a gentle, selfless one is a familiar device in Victorian literature. In novels such as

G. A. Lawrence's *Guy Livingstone, or 'Thorough,'* or Anne Brontë's *The Tenant of Wildfell Hall*, or Thackeray's subtler *Vanity Fair*, the opposition is more or less *vis-à-vis*, but in other works, such as Tennyson's *Idylls of the King*, the contrast is less schematic. In *Great Expectations*, Mrs. Gargery, among others, balances Biddy's strong will; in *Barchester Towers*, Eleanor Bold counteracts Madeline Neroni; Fanny Dorrit and Miss Wade are set against Little Dorrit and Pet Meagles in *Little Dorrit*.

Guy Livingstone offers a particularly clear instance of this conventional opposition. Flora Bellasys is equated with such figures as Penthesilea, Radigund, Sapphira and Circe, while Guy plays Samson to her Delilah. The narrator of the novel, seeing Flora dance with Guy, "thought of the old Rhineland tradition of the Wilis; then the daughter of Herodias came into" his mind. (ch. 20) Guy's proper and enduring attraction is not to the flirtatious and enticing Flora, but to Constance Brandon, who is referred to as "a saint." Her suffering and death, indirectly occasioned by Flora's designs upon Guy, become the means for Guy's redemption, enabling him to repudiate Flora, who appears to the narrator as "the impersonation of material life, exuberant and vigorous, yet delicately lovely—the Lust of the Eye incarnate." (ch. 30)[9] Just as the faithful Constance must die her saintly death, so Flora must suffer loneliness and desideration, bringing flowers of remembrance to Guy's grave. The narrator muses, "they say that great enchantresses, from Medea and Circe downward, have generally been unhappy in their loves." (ch. 35) Constance, the selfless saint, triumphs in the realm of "real" values, scattering the earthly Flora's victories as the wind will scatter her flowers over Guy's indifferent grave. The woman who attempts to commandeer physical authority discloses her own incompleteness: a beautiful flower perhaps, but one no soil can nourish fully. The saintly way is best—even in death.

WOMAN AS SAINT

Presenting the good woman as a domestic saint was a favorite stylization in Victorian literature. "The typical virtuous heroine of the Victorian novel is a softened version of Griselde—rewarded for exploitation by being venerated as a saint. Women, it is implied, are wonderfully angelic and superior to men for giving up their lives to

male happiness—but there is no question that this is what they should
do."[10] The saintly woman comes in a variety of types. Madeline Bray,
in *Nicholas Nickleby*, and Lizzie Hexam in *Our Mutual Friend*, are
identifiable Susannah figures, as is Browning's Pompilia in *The Ring
and the Book*. All are fundamentally innocent women pursued by
menacing male figures. The narrator of Thackeray's *The Adventures
of Philip* remarks that although Mrs. Woolsey was slandered by the
wicked elders at gentlemen's clubs, she was really "modest and innocent as Susannah." (ch. 34) The reference was so well known that
Thackeray could depend upon his readers to make the necessary associations.[11] Some characters, such as Tennyson's Elaine or Maud,
assume more peripheral saint-like functions, while in Dickens' Agnes
Wickfield, the Susannah figure and the successful domestic saint combine. David Copperfield outlines Agnes' saintly function in highly
emblematic, almost iconographic, terms before she is actually enshrined at his fireside.

Indicative as these examples are of Victorian attitudes toward their
secular saints, other instances are more precise and more consequential. Charles Kingsley presented the figure of the saintly woman without disguise in *The Saint's Tragedy* (1848), where his prototype was
Saint Elizabeth—obedient and loving wife, moral guide, selfless individual, and benefactress of the poor. For Kingsley, the agreeable
woman was Saint Elizabeth improved by Victorian enlightenments,
like his own character, Argemone, in the novel *Yeast* (1849), who
learns, through love and Lancelot Smith's allegorical sketch, "The
Triumph of Woman," that secular sainthood is more worthy than
celibate sanctity, though she dies of typhus before she can marry and
fulfill her womanly nature. Like many another Victorian heroine, Argemone is identifiable with a pictorial saint: "With her perfect
masque and queenly figure, and earnest upward gaze, she might have
been the very model for which Raphael conceived his glorious St.
Catherine—the ideal of the highest womanly genius, softened into
self-forgetfulness by girlish devotion." (ch. 1) Grace Harvey, in *Two
Years Ago* (1857), is another of Kingsley's saintly women. She, like
Disraeli's Sybil Gerard in *Sybil, or The Two Nations* (1845), is persuaded to exercise her virtue in the domestic sphere.

In George Eliot's works, the saintly figure was so much altered to
satisfy nineteenth-century thought that she ceased to be religious at
all. However, while abandoning theology, Eliot maintained the mor-

al purpose and moral conventions of the literature of her time.[12] Dorothea Brooke, Eliot's modern Saint Theresa, is thoroughly secularized.
Moreover, while Kingsley was satisfied to make his emblematic figure
historically believable, Eliot preferred that her moral design should
emerge out of ordinary human causes, rather than have the human
causes fulfill a presumed moral design. In this she approaches what
we now know as realism, while retaining and transmuting conventional Victorian emblems.[13] Nonetheless, Eliot was willing to retain
the use of saintly parallels, as the associations in *Middlemarch* indicate. Lisbeth Bede in *Adam Bede* (1859) says of the sweet-natured
Dinah Morris, " 'Ye've got a'most the face o' one as is a-sittin' on the
grave i' Adam's new Bible.' " (ch. 10) Donnithorne says that she looks
"like St. Catherine in a Quaker dress." (ch. 5) And elsewhere Dinah's
image is compared to the way one "feels the beauty and the greatness
of a pictured Madonna." (ch. 26) In *Romola*, too, the heroine is conceived as Madonna-like.

Later in the century, Mrs. Humphry Ward provided her own version of the same saintly emblem. Although Catherine Leyburn in
Robert Elsmere (1888) is clearly and consistently identified with Saint
Elizabeth, her qualities are systematically refined to suit Victorian
views.[14] Catherine Leyburn is the modern Elizabeth—appropriately
more liberal in her perception of moral values and behavior in the
world. Catherine's career, while recapitulating the pattern of the original St. Elizabeth's life, becomes as well a revised pattern of that life
for modern times. In this case, the heroine is a convincingly human
example of goodness, reenacting an eternal pattern as exemplified in
the life of Saint Elizabeth. What is more, she suggests in the sequence of her experiences, a greater design. Catherine Elsmere lives
her life as an individual and is yet a performer in a great moral
scheme; she is both saintly emblem and ordinary woman. This assumption is later openly mocked in H. G. Wells' *Ann Veronica* (1909),
where the traditional and 'chivalric' Mr. Manning tells Ann that
women must remain queens of beauty on their thrones. "We can't afford to turn our women, our Madonnas, our Saint Catherines, our
Mona Lisas, our goddesses and angels and fairy princesses, into a sort
of man." (ch. 3) The acceptance of this saintly convention is characteristic of the later nineteenth century in the case of Mary Collet, in
Henry Kingsley's *Ravenshoe*, who concludes her saintly life in a convent. Mary Collet prefigures a type very common at the end of the

century, as, for example, the cloistered women in the poetry and short stories of Ernest Dowson.

But certain important changes developed in the convention from the early part of the century when Warren could describe Kate Aubrey, in *Ten Thousand A-Year* (1841), as a "ministering angel" or an "angelic messenger." If Lucy Ashton, in Scott's *The Bride of Lammermoor* (1819) had something "of a Madonna cast" in her appearance, it was a visual association only, meant to suggest her essential saintliness; she is a Susannah whose chastity is lost, a saint who dies in madness, not sanctity. The numerous later stylizations of the type became more suggestive of moral values, until George Moore offered a variation characteristic of the end of the century in his early novel, *Muslin* (1886), where Alice Barton is described as "the truer Madonna whose ancient and inferior prototype stood on her bracket in a forgotten corner." (ch. 10) Moore is here quite consciously turning the tables on the conventional association, since his madonna has lost her religious faith. Her genuine human sympathy is presented as something superior to traditional formal religion. Others who claim religion are mere hypocrites concerned only with making a good marriage, whereas Alice has her eye fixed on the greater truth of human decency. Nor does Alice become a domestic saint, since she aspires to nothing more than the security of middleclass housewifery.

Stretching the convention of the saintly heroine even more is Hardy's picture of Sue Bridehead in *Jude the Obscure* (1895). Sue is a saint who wishes to be a new woman. She is Susannah throwing herself into the arms of the waiting elder, Phillotson. Sue is more akin to Dowson's little girls, nuns, and celibate women, than to Grant Allen's Herminia Barton. She is the conventional saint who never should have been touched by man, but who is violated by him and ends her days in perpetual martyrdom, not saintly queenship of the hearth.

GRISELDA

One of the most commonly used conventional saints in the literature of the Victorian period was Griselda. Mrs. Crawley, in Trollope's *Framley Parsonage* (1860) and *Last Chronicle of Barset* (1867), is a typical example of the wife who courageously endures intolerable conditions. Fanny Robarts, in *Framley Parsonage*, is a milder version of the same type, and Mrs. Scatcherd in *Dr. Thorne* (1858) is a variation of the faithful wife who must endure not only a drunkard husband, but also a son who dies of alcohol. Dickens utilized the type in the tale, "The Drunkard's Death," and in "The Stroller's Tale" in *The Pickwick Papers.* His use of the Griselda type here and in "The Convict's Return," also in *The Pickwick Papers,* is thoroughly conventional. Harriet Carker, in *Dombey and Son,* has the same attributes, but is not a wife, while Mrs. Quilp, in *The Old Curiosity Shop,* is a parody of the common type. Dickens was too fond of the simplified convention himself to offer any profound modification or amplification of it. Most manifestations of the convention resembled Barbara Fleming in Mary Howitt's poem, "Barbara Fleming's Fidelity," where the quasi-Griselda Barbara, having had a vision of her purpose in life, patiently awaits the return of her providentially determined husband, meanwhile refusing marriage, comfort, and wealth, while suffering certain emotional stresses. In the end, her patience is improbably, but necessarily rewarded.

The association of the long-suffering wife with Griselda was a familiar one from the beginning of the century. The convention was given an ironic twist as early as 1804, when Maria Edgeworth published *The Modern Griselda,* in which Griselda Bolingbroke, a young bride in love with conjugal ascendancy, is contrasted with Emma Grandby, whom she sardonically refers to as *"the pattern wife, the original Griselda revived."* (ch. 4) But Emma is a clear advance upon the original Griselda who submitted absolutely to Gaultherus' absolute demands for obedience. Emma demonstrates not dumb subservience, but reasoned obedience, and, above all, selflessness. Emma's life is benign, while the proud and aggressive Griselda Bolingbroke loses her husband and her happiness. In Susan Ferrier's *Marriage* (1818), the lightheaded and ambitious Lady Emily advises Mary Douglas to "Marry the Duke, and drive over the necks of all your relations. . . ." She warns her that a girl must be forceful. "Your patient Grizzles make nothing of it, except in little books: in real life they become perfect pack-horses, saddled with the whole offences of the family." (Vol. 2, ch. 14) Mary has sense enough to be neither rash nor obtusely obedient like Griselda.

For some writers, the Griselda figure represented, without irony, the ideal of the faithful wife, the obedient companion. She was the epitome of the conventional figure described above. In Edwin Ar-

nold's poem, *Griselda. A Tragedy* (1856), for example, the traditional tale of Griselda's suffering is recounted. The Marquis of Saluz-
zo wishes to marry a common girl, Griselda, and wins her in disguise.
Subsequently he decides that he must test his wife's love. He has her
infant children taken from her and leads her to believe that she is
hated by his subjects. For twelve years he perpetuates the deception; Griselda grieves patiently the entire time. The Marquis has Griselda learn of his supposed plans to abandon her and to remarry in
order to guarantee noble offspring. The people, who have no idea of
the Marquis' motives, are unhappy with him for his behavior toward
his wife, for whom they feel genuine affection. Griselda is ordered to
prepare the rooms for the Marquis' new bride, and she dutifully does
so. But when the new bride is to be brought in, the Marquis explains
that he has returned Griselda's children to her and the trial of her
fidelity is revealed at last. Griselda swoons, but is revived and the dramatic poem ends with the suggestion of a happy life thereafter.
Tennyson's Enid, in the *Idylls of the King*, is another Griselda type,
though she is properly assertive.[15]

Admiration for the long-suffering and faithful wife is demonstrated
in Edward Fitzgerald's letters where he praises the patience of the
painter Romney's wife and her gentle forgiveness in tending the man
who had earlier abused her when he is ill and dying. "This quiet act
of hers is worth all Romney's pictures! even as a matter of Art, I am
sure."[16]

For writers such as Charlotte Brontë, the conventional Griselda
figure served not as a model for behavior, but as a target of criticism.
Crimsworth, in *The Professor* (1857, published posthumously), says
admiringly of his self-sufficient wife, "I see you would have made no
patient Grizzle." (ch. 25) Trollope went so far as to offer, in addition
to the conventional type, a mocking contrast to it in his unsaintly
portrait of Griselda Grantley. Most men were probably just as much
deceived as Mr. Raggles, the miserly character in Robert Bell's *Ladder of Gold* (1850), who "confidently believed that he had married a
patient Grisel, whose voice would never be heard in the house, who
would tread the stairs like a mouse, do exactly as she was desired, and
never interfere with his business." (Vol. 1, book 1, ch. 3) When he
discovers his error, Raggles frightens his wife into an approximation
of the behavior he desires.

Women did not accept the conventional role easily. In Trollope's *He Knew He Was Right* (1868-69), Nora Rowley and Dorothy Stanbury are contrasted with several imperious women, but notably Nora's sister, Emily. Early in the novel, the two sisters have a dispute. Emily feels that it is crude and unreasonable of her husband, Louis Trevelyan, to demand that a certain Colonel Osborne discontinue his visits. Nora, deploring Louis' intemperate sentiments, still advises conjugal submission. Emily's response is abrupt and revealing:

> "And to endure any insult and any names? You yourself,—you would be a Griselda, I suppose."
> "I don't want to talk about myself," said Nora, "nor about Griselda. But I know that, however unreasonable it may seem, you had better give way to him now and tell him what there was in the note to Colonel Osborne." (ch. 11)

Nora no more wishes to be Griselda than did Emma Grandby or Mary Douglas. They all wish, instead, to be reasonable women, capable of demonstrating satisfactorily their respect and love for their mates, without having to endure the incredible trials that were Griselda's share.

It remained for one of the greatest ironists of the age to present the most telling twist upon the convention. In *The Egoist* (1879), George Meredith explains that when an Egoist is jealous, a woman "must be sculptured Griselda with him not in her soul to suffer the change" from saintly to murderous, so unendurable is male egoism. (ch. 23) Only by assuming and believing in the role of the obedient Griselda, Meredith says, can a woman save her own soul and keep herself from the rages that male egoism would otherwise engender. Nonetheless, the nineteenth-century Griselda may not be all she seems. Lady Busshe may exclaim over Laetitia Dale, who has come, after long years of admiration, to the point where she seems to have won Sir Willoughby Patterne's love: "I love to see a long and faithful attachment rewarded—love it! Her tale is the triumph of patience. Far above Grizzel!" (ch. 45) But Laetitia will be no saintly Griselda, nor has her patience been resignedly accepted. Sir Willoughby proposes to her out of desperate vanity, and she accepts from weariness. Sir Willoughby has lost Clara Middleton, the beauty, but "he had the lady with brains! He had; and he was to learn the nature of that possession in the woman who is our wife." (ch. 49) Patient Griselda will prove more imposing than any bold harridan might have seemed before. The toughness she has learned in her trials has given her a strength unknown to her vain wooer. And with her triumph there comes no love, but only a weary attempt at respect.

In this picture of the fatigued Griselda, Meredith indicated the falseness of the conventional image. His is only one of many such indications, for, from the very outset of the century, there had run a mocking strain to counteract the appearance of the conventional type in the literature of the Victorian period. Women may have been obedient and reticent, for the laws which put them totally under the control of their husbands, who managed their money and determined the lives of their children, left them little alternative. But this did not mean that the patient endurance of suffering was an existence that the majority of Victorian women could applaud. Throughout the century, the two images of the Griselda and her more canny opposite conflicted. In the end, the convention died of mocking laughter.

DESTRUCTIVE WOMEN

Destructive females in Victorian literature are generally motivated by pride or physical passion. Rosa Dartle is one such potentially malign figure, only aggressive because of her unrequited passion for Steerforth; but she is only a miniature. Trollope's Madeline Neroni, in *Barchester Towers*, clearly the vain seductress, is drawn in a comic manner—the limits of her enticements being established by her invalidism, itself constituting a kind of poetic justice as the consequence of her misdirected passion.[17] Miss Wade, in *Little Dorrit*, is a clear example of the Judith figure. Abandonment by Henry Gowan is the specific cause for her hatred of men, but its first cause is her own self-conscious pride. Like the jilted Miss Havisham, she attempts to eradicate her subtler feminine qualities in favor of peremptory power.

Man-destroying women are frequently and quite naturally presented as handsome, but their beauty has a peculiar quality. Lady Caroline Caversham in Samuel Warren's *Ten Thousand A-Year* "seems the exquisite but frigid production of a skilful statuary." (Vol. 1, ch. 8) Lady Roseville in Bulwer-Lytton's *Pelham* is "stately and Juno-like" (ch. 52), and Blanche Ingram in *Jane Eyre* appears as a "type of majesty" who is clearly self-involved and proud. In the charades performed at Rochester's home, she suggests the idea of "some Israelitish princess of the patriarchal days," and, although she is playing Rebecca at the well, the identification with the Old Testament Israelitish princesses hints also at other commanding females such as Judith and Jael. Although they usually exhibit astounding beauty, it is really abrupt masculinity that characterizes these conventional types. Charles Reade made an apparently conscious attempt to revise or modify the masculine woman in the aggressive females of *Hard Cash*, and more noticeably with Jael Dence in *Put Yourself in His Place*, whose threatening name indicates her physical power but belies the gentleness of her heart.[18]

Edith Dombey is a superb Judith emblem, though she is not described in those terms. She is proud and scornful of men, whose attentions she considers degrading. Unlike some Judith types, she is not moved by physical passion, though she is capable of a genuine, and conspicuously futile, maternal love for Florence Dombey. Hers is a cold, stern pride. Her beauty is mortgaged for material advantages, from which, as she has foreseen, she derives no pleasure. Her effect upon the men who pursue her is tantamount to emasculation. That Dickens saw her as a Judith figure, is evident enough despite the small number of allusions in the novel. At one point in *Dombey and Son* (1846-48), Dickens describes a prominently displayed picture in Carker's home. "Perhaps it is a Juno; perhaps a Potiphar's Wife; perhaps some scornful Nymph," but, in any case, the "supremely handsome" figure with the "proud glance," is "like Edith." (ch. 33) "Juno," of course, was a byword for the authority-usurping female, while "Potiphar's Wife" suggests both conjugal betrayal and destruction. But the picture, which is a type of Edith, is *any* "scornful Nymph." It could be a Judith or Salome. It is not the *name*, but the *type* that is significant; Juno and Potiphar's Wife were not passive scornful nymphs; they were aggressors. So too is Edith.

The culminating demonstration of her Judith-like attributes is the scene in Dijon where Edith tells Carker that she is deserting him. Her behavior is sufficient to designate her a true Judith emblem, but the task is simplified by a glance at the illustration, "Mr. Carker in his moment of triumph," that Hablot K. Browne provided for the scene. The posture of the two figures is highly suggestive of an emasculatory act. Edith's arm, extended toward Carker in a gesture of contempt, aims directly between his legs which spread laxly apart in a scarcely disguised posture of vulnerability. It is far more interesting, however, to follow the line of Edith's arm back to the impelling loci of the illustration. Directly behind Edith, balancing the line of her extended arm, is a statuette of an Amazon on horseback about to spear a fallen enemy. More interesting yet, following the arc of Edith's arm upward along her proudly raised head, one's eye strikes abruptly against the painting of Judith at the bed of Holofernes, the sword with which her deed is to be accomplished prominently evident in her hand. More provocatively, the Judith of the painting, by way of her downward-pointing sword, forces the eye back toward Edith. It is hard to ignore the suggestion that the painted Judith is pointing her sword at Edith in the same fashion that Edith directs her ominous gesture toward Carker. The Amazon's dart, moreover, could well be destined for the fallen combatant, but is just as conceivably directed at Edith herself. Such pictorial evidence testifies that the masculine, almost heroic impulses which furnish Edith with the power to "destroy" Carker and Dombey, are equally destructive to herself. When the ruinous act is over, Edith is faced with her own despair. She is like so many other Judiths, childless, though she craves Florence's love. And she is aware of her own incompleteness. Violating her true womanhood through pride in a society that values the virtue and obedience of women may provide a woman with temporary power, but ultimately, having thus betrayed her womanhood, she must suffer. The Amazon's weapon maims the maimer.

Hawthorne made a similar observation of the character of the man-destroying woman in *The Marble Faun* (1860). His novel provides a clearer and more profound observation of the conventional type, and it too is presented in pictorial terms. While visiting Miriam's studio, Donatello indifferently browses through some of the artist's sketches. The first sketch represents "Jael driving the nail through the temples of Sisera," and it is done with such force that it is as though Miriam "herself were Jael, and felt irresistibly impelled to make her bloody confession in this guise." The pattern of the drawing prefigures Miriam's own history, for, although at first "the conception of the stern Jewess had evidently been that of perfect womanhood, a lovely form, and a high, heroic face of lofty beauty," ultimately Miriam "converted the heroine into a vulgar murderess." (ch. 5) The same progression from noble to vulgar asserts itself in another sketch, "the story of Judith," in which Holofernes' decapitated head grins with "triumphant malice" at the surprised Judith. In the sketch representing "the daughter of Herodias receiving the head of John the Baptist in a charger," Miriam had "imparted to the saint's face a look of gentle and heavenly reproach," by the force of which Salome's "whole womanhood was at once awakened to love and endless remorse." In each representation, Miriam "failed not to bring out the moral, that woman must strike through her own heart to reach a human life, whatever were the motives that impelled her." (ch. 5)

Hawthorne's "Judith," in her pride, arrogance, and eventual misery, resembles a simple character such as Flora Bellasys. But Miriam offers an explanation for the self-destructiveness of the man-destroyer. Only after her critical act, which she undertakes in a proud, noble, even heroic manner, does she discover her error; only then, in conscience's glance—whether of malice or gentle reproach—does she realize that her act is in some obscure way an expression of her own incompleteness and disharmony. Only beyond reprieve is "her whole womanhood" at once awakened. Her arrogant aggression manufactures misery as inevitably as self-love harvests a loveless self. To assume the masculine, aggressive role is to violate her true womanhood, for, to Victorians, woman is not naturally aggressive, and if she insists on aggression, she "must strike through her own heart to reach a human life."

Hawthorne's saint is not so excitingly complex as his Judith. Hilda is a virgin preserved by virtue, humility, selflessness, and generosity. She is Susannah, Saint Elizabeth, and Griselda in one. Ultimately she leaves her "Virgin's shrine" to be herself "enshrined and worshipped as a household saint, in the light of her husband's fireside." (ch. 50) While the unwomanly Judith suffers a crippled femininity, the wholesome saint achieves the blessing of wedlock, and what is more, the opportunity to expand her goodness to the responsibility and joy of motherhood. We have already observed that Judiths are not child-bearers.

It is also worth observing that quite often Judith figures are seen not only emblematically, but pictorially. Though there was a long-established artistic tradition employing Judiths and Salomes, there were also recent well-known representations of the types such as William Etty's Judith trilogy and Moreau's Salome.[19] That the Judith emblem should be pictorially conceived is in keeping with the sensuous qualities of the female type representing usurped mastery fla-

vored with the sharpest delights of a sensory world. Physical beauty
and luxuriousness are persistent attributes of the Judith figure; hence
to offer the emblem in the fixed and iconographic form of a painting
or illustration is to duplicate and reinforce the intensity of the initial
image.[20] Pictorial association is evident in Trollope's *The Last Chronicle of Barset* (1867), where the Judith figure is used in a more subtle
fashion. In this novel, Conway Dalrymple, an artist, meets Clara Van
Siever at the home of Mr. and Mrs. Dobbs Broughton. His response
prepares us for a conventional emblematic figure:

> Dalrymple, when he saw her, recoiled from her, not outwardly, but in-
> wardly. Yes, she was handsome, as may be a horse or a tiger; but there
> was about her nothing of feminine softness. He could not bring himself
> to think of taking Clara Van Siever as the model that was to sit be-
> fore him for the rest of his life. He certainly could make a picture of
> her, as had been suggested by his friend, Mrs. Broughton, but it must
> be as Judith with the dissevered head, or as Jael using her hammer over
> the temple of Sisera. (ch. 24)

But our expectations are slyly disappointed, for while Clara models
for Dalrymple's painting of Jael, a significant alteration takes place,
revealing her truly feminine qualities to the artist. Clara directs her
strong will not against Dalrymple, but against her far more arrogant
and demanding mother, who wishes to force her into an undesirable
marriage. Clara's flashing eye and masculine self-will are utilized in
the defense of her feminine prerogatives, not in opposition to the prerogatives of men. Strength of character is combined with a loving
nature—cautiously but undeniably revealed—to compose a figure with
Judith's pride and passion as well as the modern Griselda's reasoned
obedience and affection. Furthermore, while Clara acts the part of
Jael in costume only, Mrs. Dobbs Broughton assumes a more authentic role as Potiphar's Wife, for she feels more than friendship toward
Dalrymple. It is this contrast between the true spirit in the guise of
destructiveness, and destructiveness in the guise of cordiality, that
determines Dalrymple's permanent image of Clara. At the moment
when his love for Clara becomes an open affection, he willingly destroys the painting of her in Jael's posture. Clara ceases to be a man-
destroyer, even potentially, and becomes Dalrymple's helpmate.
Thackeray's irony was to have Becky Sharp willingly choose, in mundane existence, the very role that she fulfilled in a greater moral de-

sign; Trollope's is to hint this much and then show us that we are wrong. It is worth recalling that it is Dalrymple who sees Clara as Jael, not Clara herself. The imposed emblematic function proves false, and Trollope gains an interesting vitality in his novel by the ironic mutation of a familiar convention.

Trollope might easily have derived the notion for his Jael from his acknowledged master, Thackeray, for there is a similar attempt in *The Newcomes* (1854-55) to combine the attributes of Judith and Griselda. Clive Newcome, like Dalrymple, is an artist, and his reflections on Ethel take a pictorial form.

> "She would do for Judith, wouldn't she? Or how grand she would look as Herodias's daughter sweeping down a stair—in a great dress of cloth of gold like Paul Veronese—holding a charger before her with white arms, you know—with the muscles accented like that glorious Diana at Paris—a savage smile on her face and a ghastly, solemn, gory head on the dish—I see the picture, sir, I see the picture!" (Vol. 1, ch. 25)

Ethel is, indeed, haughty, handsome, and scornful in her youth. But a sequence of misfortunes alters her nature dramatically, and the once arrogantly destructive Judith-Salome becomes a mild and selfless Griselda or Saint Elizabeth, assisting the poor and the infirm. Although Thackeray refuses to stipulate the conclusion to his novel, he leaves us free to suppose that Clive does marry Ethel and convert her benevolence into a domestic sainthood under his protection.

It is evident then that although Thackeray exploited the same stylization as his contemporaries, he often went beyond them in ironic utilization. In *Vanity Fair* (1847-48), for example, there can be little doubt that Becky Sharp, who chooses for herself the role of Clytemnestra, is the destructive woman represented elsewhere by Flora Bellasys or Edith Dombey. However, she is scarcely the same simply destructive type common in the literature of the period; nor is her punishment of the same magnitude as theirs. While manipulating his Clytemnestra in a detached, amused fashion, and suggesting that all men are puppets acting out the same familiar pilgrimage, Thackeray hinted as well that although we presume to elect our roles (even to fulfilling of Clytemnestrian vices), we never escape the designations of an over-arching moral drama. Amelia Sedley may have the trappings of the conventional nineteenth-century secular saint, but there has been some tampering with the mundane hagiology, for Amelia is no more saint than Becky is Satan. Both play roles only partially self-elected; primarily they enact schemes prepared for them as much by the enduring moral patterns of human existence as by the conscious artist who borrowed the title of his novel from one of the most famous schematizations of an eternal pattern.

Thackeray's characters, while approximating stylized roles in an ideal drama, remain human beings, and it is through the disparity between emblematic and human qualities in his characters that Thackeray gains his most savory effect. Our first impression is of puppets brought to life; but the puppets having elected roles themselves, our greater shock is to witness the types resume human qualities. Thackeray's characters have their homely adventures, while behind them move the shadowy emblems in their idealized design, infrequently exhibiting malign or lovely features, like Becky in her murderous guise peering from behind the draperies at the terrified Jos Sedley in Thackeray's own illustration. Thackeray does not wish us to forget, despite the verisimilitude of his style, that there is, beyond the recognizable surface reality, what we may call the super-reality of moral values. The novels demonstrate moral designs not because they require a structure, but because Thackeray himself supposed a moral order which any faithful "history" would necessarily acknowledge.

There are odd instances where the Judith emblem is not fixed and static. A curious dynamics of female aggressiveness occurs in *Great Expectations* (1860-61), when Estella, the most characteristic Judith, is prompted—indifferently now—by pride. Mrs. Gargery is the first domineering female we meet, but she is soon overshadowed by Miss Havisham, who, in turn, is softened proportionally to Estella's waxing heartlessness. All the while, behind these civilly aggressive women, is the wild spectre of Molly, to whose powerful hands Jaggers so ominously calls his guests' attention. This accumulation of female power is counterbalanced by two saintly characters, Clara Barley and Biddy. In the original version of the story, all of the destructive women suffer miserable fates, while the Griselda-like domestic saints find the harmony that their enduring characters merit. But in Dickens' revised version, even Judith, in the guise of Estella, is spared, and the unattainable star is attained. Salome improbably renovates her chastened saint, and the moral design loses its intended force to satisfy an equally insistent convention of sentimental reward.

There is a similar dynamism of quasi-Judiths in Trollope's *He Knew He Was Right* (1868-69). First the reader encounters Emily

Trevelyan, the proudly rebellious wife; but as she retires to impatient discomfort, the role of female tyrant is assumed by Aunt Stanbury who is referred to as the "Juno of the Close." Aunt Stanbury, however, is not the stern woman she seems, and the role shifts to Priscilla Stanbury, who distrusts men and is determined to remain a spinster. As she too proves relatively amiable, the role is transferred to Camilla French, who "was a Medea in spirit." Even she grows tame and Wallachie Petrie, the ludicrous American Republican, assumes the aggressive role. By thus displacing the female energy of his novel, Trollope gradually transfers the unwomanly attributes from a serious to a preposterous level. Emily Trevelyan's obstinacy is converted to a genuine concern for the husband she has injured, and she herself becomes the Griselda-like woman she earlier mocked to her sister Nora, the authentic modern domestic saint. Moreover, she represents domestic sanctity in contrast to the absurdly Judith-like Wallachie Petrie. Emily is not only a Judith reformed, but an exemplary anti-Judith as well.

Emily Trevelyan, in her growth from Judith to saint, is very similar to the reformed Griselda Bolingbroke. Such a transformation suggests that while most authors continued to use these emblems as simple indicators within their moral designs, others wished to unite them, creating the union of womanhood that was neither militant nor sentimental, but gentle and self-assured, like the estimable Emma Grandby who had offered her example at the century's outset.

We have already observed this conscious intent in Trollope and Thackeray, but an earlier and more stylized version of the approach occurred in Tennyson's *The Princess* (1847). In that poem, Florian spies on Ida's court from a delightfully appropriate position:

> Arriving all confused among the rest
> With hooded brows I crept into the hall,
> And, couched behind a Judith, underneath
> The head of Holofernes peeped and saw.

(IV)

Judith, for Ida's disciples, is one type of perfect womanhood, and under the threat of retributive power against men, they conduct their education and their justice. But Tennyson's poem implies that Judith is no fit emblem for womanhood—at least not in Victorian England. Princess Ida herself illustrates the dilemma. The Prince views her "highest, among the statues, statue-like, / Between a cymbal'd Miriam and a Jael," but in her hands she holds Psyche's baby. Her appearance is "Like a Saint's glory," but she is "No saint—inexorable—no tenderness— / Too hard, too cruel." (V) Ida, through the acknowledgement of her own womanly inclinations, frees herself from voluntary bondage between masculine Miriams and Jaels to become the saint she has the power to be. It is her discovery that love and motherhood, not power and pride, constitute feminine harmony that liberates her and brings her joy. Yet her ambition was not wholly wrong, for though a woman should be no Judith, Miriam, nor Jael, she should learn a portion of that independence of spirit that these emblems signify in the extreme. Tennyson's recommendation, when Prince and Princess finally unite, is that "the man be more of woman, she of man." (VII)

The conventional Victorian attitude toward women was expressed by Robert Bell in *The Ladder of Gold* (1850), when he wrote that "Stern and obdurate strength is not the finest characteristic of women; they are most strong and most lovable in their weakness. In this aspect we discern their humanity, which brings them nearer to our sympathies; and even their errors and failures add a grace to our devotion by leaving something for our magnanimity to forgive." (Vol. 2, book 4, ch. 6) It was against over-simplified and condescending notions of this kind that Tennyson was reacting, and which Kingsley likewise deplored. In *Yeast* (1848-49), Kingsley praised Tennyson's poem and gave his own approval of a certain masculinity in women. He too wished to see women acquire some of the intellectual and practical strength of men. It was a question of finding the proper balance between Judith and Griselda. Women themselves had reservations, and George Meredith imaged one of them in the character of the active Vittoria in his novel of that name. "She asked herself whether a woman who has cast her lot in scenes of strife does not lose much of her womanhood and something of her truth; and while her imagination remained depressed, her answer was said." (ch. 34)

Meredith's Rhoda Fleming is likened to Rachel, to the Queen of Egyptians, to Medusa, and to Judith. She is described as resembling a woman of the East, or a gypsy, and is strong as a male. And yet, Meredith clearly approves of her once she tames her own spirited nature. And Judith Marsett, in *One of Our Conquerors* (1891), acknowledging her adultery, is unhappy with the role she finds herself playing. "I did something in Scripture. Judith could again," she says, and exclaims, "I loathe my name; I want to do things." (ch. 28) The potentially destructive woman now has become aware of her resemblance to Judith and the long tradition of man-destroying women. But there is an eagerness even here to resist the impulse to destroy.

Perhaps part of women's confusion was in the traditional assigning of contradictory roles, described by Hazel Mews in *Frail Vessels*. Women were viewed both as tempting sirens and holy virgins. At times the conventional roles did not seem to serve. Carlyle, in indicating the lapse of greatness in his own times, declared that even great potentialities of character were easily lost in modern times. Speaking of a famous murder case of the Victorian period, he wrote: "A Mrs. Manning 'dying game,'—alas, is not that the foiled potentiality of a kind of heroine too? Not a heroic Judith, not a mother of the Gracchi now, but a hideous murderess, fit to be the mother of hyaenas! To such an extent can potentialities be foiled."[21] Perhaps the answer to it all is that the heroism of the past has no place in modern society. The Victorian world, its spokesmen might argue, required no Judiths, Jaels or Miriams. They required instead the gentler models of Griselda, or Saint Elizabeth. The problems of the age were not military, but domestic. Clearly most Victorians felt that women were better off out of the man's world which was less heroic than it was sordid. Thackeray's *The Adventures of Philip* (1861-62) illustrates the irony of the Biblical model. A drawing entitled "Judith and Holofernes" merely shows a woman in ordinary Victorian dress holding a handkerchief of chloroform over the face of a man, also in ordinary dress. Only the title suggests the nature of her act, which is scarcely so permanent as the original Judith's. John Cordy Jeaffreson's popular novel of 1872, *A Woman in Spite of Herself*, relates how a woman in masquerade as a man learns to be a woman again through subjecting herself to the love of a man. The next step beyond assuming a man's role is to become a man. It is that transformation that reveals the falseness of the aspiration to freedom, control and power. Judiths lose more than they gain. Their reward, most writers indicate, is pain.

If earlier in the century, Thackeray and Dickens conceived of their characters as performing parts in a larger moral design, for Thomas Hardy, characters became pawns in a great design that was either indifferently fortuitous or cruel. And this pattern is of all ages, as Hardy's allusions indicate. Eustacia Vye, in *The Return of the Na-*

tive (1878), is never called a Judith, but her aggressive qualities are suggested by similes comparing her to the Witch of Endor, or one of several pagan divinities. Her masculinity is suggested by identifications with Ahasuerus and Judas, as well as by her taste in children's names. "Had she been a mother she would have christened her boys such names as Saul or Sisera in preference to Jacob or David, neither of whom she admired." Her potentially murderous nature is implied in an equation with Candaules' wife, and Hardy judges at one point that in heaven Eustacia "will probably sit between the Heloïses and the Cleopatras." (Book 1, ch. 7)

Although Eustacia is just as beautiful, proud, and destructive as Edith Dombey, Flora Bellasys, or Annabella Lowborough, and plays Salome to Wildeve, and more metaphorically to Clym Yeobright, "a John the Baptist who took ennoblement rather than repentance for his text" (Book 3, ch. 2) (and who ironically outlives his Salome), she is different from earlier Judith figures. In other emblems, there is a suggestion that the characters, possessed of believable personalities as many are, are yet figures operating under the necessity of a moral design within the work of art. With Hardy, the work of art achieves its form through the rehearsing of causation and chance in human affairs. Eustacia is as helpless in the grip of her passions as Wildeve and Clym. Familiar patterns of moral values emerge in the novel, but the characters are less figures of a moral scheme than victims of existence itself. Hardy had planned that virtue should not be rewarded in this novel, but was unable to resist the pressures of popular convention and finally allowed Diggory Venn to win the Griselda-like Thomasin Yeobright. Here and in other novels, Hardy was inclined, not to reward, but to violate the conventional assumption of a moral design.

Hardy sought to portray his Judith figure in terms less strict than moral designs customarily allowed. For the strictness of the moral design, he substituted chance and the necessities of human fate. Eustacia is conventionally proud and passionate, plays the aggressor, and suffers a hard fate; but it is not the same stylization. Edith Dombey elected her role, as, in a far more obvious way, did Becky Sharp. But Eustacia has no real choice. Ironically, the role she performs in the ancient "Saint George" play that the mummers present, is that of a heathen destroyed by a Christian crusader. In reality, it is not a moral anticipation that requires Eustacia's death—as it is for the heathen in the play—but the consequences of existence itself. The simple and neat moralism of the day within the novel is consciously revoked by the crude moral of "reality."

Hardy seems to have been acidly aware of these conventions. At the end of the century, when other writers were describing new Saint Theresas or Elizabeths, Hardy offered fragmented protagonists like Eustacia Vye or Sue Bridehead. His female figures are not situated between Griselda and Judith, but between marginal types like Hel-oïse and Cleopatra, or saint and pagan. Hardy still had the conventional associations in mind when he equated Jude and Arabella with Samson and Delilah. But the scheme of *Jude the Obscure* (1895), exploiting the usual expectations, is stubbornly incomplete in moral terms.[22] It is a baffled Christian design which derives much of its vigor from the fact that it so closely parallels, yet so rudely and ironically offends, the customary design. Sue is both pagan and saint, but Hardy has her fail at both roles because she is a woman. The psychological reality breaks through prescriptive moral design, leaving the design of art, but in so doing it presupposes the very scheme it violates. Hardy's approach is possible because the conventions he attacked were so familiar.

Use of the Judith emblem continued throughout the Victorian period, though with different writers it took different forms, from the direct to the ironic. Moreover, there seems to have been a growing self-consciousness regarding the use of emblems, until at the end of the century a more forthright yet complicated attitude prevailed. The saint is named and openly transmuted by George Eliot and Mrs. Humphry Ward, while Judith figures become, with Hardy, destiny-driven victims themselves. The characters have become psychologically more recognizable in terms of our present concepts of personality. In Lord de Tabley's poem, "Jael," the heroine's supposedly noble act is, characteristically, occasioned by personal ambition and vanity. The consequence for Jael is a life of intense remorse. Lord de Tabley, through the device of poetic monologue, creates a "realistic" Jael, but the very fact that he selects this conventional representative of the mischance of female mastery, reinforces her emblematic significance.

Another, more artful method of utilizing the destructive or saintly type emerges near the end of the century. Heroines in Dowson's short stories, for example, actually become nuns and saintliness is no longer domestic, but cloistered. The saints, too, remain childless now. And the man-destroyers are no longer singly disastrous. Writers were adopting Swinburne's vision of the archetypal destructive woman.[23] In Arthur Symons' "Dance of the Daughters of Herodias," women are described as "the eternal enemy." Yet they are not to be punished for the havoc they wreak among men, "For beauty is still beauty, though it slay, / And love is love, although it love to death."

Oscar Wilde's *Salomé* (1892, English edition 1894) is a superb example of the use of the emblem late in the century, for here, though Salomé preserves the unexplained lustful motives of a Flora Bellasys, there is no attempt to make her psychologically or even fictionally "real." She is a type, and frankly recognized as such; accordingly, her declarations are not by innuendo, but are direct. "Jokanaan," she pronounces, "I am amorous of thy body!" Salomé is still a man-destroyer and arrogant lover of the things of this world who wounds herself by her own destructive impulse. At the end of the play she is still the scorned woman, still in love with the dead scorner, and vainly craving him still. But Wilde's emblem no longer functions in a larger moral design. Now the artist focusses on the emblem itself and makes of it another kind of design. Similarly, in Arthur W. E. O'Shaughnessy's poem, "The Daughter of Herodias," the conflict of saintliness and evil is highly concentrated in the figures of John and Salomé and is so simplified as to become merely a dialogue representing the emblematic contention of flesh and spirit.[24]

The stylized language in Wilde's *Salomé* also dissuades us from taking Salomé as a real human being. Instead, the total composition is the lesson. It is a method totally different from Kingsley's *The Saint's Tragedy*, where characters, though types, have a surface reality as well; and where the characters, not the design of the work, convey the moral import. Wilde's highly stylized drama isolates a single emblem, elaborating it in the way that a gem is elaborated by ornamental cuttings. His Salomé no longer contends with a saintly female counterpart, for, as with O'Shaughnessy's types, she and her victim are magnifications of all human nature, and she is the principle of undisciplined self-indulgence which destroys what it only seems to love, unveiling murder as self-amputation. Ironically, as the emblem becomes more obviously stylized, displaced, and elaborated, it helps the reader to discover notions of human behavior far more "realistic," as we now believe, than those suggested by the so apparently real mid-Victorian heroines.

Destructive women in Victorian literature are signalled primarily by Old Testament and classical allusions, while good women are compared to medieval personages. At the end of the century, the separation is fiercer still—barbaric women oppose saints or even the Virgin Mary. Although there were worthy and noble suffering women in the Old Testament such as Rachel or Deborah, its Hebraic atmosphere was, like the pagan climate of Greek and Roman literature, too harsh for Victorian ideals of women, though it furnished satisfactory masculine models and admirable moral paradigms. Where the Old Testament is not polygamous, it is suspiciously liberal. There are too many Miriams, Judiths, Jaels, Jezebels, and Shebas for a sensitively authoritarian gentleman to feel comfortable. The New Testament, though expressing a suitably milder morality, offered few striking women as models, except the sinning Salome or Magdalene and the exalted Mary. Victorian writers preferred to take their types of female virtue from the Middle Ages, which, for many people in the nineteenth century, represented an age of faith and security. Moreover, for Victorians, inspired by concepts of progress, virtuous models might be most suitably drawn from relatively recent historical times.

I have suggested, particularly while describing Tennyson's *The Princess*, that the Judith emblem was associated in Victorian minds with the unwomanly assumption of power by women who violate their true natures and thereby inaugurate their own despair. If women are believed to be constitutionally tender and palliative, Amazonian traits become pernicious to men, whose roles they disrupt, but also to women, whose established natures they contradict. But, while theories of character and personality altered, becoming both more behaviorist and more internally dynamic, women were more freely asserting their equality with men as human beings and denying outmoded stipulations about female nature. Intensified arguments for emancipation assumed that women were not "naturally" destined to fulfill saintly domestic roles, but might become active Saint Joans. Ibsen's women were to change markedly certain types of literary representations. Foreseeably, as women pleaded for equality with men, certain literary representations became more destructive; every breach of "real" feminine nature required a more serious punishment, and authority in women appeared savage and satanic.

It is a commonplace about Victorian society that values of the home were distinct from values of the thoroughfare, and that, while a man might marry for comfort, his passions drove him elsewhere for pleasure. This form of double standard, insofar as it was true, very likely helped to promote objections in fiction and poetry to loveless marriages. This same double standard also conveys meaning to the stylized opposition of Judiths and Griseldas. Carnality attends the Judith figures, evilly clothed in seductive graces, while saintly fiancées and wives have only a pure beauty and virtue to aid them. The desire to combine the seductive and saintly could easily lead to the fabrication of fictional types embodying both physical energy and saintly virtue. Literary emblems, in their various and subtle forms, though conventions in a public tradition, might also participate in an individual preference. Behind the admiration of a Clara Van Siever or a Princess Ida could be the yearning for an aggressive yet womanly companion. On the other hand, the tendency to separate sensuous sinners and spiritual saints, between whom a hero inevitably suffers, might indicate a curiously ambivalent readiness to accept the reduction of masculinity to servile and humiliating postures so long as ultimate redemption is available. This attitude might culminate in the peculiarly abject misogyny not unknown at the end of the century, or the subtler expressions of masculine abasement which Beardsley's punitive females constitute. And if one were to seek for the passion of a Judith, combined with the yielding saintliness of a Griselda, there remained only one major type wherein these two figures might be combined. That figure was the Magdalene, and, more particularly, the Magdalene redeemed.

THE MAGDALENE, OR FALLEN WOMAN

The Victorians were at no time unaware of their fallen sisters, as Steven Marcus' *The Other Victorians* and Brian Harrison's review of that book in *Victorian Studies* for March 1967 make clear. These works offer a better introduction to the subject of the fallen woman in nineteenth-century society than more specific books such as Martin Seymour-Smith's *Fallen Women: A Sceptical Enquiry into the Treatment of Prostitutes, their Clients and their Pimps, in Literature.*

Studies such as Michael Ryan's *Prostitution in London* (1839), William Acton's *Prostitution Considered in its Moral, Social and Sanitary Aspect* (1857), and Bracebridge Hemyng's information on London prostitution in Mayhew's *London Labour and the London Poor* in 1861 helped to make the problem fully public. In their usual typological manner, the Victorians referred to prostitutes as Magdalens. Refuges for prostitutes were called Magdalen homes, evangelical reformers published a periodical called the *Magdalen's Friend*, and William Tait wrote a study of Edinburgh prostitution entitled *Magdalenism* (1840). One of the most famous Regency prostitutes, Harriete Wilson, wrote to Bulwer-Lytton that she was *"rechristened Mary Magdalen* by my own desire at the Catholic Confirmation."[25] There was a good deal of social concern about the problem of prostitution. Tennyson wrote in "Locksley Hall Sixty Years After": "Crime and hunger cast our maidens by the thousands on the street." And many notable figures in Victorian society eagerly sought to assist these women to reformed lives—among them such men as Dickens, Gladstone, and W. T. Stead.

The prostitute and the fallen woman were not necessarily one and the same, though most popular literature tended to equate loss of virtue with moral corruption. In Hannah Maria Jones' *The Gipsey Girl* (1836-37), Eva St. Juan is seduced and abandoned by Herbert Walsingham. She lives among gypsies in a debased state and wreaks revenge on her corrupter, but is later destroyed herself. T. P. Prest, in *The Gipsy Boy*, describes Laurence Cleveland's seduction of his sister-in-law who consequently follows the traditional route from beggary to prostitution the workhouse and finally the gutter. Meanwhile, Clara, the betrayed wife, yields to temptation because of her unfaithful husband's suspicions. That these fallen women are associated with gypsies and the outcast life shows that fallen women were inevitably classed among the aliens of society. The gypsies simply add a touch of mystery and exoticism.[26]

Clearly society expressed little open sympathy for the fallen woman. And yet throughout the nineteenth century there was a contrary impetus which strove to establish a basis of sympathy for those who had sinned against purity. In Thomas DeQuincey's fable, "The Daughter of Lebanon," one of the Evangelists meets a fallen woman and offers to help her. The one thing she craves is to be able to go home. "Lord, that thou wouldest put me back into my father's house," she cries. The beautiful lady's history is a catalog of the conventional nineteenth-century circumstances of outcast women, rather than an account of Biblical times. The Prophet-Evangelist promises the woman that she can go home, but the home to which she returns is a heavenly home. After her death, "the evangelist, with eyes glorified by mortal and immortal tears, rendered thanks to God that had thus accomplished the word which he spoke through himself to the Magdalen of Lebanon" and "put her back into her Father's house."

For DeQuincey, the burden of the woman's sin falls upon an unreasonable parent and a dishonorable lover. It is a crime of society, not of an individual. In his *English Social History*, G. M. Trevelyan observed that it was Victorian economic conditions and hypocrisy about sex that made prostitution so overwhelmingly common a feature of English life in the nineteenth century.[27] So Frances Trollope suggested in *Jessie Phillips: A Tale of the Present Day* (1844), in which a rural girl is seduced by the son of the squire. The rich, it is clear, are protected, while the poor suffer and are abandoned.[28] In his pseudonymously published satirical poem, *Stone Talk* (1865), Sir Richard Burton presented a crude and forceful picture of what poverty can lead to for those who remain unprotected. Seduction leads on to child-murder and prostitution, begging and thievery, "Till, when all foul resources fail, / She dies in Magdalen or jail."

Among the most famous of all pleas of sympathy for the fallen woman was Thomas Hood's poem, "The Bridge of Sighs" (1844), which was based upon an actual incident.[29] Hood's poem depicts the pathos of the kind of life that leads young women to commit suicide rather than face a lifetime of degradation. At the same time that it reinforced the notion that sin led to suffering and sorrow, it emphasized that these sufferers were fellow humans. "The dark arch" and "the black flowing river" at Waterloo Bridge, the haunt of suicides, are repeated frequently in Victorian literature of sexual disgrace, and George Cruikshank's powerful print of the suicide of the drunkard's prostitute daughter captures the wild agony with tremendous force.[30]

A growing number of writers dared to manifest sympathy for fallen women. Effie Dean in Scott's *The Heart of Midlothian* (1818) was an early example. John Clare's "A Maid's Tragedy" is another. In this poem, a ruined maid, driven from her father's home with her illegitimate child, dies in the cold night, having vainly pleaded for admission at her faithless lover's door. The poem is altogether conventional, but offers a genuine compassion. In the 1840s, protest against other social evils was reflected in suggestions that Magdalenes were not voluntary outsiders. J. A. Froude's *The Lieutenant's Daughter* (1847) presented a sympathetic and candid treatment of a prostitute heroine, and in Dickens' novels a wide variety of Magdalenes appeared. Nancy, in *Oliver Twist* (1838), has a kind heart despite her spoiled virtue. Alice Marwood, in *Dombey and Son* (1848), though vindictive and vengeful, ends her life hoping for salvation, thanks to the unprejudiced assistance of Harriet Carker. There are other fallen women in Dickens' novels, but perhaps the most memorable occur in *David Copperfield* (1850). Little Em'ly is the most familiar example of the innocent maiden seduced deceitfully. Her life is maimed, but, through the persevering love of her guardian, Mr. Peggoty, she is saved from a life of sin and taken to Australia to begin a new life. Her dreams of grandeur end in humble toil. But more striking, if less prominent in this novel, is the figure of Martha Endell. Hablot K. Browne's illustration, "Martha," summarizes the sympathetic approach that Dickens wished to convey. Martha, the corrupted girl, crouches on her knees beside a chair, while her well-wishers, including Em'ly, look on. None seeks to condemn her, and their generous sentiment harmonizes with the Christian spirit represented by the picture on the wall above Martha—a picture of Mary Magdalen at the feet of Christ. Even Martha's posture imitates Mary's. A similar forgiveness seems in order. And, as though to counterbalance the forgiveness recommended by the example of Christ, another picture almost obscured but hovering ominously behind Em'ly suggests why such forgiveness is necessary. The picture is of Eve being tempted by the serpent, a scene which clearly implies woman's ingrained weakness to temptation.

Women are born to weakness of the flesh, Dickens seems to suggest, thereby putting himself very much at one with prevailing notions of his time, though he does not agree that this weakness merits pitiless condemnation. Dickens reflected a common attitude as well in his depiction of the end to which fallen women normally come. Martha, poised at the foul river's edge seems "a part of the refuse it had cast out." (ch. 47) She is "a prostrate image of humiliation and ruin." Dickens cannot resist the obvious parallel between the soiled river and the soiled maid, and harks back to the convention of the ruined country girl.

> "I know it's like me!" she exclaimed. "I know that I belong to it. I know that it's the natural company of such as I am! It comes from country places, where there was once no harm in it—and it creeps through the dismal streets, defiled and miserable—and it goes away, like my life, to a great sea, that is always troubled—and I feel that I must go with it!" (ch. 47)

In keeping with Dickens' own sympathies, however, Martha is spared, and given another chance at a decent life. Thus, although Dickens utilized the convention, he turned its bitterest aspect to a more generous end, trying to indicate that although the conventional view was true, it required an ameliorating Christian response, rather than downright condemnation.

The theme of the fallen woman was a persistent one in public comment, poetry, fiction, and theatre, and found expression in other arts as well. Rossetti's "Jenny" was a notable example of the subject in poetry; he also dealt with it pictorially in "Found." Millais' "Virtue and Vice," Holman Hunt's "The Awakened Conscience," Frederick Walker's "The Lost Path," and Augustus Egg's sequence "Past and Present" further demonstrate that the theme was a common subject in art.[31]

The novel *Ruth* (1853) offers an interesting modification of the convention. Mrs. Gaskell had treated the subject of the fallen woman in the short tale, "Lizzie Leigh," where the heroine, having borne an illegitimate child, becomes a nurse, hoping in this way to find redemption. And the character of Esther, in *Mary Barton* (1848) is forceful, if conventional. But in *Ruth* Mrs. Gaskell sought to understand more deeply the consequences of female frailty. The plot develops conventionally—the innocent beauty ruined by a man of higher class. Ruth's suffering and shame become a means of purification actually providing her with a spiritual opportunity she might otherwise have lacked. Coventry Patmore had similarly consoled betrayed women in *The Angel In The House* when he wrote,

> Good is thy lot in its degree;
>   For hearts that verily repent

> Are burden'd with impunity
>> And comforted by chastisement.
> Sweet patience sanctify thy woes!
>> And doubt not but our God is just,
> Albeit unscath'd thy traitor goes,
>> And thou art stricken to the dust.

("The Betrothal," canto 10)

The kindly minister, Mr. Benson, argues with his hidebound parishoner, Mr. Bradshaw, "that not every woman who has fallen is depraved," and continues, "Is it not time to change some of our ways of thinking and acting? I declare before God, that if I believe in any one human truth, it is this—that to every woman, who, like Ruth, has sinned, should be given a chance of self-redemption—and that such a chance should be given in no supercilious or contemptuous manner, but in the spirit of the holy Christ." (ch. 27) Mr. Benson identifies Ruth with the repentant Mary Magdalen, as Ruth does herself, when, refusing to accept her lover's belated offer of marriage, she says, "The errors of my youth may be washed away by my tears—it was so once when the gentle, blessed Christ was upon earth." (ch. 24) Despite her early mistake, Ruth develops into a noble example of womanhood and Christian behavior. What is distinctive in the story, is that, when given the opportunity to marry her seducer, Ruth refuses. This was a bold and unconventional attitude indeed.[32]

Mrs. Gaskell was not the first to place the greater blame for sexual offense upon the man rather than the woman; and later, George Eliot argued that men were responsible for fallen women because they lacked self-control. Henry G. Jebb presented a similar argument in *Out of the Depths* (1859). In Charles Kingsley's *Yeast* (1848-49), Colonel Bracebridge betrays his mistress, Mary, but, acknowledging guilt, commits suicide when he learns of her baby's death. And Arthur Donnithorne in Eliot's *Adam Bede* (1859) lapses into profound melancholy after his seduction of Hetty Sorrell, who is spared execution for child-murder, though she is transported for her crime. In these novels and many others, male guilt is a prominent feature of the narrative. Ordinarily the sin was mutual. Though the young women may have been misled and behaved unwisely, they did willingly participate. There was, however, another manner of fall more disturbing to those who sympathized with the fallen. In Elizabeth Barrett

Browning's *Aurora Leigh* (1857), Marian Erle's "fall" is anything but voluntary. When Aurora first sees Marian carrying an infant, she suspects her immediately of indiscretion; later she is ashamed of her suspicion when Marian recounts her real experiences. Deceived by Lady Waldemar into leaving her suitor, Romney Leigh, Marian found herself in the hands of a vicious procuress, who drugged her and gave her into the hands of professional ravishers, who hoped to add her to their stable. Angrily, Marian declares, "man's violence, / Not man's seduction made me what I am." (Book 6)

Innocent though she may be, Marian remains guilty in the eyes of society and realizes that she is forbidden even to proclaim her wrong. But, as Mrs. Browning's poem itself demonstrates, more and more writers were willing not only to speak of such matters but to take sides as well. There was not, however, a shortage of voices protesting this outspokenness. Mrs. Oliphant was representative when she complained of Mrs. Henry Wood's *East Lynne* that a runaway wife was a poor choice for the heroine. "The Magdalen herself, who is only moderately interesting while she is good, becomes, as soon as she is a Magdalen, doubly a heroine." Mrs. Oliphant concluded that "Nothing can be more wrong and fatal than to represent the flames of vice as a purifying fiery ordeal, through which the penitent is to come elevated and sublime."[33]

MAGDALENE REDEEMED

Mrs. Oliphant's caution was not heeded. While the conventional figure of the Magdalene persisted, a new type of heroine emerged who fit Mrs. Oliphant's description exactly, having been purified by the flames of vice to become an elevated and sublime penitent. A good example of the Magdalene redeemed is Ellen Horton in Henry Kingsley's *Ravenshoe* (1861), who, repairing her collapsed virtue, retreats to a life of cloistered faith. But, repentance and all, the redemption is not complete. Although, in her nun's dress, "there was really something saint-like and romantic about her . . . there was no ring of glory round her head. Poor Ellen was only bearing the cross; she had not won the crown." (ch. 65) Ellen Horton does not fully achieve sainthood though she acquires all its trappings, but Meredith's Dahlia Fleming, whose suffering is more persuasively conveyed, does achieve a definite, if secular saintliness. Meredith was praised by one reviewer for treating this difficult subject without sermonizing or sentimentalism,[34] while another wrote,

> Dahlia is a true but sad picture of the sufferings of one who has gone astray from the paths of virtue, and excites the keenest pity and admiration in the reader—the former, because her sorrows and trials are told with such deep feeling; the latter, because the sketch is so painfully and vividly real.[35]

Dahlia's story is a familiar one. She is the proud and ambitious daughter of a prosperous farmer. This combination of ambition and passion leads her to elope with Edward Blancove the squire's son. First inclined to make their love legal, Edward hesitates and then abandons Dahlia. Later he returns to offer her marriage. Seeing Dahlia wasted by illness, Edward is moved "to make her his own, if only for the sake of making amends to this dear fair soul, whose picture of Saint was impressed on him." Dahlia has "come out of her martyrdom stamped with the heavenly sign-mark." (ch. 48) Edward is surprised when Dahlia, like Ruth before her, refuses to accept the offer of a man she no longer loves:

> There was but one answer for him; and when he ceased to charge her with unforgivingness, he came to the strange conclusion that beyond our calling of a woman a Saint for rhetorical purposes, and esteeming her as one for pictorial, it is indeed possible, as he had slightly discerned in this woman's presence, both to think her saintly and to have the sentiments inspired by the overearthly in her person. Her voice, her simple words of writing, her gentle resolve, all issuing of a capacity to suffer evil, and pardon it, conveyed that character to a mind not soft for receiving such impressions. (ch. 48)

Thinking of Ellen Horton or Isabel Vane, the *Saturday Review* praised Meredith because he did not surround his "sinner with all manner of artificial saintly crowns and heavenly haloes."[36] But from the passages above, it is perfectly clear that that is precisely what Meredith did do, and in so doing, joined himself to a growing company, as the reviewer's remarks suggest, who were fabricating a new type of Magdalene convention.

Fallen women appear elsewhere in Meredith's works, and, except for the case of Mrs. Mount in *The Ordeal of Richard Feverel* (1859) and the ambivalent treatment of the faithless wife in the poem sequence, *Modern Love* (1862), Meredith tended to sympathize with women who violated sexual customs. The reasons for this sympathy are set forth in a remarkable long poem, "The Sage Enamoured and the Honest Lady," and are developed in some of the later novels. Neither Judith Marsett nor Nataly Dreighton is condemned, though the two women are significantly different. Judith is simply a lusty young woman who liked "love, blood, and adventure" (*One of Our Conquerors*, ch. 28), whereas Nataly is in all ways but one entirely respectable. She has agreed to live with Victor Radnor, though he is still married, in order to save him from spoiling his life. Nataly's way is not easy, but it is depicted as an admirable one. Aminta, in *Lord Ormont and His Aminta* (1894), leaves her husband to live with the man she really loves, apparently with Meredith's approval. But by the time these later novels appeared, the admirable Magdalene was no longer a peculiarity.

When *Rhoda Fleming* first appeared (1865), it was still unusual for respectable novelists to defend fallen women. Such defenses often did occur in sensational novels, melodramas, or in the writings of the socially committed. It is all the more surprising, therefore, to discover Anthony Trollope, among the most respectable of authors, writing a novel in which a fallen woman is clearly defended. Trollope explained in his *Autobiography* that *The Vicar of Bullhampton* (1869-70) "was written chiefly with the object of exciting not only pity but sympathy for a fallen woman, and of raising a feeling of forgiveness for such in the minds of other women." (ch. 18) Trollope describes his character as "a poor abased creature who hardly knows how false were her dreams, with very little of the Magdalene about her—because though there may be Magdalenes they are not often found—but with an intense horror of the sufferings of her position." (ch. 18) Trollope took up this theme again in *Dr. Wortle's School* (1881) in which the upright but open-minded Dr. Wortle defends the unfortunate Mr. Peacocke who discovered, after marrying Ella LeFroy that her cruel husband was still alive. Peacocke considered it his duty to continue to live with Ella as husband and wife, but their scandalous relationship comes near to destroying Dr. Wortle's prosperous establishment. Dr. Wortle admits that men must uphold certain laws, agreeing that that is why it is wrong for men and women to live together unmarried. He also realizes that there are special circumstances in which "one is forced to go beyond common rules." (Part 5, ch. 7) Attempting to persuade his respectable wife that Peacocke's "wife" is not to be condemned, Dr. Wortle asks:

> "Do you ever think of Mary Magdalene?"
> "Oh yes."
> "This is no Magdalene. This is a woman led into no faults by vicious propensities. Here is one who has been altogether unfortunate, —who has been treated more cruelly than any of whom you have ever read." (part 4, ch. 11)

Trollope's aim is to indicate that not all fallen women are the same— that they should be judged not for their circumstance, but for their character. Trollope, as well as other Victorian novelists, wished to evoke sympathy for fallen women; at the same time, the fallen women he defends are largely conventional. Mr. Peacocke, for example, eventually manages to marry Ella and settle down in proper domesticity. Unusual as it may have been for Trollope to champion fallen women, he did even this within an acceptable and conventional mode.

The same cannot be said of Wilkie Collins, who had personal experience of fallen women and their feelings. In *The New Magdalen* (1873) Collins boldly called attention to what had once been a forbidden topic, and at the same time officially announced the new version of the conventional type. No longer is the Magdalene doomed to a life of misery or even modified recovery. Collins was unwilling to say with Trollope that for the repentant Magdalene, "though there was possible to her a way out of perdition, still things could not be with her as they would have been had she not fallen." (*Autobiography*, ch. 18) When Grace Roseberry meets Mercy Merrick on the French frontier in 1870, she explains that she has few prospects and is worried about her future. Mercy responds by telling Grace her own story, confessing that she is a fallen woman. And, though she accepts the fact that she cannot recover her place in society, she is not bowed down with shame. "I sometimes ask myself," she says, "if it was all my fault. I sometimes wonder if Society had no duties toward me when I was a child selling matches in the street." (First scene) Then, asking Grace "Will you hear the story of Magdalen—in modern times?" Mercy goes on to relate how she was led to redeem herself by hearing a sermon preached by Julian Gray. (First scene)[37]

Collins' message is not far beneath the surface of his improbable tale. When Mercy, who, through strange circumstances, comes to live with Lady Janet Roy in the character of Grace Roseberry, she is introduced to Horace Holmcroft who admires his mother and sisters as models of female behavior. The disguised Mercy has other feelings. " 'It sickens me,' she thought to herself, 'to hear of the virtues of women who have never been tempted. Where is the merit of living reputably, when your life is one course of prosperity and enjoyment?' " (Second scene) This is no mere echo of Milton's "I cannot praise a fugitive and cloistered virtue," but is, instead, a revaluing of a society much given to moral intimidation. Collins' point is that those who have endured life on the dark side of experience are not only the better for it—they are stronger where the scars have formed, as Hemingway would put it—but they may even be more attractive as a result. When Julian Gray meets Mercy in her impersonation of Grace Roseberry, he admires her immediately. " 'No common sorrow,' he thought, 'has set its mark on that woman's face; no common heart beats in that woman's breast.' " (Second scene) What follows is Collins' attempt to show that the redeemed Magdalene is, in fact, a person far superior in character to the respectable Grace Roseberry. Ultimately, Mercy reveals her identity and is shunned by the "respectable" characters, while Lady Janet defends her, and Julian Gray, the most manly character in the story, wishes to marry her. After an initial reluctance, she yields. But Society is still unwilling to accept Mercy and her minister husband. When Lady Janet gives a ball for the newlyweds, Society comes, but does not bring its unmarried daughters. At last, Julian and Mercy leave for America to seek a new life.

Collins' story was not original in depicting a fallen woman as capable of thorough redemption. *Ruth* had already asserted that. What marks *The New Magdalen* is the more aggressive notion that the redeemed Magdalene is actually superior to respectable society precisely because of the experience she has endured and overcome. It is a variation upon the prevailing Victorian belief that suffering was a means to salvation and even welcome as a blessed feature of life.[38] Praising the self-reliance and courage of Mercy Merrick, Collins condemned the society which ignored her in her need and then spurned her because of the sin its indifference drove her to. The story is a development of the sentiments expressed in DeQuincey's "The Daughter of Lebanon," and is an extension of the sentiment expressed by

Mrs. Gaskell, George Eliot, and others that men were more to blame than women in most seductions. In Collins' version, the new Magdalene actually becomes a model of rectitude outshining the petty, and self-congratulatory society at whose hands she suffered.

Collins took up the theme of the reformed prostitute again in *The Fallen Leaves* (1878-79), but in this novel the type is heavily sentimentalized. The thoroughly admirable hero of the story, Claude-Amelius Goldenheart, encounters a young prostitute on the streets and seeks to help her. "The appearance of the girl was artlessly virginal and innocent; she looked as if she had passed through the contamination of the streets without being touched by it, without fearing it, or feeling it, or understanding it." (Book 6, ch. 1) Even Sally's companions, "the outcasts of the hard highway," are moved by unselfish and compassionate feelings. Amelius cares for Sally, who adores him. Gradually he comes to prefer this simple and direct young woman to the more sophisticated, but inhibited Regina Mildmay. Finally Amelius marries Sally, though he realizes that the world's religion will be sorry for her, and charitable to her, but society will not take her back. Collins approves of Amelius' good-hearted and unconventional behavior, and Amelius' choice of Sally over Regina implies a preference for passionate directness over the safe and respectable frigidity associated with Victorian ladies.

George Gissing, who was to contribute generously to the literature on women's rights, actually married a young prostitute, Marianne Helen Harrison, with whom he had fallen in love.[39] "Gissing regarded Helen as a victim of society, and he undertook the mission of redeeming her," writes his biographer, Jacob Korg.[40] This idealistic gesture was destined to severe disenchantment, for Helen proved to be crude, unsympathetic and unruly. Nonetheless, when Gissing dealt with the subject of the fallen woman in *The Unclassed* (1884), he utilized the conventionally sentimental figure of the Magdalene common at the time. Lotty Starr is a fallen woman, estranged from her stern father, yet she manages to keep up a discreet life and to send her daughter to a respectable boarding school. Upon her death, however, her daughter chooses life in the streets and prostitutes herself profitably until she meets Osmond Waymark and discovers a reason for reforming. Like Amelius Goldenheart in Collins' *The Fallen Leaves*, Waymark is attracted to two women, the physically exciting Ida Starr and the more ethereal Maud Enderby. Like Amelius, Waymark finally selects the more passionate and experienced of the two. The novel ends with a hint of their marriage, which is also prefigured in the subplot which describes the reformation of Ida's prostitute companion, Sally Fisher, to Waymark's open-minded friend.[41]

These sentimentalizations did not go uncriticized. In Samuel Butler's *The Way of All Flesh*, published in 1903, but written much earlier (1872-84), Ernest Pontifex, coming upon the quondam maid of his parents' household who had been dismissed when her illegitimate pregnancy was discovered, fancies himself in love with the girl and determines to marry her since he refuses to live in sin. "To him," we are told, "she appeared a very angel dropped from the sky, and all the more easy to get on with for being a fallen one." (ch. 71) They do marry, and it does not take Ernest long to discover that his new wife is anything but an angel, for she soon lapses into her old habit of drunkenness. Later, after considerable discomfort on both sides, Ernest and Ellen separate when it is revealed that Ellen had already been married to John, Mr. Pontifex's ex-coachman. Butler's tale reads very much like a satire upon stories by Collins and Gissing; it might even be considered a suitable comment upon Gissing's private life.

While the sympathetic Magdalene had become the more familiar conventional type in literature, there were serious writers who felt the sentimental stylization had gone too far and therefore sought to correct the impression that the convention might create. But there were also those who, recognizing the generous motive behind the image of the redeemed Magdalene, sought to reconcile a sympathetic treatment of fallen women with a realistic picture of what their lives might involve. Notable among these writers was Thomas Hardy. In "A Sunday Morning Tragedy," a girl dies from taking an herb meant to shield the shame of her fall by causing an abortion. In fact, the boy responsible would have wed her, and her death from the herb proves to be a sad and unnecessary consequence of respectable values. Similarly, in *Tess of the d'Urbervilles* (1891), common country folk accept the fallen more readily than the fastidious and cultivated Angel Clare can manage. Hardy subtitled his novel, "A Pure Woman Faithfully Presented," and, like Trollope, obviously intended to contradict the notion that those who suffer a fall are necessarily wicked. Mrs. Oliphant remarked that the subtitle was Hardy's "flag or trumpet, so to speak, of defiance upon certain matters, to the ordinary world."[42]

Mrs. Oliphant was not the only contemporary reviewer to challenge Hardy's claim;[43] but there were also those prepared to defend what now seems to be the most important contribution of *Tess* to the convention of the sympathetic Magdalene. Clementina Black, writing in *The Illustrated London News* for 9 January 1892, made the following significant observation:

> Mr. Hardy's story, like *Diana of the Crossways*, is founded on a recognition of the ironic truth which we all know in our hearts, and are all forbidden to say aloud, that the richest kind of womanly nature, the most direct, sincere, and passionate, is the most liable to be caught in that sort of pitfall which social convention stamps as an irretrievable disgrace. It is the unsuspicious and fundamentally pure-minded girl in whom lie the noblest possibilities of womanhood, who is the easiest victim and who has to fight the hardest fight.[44]

Hardy was not concerned with converting Tess into a saint-like penitent after the fashion of Ellen Horton or Dahlia Fleming. His main purpose was to convey an authentic picture of the consequences of an unfortunate circumstance upon a fundamentally good and loving woman. In *A Pair of Blue Eyes* (1873) Hardy identified Elfride, the suspected but innocent heroine of the tale, with the Madonna, Magdalene, and Jael. Although she is neither saint, sinner nor destructive woman, she appears to be all of those to different men at different times. Hardy was capable of thus toying with conventional lables while refusing to conform to the conventions himself. In *Tess* he ignored the ironic reversals of this convention to deal directly with a problem of significance. Tess is identified with Mary Magdalene in her redeemed, not her fallen state, though Angel Clare, her lover, is unaware of this dimension of her nature. Tess' real sorrows derive not so much from her fall, as from Angel's interpretation of, or reaction to it. His "conventional standard of judgment had caused her all" her later troubles. (Phase 5, ch. 44) And, though Angel, who has himself slipped in his early life, can say to a young woman he thinks of seducing, "Women may be bad, but they are not so bad as men in these things!" he still finds it impossible to return to Tess and accept her as his faithful wife. (Phase 5, ch. 40)

Hardy wished to demonstrate the hardship and injustice of Tess' suffering for an offense that was not entirely her own and which was not a voluntary offense in the first place. At the same time he indicated that the true cruelty in society was not with humble folk but with genteel society. Even the supposedly "advanced and well-meaning" Angel could not accept the ordinary fact of Tess' lost virginity, but made of it a monstrous cloud to darken his own exalted ideals. Coventry Patmore had described woman's loss of chastity as the tragedy of tragedies in a poem entitled "The Tragedy of Tragedies," thereby indicating the extreme importance placed upon virginity by Victorians. Hardy, like others before him, such as Charles Dickens, Mrs. Gaskell, and Anthony Trollope, wished to assert the importance of individual cases and to correct the common tendency to assume that all fallen women were tainted or depraved. Hardy's was a realistic and rational attempt to describe a circumstance in which a simple human being, without becoming transformed into a saint, recovers from her misfortune only to be destroyed by her lover's unwise scruples. It is in a novel such as this that the literary convention and the social reality most nearly approach one another, rather than in those too familiar tales of fallen women succeeding finally in achieving respectability and marrying their liberal-minded lovers.

SENTIMENTAL TYPE

As we have seen, there was, in the later part of the nineteenth century, a growing tendency among English writers to sentimentalize the figure of the Magdalene. In Kipling's poem, "Overheard," for example, the persona tells how he overheard a young girl speaking to her friend, "A sort of overgrown brute":

I heard it out to the end—.
    A story of pain.
    Here you have it, in fine
        (Her words, not mine):
"Tried for luck in London—
            Voila tout!
Failed, lost money, undone;
Took to the streets for a life.
            Entre nous,
It's a terrible uphill strife,
Like all professions—too filled."

The reflective persona then muses, comparing the girl to a child who has broken a toy, "Or, was it a life gone bad?" The irony of the girl's brief account is spoiled by the poet's sentimental conclusion.

So commonplace had the notion of accepting erring women become that George Moore need not have feared much abuse for having his highly respectable Alice Barton, in *Muslin* (1886), actually finance her fallen friend's withdrawal to Dublin to bear her illegitimate child secretly. Though Alice is never remotely connected with seduction, she is capable of genuine sympathy for her friend. Moore's is not, in itself, a grossly sentimental depiction, though it counts on a cultivated sentimental response from its readers. In George du Maurier's *Trilby* (1894), it is the character of Trilby herself that is blatantly sentimental. Trilby is a good-hearted girl with loose morals who never really does anything wrong, and who only feels shame and sorrow when she falls in love with a prudish young artist of good family. Cigarette, the promiscuous mascot of the French foreign legion is another such rough diamond in Ouida's *Under Two Flags*. The public's acceptance of Trilby and Cigarette indicates that society was no longer inclined to denounce books about fallen women, whatever its day-to-day attitude might be.[45] For, in reality, fallen women were not such sentimental favorites as the fiction and poetry at the end of the century might suggest. In large part, the literary convention predominated as it did in order to improve the general attitude, and suggest that fallen women might be acceptable as human beings. George Bernard Shaw, in *Mrs. Warren's Profession* (1894), advanced the idea that not only might the prostitute be a suitable member of society when redeemed, she might be equally suitable, even valuable—if for no other reason, from an economic point of view —when unredeemed. Vivie Warren is obliged to realize what many Victorians did not wish to admit: that their society was buttressed by sins worse than prostitution, and by people worse than Mrs. Warren.[46]

Henry Arthur Jones in *Michael and his Lost Angel* (1896) offers a unique twist on the fallen woman—the fallen man. Audrie Lesden would have been familiar to Jones' audience. A handsome woman with a questionable character, she cannot help teasing the earnest minister, Michael Feversham. Before long this unlikely pair find themselves deeply in love with one another, and despite Feversham's high intentions, they consummate their love. Feversham is appalled to learn, soon after, that Audrie's good-for-nothing husband is still alive and that he is guilty not only of fornication, but of adultery. After a public confession, Feversham becomes a wanderer, but returns to his Roman Catholic uncle's monastery in Italy just in time to embrace Audrie once more before she dies. After her death, Feversham offers to submit himself wholly to his relative's religious guidance, wishing only that he may meet Audrie again in the next life. Although Audrie is a fallen woman of a familiar stamp, Jones' play is really about the fallen clergyman. But, most significant is the notion underlying their sin, that their fall redeems each from a false mode of life— Audrie from her cynicism and Michael from a too strict morality. The story is thick with echoes of fallen women converted to saints and other familiar trappings of the convention, but there is no genuine import in the work, and its "controversial" subject seems merely a device for attracting an audience.

If Jones' play may be seen more as a theatrical gesture than a serious plea, Grant Allen's best-selling novel, *The Woman Who Did* (1895), may be called "an attempt to treat love and marriage frankly and honestly."[47] In a way, this novel truly represents the apotheosis of the Magdalene convention. Herminia Barton, the heroine of Allen's story, announces that "Other women have fallen, as men choose to put it in their odious dialect; no other has voluntarily risen as I propose to do." (ch. 3) [48] What Herminia proposes to do is live as though married to her lover, Alan Merrick, without marrying him. Her reason for refusing marriage is to indicate to all women who follow that they may have a life of their own, free from legal enslavement, without renouncing love.

If earlier fallen women had been associated with sainthood because they were redeemed and saved from their unwise course, Herminia's martyrdom consists of not yielding to conventional views. "Our hearts against the world," she says to Alan; "love and duty against convention." (ch. 5) Herminia knows that her course of action will mean suffering for her, but she declares that "Every great and good life can but end in Calvary." (ch. 3) Throughout the novel Herminia is associated with sainthood and martyrdom. Her action is called "her willing martyrdom for humanity's sake," (ch. 1) and Alan, who is somewhat more timid than his beloved, respects her "ideal world of high seraphic harmonies," and her "stainless soul." (ch. 4) In her idealistic behavior, Herminia is clearly presented as superior to the Philistine life that surrounds her in the same way that Hardy's Tess had been the year before. The narrator states that for ordinary society, "A life-time would have failed it to discern for itself how infinitely higher than its slavish 'respectability' was Herminia's freedom." (ch. 7)

There is no doubt about Herminia's high motives in opposing society's conventions, and yet she is not saved from the consequences of her unusual behavior. When Alan dies, Herminia is forced to labor at hack journalism in order to support herself and Dolly, her daughter. The great irony is that Dolly grows up revering traditional values and therefore despises her mother when she learns the truth about her own birth. But, whatever society's judgment upon Herminia, Allen is clear in his estimate of Herminia's behavior. We are told that Herminia loved a madonna and child by Inturicchio. "To her it was no mere emblem of a dying creed, but a type of the eternal religion of maternity. The Mother adoring the Child! 'T was herself and Dolly." (ch. 23) Dolly does not choose to play the role that Herminia assigns her; thus, to insure Dolly's safe marriage to the wealthy young man she loves, Herminia commits suicide by taking prussic acid. But even in this act she reveals the nobility of her fallen nature which is superior to ordinary individuals, for she dies "with hand folded on her breast, like some saint of the middle ages." Allen goes on to proclaim: "Not for nothing does blind fate vouchsafe such martyrs to humanity. From their graves shall spring glorious the church of the future." (ch. 24)

Despite the sentimental nature of this novel, it must be viewed as a serious presentation of the Magdalene convention. Allen declared that he had written *The Woman Who Did* "wholly and solely to satisfy my own taste and my own conscience." And yet, in historic perspective, his utilization of the convention appears as a predictable culmination of the Victorian taste for mingling saintly and sinful femininity. After this, the type could develop no further, and extreme stylizations or parodies followed.

Oscar Wilde's incomplete *La Sainte Courtisane, or The Woman Covered With Jewels,* is an ironic version of the tendency to combine the sinner and the saint. Wilde uses the emblem of the Magdalene, refashioning it in a characteristic manner. In Wilde's composition, the sinful Myrrhina comes to the wilderness from corrupt Alexandria to tempt the saintly recluse, Honorius, to the things of the world.

When, after angry resistance, he yields, the two characters reverse roles and Myrrhina refuses to accompany the fallen saint to Alexandria, saying, "I have repented of my sins and I am seeking a cavern in this desert where I too may dwell so that my soul may become worthy to see God." Wilde has converted the conventional figure of the redeemed Magdalen-Judith to a Magdalen-Saint, but in the process the moral world suffers a strange isostasy. Myrrhina is no Ethel Newcome nor Princess Ida, combining the best of male and female and thereby completing a larger moral design. Wilde's concentration upon the emblem and what happens to it creates from the emblem a design with its own significance. Myrrhina is the sensuous, predatory instinct converted to morality, while Honorius embodies man's defensive asceticism powerlessly sliding to indulgence. Like another sensualist, Dorian Gray, Myrrhina has taken a dangerously rich byway to virtue; unlike him, she will probably enjoy her redemption. Honorius, in his coldly proud and frightened virtue, once having glanced up from his straight road, is irrecoverably inflamed and lost. It is a peculiar moral perhaps—that indulgence is as sure a way to grace as denial, probably surer—but it is a moral nonetheless, at one with its unlikely stylization, not merely a design given flesh by surface detail.

Wilde's brief dramatic fiction epitomizes the change that had overtaken the convention of the fallen woman. From pitiable, to sympathetic, to sanctified, the Magdalene had become one of the most remarkable literary types. Even respectable fiction could employ a redeemed Magdalene to good effect—the type was in favor in fiction, though except in certain circles, she remained deplored and even denounced in actual life.

The convention was common enough to call up a certain amount of mockery. Thus Thomas Hardy, who had developed the subject amply in *Tess of the d'Urbervilles* and to some extent in other novels, made fun of the topic of the fallen country wench in his poem, "The Ruined Maid," wherein the supposedly miserable young rustic girl who has been ruined turns out to be more comfortable and happy than her virtuous friend. And, the playwright St. John Hankins converted the same theme into comedy in his play *Last of the de Mullins* (1907), where "the melodramatic situation of *The Woman Who Did*" becomes a "light-hearted comedy in which the ruined maid and her bastard son reach a happy ending."[49]

SUMMARY

Literary conventions concerning women may reveal certain fears, anxieties and desires of Victorian men. It is difficult to determine how conscious most writers were of the conventions they used, but surely the fact that gentle, lovable women were for the most part sexless and yielding Griseldas, while desirable women were aggressive and often destructive Judiths, tells us something about the age. Most revealing of all is the attempt to combine in the conventional type of the Magdalen the sensuousness of the Judith and the saintliness of the Griselda. Perhaps a good part of Victorian manhood lusted after a woman whose experience qualified her as a lover, while her repentance sanctioned her as a wife and mother.

\Throughout the century, women were seeking to establish a new image of themselves, while men in their literature and their art were attempting to fix them in suitable types.\Perhaps the many denunciations of the suffragettes were less honest than they seemed, as were sympathetic reinforcements of women's rights. John Davidson's "To The New Woman" (1894) may suggest the Victorian male's authentic, if confused, response:

Abler than the man to vex,
Less able to be good,
Fiercer in your sex,
Wilder in your mood,
Seeking—who knows what?

This was the aggressive, liberated woman, seeking ideals of her own and the freedom that would enable her to pursue those ideals. But Davidson adds:

Soon again you'll see,
Love and love alone,
As simple as can be,
Can make this life atone.

Here Davidson acknowledged that woman was the object of physical and spiritual love, that her true nature resided in her knowledge of the emotional life, that she was an ennobled Eve, a Judith whose instincts were subdued from the wild Magdalen's excess to a saintly function. And, at last, she would assume her saintly function:

> And meet your splendid doom,
> On heaven-scaling wings,
> Women, from whose bright womb
> The radiant future springs.

This does not sound a great deal different from Tennyson's pronouncements in *The Princess*, and perhaps the truth is that attitudes did not change all that much throughout the century. Yet in the conventions of nineteenth-century English literature a strange psychological battle is acted out, in which changing types contain the hostile and attractive energies that men felt for women, and beneath the respectable surface there lurked a subtle yearning for the untrammelled spirit which, though it clearly exerted a strong appeal, could not be openly acknowledged. Moreover, the appeal thus embodied in female types may, with justification, be considered as a manifestation of a broader discontent, of a restless desire to possess the comforts of an orderly society without renouncing the lustier and more adventurous qualities of life. As discontent with society increased near the end of the century, it was the outcast type, the rebel, the champion of the senses, who became more attractive. The Magdalene was experienced and free, and her narrow domestic sisters could no longer compete for the affections of men who yearned for escape.

CHAPTER THREE

MALE TYPES

JACOB

Some conventions had only the aura of traditional morality about them, being principally materials of popular romance. Nonetheless, upon occasion, even the most commonplace figures bore a moral significance, playing a part in a larger moral design. The faithful lover is one such type. His Biblical prototype was Jacob, whose patient labor to earn the woman he loved made him a model for true lovers. The figure of the patient, faithful lover was agreeable to Victorian taste partly because the suffering associated with frustrated love had the same value as did other forms of suffering which were viewed as means to moral improvement. Also, Victorians seemed to find indications of constancy, whether in institutions or in love, comforting.

Frederick Graham, in Coventry Patmore's *The Angel in the House* (1854-63) is a well-developed example of the Jacob figure. In love with his cousin Honoria Churchill, he does not declare his love because he finds that she loves Felix Vaughan, to whom she is soon wed. Frederick's love for Honoria is constant however. His mother, recognizing her son's nature, warns him against marrying a less worthy woman out of desperation:

Besides, you dread,
In Leah's arms, to meet the eyes
Of Rachel, somewhere in the skies,
And both return, alike relieved,
To life less loftily conceived.

("Faithful For Ever," sec. 11)

But Frederick does marry a common girl, who, after years of marriage, receives her full portion of his love, which she has deserved by her own faithfulness and good nature. Still, Frederick retains his love for Honoria, though now this love has come to include a general love of mankind and of all that is good and true. In "The Espousal," Felix Vaughan had "thought with prayer how Jacob paid / The patient price of Rachel" ("Epitaph," sec. 10), but he won his Rachel and did not suffer as Frederick must. Felix's love is mainly human and domestic, whereas Frederick's role as Jacob has led him beyond the merely physical. His fidelity now is to a higher object even than Honoria. In describing his faithfulness, Frederick writes to Honoria of this higher object.

Not on the changeful earth alone
Shall loyalty remain unmoved
T'wards everything I ever loved.
So Heaven's voice calls, like Rachel's voice
To Jacob in the field, "Rejoice!
"Serve on some seven more sordid years,
"Too short for weariness or tears;
"Serve on; then, oh, Beloved, well-tried,
"Take me for ever as thy Bride!"

("Victories of Love," sec. 11)

Frederick is the model Jacob who never achieves his earthly Rachel, but who is happy with Leah. His is not the usual pattern of the faithful lover, for his constancy transcends human love and places the true object of fidelity beyond the chances of human passion. Few writers employed the Jacob convention so elaborately as this to so definite a conclusion. In general, the type was used to emphasize a narrative circumstance, point a moral, or later in the century, deliver an ironic observation.

There are two Jacob figures in George Eliot's *Adam Bede* (1859), illustrating two approaches to the type. Adam is associated with Joseph the provider, though he resembles Jacob as well. Seth, his brother, is identified entirely with Jacob. He realizes this himself and describes his feeling to Dinah Morris:

> "It's a deep mystery—the way the heart of man turns to one woman out of all the rest he's seen i' the world, and makes it easier for him to work seven year for *her*, like Jacob did for Rachel, sooner than have any other woman for th' asking. I often think of them words, 'And Jacob served seven years for Rachel; and they seemed to him but a few days for the love he had to her.' I know those words 'ud come true with me, Dinah, if so be you'd give me hope as I might be win you after seven years was over." (ch. 3)

Seth is among those faithful lovers destined to disappointment, though he has placed his affections prudently and not in passion. Though his love may be true and enduring, Dinah does not return it; she can respond only to his brother, Adam. Yet Adam's first love is for Hetty Sorrell; an affection that is gravely misdirected. Later, realizing the true direction of his feelings, he resembles Seth in his silent love for Dinah. However, he and Dinah ultimately acknowledge their love for one another. In this regard, Adam is unlike many of the faithful lovers of popular romance whose secret love is unrequited and consequently more poignant.

Richard Burnell, in Mary Howitt's "The Ballad of Richard Burnell," is of this order. Burnell, who loves Alice deeply, decides not to mention his love when he learns that Alice loves Leonard Woodvil. Instead, upon their marriage, Burnell abruptly leaves his home. It is only years later, when he returns, that he can confess to Alice:

> "Yes, I loved thee, long had loved thee,
>   And alone the God above,
> He, who at that time sustained me,
>   Knows the measure of my love."

But no consummation rewards Burnell's patient love; there is only the opportunity for a further dedication. And so Alice advises him:

> "'Tis alone of His appointing,
>   That thy feet on thorns have trod;

Suffering, woe, renunciation,
     Only bring us nearer God."

Here and in many other works of the time, a quiet, sustained love resembles religious devotion. Just as silent dedication to a moral idea may strengthen and sustain a man, so may a noble fidelity fortify a man's sense of what is admirable in his own view of the world. Possession, this attitude implies, is less important than dedication. In a way, this convention represents a domestication of Keats' sentiment expressed in the "Ode on a Grecian Urn," that the highest delight is the untasted, but, at the same time, is entirely at one with the commonplace Victorian belief that renunciation was a guaranteed way to nobleness and sanctity. In Tennyson's *The Lover's Tale*, the faithful lover, Leolin, having remained silent and lost his beloved to his friend, later acquires proprietary rights over her by recovering her from the tomb where she had been placed after she had presumably died. But, in an act of oriental and Christian resignation, Leolin resigns the object of his love to her husband once more. Faithful, unrequited love here signifies the ultimate power of renunciation, as well as its ennobling character.

There are amusing characterizations of the unrequited lover in the literature of the time, several of which—such as Toots in *Dombey and Son*, and Smike in *Nicholas Nickleby*—appear in Dickens' novels. But Dickens also employed the Jacob figure more seriously. Kit Nubbles, in *The Old Curiosity Shop*, is dedicated to Little Nell and seems to love her in the same way that Walter Gay loves Florence Dombey. Actually, Kit is dedicated to Nell as an ideal, not as an object of desire, and therefore he may continue to cherish her after her death. Other faithful lovers, such as Arthur Clennam or Pip, learn that their constancy has been misplaced. Arthur discovers a more suitable recipient for his love in Little Dorrit, and Pip, thanks to Dickens' advisers, fulfills his desires by winning the unapproachable object of his dubious attachment, Estella. Some, like Tom Pinch, in *Martin Chuzzlewit*, are content to see the object of their love safely happy and married to someone else, in the manner of Seth Bede. Ham, Emily's faithful lover in *David Copperfield*, is a notable example of the simple, unwavering soul, unable to transfer his affection from its one object even when his Rachel proves more of a Magdalene.

The more familiar destiny for the Jacob figure was eventual gratification and reward for constancy. Edward Lyndsay, in Susan Ferrier's

Inheritance, is so patient and reserved in his love that Gertrude St. Clair is scarcely aware of it. Ultimately, his virtue and love manifest themselves, Gertrude acknowledges her own growing feelings for him, and their acquaintance culminates in marriage. Gilbert Markham, in *The Tenant of Wildfell Hall*, is less reserved, but equally faithful in his love. He suffers agonies of jealousy and uncertainty, but because he never truly loses faith in his beloved, he is rewarded not only with her love, but with a small fortune as well.

The literature of the time abounds with faithful, patient lovers of this sort, such as Anthony Tourneur in Anne Thackeray Ritchie's *The Story of Elizabeth*, Arabin in *Barchester Towers* who is prevented from declaring his love for ecclesiastical reasons, Louis Moore in *Shirley* whose hesitation in declaring his love is caused by financial circumstances, and Will Ladislaw in *Middlemarch*. All of these figures are willing to forego consummation of their love. In their hearts, some of these lovers are convinced that their love would be returned if circumstances were right; others, like Jem Wilson in Mrs. Gaskell's *Mary Barton* (1848), can only hope.

Trollope used two contrasting Jacob figures in *The Way We Live Now* (1874-75). John Crumb is a plodding, but devoted rustic lover somewhat in the mold of Dickens' Ham, but Roger Carbury is the genuine example. He remains constant in his love for Hetta Carbury even when it is clear that she prefers his young friend, Paul Montague. Only after a severe internal struggle is the good Roger able to accept Paul as his friend once more and modify his passion for Hetta to a more discreet friendship. However, if the mild Roger loses his Rachel, the more persistent Crumb succeeds in marrying his, though his success is a modest one. Major Campbell, in Kingsley's *Two Years Ago* (1857), is the faithful lover of Lucia St. Just, though she never knows. He is very discreet and restrained and is outraged when Lucia's husband, Elsley Vavasour, suspects his intentions. When he dies in the Crimea, he sends home a memento of Lucia that he has carried with him for years. George Martin, in Dutton Cook's *A Prodigal Son* (1863), loves his friend Wilford's wife, and, though he doubts his own capacity for disinterestedness, does manage to reconcile the couple after a misunderstanding. Having done so, he realizes that he loves Violet even more for her fidelity to Wilford. In the end, George is not left alone, however, but is in love with Violet's younger sister.

As has already been suggested, the faithful Jacob was not always treated with full seriousness. Many writers chose to present their characters without the usual romantic coloring. In Meredith's *The Ordeal of Richard Feverel* (1859), it is not Richard who is the unrequited, devoted lover, but the comical Ripton Thompson. Jacob is reduced, in this case, to a household pet, for Ripton's devotion to Lucy Desborough is of the "Old Dog" variety, faithfully worshipping and wishing to be near the object of admiration. Other Meredith Jacobs are more traditional, but never fully conventional. In characters such as Shibli Bagarag, Robert Eccles, and Vernon Whitford, there is a realistic swerving from the true plumb of Jacobness that makes the conventional pose more credible. Still, there is always something of the family pet about these lovers, even in that staunchest of undeclared suitors, Thomas Redworth, in *Diana of the Crossways* (1885), who tells Diana finally, "I taught this old watch-dog of a heart to keep guard and bury the bones you tossed him." (ch. 43) Despite their variation from the commonplace types they approximate, Meredith's Jacobs generally remain true to the pattern. They silently admire, and in most cases are rewarded with reciprocal love that satisfies them and terminates the plot. Earlier, however, a variation on this model had appeared that made a very important distinction. In Thackeray's *Vanity Fair* (1847-48), William Dobbin, devoted to Amelia Sedley, serves her as faithfully as an old dog through her romance and marriage with George Osborne and beyond. But Thackeray is unwilling to indulge the normal expectations of his audience, and, though he permits Dobbin to win Amelia in the end, it is on terms not many aspiring Jacobs would consider worth the long years' wait, for Thackeray is at pains to show that, though Jacob may be sincerely devoted, Rachel may not always be worthy of that devotion.

Thackeray's friend and admirer, Anthony Trollope, chose to emphasize a similar realism on both sides of the Jacob convention. As is often the case in these situations, the impediment to an exchange of affection is not a demanding father, but another man. In *The Small House at Allington* (1864), Lilian Dale bestows her affections on Adolphus Crosbie, and Johnny Eames must endure his hidden love for her. Eames has "the constancy of a Jacob," though he must make an effort to free himself from the not entirely unwelcome attentions of Miss Amelia Roper. Again, in *The Last Chronicle of Barset* (1867), Eames' fidelity is described as "the constancy of a Jacob," (ch. 70) and we are told that he "believed himself to have out-Jacobed Jacob." (ch. 15) And yet Eames has indulged in some rather advanced dalliance with the aggressive Madalina Demolines. Unlike Dobbins, Eames is not stainless, and also unlike the good major, he does not achieve his love in the end, for, despite her high regard for him, Lilian refuses Eames after all, sentimentally viewing herself as a storm-shattered tree, a victim of romance.

The use of the Jacob convention was basically sentimental, and there were as many sentimental versions of the faithful lover at the end of the century as there had been at its beginning, indicating that the type, despite irreverent treatment of it by major writers, was not likely to die out, though, for the most part, its moral implications did. Trilby, the bohemian charmer of du Maurier's novel of that name, has not one, but three faithful lovers, none of whom enjoys her after all. Equally sentimental is a later manifestation of the Jacob convention in Hall Caine's *The Prodigal Son* (1904). Magnus, the good but misunderstood brother, relinquishes his beloved Thora to Stephen. She is touched by his gesture:

> "Magnus, I think—I really think you would do anything in the world for me."
> A gruff laugh came back to her, half smothered as in a man's beard, and then a choking voice said, "I believe I would, Thora."
> "And if I wanted you—or baby wanted you—I think you would follow us to the ends of the earth."
> "Only say 'Come' and I'll come, Thora." (Part 3, ch. 10)

Magnus' love is conventional and sentimental, and extreme according to the needs of popular romance, and, predictably, he and his brother Stephen are compared to Jacob and Esau. As it turns out, the reference to Jacob and Esau has a double edge, for, Biblically it was Jacob who deprived Esau of his birthright. In *The Prodigal Son*, which obviously does not lack for Biblical parallels, the typological associations of the two brothers are confused. Both brothers may be viewed as deprived Esaus, both may be viewed as prodigals, and in an ironic fashion both may be viewed as Jacobs. Magnus is the more faithful lover, but he is also the dispossessed elder son, and in the end he requires God's forgiveness as a wavering prodigal. Stephen is the more obvious prodigal who requires a long process of redemption, loses his birthright through his sins, yet loves his childhood home and friends. Caine seems consciously to be playing upon the familiar conventions of his reading public, and though he is willing to exploit the sentiment of the Jacob emblem, does not overlook the moral complications that had become fully apparent in the writings of his contemporaries.

If the sentimental version of the Jacob figure is most common, it is the antithetical use of the Jacob convention that is most interesting. Reluctance to credit the simple romantic convention led many writers, such as Meredith, Thackeray and Trollope, to employ a contrary pattern in the emblematic figure. They wished to indicate that few modern men would engage in Jacob's folly, or maintain so purely Jacob's dedication. In Robert Louis Stevenson's *The Master of Ballantrae* (1888-89), Henry Durie is a faithful lover, unwearied in the service of his beloved. However, he is viewed not as the devoted Jacob that Seth Bede so warmly recalled, but as the Jacob whose duplicity robbed his brother of his birthright. There is a massive irony at work in Stevenson's story, for James Durie, Henry's older brother, is the one who accuses Henry of playing thieving Jacob to his Esau; whereas, it actually is James who secretly wastes the wealth of the estate that Henry has been left to govern. Moreover, it is toward James that Henry's wife Alison's affections are directed. The deceitful James appears to Alison as the faithful but outcast lover, while the true romantic Jacob, Henry, has won his beloved only to find her unable to respond. Stevenson saw no virtue in the long-suffering Jacob. He was not a model to be imitated in a world where good and evil were so confusedly intertwined.

A curious variation of the Jacob motif occurs in Ernest Dowson's short story, "The Statute of Limitations" (1893). Michael Garth leaves England to make his fortune in Chili so that he may return to marry the woman he loves. But his stay in Chili is prolonged, his return delayed, until fifteen years have passed. When he finally sets forth on his homeward journey, Garth begins to have doubts about the marriage that he has so long anticipated. He has been the faithful and industrious Jacob, but he now realizes that his Rachel will not be the same woman that he left behind. Their marriage would be a marriage of strangers. Unable to face this situation, Garth apparently commits suicide. It is Jacob at the end of his tether.[1]

Several of the examples that I have noted indicate a growing doubt concerning the virtue of a Jacob-like devotion. The novels of Thomas Hardy provide instances bleaker still. In *A Pair of Blue Eyes* (1873), there are two Jacob figures—Stephen Smith and Henry Knight, and both become prematurely disillusioned with the woman they both love. Their devotion lasts only so long as they can feel that they alone are destined to enjoy Elfride's love. When their images of her are stained, they both abandon her. Neither lover has genuinely understood the woman they both romantically cherish. Elfride is, in a sense, the victim of their lack of faith, but even more, they themselves recognize the violation of human affection that their mutual distrust represents. In his pursuit of Rachel, Jacob had been considered notable for his elevated sentiments and his moral dedication. But Hardy suggests that anything resembling such a traditional severity is dangerous, not ennobling. What he says of Knight applies as well to Smith:

> The moral rightness of this man's life was worthy of all praise; but in spite of some intellectual acumen, Knight had in him a modicum of that wrongheadedness which is mostly found in scrupulously honest people. With him, truth seemed too clean and pure an abstraction to be so hopelessly churned in with error as practical persons find it. Having now seen himself mistaken in supposing Elfride to be peerless, nothing on earth could make him believe she was not so very bad after all. (ch. 35)

All too often in Hardy's novels the high-minded, faithful lovers come to bad ends. Giles Winterbourne, in *The Woodlanders* (1886-87), is faithful to a fault. Grace Melbury realizes only after Giles has sacrificed his life for her that "Her timid morality had, indeed underrated his chivalry till now, though she knew him so well. The purity of his nature, his freedom from the grosser passions, his scrupulous delicacy," had never been fully apparent to Grace. (ch. 42) And yet, Giles himself has not been deceived in his passion. He had imagined his hopes vain and had sought in a very practical way to suppress them. Later, when those hopes were flattered once more, Giles was not so naive as he had been; he "was not quite so ardent as heretofore." This, Hardy suggests, is in the nature of things, for "There is no such thing as a stationary love: men are either loving more or loving less." (ch. 38) Thackeray's Dobbin achieved his Rachel only to learn that the value of his constancy was in the faithfulness itself. Hardy's characters are generally spared this bitter realization in the equally bitter denial of their desires. Gabriel Oak's love ends sadly as would Diggory Venn's without Hardy's artificial happy ending, which is not compatible with Hardy's world, not because men are incapable of such dedication, but because the nature of things is to frustrate that dedication, as Jude Fawley's life illustrates. Jude can declare honestly to Sue Bridehead, "All that's best and noblest in me loves you, and your freedom from everything that's gross has elevated me, and enabled me to do what I should never have dreamt myself capable of, or any man, a year or two ago." (Part 5, ch. 2, *Jude the Obscure*) And later, Sue can declare, "Your generous devotion to me is unparalleled, Jude!" (Part 6, ch. 4)

But this devotion is of no consequence, for the "predestinate" Jude and Sue are bound for disaster. Faithful lover though he may be, Jude is troubled by the reappearance of his first wife, Arabella (clearly illustrative of the flesh and of man's fall), despite his impulse toward a higher form of love. Jude's Leah will not permit a comfortable Rachel with her Jacob. Moreover, to fulfill the exalted love he feels for Sue, Jude must violate the rules of society, going so far as to take her from an unoffending husband. Jude cannot live by his code and society's as well. Nor does his ideal remain constant, for Sue also is human, subject to the altering forces that play upon all men and place the simple fable of the enduring Jacob and the unchanging Rachel beyond credibility. Not in this world, Hardy declares; and after him it seems that the Jacob figure passes out of the first rank of fiction to reside once more in the less demanding atmosphere of popular romance.

I have not chosen to examine the Jacob figure in depth because it is too much a part of all narrative art. I have merely sought to indicate briefly that even such a hackneyed type as this had moral associations for nineteenth-century writers that transcended ordinary sentimental conventions. Equally important was the persistent recognition throughout the century of the invalidity of the image. While popular fiction promoted the picture of a Jacob pining for his Rachel, certain acute authors were indicating that Jacob's pining and his probable home life would scarcely be, in their world, what it was purported to be in Biblical times. Victorians longed to believe in the value of a constant and self-renouncing love, such as that described by Coventry Patmore, and hoped that it would have its final reward, either in the flesh or in the spirit. At the same time, it was all too clear to many, that not only was the constant love unlikely to persevere, but its reward was more likely to be disenchantment than joy.

There is another, less obvious explanation for interest in Jacob's plight which is directly related to the social customs in Victorian England. In *Guy Livingstone; or "Thorough,"* (1857) George Alfred Lawrence offered another perspective on the familiar story.

> Yes, many men have their Rachel; but—there being a prejudice against bigamy—few have even the Patriarch's luck, to marry her at last. For the wife *de convenance* generally outlives her younger sister; and so, one afternoon, we turn again from a grave in Ephrata-Green Cemetery, somewhat drearily, into our tent pitched in the plains of Belgravia, where Leah—(there was ever jealousy between those two) —meets us with a sharp glance of triumph in her "tender eyes." (ch. 7)

If the faithful lover represented for some Victorians a constancy and nobility desirable in their world, and for others a model of a more spiritual dedication, for yet others the yearning of a frustrated lover may have called to their minds the compromises they had made with the conveniences of their society; and, in the ordeal of Jacob, the Victorians may have seen their own romantic natures freed to feel the passions they had not permitted themselves to declare. Even Jacob may have seemed a means of vicarious escape from what many felt to be an oppressive climate of convention and respectability.

THE SAMARITAN

The use of some conventional types is so obvious that it requires only a brief discussion. The Good Samaritan is one such type, though its obviousness of application belies the purpose it came to fulfill. References to this figure are mainly incidental and do not represent a highly developed concept largely because the mere allusion was enough to call up the appropriate sentiment. In *John Halifax, Gentleman*, (ch. 31) one doesn't question the excellence of John Halifax's behavior when he alone takes the risk of saving good Mr. Jessop's bank from failing. Mrs. Jessop blesses Halifax, who responds with a modest "Thank you" and a handshake. Impressed by John's good deed, Phineas Fletcher thinks to himself, "watching the many that came and went, unmindful, '*only this Samaritan!*'" The model of the Good Samaritan here is precise and serious. Elsewhere it is only a convention of speech. For example, when Carinthia in Meredith's *The Amazing Marriage* is referred to casually as a Samaritan, or when a kind neighbor, in du Maurier's *Trilby*, tends Little Billee after an evening of unaccustomed excess, "putting him to bed and tucking him up like a real good Samaritan." (Part 4)

Thackeray developed the Samaritan convention with some thoroughness, not only in his novels, but in the illustrations for them as well. John Harvey remarks that "In Thackeray's capitals, the Good Samaritan is introduced both in *The Newcomes* (Vol. 2, ch. 39) and *The Virginians* (ch. 21); the latter example is one of the largest capitals in the novel, and the evident seriousness of the subject has brought out an unusual strength of drawing in Thackeray."[2] One of Thackeray's noblest heroes, Colonel Newcome, is characterized by Frederick Bayham, who has benefitted from his generosity, as "that good Samaritan." (Vol. 2, ch. 6) There is no irony in this reference, for, although Thackeray was no blind worshipper of his society, he still believed in the beneficial operation of good example. In *The Newcomes*, for example, Ethel's musing upon the penury of her "dear, kind, generous uncle," Colonel Newcome, prompts her to play the part of good Samaritan herself. (Vol. 2, ch. 40) Thackeray's system of values implies the importance of conventional models of behavior, and though he frequently mocked artificial stylizations in literature, he did not hesitate to use them himself when they seemed suitable.

Thackeray believed that imitation of the worthy Samaritan, like the imitation of Christ, could have a favorable effect, and that Samaritans were needed in a society well populated with thieves and victims. Thackeray specifically suggested this in the full title of his later novel, *The Adventures of Philip on his way through the world, showing who robbed him, who helped him, and who passed him by* (1861-62). Despite the abundance of thieves and indifferent passersby in the world Thackeray here described, there is also a sufficient number of Samaritans to make the pilgrimage worthwhile. References to wayfarers, thieves, and Samaritans occur frequently enough to make Thackeray's parallel clear. One chapter is even entitled, "Samaritans," possibly ironically because it is in this chapter that a most important Pharisee, Lord Ringwood, decides to pass Philip by in his difficulties. " 'Hang the fellow! he will, of course, be coming for money. Dawkins, I am not at home, mind, when young Mr. Firmin calls.' So says Lord Ringwood, regarding Philip fallen among thieves. Ah thanks to Heaven, travellers find Samaritans as well as Levites on life's hard way!" (ch. 15) Mr. Twysden, Philip's uncle, is another "Levite," who would "neither give wine, nor oil, nor money" to a fallen man. (ch. 3) Thackeray observes of Philip's friends, "The Samaritan who rescues you, most likely, has been robbed and has bled in his day, and it is a wounded arm that bandages yours when bleeding." (ch. 25) In the novel, Samaritans constitute a small, initiated group, recognizing the importance of their own generous activity, but they are also an unconventional lot, for their behavior is not common. "The religious opinions of Samaritans are lamentably heterodox," Thackeray observes dryly, and then adds, "O brother! may we help the fallen still though they never pay us, and may we lend without exacting the usury of gratitude." (ch. 23)

This adjuration is straightforward enough, and so is Thackeray's charge against the foremost thief and Levite of them all.

> Who scorns? who persecutes? who doesn't forgive?—the virtuous Mrs. Grundy. She remembers her neighbour's peccadilloes to the third and fourth generation; and if she finds a certain man fallen in her path, gathers up her affrighted garments with a shriek, for fear the muddy bleeding wretch should contaminate her, and passes on. (ch. 8)

Yet it is not only in the society of nineteenth-century England that thieves waylay wanderers, and Levites pass sufferers by, and Samaritans are in demand. The conditions which required the Biblical Samaritan to serve indicate that man has always found something lacking in his societies. Thackeray declares that it is because life itself is a risky journey. The parable of the Samaritan being a good one, it therefore ought not to be forgotten and the novel serves to remind us. His hero, Philip, may trip and fall and require help, but he is in no way unusual. It is Thackeray's unambiguous application of the Samaritan convention which demonstrates the emblematic and even typological frame of thought that might underlie even the most casual utilizations of the convention. Thackeray's novel is very much in the "realistic" mode of nineteenth-century fiction, but this does not prevent him from enlarging its meaning through the correlative of a scriptural parable, any more than Joyce's naturalistic *Ulysses* is disqualified as an authentic record of life because it exploits a classical fable.

As one might suppose, in Victorian novels the Samaritan's assist-

ance consists to a great extent of providing money rather than wine
or oil. Concentration upon the financial charity of the Samaritan reveals how thoroughly commercialized much of Victorian morality
was, and how distant from the immediacy of human suffering the
solution seemed to be drifting. Dickens was fully aware of this tendency of his age. Attacking the Malthusian philosophy, he quipped
that unfortunately the Good Samaritan was a bad economist. (*Hard
Times*, Book 2, ch. 12) He referred elsewhere to the "ragged Samaritan" who, living among the poor himself, was among the few to offer
succour.[3] And old Betty Higden's case in *Our Mutual Friend* (1864-
65) signifies the degree to which the Samaritan ideal had been disfigured. "It is a remarkable Christian improvement," Dickens writes,
"to have made a pursuing Fury of the Good Samaritan; but it was so
in this case, and it is a type of many, many, many." (Book 3, ch. 8)
The Samaritan that Betty flees from is institutionalized welfare,
which, to her, means the workhouse. In her flight, Betty encounters
another, baser modification of the type in Rogue Riderhood, who
extorts money by assuring Betty that she will *not* be helped. Betty's
journey, which ends in death, is a prolonged escape from the Samaritan. What Dickens suggests is that bureaucratic goodwill is as likely
to be harmful as helpful to those it insists upon aiding. But, in addition, he describes a situation so deplorable that the harried victim
must turn for assistance to the thief to protect her from the loathsome
Good Samaritan.

The very emphasis upon money, business, and worldly advancement made the outstretched helping hand suspect. Just as the apparently honest and God-fearing society of nineteenth-century England
was, underneath, a turmoil of conflict involving both rich and poor,
characterized by dishonesty and swindling, so the genial Samaritan
might all too often be the true thief. In *Martin Chuzzlewit* (1843-44),
the unscrupulous American, General Choke, having led Martin to
his crony, Mr. Scadder, to be swindled, assumes indifference and
withdraws from the negotiations and looks "at the prospect, like a
good Samaritan waiting for a traveller." (ch. 21) Needless to say, it
was not the good Samaritan who sat in wait for the traveller; his was
a spontaneous gesture. It was the thief who kept an alert eye on traffic. In Meredith's *Evan Harrington* (1860), Louisa, the Countess de
Saldar, caustically refers to her generous brother Evan as "the modern

Samaritan." (ch. 15) For Louisa, being a Good Samaritan is scarcely a wise or practical occupation in a society devoted to individual advancement. She can see no place for compassion and generosity because it is not advantageous. That Evan, despite her sarcasm, adheres to his line of conduct, indicates that, for Meredith, the traditional model of selfless generosity was even more necessary in a world increasingly unappreciative of, and even hostile to it.

If Evan can privately determine to maintain his role as a true Samaritan despite the ridicule of the world, as represented by his sister, for others it was not so easy to trust the traditional figure. For example, in Wilkie Collins' *The Moonstone* (1868), the arch-hypocrite, Godfrey Ablewhite is described as "a barrister by profession; a ladies' man by temperament; and a good Samaritan by choice." (First Period, ch. 8) Not only does Collins imply that the Good Samaritan is out of place in this sequence, but he reveals that undoubtedly Ablewhite's apparent charity merely conceals a corrupt way of life. Like Dickens' General Choke, he is the thief disguised as Samaritan the more effectively to rob those who foolishly place their trust in him. It is a sad society in which it is no longer possible to trust the old emblems of charity and humanity. Even these have been appropriated by the very forces they once sought to counteract.

The history of the Good Samaritan convention reveals a subtle depth of depression among Victorian interpreters of their age, for it shows that these writers were aware of how the commercialism of their time had not only vitiated the principles of Christianity upon which modern culture supposedly rested, but had corrupted and at the worst transformed the very emblems of that Christianity, first by identifying Samaritanism with cash and then by using Samaritanism as a mask for extorting money. Capt. Grog Davis, in Charles Lever's *Davenport Dunn* (1857-58)—a stern indictment of the Victorian cash society—sums up the situation. Clergymen, lawyers, and everyone else, he observes, use money as a means of evaluating worth, and therefore he feels himself entitled to employ the same standard. After all, he adds, selecting the most telling example, "take the doctors, and you'll see that their humanity has its price, and the good Samaritan charges a guinea a visit." (Vol. 2, ch. 77) Little more need be said to indicate the extent to which the conventional figure of human compassion had come to suggest the debasing commercialism of the age.

THE POOR SCHOLAR

Conventional characters based upon scriptural types were not the only stylized figures in Victorian literature. The figure of the poor scholar, from Chaucer's Clerk of Oxford onward, had become a familiar, secular figure in English literature. Though often a figure of fun, the poor, proud scholar is a sympathetic type as well; and in nineteenth-century English literature this conventional character became a vehicle for certain important attitudes.

Sir Walter Scott's Dominie Sampson in *Guy Mannering* (1815) is a peculiar-looking individual, and his physical attributes "all added fresh subject for mirth to the torn cloak and shattered shoe, which have afforded legitimate subjects of raillery against the poor scholar, from Juvenal's time downward." (ch. 2) Yet, despite the humor he provokes, Dominie is a sympathetic, even admirable character. It is his poverty, coupled with his learning, that makes him so attractive, indicating a certain unworldliness that might have appeared attractive to sincere Christians and all those who felt uncomfortable in an increasingly acquisitive culture.

Dominie occasionally extends his sympathies and affections beyond his books, but other scholarly types in the literature of the time were less appealing. The dedicated scholar appears as a lamentable type of wasted power in Eliot's Casaubon, or in Christopher Clutterbuck in Bulwer-Lytton's *Pelham*. Pelham describes Clutterbuck as a good fellow who drifted into the clerical profession and an uncomfortable marriage because his whole attention was concentrated on his beloved classics. He is Carlyle's dry-as-dust scholar, preoccupied with dead matter and vain of his preoccupation. Unlike Casaubon, Clutterbuck expresses no great objective in his scholarship. Pelham laments that "beyond the elucidation of a dead tongue he indulges no ambition; his life is one long school-day of lexicons and grammars . . . elaborately useless, ingeniously unprofitable." (ch. 63) Still, Clutterbuck is not entirely unappealing, and in another early novel, *The Disowned* (1828), Bulwer-Lytton provides a wider view of the type. Algernon Mordaunt, deprived of his wealthy inheritance, assumes a new identity as a poor student, attempting to make an honest living from his great store of knowledge. His position is courageous, but not hopeful. By contrast, the effete son of the man who has usurped Mordaunt's rights degenerates into a peevish, invalid, dry-as-dust schol-

ar, seeking no use for his knowledge beyond a tetchy self-indulgence. To Bulwer-Lytton, poverty may enhance the value of the
scholar by driving him into the practical world and obliging him to
consider his learning in relationship to it. When abstruse learning is
valued for its own sake, however, the scholar, poor or not, is more
likely to become a subject of criticism or satire.

There was a whole series of poor scholars in the school novels of
the Victorian period. From Matthew Scrawler in Joseph Hewlett's
College Life: or The Proctor's Notebook (1843) to Beerbohm's
Noakes, in *Zuleika Dobson* (1911), the student short of money but
long on brains or shrewdness worked his way successfully through
public school or university. Matthew Scrawler is the admirable version of the type; Noakes is Beerbohm's satirical comment upon it.
One of the more notable examples was Frederic Farrar's schoolboy
hero in *Julian Home: A Tale of College Life* (1859) who goes to St.
Werner's as a sizar to suffer humiliation before making his way as a
first-rate scholar to better academic circumstances.

It is surprising how slight is the reference to the actual learning
of the poor scholar. Carlyle's Diogenes Teufelsdröckh is one exception because he is created to be a vehicle for ideas derived from
profound learning. In this sense, Teufelsdröckh is a distinctly Victorian variation upon the conventional type. The poor scholar as mysterious sage may owe something to the romantic mood of the age in
which he was created, but he was drawn from life as well. Carlyle
himself was an apt model. George Borrow did not hesitate to describe himself as a scholar, and his adventures as a latter-day wandering scholar among tinkers, gypsies, and alien peoples afforded yet
another perspective on a type which demanded some attention and
even admiration. Still, it is the *state* of impoverished scholarship that
is important, rather than the nature of the learning involved. In
Dickens' *The Old Curiosity Shop*, for example, the poor schoolmaster who helps Little Nell and her grandfather is notable not for his
learning, but for his compassion, and it seems evident that poverty
and compassion, in his case, complement one another.

A prominent feature of the poor scholar is his retiring and un-
worldly nature. In "George Silverman's Explanation," Dickens utilizes this conventional association to create a character of extraordinary self-suppression. Silverman describes his early schooldays and
his desire to be discreet.

> It was in these ways that I began to form a shy disposition; to be of a timidly silent character under misconstruction; to have an inexpressible, perhaps a morbid, dread of ever being sordid or worldly. It was in these ways that my nature came to shape itself to such a mould, even before it was affected by the influences of the studious and retired life of a poor scholar. (ch. 5)

Silverman's entire life is one of confinement and self-denial. His aspirations are modest, his love is futile and must remain a secret. Although he loves his pupil, Adelina, he does not permit himself to consider the attachment, because of his humble circumstances, and takes pleasure in seeing her happily united with another of his pupils. Having suffered unjustified suspicions, he eventually finds peace when he is "presented to a college-living in a sequestered place." (ch. 9) Dickens has made his poor scholar admirable, according to his lights, making his learning and withdrawal signs of sensitivity rather than indifference. His unworldliness is not impracticality, but self-denial and a manifestation of his generous nature. He is, in his retirement, intelligence, and renunciation, a type of the self unstained by a sordid world; a model to be admired according to the moral assumptions of the age. To some extent this is what the poor scholar represented, though rarely in so pure a form as Dickens' Silverman. William Crimsworth, in Charlotte Brontë's *The Professor*, is more self-conscious and more prudish in his attempt to preserve himself from a corrupting world, while Louis Moore in *Shirley* is tempted to deny his true love in order to derive some material benefit from the society his intelligence prompts him to scorn. The generous and considerate Job Legh, in Mrs. Gaskell's *Mary Barton*, is the working man variation of the same essential figure.

It was not unusual that the poor scholar was also a cleric since education at Oxford or Cambridge frequently indicated a preference for holy orders. Well-educated but poorly financed young men attempting to make their way in an uncongenial world occur in Trollope's novels. Two characteristic examples are the Reverend Francis Arabin in *Barchester Towers* (1857), and the Reverend Josiah Crawley in *Framley Parsonage* (1860) and *The Last Chronicle of Barset* (1867). Arabin left the university after a religious struggle that drew him dangerously near to the Catholicism of Newman, but finally brought him to a sound Anglican faith and "humility of spirit." Although in his earlier days he had disdained the ordinary attractions of middle-

class existence, now, at forty, he finds himself envying the comforts
of life and yearning for a wife and family. His position is all the more
uncomfortable in that he has acquired no wealth and is obliged to
live on nothing more than a competence. Arabin's situation is scarcely
an ordeal, though, since he enjoys all the advantages of good station
in society. It is mainly in his refusal to declare his love for Eleanor
Bold that he resembles other similar types. Unlike George Silverman, however, he does finally announce his love and win the attractive widow. In addition, he is soon after named Dean of Barchester
and his lonely, intellectual life is transformed to an affectionate, domestic existence, concerned mainly with routine affairs, not thoughtful and tortuous speculation. In a way, Arabin may be seen to have
been "cured" of scholarship. The case is different for Josiah Crawley, who has been embittered by his poverty and has come to take a
perverse pride in indigence. He refuses to accept innocent gifts and
assistance of any kind, though his wife receives some aid secretly
to support the family. It was Crawley who had helped Arabin to
overcome the temptation of Catholicism, and Arabin, in return, has
rescued the Crawleys from a hard life in Cornwall to a scarcely more
profitable living in Barset. Crawley's bitterness is aggravated by his
sour pride, and eventually Arabin takes it upon himself to criticize
his mentor, and aid him thereby to a happier life.

It is in the later novel, *The Last Chronicle of Barset*, that Trollope
explores this conventional type most fully and presents the pathos of
it directly. As the novel opens, Crawley is under suspicion of having
misappropriated a check for £20, but his inability to account for the
check is characteristic of his impracticality and indifference to material things. Isolated and embittered, Crawley feels the pain of
poverty deeply. He has labored in the ministry for a pittance until
his reason has momentarily failed him. Knowing himself to be a finer
scholar than his colleagues he laments that, "with these acquire-
ments, with these fitnesses, [he] had been thrust down to the ground."
(ch. 61) Crawley identifies himself with heroic sufferers such as Samson, Milton or Belisarius, because he sees that "the impotency, combined with the memory of former strength and former aspirations, is
so essentially tragic!" (ch. 62)

Trollope's stern and unpleasant picture is made all the more so
because Crawley's faithful and loving wife and daughter are unable
to comfort him despite his reciprocated affection. But the grim picture

brightens at last. Crawley is proved innocent of any impropriety and is rewarded with a better living and the friendship of his superiors in the church. Nonetheless, although Trollope provides a conclusion not likely to jar the sympathies of his readers, Crawley's is not a simple happy ending. His learning has brought him nothing; it has only deepened his vision of suffering. The cruelest of ironies lurks in this grim character—that profound learning only intensifies and even elaborates through allusion and contrast the agonies of poverty which the ignorant might also suffer, though with less precision.

George Eliot was also interested in the conventional figure of the poor scholar, against which she was prepared to set a more comfortable, but less appealing type, such as Mr. Casaubon in *Middlemarch* (1871-72). If figures such as Dominie Sampson or Christopher Clutterbuck were saved from being offensive largely because they were poor and made aware of necessities and feelings beyond their studies, Casaubon, in being financially secure, is able to concentrate all the more egotistically upon his scheme. But, for the most part, Eliot's poor scholars are favorably presented. There is a certain honor that accompanies their hardship, as though they had accepted indigence as one of the concomitants of intellect. This impression is not always justified. Rufus Lyon, the dissenting minister of *Felix Holt, The Radical* (1866), lives in reduced circumstances. His dwelling is "not quite so good as the parish clerk's," for the prosperity of his congregation "had led to an enlargement of the chapel, which absorbed all extra funds and left none for the enlargement of the minister's income." (ch. 4) However, this way of life does not result from his devotion to his studies, which are mainly theological, but is the consequence of his one deviation from a steady life—his love for Annette, Esther's mother. Nonetheless, Rufus fulfills the main expectations of his type. He is essentially humble in all things except his learning, about which he has a confidence approaching vanity. Also, he is timid about himself, though politically active where politics touch upon religion—the substance of his life. While fulfilling the type, Rufus is still a realistic figure with more than a typical role to play.

Mordecai, in *Daniel Deronda* (1876), is another dedicated man, also impoverished, also a great scholar,

a man steeped in poverty and obscurity, weakened by disease, consciously within the shadow of advancing death, but living an intense life in an invisible past and future, careless of his personal lot, except for its possibly making some obstruction to a conceived good which he would never share except as a brief inward vision. (ch. 42)[4]

Like George Silverman, Francis Arabin, or Algernon Mordaunt, Mordecai's learning will achieve little more than an internal discovery, though there is some suggestion that Deronda will carry on his intellectual ideal and attempt to make it material. Yet such internal discovery is by no means despicable in itself. It is, perhaps, as important as the equally high-minded pursuit of knowledge presented in *Romola* (1862-63). Eliot there describes Bardo de' Bardi as "a man with a deep-veined hand cramped by much copying of manuscripts, who ate sparing dinners, and wore threadbare clothes, at first from choice and at last from necessity; who sat among his books and his marble fragments of the past, and saw them only by the light of those far-off younger days which still shone in his memory: he was a moneyless, blind old scholar." (Book 1, ch. 5) When he first appears in the novel, it is with his daughter, Romola, who is reading to him of Teiresias, blinded for having viewed the unclothed goddess Minerva, but compensated for his loss with the gifts of prophecy and long life. Bardo is no Teiresias, for he has lovingly devoted his life and his sight to his studies, admitting "even when I could see, it was with the great dead that I lived, while the living often seemed to me mere spectres— shadows dispossessed of true feeling and intelligence." (Book 1, ch. 5) He has no gift of prophecy nor does he live a remarkably long life. The image of Teiresias provides only an irony by which to judge the blind old scholar.

Yet Bardo had "led a pure and noble life," Romola declares to her brother and "sought no worldly honours; he has been truthful; he has denied himself all luxuries; he has lived like one of the ancient sages." In fact, he has lived "according to the purest maxims of philosophy." (Book 1, ch. 15) But his dedication has, after all, benefited little. His son has lived estranged from him and his beliefs, and his daughter cannot be spared the suffering from which she learns her own way of life. For Eliot, it seems, though learning and knowledge are much, they are of small importance to most men unless coupled with a willingness to utilize that knowledge among men in a world of events.

For George Meredith, as for George Eliot, the scholar is essentially a student of literature. Vernon Whitford, in *The Egoist* (1879), is not actually in want, though he is dependent. As a consequence, Sir Willoughby, who provides Vernon's pension, views him as the typical stuffy scholar, incapable of the sentimental communication that he believes he shares with Clara Middleton. In reality, the poor scholar, Vernon, is vastly more capable of expressing his *true* sentiments, and, in the end, succeeds in winning Clara and achieving a happy and independent existence. The poor scholar at this point begins to resemble the garret-dwelling poet—another familiar figure in the literature of the time. But, while Meredith's scholars may suffer some modest deprivations, especially in regard to their social station, they are never morally or physically threatened by genuine want. Arthur Rhodes, in *Diana of the Crossways* (1885), is a struggling student and poet, but his privations involve nothing more than having to work as a clerk. Gower Woodseer, patterned on Robert Louis Stevenson, is described in *The Amazing Marriage* (1895), as "Nature's poor wild scholar." (ch. 46) Although somewhat absentminded, after the fashion of scholars, and with little cash, he is scarcely the same type that appears in the darker novels of the time. For the most part, Meredith does not conceive of knowledge as separate from use, and hence he has no doubts about the cloistering of learning. His poor scholars are neither very poor, nor very devoted to actual scholarship—they are basically intelligent individuals living in modest circumstances and given to habits of reserve. In this regard, Meredith was not quite in the current of his time, for although his unsoiled genteel types reproduced a social reality, in the literature of the late nineteenth century the poor scholar was being used to indicate a different truth.

In William Hale White's *The Autobiography of Mark Rutherford, Dissenting Minister* (1881), neither the poverty nor the scholarship of the scholar is emphasized. The novel is really about the religious struggles of a sincere intellect. Like many similar stories of its time, it describes the gradual liberation of an individual mind from strict doctrine to freer principles—in this case, agnosticism. What is of interest concerning the figure of the poor scholar is that now qualities traditionally attached to that type are carried over to the germane figure of the religious doubter. Rutherford never really suffers serious want, but, on the other hand, his unpopular religious views force him to abandon the ministry and work in other areas where his scholarly training can assist him. The barren material existence once associated with the quester after knowledge now becomes part of the landscape of spiritual inquiry.

In Mrs. Humphry Ward's *Robert Elsmere* (1888), there are two scholarly characters of special interest. Robert Elsmere himself, like Mark Rutherford, searches for and ultimately discovers a personal spiritual code. Elsmere's code is more satisfactory than the doubtful Rutherford's, but it is also the product of a serious personal struggle. Elsmere is never reduced to real poverty. There is nothing here resembling the squalid conditions that Bulwer-Lytton's Algernon Mordaunt endured. Even indigence is genteel, resembling in this respect the easeful need of Meredith's intellectual recluses.

If Elsmere endures a modest privation in the accomplishment of his spiritual journey, his friend, Edward Langham, is doomed not to triumph over the wearing influences of his society. Langham sees himself as a "poor, silent, insignificant student" (ch. 36), but he is poor only in relation to the class in which he moves, and does not suffer from genuine want. Langham was supposedly modeled on Amiel, and his personal qualities, like that morose journal-keeper's, are a curious perversion of the very attributes associated with earlier and simpler versions of the poor scholar type.

> The uselessness of utterance, the futility of enthusiasm, the inaccessibility of the ideal, the practical absurdity of trying to realise any of the mind's inward dreams: these were the kind of considerations which descended upon him, slowly and fatally, crushing down the newly springing growths of action or of passion. (ch. 5)

At one time, the scholar suffered privations because he valued utterance, cherished a literary or scholarly enthusiasm, strove to imagine if not possess an ideal, and eagerly aspired to realizing the mind's inward dream. But all of this is at an end in Langham. He is a poor scholar indeed, but his is an impoverishment of the spirit, not of the pocket. There is no sympathy for him, no pathetic romance associated with his condition. The flame of interest that kept the former type alive and attractive has died out in the Langhams and Rutherfords of the century's end. If earlier scholars failed too often to apply their knowledge to the real life around them, they yet preserved a certain authenticity in their love of scholarship itself. In Langham, love of study and of life sink to a low and perilous level. He signifies the betrayal of what the earlier convention stood for. Not only does his learning isolate him from his own times, other men, and application in the society around him, it isolates him from his own impulses. His knowledge, turned in upon himself, feeds there. He is like the aged and desponding Merlin, lost at last to use and name and fame, the sad wreck of the earlier sage who cared for nothing but knowledge and the truth. Tennyson's image of the lost sage could stand as a model for all that Langham represented.

There were some characters who hoped to bring their learning to bear on their times. Edwin Reardon, in Gissing's *New Grub Street* (1891), is a highly intelligent man, ambitious to achieve something through his idealistic novels. Unfortunately, the time seems to have passed for such application. Now what society wants is the superficial pabulum that Jasper Milvain is only too happy to provide. Gissing was probably conscious of the irony in his use of the poor scholar convention, for Reardon is driven into sordid poverty by attempting to communicate his knowledge to society at large, and, in the end, longs for the life of an obscure scholar, content to teach little children in a small town. It is the exact reverse of what was amiss with figures such as Clutterbuck or George Silverman. "My strongest desire now," Reardon tells his friend, Biffen, "is for peaceful obscurity." (ch. 31) He has found that the desire for fame and utility are will-o-the-wisps that delude eager and talented young men. "They come here to be degraded, or to perish, when their true sphere is a life of peaceful remoteness. The type of man capable of success in London is more or less callous and cynical." (ch. 31)

That Gissing was aware of the irony in his use of the convention may be indicated in a second example from the novel. Alfred Yule is typical insofar as he is a learned scholar reduced to marginal poverty. He has been embittered by his poverty, behaves cruelly to his long-suffering daughter, Marian, and descends to a coarse self-pity when he learns that he may become blind for life, a forecast that proves true. There is none of the cosy association of scholarly father and loving daughter suggested by Eliot in *Romola* or *Felix Holt*, where financial need made the affections more firm. Instead, poverty eats away at affections, health, and spirit; and, for the characters in Gissing's novel, there is no last minute redemption as there is for Trollope's poor scholars. The illusion, Gissing seems to say, is at an end. Better to be that obscure and reclusive scholar, living in tatters and in love with his studies, than the debased creatures cast off by a fickle and tasteless public.[5]

The illusion of poverty and knowledge exposed in Gissing's novel was examined in detail in Hardy's *Jude the Obscure* (1895). Hardy took delight in contradicting or transforming the conventions he encountered, and in Jude Fawley he created an anti-type of the poor but enduring scholar. Jude, despite his intense longing, never achieves the scholarly competence of other fictional poor scholars. If the utilization of knowledge proved difficult in *New Grub Street*, in *Jude the Obscure* its mere acquisition is almost impossible. But those who shut Jude out are not themselves to be admired. Hardy undoubtedly sympathized to a great extent with Sue Bridehead's opinion that Christminster, far from being "a great centre of high and fearless thought," was merely "a nest of commonplace schoolmasters whose characteristic is timid obsequiousness to tradition." (Part 5, ch. 7)

Previously, the object of scholarship at least seemed worthwhile, though the failure to apply accumulated learning might be reprehensible. Now, not even the object merits interest. Phillotson's part in the novel is to indicate the stultification of what is called learning. Like other poor scholars, he suffers privation through an unwise placement of his affections. He verifies Sue's opinion that traditional learning is confining and deadly to the spirit. Scholarship is part of a futile past with no place in a bleak future. Jude's long struggle to educate himself in Latin and Greek culminates in little more than blasphemy and an ability to recognize inscriptions and epitaphs. His whole career of self-education is a parody upon the yearning to acquire what most considered a valuable acquisition—the accumulated wisdom of the past. For Hardy, that tradition meant little, and the poor scholar was all the poorer because, not only might his preoccupation leave him financially in need, but his possession, for which he was willing to sacrifice so much, was an empty purse as well.

It is not surprising that the figure of the poor scholar became, during the Victorian period more a figure of pity and despair than of comedy. All too often such conventional literary types had real prototypes. George Eliot might think of an Emanuel Deutsch while describing her Mordecai, or William Hale White might have his own career in mind while relating the autobiography of Mark Rutherford. There had been all too many talented young men, such as James Anthony Froude or Arthur Hugh Clough, who had been driven by their intellectual convictions into at least a temporary poverty. The type, in short, was not unfamiliar either in literature or society itself. And this was a society in which the traditional arcane knowledge of the past was being challenged by a new, science-defined learning, and being told that it was useless and out of date.

The gradual transformation of the poor scholar in fiction did more than present a history of alteration in a literary convention, it reflected a growing distrust of traditional and institutionalized knowledge in general. Now it was not the scholar who was an object of criticism so much as his scholarship. Any scholar seemed a poor scholar who invested his energy in worn-out ideas of the past. Merlin, the arch-scholar and sage, had feared the loss of his use and name and fame, and doubt and self-indulgence had made fact of his fear. Tennyson was perhaps more prophetic than he would have wished to be in foreseeing the cancellation of use and name and fame because men could no longer believe that dedication to the truths of the past was worth the necessary abnegation. It was another avenue of escape sealed shut.

CHAPTER FOUR

MARRIAGE

BACKGROUND

Since the institutionalization of marriage, it has been a favorite subject for writers of all ages. The Victorians were no different. There were traditional ways of treating marriage, but there were peculiarities of the institution as it existed in nineteenth-century England that also affected its representation in fiction. The fundamental attitude was that marriage was an unquestioned goal, though there was substantial difference regarding that goal. In 1841, one author of a book on feminine perfection wrote: "A female's real existence only begins when she has a husband," expressing the representative Victorian viewpoint. "Getting settled," was woman's goal; any other future was bleak.[1] Popular fiction presupposed marriage as the happiest state in life, implying that most marriages were successful, save only those where an obvious vice upset domestic order. But many saw that marriage was not accurately represented in tales of this sort. G. R. Drysdale remarked in 1854 that most marriages were the result of some interested motive other than love, and that romantic love could be found only in fiction.[2] Other writers demonstrated an alertness to the real state of marriage. Although the *mariage de conve-*

nance may have been accepted as natural in the novels of the twenties and thirties, it became a major target of criticism later in the century.

Even in the Victorian era marriage was complicated by the women's rights question. In 1859 *The What-Not or Ladies' Handy Book* included the following observation:

> It is probably not generally known that when once a woman has accepted an offer of marriage all she has or expects to have becomes virtually the property of the man she has accepted as her husband and no gift or deed executed by her is held to be valid; for were she permitted to give away or otherwise settle her property between the period of acceptance and the marriage he might be disappointed in the wealth he looked to in making an offer.[3]

The Marriage and Divorce Act of 1857 rendered divorce less costly insofar as it became available through the law courts, but it was still very difficult for a woman to obtain. And not until 1882 were married women declared mistresses of their own property. Until then, "at common law the wife's personal chattels vested absolutely in her husband on marriage and any personalty which she acquired during marriage (such as money earned by or bequeathed to her) followed the same course."[4]

Marriages, especially in the well-to-do classes, were frequently arranged by parents, and strict parental supervision was less a matter of prudery than a concern to protect girls from adventurers who might try to marry them before they could be legally protected by proper settlements.[5] A major dilemma facing the young woman, instructed that love and marriage were her purposes in life, was the attempt to combine the two. Young women were encouraged by plays, novels, and romances, to behave like coquettes and dream of love, Sir Richard Burton noted acidly in *Stone Talk* (1865), but they ended by following Mama's advice:

> No shame to know, to feel no fear
> In hunting rent-roll or a peer;
> Who limit wedlock's full extent
> To diamonds and settlement;
> Who views the matrimonial mart
> With stony eye and callous heart,

Trots out from her paternal stall
As nag for sale by Tattersall,
To highest bidder is knocked down
Like any slave in Stamboul town,
And swears to honour, love, obey,
The while her heart has gone astray
With some old flame who bides his day.

A woman might find herself confronted with one of the two sorrows of love described by Tennyson in an early poem, "A Contrast." On the one hand, there was sorrow from the heart given without the hand, and on the other, the hand without the heart.

Susan Ferrier's *Marriage: A Novel* (1818) summed up several of the fundamental attitudes toward the institution of marriage. In this story, Miss Ferrier describes most familiar types of marriage—the runaway love match, the ambitious marriage of convenience, the sacrificial second-best marriage, and the authentic marriage of mutual minds. The novel reflects the author's belief in the importance of love in marriage, though she is eager to air other attitudes as well. When the romantically vapid Lady Juliana expresses a desire to marry the man she loves, her domineering father, Lord Courtland, responds with a set piece.

> "There's no talking to a young woman now about marriage, but she is all in a blaze about hearts and darts, and—and—But hark ye, child, I'll suffer no daughter of mine to play the fool with her heart, indeed! She shall marry for the purpose for which matrimony was ordained amongst people of birth—that is, for the aggrandisement of her family, the extending of their political influence—for becoming, in short, the depository of their mutual interest. These are the only purposes for which persons of rank ever think of marriage. And pray, what has your heart to say to that?" (Vol. 1, ch. 1)[6]

Ironically, Lady Juliana later repeats this sentiment when she advises her own daughter, Mary, to accept the convenient marriage arranged for her. The sensible Mary protests that she is scarcely acquainted with Mr. William Downe Wright and would prefer to know "something of his character, his principles, his habits, temper, talents—in short, all those things on which my happiness would depend!" (Vol. 2, ch. 18)

Lady Juliana had found only unhappiness by refusing to marry the lord her father had acquired for her and by running off with her beloved Henry Douglas. She does not intend that her beautiful daughter, Adelaide, should similarly mistake her interests. Adelaide gives up her handsome cousin Frederick to marry a stupid but rich lord. "Amidst pomp and magnificence, elate with pride, and sparkling with jewels Adelaide Douglas reversed the fate of her mother; and while her affections were bestowed on another, she vowed, in the face of heaven, to belong only to the Duke of Altamont!" (Vol. 2, ch. 21) Despite the social triumph represented by this marriage, the reader has no doubt that the decision has been unfortunate.

The admirable Alicia Douglas recounts another unfortunate romance. Though she loved Edmund Audley, she could not marry him, for Lady Audley, his mother, to whom Alicia owed a great deal of respect and gratitude, disapproved of the union. To avoid the temptation of yielding to Edmund's love, Alicia married Archibald Douglas. Her life thereafter was satisfactory, but not fully happy. Happiness can follow only from a model marriage, and it is Mary Douglas' marriage that must serve as the correct example. To begin with, Mary has a well-equipped and religiously sound mind. Moreover, riches and great estates mean nothing to her. She even surprises her impetuous cousin Emily by explaining that she can only marry a man she loves. "Prudence, I thought, had been the word with you proper ladies," Emily responds, "a prudent marriage!" (Vol. 2, ch. 14) And prudent Mary's marriage is, for she weds Charles Lennox, a man whose character she admires and who offers her no more than love and a comfortable home; though subsequently they inherit a substantial fortune and estate. Meanwhile, her sister Adelaide's high connection disintegrates into disgrace, for "in something less than a year from the time of her marriage, this victim of self-indulgence again sought her happiness in the gratification of her own headstrong passions, and eloped with Lord Lindore, vainly hoping to find peace and joy amid guilt and infamy." (Vol. 2, ch. 32)

CRITICISMS OF COMMERCIAL MARRIAGES

What is peculiarly Victorian in much of the literature to follow Susan Ferrier's novel is the protest against forced, loveless, commercial marriages. Some writers were not untouched by the reality of loveless marriages in their own lives. Bulwer-Lytton's early sweetheart was forced into an unwanted marriage and died within a couple of years.[7] Tennyson presumably suffered acutely by losing Rosa Baring, who married a man of position and wealth favored by her parents.[8] He later used the conventional circumstances of the arranged marriage in several poems besides *Maud*, always with negative sentiments. "The Flight" presents a young woman telling her sister that she would rather run away from home than marry the man her father has chosen in order to save his property. "This father," the girl says, "pays his debts with me, and weds me to my grave." She cannot face the prospect of marrying a man she loathes and of going through the church ceremony with him. "To lie, to lie—in God's own house—the blackest of all lies!" she exclaims, and decides to flee, no matter what the consequences. In other poems, the young lady, though similarly reluctant, marries; the disappointed lovers are left to lament their states in "Locksley Hall," and "Edwin Morris." "Aylmer's Field" contains a well-known denunciation of parental vanity that breeds only disaster for a daughter and her faithful lover. Although Sir Aylmer Aylmer had not yet "set his daughter forth / Here in the woman-markets of the west, / Where our Caucasians let themselves be sold," he does attempt "to sell" Edith and only brings about young Leolin's suicide and Edith's death. But, opposed as Tennyson was to "Wealth with his wines and his wedded harlots" ("Vastness"), he did not countenance wifely infidelity once the marriage was complete, as his late poem, "The Wreck," indicates. Here, a young woman is ignorantly wed to a wealthy and impressive man with whom she shares no interests. She elopes with a more congenial partner, but he dies in a wreck at sea, while she survives only to learn that the infant she has left behind has died. She accepts these catastrophes as retribution for her sin.

Marrying for money, or to satisfy a parental wish is a familiar theme in Dickens' novels. But only sorrow comes of marriages such as Edith Dombey's, Louisa Gradgrind's, or Lady Dedlock's. Thackeray's *The Newcomes* (1853-55) made a similar point about marriage, utilizing as its model Hogarth's subject in "Marriage á la Mode."[9] Thackeray, like Sir Richard Burton after him, declared that commercial marriages were the normal, not the exceptional thing. Since "women sell themselves for what you call an establishment every day, to the applause of themselves, their parents and the world, why on earth should a man ape at originality and pity them?" he asks. Despite "the lies at the altar, the blasphemy against the godlike name of love, the sordid surrender, the smiling dishonour," he says such marriages are often more satisfactory than the most brilliant love matches. (Vol. 1, ch. 28) Lord Kew, in a similar vein, derides love marriages. They are "good for romances, and for Misses to sigh about; but any man who walks through the world with his eyes open, knows how senseless is all this rubbish." Only Baucis and Philemon will enjoy instant love and long endurance of it, he adds. "As for the rest, they must compromise; make themselves as comfortable as they can, and take the good and the bad together." (Vol. 1, ch. 30)

Describing the mercenary attitudes of young ladies toward marriage, Thackeray indicates playfully that Ethel Newcome is in an awkward position as a heroine, since she submits entirely to the same crass conventions of the marriage mart. But she has the opportunity to learn better. Madame de Florac, herself a victim of an unfortunate marriage of convenience, tries to prevent Ethel from repeating her mistake. It takes more than a simple warning to reveal the truth of Madame de Florac's argument, but, persuaded at last, Ethel is spared her sorrow. Others, like Lady Clara and Barnes Newcome, are not so fortunate.

> A bad selfish husband had married a woman for her rank: a weak, thoughtless girl had been sold to a man for his money; and the union, which might have ended in a comfortable indifference, had taken an ill turn and resulted in misery, cruelty, fierce mutual recriminations, bitter tears shed in private, husband's curses and maledictions, and open scenes of wrath and violence for servants to witness and the world to sneer at. We arrange such matches every day; we sell or buy beauty, or rank, or wealth; we inaugurate the bargain in churches with sacramental services, in which the parties engaged call upon Heaven to witness their vows—we know them to be lies, and we seal them with God's name. (Vol. 2, ch. 19)

Thackeray's had been an unfortunate marriage and the subject recurs in his fiction. He does not suggest that the sorrow that follows from unwise unions is unforeseen. Pendennis, narrating *The Adventures of Philip* (1861-62), laments in customary fashion the marriage "sacrifice" of Agnes Twysden. Later, we learn that Agnes chose the sacrifice because of the wealthy prize. Subsequently, we are warned that since mothers sell their daughters for marriage in the same way that horse dealers peddle their horses, every chance exists that a buyer may be deceived in his purchase. (ch. 20)[10] But, if Thackeray was thus able to warn prospective buyers about the cattle at market, he was not much inclined to recommend efficient courses. Love marriages, too, had a way of lapsing into withered romance, as more than one history in *Vanity Fair* illustrates.

Trollope was readier to offer a suitable remedy than Thackeray. But love, not money must be the motive for marriage. The subject of money marriages occurred often in his fiction, for example in *Doctor Thorne*, where both Frank and Augusta Gresham feel the need to marry for money. The convention is treated more seriously in *Can You Forgive Her?* in which a forced marriage is the central concern, and in *The Claverings*, which is practically a tract on the sin of marrying for money, a theme which is everywhere present in *The Way We Live Now* (1874-75). For the impecunious rascal, Fred Carbury, money is the one value in marriage, and he considers it "his business to marry an heiress." (Vol. 1, ch. 2) And he soon becomes interested in the tycoon Melmotte's daughter, Marie, whom he considers "simply as the means by which a portion of Mr. Melmotte's wealth might be conveyed to his uses." (Vol. 1, ch. 17) Marie is inexplicably attracted to Fred, but their elopement is scotched by her dreadful father who wishes Marie to marry Lord Nidderdale, who also views her as a financial acquisition. The old marquis, in going over possible partners for his son, Nidderdale, reveals his blatant mercantile attitude toward marriage; "I don't think that a woman of forty with only a life interest would be a good speculation," he observes. (Vol. 2, ch. 85) Being frustrated in her attachment to Fred Carbury, Marie agrees to marry Nidderdale on the understanding that it is strictly a commercial arrangement not involving love. Greater commercial circumstances, involving the collapse of her father's financial empire and his subsequent suicide, prevent the marriage after all, and Marie ends up marrying the canny American promoter, Mr. Hamilton K. Fisker.

Georgiana Longstaffe's principal aim is to marry well, but her father is unable to provide her with the appropriate settings in which to encounter proper and eligible men. Georgiana becomes desperate as she sees her opportunities diminishing:

> At twenty-two, twenty-three, and twenty-four any young peer, or peer's eldest son, with a house in town and in the country, might have sufficed. Twenty-five and six had been the years for baronets and squires; and even a leading fashionable lawyer or two had been marked

by her as sufficient since that time. But now she was aware that hitherto she had always fixed her price a little too high. On three things she was still determined,—that she would not be poor, that she would not be banished from London, and that she would not be an old maid. (Vol. 2, ch. 60)

Georgiana is finally driven to consider marriage with a proper and well-to-do city Jew, Mr. Brehgert, but her father's prejudice and her own calculating nature prevent the match and she consoles herself later by running away with a lowly curate.

Marie Melmotte and Georgiana Longestaffe are counterbalanced in the novel by Henrietta Carbury. Henrietta's mother has chosen as the intended Roger Carbury, Henrietta's second cousin. Roger loves Henrietta, but Henrietta loves Paul Montague. She muses at one point, "Could it be right that she should marry one man when she loved another? Could it be right that she should marry at all, for the sake of doing good to her family?" (Vol. 2, ch. 52) Her answer is no, and she persists in refusing Roger and eventually marries Montague. Her fidelity to passion rather than comfort and convenience obviously meets with Trollope's approval.

The condemnation of marriages of convenience was by no means limited to major writers. A poem by James C. Patterson, entitled "Sold," appeared in *The Cornhill Magazine* for May 1861. It summarizes what was apparently a widespread sentiment in English society. In the dramatic monologue a discarded lover explains to a friend how his beloved was forced to marry a suitor preferred by her parents while he was at sea. When he sees her again, she is ill and dreadfully altered. The despairing lover cannot restrain himself, recalling the picture of his once beautiful sweetheart, and breaks out with Tennysonian fervor, "They have sold her: by heaven! they have sold her, to the slavery of wealth and position." Bitterly he observes that women write petitions and say prayers to free the slaves, but do not recognize their own plight. "Worse than slaves are those women of England who barter their souls for a carriage" and "calling the purchase a marriage, / Live on in their legalized sin."

This sentimental but representative poem was fully conventional. Yet the convention was based upon a social reality and was depicted in other arts as well, for example in Sir William Quiller Orchardson's painting, "Mariage de Convenance." By the end of the century, it was no longer possible to distinguish the literary convention from the social tract, and, in his sermonizing novel, *The Woman Who Did* (1895), Grant Allen says of his nobly rebellious heroine, Herminia Barton, that "the mart was odious to her where women barter their bodies for a title, a carriage, a place at the head of some rich man's table." (Ch. 13)

In 1897, *The Lady's Realm* published a series of four articles on "The Modern Marriage Market." The first, and least temperate of these articles was by the popular novelist, Marie Corelli. "Taking the whole of London Society in a sweep of generalisation, she declared that the London market opened in May, and that the 'season' when girls were brought out was as barbaric as the slave-market of Stamboul. The bargain and sale of young girls was in her opinion the *raison d'etre* of all the balls, dinners and parties to Hurlingham and Ascot."[11] Tract and fiction here combine. The convention, long a part of the literary tradition had grown impertinent. The social convention and the literary convention stood directly at odds. What society most valued was what much of the literature of the time condemned. It is difficult to assess what effect one convention had upon the other, but whether slight or great, the literary convention of the marriage of convenience is one example of the direct penetration of social reality by literature.

But direct castigation was supplemented by more involved forms of criticism. Wilkie Collins, seeking to heighten the dilemma of his heroine, in *The Woman in White* (1859-60), had Laura Fairlie, out of respect for her father's dying wish, marry Sir Percival Glyde, who later reveals himself as an evil conniver. From the start it is clear that this is "an engagement of honour, not of love," ("Narrative of Walter Hartright") for Laura really loves Walter Hartright, whom she must renounce. Collins has merely increased the extreme conflict in Laura. She might have ignored her father's request, if she had known Sir Percival's true nature, but, assuming that he is a good man, she accepts him from the highest of motives—filial obedience. Collins' bitter touch to the familiar convention is to make the noblest feelings lead to the greatest evil and suffering. Laura is impelled to the arranged marriage by her own high principles, not by family pride or the need for money, but the consequence is no less cruel and demeaning. Less nobly, Helen Vavasour, in G. A. Lawrence's justly obscure novel, *Barren Honour* (1868), having, by the author's laborious contrivances, been separated from her true love, contracts a much-admired match with the wealthy but savage Lord Clydesdale, which saves the family fortune, but debases Helen's nature and leads ultimately to melancholy and a wasting death. In the same author's *Sans Merci; or Kestrels and Falcons* (1866), women are generally predatory. Bessie Standen, cold-bloodedly deceives Brian Maskelyne into a marriage for his money, though she loves another man, Flora Bellasys marries Lord Dorrillon to satisfy his vanity and her desire for status, with the clear understanding that there is to be no sexual connection.

The extreme sense of duty manifested by Laura Fairlie and the reckless martyrdom of a Helen Vavasour were not likely to affect most young ladies in love so much as a mansion, equipage, and a sumptuous income. In fact, it was frequently the mothers, not the girls themselves, who conducted the search for these desirable matrimonial qualifications. In Laurence Oliphant's *Piccadilly* (1865), a Negro gentleman, John Chundango, asks for Ursula Broadhem's hand, offering to purchase it with jewelry, stock and "royal blood." Ursula will have nothing to do with this arrangement, though her mother accepts it. Frank Vanecourt then makes an offer to spare Ursula further annoyance and to save her from Chundango, though he realizes that she does not wish to marry him, nor does he really intend to persuade her to do so. Behind the frivolous satire, Oliphant clearly intended a bitter moral.

In *Marriage*, Mary Douglas refused Lord Glenallan—a handsome, if insipid man with £ 20,000 a year—because she could not love him. In *Piccadilly*, half a century later, existence of the money is not so certain, and is in the hands of an offensive black man. As in Thackeray's *Adventures of Philip*, where one of Agnes Twysden's suitors is the rich mulatto Grenville Woolcomb, the racial prejudice is undisguised, serving as yet another indicator of how crass and loathsome the marriage of convenience had become to Victorians. At one time, the proposed husband may have been old or stuffy; he was rarely so glaringly unsuitable as these representatives of a muddled society's corrupt standards.

It remained for Thomas Hardy to add an ironic and ludicrous touch to the use of this convention. In *The Hand of Ethelberta. A Comedy in Chapters* (1876), the young heroine, faced with the choice of giving her hand without love to acquire wealth and social status, or marrying one she loves with no hope for riches, makes her choice not in the traditional method of bibliomancy, but by turning to the pages of

Mill's *Utilitarianism* for guidance. Reading that one should choose the greatest good for the greatest number, she accepts this dictum as a rule and determines to forget her romantic love and wed a repulsive peer, thereby benefitting her impoverished family. The peer may not be repellent in the same way as Chundango and Woolcomb, or even Trollope's Mr. Brehgert, but the crudity of the arrangement is even more openly evident. Hardy could not ignore the ironies associated with Ethelberta's marriage of convenience. She had, after all, selected the most promising of three such opportunities. When she discovers that her new husband has kept a mistress on his estate, she first rebels and then accommodates herself so well to circumstances that she concludes by obtaining complete dominance over Lord Montclere and his estate. In short, the marriage of convenience is convenient indeed, and Ethelberta scarcely misses her erstwhile lover, who happily marries her humble sister, Picotee.

Despite Hardy's fundamentally comic approach a certain flavor of ironic criticism remains. Ethelberta's commercial view of marriage is unappealing, but at the same time, it is occasioned by the lovelessness and mammonism of the entire nation. Ethelberta justifies her behavior not by obedience to a parental wish, but by adherence to a social law created by men who were frequently viewed as emotionless technicians of thought. Hardy here mocks the convention so central to many serious writers of his time, but his mockery confirms their serious charges against the Victorian marriage customs. By the end of the century, the marriage of convenience implied far more than a mere romantic mistake. From its place as a legitimate and accurate depiction of a social phenomenon, this marriage convention in literature had become an emblem of an entire society's corruption by deceptive rules of number, convenience, and cash. That writers so vehemently opposed what they thus viewed as corruption is an obvious indication of a severe discontent with their world.

COPHETUA

Part of the romance of marriage in nineteenth-century literature is in the overcoming of one or another barrier to its accomplishment. "A major cause of trouble between lovers was the misunderstanding based on false information or mistaken suspicion," Margaret Dalziel writes, going on to list as other common difficulties, parental opposition, reverse of fortune, and infrequently difference of station.[12] But difference of station was more common a theme than her comment suggests. Moreover, this difference was frequently seen in emblematic terms for which the example was King Cophetua and the Beggar Maid.[13] Tennyson employed this motif more than once, beginning with his early poem, "The Beggar Maid," a straightforward rendering of the legendary incident.

There are fortunate and unfortunate versions of the Cophetuan convention in Tennyson's poetry and elsewhere in the literature of the time. Thomas St. Clair, in Susan Ferrier's *The Inheritance*, marries beneath his station with unfortunate consequences. In Trollope's *Dr. Thorne* (1858), Frank Gresham, despite elaborate opposition, succeeds in marrying Mary Thorne, a girl of lower station. When Frank's father yields and Frank is free to claim Mary, Dr. Thorne informs the Greshams that Mary is heiress to a large fortune. Trollope avoids any consideration of the foul consequences that might have succeeded Frank's marriage with this clumsy though thoroughly popular device. Trollope's inheritor of blood does not stoop so low as he at first seems to do, and his beggar maid brings her needy king a handsome dowry.

It is not always so with Trollope, though his beggar maids are invariably discreet, being mainly little more than one or two steps below the men who love them on the social scale. In *Framley Parsonage* (1860), Lucy Robarts is of the respectable middle class and her lover is Lord Ludovic Lufton, the local aristocrat. Lady Lufton is opposed to their union on the grounds that Lucy is "insignificant." In fact, Lady Lufton has been impressed by her interview with Lucy and knows that she must relent if she is to preserve her son's love. Lucy is a young woman of character and humor, and she foresees the conventional difficulties. When she learns that Lady Lufton wishes to see her, she says to her sister-in-law, Fanny, that she'll go immediately and get it over with.

> "But, Fanny, the pity of it is that I know it all as well as though it had been already spoken; and what good can there be in my having to endure it? Can't you fancy the tone in which she will explain to me the conventional inconveniences which arose when King Cophetua would marry the beggar's daughter? how she will explain what Griselda went through;—not the archdeacon's daughter, but the other Griselda?"
> "But it all came right with her."
> "Yes; but then I am not Griselda, and she will explain how it would

certainly all go wrong with me. But what's the good when I know it all beforehand? Have I not desired King Cophetua to take himself and sceptre elsewhere?" (ch. 35)

The title of the chapter is "The Story of King Cophetua."

In the event, Lucy does not get the lecture she expects, but she does get Ludovic. Similar situations occur elsewhere in Trollope's stories, as with Henry Grantly and Grace Crawley in *The Last Chronicle of Barset*. Despite its prominence, however, the Cophetua convention is not used seriously by Trollope, as a scene from *He Knew He Was Right* (1868-69) demonstrates. When Sir Marmaduke learns of Mr. Glascock's intention to marry an American, he reckons that she will be able to make her way in society. Trollope adds that "he would have been bound to say as much had Mr. Glascock intended to marry as lowly as did King Cophetua." (ch. 78) The reference came easily to Trollope, and was insignificant after all in his fictional world where genuine poverty and thorough aristocratic domination do not appear, and where the observation of social graces generally makes it impossible to object to even this extraordinary line of conduct.

The Cophetua image was of course only a stylized way of representing a broader conventional figure. Lady Dedlock, raised from a relatively humble station to a place of eminence, must abandon the man she really loves. This is one basic form of the convention. A more complex variation occurs in Charles Lever's *Davenport Dunn* (1857-59), where Captain Davis entices the impoverished but aristocratic Annesley Beecher into marrying his daughter Lizzie. Beecher is led to imagine how nobly he would defend his marriage to a humbly born girl before his fellow aristocrats. He views himself in heroic terms. When he later inherits his brother's estate and becomes a peer, he is deeply ashamed of his connection. Meanwhile, Davis has loathed having to sacrifice the daughter he loves to the foolish Beecher, but he views the marriage mainly as a financial necessity. Lizzie, on her part, agrees to the arrangement, despite her low estimate of Beecher's character, in order to help her father, but also because her pride urges her to accept the challenge of society's potential disapproval. She is confident that she can behave in a manner suitable to the position she will hold. Though her confidence proves true, it does not cancel the fact of her low parentage, and it is this that shames her weak husband.

The Cophetua convention was often used ironically. Lady Caroline, learning of Ursula's marriage to John in Miss Mulock's *John Halifax, Gentleman* (1856), observes with all affectation about the modestly circumstanced pair, "*Ma foi!* this is the prettiest little episode I ever heard of. Just King Cophetua and the beggar-maid—only reversed. How do you feel, my Queen Cophetua?" (ch. 19) Dickens was sentimental but serious in his version of the Cophetua convention. When he described the potential union of Eugene Wrayburn and Lizzie Hexam, he first indicated how random this King Cophetua was in his passions before he proceeded to elevate the object of his affection to his dubious level. Nor did Dickens offer any guarantee that the *mésalliance* would work. For him, the beggar maid, not the king, was the more generous of the pair.

The Cophetuan marriage seemed obsolete as time passed because many erstwhile kings were now in the marketplace. If the circumstances that Lever described in the 1850s were probable, by the end of the century unusual marriages by men of aristocratic station were quite common. American heiresses, for example, became familiar partners for noblemen late in the century.[14] But there were even less acceptable unions; George Bullock refers to "the alarming frequency with which young men introduced chorus girls into the Peerage."[15] The social fact, then, was not uncommon, and the literary convention merely played various changes upon it. In *The Woodlanders* (1886-87), Thomas Hardy indicated that the adaptation to financial necessity did not prevent needy young men of good family from preserving aristocratic sentiments. In Hardy's novel, Mr. Melbury urges his daughter Grace to break off her understanding with Giles Winterborne and marry Edgar Fitzpiers on the strength of Fitzpiers' respected family name and superior education. It is soon evident that Fitzpiers' instincts remain patrician, though his finances are not. He is strongly attracted to the wealthy and elegant Mrs. Charmond and runs off with her, leaving the Melburys shamed and embarrassed. In the end, Fitzpiers returns to beg his estranged wife to rejoin him. That she agrees by no means signifies a happy ending in Hardy's world. Mainly the reunion emphasizes the ease with which Giles' death is forgotten and the malleability of human emotions and values.

If Hardy demonstrated the insignificance of station and thereby the pointlessness of the Cophetuan gesture, George Moore, in his novel, *Muslin* (1886, largely rewritten 1915), implied a condemnation of the continuing fantasy reflected in the old legend. *Muslin* is about the female pursuit of good matches, and offers as its model union a quiet, commonplace, middle-class marriage. From the opening of the novel, when Alice Barton's play based upon the legend of King Cophetua is performed at her girls' school on graduation day, the legend serves as a thematic counterpoint to the events of the plot. Violet Scully, who plays the beggar-maid in Alice's play, later captures the Marquis of Kilcarney, a man she does not love, but who, because of his position, has been the principal prize of the Dublin Season. Gossips go so far as to attribute her success with the marquis to the fact that Violet had played the beggar-maid role. (Ch. 25)

The Cophetua dream, Moore suggests, is a pernicious one. It confuses young women with false values. It seems to suggest that every beauty, regardless of her station, can marry a "king." But Moore's novel shows that Cophetua is won by guile playing upon his own foolishness and susceptibility. A Cophetua of this character thus won could be of no real interest to a true woman. But Moore leaves his outmaneuvered beggar-maid, Olive Barton, uninstructed by her disappointment. Only Alice understands fully what her instincts and principles had suggested to her all along, and hers is the happy marriage, based on "honest materialism," and free of illusions. (Ch. 29)

Theodore Watts-Dunton took another approach, yet more ironic, in his novel, *Aylwin* (1898). Henry Aylwin, wishing to raise Winifred Wynne up to his station in life, encounters predictable resistance from his proper mother; more surprisingly, he meets with even stronger objections from Winifred herself. She does not trust wealth, all of her values being associated with nature and the simple pleasures of life. Consequently, she puts Henry on a year's probation, allowing him time to demonstrate that he has not been corrupted by money. By the time the lovers are reunited, both have sufficiently evidenced their freedom from all notions of caste, to permit their marriage.

Among the most ironic employments of the Cophetua convention is that of George Gissing in *Demos* (1886). In this bitter novel, a working-class youth, Richard Mutimer, is elevated to a lofty station when he unexpectedly inherits a wealthy estate. He is idealistic and hopes to put his radical economic notions into practice. However, he soon discovers that with social elevation, his tastes change and he prefers the polished, appealing Adela Waltham to his former working-class sweetheart, Emma Vine. King Cophetua now scorns his beggar maid and eyes the ladies of the court, an act all the more ironic in that he is himself only recently ascended to the throne.

The convention of the elite figure raising up his, or sometimes her, beloved to a higher station in the manner of King Cophetua with his beggar maid, was prominent in the imagination of writers in nineteenth-century England. However, while it frequently served as little more than an embellishment of popular romance—and we have not really examined that all too common feature—in more memorable works, the convention came to signify an imbalance in society productive of serious and undesirable consequences, and was therefore used more to chide than to enhance.

MARRIAGE ENDINGS

The last-chapter marriage (or marriages) is a thoroughly accepted convention of Victorian literature. But here, as with other subtler conventions, there are antithetical qualities. Although terminal marriages were commonplace, they underwent a good deal of modification. Lionel Stevenson notes correctly that the cumulative effect of many forces tending toward the amelioration of the woman's condition in nineteenth-century England "destroyed the conventional literary picture of innocent maidens needing the protection of generous men and achieving it by matrimony in the last chapter."[16] Robert Bell, in *The Ladder of Gold* (1850), was only one of many writers who took direct offense at the matrimonial convention. Having at the end of his second volume described the arranged marriage of his desolate heroine, Margaret Rawlings, to Sir Charles Eton, he begins his third volume with a direct address to his readers. Assuming that they are upset by his marrying Margaret off, he wishes to justify himself.

> What could happen after that in which a novel-reader could be expected to feel any sympathy? The young lady was married, and made wretched for life, and there was an end of her. Romance is over, and vegetation begins when people marry. Hence it is that the established and legitimate law of novels is to reserve the matrimonial incidents for the consummation of the story. You may do anything else you please with your characters during the course of the plot—hang or assassinate them, or let them run away with people's wives—but you must not marry them till the last page. The clergyman in a novel may be regarded as the undertaker of the story, and when he makes his appearance, the

play is played out, and nothing more remains to be said or done but to bury the dead. (Vol. 3, Book 1, ch. 1)

Bell argues against this conventional view, declaring that "A novel is a picture of real life," and since life does not stop with marriage, the novelist is entitled to pursue subjects beyond matrimony. At the same time, marriage is an important subject throughout Bell's novel.

Far from the end of *The Adventures of Philip* (1861-62), Thackeray observes, concerning the approaching marriage of Philip Firmin and Charlotte Baynes, "the end was approaching. That event, with which the third volume of the old novels used to close, was at hand." (Ch. 32) But the novel goes on and Philip has a good deal more to endure before he inherits a fortune and fades from the picture at the novel's end. In *The Newcomes* (1853-55), Thackeray makes his point more clearly through the character of Mrs. Mackenzie who addresses herself to the narrator of the story. "You gentlemen who write books, Mr. Pendennis, and stop at the third volume," she says, "know very well that the real story often begins afterwards. My third volume ended when I was sixteen, and was married to my poor husband. Do you think all our adventures ended then, and that we lived happy ever after?" (Ch. 23)[17] Quite in keeping with this sentiment, Thackeray describes the misadventures that succeed marriage both in this novel and elsewhere. The marriage of Clive Newcome and Rosa Mackenzie is no more successful than David Copperfield's with his Dora in Dickens' novel, or Thackeray's own Amelia Sedley and George Osborne in *Vanity Fair*. Clive and David both have a second opportunity to end their stories with traditional wedding bells, the only variant in the basic convention being that it is for the second, rather than the first time. In *Vanity Fair*, Colonel Dobbin finally wins the woman for whom he has waited; however, the perfunctory marriage is not the usual cheery conclusion, but the beginning of a formal disenchantment.

Anthony Trollope may not have had the same personal reasons for distrusting the notion of marriage as a solution to life's troubles that Thackeray had, but he shared the superior novelist's views so far as the convention applied to fiction. It is, he remarks in *Barchester Towers* (1857), the ordeals of characters that delight the public. "When we begin to tint our final pages with *couleur de rose*, as in accordance with fixed rule we must do, we altogether extinguish our own powers of pleasing." (Ch. 51) Later he adds the famous observation that "the end of a novel, like the end of a children's dinner-party, must be made up of sweetmeats and sugar-plums." (Ch. 53) And the sweetest of these is the marriage that resolves all complications. With not a little wryness in his remarks, Trollope resumes his tabletop metaphor in a later novel of the Barchester series, *Framley Parsonage* (1860). This novel, too, ends with marriages, but in this instance Trollope defends the convention.

> Nevertheless, is it not the fact that the sweetest morsel of love's feast has been eaten, that the freshest, fairest blush of the flower has been snatched and has passed away, when the ceremony at the altar has been performed, and legal possession has been given? There is an aroma of love, an undefinable delicacy of flavour, which escapes and is gone before the church portal is left, vanishing with the maiden name, and incompatible with the solid comfort appertaining to the rank of wife. To love one's own spouse, and to be loved by her, is the ordinary lot of man, and is a duty exacted under penalties. But to be allowed to love youth and beauty that is not one's own—to know that one is loved by a soft being who still hangs cowering from the eye of the world as though her love were all but illicit—can it be that a man is made happy when a state of anticipation such as this is brought to a close? No; when the husband walks back from the altar, he has already swallowed the choicest dainties of his banquet. The beef and pudding of married life are in store for him;—or perhaps only the bread and cheese. Let him take care lest hardly a crust remain—or perhaps not a crust. (Ch. 48)

Obviously the compliment to marriage as the crowning act of love is two-edged since Trollope implies that love is not worth examining in its subsequent domestic phase. In *The Small House at Allington*, that phase is put off entirely for the central characters, John Eames and Lilian Dale, who do not wed, though a couple of other marriages are introduced at the novel's end to pacify any readers deeply offended by Trollope's overt frustration of a favorite convention.

But Trollope was prepared to go further yet. He begins *He Knew He Was Right* (1868-69) with a courtship and a marriage and what follows is basically the history of an unwise union of two proud and stubborn natures. It is perfectly evident in the case of Louis and Emily Trevelyan that marriage does not necessarily solidify the love that led up to the ceremony. Indeed, it is that very ritual that dooms what affection the two genuinely feel for one another. Near the end of the novel, with its sad history nearly over, Trollope almost bitterly confronts the subject of nuptial conclusions. He apologizes for taking his readers from one wedding to another, but explains that "it is the nature of a complex story to be entangled with many weddings towards its close. In this little history there are, we fear, three or four more to come." Despite Trollope's playful forecast, no hymeneal avalanche occurs, and in due course the central characters marry. The convention, having been much assailed and mocked, asserts its dominance after all.

George Eliot's *Middlemarch* (1871-72) is most certainly concerned with marriage, though its approach is far from conventional. Mainly it describes the failure of marriage. Dorothea's marriage to Casaubon leads to a rapid disillusionment, and Lydgate discovers, somewhat more gradually, the nature of his mistake in marrying Rosamond Vincy. But if these unfortunate marriages stand as caveats to hasty lovers, the marriage of Fred Vincy and Mary Garth manifests a wise union, and Dorothea's marriage to Will Ladislaw represents a satisfactory accommodation though it is too ambiguous to serve as a model. Still, the novel is not a discourse upon marriage, and, rather than quarrel with the convention, Eliot sought to avoid it.[18]

George Meredith, on the other hand, was deeply concerned not only with the subject of marriage, but with its place in fiction as well, and his highly self-conscious attitude toward the convention is representative of feeling in the later part of the century. Meredith complained that, having disposed of the subordinate "heroine Constance and her young Minister of State," Percy Dacier, by marriage in his novel, *Diana of the Crossways* (1885), he was led to feel that there was little reason for continuing his story. "When we have satisfied English sentiment, our task is done," he mocks, apparently abandoning the convention of the hymeneal conclusion. (Ch. 39) Yet even the title of the last chapter, "Nuptial Chapter; And Of How A Barely Willing Woman Was Led To Bloom With The Nuptial Sentiment," shows how selfconsciously and ironically Meredith yielded to the prevailing sentiment.

In *Beauchamp's Career* (1876), Meredith goes further and describes how Rosamund Romfrey, concerned for Nevil Beauchamp's happiness and conditioned by "readings in the fictitious romances which mark out a plot and measure their characters to fit into it," expects that Renée "would have seen her business at this point, and have glided melting to reconciliation and the chamber where romantic fiction ends joyously." (Ch. 48) But Meredith disappoints this expectation of popular romance. Although he does convert his last chapter into a nuptial chapter—for Nevil marries Jenny Denham after having skirted more than one other possibility—it is a funereal chapter too, since it concludes with Nevil's death soon after his marriage. Meredith was willing to mock the obligatory nuptial convention, but his regular practice was to yield to it after all, even if reluctantly. However, in his later novels, his nuptials become less and less regular, verging even on the outrageous, as in *Lord Ormont and His Aminta* or *The Amazing Marriage.*

Some authors, such as Charles Reade, remained unashamedly content to conclude their novels with nuptial orgies. In *Put Yourself in His Place*, Reade ends by marrying off not only Henry Little and Grace Carden, but more improbably old Mrs. Little and Dr. Amboyne, and more improbably yet, Squire Raby and Jael Dence (the last is a version of the Cophetua convention). However, in the face of changing social conditions, Robert Bell's complaint that novels should be faithful to life even in marriage, and George Eliot's attempt at that fidelity, made the continuance of the nuptial convention more galling than satisfactory for many writers. Even the popular novelist, Mrs. Oliphant, declared that she would have preferred to leave the hard-working heroine of *The Curate in Charge* struggling in poverty, but she felt it expedient to marry her off to the hero instead.[19]

There were, of course, authors willing to give their own versions of the "more legitimate conclusion," none more so than Thomas Hardy. Hardy clearly objected to the happy hymeneal ending, and although he yielded the point in *The Return of the Native* in the same way that Dickens had earlier with *Great Expectations*, he did not always give way. In novels such as *The Mayor of Casterbridge, The Woodlanders*, or *Tess of the d'Urbervilles*, marriages do not work out well, and are treated bitterly or ironically, while in *Jude the Obscure* Hardy put a chilling finish to the no longer credible convention of the nuptial ending.[20] Marriages initiate the difficulties of the characters in this novel. Jude's marriage to Arabella is no rural romantic idyll; it is the ruin of a dream. Likewise, Sue's marriage to Phillottson is wrong-headed from the start, and is based on a false view of what marriage entails. Hardy emphasizes relentlessly that a legally correct marriage can, because of the partners' feelings, be actual adultery, while an illicit relationship can be the truly spiritual connection. The tragedy is that society, with its many prohibitions, will not permit the more natural connections and crushes humanity with rules. The wedding bells that once brought joy and happy endings here bring only agony and regret.

The misgivings had begun early, and such notable characters as David Copperfield, Clive Newcome, and Richard Feverel learned from rash marriages early in their fictive histories what error could reside in matrimony. David and Clive were given second opportunities; Richard was not. The first two had merely seen that their choice had been unwise; Richard discovered too late that his choice had been right. His was the sorrier discovery. But in *Jude the Obscure*, each new rearrangement of partners only indicates more and more savagely Hardy's conviction that the institution was pernicious, and his closing chapters constitute a monumental parody of the nuptial convention. Many novels, such as *Barnaby Rudge*, ended with double weddings or more; it was often expected not only in cheap popular romances, but in creditable novels. But Hardy brutally drives his characters back to their first errors. Jude and Sue had had second chances, now those chances return upon them. Sue willingly remarries a man for whom she feels a physical aversion, and Jude drunkenly lapses back into his foolish marriage with Arabella. Here is the romantic conclusion inside out. Although the convention might survive this crushing assault in the more thoughtless literature that followed, serious writers found it necessary to take into account the clear distinctions that existed between those nuptial chapters that seemed to close such jolly careers and the sadder and sadder realities.

CHAPTER FIVE

COINCIDENCE

COINCIDENCE AND PLOT

Nineteenth-century writers commonly introduced the most improbable coincidences into their narratives. This device was, in large part, an inheritance from earlier literary tradition. How unlikely it is that David Copperfield should journey to Yarmouth just when Steerforth's ship is wrecked by a wild tempest and Ham dies attempting to save his scapegrace rival. But who objects to this coincidence?

For Dickens, such crossings and intertwinings are part of his art, not merely representations of what he felt life to be. Hence, although there are numerous coincidences in *Bleak House*, the book is satisfying. We enjoy "The ingenuity of the whole structure and the illusion of god-like superiority that discovers a tight web of cause and effect beneath the apparent chaos of daily affairs."[1] It is unlikely, to take a random instance, that in the whole population of London, including its rogues, beggars and scamps, Mrs. Brown should come to know Rob the Grinder, just as it is improbable that Alice Marwood should unwittingly knock at Harriet Carker's door to beg for help from a relation of the man who has ruined her. "Nothing is introduced at random," John Forster said of *Bleak House*, "everything tends to the catastrophe."[2]

For Dickens, E. D. H. Johnson observes, "the apparent randomness of existence conceals an underlying providence."[3] Forster wrote that Dickens delighted in "the coincidences, resemblances, and surprises of life,"[4] but he found a more suggestive use for them in his fiction. In *Little Dorrit*, Dickens closes the second chapter of Book One with the well-known reflection:

> And thus ever, by day and night, under the sun and under the stars, climbing the dusty hills and toiling along the weary plains, journeying by land and journeying by sea, coming and going so strangely, to meet and to act and react on one another, move all we restless travelers through the pilgrimage of life.[5]

The interaction of men's lives signified something more profound than mere democratic agreeableness. "The coincidences in *Oliver Twist* are of too cosmic an order to belong in the category of the fortuitous," Steven Marcus says, going on to explain that the various characters of the novel represent various virtues. "For the population of *Oliver Twist* consists only of persons—the wicked and the beneficent—involved with the fate of the hero. There are, almost, no other sorts of people in it; and in a world where there is no accidental population, no encounter can be called a coincidence."[6] Dickens himself defended his use of coincidences in *A Tale of Two Cities*: "I think the business of art is to lay all that ground carefully, not with the care that conceals itself—to show, by a backward light, what everything has been working to—but only to *suggest*, until the fulfilment comes. These are the ways of Providence, of which ways all art is but a little imitation."[7]

A variety of coincidences appeared in poems and novels to emphasize a point or point a moral. In Bulwer-Lytton's *The New Timon*, Morvale coincidentally encounters Arden, a man who, Morvale later discovers, has injured him deeply. That Arden should be the father of Lucy, the orphan girl that Morvale had previously taken under his care, only compounds the improbability. Given these coincidences, it is not astonishing that Morvale and Lucy should happen, after a long separation, to visit Lucy's mother's tomb at the same moment and thereby become happily united once more. Coincidences here are unlikely, but demonstrate a scheme of moral cause and effect. Coincidences operate fortuitously in *Jane Eyre* (1847) as well. Mr. Mason happens to be in Jamaica where he learns from Jane's uncle that she is to marry Rochester. Mason, with his important knowledge of

Rochester's wife, returns in time to prevent the marriage and occasion Jane's flight from Thornfield. It is on this flight, in turn, that Jane falls in with the Rivers family, who, by coincidence, turn out to be her relatives. So frequent was Charlotte Brontë's use of coincidence in *Villette* (1853), that the reviewer in the *Athenaeum* complained of it. And yet these unlikely conjunctions were quite acceptable in Victorian fiction.[8]

Bizarre coincidences did occur in life, as Richard Altick has indicated,[9] but in fiction they were commonplace. By chance, Harry Carson, in *Mary Barton*, is murdered exactly where Jem Wilson had quarrelled with him earlier, and this unfortunate coincidence leads the authorities to believe Jem guilty of the crime. Contrarily, John Halifax happens to save a Mr. March, and later falls in love with his daughter, though there has been no communication in the meantime. John's close friend, Phineas Fletcher, notes the connection:

> "By-the-bye, did not the father's name strike you? *March*—suppose it should turn out to be the very Mr. March you pulled out of Severn five years ago. What a romantic conjuncture of circumstances!" (Ch. 10)

There are other similarly benign coincidences of this sort in *John Halifax, Gentleman* (1856), not all of them so romantic, but all quite fitting for Miss Mulock's purpose of describing a morally sound hero.

Many Victorian novels were structured by coincidences; Mrs. Gaskell's *Ruth* (1853) is a clear example. By chance Ruth is passing by just as Mr. Bellingham saves a young boy from drowning. Their friendship begins under these extraordinary circumstances. Coincidentally, Mrs. Mason, Ruth's employer, later comes upon Ruth and Mr. Bellingham out strolling and charges the young girl with impropriety, thus prompting Ruth to place herself in Mr. Bellingham's care. Ruth's fall is surrounded by unusual coincidences, and a "romantic conjuncture of circumstances" precipitates the climax of the tale. By coincidence, the Mr. Donne who is Mr. Bradshaw's chosen candidate for Parliament is really Bellingham, who recognizes Ruth, now in Mr. Bradshaw's employment. Meanwhile Mrs. Pearson appears in Eccleston in time to reveal Ruth's history and bring about new trials for the penitent woman.

There is no special irony in these coincidences; they merely serve the development of plot, for coincidence in nineteenth-century fiction was mainly a convenience of plot, as in Prest's *The Gipsy Boy* or

Charles Lever's *Davenport Dunn*. How unlikely, and yet useful to the plot, that Paul Classon, in the latter novel, should encounter Grog Davis at an obscure inn in Holbach and provide him with important information about the Lackington estates, about which Davis is deeply concerned. Such coincidences are common in Trollope's novels, as well. In *The Way We Live Now* (1875-76), for example, Ruby Ruggles comes to stay with her relative, Mrs. Pipkin, at the time that Mrs. Hurtle is lodging there. By this device, Trollope is able to draw together two otherwise disparate strands of his narrative.

Some works used coincidence for special effects. George Borrow did not consider it out of place in *Lavengro*, which purported to be autobiography. But, since he claimed that his work was a "dream of life" rather than a strict autobiography, the uncanny coincidences are explainable in those terms. In *The Romany Rye* it is incredible, unless one reads a certain crude moral allegorizing into the account, that Borrow should encounter the papist priest, the postillion, and his old friend Murtagh, all three of whom were involved in a peculiar adventure in Italy. Similarly, it is most unusual that Borrow should become acquainted with Jack Dale only to discover that he is the son of a forger whose activities produced inconvenience and trouble years before for the kindly collector of China who tended Borrow when he was injured. Only by viewing life as a form of fantasy or dream, open to manipulation, could such coincidental combinings of individual fates, and such neat unitings of disparate tales, become acceptable.

Most writing of the time, however, presented a more authentic picture of life—without excluding coincidence. Robert Bell warned his readers in *Ladder of Gold* against the hasty dismissal of odd conjunctions of circumstance:

> Let nobody despise coincidences. There is not so much of chance in them as we are apt to imagine. The universe is a system of such perfect order that everything strikes in its proper place at the right moment. . . . Most events, from the founding of empires to the bursting of steam boilers, are inevitable results of an absolute chain of causation. (Vol. 1, Book 2, ch. 1)

In a realistic novel such as *Felix Holt, the Radical* (1866), George Eliot employed a surprising number of coincidental events. It is unlikely that Felix should discover Maurice Christian's pocketbook containing the chain identifying Esther's parentage, and that he should take it to the one man, Rufus Lyon, who knows of that connection because he married Esther's mother. Christian's encountering Dominic Lenoni, an old acquaintance from Italy is equally unlikely; but most coincidental is Esther's history involving her with the Transome estate to which she is heir. R. T. Jones remarks of this latter set of complications that Esther ultimately finds herself in a position to have Transome Court with or without Harold Transome, the present owner, and that "all the coincidences and legalities have been contrived to put her in that position."[10] All of the manipulations of events are designed, by Eliot, to place Esther in a dilemma where she can demonstrate her moral strength.

There is an ample dosage of coincidence in *Middlemarch* as well. Here Eliot defends the manner in which Raffles happens upon Bulstrode's letter, thereby leading him back to his confederate in deceit and precipitating a major catastrophe in the novel. Small accidents and large are equally likely in a random existence, Eliot explains. "To Uriel watching the progress of planetary history from the Sun, the one result would be just as much a coincidence as the other." (Book 4, ch. 41)

If coincidences appeared so unashamedly in what were supposedly matter-of-fact tales, it is not surprising that coincidence was used in the more sensational Victorian novels too. For example, an awkward twist of plot is required in *East Lynne* to manage Isabel Carlyle's return to her former home and family in the disguise of a governess, thereby creating the heart-rending central circumstance of the story. This is possible in the novel because Afy Hallijohn, also involved with the unscrupulous seducer, Levison, and with the unjustly condemned Richard Hare, happens to meet Isabel in Germany, and tells her that a governess' position is open at East Lynne. In *Lady Audley's Secret* it is coincidental that George Talboys knows Robert Audley and meets him immediately upon his return from a long absence overseas, and that it is to Audley's own uncle that Talboys' missing wife is married. Audley's bringing Talboys to his uncle's estate occasions the meeting between George and his wife Helen, and begets the entire mystery that follows. The whole story, in short, turns upon a coincidence. And if coincidences did not provide the foundation of a plot, they did, as we have already seen, serve to unravel mysteries or save endangered heroes, as in Charles

Reade's *Hard Cash*, where two minor characters merely happen to walk into the courtroom where Alfred Hardie is on trial, and, by their testimony, swing the decision in his favor. Crude plot conveniences of this sort are not worth enumerating, but there were other sensational novelists who made more of this convention than a mere hinge for a creaky fable. As David Goldknopf observes, "though sheer artifice at times, coincidence at other times makes a tacit metaphysical statement."[11]

Wilkie Collins made ample use of coincidence in his stories. Though he used coincidence for plot convenience, he also sought to unite moral and thematic purposes with this device. In *Hide and Seek* (1854), Zachary Thorpe's fortuitous encounter with old Mat Grice leads to the latter's acquaintance with Valentine Blythe, who happens to be the protector of Mat's dead sister's illegitimate child, of whom it is finally revealed that Zachary's father is the parent. Similarly, Captain Kirke, in *No Name* (1862), returning from China, happens by accident upon the destitute and seriously ill Magdalene Vanstone. Frustrated love for Magdalene was Kirke's reason for going to China in the first place; thus he is her appropriate savior. Naturally, the ship in which Kirke returns is called *The Deliverance*. In a later story, *The New Magdalene* (1873), Collins again employs benevolent coincidence to effect the proper transfer of confused identities. But at times Collins' coincidences can be downright offensive, as, for example, in *The Fallen Leaves* (1878), where the rascal Jervy is acquainted with both Phoebe and Mrs. Sowler, the only persons who possess essential details about Mr. and Mrs. Farnaby's secret of a lost child. More astronomically improbable is Amelius Goldenheart's encountering the lost child as a streetwalker on his very first stroll through the London slums!

Collins was not merely belaboring a convention of fiction by his use of coincidences. In *Armadale* (1864-65), Ozias Midwinter appears in the village where Allan Armadale, the son of his father's great enemy, lives. They become friends and, while sailing near the Isle of Man, are stranded on an abandoned timber ship, *La Grâce de Dieu*, the very ship on which Ozias' father permitted Allan's father to drown years ago. Allan has a dream which prefigures the action to come. Other strange coincidences follow, leading Ozias to believe that Fate has determined that he and Allan must be forever opposed. However, the dream and the coincidences prove that a greater power for good has been guiding events. Ozias confesses that he still cannot view Allan's dream in ordinary rational terms. "Though I know what extraordinary coincidences are perpetually happening in the experience of all of us," he says, "still I cannot accept coincidences as explaining the fulfillment of the Visions which our own eyes have seen. All I can sincerely say for myself is, what I think it will satisfy you to know, that I have learned to view the purpose of the Dream with a new mind." ("Epilogue," ch. 2)

There is a similar situation in *The Woman in White* (1859-60), in which Marian Halcombe dreams that Walter Hartright speaks to her, promising to return from his long absence. He adds a more imposing note. "The night when I met the lost Woman on the highway, was the night which set my life apart to be the instrument of a Design that is yet unseen." ("Marian Halcombe's Narrative") Hartright sees the design as a retributive chain of circumstances leading from a parent's wrong to his child's suffering. The destiny here is no unusual or novel fate; it is the fulfillment of a familiar scriptural assertion by the Power who was believed to design all things. The mystery and the marvellous coincidences now are part of the providence of God.[12] Hartright asserts his belief that "the Hand of God" directed the actions of individuals concerned in the adventure. An assertion of this kind supports David Goldknopf's contention that "the purpose of coincidence, in short, is to make God a character in the novel."[13] And certainly there is more than a hint of divine retribution active in immediate circumstances in such outlandish coincidences as that which occurs in Kingsley's *Alton Locke*, when Alton's greedy cousin George contracts typhus from a coat which had covered a dead laborer in a sweatshop he himself helped to sustain. The suffering of the oppressed makes itself felt with bitter irony. Nor was it peculiar for nineteenth-century writers to incorporate divine purposes in their works, for throughout society there existed a more or less accepted notion that God did act upon the lives of men.

PROVIDENCE

Victorians frequently attributed accident, chance and coincidence —all involving unexpected events—to providence. Even so apparently alienated a spirit as Edward Fitzgerald included in the *Rubai-*

yát of Omar Khayyam (1859), a sentiment acceptable to most Victorian minds:

And the first Morning of Creation wrote
What the last Dawn of Reckoning shall read. (stanza 73)

For Martin Tupper, there could be no doubt regarding the workings of Providence. "The little hints of Providence are dropped as millet seed," he says, waiting for men to recognize them in all things, even in "the right man casually met, the curious coincidence of matters." ("Of Little Providences") What appears disastrous to us is "the will of Heaven, not the whim of chance," for "Many things marvellous to us, until we know their causes, / Justify the government of Providence, with those their causes known." ("Of Circumstance") Finally, he summarizes a position thoroughly familiar to his readers. A wise man, he says, will acquiesce in "all the will of Providence" because he knows that "Circumstance is the servant, not the master of his soul," and enables him to prepare himself for heaven. ("Of Circumstance")

In Scott's *The Bride of Lammermoor* (1819), the squeamish villain, William Ashton, thoughtlessly involves his beloved daughter in a selfish scheme that will harm her as much as its intended victim, young Ravenswood. "But," Scott explains, "Providence had prepared a dreadful requital for this keen observer of human passions, who had spent his life in securing advantages to himself by artfully working upon the passions of others." (Vol. 2, ch. 1) It is his own family that will reap the whirlwind. Meanwhile, Susan Ferrier could confidently assert in *Marriage* (1818) that "In the arrangements of an all-wise Providence there is nothing created in vain. Every link of the vast chain that embraces creation helps to hold together the various relations of life; and all is beautiful gradation, from the human vegetable to the glorious archangel." (Vol. 1, ch. 27) Providence thus became the explanation and excuse for coincidence, both in life and in fiction. But, in addition to providing an overall design, the belief in Providence offered a reassurance of the mysterious accidents of life. In "Providence (I)," John Clare cautioned against a selfish view of God's purpose.

Folks talk of providence with heedless tongue
That leads to riches and not happiness,

Which is but a new tune for fortune's song,
And one contentment cares not to profess.

Providence is really, he explains, what provides a knowledge of how good grows out of evil and gives peace to the heart. And, in "Providence (II)," he adds that Providence fortunately keeps us ignorant of the future and therefore willing to continue life's struggle. "Kind providence amid contending strife / Bids weakness feel the liberty of life."

Clare's view implied that lives were predetermined and that freedom was only an illusion; others felt that Providence attended to each life, which was determined by individual freedom. But it was not always easy to reconcile the strange accidents and coincidences of life, as directed by God, with the concept of free will, essential it would seem in fiction as much as, or more than, in life. Robert Plumer Ward explained, in *Tremaine, or The Man of Refinement* (1825), that although God may have designed coincidences—such as those of natural phenomena—to operate in a particular way on the plans of men, the wills of those men were untouched. "Action," he concludes, "may be controlled, yet the will left free." (Ch. 36) This was but one of many similar arguments to justify human exertions leading toward salvation in the face of a predetermined scheme.

But more important, as Tupper's verse indicates, was the ability to accept strange occurrences, including extraordinary coincidences, whether favorable or unfavorable, as the correct scheme of things. Thus, the outrageously upright and unimpeachable Charles Aubrey in Warren's *Ten Thousand A-Year* (1841) expresses his great confidence in providential design through his noble resignation to a brutal series of misfortunes and coincidences.[14] He frequently comforts himself with the reflection, "What know we of the ultimate scope and end of His workings?" (Vol. 3, ch. 8) Deprived of his family estates by a fool, impoverished, left to care for his helpless family, faced with grave debts and grave cares, Aubrey can still find consolation:

"And what, now, have I really to complain of?" said he to himself; "why murmur presumptuously and vainly against the dispensations of Providence? I thank God that I am still able to recognize His hand in what has befallen me, and to believe that *He hath done all things well*; that prosperity and adversity are equally, from Him, means of accomplishing *His* all-wise purposes!" (Vol. 2, ch. 2)

Certainly Aubrey's case is an extreme one, but popular Victorian fiction abounds with equally extraordinary sufferings accepted by equally virtuous heroes and heroines as the will of Providence. It was even possible, outside of fiction, to offer to the lower classes the comforting information that the laws of property by which they suffered were the laws of Providence, as William Paley did in his *Reasons for Contentment Addressed to the Labouring Part of the British Public* (1793), a consolation reiterated by other commentators in following years. Even romance was providential. In Kingsley's *Yeast*, Lancelot Smith not only wins Argemone's love by persuading her that their meeting is the plan of Providence, but he is also able to comfort himself with the belief that his financial ruin is an expression of providential will.

Of course, many writers mocked the tendency to blame or praise Providence for what were mere coincidences or unexpected circumstances. George Eliot's Arthur Donnithorne, in *Adam Bede* (1859), unable to find a horse that can carry him away from temptation, feels a certain irritation, for "it seemed culpable in Providence to allow such a combination of circumstances." (Ch. 12) Later, having failed to escape temptation, and therefore faced with the consequences of his offense, Donnithorne still finds his position unjust, since he believes himself such a good fellow at bottom that "Providence would not treat him harshly." (Ch. 29) *Middlemarch* provides further examples of this egoistic confusion of the convenient and the ordained. Rosamond Vincy feels that she has "a Providence of her own who had kindly made her more charming than other girls," and arranged events in her favor. (Book 3, ch. 27) And Mr. Casaubon considers that "Providence, in its kindness, had supplied him with the wife he needed." Eliot adds that "Whether Providence had taken equal care of Miss Brooke in presenting her with Mr. Casaubon was an idea which could hardly occur to him." (Book 3, ch. 29) These characters are deluded in their preempting of providential concern as is Mr. Bulstrode later in a more egregious act of presumption, for Bulstrode presumes that it is the will of Providence that Raffles should die rather than reveal his secrets, and when he does die, with some slight assistance from Bulstrode, the pious banker can "go to bed and sleep in gratitude to Providence." (Book 7, ch. 70) There can be no doubt, with Eliot, that Providence has lost its divine association and has been revealed as egoism—the projection of selfish designs upon a re-

calcitrant universe and a form of justification for actions of doubtful morality.

George Meredith also examined the peculiar tendency to appropriate Providence to personal interests. In *Evan Harrington* (1860),
Evan's sister, the Countess de Saldar, accepts the death of a Sir Abraham Harrington "as a piece of Providence,"since it enables her to
maintain the fiction of her high social caste by pretending relationship to the aristocrat. (Ch. 9) When necessary for her schemes, the
Countess assists "Providence to shuffle the company into their proper
places" places, that is, which suit her purposes. (Ch. 16) The Countess,
who has appropriated the functions of Providence through her cal-
culated scheming, nonetheless does, like Arthur Donnithorne, suppose that circumstances are being supervised for her. Meredith
indicates how egoistic and foolish this assumption is by observing its
triviality: "Providence, she is sure, is keeping watch to shield her sensitive cuticle." (Ch. 18) The Countess, in her unscrupulous way, acknowledges that "any means that Providence may designate, I would
employ," and she is confident that Providence will inflict vengeance
on her enemies. (Ch. 19) Still, it is not likely that Providence, or even
chance, can favor any individual's complicated designs based on
falsehood. Although she can declare, "Let your conscience be clear,
and Providence *cannot* be against you," the Countess forgets that her
conscience is, if examined, not clear. (Ch. 27) Hence, when her
schemes begin to sour, she does not "ruffle well," as Lady Jocelyn
expresses it. "But," Meredith explains, "a lady who is at war with two
or three of the facts of Providence, and yet will have Providence for
her ally, can hardly ruffle well." (Ch. 21) Ultimately, this kind of
Providence backfires. Like Eliot, but more playfully, Meredith mocks
those hypocrites who would console the sufferings of others, and defend their own devious manipulations of events with the old saw that
whatever is is the will of Providence. But Meredith does not intend
merely to mock what he considers an atrociously false perception of
reality. Early in his story, he enunciates an equally imprecise, but
more credible view of the nature of circumstance and human desire:

> they to whom mortal life has ceased to be a long matter perceive that
> our appeals for conviction are answered,—now and then very closely up-
> on the call. When we have cast off the scales of hope and fancy, and
> surrender our claims on mad chance, it is given us to see that some plan
> is working out: that the heavens, icy as they are to the pangs of our

blood, have been throughout speaking to our souls; and, according to the strength there existing, we learn to comprehend them. But their language is an element of Time, whom primarily we have to know. (Ch. 10)[15]

The design that men fail to see working itself out in their actions is no longer the will of God, but a natural process, which men must recognize and adapt to. This adaptation involves the control of egoism and a consequent recognition that Providence does not trail us lovingly through all accidents.

DESTINY

By the end of the century, it had become difficult to accept notions of providential guidance. Somehow divinity had moved to a greater distance or disappeared altogether. David Goldknopf remarks that "as the Victorian age matured, the growing prestige of scientific determinism and its intrusion into the realm of biblical revelation allowed God less and less maneuverability in the realistic novel."[16] Though occultists might feel the nearness of supernatural forces, few of them saw the hand of Providence in the affairs of men. Symptomatic of the change that had been taking place, is Oscar Wilde's tale, "Lord Arthur Savile's Crime" (1887). Lady Windermere, when told that she is tempting Providence, replies, "surely Providence can resist temptation by this time." This irreverent remark, like so many others of Wilde suggests a more serious intellectual transformation; for indeed, it is not Providence that is operating to influence the lives of men in this story, but destiny. When Lord Arthur Savile has his hand read, he makes a shocking discovery; "for the first time he had become conscious of the terrible mystery of Destiny, of the awful meaning of Doom." Providence, which was beneficial, even in its apparent evil, and encouraged trust and resignation through confidence in a greater good is replaced by Destiny, a force which men struggle against or *must* accept. Men had spoken of destiny before, but it had been chiefly identified with Christian concepts of providential design, as in the poems of Browning or Tennyson. Wilde would not have it so. In his morality tale, Lord Arthur, in laboring to fulfill his destiny under his own direction, and thereby spare himself unforeseen consequences, brings about that very destiny. It is his conviction that he has a destiny that makes it real.[17]

Even popular literature incorporated notions of Fate replacing Providence. But often no clear distinction was made. Rider Haggard has Holly speculate in *She* (1886-87) that Ayesha "was now about to be used by Providence as a means to change the order of the world." (Ch. 22) Later, when Ayesha has been destroyed, Holly asserts that "it requires no great stretch of imagination to see the finger of Providence in the matter," for Ayesha "opposed herself to the eternal law, and, strong though she was, by it was swept back into nothingness —swept back with shame and hideous mockery!" (Ch. 26) And yet, for all this moralizing about Providence and its purposeful guidance of events, Holly concludes his narrative with the conviction that the final development of Ayesha's story will be "in obedience to a fate that never swerves and a purpose which cannot be altered." (Ch. 28) Fate and Providence are entangled in such a way that both the longing for a guiding hand in human events, and a doubtful conviction that an iron fate relentlessly demands a working out of its purposes, coexist. This confused state was characteristic of much late Victorian literature, where questions of destiny, free will and divine guidance were implied, though seldom examined.

Many late Victorian writers agreed with Wilde's substitution of an inscrutable destiny for a mysterious Providence. But some were eager to elaborate upon the change. Hardy's novels, for example, are notorious for their coincidences. "Often, to point his moral and bring about the tragic climax," Frank Chapman says of Hardy, "he has to resort to a long chain of improbable coincidences, Tess' confession slipped under Angel's door, goes under the carpet, Winterborne's team meets Mrs. Charmond's carriage in a narrow lane, and forces it to turn back: these are well-known instances. But there are even more flagrant examples."[18] For Lionel Stevenson, "the ascendancy of blind chance . . . gives Hardy's major novels the fatalistic dignity of Greek tragedy."[19] But Stevenson also observes that blind chance operates with overwhelming frequency to spoil happiness and doom characters to bitter fates. From one point of view, the coincidences of Hardy's novels, from the improbable meeting of the two returning lovers of the same girl in *A Pair of Blue Eyes*, to the more credible coincidences that Henchard's character prompts in *The Mayor of Casterbridge*, exist to prove that man is no more than a grain caught in a huge machine of time. His only destiny is to be destroyed. At its grimmest, this is the pessimistic side of Schopenhauerian philosophy.

Its more favorable manifestation was in the numerous schemes propounded for comprehending the universe, of which William Butler Yeats' is the most familiar to students of English literature. Yeats' *A Vision* projected massive, all-encompassing, elaborate schemes, determining the destinies of all men for all time. By its very elaborateness, it reduced the question of destiny and predetermination to a peripheral consideration.

It is possible to maintain, as Bert G. Hornback does in *The Metaphor of Chance*, that "Coincidence is frequently Hardy's way of expressing, dramatically, the idea of the intensity of experience."[20] Hornback argues convincingly that coincidence may be viewed as a modified convention in Hardy's novels, fully conscious and carefully employed. Although coincidences mainly serve to discomfort or even destroy men, through historical reference and metaphorical setting, they may suggest larger truths that transcend man's immediate fate. Coincidence can be a part of a positive assertion. Hardy, Hornback argues, "believes in the potential of man to live intensely and heroically, and this belief makes possible his use of coincidence as an aesthetic and philosophical convention."[21]

But whether or not one agrees that the ever-present coincidences in Hardy's fiction and poetry indicate a hopeful or a pessimistic intent; whether or not one agrees that they are esthetically acceptable, or constitute deplorable flaws, it is undeniable that Hardy uses them in a highly stylized manner. He is not, as David Goldknopf suggests, "simply trying to suborn a characteristic feature of early Victorian novels,"[22] but is creating his own convention, consciously exploiting a traditional device. Hardy may not have succeeded in transforming the function of the familiar convention of coincidence, but he made a determined effort to do so. If, for Eliot, all accidents of human experiences were equally coincidental when seen from the sun, for Hardy all of human experience itself was accident within a larger movement. Meredith had suggested that men strip themselves of egoism to see nature's operations more clearly, but Hardy sought to strip mankind of ego by showing him as a pitiful figure in a vast, indifferent scene where accidents which once signified the consoling evidence of divine guidance now merely mocked human pride by engendering dismay and disappointment.

There were yet other ways of looking at destiny. Theodore Watts-Dunton, in *Aylwin*, offered a Renaissance of Wonder, a quasi-spiritual revival of romantic appreciation of the natural world and the possibilities of the spirit to combat the dismal pessimism that "The Revolving Cage of Circumstance" would otherwise beget. Watts-Dunton's novel includes references to several different forms of destiny, from blind circumstance, to gypsy dukkeripens, to pagan fates, and mystic governance. What is important in every case is that these various forms of destiny can be altered by the exertion of human will. In stressing this feature of man's relationship to destiny, Watts-Dunton was representative of many other writers of the time as profound as Tennyson, or as superficial as Henley. Tennyson and Watts-Dunton were champions of the power of the human will, and like Elizabeth Barrett Browning, believed in a spontaneous relationship to the universe. Aurora Leigh is discontented with Romney Leigh's tendency to cross out "the spontaneities / Of all his individual, personal life / With formal universals." (*Aurora Leigh*, Book 3) She even supposes that God may be in a continuous process of spontaneous development, and later asserts that

> What we choose may not be good;
> But that we choose it proves it good for *us*
> Potentially, fantastically, now
> Or last year, rather than a thing we saw,
> And saw no need for choosing. (Book 8)

Charles Aubrey in Warren's *Ten Thousand A-Year* had been able to sustain himself in adversity by confidence both in his own "unconquerable WILL—and also by a devout reliance upon the protection of Providence." (Vol. 2, ch. 11) Tennyson echoed this belief in "Will," where he declared that those who used their will gained more control over their lives and put themselves more at one with divine purpose; and James Hinton simplified the problem even further by asserting that "Man is free when sin is impossible to him," adding that "Action, freedom, necessity, holiness all are one. Necessity and freedom are one in love."[23]

But assertions of this kind were less common at the end of the century, when a less confident spirit prevailed. Wilde's *The Picture of Dorian Gray* describes a world in which man seems incapable of willing what will happen to him, largely because he has ceased to believe in the power of his will. "You and I are what we are, and will be what we will be," Lord Henry says to Dorian. (Ch. 19) This is an attitude that reaches its low ebb of energy in the coy urbanity of a Beerbohm aside.

> No martyrdom, however fine, nor satire, however splendidly bitter, has changed by a little tittle the known tendency of things. It is the times that can perfect us, not we the times, and so let all of us wisely acquiesce. Like the little wired marionettes, let us acquiesce in the dance. ("A Defence of Cosmetics")

Whether relatively benevolent, or decisively nihilistic, the various projections of huge deterministic schemes or of private spiritual promise effectively altered the traditional Victorian convention. Coincidence had once lubricated a sensational plot or saved a hero. Odd chances had caused temporary sufferings inevitably reprieved by equally surprising accidents. But when Providence ceased to promise eventual reward, more thoughtful Victorians ceased to close with unqualified happy endings. Dickens, among others, had viewed his art, in all its intricacy, as an imitation of the ways of Providence. But with Providence gone, novelists did not abandon intricate plotting. If anything, artistic control became more severe, more precise, as though the plotting itself might in a way replace the external order no longer guaranteed. If existence was to be interpreted as a set of discoverable laws, then the novel would be written along the lines of scientific examination. If the associations discovered by science proved spurious, it did not matter to the worlds of fiction and poetry, for, even in the realistic mode, coincidence held its place. But though coincidence remained an active ingredient in English fiction, its transformation had been significant and the implications profound.[24] So long as Providence had guided men and free choice of good and evil lay open to them, dramatic opportunities remained, and each coincidence promised rich meaning. The gradual replacement of Providence by more deterministic views reflected a widespread conviction that man was a prisoner not only of the flesh and of a particular society, but of existence itself, where all coincidences were interchangeable, all happenstance equal to the most careful plan.

CHAPTER SIX

DUELLING

Some nineteenth-century literary conventions, such as duelling, served trivial ends and never truly developed into significant tools for writers of the time. Nonetheless, their survival through the century reveals a gradual hollowing out of once serviceable devices. Duelling was a true part of life in the eighteenth century and continued to be into the early nineteenth century. But, as duels ceased to be a part of real experience, they became crude devices for producing dramatic effects in literature.

THE SOCIAL REALITY

Since British law in the Victorian period did not distinguish between duelling and murder, it was difficult to obtain a conviction because the two offenses were not considered comparable. Thus there were no adequate legal restraints upon the practice before Victoria's reign. Duelling was most common among military men; in fact, "in 1814 an ensign was dismissed from the service by sentence of a general court-martial" for *refusing* a duel.[1] The relative acceptability of duelling is indicated by a list of names of notable public figures who participated:

Lord Byron killed Mr. Chaworth in 1765; Charles James Fox and Mr. Adams fought in 1779; duke of York and Colonel Lennox, 1789; William Pitt and George Tierney, 1796; George Canning and Lord Castlereagh, 1809; Mr. Christie killed John Scott, editor of the *London Magazine*, 1821; duke of Wellington and earl of Winchelsea, 1829; Mr. Roebuck and Mr. Black, editor of *Morning Chronicle*, 1835; Lord Alvanley and a son of Daniel O'Connell in the same year; Earl Cardigan wounded Captain Tuckett, was tried by his peers, and acquitted on a legal quibble.[2]

Aubrey de Vere commented in his *Recollections* (1897) that duelling was still a favorite diversion in the Ireland of his youth. Nor was duelling limited to England and the Continent. The famous duels of Clay and Randolph, Burr and Hamilton, and Commodore Barron and Captain Decatur attest that Americans maintained the practice also.

There was considerable opposition to the practice of duelling. Napoleon was its outspoken foe. Bentham had written on the subject in *An Introduction to the Principles of Morals and Legislation* (1789), and he was not the first. William Hunter, in *An Essay on Duelling* (1792), presented his plea for legislative interference to correct the then growing acceptance of duelling. His arguments were to be repeated frequently thereafter. Single combat he traced back to the pagan Goths, but suggested that in modern society, a man's honor could be protected by law. Furthermore, Hunter argued, men are not equal in the use of weapons, since some men train themselves to the deadly skills. If a man is truly honorable he can afford to refuse a duel, since only those whose characters are in question fear shame. Above all, Hunter suggested that duels did not enforce observation of the rules of politeness and generate courage as they were reputed to do, but promoted bullying and aggression. Far better, he observed to establish a law that shames offenders in duels. Hunter's picture of the duellist presents him stripped of romantic glamor.

The systematic duellist is one of those monsters, whom Nature, in her wrath, now and then produces, in order to exhibit the height of human profligacy. He is a wretch, without shame, without morality, without religion; in whose breast every degrading passion is constantly in action, and propelling him to the vilest and most nefarious purposes. His heart is uniformly callous to the softer emotions of pity and forgiveness, and all the faculties of his soul are perverted and contradictory. His only glory consists, in rendering himself contemptible, and others miserable. He prides himself on the number he has murdered in cold blood, and the many families he has plunged into affliction, or want; and is ever on the watch for some unfortunate victim to add to his trophies.[3]

Not all those involved in duels appeared as monsters. Abraham Bosquett asserted in his *The Young Man of Honour's Vade-Mecum, Being A Salutory Treatise on Duelling, Together with the Annals of Chivalry, the Ordeal Trial, and Judicial Combat, from the Earliest Times* (1817) that he himself had been four times a Principal and twenty-five times a Second in duels, yet "life or honour were never lost in [his] hands."[4] Bosquett emphasizes the palliative aspect of duelling, indicating that the principal duty of seconds is the avoidance of combat, rather than its accomplishment. He argues that "the practice of duelling, though in general as pernicious as absurd, has been followed by some beneficial effects." The beneficial effects he cites were familiar justifications for duelling, but were, as we have seen from Hunter's essay, denied by opponents of the practice. Bosquett and others believed that duelling had "tended to make men more respectful in their behaviour to each other, less ostentatious in conversation, and more tender of living characters, but especially of female reputation; and the gentleness of manners introduced by this restraint, at the same time that it has contributed to social happiness, has rendered duels much less frequent, by removing the causes of offence."[5] Nonetheless, despite his practical advice on how to stand, how to know one's weapons, and so forth, Bosquett agreed that "the generality of duels result from futile causes,"[6] and he cited many instances of disastrous consequences from recent duels. He recommended the establishment of a Court of Honor to adjudicate quarrels that might lead to duels, thereby avoiding civil law.[7]

In a fugitive pamphlet, "On Duelling," printed privately for his friends, Charles Hay Cameron argued the irrationality of the practice.[8] Far from being a means of refining manners, duelling was, Cameron observed, a reversion to savagery and a confession that wisdom cannot solve the problems involved. To support duelling was to support in principle "the unrestrained privilege of maiming and murdering."[9] In fact, Cameron continued, duelling aggravates the evils it is intended to suppress, "for the quantity of pain which one man can inflict upon another by an insult where duelling is not permitted, is in reality very minute compared with the quantity of pain which one man can inflict upon another by an insult where duelling is established."[10] Supposedly duelling served to repress insults, but instead, Cameron noted, it made insults more significant. One who does not fear public disapprobation would not refrain from insulting others, for he would be equally indifferent to the insistence that he clear his honor by combat. If men truly feared the disapproval of society, that disapproval, without duelling, would be enough to repress insults. The real function of public censure was to prohibit not encourage barbarism. Cameron concluded his argument by pointing out that all men do not require the practice of duelling to behave, and he cited clergymen as an example. His hope, like that of other opponents of duelling, was to change the public image of the practice and bring it under strict legal control.

Gradually duelling came under legal control. It had not always been so, for "in 1816 Day, J. summing up in the trial of Rowan Cashel, an attorney, at Cork, regretted that the law of honour 'should countervail the law of the land; and that we cannot unfortunately oppose this despotic law which, if a gentleman deny to accede to, he must be stigmatized as a coward.' "[11] In 1808, Major Alexander Campbell was sentenced to death for killing Captain Alexander Boyd in a duel. It was a memorable decision. In 1813, the surviving principal and his seconds were accused of the murder of Lieutenant Blundell in a duel. And, in 1843, public attention was drawn to a duel in which Colonel Fawcett shot his brother-in-law, Lieutenant Monroe, having gone out reluctantly in obedience to the prevailing code.[12] And "by the eighteen-forties a favourable verdict from a jury was apparently sufficiently improbable as to make flight from the country preferable."[13] Nonetheless, in 1855, Lorenzo Sabine, in a history and examination of duelling, could declare that duelling was not generally punished in England and that "it is scarcely an exaggeration to add, that witnesses, judges, juries, prosecuting officers, and the higher advisers of the crown, have united to *prevent* punishments under the laws against duelling."[14] Fortunately, Sabine added, duels had become rare in England. Meanwhile, an association for the suppression of duelling was formed in London in 1842 and made its report in 1844, the year in which the subject was debated in the House of Commons. The result was an amendment to the articles of war (April, 1844) making severe the penalties for military men caught duelling.[15] The Queen, along with the Prince Consort, specifically wished to see duelling suppressed, as Justin McCarthy pointed out, not neglecting to boast a little in regard to the progress that had been made in his day.

> One reform which Prince Albert worked earnestly to bring about, was the abolition of duelling in the army. Nothing can testify more strikingly to the rapid growth of a genuine civilisation in Queen Victoria's reign than the utter discontinuance of the duelling system. When the Queen came to the throne, and for years after, it was still in full force. The duel plays a conspicuous part in the fiction and the drama of the Sovereign's earlier years. It was a common incident of all political controversies. It was an episode of most contested elections. It was often resorted to for the purpose of deciding the right or wrong of a half-drunken quarrel over a card table. It formed as common a theme of gossip as an elopement or a bankruptcy. Most of the eminent statesmen who were prominent in the earlier part of the Queen's reign had fought duels. At the present hour a duel in England would seem as absurd and barbarous an anachronism as an ordeal by touch or witch-burning.[16]

Charles Mackay, in his *Extraordinary Popular Delusions and the Madness of Crowds* (1841), concluded that the general causes of duels were "of the most trivial or the most unworthy nature."[17] Mackay recommended Bosquett's solution—a court of honor to take cognisance of offenses likely to precipitate duelling; "a custom," he adds, "which is the disgrace of civilisation."[18] In the same year, J. G. Millingen's *History of Duelling* appeared and became a standard source on the subject, providing most of the information for two articles on duelling in England and duelling in France that appeared in the June 6 and June 27 issues of Dickens' *Household Words* of 1857. But by 1857, duelling in England was almost entirely a matter of history. The last notable duel on English soil was fought between George Smythe and Colonel Frederick Romilly in 1852.[19] Thereafter, duellists were generally obliged to settle matters abroad. That, however, did not prevent the topic from remaining a current subject of discussion and opinion. Arguments as cogent as Cameron's ignored only that an established usage is not so easy to expunge as a mere rule or habit, especially when that custom is cloaked with glory and associated with a privileged caste. The eleventh edition of the *Encyclopaedia Britannica* summarizes the issue by stating that the duel "survived in more civilized times as a class distinction and as an ultimate court of appeal to punish violations of the social code. In a democratic age and under a settled government it is doomed to extinction."[20] It was, after all, manly to defend one's honor in that way, and some, including Queen Victoria (who had had second thoughts by 1852), felt the loss of such a decisive assertion of gentlemanly rights. "By the time the Liberals were pushing Army reform the Queen was against it. Duelling, which [Albert] had helped to abolish, she now felt was needed to keep chivalry alive: 'There *are* positions which require Duels, I really think & many Gentlemen have said the same.' "[21] To many, the passing of duelling indicated the passing of an age. "The end of duelling in England weakened the concept of the gentleman as the follower of an heroic, pagan code and helped to make way for a somewhat different one," writes W. L. Burn.[22] Not everyone was happy to see the change.

While duelling came to be viewed as a defunct social practice, it enjoyed a revived romantic glamor—and numerous accounts of famous historical duels appeared, among them, Lorenzo Sabine's *Notes on Duels and Duelling* (1855) and Andrew Steinmetz' more elaborate *The Romance of Duelling in All Times and Countries* (1868). These and other books revealed the many bizarre circumstances in the duels especially of famous men. A bizarre duel involved Sir Richard Burton's father who shot a man in a duel, nursed him back to health, and then shot him again in another duel.[23] Several accounts included the duel of Lord Byron, relative of the poet, and Mr. Chaworth, which occurred in 1765. The combat was with swords in a room lighted only by a tallow candle. Chaworth died and Byron submitted to trial by his peers. He was found guilty of manslaughter, but being a peer, paid his fee and was freed. Another frequently cited encounter was the Scott-Christie duel in 1821, at Chalk Farm, a famous duelling rendezvous near London. Before the duel, Mr. Christie called out to his antagonist, "Mr. Scott, you must not stand there; I see your head above the horizon; you give me an advantage."[24] In the duel itself, Christie aimed his first shot away, but Scott's seconds did not tell him and both parties fired a second time. Scott was killed. Christie was acquitted. The seconds in this lamentable incident were, for Christie, a Mr. Trail, and for the unfortunate Scott, Peter George Patmore, friend of Hazlitt, Lamb and other notable literary figures, and father of the prominent Victorian poet, Coventry

Patmore. Overcome by remorse, Patmore fled England. He was greatly reviled by society at large for his part in the affair and never truly
lived down the shame associated with it.[25]

Most duels were not pictured as noble, and many were likewise
not brutal. Many were not dangerous at all, but, like the Duke of
Wellington's with the Earl of Winchester in 1829, were formal modes
of settling a quarrel, with parties either not firing at all or firing at
random. Some duels were comic, as was Moore's abortive encounter
with Jeffrey. As often as not, projected duels were tactfully avoided.
In his *Autobiography*, C. J. Mathews, the famous stage performer,
recounted how, in 1823, he and Count D'Orsay, otherwise agreeable
companions, nearly came to a duel over a trivial difference of opinion.
The misunderstanding was resolved quite simply by the potential
combatants' seconds—both gentlemen of station.[26] This incident demonstrates both how easily offense could be taken, and also how convenient a withdrawal from actual confrontation could be. On the
whole, the ritual of duelling involved far more negotiation and diplo-
macy than it did authentic violence.

THE LITERARY CONVENTION

Duelling had been a literary staple for some time. The drama of
the Restoration abounds with duels. Duelling was so common in the
literature of the nineteenth century that it is perhaps necessary to
provide only a few examples. In Scott's novels, there is a duel between Lovel and Captain M'Intyre in *The Antiquary* (1816), between
Sir Piercie Shafton and Halbert Glendinning in *The Monastery*
(1820), and in *Kenilworth* (1821) between Tressilian and Varney.[27]
Duelling was expected in melodrama, and in a popular thriller like
T. P. Prest's *The Gipsy Boy* was a convenient device for getting rid
of unneeded characters. There is a perfunctory duel in Disraeli's *Vivian Grey* (1826-27), when Grey, for very slim reasons, becomes involved in contest of arms with Frederick Cleveland, an intelligent
man whom he admires, but nonetheless unintentionally murders. The
duel is an unexpected commonplace of the university novel, beginning with Gibson Lockhart's *Reginald Dalton: A Story of English
University Life* (1823).[28]

As in Disraeli's novel, duels were often associated with political
intrigue, and, with the convenient, if not plausible movement of plot.

But equally productive of duels were romantic intrigues. Pelham, in Bulwer-Lytton's novel of that name, fights one duel over a ludicrously trivial issue because it allows him an opportunity to act grandly by sparing his opponent. He engages in a second duel, however, as a result of the vindictive Duchess de Perpignan's machinations. Once more Pelham succeeds easily, leaving his opponent wounded. His duels merely indicate Pelham's mastery of all those skills considered necessary in a complete and accomplished man. In *The Disowned* (1828), published about the same time as *Pelham*, Lord Ulswater, by challenging the pacific and noble-hearted Algernon Mordaunt, suggests the manner in which aggressive individuals often attempted to intimidate those less inclined to prove their points by violence. The duel never takes place because Ulswater himself is attacked and injured by political opponents. He suffers from a base version of his own violent methods.[29]

What is interesting in these novels is that duelling is not condemned. It is, on the contrary, used to demonstrate the ability and manliness of the characters. Although the duels may have unfortunate consequences, these consequences do not emphasize the folly of duelling. In *Guy Livingstone*, Lawrence seems to express a virtuous delight in Colonel Mohun's victory over the vicious Horace Levinge in a duel. Even Levinge's maimed corpse is described with vengeful appreciation, and the reader is left with a favorable impression of Mohun's action. Later, in *Barren Honour*, Lawrence's central character briefly considers challenging his enemy to a duel—necessarily on the Continent—but realizes that, not only would his opponent be too cowardly to risk his life, but it would not be an entirely Christian resolution to his situation.

There was a sufficient body of imaginative literature that did openly condemn duelling, of which Samuel Warren's "Duelling," in *Passages from the Diary of a Late Physician* is typical.[30] In this story, a certain Captain ——— and a Mr. Trevor quarrel over the affections of Beautiful Mary, "The Blue Bell of ———." In an attempt to prevent bloodshed, the combatants' friends leave the powder out of the pistols that the two men have determined to fire at one another's breasts across a table. Although all honorable aspects are lost in the lunatic duel the antagonists propose, the two men are nonetheless enraged by their friends' interference. They persist in their intention, carrying out their duel with swords. The young captain is killed, cloven to the heart. Mr. Trevor, appalled by his deed, flees to France, the inevitable refuge of duellists. He does not survive long, dying five years later, still haunted by his crime.

If some accounts condemned the madness of duelling, others demonstrated its ludicrous side. Everyone remembers Dr. Slammer of the Ninety-seventh calling out poor Mr. Winkle in *The Pickwick Papers* (1836-37). Mr. Winkle, with good reason, supposes that there are many ways to avoid the actual combat without being dishonored. But no one does intervene, and Winkle is only saved from the embarrassment—or worse—of a duel when Slammer discovers that Winkle is not his man. The misunderstanding is comic enough, but Dickens added a further jibe at those who encouraged duelling. When it is clear that no duel is to take place, the aggressive Dr. Payne offers Winkle a chance to satisfy himself, if he is aggrieved by the incorrect challenge. Winkle declares himself satisfied, and Payne continues, "'the gentleman's second may feel himself affronted with some observations which fell from me at an earlier period of this meeting; if so, I shall be happy to give *him* satisfaction immediately.'" (Ch. 2) This is outright slapstick. Dickens used the same situation in "The Great Winglebury Duel," in *Sketches by Boz*, where Alexander Trott and Horace Hunter comically approach a duel that does not occur. There is an amusing scene in Kingsley's *Two Years Ago* (1857) when Tom Thurnall terrifies a raw second, who comes to deliver a challenge from Squire Trebooze, by saying that he'll duel the Squire across a handkerchief and then take the second himself. The intimidation works, and no duel is planned. The method could be somewhat subtler. Thackeray, in *The Adventures of Philip* (1861-62), describes how Colonel Bunch, backing Philip in his romance with Charlotte Baynes, comes into conflict with his old friend, Charlotte's father. General Baynes seeks Major MacWhirter's assistance as his second. Out of keeping with the duelling tradition, MacWhirter refuses to act in that office for the simple reason that he supports Bunch. It is a notable example of a non-duel in literature. (ch. 27)

Objections to duelling were generally of a more serious nature. Hence, Browning depicts in the companion poems, "Before" and "After," first the rash aggression and then the remorse of the surviving duellist. "Ha, what avails death to erase / His offence, my disgrace?" the narrator asks. In *The Small House at Allington* (1864), Trollope lightly dismissed the idea of duelling altogether. But the condemnation could be more telling than that; it could come from the lips of a beautiful woman. Thus, in Owen Meredith's *Lucile* (1860), when Duke Luvois plans to force Lord Alfred Vargrave to a duel, Lucile upbraids him.

> No! you can have no cause, Duke, for no right
>   you have
> In the contest you menace. That contest but
>   draws
> Every right into ruin. By all human laws
> Of man's heart I forbid it, by all sanctities
> Of man's social honor. (Part 1, canto 6, sec. 14)

When duelling could thus be denounced in a tale concerned with love and honor, it is clear that the notion was genuinely defunct.

That duelling should have ceased in fact did not prevent writers from continuing to employ it in their fiction. A novelist concerned with an earlier historical period might employ duelling as a legitimate part of his narrative. Thus the duel between Haredale and Chester in *Barnaby Rudge* and Lord Mohun's duels with the duke of Hamilton and Castlewood in *Henry Esmond* are justified by their historical settings, as is the memorable duel between James and Henry Durie in Stevenson's *The Master of Ballantrae*, which is in keeping with its historical setting and achieves the plot purposes of its author.

Some authors continued to employ the convention because it offered a form of contest between male antagonists unlike any other. In Tennyson's *Maud* (1855), the duel is an emblematic event in a highly stylized fable, despite its direct application to contemporary society. Other writers sought to employ duels in a realistic manner. In Robert Bell's *The Ladder of Gold* (1850), much of Book Six is devoted to a duel between Henry Winston and Lord Charles Eton. From what one can learn of the actual circumstances of duels in the early part of the century, Bell's account appears to be remarkably faithful. Lord Charles' second, Colonel Mercer Beauchamp, disapproves of duels and seeks some other means of settling the argument, but Henry is intransigent and insists on a duel. Michael Costigan, a hot-blooded Irishman, in making arrangements on Henry's behalf, is equally unwilling to consider an amicable agreement. The duel is set to take place at Chalk Farm (the famous setting of the Christie-Scott duel, among others), and before the time the experienced Costigan gives Henry some practical advice, warning him not to wear anything that might prove a useful target for his antagonist —no white waistcoat, no tie, no bright buttons. He advises him to wear unpolished boots, and keep his watch in his right-hand pocket. The directions here sound like Bosquett's in *The Young Man of Honour's Vade-Mecum*. In the duel, Henry is not hit, but Lord Charles is wounded. Taken to his uncle's home, he lingers for a time and then dies. Henry then feels the full burden of remorse, for it has separated him from the woman he loves, Lord Charles' widow. Although he receives her forgiveness, he is obliged to go abroad. Only at the very end of the novel is there a suggestion that after many years Henry is expected to return.

It is perfectly clear that Bell disapproves of duelling and is happy to record its passing as a custom. His digression on the subject is worth quoting at length. After lamenting the human tendency to set up false gods, such as Honor, which sacrifice everything to self-love, Bell continues:

> Happily for the progress of rational civilisation, public opinion has undergone a revolution on this question, and duelling is regarded in all influential quarters merely as a relic of the barbarous ages, and as affording a proof of nothing on earth but want of sense. Even the few faded and emaciated fire-eaters who yet infest society, are giving up the practice because they can earn no credit by it. No man is now amenable to the imputation of cowardice who declines upon every slight occasion to stand up to be shot at, and to suffer, through his folly, the hopes and affections of many innocent people to be slain at the same moment. As to the courage exemplified in a duel, it is sheer imposture. The rankest cowards have fought duels, and frequently found a convenient escape in them from their real pusillanimity. (Book 6, ch. 2)

Bell's treatment of duelling is realistic in most ways, though it seems an intrusion into his loosely organized novel.

George Meredith, in many ways a remarkably realistic novelist, was oddly fascinated by the convention of the duel. Meredith employed duels prominently in several of his novels. In *The Ordeal of Richard Feverel* (1859), Richard is seriously wounded in a duel with Lord Mountfalcon. The duel is foolish from the start, but Richard is

driven to it by an exaggerated sense of his own honor. Here as elsewhere in Meredith, unwise dedication to chivalric notions leads to
no good end. For Richard, the consequence is the loss of his beloved
Lucy, who goes mad and dies believing Richard mortally injured.
Duelling plays a large part in *Vittoria* (1866), but is more fitting in
that historical account of the struggle between the Austrian army and
Italian insurgents. The Austrian Captain Weisspriess represents all
of the accomplishments and offenses of the ruling Austrians, and he is
not surprisingly an accomplished duellist. It is altogether fitting that,
at the end of the novel, the Italian rebel, Carlo Ammiani, should
murder Weisspriess in a duel.

If duelling was a reasonable feature of *Vittoria*, it was integral to
The Tragic Comedians (1880), for this story was based upon real facts
in the life of Ferdinand Lassalle. In the novel, the brilliant politician,
Sigismund Alvan, becomes romantically involved with young Clotilde von Rüdiger. The involvement leads to numerous misunder-
standings that culminate in Alvan's challenge to Clotilde's father.
Prince Marko, an absolute amateur with pistols, accepts the challenge
in General Rüdiger's place against Alvan, who is an accomplished
marksman. So certain does the outcome of the duel seem that Clotilde
supposes Providence to be acting savagely on her behalf to dispose
of Marko, who is an obstacle to her love. Amazingly, it is Alvan who
dies from wounds received in the duel. Meredith suggests that he
suffers punishment for his rashness. Having failed to subdue his
blood, his passion has made him a tragic fool.

Although Meredith used the duelling convention frequently
enough to indicate his fascination for the practice, he recognized
the folly of the veritable act. In *The Adventures of Harry Richmond*
(1871), Harry and Prince Otto fall into a misunderstanding and have
a duel, which Harry describes as "a silly business on all sides." (Ch.
32) Later he adds: "The utterly unreasonable nature of a duel was
manifested by his [Otto's] declaring to me, that he was now satisfied I did not mean to insult him and then laugh at him. We must regard it rather as a sudorific for feverish blood and brains." (ch. 33)
Again, in *Beauchamp's Career* (1876), when reviewing gossip of
Beauchamp's having been involved in a duel in France, Mrs. Gran-
cey Lespel remarks, "Duelling is horrible. . . . It was an inhuman practice always, and it is now worse—it is a breach of manners." (ch. 26)

In the society that Meredith was addressing, nothing could be worse than a breach of manners. It is clear that duelling had fallen very low indeed.

In his late novel, *Lord Ormont and His Aminta* (1894), Meredith again employed the duel convention. Lord Ormont himself is a warrior and a practiced duellist, and throughout the novel there is a hovering threat of the aggressiveness that Lord Ormont represents. But the tough old battler subdues his combative instincts and ends up sending his own grand-nephew to the school operated by his runaway wife, Aminta, and her lover. Instead, it is Adolphus Morsfield, a persistent suitor of Aminta's, and an accomplished duellist, who dies at the hands of Captain May, who must, of course, flee to France. The reviewer for the *Saturday Review* observed that this duel takes place in a fencing school "with foils of which the duellists [knock] off the steel buttons. This is a feat so hopeless to perform that it exists only in novels, though it is said to be forbidden in the French army."[31] The reviewer was obviously not satisfied with Meredith's use of this and other romantic conventions, yet Meredith had lent the convention about as much significance as it would bear.

For the most part, writers merely employed duels as fine pieces of action, as convenient dramatic conflicts, or as a neat method for disposing of obstreperous characters. In Gissing's novel, *Demos* (1886), Hubert Eldon returns home from France, having suffered a wound in a duel occasioned by a romantic entanglement. The event is scarcely credible and is useful only in creating a specious romantic background for Eldon, while providing Mrs. Waltham a good reason for disapproving of him and extinguishing her daughter's interest in him. Gissing's employment of the convention is awkward and ineffective. It is a borrowing from an already stale tradition with no new import to give it spice. Meredith, at least, made the convention a part of his own philosophical scheme. Duelling, for him, was an attractive but clearly outmoded form of intercourse. It represented the triumph of the passions over reasonable will. It was, as Harry Richmond put it, mainly a sudorific for feverish blood and brains. And in his scheme, it was just another of those activities prompted by unreasoned passion, which brought mainly misery. Despite Meredith's attempt to give the tired convention meaning, it did not really work. The duel as literary convention failed to achieve any profundity mainly because the social convention upon which it was based was already waning before the middle of the nineteenth century. Duels served simple purposes of plot sensation, and were occasions for moral denunciation, but the convention never became a complex literary device.

CHAPTER SEVEN

DEATHBEDS

ATTITUDE TOWARD DYING

E. M. Forster observed that the Victorians had a strong affection for deathbeds,[1] and Elizabeth Longford in her biography of Victoria explained that "Frank interest in death-bed scenes was quite normal. Partly because Victorians cared passionately about religion, the moment of passing from this world to the next was not one to be hushed up. Only paupers died in hospital so opportunities for study were plentiful." She adds that "The young Victoria collected from Queen Adelaide the 'painfully interesting details of the King's last illness'."[2] J. F. Stephen was among those critics of the literature of his time who felt that deathbed scenes were abused, especially by a writer such as Dickens.[3] But on the whole deathbed scenes were common in Victorian literature because they were an important practical and moral feature of life. "The fetish of deep family mourning was encouraged by the tradesmen concerned; but it was also one of the most strongly entrenched customs of the age. Mourning the dead is an instinct as old as man, but in no era had it become such an iron-bound convention as in the Victorian age."[4] And deathbed scenes were a central part of the mourning tradition, which extended of course well beyond the actual interment.

George Eliot, identifying the books that Adam Bede read to improve himself, lists works that one might expect to have found in many an English home well into the nineteenth century. Among these books is "Taylor's 'Holy Living and Dying.'" (*Adam Bede*, Ch. 19)[5] In *The Rule and Exercises of Holy Dying* (1651), Jeremy Taylor provided prayers, forms of conduct, and attitudes of mind to meet the difficulties of one's own or another's temporary or fatal illness. At one point he gives a list of "Arguments and Exhortations to move the Sick Man to Confession of Sins," that a minister or other concerned person might employ. There are twenty-four separate items in the list; and most of those he mentioned would reappear often in some of the moving or bathetic deathbed scenes of Victorian literature.

In a subsection of *Holy Dying* entitled "The Circumstances of a Dying Man's Sorrow and Danger," Taylor also presented the traditional belief that a man who has led a sinful life will experience a painful and arduous death, accompanied by fear and remorse. "But when a good man dies," he says, "angels drive away the devils on his deathbed," and thus "joy breaks forth through the clouds of sickness" which does "but untie the soul from its chain, and let it go forth, first into liberty, and then into glory." (Ch. 2, sec. 4) Martin Tupper, in "Life's End," rephrased Taylor's thoughts for his own audience, declaring that "when the bad man dieth, all his sins rise up against him, / Clamouring at his memory with imprecated judgments; / But when the good departeth, all his noble deeds / Surround him like a cloud of light to sphere his soul in glory." George Borrow, describing his father's death in his arms, had similar traditional views in mind. "I make no doubt," Borrow declares, "that for a moment he was perfectly sensible, and it was then that, clasping his hands, he uttered another name clearly, distinctly—it was the name of Christ. With that name upon his lips, the brave soldier sank back upon my bosom, and, with his hands still clasped, yielded up his soul." (*Lavengro*, Ch. 28) This is the tone of most virtuous deathbed scenes. But upon occasion, it is not the Bible, or Christ, that is prominent, as in Dr. Dabbs' account of Tennyson's last moments.

Nothing could have been more striking than the scene during the last few hours. On the bed a figure of breathing marble, flooded and bathed in the light of the full moon streaming through the oriel window; his hand clasping the Shakespeare which he had asked for but recently, and which he had kept by him to the end; the moonlight, the majestic figure as he lay there, "drawing thicker breath," irresistibly brought to our minds his own "Passing of Arthur."[6]

The sentimentalizing of a great poet's death might easily draw upon the secular deity of poetry, rather than the divine, but the scene is, one way or the other, clearly staged, as were so many deathbed scenes of the time. Henry Peach Robinson's popular photograph, "Fading Away," represents, perhaps, the common pictorial version of the scene. It is, therefore, refreshing to find a description such as Edward Fitzgerald's record of his father's death. There is no mention of Christ, Shakespeare, noble features, moonlight or other traditional trappings. Instead, Fitzgerald notes, of the father he loved, "He died in March, after an illness of three weeks, saying 'that engine works well' (meaning one of his Colliery steam engines) as he lay in the stupor of Death."[7]

Dickens employed the traditional warning tales of dying profligates in *Pickwick Papers*, but also utilized types who would reappear later in different guises. The Chancery prisoner's death in *Pickwick Papers* anticipates the death from inanition of Mr. Gridley, the man from Shropshire, and Richard Carstone, both victims of Chancery in *Bleak House*. Some deathbed scenes combine the innocence of childhood and pathos of adulthood, as with David Copperfield's mother, who "died like a child that had gone to sleep" in Peggoty's arms. (*David Copperfield*, Ch. 9) And other deathbed scenes, while being serious, also have a touch of the comic in them, like the death of Mr. Barkis. Hablot K. Browne captured this combination of sentiments in his illustration entitled "I find Mr. Barkis 'going out with the Tide' " in *David Copperfield*, where Barkis ludicrously embraces the chest containing his valuables, while the onlookers are all serious and sympathetic, and on the wall behind Barkis a picture shows Christ ascending into heaven.

DEATHBED SCENES IN LITERATURE

In Victorian literature, deathbed scenes served every conceivable purpose. In Susan Ferrier's *Marriage*, Mary Douglas and Charles Lennox realize the depth of their love over the deathbed of Charles' blind mother. Deathbed scenes occur regularly whenever a moral pause is required in T. P. Prest's *The Gipsy Boy*, and Samuel Warren's "A Scholar's Death-Bed" is a typical sentimental set piece. Deathbed scenes are common in the poetry of the period, from Thomas Hood's thoroughly conventional, "The Deathbed," to Rossetti's subtley related poem, "My Sister's Sleep." The verse of "A Vagrant's Deathbed," describing the contrast between affluence and poverty, in *Household Words* (Vol. 3, no. 53) was complemented by more accomplished poems of established poets. Browning exploited the deathbed setting in "Evelyn Hope" and "The Bishop Orders His Tomb," while his wife wrote "A Thought for a Lonely Death-bed," a prayer requesting that nothing be interposed between the speaker and Christ when she comes to die. Tennyson used the device comically in "The Northern Farmer: Old Style" and melodramatically in "Rizpah."

The convention was obvious, in fiction as well as in poetry, though in fiction it appeared as part of a larger narrative, and therefore had a different function. In novels, for example, deathbed scenes are frequently instrumental in revealing the moral direction of the narrative. They become tests of character and turning points in action as much as dramatic scenes in their own right. The sentimental deathbed scene of Isabel Vane in *East Lynne* made a heavy moral point. Charlotte Brontë used a traditional deathbed scene to describe Helen Burns' passing in *Jane Eyre*, but was capable of a subtler utilization of the convention when, in *Shirley*, she employed all of the tricks of the deathbed scene and then had her heroine, Caroline Helstone, recover. Anthony Trollope was content to indicate predictable conditions in his deathbed scenes, and consequently, while the questionable Mrs. Proudie dies in bizarre circumstances, the good Mr. Harding dies mildly, and Bishop Grantly, in *Barchester Towers*, displays in death the attributes of his life, expiring in a mild and serene manner. Much of the last chapter of Froude's "The Spirit's Trial" (1847) is, in effect, a prolonged deathbed scene, at the end of which Edward Fowler has his friend read an account of a deathbed scene to him. As Edward is dying at Eastertime, the sun breaks out, and he exclaims, "See, see! he is coming!" (ch. 9) Playing to a somewhat different audience, Ouida employed deathbed scenes of a more piquant, though less meditative nature as with the death of Leon Ramon, or Rake's death in the desert in *Under Two Flags* (1867). And Allan

Quatermain's prolonged deathbed scene in Rider Haggard's *Allan Quatermain* (1887), provides a typical picture of the clean-living adventurer's resigned and trusting acceptance of the end.

One commonplace use of the deathbed scene was to give a fallen sinner the opportunity to demonstrate rehabilitation and repentence. Dickens gave even the most conventional of these scenes his own transforming touch. Thus, although Alice Marwood's dying moments are little different from many others, they are nonetheless particularly Dickensian. Repenting her former life, and brought to an appreciation of Christian truths by Harriet Carker, Alice dies thankful of her friend's help. Alice's eyes follow Harriet as she leaves the room:

> and in their light, and on the tranquil face, there was a smile when it [the door] was closed.
>
> They never turned away. She laid her hand upon her breast, murmuring the sacred name that had been read to her; and life passed from her face, like light removed.
>
> Nothing lay there, any longer, but the ruin of the mortal house on which the rain had beaten, and the black hair that had fluttered in the wintry wind. (*Dombey and Son*, ch. 58)

If Alice's death demonstrates the redemption of a sinner on a personal level, Magwitch's death in *Great Expectations* indicates broader meanings, for his "deathbed scene" actually includes his courtroom denunciation of man's faulty justice and God's greater judgment. Afterward, Magwitch dies quietly, his last act being to kiss Pip's hand—a form of blessing and thanksgiving combined.

Deathbed scenes could also reveal the dreadful state of those who were remorseful, though not reformed. The drunkard tumbler's death in the "Stroller's Tale" in *Pickwick Papers* is a typical example. In this case the dying man is overcome with guilt, he fears the wife he has abused so long, and raves about the theatre and the public house. Finally he lapses into a fit of delirium tremens, and dies a convulsive and painful death. Similarly, in Anne Brontë's *The Tenant of Wildfell Hall*, Arthur Huntington's short, brutish life of intemperance leads to death, and his abused wife, Helen, returns to tend him in his final illness, happily reporting that on his deathbed Huntington was penitent at last.

There is a conscious exploitation of the deathbed scene in Miss Braddon's *Charlotte's Inheritance* when Captain Paget, who has been a petty swindler and rascal all his life, faces his last moments.

> Later, when the doctor had felt his pulse for the last time, he cried out suddenly, "I have made a statement of my affairs. The liabilities are numerous—the assets *nil*; but I rely on the clemency of this Court." (Book 10, ch. 6)[8]

And in G. P. R. James' *The Gipsy*, we learn something of why rascals might feel penitence on their deathbeds, though nowhere else. When Sir Roger Millington, a parasite who has assisted the evil Lord Dewry in his schemes, is dying, the local parson encourages him to repent and to help, with his dying breath, to undo some of his mischief. He fortifies his persuasion by reminding the dying scoundrel that man closes his eyes in death and wakes instantly in the other world stripped of his body, where the sins of his life are naked for all to see. Not surprisingly, the parson's argument succeeds. In Rossetti's "A Last Confession," a dying Italian, without repenting, regrets the loss of the woman he loved, but murdered. Still, the deathbed convention of the period contributes greater force to Rossetti's poem simply because his audience anticipates penitence. When it does not come, the poem becomes something sharper, perhaps more believable, than a mere deathbed confession with the normal pieties.[9] Roger Scatcherd, in Trollope's *Doctor Thorne*, is a forceful example of the debauchee who dies penitent. Despite being worth a half-million pounds, Scatcherd regrets his entire life of vindictiveness and intemperance. Nothing, the obvious moral shows, can shield a man from the truthful last moments of the deathbed.

Another example of deathbed remorse draws the theme of misspent and misvalued life closer to the artist himself, for Tennyson's "Romney's Remorse" deals with the painter George Romney's deathbed regret that he had abandoned his wife in order to pursue his career. His debauchery was an indulgence not of the body, like Dickens' pathetic tumbler, but of the spirit. At last, he has "stumbled back again / Into the common day, the sounder self." But he is dying and his humble wife returns to tend him at the last. Now he hates the word art and exclaims: "My curse upon the Master's apothegm, / That wife and children drag an artist down!" He now sees his error

in leaving his wife to seek artistic fame, and fears that he has "lost /
Salvation for a sketch." He has no alternative but to lament and
hope for forgiveness. In Kingsley's *Two Years Ago* (1857), the poet
Elsley Vavasour dies repenting his vanity and false jealousy. He urges
his friends to burn all of his poems and to prevent his children from
making verses. The poet in Owen Meredith's poem, "Last Words,"
also laments a life devoted to the pursuit of fame through art. He
tells his friend Will, who attends him at the end, that death is actually
easier than life, and, he begins to feel hope beyond this world in
which he has known only failure.

> Already I feel, in a sort of
>   still sweet awe,
> The great main current of all that I am beginning
>   to draw and draw
> Into perfect peace. I attain at last! Life's a
>   long, long reaching out
> Of the soul to something beyond her. Now comes the
>   end of all doubt.

The poet in "Last Words" has failed in his ambition to fashion from
common men, "Man, with his spirit sublime, / Man the great heir of
Eternity, dragging the conquests of Time!" just as Browning's Paracelsus failed in his extravagant aims. But on his deathbed, Paracelsus conveys to his faithful friend, Festus, his hopes for the progress
of Man. He dies not lamenting his wasted life and his obscurity, but
hopeful that, in the future, men will come to understand the message
of love he has won with such effort.

Customarily deathbed scenes sought to show the importance of
being ready for death, and to justify the existence of this overpower-
ing mystery. Consciousness of death runs throughout Charlotte
Yonge's *The Heir of Redclyffe*, climaxing in Guy Morville's deathbed
scene. Aware that death is imminent, he has Amabel recite some
verses from *Sintram*, which conclude hopefully.

> Death comes to set thee free,
> Oh! meet him cheerily,
>   As thy true friend:
> And all thy fears shall cease,

And in eternal peace,
    Thy penance end. (vol. 2, ch. 13)

Guy, who has proved his noble and generous nature throughout his life, now dies a noble death. It is a typical picture.

> At that moment the sun was rising, and the light streamed in at the open window and over the bed; but it was "another dawn than ours" that he beheld, as his most beautiful of all smiles beamed over his face, and he said, "Glory in the Highest!—peace—good will"—a struggle for breath gave an instant's look of pain; then he whispered so that she could but just hear—"The last prayer." She read the Commendatory Prayer. She knew not the exact moment, but even as she said, "Amen," she perceived it was over. The soul was with Him, with whom dwell the spirits of just men made perfect; and there lay the earthly part with the smile on the face. She closed the dark fringed eyelids—saw him look more beautiful than in sleep,—then, laying her face down to the bed, she knelt on. (vol. 2, ch. 13)

In many deathbed scenes a dying one passes on a moral responsibility to others. Constance Brandon, in *Guy Livingstone*, conveys to her saddened lover both remorse for his behavior and a yearning to seek a higher meaning in life. In Kingsley's *Yeast*, Argemone Lavington on her deathbed not only acknowledges the appropriateness of her death from a fever contracted while tending the poor her wealthy family has hitherto neglected, but passes on a legacy of moral duty to her faithful lover, urging him to remember her and labor to achieve the noble aim of seeing the slums cleared and disease brought under control among the poor.

The death of a good woman, especially a mother, often called for a sentimental tableau in the popular literature of the Victorian period. Mrs. Aubrey in Samuel Warren's *Ten Thousand A-Year* recovers from a brand of madness just in time to die a good and inspiring death. On the other hand, Alice Wilson, in Mrs. Gaskell's *Mary Barton*, having lived a pious life, glides into death by way of a second childhood. "The firm faith which her mind had no longer power to grasp, had left its trail of glory; for by no other word can I call the bright happy look which illumined the old earth-worn face. Her talk, it is true, bore no more that constant earnest reference to God and His holy word which it had done in health, and there were no deathbed words of exhortation from the lips of one so habitually pious."

(Ch. 33) Instead, Alice's mind dwells in the happy memories of her childhood. "And death came to her as a welcome blessing, like an evening comes to the weary child." (Ch. 33) The virtuous and long-suffering mother of the prodigal Paul Tatnall in Joseph H. Ingraham's *The Gipsy of the Highlands*, manages, on her deathbed, to convert the young woman who loves her son with forceful and sustained arguments. Having accomplished this, she prays that her son may repent and be saved, but "here her voice failed her, and her eyes, after steadfastly regarding heaven, slowly closed, while a smile came like sunlight to her features, and then a shadow passed slowly across her falling countenance—a sigh! and the pure spirit of the broken-hearted and pious widow took its flight to heaven!" (Ch. 9) In the popular literature of the time, "Purity and innocence always triumphed over the powers of evil, and the story ended with a betrothal, or, quite as often, with the sinner repentant on his deathbed," Janet Dunbar observes.[10]

In *The Ring and The Book* Browning wrote a memorable death-bed scene which, like Magwitch's in *Great Expectations*, was less the expression of an individual spirit than the exemplification of a way of life, correcting a faulty world with the intensity of vision given to those who are on the verge of a presumably higher and finer realm. Pompilia is the embodiment of innocence, and her proper home is not this world, but the next. "The hovel is life," she says, anticipating liberation from it. Like Little Nell, she does not fear death, but looks forward to it almost gladly, certainly with relief. Her last words are for those who must remain in the world, and, although she does not, like Kingsley's Argemone, have any specific social labor to recommend, she does cheer on the laborers left in the vineyard.

> So, let him wait God's instant men call years;
> Meantime hold hard by truth and his great soul,
> Do out the duty! Through such souls alone
> God stooping shows sufficient of His light
> For us i' the dark to rise by. And I rise. (Book 7)

Although Pompilia's virtue has earlier been questioned, there is little doubt in the reader's mind of her virtue. The same can be said of Mrs. Gaskell's Ruth. Although Ruth had lapsed from chastity in her youth, her adult life has been a series of virtuous triumphs, and her death represents the achievement of a higher virtue than that found in most of her neighbors, for she has contracted her own fatal illness while tending epidemic victims whose health concerns the entire community. Her death is an apotheosis of selfless dedication and it enjoys the appropriate furnishings.

> "I see the Light coming," she said. "The Light is coming," she said. And, raising herself slowly, she stretched out her arms, and then fell back, very still for evermore. (ch. 35, *Ruth*)

Less theatrical, but equally indicative of feminine virtue is the long "deathbed" letter that Jane Graham leaves for her husband to read after her death in Coventry Patmore's *The Angel in the House* (sections 7 through 9 of "The Victories of Love"). Jane includes expressions of her love for Frederick and her hope for their future, as well as a record of her vision of heaven. Although this is not a genuine deathbed scene, it achieves the same effects and draws upon the same conventional materials. In some ways it is even more demonstrative of what the virtuous deathbed scene meant to Victorians, since it avoids entirely the actual physical death by concentrating on the thoughts recorded while Jane gradually weakened, thus making her posthumous letter resemble a private prayer.

THE CHILD

If Charlotte Yonge had captured a prevailing sentiment about death in her picture of Guy Morville's end in *The Heir of Redclyffe*, she touched an equally evocative chord in her conventional account of the child, Felix Dixon's death. Gillian Avery has written that whereas Georgians tried to shock their readers into good behavior through the use of death, "the early Victorians strove to edify by recording pious deaths," and later Victorians became sentimental. In all cases, childhood death "tended to be linked with the themes of punishment and reward."[11] A disobedient child could be instructive to others. In tract stories, a child's death is quite openly a "holy example" required for the conversion of the remaining characters of the tale.[12] As the century progressed, the death of innocence was more markedly associated with the death of children. Peter Coveney writes of two popular novelists of the later Victorian period, "with Marie

Corelli, as with Mrs. Henry Wood, death is never very far removed from her image of the child."[13]

Dying children were clearly representatives of innocence, but although "the child may die talking of heaven and angels, he does not seem to have heard of sin."[14] In *Misunderstood* (1869), Florence Montgomery exploited both the punishment of the disobedient child and the innocence of his death, combining them both into one character, young Humphrey Duncombe. Humphrey is not a bad boy, though he is thoughtless. Yet, when he is dying, the narrator remarks that "natures like Humphrey's are not fit for this rough world. Such a capacity for sorrow has no rest here, and such a capability for enjoyment is fittest to find its happiness in those all-perfect pleasures which are at God's right hand for evermore." (Ch. 16) Humphrey has been capable of one profound emotion—love for his dead mother, and, on his deathbed, beneath his mother's picture, he imagines she has come to claim him.

> Those who were standing round saw only the expression of pain change to the old sunny smile. His lips moved, and he lifted his arms, as his eyes were raised, for a moment, to the picture above him, on which the sun was pouring a dazzling light. They closed: but the smile, intensely radiant, lingered about the parted lips; the short breathing grew shorter . . . stopped . . . and then . . .
> "It's no use my saying the rest," said little Miles in a whisper, "for Humphie has gone to sleep." (ch. 17)

Gillian Avery comments that the death of Humphrey in *Misunderstood* is "shamelessly derived from the death of Paul Dombey,"[15] while Peter Coveney remarks that "William Carlyle of *East Lynne* is perhaps the most notorious of the Victorian dying children, whose ancestry lay in Little Nell and Paul Dombey." Coveney adds, however, that whereas such figures as Paul Dombey, and Eppie in *Silas Marner* are serious creations, William Carlyle's context "is no more than a moralizing melodrama, declaring the inevitable retributions of carnal sin."[16] Little Paul's death in *Dombey and Son* was one of the most famous deaths in Victorian fiction. The dying is prolonged, but the deathbed scene is relatively brief, terminating with the suggestion that little Paul already views his dead mother and his Savior before he dies. "Mama is like you, Floy," he says to his sister. " 'I know her by the face! But tell them the print upon the stairs at school is not divine enough. The light about the head is shining on me as I go!'" (Ch. 16) A scene such as this could be viewed as moving and moral, or merely as sentimental trash, but it sold.

Dickens made frequent and varying use of the dying child. Little Johnny, in *Our Mutual Friend*, dies in a spirit of charity, bequeathing his toys to the ailing child in the bed near his own, but his death is merely one more in a sequence of touching childhood deathbed scenes. Dickens had used a child's deathbed to point a moral as early as *Pickwick Papers*, when Gabriel Grub was forced to witness the pathetic event. Later, Scrooge, though obliged to witness a similar scene, had the opportunity to forestall it. There are, of course, other dying youngsters of various ages in Dickens' works, including Smike in *Nicholas Nickleby* and Jo in *Bleak House*, but the most memorable children's deathbeds, aside from Paul Dombey's, appear in *The Old Curiosity Shop*. Long before her own decline, Little Nell witnesses the death of a young schoolboy, his schoolmaster's most promising student. The meaning of this death is not lost on Nell.

> But the sad scene she had witnessed, was not without its lesson of content and gratitude; of content with the lot which left her health and freedom; and gratitude that she was spared to the one relative and friend she loved, and to live and move in a beautiful world, when so many young creatures—as young and full of hope as she—were stricken and gathered to their graves. (Ch. 26)

There are other advantages to an early death that Nell does not consider, but some of them are indicated to her later by the schoolmaster who has learned to accept the death of the young and innocent through his faith in the triumph of good. "If the good deeds of human creatures could be traced to their source," he says, "how beautiful would even death appear; for how much charity, mercy and purified affection, would be seen to have their growth in dusty graves." (Ch. 54) Although we do not witness Nell's death, we see her soon after on her deathbed. She signifies death of innocence and her travail in this world is ended. "Sorrow was dead indeed in her, but peace and perfect happiness were born; imaged in her tranquil beauty and profound repose." (Ch. 71)

The consolation suggested by the schoolmaster's words and implied in Dickens' portrayal of Nell, is echoed in Archbishop Trench's poem, "On An Early Death": "Nothing is left or lost, nothing of good,

/ Or lovely; but whatever its first springs / Has drawn from God, returns to Him again." This view was commonplace, and yet, it is possible, beyond the Christian comfort for the loss of youth and innocence, there is a more ominous implication. Peter Coveney sees in
the transformation of the image of the child, from life-bearer, to
death-borne, a grim indication about the Victorian age. "It is as if so
many placed on the image the weight of their own disquiet and dissatisfaction, their impulse to withdrawal, and, in extremity, their own
wish for death. . . . It is a remarkable phenomenon, surely," he adds,
"when a society takes the child (with all its potential significance as
a symbol of fertility and growth) and creates of it a literary image, not
only of frailty, but of life extinguished, of life that is better extinguished, of life, so to say, rejected, negated at its very root.[17]

For many writers, and doubtless some portion of their audience,
the deathbed became a sanctuary, where the qualities of childhood
could escape the effects of time and suffering. The poems of poets
such as Francis Thompson and Ernest Dowson suggest the wistful
desire to worship what children stand for, while hoping that life will
not touch them. On a gayer note, but no less exclusive, the world of
children is largely removed to the province of fantasy in the works
of R. L. Stevenson, Sir James Barrie, Rudyard Kipling, and George
MacDonald. This exclusion of the child from the corrupting ways of
adulthood, suggests a growing conciousness of the nature of that society's failure and is, to a large extent, a confession of decline.

CONCLUSION

Despite its apparent sentimentality, the deathbed convention was
much in keeping with the Victorian attitudes toward death, which,
in general, would appear exaggerated and mawkish today. But
some manifestations of the convention are truly memorable. It was
not only women and children who could die deaths remarkable for
their innocence and sweetness, for example. Though most adults were
somehow qualified in their virtue by mere exposure to the world,
some could transcend that sullying influence. Thackeray transformed
the customary image of adult reconciliation with death into one of
innocence more commonly associated with the deaths of children,
and, in doing so, created one of the most famous deathbed scenes in
Victorian literature. Old Colonel Newcome is wandering in his mind

as the end draws near. He is a pensioner now of his old school, Grey Friars, but he feels no shame in his humble position. His concerns, even in his hallucinations, are for those he loves. Finally, the end comes.

> At the usual evening hour the chapel bell began to toll, and Thomas Newcome's hands outside the bed feebly beat time. And just as the last bell struck, a peculiar sweet smile shone over his face, and he lifted up his head a little, and quickly said, "Adsum!" and fell back. It was the word we used at school, when names were called; and lo, he, whose heart was as that of a little child, had answered to his name, and stood in the presence of The Master. (*The Newcomes*, Vol. 2, ch. 42)[18]

There is a general resemblance here to other concluding deathbed scenes. Mordecai's death, for example, closes *Daniel Deronda* like a sort of benediction.

The traditional moral significance of deathbed scenes persisted beyond the nineteenth century. The dying curses that echoed through the popular romances of the time, and modifications of them, as in Bulwer-Lytton's *A Strange Story*, where the dying Dr. Lloyd angrily foretells his professional antagonist, Dr. Fenwick's, suffering and doubt, did not disappear from adventure tales. And religious significance remained in such stories as Mrs. Opie's novel, *Adeline Mowbray* (1905), where a freethinker recants on his deathbed.[19] Some writers employed the convention merely as a technical convenience. Wilkie Collins opened *Armadale* with a prolonged deathbed scene, in which the older Allan Armadale, dying of a creeping paralysis, recounts the history of his misadventures with his antagonist, the other Allan Armadale. Collins realized that this was a strong scene, and used the technique in *The Dead Secret* as well. The device provides a forceful initiation to the story, but, aside from hinting of malign agencies at work and impending disasters prescribed by destiny, Collins did little to exploit the convention. There is a little more irony in Dutton Cook's *A Prodigal Son* (1863), where the first five chapters are taken up by the death of old George Hadfield. The tough old man dies with a smile on his lips and his doctor remarks that "He looked so grand and handsome, it was difficult to believe that he died cruel, and relentless, and unforgiving." (Vol. 1, ch. 5)

The deathbed convention was not a mere literary contrivance. Most families were acquainted with the fact of death near at hand.

In "The Lifted Veil" (1859), George Eliot acknowledged, through the narrator of her story, the monumental importance of witnessing the dying moments of another being. Latimer, recounting how he had watched at his father's deathbed, exclaims, "What are all our personal loves when we have been sharing in that supreme agony? In the first moments when we come away from the presence of death, every other relation to the living is merged, to our feeling, in the great relation of a common nature and a common destiny." (Ch. 2) Possibly it was this sense of a common destiny, more than the attempt at moral persuasion, that was most captivating in the convention of the deathbed. Walter Houghton is, perhaps, too hasty in declaring that death scenes in Victorian novels "are intended to help the reader sustain his faith by dissolving religious doubts in a solution of warm sentiment."[20] A powerful passage from Robert Bell's *The Ladder of Gold* (1850) demonstrates that the Chamber of Death signified more to Victorian readers than a consoling reassurance about the next life. It was, as much or more, a reminder of the vanity of this life.

> Rich and poor, proud and humble, the wronged and the wrong-doer, are here brought to a common level. Their stormy passions, their grand projects, their great revenges,—what are they here in the Presence of the Dead—a breath of air which thrills a leaf and passes on. What are our loves and hates here? our honours, our humiliations?—a poor fading dream! Upon this threshold the unreality of life is made clear to us, and we see the pageant vanishing before our eyes. (Book 1, ch. 4)

Not all deathbed scenes were conventional. Many still appear faithful to the reality. There is the justly famous dramatic and realistic decease of Peter Featherstone in *Middlemarch*, where George Eliot actually seems to be taking pains to contradict the saccharine deathbed scenes which she herself was not totally innocent of using, as the death of Eppie in *Silas Marner* testifies. And Eliot's realism was in keeping with a growing tendency to resist the conventional form of the deathbed scene. As was so often the case, when conventions came to be attacked, Thomas Hardy was prominent in the assault. Not only does he introduce the bizarre deathbed sequence of old John South (who dies when the elm tree that has terrified him is cut down) into *The Woodlanders*, but in the death of Giles Winterborne in the same novel he presents a matter-of-fact exit, not a sentimental diminuendo. After becoming ill from exposure, Winterborne loses consciousness. "In less than an hour the delirium ceased; then there was an interval of somnolent painlessness and soft breathing, at the end of which Winterborne passed quietly away." (Ch. 43) This plain demise is in contrast to the brutal deathbed scene of Jude Fawley in *Jude the Obscure*. There Jude lies abandoned on his deathbed reciting to himself the lamentations of Job, while outside the crowds cheer on a festival day, and his wife sports with some gay associates. He dies alone and unheeded with only a wish never to have lived upon his lips. It is a bitter termination for a convention that had held the conviction of its readers throughout the century.

Deathbed scenes in Victorian literature could be moving or bathetic; they could be technically convenient or structurally important; but they were generally accepted and appreciated. The deathbed presented the last preserve of truth; it was a final opportunity to repent, admonish or encourage. As a result, it customarily bore, for Victorians, an importance far greater than what we place upon it. Very likely there were few of those staged deliveries of touching last words in reality. Perhaps those mortal scenes were uglier than writers cared to admit. But in literature they were an automatic means for conveying clearly and without reserve, the basic importance of the moral scheme which underlay so much of the writing of the time. As faith in a life after death waned, death could still be viewed as the touchstone of human vanities, but the deathbed scenes disappeared as mortuary practices changed and most deaths began to occur in hospitals rather than homes.[21] Offensive as many modern readers now find the deathbed convention, it was, for its time, a truly immediate reality that bound fictional convention and social fact together.

CHAPTER EIGHT

SWINDLES

MONEY AND SOCIETY

Victorian England has often been characterized for its interest in getting and spending. Much of that getting was only marginally legal, and even then, it was not entirely sound. Especially in the first half of the nineteenth century, financial speculation was a doubtful enterprise. G. M. Young has remarked that, not finance, but production was the governing notion for Victorian moneymakers;[1] nonetheless, there was sufficient interest in speculation to bring on, after the lean years following the war, a financial boom in 1824-25. "Certainly at that time there was a stock market boom as well as a peak of industrial activity, and a wave of speculation as well as a burst of real investment. While the market value of Mexican and South American shares soared and the daring turned to South America as a new Eldorado, the volume of domestic building broke all previous records."[2] At the same time that Lord Liverpool warned the public against speculators and company promoters, he informed them that the government would not interfere, and Parliament repealed the Bubble Act of 1720.[3]

The difficult years after the Napoleonic wars were followed by economic crises in 1825, 1836-37, 1847, 1857, and again in 1866.[4]

Joint-stock companies, and other large financial concerns were not entirely trustworthy, though they enticed many with their promises of high dividends. D. Morier Evans tells us that even the most respected firms were less stable than they seemed and when the eminent Messrs. Harman & Co., Russian merchants and agents to the Imperial Court at St. Petersburg failed, it was discovered that the firm "had been utterly insolvent for nearly a quarter of a century; its debts and liabilities were enormous, and the assets barely capable of paying a respectable dividend."[5] Many reputable firms invested unwisely, and wild speculation, coupled with other financial shocks, including bad harvests and European upheavals, brought on renewed crises. E. L. Woodward, in discussing the cyclical return of economic troubles in nineteenth-century England, says that the intervals between crises was regular, but speculators failed to learn from them. Still, "there were also special reasons for each crisis."[6] The Bank Charter Act of 1833 aimed at controlling imprudent extension of credit by small banks. But a sudden increase in the number of joint-stock banks occasioned an expansion of credit just when the railway boom was encouraging speculation. The result was more bank failures both in England and America. A later Bank Charter Act (1844), also failed to have a lasting effect upon unwise extension of credit and speculation. The 1866 failure of the firm of Overend and Gurney resulted from risky speculation, and the fall of this reputable company started a run on the banks and the ruin of many speculative ventures which had come into existence since 1856.

Attempts had been made to control the disorderly financial situation of various speculating organizations. A prominent move in this direction was the Companies Act of 1844, which set out "to tidy and to systematize" speculation.

> The 1844 Act laid down that all companies had to be registered, and that they had to publish their prospectuses and balance sheets. Although most English business was not organized in incorporated companies in 1844, the reforms were rightly regarded as guarantees of business 'improvement.'[7]

But there were some forms of investment that eluded all control, among them, railway speculation, which saw two major periods of speculation mania, in 1845 and again in 1864-66. Railway speculations, along with many others, were suddenly abridged by the crisis of 1866. Railway investment was particularly volatile largely because railway business was so chaotic. It was Thomas Brassey who brought sound organizing principles to the railway contracting business. Before him contractors were notable only because they so often went bankrupt. Brassey's success in making railway contracting a reputable branch of the profession did not prevent some major contractors, such as Sir Morton Peto or Thomas Savin from going bankrupt when times were bad. Furthermore, accounting methods were deplorable among railway companies before the Regulation of Railway Act of 1868 brought some order to them. Railways were not, as it seemed, trying to mystify the public with their records, it was simply that they "were inventing new techniques of financing, and they were running well ahead of any existing auditor's technique of control."[8] Sometimes this financial slovenliness could be costly, as when the Great Northern Railway company discovered in 1856 that they had been defrauded of something like a quarter of a million pounds by one of the clerks in their stock transfer office, a certain Leopold Redpath.

Given this loose financial climate, it is not surprising that railway companies, and particularly speculators in them, were viewed with some suspicion. George Hudson is typical. His dazzling career was based on disregard for ordinary financial rules and some plain dishonesty; "by 1859 he was exhibited as the principal character of a rogues' gallery in a book by D. Morier Evans called *Facts, Failures, and Frauds.*"[9] But Hudson was not so clearly objectionable in the Forties as later critics might assume, and although he was accused of misappropriation of shares, falsification of accounts and balance sheets, and bank malpractices, he was never criminally prosecuted for his offences. Hudson's biographer, Richard S. Lambert, notes that "The coming of railways during the 'thirties and 'forties of the last century was probably the most upsetting and stimulating single economic phenomenon that society in this country has ever experienced."[10] In the confusion of this new phenomenon it was easy to deceive and be deceived. Hudson became the model of financial "rockets" not only because his success and failure were rapid—rising from the respected Mayor of York in 1837 to the zenith of his power in 1844 and collapsing in the crisis of 1847—but also because it had been extensive as well, involving banking and finance, landed property, and the railway. At the same time, his gaudy social life attracted attention, while his common birth made him seem all the more an anomaly in the circles he frequented. In the end, Hudson lost his money and his power and was forced to live a shabby life on the Continent. After an attempt at reelection in Whitby was frustrated by his arrest, Hudson retired to obscurity, dying in 1871.

Although Hudson's practices were far from proper, there were few regulations to govern him. Moreover, his business conduct was made possible by the greed and gullibility not only of the uninformed many, but the powerful few. Hudson's contemporary, D. Morier Evans, wrote in *The Commercial Crisis of 1847-1848* (1848), "It will thus be perceived, that throughout the several phases of the mania, the distinctive features of fraud and chicanery were prominently presented, and that in the grand drama, each change of scene was accompanied by incidents as remarkable as any which had already preceded them."[11] Indicating how involved the influential classes were in the mania, R. S. Lambert states that, "A return called for by Parliament, to show the number of persons who had subscribed more than £ 2,000 in railway undertakings, included the names of 900 lawyers, 364 bankers, 257 clergymen, and 157 Members of Parliament, besides large numbers of noblemen, merchants, and manufacturers."[12] Hudson was assisted in his financial schemes because few people understood how manipulation of railway funds might occur. First a provisional committee of backers, composed of men with some reputation, was established. D. Morier Evans indicates how eager men were, in 1845, to be on the provisional committees: "Earls and Marquises struggled with London capitalists and rustic landowners to add attractiveness by the sanction of their names; the needy barrister professed affection for a seat at the councils of boards, which seemed likely to bring more profit than the law, and was as importunate as most persons to be ensured that position."[13] When the bill came before Parliament, lawyers and engineers were consulted on problems such as clearing rights of way. An Act of 1842 required a deposit of one-tenth of a proposed company's capital while the Board of Trade reported on the advisability of all proposals. The method of approval in the House of Lords was swifter than that in the Commons, but, in any case, directors of companies, so long as new building was under way, could keep the capital account of their company open, thereby permitting them to use the cash as they pleased.

Though he was the most notorious, Hudson was only one of many men who exploited these financial circumstances. Although the most dramatic, railroads were not the only targets for reckless speculators.

Charles J. Mathews told of his experiences as an employee of the Welsh Iron and Coal, "one of the many companies conjured into life by the magic wand of the celebrated (notorious?) John Wilks—not the John Wilkes of No. 45, but the John Wilks of forty-five bubble companies—producing a rage for speculation in London almost equal to the famous South Sea Bubble of years gone by."[14] Wilks' Welsh Iron and Coal company did not fail, though it was also no remarkable success, for Wilks had little interest in the operation as an industry, being concerned only with its value as a speculation. What was important to Mathews was Wilks' deplorable conduct and apparent social ignorance. Generally men such as Wilks and Hudson were loud and brash, not the smooth swindlers who so frequently appear in the fiction of the period.

If various joint-stock companies suffered clumsy or unscrupulous management, it was frequently the banks who invested or extended credit unwisely and therefore often came to grief, bringing the nation into difficulty as well. Furthermore, as the article, "Savings' Bank Defalcations," which appeared in *Household Words* in 1850 indicated, crimes of simple misappropriation of funds were so common as to engender serious public concern. Throughout the century, genuine misgivings persisted in regard to banks, joint-stock companies, and businesses in general. Economic crises did not end in 1866, but continued to recur, and business practices did not improve with time. Even in 1875, *The Times* (11 Aug. 1875) expressed alarm at the extensiveness of dishonesty in private enterprise.

FINANCE IN LITERATURE

Considering the prevailing economic conditions and attitudes in nineteenth-century England, it is not unusual that financial failure was a major theme in Victorian literature. Most examples of bankruptcy and ruin were merely faithful reflections of the times, but they also served to point a moral. Ivan Melada, in *The Captains of Industry in English Fiction, 1821-1871*, indicates how common the criticism of joint-stock companies was in literature from the writings of Harriet Martineau and the *Chamber's Miscellany*, to Dickens' novels, Thackeray's *The History of Samuel Titmarsh and the Great Hoggarty Diamond* (1841), and Charles Lever's *Davenport Dunn: A Man of Our Day* (1859).

In Samuel Warren's *Ten Thousand A-Year* (1841), the "Gunpowder and Fresh Water Company," and the "Artificial Rain Company," are fraudulent joint-stock companies. In revealing the criminal nature of these enterprises, Warren describes one of the familiar techniques that their promoters employed. Playing upon the vanity of the foolish Lord Dreddlington, these promoters coax the peer into lending the dignity of his name to their undertakings. The peer's friends try in vain to warn him. The dishonest nature of the enterprise becomes evident only when the chairman of the Artificial Rain Company, Sir Sharper Bubble, absconds with the company's available funds, leaving Dreddlington and many others to suffer the consequences.[15] Even the arch-villain, Mr. Gammon, loses money at the hands of his equally unscrupulous associate. Warren's main purpose here is to demonstrate the folly of Lord Dreddlington's vanity. And for an age preoccupied with money, what more convincing manner of indicating pride's necessary fall could there be than a genuine financial collapse?

Personal bankruptcy was a familiar convention in nineteenth-century literature, and was often associated with speculation or financial betrayal, as is the case with the Rivers family in *Jane Eyre*. The dangers of speculation are frequently stated in Victorian fiction. Writing about Geraldine Jewsbury's *Marian Withers* (1851), Ivan Melada remarks that "because his success was the result of hard work accompanied by near starvation, Withers has little use for the get-rich-quick aspects of joint stock company operations, and much less for the speculator."[16] A similar contempt for the "City Man" living upon speculation is exhibited in G. W. M. Reynold's *The Mysteries of London* (1845), where George Montague is not only responsible for ruining a friend, but corrupts his daughter as well when she is left in need.

Writers did not use bankruptcy only in a negative way, but showed that definite benefits could follow from financial disaster. In Charles Kingsley's *Yeast* (1848-49), the failure of Lancelot Smith's uncle's bank, as a result of unwise speculations, ruins Lancelot, among others. In condemning the credit system, and speculation in particular, Kingsley does not condemn Lancelot, for, as his uncle says to him, "you are just the innocent one among us all. You, at least, were only a sleeping partner." (Ch. 14) But Lancelot derives moral benefit from his material failure:

"No," he said, "no more pay without work for me. I will earn my bread or starve. It seems God's will to teach me what poverty is—I will see that His intention is not left half fulfilled. I have sinned, and only in the stern delight of a just penance can I gain self-respect." (Ch. 14)

Similarly, when Alfred Vargrave is ruined by Sir Ridley's financial maneuvers in Owen Meredith's *Lucile* (1860), the catastrophe has a beneficial effect, for it draws Alfred and his wife together again in an intimacy that promises well for their future. "And thus," the narrator observes, "loss of fortune gave value to a life." (Two. VI. viii) But despite the hopeful moral consequences of financial ruin—closely related to the notion in Victorian fiction that suffering strengthens virtue by testing it and leads to an eventual reward—most examples of swindling and economic failure are indicators of the moral corruption of the age. In Tennyson's *Maud* (1855), for example, it is only necessary for the narrator to mention that "a vast speculation had failed," to indicate long perspectives of dishonesty and even criminality on the part of those responsible for his father's death. And clearly, the details of Tennyson's poem reveal how pervasive consequences of the greed typified by the "vast speculation" could seem.[17]

As one might expect of a novelist deeply concerned about social habits, Thackeray also employed the swindle convention to good purpose. John Sedley's bankruptcy in *Vanity Fair*, clearly related to the unsteady economic circumstances of the Napoleonic period, is more pathetic than instructive. But Thackeray knew how to utilize the convention for moral purposes and the Bundelcund Banking Company in *The Newcomes* (1853-55) is more in the customary manner. Of course, Thackeray was fully aware of the conventionality of the subject, and, when the time came to describe the company's collapse, remarked to his readers: "Yes, sir or madam, you are quite right in the opinion which you have held all along regarding that Bundelcund Banking Company, in which our Colonel has invested every rupee he possesses." He admits further that he has found it difficult, as narrator, not to denounce the speculation sooner; "and whenever I have had occasion to mention the company, [I] have scarcely been able to refrain from breaking out into fierce diatribes against that complicated, enormous, outrageous swindle." (Vol. 2, Ch. 32) Worse yet, Thackeray adds, it was only one of many similar swindles practiced on the innocent. And yet, the effect of the ruin that the bank failure brings upon Colonel Newcome and his son is far

from deplorable. Clive feels only hope for the future and relief that
the speculation and its complications are over. Colonel Newcome's
ruin brings him to the Grey Friars almshouse, but this humbling only
demonstrates the old man's genuine virtue, and Clive, meanwhile,
though brought low, reveals his strength of character in adversity.
Eventually, his way is made easy again by a timely inheritance. For
Thackeray, much concerned as he was about money and its power,
the loss of great fortune could serve a moral purpose in the larger design of his fiction. The convention of financial ruin was only one more
method of testing virtue, of placing demands upon the individual
moral will. Stripped of worldly fortune, the hero must reveal his basic
strength of character. Financial ruin thus becomes a secular version
of the *felix culpa*.

The emblematic nature of this convention is fully evident in a novel
like *The Adventures of Philip* (1861-62), where Dr. Firmin, by wasting
his son Philip's fortune, has, in effect, sacrificed him to his own God,
Mammon. The point is all too ironically apparent when Dr. Firmin
directs in a letter: "My will, made long since, will be found in the
tortoiseshell secretaire standing in my consulting-room under the picture of Abraham offering up Isaac." (Ch. 14) Philip himself is aware
of the irony. "His father was his fate, he seemed to think, and there
were no means of averting it. 'You remember that picture of Abraham and Isaac in the Doctor's Study in Old Parr Street?' he would
say. 'My patriarch has tied me up, and had the knife in me repeatedly. He does not sacrifice me at one operation; but there will be a final
one some day, and I shall bleed no more.'" (Ch. 37) But, just as Isaac
is eventually spared, so Philip survives his "ruin." In fact, Thackeray
here carries the convention a step further, describing the relatively
impoverished Philip as thoroughly happy in his condition. Philip
has never desired wealth, and the lack of it does not destroy his happiness, but actually places it upon a firmer foundation of self-knowledge and self-confidence.

During the years when Thackeray was writing these novels, large-
scale swindles were much in the news, and more than one novelist
founded a tale upon the popular scandal of the day. Robert Bell's
The Ladder of Gold. An English Story (1850) is based on the career
of George Hudson and is a better novel than its obscurity suggests.[18]
Bell's story describes the career of Richard Rawlings from poor assistant, to miserly merchant, to emperor of the London financial world.

Rawlings' rise follows from his fundamental discovery at the funeral of his employer that the mourners display obviously false sentiments. Rawlings asks himself, "How is it that men can thus be brought to dissimulate their real convictions, and prostrate themselves before an object they despise?" His answer is immediate. "Why, gold does it all!" (Vol. 1, Book 1, Ch. 5) Rawlings promptly marries his employer's widow for her fortune and soon learns, through the help of Tom Chippendale, a lawyer, to increase his fortune through investment. The first major step in his advance is in the exploitation of the financial needs of the likes of Lord Valteline, a thoughtless aristocrat.

As the years pass, Rawlings' growing ambition and avarice harden his heart. He becomes involved in the new business of railway speculation and finds that he is particularly suited to it. He involves himself in politics in order to compass his financial plans; and he begins to entertain lavishly. Bell explains that the apparent magic of Rawlings' money miracles was attributable not to the skill of the sorcerer, but to the credulity of his public.

> His name was a tower of strength, and whenever it appeared the shares were instantly quoted at a premium, that made the grovelling world at his feet look up to him with a feeling of confidence, not such as men repose in the known and tested powers of their fellow-men, but such as a slavish superstition accords to Juggernaut or Joss. (Vol. 2, Book 3, ch. 1)

Rawlings forces his daughter Margaret into an unhappy marriage with Sir Charles Eton to satisfy his lust for social distinction, now possible through his wealth. In the meantime, he stacks his committees with "flunkies" to guarantee his own freedom of action. Finally the crash comes: "The mass of speculators were ruined; and a few crafty hands had amassed enormous wealth." (Vol. 3, Book 1, Ch. 1) Rawlings survives the crash, but Sir Peter Jinks, convinced that Rawlings is a consummate swindler, resolves to expose him. Although much that is improper is disclosed, nothing absolutely dishonest can be proven. Nonetheless, Rawlings' financial empire collapses. He is not greatly moved by his disaster, however, for he has achieved the luxury and social position that he sought and found them savorless. Afterward, he is content to pursue a modest career in industry. This prolonged account of financial chicanery is only one thread in Bell's complicated novel, but it is the most fascinating and surely was what occasioned its large, if temporary, success. Bell had been easier on his financial villain than other writers, for he fully acknowledged that it was public greed and credulity that turned men like Rawlings—or George Hudson—into successful swindlers. The offense, though clearly individual, was also social. In this context, the swindle convention suggests a more profound moral purpose than the mere testing of individual character by adversity.

Charles Lever's *Davenport Dunn: A Man of Our Day* appeared during the years 1857 to 1859, when the effects of the 1857 financial crisis were still prominent in readers' minds. Lever's central character, like Bell's, rises from humble origins to a position of extensive financial and political power. Dunn, however, realizes how limited his gifts are, and how much he depends upon the credulity of others. His great opportunity came with the Irish Encumbered Estates Bill, which permitted him to manage the acquisition, for himself and for others, of Irish estates embarrassed by debts. This Act, coming into effect in 1849, was designed to attract English investors to Ireland, but suggestions in Lever's novel notwithstanding, the overwhelming number of buyers were Irish, not aliens.[19] Dunn had been clever enough to take advantage of these circumstances in Ireland, and, by shrewdness and deception, constructed a financial empire. Although Dunn is involved in general schemes to acquire money, property and influence, one that is developed at length and proves most consequential is "The Grand Glengariff Villa Allotment and Marine Residence Company," a land development supposedly intended to benefit the local populace. Sybella Kellett, the highly efficient heroine of the novel, while working with Lord Glengariff and Dunn's creature, Simpson Hankes, gradually realizes that the scheme is a fraud, and with the end of the Vienna conference, followed by panic on the exchange, and the coincidental misdirection of a letter from Dunn revealing the precarious nature of his many schemes, Sybella finally conceives the truth. "This great venture is a swindling enterprise! All these poor people whose hard-earned gains have been invested in it will be ruined; my own small pittance, too, is gone. Good heavens! to what a terrible network of intrigue and deception have I lent myself?" (Ch. 60) She threatens to expose the entire scheme, denouncing Dunn as "a man of nothing, living the precarious life of a gambling speculator, trading on the rich man's hoard and the poor man's pittance, making market of all, even to his patriotism." (Ch. 60)

Hankes manages to prevent Sybella from carrying out her threat, and in the meantime, Dunn is honored by the government as a "man of successful industry." (Ch. 61) Lever interrupts to condemn the popular "worship of the golden image of Gain," and to declare Dunn "the incarnation of this passion." (Ch. 61) Dunn is also representative of crude ambition, since he aspires to marry the aristocratic Lady Augusta Glengariff and to achieve a Peerage. His plans are foiled, however, by the violent intervention of Capt. Grog Davis, who is interested in another scheme that Dunn has been pursuing. Both men are eager to control the settlement of the Lackington-Conway dispute over the rights to a huge and wealthy estate and title. In a struggle, Davis, a gambler and adventurer, kills Dunn and is arrested. In conducting his own defense, Davis voices Lever's chief moral point in the novel. Comparing himself to Dunn, Davis concedes that "we were both adventurers, each of us traded upon the weakness of his fellows; the only difference was, that he played a game that could not but win, while I took my risks like a man, and as often suffered as I succeeded." (Ch. 78) Davis, we are told, preyed upon young men of fortune, whereas Dunn robbed the poor, the orphaned and the helpless. Sentiment turns against the once-venerated Dunn, while Davis is convicted of manslaughter with a recommendation of mercy. But Lever's point has been amply made. The swindles and chicaneries of Dunn and his cronies are played out against the background of the Crimean war. Lever's conviction that the war, or at least the soldiers fighting in it, represented genuine honor and glory, only makes the spurious glory of the hypocritical swindler more ignominious. The convention of the swindle is here far more than a mere device to move forward the action of a plot, to separate lovers, or inconvenience a hero, it has been expanded and constitutes now a general indictment of the way men lived in the prosperous mid-century in England. The nation as a whole, not merely one man, is held to be responsible here as in Bell's *Ladder of Gold* because it has buttressed financial deceit with its own greed for money. About this same time, Richard Burton remarked in *Stone Talk* (1857) that England had sold out to Mammon. The charge was a common one, and in journalism too the subject was popular, as in Henry Morley's article, "The Predatory Art," in the 14 March 1857 issue of *Household Words*. But one of England's greatest writers, Charles Dickens, had been sounding the tocsin on this very topic for some time.

Grahame Smith has shown, in *Dickens, Money, and Society,* how skillfully Dickens used money as a feature of his writing, concluding that "The details of plot, character, and action which make up the complex structures of Dickens' later novels reflect the web of financial interdependence that holds individuals and classes in modern society in a grasp as isolating as it is inescapable."[20] But Dickens' consciousness of the world of finance as a type of moral risk is evident before the late novels. Dickens had always been aware of the manner in which the innocent could be injured by the swindling that also eventually maimed the swindler. If Ralph Nickleby is a successful money-getter, his unfortunate brother is not. "Speculation is a round game," Dickens observes early in *Nicholas Nickleby* (1838-39), "the players see little or nothing of their cards at first starting; gains *may* be great—and so may losses. The run of luck went against Mr. Nickleby. A mania prevailed, a bubble burst, four stockbrokers took villa residences at Florence, four hundred nobodies were ruined, and among them Mr. Nickleby." (Ch. 1) Because of Mr. Nickleby's error, Nicholas and Madeline, his children, find themselves left to fashion their own careers. No inheritance provides them with the means to help themselves or others; but, on the other hand, no immediate wealth tempts them to idleness and vanity. They must make their own way. This is the most conventional utilization of the swindle, the forcing of characters onto their own resources. It is another way, as we have already seen, of testing their characters. It goes no further in this novel, but is a busy author's convenient device.

Swindling is more prominently used in *Martin Chuzzlewit* (1843-44). Martin's naive investment in the Eden Land Corporation is an example of self-concern leading only to a downfall. So proud is Martin of his own abilities, that he does not recognize the highly suspicious nature of the American development scheme. Fortunately, as Martin's investment is slight, so is his failure, and his moral profit outweighs his financial loss, for he learns an important lesson in humility. The Anglo-Bengalee Disinterested Loan and Life Assurance Company in the same novel demonstrates how easily the vicious and greedy may be duped. All is attractiveness, neat appointments, and flashy surface to entice the ordinary customer. But Montague Tigg induces Jonas Chuzzlewit and Mr. Pecksniff to invest in his company not because of its apparent prosperity, but simply because they are convinced that he is a knave, and they hope to profit by his knavery. Rascality, if profitable, was too frequently condoned, Dickens implied here and was to state clearly later.

Mr. Dombey, in *Dombey and Son* (1848), learns the extent and terrible vulnerability of his pride when he discovers that his trusted subordinate, Carker, has run off with his wife and his fortune. Mr. Morfin explains that Carker had left his activities quite evident, "as if he had resolved to show his employer at one broad view what has been brought upon him by ministrations to his ruling passion." (Ch. 53) There is no danger to Dombey's firm if he will make the necessary adjustments, but the enraged merchant is too preoccupied with his own injuries and too obstinate about his business to do so, and the result is bankruptcy. Clearly, Dombey has been punished for his pride and arrogance; he is the embodiment of Mr. Morfin's judgment upon an increasingly inhumane society: "We are so d———d business like." (Ch. 33) But Dombey's loss of position and fortune is only one indication of the rewards that await men who involve themselves in unwise enterprises. For Dickens, Dombey's fall is emblematic of far more than financial ruin.

> The world was very busy now, in sooth, and had a deal to say. It was an innocently credulous and much ill-used world. It was a world in which there was no other sort of bankruptcy whatever. There were no conspicuous people in it, trading far and wide on rotten banks of religion, patriotism, virtue, honour. There was no amount worth mentioning of mere paper in circulation, on which anybody lived pretty handsomely, promising to pay great sums of goodness with no effects. There were no shortcomings anywhere, in anything but money. The world was very angry indeed; and the people especially, who, in a worse world, might have been supposed to be bankrupt traders themselves in shows and pretences, were observed to be mightily indignant. (Ch. 58)

Dickens saw clearly what other writers would come to assert more and more loudly in the following years. Bankruptcy in the courts was often a real consequence of bankruptcy of values, but more important for Dickens as an artist, the one became a working symbol for the other.

By the time Dickens came to write *Little Dorrit* (1855-57), he had a full understanding of how his symbol could work and a clear view of the extent of the grand manner of swindling. The lust for money appears in this novel as a disease, and among the most diseased is

Mr. Merdle, who seems to be a clever and successful financier, but who is "simply the greatest Forger and the greatest Thief that ever cheated the gallows." (Book 3, Ch. 25)[21] Dickens is more clever in presenting Merdle than he had been with swindlers in his earlier novels, and he is subtler and more devastating than Bell or Lever insofar as he makes Merdle not a commanding presence, but an insignificant individual magnified only by the illusion of his wealth. His vain wife even suggests that he not go into Society. Merdle, with uncharacteristic spirit, responds, "And yet will you tell me that I oughtn't to go into Society? I, who shower money upon it in this way? I, who might be almost said—to—to—to harness myself to a watering-cart full of money, and go about saturating Society every day of my life?" (Book 1, Ch. 33) Merdle is as much a victim of his dishonesty as anyone else, for the great swindler realizes that he is a prisoner of his crimes. And all of society participates in that crime by exalting Merdle to a position of trust and influence, merely because he has demonstrated a knack for making money. Believing Merdle to be immensely rich, people "prostrated themselves before him, more degradedly and less excusably than the darkest savage creeps out of his hole in the ground to propitiate, in some log or reptile, the Deity of his benighted soul." (Book 2, Ch. 12) Even the good-hearted and the innocent, like Pancks and Arthur Clennam, are seduced into investing their money in certain schemes through their confidence in the Merdle name.

Everyone suffers from "Mr. Merdle's complaint." It is a malady that infects the innocent as well as the guilty. What Dickens implies in this masterful utilization of the swindle convention is that when an entire society falls ill with the lust for gain, everyone will suffer. The lust for gain was represented for Dickens by financial speculation. "As is well known to the wise in their generation," he wrote in *Our Mutual Friend* (1864-65), "traffic in Shares is the one thing to have to do with in this world. Have no antecedents, no established character, no cultivation, no ideas, no manners; have Shares." (Book 1, Ch. 10)

But in *Little Dorrit*, Dickens saw beyond the familiar device of financial ruin as a personal punishment and moral corrective, to a broader perspective of bankruptcy as the inevitable outbreak of the lingering disease that he had described earlier in *Dombey and Son*. The infection was moral; the manifestation, though apparently material, was equally moral; and, if read correctly, instructive. Financial ruin was the most forceful metaphor Dickens could find to indicate to his society that they had misplaced their values and would surely suffer from the false investment of their energy in specious properties.

LATER ATTITUDES

Unlike the social conventions of duelling or gypsies, dishonest speculation did not gradually fade away. Accordingly, it was less likely—except for a certain amount of sentimental embroidery as represented in Thackeray—to become romanticized. It was too immediate. The crimes of early days were bad, D. Morier Evans admitted in 1864, but added, "it is evident that the tone of financial morality has experienced considerable deterioration since the ever-memorable railway mania of 1845."[22] Bad as the knavery of that time was, Evans repeats, "it scarcely approaches, in open trickery, and lucre-hunting, the promotion system, and share rigging of the present day."[23] And he proceeds to describe the "unholy alliance" between promoters and directors of joint-stock companies at mid-century.

William Ashworth, in *An Economic History of England 1870-1939*, asserts that only a small minority of financiers dealt in speculations until late in the century, and that, among other things, "to save abundantly and invest prudently" was the true aim of mid-Victorians.[24] Evans would have agreed with Ashworth's assertion that joint-stock banks were an improvement upon private banks. But, he did not declare his view regarding a state bank, though the emergence of the Bank of England as the central institution for controlling reserve became the main economic fact of late Victorian England. Moreover, there was a steady growth in the stock market. "The changes in company law between 1855 and 1862 made incorporation with limited liability available to any firm of more than six partners which was willing to comply with a set of not very onerous conditions, and thus removed one of the obstacles to a public issue of shares."[25] In retrospect, Ashworth could observe that movements of this kind had been for the best. But in mid-century, with memories of earlier crises still acute, current crises not entirely sped, and future crises yet probable, it was not so easy to be complacent; especially when the evidences of suffering and viciousness were so immediately visible. Having described the lamentable circumstances of the victims of the 1857-58 crisis, Evans continued to expose a sadder feature of the catastrophe.

> Scarcely less melancholy than this exhibition of physical distress was the aspect of a widely spread commercial immorality presented by the revelations of the crisis. Cases of mere over-speculation form the most agreeable part of the picture; the darker portion being filled with the records of fraud, and of a recklessness which was equivalent to fraud. A long succession of firms could be passed in review, in which assets and liabilities seem like so many figures, selected for no other object than that of illustrating a strong disproportion. And these "irregularities" reflected alike on creditor and debtor, who seemed, as it were, leagued together to keep up a rotten system of accommodation. For instance, when it appeared that a house which offered two shillings in the pound was a debtor to the Liverpool Borough Bank for £ 30,000, unsecured, who could say which was the more culpable party?[26]

Evans proceeds to give a "striking illustration of the manner in which the credit system was worked" by a "daring genius" of 1855, whose methods were both reckless and dishonest.[27] More ominously, Evans continued, "just before all these revelations of vice and wretchedness took place, the country was supposed to be in a remarkably prosperous condition, because, forsooth, the export trade had greatly increased. No inference could possibly be more fallacious."[28]

It is obvious from much of the writing of the time that beneath the apparent prosperity of middle and late Victorian England, there lurked a dread of certain frightening truths: that the seemingly abundant system was rotten at the heart, and what was worse, inhabited by the vicious and unscrupulous. Novels such as Bell's *The Ladder of Gold* or Lever's *Davenport Dunn*, indicated the continuing interest in finance and speculation which was common to both England and America at this time, as Twain's *The Gilded Age: A Tale of To-Day* (1873) and William Dean Howells' *The Rise of Silas Lapham* (1885) demonstrate. Continental literature also abounded in similar themes, as in the novels of Balzac and Stendhal. The continuing reference to swindling and financial ruin in nineteenth-century literature shows that the profits and disasters of financial trickery and chicane were never far from the popular imagination.

In many novels of the second half of the century, financial failure continues to be used incidentally in a highly conventional manner;

thus the collapse of Major Strike's questionable company in Meredith's *Evan Harrington* (1860) and the awkward subplot of the pretended bankruptcy of the Cogglesby brothers add little to the novel beyond providing a villain who will compromise his wife's honor for profit, and two benevolent figures who represent commercial sanity. James Little, in Charles Reade's *Put Yourself in His Place* (1870), commits suicide after overspeculating, thereby setting the wheels of plot moving and leaving his son, Henry, the hero of the novel, to fashion his own career. In Mrs. Oliphant's *At His Gates* (1872), obscure disastrous financial speculations lead a mediocre artist to abandon his family, again leaving dependents, a wife and daughter, to make their own way in the customary fashion. The collapse of Grapnell and Co. in *Daniel Deronda* (1876) is the motivation for Gwendolen Harleth's decision to marry Grandcourt.

In other novels, financial speculation is an abiding presence. The entire social existence of the Pole family in Meredith's *Sandra Belloni* (1864) is threatened by Mr. Pole's impending business ruin as the result of certain unscrupulous practices by his associates. His cry is one that would touch the heart of any paterfamilias. Speaking of his daughters, he exclaims, "They are beggars, both, and all, if they don't marry before two months are out. I'm a beggar then. I'm ruined. I shan't have a penny. I'm in a workhouse. They are in good homes. They are safe, and thank their old father." (Ch. 26) Philip Sheldon, in Miss Braddon's *Birds of Prey* (1867), after murdering his friend, Tom Halliday, and marrying his widow for her money, becomes a stockbroker and devotes himself to speculation. Miss Braddon may have had in mind the swindler Montague Tigg's description of his business in Martin Chuzzlewit: "We companies are all birds of prey," he says, "mere birds of prey" (Ch. 27) for the speculations in the novel and its sequel, *Charlotte's Inheritance* (1868), are predatory in nature. For example, when Sheldon's speculations, which are described as paper boats upon the sea, founder through the collapse of the stock market in a period of national crisis, he determines that his only salvation is to murder Charlotte, his step-daughter, for her inheritance. He fails in this scheme and flees to New York, a frequent haven for scoundrels of nineteenth-century British fiction. He later returns, impoverished, to die at Charlotte's door.

Dickens aimed to present Merdle as an emblem of the destructiveness of greed, but Trollope's Melmotte in *The Way We Live Now*

(1874-75) is a caricature of a veritable type. Trollope meant Melmotte to be representative, but not symbolic. He was telling a story; Dickens was sketching a fable. Verisimilitude was far more important to Trollope than to Dickens. And, after all, says Max K. Sutton, "Melmotte holds no more of a monopoly on selfishness than did his historical prototypes—George Hudson, the railway king whom Carlyle called "the big swollen gambler," "Baron" Grant, who floated companies such as the Central Uraguay Railway which did nothing, and Lionel Nathan de Rothschild."[29]

As the century drew to a close, the invidiousness of dishonest speculation was portrayed in realistic terms. A decade before Trollope's novel, Charles Reade had treated this subject realistically in *Hard Cash* (1863), where the dishonest banker, Richard Hardie, is all too credible. Hardie has used the money from his son Alfred's trust fund to speculate in railway shares and, to forestall discovery, has his son unjustly committed to an asylum. Later, when his bank is threatened with failure, Hardie is forced to accept his unscrupulous clerk, Noah Skinner, as a partner because Skinner has evidence of his misdeeds. Hardie laments his lost rectitude, but nonetheless sinks further and further into disreputable dealings, declaring bankruptcy while still exploiting the victims of his swindling. Although he escapes prosecution for his crimes, they prove too much for his conscience, and his punishment is utterly fitting, for, although he is actually well-to-do, he lives under the protection of the son he abused, firmly believing that he is on the verge of ruin, and suffering from an anxiety that soon kills him. *Hard Cash* is by no means a fine novel, but it is a convincing picture of the all too plausible conduct that the lust for money could occasion in the cash-oriented society of Victorian England.

As Trollope's title suggests, he is depicting a corrupt society. He explained in his *Autobiography* that he was instigated to write his novel "by what I conceived to be the commercial profligacy of the age." (Ch. 20) He dreaded the gradual acceptance of dishonesty in high places, "fearing that men and women will be taught to feel that dishonesty, if it can become splendid, will cease to be abominable." (Ch. 20) In the novel, it is Roger Carbury who voices this sanity. He views Melmotte as "a miserable imposition, a hollow vulgar fraud from beginning to end,—too insignificant for you and me to talk of, were it not that his position is a sign of the degeneracy of the age." Because society accepts a person like Melmotte, it encourages swindling. His conclusion is that "the existence of a Melmotte is not compatible with a wholesome state of things in general." (Vol. 2, Ch. 55)

Money is the overwhelming value for most characters in the novel except for a few like Roger or Henrietta Carbury. Melmotte, like Merdle, and other precursors, is worshipped by those who admire his skill at making money. But Trollope's view of society's implication in the Mammonism of the time is somewhat more sour than earlier writers', for Melmotte is openly supposed to be a rogue and swindler, and nonetheless, is courted and sought out by the public at large, who hope to profit from his deviousness. When Paul Montague suggests to Mrs. Hurtle that Melmotte is probably a swindler, she replies: " 'Such a man rises above honesty . . . as a great general rises above humanity when he sacrifices an army to conquer a nation. Such greatness is incompatible with small scruples. A pigmy man is stopped by a little ditch, but a giant stalks over the rivers.' " (Vol. 1, ch. 26) Respect for Melmotte's scheming begets further unscrupulousness, reflected in the cheating at cards at the Beargarden Club, and the swindling of the same club by its manager, Vossner. Trollope likens Melmotte's ambitious swindles to the gambling of Felix Carbury and his cronies. Although Melmotte's crimes end in drunken muddling toward suicide by prussic acid, the American sharper, Hamilton K. Fisker's intention to continue his railway scheme in San Francisco indicates that the demise of one scoundrel does not inhibit the rascality of those who survive.

Trollope's elaborate use of the swindle convention, though realistic, is still squarely in the moral tradition, as was George Eliot's. Mr. Lassmann of Grapnell and Co. in *Daniel Deronda* (1876) is not symbolic, despite his company's revealing name, but he does represent the same moral problem as Trollope. Although Lassmann never actually appears as an actor in *Deronda*, his probable fraud has important consequences. Eliot made clear her views on the subject in "Moral Swindlers" in *The Impressions of Theophrastus Such* (1879), where Melissa pities the disgrace of Sir Gavial Mantrap after the exposure of his financial misbehavior. Theophrastus suggests that it might be more fitting to pity the victims of Mantrap's swindle, but Melissa replies that Mantrap is a moral family man. Theophrastus recommends that such men be recognized as immoral, regardless of their domestic virtues, and that the use of the term moral come in for closer examination. Eliot's caution suggests that what Dickens and Trollope had feared—that worship of money and money getters would induce a tolerance of their offences—was indeed coming to pass. When chastity can cover a multitude of pecuniary sins, values have surely reached their nadir.

So common were references to frauds, swindles, and bankruptcies in literature that, by the end of the century, only a peculiar variation upon the convention could guarantee a response. Thus, George Gissing, with characteristic irony, relates Richard Mutimer's disastrous error in *Demos* (1880). This enthusiastic leader of the working class, who has already had a taste of capitalist methods, invests the funds of a working man's savings association in a fraudulent company called the "Irish Dairy Company." Ironically, the unknown promoter of this swindle is actually Willis Rodman, Mutimer's former business associate, but now his shrewd though despised brother-in-law. Mutimer, Gissing makes clear, has been tainted by the possession of money because he has not been prepared for its use. Only when he is deprived of wealth does he resume his best nature. It is, therefore, poetic justice that he should innocently meet his end as the result of a financial speculation of the most fraudulent description.

The speculation, swindle, or other occasion of financial ruin was too immediate a reality of nineteenth-century England to operate strongly as a symbolic or emblematic convention in literature. For the most part, it depicted things as they were. Nonetheless, that appearance was conventional, and certain authors were able to indicate a greater meaning in financial failure than mere poverty. It could be used as an indicator of moral worth by serving as a test or punishment. Only a few writers, Dickens most notable among them, were able to view individual peculation as symptomatic of a greater moral obliquity in the seemingly respectable society. But through commonplace and profound applications of the convention, Victorian writers revealed an extensive distrust of the cash values upon which their society was founded. Even in their writings that doled out moral rewards in the form of business success or rich inheritances, the ever-present threat of financial ruin indicated that the vaunted Victorian security was never beyond suspicion. Wilkie Collins could have his character, Amelius Goldenheart, refer to "those organized systems of imposture, masquerading under the disguise of banks and companies" run by supposedly respectable men, associated, "year after year, with the shameless falsification of accounts, and the merciless ruin of thousands on thousands of victims." (Book 5, Ch. 3, *Fallen Leaves*) But it was not only straightforward critics of society like Collins who hinted at the frightening emptiness beneath the façade of Victorian economic security and pride. Perhaps the last "Victorian" novel to employ the swindle convention extensively was H. G. Wells' *Tono-Bungay* (1908), in which the rise and fall of Edward Ponderevo, by means of a patent medicine and false advertising, symbolizes the decay and imminent collapse not only of England, but of all western culture.[30] That financial ruin was so little romanticized and yet so much a part of the literature of the age suggests that even the most complacent writer inadvertently signalled the instability of his society by employing with ease the familiar and credible convention of financial ruin.

CHAPTER NINE

MADNESS

In *Madness and Civilization*, Michel Foucault described the signal transformation that occurred in Western civilization's conception of madness as a shift from a philosophical to a pathological outlook; "that is, the reduction of the classical experience of unreason to a strictly moral perception of madness, which would secretly serve as a nucleus for all the concepts that the nineteenth century would subsequently vindicate as scientific, positive, and experimental."[1] In Foucault's view, the eighteenth-century attitude toward madness depended upon the assumption that it was "the negation of reason." It is a philosophical paradox which itself would be agreeable to the classical taste for order and balance:

> For madness, if it is nothing, can manifest itself only by departing from itself, by assuming an appearance in the order of reason and thus becoming the contrary of itself. Which illuminates the paradoxes of the classical experience: madness is always absent, in a perpetual retreat where it is inaccessible, without phenomenal or positive character; and yet it is present and perfectly visible in the singular evidence of the madman.[2]

193

This attitude ultimately engendered a fear of madness. What was unlike reason, if left uncontrolled, became evil. Earlier, madness had its acknowledged, if eccentric, place in the pattern of social existence, being treated openly. But by the eighteenth century, it had become a feature of human nature to be hidden and confined. The secrecy surrounding madness helped to cultivate the belief that it was a moral pollutant. "Moral condemnation of the mentally abnormal was as strong a component of eighteenth-century rationalist theology as it was of medical thought, or the inarticulate beliefs of the labouring classes."[3] Only an age that admired the complete order of the mind through reason could so deeply fear what it had defined as the principal threat to reason. Samuel Johnson was not alone in his belief that madness was occasioned by too great an indulgence of the imagination; nor was he peculiar in his conviction that the exercise of reason was the means to restrain imagination's whimsy.[4]

Nigel Walker, concerned with insanity in relation to English law, observed that, since there were no provisions for housing the insane in the eighteenth century, madmen were necessarily confined in jails which "was neither as unjust nor as inhumane as it sounds to modern ears. Private madhouses were few until the end of the eighteenth century, and in any case were beyond the means of all but the well-to-do."[5] These madhouses were custodial rather than remedial; haphazardly employing old and new techniques for curing inmates such as surprise baths, emetics, and restraints. About 1755-69 notable changes occurred in the treatment of the insane because of an increased public awareness of social problems raised by the mentally disordered.[6] The first real successes with pleas of insanity in court trials began at this time, and voluntary subscription hospitals for the insane were founded.

The only official institution for the insane in England, from 1547, when it was given to the city of London as a hospital for poor lunatics, until 1751, when St. Luke's Hospital for Lunaticks opened, was Bethlehem Hospital. Conditions at Bethlehem had been brutal, but St. Luke's, proposed and operated by William Battie, was to be of a new character. In his *A Treatise on Madness* (1758) Battie defined madness as "deluded imagination," and distinguished two basic forms of the malady; original madness, which he felt was owing to disorders of the nervous substance, and Consequential Madness, which he attributed "to some remote and accidental cause." He noted that a medical man should not ignore the stomach, intestines or uterus as seats of madness, because of their effect upon the nervous fiber. Battie's innovations were little more than assertions that human beings suffering from madness were much like those afflicted with other diseases, and, though he objected to devices such as opium and induced vomiting to treat madness, he agreed that much madness was as unmanageable as other illnesses. James Monro, who was the physician at Bethlehem, disputed Battie's assumptions and, in his *Remarks on Dr. Battie's Treatise on Madness* (1758), asserted that madness would be forever incurable and never understood. He defended the time-honored practices of bleeding, purging, and evacuation by vomiting, as means of treating the insane. Despite Monro's response, Battie's book "came to have a considerable influence, especially on nineteenth-century judges."[7]

The *Gentleman's Magazine* of January, 1763, published an influential article which criticized the abuses suffered by the insane under confinement,[8] and in 1774 an Act for Regulating Private Madhouses was passed though it had little effect. By 1789, "the nature of the King's [George III] illness became generally known, and the topic of insanity was widely discussed in a context which excluded the attitude of moral condemnation."[9] With the model of the Retreat, run by the Tuke family at York, lunacy reform began on a national scale with the establishment of county asylums following the Act of 1808.[10]

Nineteenth-century England was given to superstitions and strange theories about madness, but unlike the eighteenth century it did not so much fear madness as pity it. Moreover, the Romantic movement was in large part a reaction against rationalism.[11] If Johnson's contemporaries feared excesses of the imagination, the Romantics exalted them. The ordered existence proposed and desired by neoclassical minds had little appeal for those who sought to emphasize the uniqueness and multiplicity of the individual and the mutability of all existence. The Romantics plunged eagerly into the subjectivism their predecessors had so warily skirted.

Too much of what the Romantics admired smacked of mental imbalance and melancholia for them to feel alien toward the insane. Much of Romanticism was a flirtation with all that had formerly been deemed madness. It is appropriate that the great encyclopedist, Diderot's, subversive sketch, *Rameau's Nephew*, should have been brought to light by the most classical of Romantics, Goethe, who translated the work and saw it published in 1805. The character of Rameau's nephew represented forces of disorder, immorality and subversion in a society that valued order, and marked a decisive change in attitude toward madness and unreason. It is not so great a step as one might imagine from Diderot's exchange to the nineteenth-century dialogue of the mind with itself that concludes with the mind finding itself disintegrating into antagonistic parts. From Diderot and Rameau's nephew to Byron's Manfred, to Dr. Jekyll and Mr. Hyde, Dorian Gray, or Conrad's Secret Sharer, is not a long, nor a complex journey.

By the eighteen thirties, English medicine viewed madness not as a manifestation of evil but as a consequence of social conditions, all too likely to strike nearby and unexpectedly. In *A General View of the Present State of Lunatics and Lunatic Asylums, in Great Britain and Ireland, and in some other Kingdoms* (1828), Sir Andrew Halliday declared that insanity was a result of the refinement of the organs. "The finer the organs of the mind have become by their greater development, or their better cultivation, if health is not made a part of the process," he averred, "the more easily are they disordered."[12] At the same time, George Burrows suggested, in *Commentaries on the Causes, Forms, Symptoms and Treatment, Moral and Medical, of Insanity* (1828), that intellectual derangements were induced mainly by society at large. "The vices of civilization, of course, must conduce to their increase," he said, "but even the moral virtues, religion, politics, nay philosophy itself, and all the best feelings of our nature, if too enthusiastically incited, class among the causes producing intellectual disorders."[13] For Burrows, as for Battie before him, madness was both constitutional and educational. It was no longer the simple result of too much scholarship or precarious religious convictions, it was now another aberration of a humanity that was, more and more, emerging as multiple and mysterious.

John Conolly wrote in his study, *An Inquiry Concerning the Indications of Insanity with suggestions for the better protection and care of the insane* (1830):

Insanity is often but a mere aggravation of little weaknesses, or a prolongation of transient varieties and moods of mind, which all men now and then experience; an exaggeration of common passions and emotions, such as fear, suspicion, admiration; or a perpetuation of absurdities of thought or action, or of irregularities of volition, or of mere sensation, which may occur in all minds, or be indulged in by all men, but which are cherished and dwelt upon only by a mind diseased. (pp. 166-67)

Allowing that mental disorders were ascribable to "corporeal disease," Conolly nonetheless admitted that there was no clear relationship. And he declared that the error, thus far, of medical men was that they "sought for, and imagined, a strong and definable boundary between sanity and insanity, which has not only been imaginary, and arbitrarily placed," but hurtful to those so segregated. (pp. 295-96) No longer was madness in a realm clearly discrete from that of reason. Reason and unreason could abide together in a constantly changing climate of human unpredictability. The extraordinary having become attractive, it was no longer necessary to fear the outrageous or unusual in human behavior. It was only necessary to appreciate it and correctly estimate its effect. "Every man is interested in this subject," Conolly says, "for no man can confidently reckon on the continuance of his perfect reason." Any departure from sound mind might occasion the loss of property and liberty, and subject the individual to sufferings and wrongs, passing "his melancholy days among the idiotic and the mad." (pp. 8-9) It was an ominous possibility that was, as we shall see, too often enacted.[14] But, if madness was now no stranger to the community, but a near companion of simple eccentricity, it remained to distinguish just what the difference was. For Conolly, and many in his time, insanity became "the impairment of any one or more of the faculties of the mind, accompanied with, or inducing, a defect in the comparing faculty." (p. 300) From this point on, consideration of the insane was in the realm of the positivists, or, as we have them today, the clinical psychologists, the behaviorists.

Among the first who sought to apply clinical methods to the understanding of aberrant states of mind, were the phrenologists. Foremost among these was Johann Christoph Spurzheim, who, in *Phrenology, or the Doctrine of the Mind; and of the Relations between Its Manifestations and the Body* (1825), set forth his theory concerning the parts of the brain and their influence upon human behavior. More directly concerned with the problem of madness was his later study, *Observations on the Deranged Manifestations of The Mind, or Insanity* (1833), where he argued for improved training of medical men to treat insanity. Although Spurzheim was largely concerned with derangements of external functions of the mind, he believed that "no branch of medicine is so intimately connected with the philosophy of the mind as insanity." (p. 49) He was fully convinced that the causes of insanity were corporeal and declared that, "The soul cannot fall sick, any more than it can die." (p. 75) In his opinion, *"the incapacity of distinguishing the diseased functions of the mind,* and the irresistibility of our actions," constituted insanity. (p. 53) Spurzheim's views of the various causes of insanity became common in the nineteenth century. Affections and passions, or intense study were popularly accepted as causes of insanity. The crime of seduction, Spurzheim said, was also a fertile source of insanity, as were religion and intemperance. He declared women more inclined to madness than men, and added that "the greatest number of insane females are the victims of amativeness." (p. 126) He attributed the high proportion of insane people in England and Ireland, compared with other countries, to the excessive indulgence in "the sentiment of self-esteem and independency." (p. 124) He proposed, therefore, that the treatment of the insane was primarily moral.

Concern for the problem of madness coupled with a suspicion that insanity was on the increase, led to the establishment of the Metropolitan Commission in Lunacy, which issued an impressive series of reports between 1829-1844, at which time their report acknowledged "that insanity comprises a complex of causes and effects—not merely one disease with a single cause."[15] The stringent Lunacy Act of 1845 followed; and, thereafter, insanity was increasingly viewed as a social and medical, not a moral problem. In 1859, a Select Committee under the guidance of Lord Shaftesbury was formed to study the lunacy laws, and it found many instances of abuse, particularly in workhouses. But despite these advances, treatment of the insane was a difficult issue and a controversial subject preceding the Lunacy Act of 1890.

MADNESS IN LITERATURE

In the literature of the nineteenth century, the subject of madness was gradually liberated from its frightening associations, and was treated with interest, and in some cases, even admiration. In Gothic fiction, insanity had enhanced supernatural effects and was primarily a terrible prospect, a curse imposed by gods or devils. With the Romantics, a new notion appeared, indicated benignly in Wordsworth's "The Idiot Boy." But beyond acceptance, admiration was possible.

In Byron's "The Dream," for example, an unhappy marriage and frustrated love lead to madness. But this disturbance of normal intellectual life hardly seems, in the circumstances, so terrible. Of the distracted lady, Byron writes:

> oh! she was changed,
> As by the sickness of the soul; her mind
> Had wander'd from its dwelling, and her eyes,
> They had not their own lustre, but the look
> Which is not of the earth; she was become
> The queen of a fantastic realm; her thoughts
> Were combinations of disjointed things;
> And forms impalpable and unperceiv'd
> Of others' sight familiar were to hers.
> And this the world calls phrenzy; but the wise
> Have a far deeper madness, and the glance
> Of melancholy is a fearful gift;
> What is it but the telescope of truth?
> Which strips the distance of its fantasies,
> And brings life near in utter nakedness,
> Making the cold reality too real!

There is no fear of the insane here, only pity and respect. To have been driven mad through the frustration of a passionate love was not among the crimes or offenses of the nineteenth century.

Likewise, it was not shameful to have had one's reason unseated by other severe shocks. Hence, the pious and cordial Mrs. Aubrey in Samuel Warren's *Ten Thousand A-Year* loses her reason when she learns that her family must abandon the family estate, Yatton. Her reason returns just in time for her to die a peaceful death. In the same novel, however, Warren draws a picture of a despicable form of lunacy. The ludicrous central character, Tittlebat Titmouse, who is constantly provoked by minor annoyances to exclaim that he shall go mad, eventually does lapse into lunacy after having indulged in various debaucheries and having been deprived of Yatton. In the end, he is "admitted an inmate of a private lunatic asylum." (Vol. 3, ch. 12) This use of lunacy in fiction was, of course, a cautionary device. A relationship between dissipation and madness is frequently assumed, as in Thackeray's early work, *The Adventures of Barry Lyndon*. Graphic works such as Hogarth's "The Rake's Progress," or Cruikshank's "The Bottle," offered similar warnings and paralleled later medical caveats, such as those Walter describes in *My Secret Life*, that masturbation would surely result in madness.

Dissipation and debauchery were not the only deviations that might lead to madness. The innocent might also suffer as Mrs. Aubrey's case suggests. Duels were frequently presented as sources of madness, especially for the bereaved survivors. If the historians of duelling can be trusted, there seems to have been a good deal of truth in such portrayals. Lorenzo Sabine quotes one such event, "Duelling: A Tale of Woe," in his *Notes on Duels and Duelling* (1856), and Andrew Steinmetz, in recounting the details of a duel between a Mr. McLean and a Mr. Cameron in Scotland in 1772, in which Mr. McLean was killed, says that "His mother hearing of this melancholy event, was instantly deprived of her senses, and Miss McLeod, a young lady to whom McLean was soon to be married, was seized with fits and died three days later."[16] Such historical incidents make Lucy's madness at the end of *The Ordeal of Richard Feverel* more credible.

In *Lavengro*, George Borrow relates the history of a gentleman who, through his and his family's foolish attraction to the Roman Catholic faith, ended in lunacy. (ch. 100) Clearly any folly might devolve into madness. The folly need not be one's own. The father in T. P. Prest's novel, *The Maniac Father* (1844), was not an unfamiliar type. His madness was consequent upon his daughter's loss of virtue.[17] Prest used the same figure in *Vice and Its Victims: Or, Phoebe, the Peasant's Daughter*, in which Mr. Mayfield goes insane when his daughter, Phoebe, elopes with a profligate lord. Mayfield recovers abruptly, however, when he learns that Phoebe's marriage was legal. Loss of virtue could occasion madness in the violated party as well. In Bulwer-Lytton's popular novel, *Pelham* (1828), Gertrude Douglas, beloved by Reginald Glanville, is driven mad as a consequence of being raped by the unscrupulous Tyrrell. Fortunately, she dies. Glanville, in his grief and revenge, comes close to madness himself, but never is this excess criticized. It is clear in the novel that this authentic insanity and near-madness follow from an excess of admirable qualities.[18] When a noble mind is faced with insupportable emotions, it cannot bend or wheedle; it cracks. Throughout the century, madness took one of two fundamental literary routes: either it was the result of a sinful, ruined life, or it was the necessary consequence of a passionate nature trapped in unbearable circumstances.

Among the earliest and most memorable instances of madness resulting from offended virtue was Scott's Lucy Ashton in *The Bride of Lammermoor* (1819). The sensitive but too highly susceptible imagination of young Lucy leads her to the violent and tragic loss of reason that a stronger but less passionate nature might have overcome. Lucy goes mad on her wedding night, when her unwanted husband enters her bedchamber. The theme of offended love begetting madness was persistent, but Scott provided other memorable models of insanity as well. The innocent madness of Davie Gellatley in *Waverley* or Madge Wildfire in *The Heart of Midlothian* reappeared in Dickens' innocently haunted Barnaby Rudge, whose simple-mindedness results directly from the criminal violence of his vicious father. And the insane Bertha Mason's death in the blazing destruction of Thornfield Hall in Charlotte Brontë's *Jane Eyre* had as its model a similar death of a maniac in a burning tower in Scott's *Ivanhoe*. Kathleen Jones finds Bertha Mason thoroughly conventional, describing her as Charlotte Brontë's "figment of the imagination stimulated by the horror novels of the late eighteenth century. Mrs. Rochester is a figure from *The Castle of Otranto* or the later 'penny dreadfuls' —not a personification of an existing social problem."[19] But the public would have been far more prepared to accept this conventional view than any realistic social characterization. Still, in utilizing the conventional type, Charlotte Brontë implied psychological realities that social comment might not have explored. The hidden Bertha is a symbol of confined passion, representing the powerful and destructive urges in man that Jane Eyre's self-control promises to remedy. Images of fire and violence prepare for the final destruction of Rochester's guilty secret, after which, a subdued man, he is fit to share his life more temperately with the disciplined Jane.

Madness for Scott was a means of advancing and complicating his plots; he rarely stopped to preach or offer symbolic overtones. His practices were imitated in much of the popular literature of the nineteenth century where certain stereotyped situations recurred regularly. Dickens' "A Madman's Manuscript," one of the interpolated tales of *Pickwick Papers*, offers splendid examples of all of the conventions. There is a history of madness in the narrator's family, though an editorial note to the manuscript describes this history as the narrator's "delusion." The madman himself is described as "a melancholy instance of the baneful results of energies misdirected in early life, and excesses prolonged until their consequences could never be repaired. The thoughtless riot, dissipation, and debauchery of his younger days, produced fever and delirium." (ch. 11) The predictable moral is not lacking, nor is the customary inclusion of an unfortunate romance. There is an echo of Scott's *Bride of Lammermoor* in the madman's account of his relationship with a young lady who eventually becomes his wife and dies by his hand. This young lady is, like Lucy Ashton, a victim of family interests, but unlike Lucy, is the target for insane violence rather than its vehicle. After his homicidal outbreak, the madman ends where all who permit their appetites unbridled sway are in danger of ending, in an asylum, haunted by a spectre of his crimes.

This crude tale is thoroughly in the conventional mold but Dickens attempted other modifications of madness in other novels.[20] Barnaby Rudge, who, as Poe was quick to observe, was hardly a successful character, recalled, as Kathleen Tillotson put it, "the theatrical stereotypes of lunacy."[21] Gordon, in the same novel, is more plausible but so much more subtle as to constitute less an example of madness than of eccentricity or deviation. Dickens does, however, manage to equate the madness of society with Gordon's deviation and indicates how different it is from Barnaby's innocent symptoms. It is a segment of society that is mad in this novel, and it is this lunacy that is more aptly depicted by Dickens than any specific individual instance. Moreover, this madness is itself associated with forces long restrained that must, after all, break loose in wild abandon. For Dickens, madness becomes a form of social infection that must be lanced before it can be cured.

Less conventional, but also less clearly related to what may genuinely be considered madness are Mr. Dick in *David Copperfield*, and Mr. Dorrit in *Little Dorrit*. In Mr. Dick, Dickens is able to present an amusing, if not medically convincing picture of benign lunacy growing out of a shock to a good man's sensitive nature and resulting in an *idée fixe*, both pathetic and diverting. Mr. Dorrit's case, on the other hand, demonstrates the way in which a mind, unused to the burdens of liberty, relapses into the comforting familiarity of strictly defined regulations. If the public madness of *Barnaby Rudge* indicated a festering illness demanding release, the mental collapse of Mr. Dorrit indicates a central vacuity, too long preserved by a surrounding shell, that must, in normal conditions, give way. Mr. Dorrit's breakdown signifies a physical decay as much as a mental failure, and his death follows close after it. Clearly Dickens was mainly concerned with madness as a metaphor for aspects of the human condition. He made no more attempt at precise delineation than did Scott or Charlotte Brontë. But more suggestively than either, he implied through the convention of madness some monstrous consequences of conduct that violated a natural moral order. Still, Dickens never was persuasive in his descriptions of madness, which seemed related to theatrical and literary sources. This is all the stranger with him since he was acquainted with the famous Dr. John Conolly. Moreover Dickens' close friend and professional adviser, John Forster, was himself an official of the Lunacy Commission, and an article entitled "The Treatment of the Insane" appeared in *Household Words* in 1852. Despite these connections with the practical details of insanity, Dickens' use of the subject remained primarily suggestive and evocative rather than descriptive and realistic.

EXPLOITATION OF THE THEME

If, for the most part, Dickens failed to exploit madness as a theme, his contemporaries made good use of it. In Henry Cockton's *The Life and Adventures of Valentine Vox, the Ventriloquist* (1840), Grimwood Goodman is falsely confined in a private lunatic asylum by his brother and nephew, who have designs upon his money and property. There is no problem in getting corrupt medical men to sign the necessary papers and once Grimwood is confined, escape is almost impossible. In addition to brutal restraint, Dr. Holdem and his cohorts change Grimwood's name and transfer him to a different asylum to keep him hidden. Ultimately Grimwood is rescued from the asylum, but his health is so reduced that he dies soon after. Meanwhile retribution is visited upon his conscience-stricken brother who goes mad and commits suicide. Vox introduced this novel with a preface denouncing the system of private lunatic asylums as pernicious and cruel, emphasizing the ease with which sane men might be confined and kept isolated from any suitable source of assistance.

In 1859, Wilkie Collins began the serial publication of his novel, *The Woman in White*, which called attention to the abuses practiced by owners of private lunatic asylums. Although there was no elaborate examination in this novel of what constituted madness, Collins, like Vox, clearly signified that the sane might easily be taken for insane on the assertion of persons scarcely qualified to determine such an important issue. Collins made no profound statement about madness, and he only implied that society itself was not free from delusion if it could be so duped and deceived by men such as Glyde and Count Fosco. In *Armadale*, Collins repeated his point about illegal confinement. The disreputable Dr. Downward changes his name to Dr. Le Doux and establishes a private asylum subject to no inspection or control, despite his lack of any professional skill. In this novel, as in *The Woman in White*, the asylum, designed for the assistance of the mentally deranged, serves as an illegal prison to confine an innocent individual likely to upset mischievous plots. In neither of these novels did Collins deal with absolute insanity, for he was more concerned with abuses of the law which permitted sane individuals to be confined.[22] Moreover, he tried subtly to demonstrate the tenuous distinction between sanity and madness that prevailed in his time.

Charles Reade was even more determined to reveal the unjust and outrageous practices allowed under the heading of treatment for the insane in his novel, *Hard Cash* (1863). Kathleen Jones suggests that the book "was probably inspired by the Report of the Select Committee of 1859-60. It was published at a time when public feeling on these issues ran high; and it enjoyed considerable financial success."[23] Reade satirized the respectable John Conolly as Dr. Wycherley, a man of little intelligence and less scruple. Dr. Wycherley, at the dishonest Mr. Hardie's request, has the banker's son, Alfred Hardie, confined in an asylum as supposedly suffering from "Incubation of Insanity." Wycherley has not even met or interviewed Alfred, and the symptoms described—headache, insomnia, melancholy—would fit any sane but temporarily distressed individual. Yet Alfred is forcibly detained in the madhouse; and, the government inspectors remain unconvinced of his sanity since they themselves are either senile or totally prejudiced by the madhouse keepers.

Alfred is not the only sane individual restrained in the asylum managed by the lascivious Mrs. Archbold. David Dodd, a victim of Richard Hardie's chicanery, is another. Both ultimately escape from their confinement, but not before Reade delivers a lecture on how easily unsuspecting individuals may be committed. Later, when Alfred has an opportunity to denounce the regulations governing such confinements, he explains to his solicitor that he was not even permitted to see the certificates that occasioned his confinement:

> "Not I," said Alfred. "I have begged and prayed for a sight of them, and never could get one. That is one of the galling iniquities of the system; I call it 'THE DOUBLE SHUFFLE.' Just bring your mind to bear on this, sir: The prisoner whose wits and liberty have been signed away behind his back is not allowed to see the order and certificate on which he is confined—until *after* his release: that release he is to obtain by combating the statements in the order and certificates. So to get out he must first see and contradict the lies that put him in; but to see the lies that put him in, he must first get out. So runs the circle of Iniquity. Now, is that the injustice of Earth or the injustice of Hell?" (ch. 44)

It is all too easy for a modern reader to understand this dilemma, but for a Victorian audience, the moral impact was appalling. Reade sought to increase the impact of his tale by a large dose of irony. The genuinely unbalanced James Maxley cannot persuade Hardie to have him committed to an asylum and later Maxley beats Hardie's beloved daughter, Jane, to death. Moreover, it is eventually Richard Hardie himself—the avaricious and unscrupulous money monger—who declines into semi-madness. He dies believing that he is on the verge of ruin, though he is, in fact, wealthy.

Although here, as in his later novel, *A Terrible Temptation* (1870-71), Reade is more concerned with demonstrating abuses in the treatment of the insane than he is with the problem of insanity itself, his novels, like those of Collins, do indicate the degree of interest expressed during the mid-Victorian period in the social and practical problems of madness. A passage from *Lady Audley's Secret* (1862) indicates how glibly the subject of confinement for insanity could be tossed about. When Robert Audley openly challenges Lady Audley with deceiving her husband about her past, she responds by threatening to charge him with madness. That such a threat could be seriously entertained shows how far fiction had gone to accept the contemporary social concern about the mismanagement of the laws dealing with the insane. It is both fitting and melodramatic that later in this popular sensation novel, Lady Audley confesses her own fear that she might have inherited madness from her mother. (ch. 34)

Anthony Trollope, in *He Knew He Was Right* (1868-69), also described the unjust circumstances which permitted the confinement of a man supposed mad; but, in the development of his character, Louis Trevelyan, failed to convey a plausible madness. Trevelyan's aberration proceeded from his jealousy and willfulness. In effect, madness, for Trollope, is what happens to people who cannot resolve the various demands of their passional natures. In the background of Trollope's story there always hovers the amiable or aggressive eccentricity of a Miss Jemima Stanbury or a Wallachie Petrie. Madness is only a further stage of such eccentricity—a stage which is frightening only insofar as it concerns the innocent.

Unjust confinement is a melodramatic device in Joseph Sheridan LeFanu's *The Rose and the Key* (1871), where Maud Vernon is confined at the avaricious Dr. Antomarchi's asylum, Glarewoods, by means of a ruse and for motives of her mother's which are never fully explained. Maud is unable to communicate with anyone outside the asylum and is warned not to make trouble, being forced to witness another inmate's subjection to a monstrous showerbath for thirty-five minutes, followed by the administration of an emetic. This incident, Le Fanu explains, was taken from a documented case. (ch. 74) Before the Lunacy Commissioners, Maud is too overwrought to respond properly, and they see no reason to release her. This is subtler than Cockton's description in *Valentine Vox* of attendants tickling Grimwood's feet until he becomes hysterical just before the Commissioners make their visit. Maud is finally freed through Dr. Damian, Antomarchi's superior, and an honest man.

MEREDITH

For many Victorian writers, like Meredith, madness was more clearly a literary convention and less of a social consideration. In *The Ordeal of Richard Feverel* (1859), the impulsive Richard's behavior leads not only to his own temporary madness, but also to that of his wife Lucy. "The shock," Lady Blandish explains to Austin Wentworth, referring to Richard's injury in a duel, "had utterly deranged her." (ch. 49) For Meredith, mental imbalance is a dreadful, yet likely possibility when men are so slow to learn the value of genuine self-discipline. How easy the disintegration of the mind can be is illustrated in *Rhoda Fleming* (1865). Dahlia Fleming's two great passions meet in her illicit love for Edward Blancove; both her physical desires and her proud ambitions are temporarily gratified and then destroyed in the progress of her painful romance. The result is that Dahlia sinks into a "semi-lunatic" state, feeling that she is "a living body buried." (ch. 41) Her frenzy declines into stupor, her passion to melancholy. After an attempted suicide and a renunciation of her lover, she settles down to a calm life devoted to caring for her sister's children. "She had gone through fire, as few women had done in like manner, to leave their hearts among the ashes; but with that human heart she left regrets behind her." (ch. 48)

Dahlia's obsessions led her close to insanity and back through its purging fire to a saner existence. Meredith, to intensify his point and establish a certain parallelism in his novel, describes a similar pattern in the character of Anthony Hackbut, the uncle of the Fleming girls. Uncle Anthony has deceived his brother-in-law, Farmer Fleming, into believing that he is a wealthy and influential representative of a London bank, whereas he is merely a bank porter. Nonetheless, his whole preoccupation is with money, and, after a long career in which his honesty and dependability have been his major acquisitions, he unaccountably carries off money belonging to the bank. He has, for too long a time, permitted his imagination to fabricate this scene; finally, the event transpires and he crumbles under the realization of it.

Uncle Anthony's collapse immediately precedes the chapter entitled "Dahlia's Frenzy," in which Dahlia affirms her passion for Edward Blancove, reemphasizing both that Dahlia and Anthony have allowed their central preoccupations to overcome them and that the consequence is mental collapse. Only through self-government and self-abnegation can the valuable experiences of life be assured and preserved.

The association of madness and excess is more clearly drawn in *One of Our Conquerors*, in the character of Victor Radnor. Radnor is a successful and contented man, but beneath his happy home life and his public position is an early "error"—marriage to an elderly woman now hateful to him—which has resulted in a life of bigamy and necessary disguise. This is the tension of his life, but what is more important is that his ambitions for influence, social position, and wealth have caused him to underrate the significance of small details of his own behavior. At the opening of the novel, Radnor slips on a piece of fruit or vegetable and falls. The "sly strip of slipperiness" that has thus overthrown him, is emblematic of the way in which all of his great plans are overthrown by small details.[24] Just as Radnor refuses to acknowledge the true nature of his early slips, he now ignores the nature of his fall, for, as Meredith remarks, "Sanity does not allow the infinitely little to disturb us." (ch. 2) In this case, however, the infinitely little upsets Radnor's sanity, for at the climax of all his ambitions, he is forced to realize that "there had been a moral fall, fully to the level of the physical" along the way. (ch. 41) And ultimately, he is left "the wreck of a splendid intelligence," when his beloved companion, Nataly, dies, and his schemes fail. (ch. 42)

Meredith employed madness in his novels not as a medical reality, but as a sign of moral qualities. Yet, in the time at which he wrote, it was not uncommon to view madness as the result of lost moral control. William B. Carpenter wrote, in his *Principles of Mental Physiology* (1874), that "It is, in fact, in the *persistence* and *exaggeration* of some emotional tendency, leading to an erroneous interpretation of everything that may be in any way related to it, that Insanity very frequently commences; and it is in this stage that a strong effort at self-control may be exerted with effect, not merely in keeping down the exaggerated emotion, but in determinately directing the thoughts into another channel."[25] For Meredith and his contemporaries, this would have seemed a sound explanation. Carpenter explained that early discipline would strengthen the will to resist the chaotic impulses leading on to madness. In a sense, madness was the punishment for an unregulated will; it was the necessary moral collapse fully predictable through the indulgence of the emotions. To let the emotions run unbridled was the first "slip" toward an imbalance that might end in lunacy.

Numerous uses of the convention of madness near the close of the century can be found, varying from Boldwood's rage in *Far From the Madding Crowd*, to Winifred Wynne's hysteria upon learning of her father's crime in Watts-Dunton's *Aylwin*,[26] to the amazing case of Renfield's madness, caused by Count Dracula's vampirism in Bram Stoker's *Dracula*. In most such cases, madness served mainly as a convenience of plot, a way of providing a natural retribution, a probable or improbable shock to the mind involving complications of narrative, and so on. In this way, the usage resembled the modern convention of amnesia. It is difficult to believe that so many subjects of private investigation could suffer partial or total amnesia from a blow to the head or a shock to the sensibilities, and yet, the numbers of these amnesia victims does not decrease, and the convention continues to flourish in fiction, film and television drama of the lower order. To the Victorian novelist, madness served, at its most rudimentary level, just this purpose.

But there was another more profound, side of the Victorian attitude toward madness. In the first volume of *Passages from the Diary of a Late Physician*, Samuel Warren included a story entitled, "Intriguing and Madness" which recounted the history of a Mr. Warningham, who, becoming infatuated with a popular actress, pursues her passionately, though he is already the accepted suitor of another lady. Upon the presentation of an emerald ring, Mr. Warningham is received at breakfast by the actress, but her lover, a military man, appears, quarrels with Warningham, and beats him. This physical punishment, combined with his frenzy, leaves Warningham in a dangerously unhealthy mental state. A doctor finds Warningham in a "state of madness" and deals with him cautiously, noting that a madman is never to be contradicted. Gradually Warningham's fit abates and his ravings end; he is disgusted with himself and with his past dissipations and resolves to lead a virtuous life. The doctor then observes that "These salutory thoughts led to a permanent reformation; his illness, in short, had produced its effect." (ch. 7)

Although his story makes familiar employment of the convention of madness, what is different is that the madness resulting from reckless conduct actually operates as a cure for the victim's moral obliquity. It is as though madness were still conceivable as an accumulated humor which, having been afforded release, leaves the body and mind purified. But in the nineteenth century it is an energy of the spirit not a humor of the body that is involved. In a way, immorality acquires a materiality affecting the self, independent of physical causes. Madness is brought on by physical conditions, but not only by physical conditions. In certain cases, madness is a malady of the soul. So often associated with evil, crime and sin, it becomes a means of curing and controlling the very condition that it has engendered. So Julius and Augustus Hare, in their *Guesses at Truth by Two Brothers* (1827) could suggest, "Temporary madness may perhaps be necessary in some cases, to cleanse and renovate the mind; just as a fit of illness is to carry off the humours of the body."[27] The notion that an outburst of madness could serve as a purgative found broader applications. The madness of Bertha Mason, which represents the recklessness of mankind—and of Rochester in particular—leads to the blazing end of Thornfield in *Jane Eyre*, and with it the extermination of its begetting madness. Similarly, the mad outbreak of the Gordon Riots in *Barnaby Rudge* expends the accumulated pressure of the society there described, and a more moderate climate prevails. Other outbreaks and holocausts serve similar purposes throughout the literature of the period.

Later in the century, the notion that madness could be beneficial led to a further recognition that it might, in a mad world, be necessary to feign madness in order to do good. So Frank Vanecourt concludes in Laurence Oliphant's *Piccadilly* (1870). At the end of this work, Vanecourt decides that the world in its present form is a madhouse, mainly because people do not act in accordance with their stated beliefs, and therefore are in a state of hallucination.[28] His recommended cure is a conversion to genuine faith which most men are unable to achieve because "they can't face the severe training which the perfection of self-sacrifice involves." (ch. 6) Oliphant's expression of this sentiment was by no means the first, nor the last. Earlier in the century, the poet laureate had produced a poem, troubling to many of his contemporaries, which summarized in a superior artistic manner the several functions of the theme of madness.

TENNYSON

In a review of Tennyson's *Maud* (1855), in *The Asylum Journal of Mental Science*, of which he was the editor, John Charles Bucknill, M.D., described the poem as "the history of a madman depicted by the hand of a master."[29] Bucknill praised Tennyson's accuracy in such details as hereditary tendency, misanthropic opinions, early hallucinations, and foreknowledge of possible madness. In the doctor's view, "the common medley of reason and unreason is truthfully given. A less skillful artist would have left this portion of the picture without any light, and would thus have missed the truth."[30]

Although Tennyson might have been pleased to have his poem praised for psychological accuracy, he would probably have urged other features of the poem as more central to his purpose. He was intimately acquainted with madness, since his father was surely unstable and one of his brothers went insane. Moreover, he had used the convention of insanity elsewhere in his poetry. Edith, in "The Sisters," goes mad from frustrated love, and Sir Aylmer Aylmer ("Aylmer's Field") after driving his daughter to death by his resistance to her love for Leolin Averill, lapses into madness ("the man became / Imbecile") and later commits suicide. Obviously, Tennyson used the madness convention with full awareness of its literary function. But in *Maud* he sought to elevate that function.

The narrator in *Maud* does not differ much in outline from common types in the literature of the time. Dickens' madman, for example, has a roughly similar career.[31] For Tennyson, however, madness serves a larger purpose as his own familiar summary indicates. He says of the narrator:

> He is the heir of madness, an egotist with the makings of a cynic, raised to sanity by a pure and holy love which elevates his whole nature, passing from the height of triumph to the lowest depth of misery, driven to madness by the loss of her whom he has loved, and, when he has at length recovered his reason, giving himself up to work for the good of mankind through the unselfishness born of his great passion.[32]

Tennyson demonstrates in his poem several uses of the madness convention. The most obvious is that of plot: a frustrated love leads to madness, which that love, enduring, cures. This is a far more sophisticated form of the model proposed by Samuel Warren in "Intriguing and Madness." But Tennyson's madman does not merely purge his mind of an unhealthy lust. Instead, a mind preoccupied with strong but morbid emotions manages to transfer its passions to a nobler object. The temporary insanity caused by the loss of that object is a form of purgation since it fastens the victim's mind upon the lost but elevated love. The madman's attention focusses more surely on his lost love, his mind regains its balance, and he is brought from morbid inaction "to fight for the good" as he sees it. William B. Carpenter was to explain the medical significance of this transfer of attention and the subsequent reassertion of the healthy will in his standard study, *Principles of Mental Physiology* (1874), where he wrote that many men were saved from an attack of Insanity by "the direction of the Mental activity towards any subject that has a healthful attraction for it."[33] But the moral significance of the events in *Maud* scarcely requires expression, since it is fundamental to Christianity—redemption through love and escape from the confinement of the self.

The world of *Maud* is, like that described in *Piccadilly*, characterized by false seemings and maddening offenses. The motif of madness in the poem, although indicating the condition of the narrator, implies as well some cause in society that makes insanity a predictable end for engaged feelings. If, for example, young women can be sold to high bidders despite their feelings, then love is indeed a "cruel madness." Thus, when the narrator of *Maud* emerges finally from "cells of madness, haunts of horror and fear," and awakes "as it seems, to the better mind," he fulfills a pattern which the nation also seems to be following as it unites itself to prove, in what appears to be a just war, that "we have hearts in a cause, we are noble still."

In this poem, which Tennyson had considered entitling *Maud, or the Madness*, the convention of insanity is used in a factual, accurate way, as a convenience of plot, as an agent of moral recovery, and as an emblem of a diseased and endangered society. Tennyson was thus able to convey meaning without producing a mere tract or sermon, because, understanding the convention for what it was, he used it with precision and effect.

LATER USES OF THE CONVENTION

Late into the century madness continued to be utilized traditionally; hence, Mary Backhouse, in Mrs. Humphry Ward's *Robert Elsmere* (1888), loses her mind after losing her virtue. But apparent madness came to be associated as well with spiritual states. Lady Alice, in George MacDonald's *The Portent* (1860), is considered a lunatic, though she is simply in a waking trance for twelve years. Similarly, Lilian Ashleigh, in Bulwer-Lytton's *A Strange Story* (1862), loses her senses and lapses into a state of suspended consciousness resembling madness, after reading a letter imputing dissolute behavior to her. During her apparent madness, Lilian lives in her imagination, dwelling close to the world of spirit. Recovering from her malady, she exclaims, "in the awful affliction that darkened my reason, my soul has been made more clear." (ch. 78) As in Tennyson's *Maud*, madness serves as a beneficial cleansing of error. It is, like the salubrious illness described earlier, an automatic indication of the limits of human expectation.

Not all writers felt that the consequences of ambitious human expectation were totally reprehensible. The many new and challenging ideas that became inescapable by the late nineteenth century called up certain predictable responses. Most prevalent of these, according to John A. Lester, Jr., was that of pessimism.[34] Among those who sought more positive escapes from the threatening revelations in science and philosophy, there was a spirited interest in examining nonlogical faculties of cognition through psychical research or exotic forms of religious belief. There was a profound desire to find a source of certainty within the human mind. In art this desire led mainly to an exaltation of the imagination and the more "esthetic" qualities of artistic production. But whether in art or in life, the escape into the mind brought the individual closer to the state of insanity than men had been willing to acknowledge for some time. Dryden could remark, "Genius and Madness are near allied, / And thin partitions do the bounds divide"; but this view had been largely dormant during the nineteenth century, though admiration for poets such as Blake and Chatterton indicated a simmering recognition of the notion.

Late in the century, the desire for escape became pronounced enough to make the madman's case almost enviable. In George du Maurier's *Peter Ibbetson* (1892), Ibbetson himself is considered mad because of his curious behavior and his strange assertions, but we quickly learn that his contempt for the madmen with whom he is confined is justifiable—if his experiences are true. For Ibbetson believes that he has lived a substantial life with the woman he loves in his dreams, and the more prominent features of his madness are merely signs of his impatience as he awaits his "translation to another sphere," that is, to existence in eternity beyond death. (Part 6) If Ibbetson's dreams are true, he is not mad and knows a life far richer even than the most remarkable imagination might attain. If they are not, he is mad, but his experiences have been none the richer for that, since he believes them. In any case, real or reputed madness provides experiences beyond the humdrum existence of most men. The intensity and beauty of the experience, even if it is ultimately false, is more pleasurable to the madman than ordinary life is to the monotonously sane.

Perhaps the most succinct and moving statement of this attitude occurs in Ernest Dowson's elegant poem, "To One in Bedlam." The lunatic's "delicate, mad hands" are more appealing than "the dull world" that stares at him. "Oh, how his rapt gaze wars / With their stupidity!" The madman's world, though actually miserable, does not seem so to him. His world is more alluring than that of all the crude and unfeeling multitude considered sane.

> Know they what dreams divine
> Lift his long, laughing reveries like enchaunted wine,
> And make his melancholy germane to the stars'?

Sadder yet for the poet who speaks is the recognition that his portion is even less attractive than the unenlightened mass, since he can yearn like the madman for the ideal. Like his "lamentable brother," he can imagine exquisite beauty. But he can have only "Half a fool's kingdom," because he is sane and must always know that the madman holds "scentless wisps of straw" not "posies" in his hands. Nonetheless, for one forced to live in a region between dreams and the vanity of the world, the madman's case seems best.

> Better than mortal flowers,
> Thy moon-kissed roses seem: better than love or sleep,
> The star-crowned solitude of thine oblivious hours!

SUMMARY

Throughout the nineteenth century madness was a real part of every man's consciousness. There were extraordinary historical cases, such as Madame Lavalette's loss of reason after the ordeal of managing her husband's escape from a French prison and the death sentence in 1815; or Georgiana Weldon's escape from confinement for insanity in 1884, which became a popular issue, containing all the ingredients of a *cause celèbre*: "the society background, the wealthy and beautiful lady under threat of duress, the dramatic escape in disguise."[35] Literary minds too could scarcely forget that such luminaries as William Cowper, Christopher Smart, and William Collins had not been entirely sane. Some, like Hazlitt, knew madness in their own families, and others, like John Clare or Arthur Symons, in themselves.

In literature, madness had first served primarily as a device to provide sensation, drama and intense climaxes. It was a convenience of plot, a quick way to explain reckless or imprudent behavior. It served the moral purpose of indicating the just termination of a dissolute life. Gradually, however, it came also to serve as a convenient emblem of more than individual madness. As insanity figured more and more readily not as evil, but as purgative good—a necessary trial by fire—it came to refer to society at large, also hopefully susceptible to cure by some species of brain fever. This hope proving vain, one last service was left to the mad. They could stand as lonely, outcast figures who preserved in their mad kingdoms the riches of the imagination so wantonly abandoned by the world about them. Although in society itself the madman, like the gypsy, was undergoing a steady domestication; in literature, like the gypsy, the madman came to represent an unreal, but earnestly desired, preserve of values no one hoped to see so purely again. The literary convention departed from social reality, creating a new, enhanced region of experience, which with the discoveries of Freud and other investigators of the human psyche, seemed even more necessary. As human nature became more and more the subject of scientific analysis, writers ventured more and more to sentimentalize and ennoble a state that men still feared, but which seemed as attractive as the alternatives facing them in a world of growing ugliness and declining values.

CHAPTER TEN

THE RETURN

Everyone remembers the moment in a favorite tale when the long-lost son, or daughter, or parent, or friend returns and all that had been suffering and confusion is resolved. The hero does not die in a shipwreck, but returns home at last to rejoin the woman who has long awaited him. The father does not die in battle, but returns to protect his threatened brood. This device was familiar to Victorian literature, as it had been since the time of *The Odyssey*. But after the Romantic period, the theme of the return had acquired an additional meaning, for in poems and tales of that period, many heroes found it necessary to withdraw to nature in order to soothe their troubled souls before returning to challenge the civilized world once more. Also, in poems from Gray's "Ode on a Distant Prospect of Eton College," to Wordsworth's "Tintern Abbey," the return of the poet himself to some remembered locale occasioned reflections on time and human change.

CONVENTIONAL VIEWS

Victorian writers continued to think of the return in these terms. Following the Romantic convention, Richard Feverel sought out nature as a retreat and there found the healing example that gave him confidence to return to his wife, seeking forgiveness and offering a renewed love. Arthur Hugh Clough describes this impulse clearly in the third stanza of his poem, "Blank Misgivings of a Creature moving about in Worlds not realized."

> Enough of this already, now away!
> With silent woods and hills untenanted
> Let me go commune; under thy sweet gloom,
> O kind maternal Darkness, hide my head:
> The day may come I yet may re-assume
> My place, and, these tired limbs recruited, seek
> The task for which I now am all too weak.

Nor did the tradition represented by Gray and Wordsworth disappear. Matthew Arnold's "Resignation," in fact, has been read as a conscious answer to Wordsworth's poem.[1]

Although nineteenth-century writers maintained the conventional use of the return as it occurred in popular romance and artistic speculation, they also had a more peculiar interest in the return motif, converting it into a dynamic emblem, rich in special meanings. John Clare's "The Returned Soldier" for example is a thoroughly conventional poem in which an aged soldier returns to his home town where he finds all of the people changed, but where he is still able to delight in the familiar old surroundings. Home itself is valued for its agreeable associations, even though all human consolation is past. An obscure poet, John Harris, in "The Love of Home," presents several accounts of pathetic returns.[2] One is the story of the aged soldier returning to his birthplace. In youth, the soldier ran away from home following a trivial argument with his parents. Never since had he communicated with his family; now, after many years of battle experience, during which he had often thought of home with longing, he has returned; but it is too late.

> He hastened on, leaning upon his staff;
> Inquired for those he loved,—but they were dead.
> A pair of stranger-eyes in his white home
> Froze the old man to sadness, and he wept.

The moral, if it may be called that, is clear: no man can ignore the influences of his tender years. Ultimately they will call to him and draw him home, and it is a sacred call to be heeded. Only sorrow waits for those who delay too long. In presenting other examples of this theme, Harris offers one to balance the sorrow of the aged soldier. He tells the story of a young man who leaves home to make his fortune in the wilderness of America. Through all his difficult labors there he never forgets his home but is warmed and encouraged by the memory of those left behind. Finally, his fortune made, he returns to find everyone well and happy, and marries the orphan girl he had never forgotten.

Harris' versions of this familiar pattern are poorly written and all too blatant in making their points. They are akin to the many cheap magazine verses that exploited the convention throughout the century, a typical example of which is the poem, "Return," in *Household Words* for 23 May 1857, which tells the hackneyed tale of a soldier's return from prolonged adventures to seek his sweet young maiden, only to learn that she is dead. Elizabeth Barrett Browning tells a similar tale of separation and return to the discovery that the beloved is dead in "The Exile's Return." And Martin Tupper in his prosy way treats this aspect of the convention in his "proverbial" poem, "Of Home."

> An exile yearneth over Home in long romancing
>   absence,
> But oft his yearnings are fulfilled by realized
>   disappointment;
> The dreaming soldier longeth for his mother's
>   wayside cottage,
> The sailor museth on his watch about the wife
>   ashore:
> But what if crime and penury, if shame and sin
>   be there?
> How saddened into wormwood is the honied thought
>   of Home!

A more accomplished version of the standard convention appears about the same time in Wilkie Collins' *Hide and Seek* (1854) in which Matthew Grice, returning from his wanderings in the American wilderness and elsewhere, discovers all his loved ones gone. He, too, had left home rashly and now pays for his thoughtlessness with deep sorrow. His return initiates a search for his sister's child that eventually reveals his friend Zachary Thorpe's father as the betrayer of his sister, Mary Grice. Not content with this dramatic use of the return, Collins sends both Zachary and Matt off to the wilderness of the New World again, only to bring them home a few pages later, this time fulfilling the formula of the happy return.

MORALITY OF THE RETURN

The device of the return was an excellent method for evoking reader sentiment, but equally important, it had sufficient energy, even in its crudest form, to convey a moral. In Felicia Hemans' poem, "The Return," the narrator visits again the place of his birth and the revered locale asks him: "Hast thou come with the heart of thy childhood back? / The free, the pure, the kind?" It asks as well if he has been true to his early love, or adhered to his "first high dreams," or if he has kept his faith "with the faithful dead" or with the parental blessing. Sadly, the narrator confesses that he does not bring his childhood heart back again, that he turned from his first pure love, and that light after light in his soul has died. Worse yet, he has forgotten the prayers he learned at his mother's knee. "Darkened and troubled I come at last, / Home of my boyish glee." It is this return that will itself redeem the tainted spirit. The narrator's previous failure to keep his spirit pure may be reversed by one simple act—the return to the province of purity. It is an alluring, if patently false, ideal. For the weary and besmirched spirit, what could be more appealing than the prospect of complete redemption merely by taking the path back to one's childhood home, so fine and free and innocent?

Home represented surcease for those sinned against as well as for sinners. Eva, in Bulwer-Lytton's poem of that name, leaves her pleasant home to marry a "Stranger from a sunnier clime," but suffers wrong, perjury and shame, for "Before the bride had left her veil, / Another bore the nuptial name." Meanwhile, an idiot who had loved Eva, and whose mind was wakened by his jealousy, lives now at Eva's old cottage, a hermit devoted to her memory. Eva's sorrows eventually drive her mad and she flees from her agony to her childhood home.

> Yet still the native instinct stirr'd
> The darkness of the breast—

> She flies, as flies the wounded bird
>> Unto the distant nest;
> O'er hill and waste, from land to land,
>> Her heart the faithful instinct bore;
> And there, behold the Wanderer stand
>> Beside her Childhood's Home once more!

Here she remains, her mind still obscured, but comforted by the old memories and by the proximity of someone to trust. It is a peaceful stopping place before "The grave the only goal" of her spirit.

Susan Ferrier expanded on the theme of the return in her novel, *The Inheritance* (1824), declaring, "There are few minds so callous as to revisit the scenes of their childhood without experiencing some emotion." These scenes are moving because of their associations with early ideals, family and friends, and because they may speak to us of "time mispent, of talents misapplied, of warnings neglected, of blessings despised, of peace departed," or of violations of God's holy law. More moving still is the thought of returning to a father's house, even if those we loved are long since dead; for a parent's love cannot be forgotten. "Even when steeped in guilt or seared in crime, one spot —one little spot—will still be found consecrated to the purest—the holiest of earthly affections." (Vol. 1, ch. 12)

Although the most common form of the return was that of a wanderer or traveller—as often as not a sailor or soldier—making his way home to solve a mystery or bring joy, as in Douglas Jerrold's popular play, *Black-Eyed Susan,* or such tales as Mrs. Gaskell's *Sylvia's Lovers* or Dickens' *Dombey and Son,* there were many variations upon this form. In Adelaide Proctor's "Homeward Bound," for example, the seagoing narrator of the poem recounts his years of imprisonment among the Moors, his eventual release, and his return home, where, like Enoch Arden, he finds his wife wed to a comrade of the old days. Unlike Enoch, he reveals himself to the couple, and then departs once more. His return home brought only sorrow and disappointment; he must set out wandering again, thinking only of his final heavenly return.

> All my comrades, old and weary,
>> Have gone back to die at home.
> Home! yes, I shall reach a haven,
>> I, too, shall reach home and rest.

Like Bulwer-Lytton's Eva, Proctor's wanderer will find his final home only beyond the grave.

ELABORATION OF THE CONVENTION

Victorian writers continued to use the return convention as a traditional plot convenience. It could be crude and sensational as in an early chapter of Ainsworth's *Rookwood* (1834) entitled "The Return," in which Ranulph Rookwood is called home by a spectral voice to discover that he is in danger of losing his inheritance. The numerous complications of the novel's plot follow. In G. P. R. James' *The Gipsy* (1835), there are two basic returns: that of Edward De Vaux to his family's estate, and that of the first Lord Dewry, who, though presumed dead, returns in disguise to bring about the necessary revelation of his brother's crime. The first return initiates the action of the novel; the second brings about the climax of the tale. In Charles Reade's *Hard Cash* (1863), David Dodd returns from his sea-going career with a fortune of £ 14,000, but is defrauded of the money by his banker. This crime begets the subsequent difficulties to be resolved through the progress of the narrative.

These straightforward manifestations of the return convention involve little more than mechanical convenience. Something more is concerned in Miss Braddon's *Lady Audley's Secret* (1862). This novel opens with George Talboy's return from Australia, where he has made his fortune. Exploiting the traditional sentiments, Miss Braddon emphasizes Talboy's impatience to be reunited with the wife he had left abruptly years before. The expectation is clear: the long-absent husband returns; his joy should be great. But he returns to be told that his wife has died. Here again, the reader's emotions are wrung. What is more sorrowful, though not unfamiliar, than the wanderer's return to an empty home? The pattern thus far is familiar. But in *Lady Audley's Secret*, the plot is complicated because George Talboy's wife still lives, though she lives in disguise married to another man.

Miss Braddon modified the traditional pattern for a new effect, as did many writers. In Proctor's "Homeward Bound," in "The Lawyer's Second Tale," of Clough's *Mari Magno*, and in Tennyson's *Enoch Arden*, individuals return to find their mates re-wed, but in Miss Braddon's novel, this circumstance has a sinister cast. The return of the absent loved one begets not joy, but fear of discovery, and the moment of recognition is not one of delight, nor even surprise, but of violence. Lady Audley pushes her first husband into a well, and assumes that he is dead. Robert Audley is thus prompted to begin his search for his missing friend, the main action of the story. Later, Talboys returns again. He has not been murdered, but has fled from the horrible truths he has discovered. His second return, after his wife has been safely confined, is favorable and pleasant. Miss Braddon cleverly exploited the two basic forms of the return in her narrative. She recognized the emotional potential of the return convention, but she used it in a sensational manner, playing slight, but important variations on a well-worn scheme; and the variations served her well.

There had been interesting exploitations of the return before Miss Braddon's, and most commonly it was the use of irony that distinguished these variations. In *Guy Mannering* (1815), for example, young Harry Bertram lands at his family's ancestral property, having returned from India by way of England. Knowing himself only as Captain Vanbeest Brown, he does not realize that the property he views is his own inheritance. To sharpen the irony, Scott has Harry reflect upon the possible fate of the heirs of this land and then concludes:

> And thus, unconscious as the most absolute stranger, and in circumstances which, if not destitute, were for the present highly embarrassing; without the countenance of a friend within the circle of several hundred miles; accused of a heavy crime, and, what was as bad as all the rest, being nearly penniless, did the harrassed wanderer for the first time, after the interval of so many years, approach the remains of the castle, where his ancestors had exercised all but regal domain. (ch. 40)

A cruel use of ironic circumstance in the return convention is that of Isabel Vane in Mrs. Henry Wood's *East Lynne* (1861). Having fled from her home and fallen from virtue, Isabel Vane returns to that home in the disguise of Madame Vine, a governess. Like many another returning fictional parent, she enjoys proximity to her loved ones once more, though Mrs. Wood has created a circumstance which extorts the maximum of sympathetic emotion from the credulous reader, for Madame Vine must silently witness her husband offering his love to a new wife, and she must see her own children brought up according to the practices of another, less sympathetic mother. In short, all those associations that should have brought her joy, bring the disguised Isabel Vane only agony. The return is not to paradise, but to purgatory.

There were innumerable unexpected returns of virtuous characters, such as Charles Ravenshoe's return from the battlefields of the Crimea after being supposed dead. A more interesting variation involved the return of the unvirtuous. Sometimes the tainted spirit returns largely unaltered, as with Alice Marwood in *Dombey and Son*. But it is just as likely that reappearance of the fallen may occasion a benign effect, as it does when the sinful Esther returns to Manchester in *Mary Barton*. Esther wishes to warn her young relative of the gruesome life that may follow from one mistake. Contrarily, Alice Marwood represents the haunting effect of sin, for she is the walking and speaking incrimination of Carker's early life.

THE CONVICT'S RETURN

Convicts' or outcasts' returns were among the most familiar. Often these characters reappear at crucial moments in a plot to disclose important secrets. Brooker, in *Nicholas Nickleby*, provides the information that reveals Smike as Ralph Nickleby's child. Steggars, in Samuel Warren's *Ten Thousand A-Year*, serves a similar revelatory purpose. Others are sinister reminders of misplaced love or trust, like Aunt Betsey's albatross, her degraded husband, who surfaces periodically only to beg money from her in *David Copperfield*. More familiar, however, was the genuine convict's return, in which the outlaw's crimes have—either officially or unofficially—been expiated. The convict's return to his home usually represents a recovery of grace, though it may nonetheless be a painful experience.

Dickens utilized this typical figure as early as *The Pickwick Papers* in "The Story of the Convict's Return," in which the son of a hated and dissolute father falls into bad ways, is caught and transported for his offenses, but returns years later to the neighborhood for which he feels a strong attachment to learn that his mother has died from abuse. Dickens adds the improbable and melodramatic twist of having the young man accidentally encounter his father, who dies at the shock of meeting him. A more benevolent version of this stereotype appears in George Borrow's *Lavengro*, when Borrow, tramping along the English roads, encounters a young man who freely admits that he is a former convict returned from penal servitude in New

South Wales. The young man feels certain that he has reformed and confesses his hope of seeing his dear old mother once more, fearing however that she may have died. Happily Borrow can assure the young man that his mother lives still, for by extraordinary coincidence she is the apple woman on London Bridge with whom he has enjoyed cordial acquaintance.

The intriguing motif of the malefactor's return has several variations. In Meredith's "The House on the Beach" (1877), it is more or less lighthearted. Philip Ribstone is not a convict, but he is a deserter from the military. Martin Tinman, who is aware of Ribstone's history, has the power to inform on him or force him to leave his seaside hometown. Ribstone has returned bearing the name Van Diemen Smith, acquired along with an honestly earned fortune from his benefactor, a former convict. Although the motif of the reformed convict is associated with this return, it is Ribstone in his new name, not the original Van Diemen Smith, who returns to England virtuous and benevolent. Actually, it is the ambitious and trivial Martin Tinman, content to have stayed at home making his fortune in his petty way, who is reprehensible. Smith, on the other hand, is courageous and has proven himself in many severe tests. He is the nobler and grander man, despite the shadow upon his character. In the end, it is the pretentious and traitorous Tinman who is discomfitted, and Smith who can overlook with disdain such treachery from a man for whom he felt only friendship.

This ironic manipulation of the return convention is a slight, though interesting one, and it plays upon conventions long established in the literature of the time.[3] Tom Taylor's successful play *The Ticket-of-Leave Man* (1863) utilized the same convention, drawing upon predictable audience reactions. There was, however, a far more significant utilization of the device in Dickens' *Great Expectations* (1860). When Abel Magwitch returns to England, he knows the risk he is taking. "I was sent for life," he explains to the astonished Pip. "It's death to come back. There's been overmuch of coming back of late years, and I should of a certainty be hanged if took." (ch. 39) But he has returned nonetheless because his whole life in exile has been devoted to the career of the young boy who once showed him kindness. Finally, he can acknowledge to his beneficiary, "Yes, Pip, dear boy, I've made a gentleman on you!" (ch. 39) Ordinarily, it is the benevolent and honest gentleman, like David Dodd, who returns home with a fortune, while the convict returns only to sorrow or repentance. But Dickens skillfully combines the two devices. With slicing irony, he makes the outcast of society also the generous benefactor. As in Meredith's later tale, the returned exile proves kinder and more noble than many bred at home in the shadow of civilized institutions, a fact that Dickens accentuates in the final court scene when Magwitch receives his sentence of death. A shaft of light in the courtroom connects judge and spectators, "reminding some among the audience, how both were passing on, with absolute equality, to the greater Judgment that knoweth all things and cannot err." Then Magwitch responds to his sentence. "Rising for a moment, a distinct speck of face in this ray of light, the prisoner said, 'My Lord, I have received my sentence of Death from the Almighty, but I bow to yours,' and sat down again." (ch. 56)

Magwitch may represent the leavings of a troubled social order, but he cannot be denied. Like James Durie, in *The Master of Ballantrae* (1888-89), he represents a principle that inevitably returns. Magwitch is more intimately associated with the social order that has outlawed him than at first appears, for he accepts that order, and his labors are to promote and exploit, not to challenge it. In all of his efforts, there has been a large portion of selfishness as well. In offering his fortune to Pip, he adds, "I've come to the old country fur to see my gentleman spend his money *like* a gentleman. That'll be *my* pleasure. *My* pleasure 'ull be fur to see him do it." (ch. 40) Magwitch may not be evil like James Durie, but he is the inseparable other half of Pip's ambitions. One cannot live exempted from work without being born to wealth or trained to theft. It was Dickens' impression that those who were born to wealth as often as not inherited money that was initially no more respectable than what a thief might give to educate a boy. It has frequently been noted that Magwitch's being chained to Pip is symbolic of more than a financial connection. Their aspirations are the same, the roots of their expectations the same. Thus, eventually Magwitch must return to manifest the inescapable connection. The returned convict convention here implies a broad indictment of an entire culture and transcends the usual narrow function of the device.

DICKENS

Dickens exploited the return convention to very good purpose by making a familiar situation rich through amplification. Although the convention may be most successfully exhibited in *Great Expectations*, Dickens used it frequently elsewhere. A sinister return occurs in *Barnaby Rudge*, when the evil Rudge himself reappears to the sorrow of his family. But there are more agreeable returning figures, such as Martin Chuzzlewit, altered for the better after his American adventure; the single gentleman in *The Old Curiosity Shop*; or Captain George in *Bleak House*, who after a long and melancholy separation returns to his heartsore mother. There is more meaning, however, in Arthur Clennam's return from China in *Little Dorrit* (1855-57). Arthur knows that his nature is maimed; he does not pretend to have "Will, purpose, hope," or any other positive desire. (ch. 2) Without hope, he returns to his mother's house, a return representative of both his emotional state and of society. The house is presented as "leaning on some half-dozen gigantic crutches" and his mother's room is furnished with "a threadbare patternless carpet, a maimed table, a crippled wardrobe, a lean set of fire-irons like the skeleton of a set deceased," all furnishings reflecting Arthur's maimed spirit and his mother's supposedly crippled condition. (ch. 3) But Arthur learns that "home" is not simply a diseased structure, it is a cold, confining prison—an apt projection of the spirit pervading the land he returns to. The chapter describing Arthur's return to his mother is entitled "Home," but it is far different from those other domestic scenes so frequent in Dickens and other writers indicating the importance of the English hearthside. Dickens expressed what love of home meant in the "Conclusion" to his *Sketches of Young Couples*:

> Before marriage and afterwards, let them learn to centre all their hopes of real and lasting happiness in their own fireside; let them cherish the faith that in home, and all the English virtues which the love of home engenders, lies the only true source of domestic felicity; let them believe that round the household gods, contentment and tranquillity cluster in their gentlest and most graceful forms; and that many weary hunters of happiness through the noisy world, have learnt this truth too late, and found a cheerful spirit and a quiet mind only at home at last.

In *Nicholas Nickleby*, the home still represented those positive values of society and individual; but, by the time he came to write *Little Dorrit*, Dickens expressed uncertainty that a return home would be joyful and conducive to peace for the restless wanderer. For Magwitch it meant fear and death; for Arthur Clennam, it meant facing old wounds of the heart, but no old joys. His physical return is, in fact, a spiritual breaking away, and when he has succeeded in his liberation, the house that has so dominated his imagination collapses. For John Harmon in *Our Mutual Friend* (1864-65) return to his childhood home also signified not joy but pain. It meant discovering beyond the apparent home to which he returned, a truer, but less substantial haven not to be reached by purchase of a steamship ticket. Harmon realizes that his motives for returning to England are unsatisfactory:

> "When I came back to England, attracted to the country with which I had none but most miserable associations, by the accounts of my fine inheritance that found me abroad, I came back, shrinking from my father's money, shrinking from my father's memory, mistrustful of being forced on a mercenary wife, mistrustful of my father's intention in thrusting that marriage on me, mistrustful that I was already growing avaricious, mistrustful that I was slackening in gratitude to the two dear noble honest friends who had made the only sunlight of my childish life or that of my heart-broken sister." (Book 2, ch. 13)

After an assault on his life, Harmon decides that John Harmon is "dead," and he asks, "Should John Harmon come to life?" (Book 2, ch. 13) He then decides that his reappearance as Harmon would only injure those he loves; therefore, in a mood of self-sacrifice, he declares that "John Harmon shall come back no more." (Book 2, ch. 13)

When Mortimer Lightwood summarizes the history of John Harmon to the gathered company at the Veneering's dinner table, it sounds very much like all those other penny-press tales about alienated parents and children. After a quarrel with his father over his sister, young Harmon suffers his parent's abuse. "Venerable parent promptly resorts to anathematisation and turns him out. Shocked and terrified boy takes flight, seeks his fortune, gets aboard ship, ultimately turns up on dry land among the Cape wine: small proprietor, farmer, grower—whatever you like to call it." (Book 1, ch. 2) The stereotyped circumstances of the return would have been familiar to Lightwood's audience: a long absent heir to a large fortune, which is controlled by a peculiar condition—in this case marriage to a woman selected by the deceased parent. But Dickens has here added powerful and complicated themes: John Harmon returns in disguise, harmonizing with a society concerned with appearance and reality; the disclosure of his return constitutes a purgatorial experience reenacted in the many drowning sequences—with Rogue Riderhood's near death, Wrayburn's narrow escape, and Wegg's comic variation, being cast into the "dust" cart with a splash.

The most symbolic, most obvious return in *Our Mutual Friend* (1864-65), is that of buried, submerged, or discarded matter. Both John Harmon and Bradley Headstone, for example, keep themselves down "with infinite pains of repression" (Book 2, ch. 14), while Mortimer and Eugene, afraid to reveal any compassion, keep all sentiment "hidden with great pains." (Book 1, ch. 2) But the opening chapter reveals that what has been submerged, whether of the body or the soul, inevitably floats to the surface.

While Rokesmith has buried his past and the identity of John Harmon with it, others struggle with equal energy to extricate themselves from the swamp of their origins. Bradley Headstone has spent his life struggling to be free from commonplace beginnings, and his ambition is mirrored in young Charley Hexam who must ultimately renounce Headstone because, as he declares, "I have made up my mind that I will become respectable in the scale of society, and that I will not be dragged down by others." (Book 4, ch. 7) These struggles are doomed to failure; for Headstone's underlying passions break forth and Charley's basic selfishness stands exposed. Conversely, the humane sentiments of Lightwood and Wrayburn cannot be stifled indefinitely and finally manifest themselves in good actions.

Bradley Headstone represents two different struggles. He wishes to suppress the passions of a man in order to be a gentleman, and at the same time desires to hide his origins and raise himself above the conditions of his birth. His is a struggle both of suppression and emergence which is reflected in the general contrasting forces in the novel. Throughout *Our Mutual Friend* there is a contrast between the brand new, the methodized, the socially suitable appearance, and the ancient, chaotic and low features of human existence. As the novel proceeds, it becomes evident that that gleaming new respectability is as much of a dismal swamp as the old scavenging society of the river. Into this complex tangle of contending elements in man's nature, Dickens introduces several traditional devices, only one of which is the theme of the return. For what Dickens is largely concerned with is man's need to acknowledge his multiple nature, to accept and not repress impulses that, when totally denied, only create more and more terrible consequences. True restraint requires a courageous recognition of all features of the self. Hidden, outcast emotions will otherwise return like unwanted malefactors to spoil the orderly everyday world.

The recurrence of repressed or hidden feelings, of reappearing persons, of near death and recovery, of collapsing systems, all help to carry the controlling themes of birth and dissolution in the novel. Behind the simple convention of a return to unloved origins in *Our Mutual Friend* is the ominous theme of man's return to dust. But the hope that always accompanies this inevitable end is indicated in the history of John Harmon, who, partly by chance and partly by an act of the will, discovers that there is a home and that there are affections to which he can return in his proper identity. The Boffins, who cared for him as a lonely child, love him unselfishly in his return as well. "These two," Harmon declares to Bella when she first learns the secret, "whom I come to life to disappoint and dispossess, cry for joy!" (Book 4, ch. 13) Thus, beyond the more gruesome human destiny of simple extinction, is a hopeful promise of a reward and reunion transcending all of the horrible facts of existence. If appearances cloaked menacing and malicious plots prompted by greed or passion, they also veiled a benevolence acting for virtue and truth. In the end, John Harmon can return from the dead, and return to a home that is both happy and secure. Through love, he has been able to fashion from the fragments of his life this final objective. (This may be the significance of Mr. Venus, whose name represents love, and whose nature yearns for it, while his occupation of articulating the deceased keeps him from the fulfillment of his desires.) Love, it is clear, is the story's regenerative force. And, although love did not bring John Harmon home, love did save him from his phantom death. It was not his arrival in England that was John's real return, but his discovery of love in Bella and the Boffins. Only then was the lonely child who had known some moments of affection resurrected.

This resurrection, and the overall theme of rebirth and return is conveyed throughout the novel by the ship and sea motifs. John Harmon's return by ship is the basic initiating force in the story. Bella knows that his return signifies that her "ship has come in." However, when Harmon is presumed dead, Bella entertains other fancies—mercenary, as she herself declares—about the vessels she sees on the river being the property of her wealthy husband. (Book 2, ch. 8) Later, when she and her Pa, and her newly acquired husband, John

Rokesmith, are dining together at Greenwich, the scene of her former fancies, Bella recalls her earlier feelings.

> "You remember how we talked about the ships that day, Pa?"
> "Yes, my dear."
> "Isn't it strange, now, to think that there was no John in all the ships, Pa?"
> "Not at all, my dear."
> "Oh, Pa! Not at all?"
> "No, my dear. How can we tell what coming people are aboard the ships that may be sailing to us now from the unknown seas!" (Book 4, ch. 4)

This may seem like little more than a misty general speculation, but Dickens has not introduced it accidentally, and later it becomes significant. One day Bella has a serious talk with her husband:

> "Do you remember, John, on the day we were married, Pa's speaking of the ships that might be sailing towards us from the unknown seas?"
> "Perfectly, my darling!"
> "I think . . . among them . . . there is a ship upon the ocean . . . bringing . . . to you and me . . . a little baby, John." (Book 4, ch. 5)

Finally the match has come full circle, for "the winds and tides rose and fell a certain number of times, the earth moved round the sun a certain number of times, the ship upon the ocean made her voyage safely, and brought a baby Bella home." (Book 4, ch. 12) Birth and rebirth are thus intimately interwoven through the motif of ships and voyages.

Vessels upon the water, as the opening chapter of the novel makes clear, do not only bring home strangers, heirs, and babies, they dredge up as well beings of the slime and mud. While the spirits of Riderhood and Headstone are cast back into the slime from which all matter emerged, and lose their identity forever, a new spirit is drawn into the world of identities and distinguished from the mutable dust and water of which all life consists. The motif of the return signifies not only man's necessary merging with the dust from which he came—for he is made of dust—but also indicates his possible reunion beyond that blending, in a world of spirit—for he is also made of that. Between the mystery of birth in the ship upon the ocean, and the mystery of death in the river and mud below, there is a pattern of dissolution and return in which man may find reason to grieve, or, through love, in which he may discover reasons for hope and happiness.

TENNYSON'S USE OF THE RETURN

Tennyson used the convention of home and the return as early as in the poem "Home." He soon modified the convention, conceiving it in moral and metaphysical terms. Thus, in "The Palace of Art," the soul leaves the palace to dwell in a humble cottage, hoping to return to the more elegant domain when she has purged her guilt. When Arthur Henry Hallam returns to England in *In Memoriam*, he returns only as a spiritless corpse, and the mourning poet must learn to accept this false homecoming, while discovering that Hallam's death on earth is a return to his spiritual home. Tennyson subtly used these and other modifications of the return motif in his poetry. But in *Enoch Arden* (1864), the convention is simple and overt.

Christopher Ricks and P. G. Scott have pointed out that there was no shortage of analogues for Tennyson's *Enoch Arden*.[4] "The number, the variety, and the popularity of these analogues shows, then, that the general situation on which *Enoch Arden* was based had become a commonplace, if a peculiarly fascinating one, for mid-Victorian writers"[5]—the long-absent husband returns to find his wife remarried. Whereas most Victorian heroes return openly, Enoch Arden does not, and it is this detail that distinguishes Tennyson's treatment of the convention. "The real moral centre of the story," Scott says, "is Enoch's decision not to break up Annie's second marriage by revealing his return, until it is too late to make any difference."[6] It is this self-sacrifice that justifies "treating him in poetry as a strong, heroic soul."[7]

Enoch Arden supported the traditional moral values of Victorian England, yet confronted those values with a moral dilemma, for which the only answer was self-abnegation. Like other long-absent voyagers, Enoch expresses doubts when he finally returns to his village. "There Enoch spoke no word to any one, / But homeward—home—what home? had he a home? / His home, he walked." And, indeed, it is in the familiar setting of this neighborhood that he is most lonely and devastated by altered circumstances. In his lonely island exile, Enoch learned patience; now "the dead man come to life" must, like John Harmon, repress the identity that could only injure others. Seeing his erstwhile wife happily wed to his old friend, Philip Ray, he feels his grief as never before, yet determines to remain silent. This determination provides the one gratification of his last days and also their glory.

> He was not all unhappy. His resolve
> Upbore him, and firm faith, and evermore
> Prayer from a living source within the will,
> And beating up through all the bitter world,
> Like fountains of sweet water in the sea,
> Kept him a living soul.

But with no aim beyond himself to work for, Enoch falls into a languor that leads to death, and he closes his life with blessings upon his wife, children and old friend, allowing the disclosure of his identity at the end only because it will give Annie the consoling certainty that he is dead.

Tennyson enriched this conventional tale with ironies of circumstance and with moral intricacies, but his chief purpose was to demonstrate the strength and nobility of spirit in a man under one of the most harrowing of conditions. Isabel Vane, as Madame Vine, had deserved the suffering she endured in a similar situation, but Enoch Arden had been a good man all his life and did not merit the agonies of having to witness those he loved without being able to convey his love to them. For Tennyson, this conventional situation was not retributive; it was an opportunity for the development of man's highest qualities. Other utilizations of this version of the return convention were, like Mrs. Gaskell's *Sylvia's Lovers*, more complicated, or, like Trollope's *Dr. Wortle's School*, more openly concerned with the moral complexities occasioned by the return of a husband to a remarried wife, but none touched the popular heart so profoundly as *Enoch Arden*. In his poem, Tennyson boldly chose one of the most commonplace literary conventions of his time and transformed it from a mere sentimental statement, as it was in so many contemporary poems, to a depiction of the inescapable misery possible even to the innocent in human existence, and the greatness of human nature that may arise from that suffering. In doing this, he offered for his time an emblem of the dignity and value of self-sacrifice.

The convention of the return could be exploited with equal significance, but greater irony, by writers such as Thomas Hardy, whose
views were less positive than Tennyson's. Peter J. Casagrande asserts
that "The return motif may well be said to be the dominant motif of
Hardy's fiction."[8] In *A Pair of Blue Eyes* Stephen Smith returns to
find his beloved significantly changed during their separation. Here,
and predominantly in Hardy's use of conventional characters or situations, there is a strong sense of irony. The device occurs in the short
story, "A Few Crusted Characters," Michael Henchard's wife returns inconveniently in *The Mayor of Casterbridge*, Grace Melbury
returns from a sophisticated school to her rural home in *The Woodlanders*, Angel Clare returns from Brazil in *Tess of the d'Urbervilles*,
and Arabella returns unexpectedly to complicate Jude's life in *Jude
the Obscure*. In *The Woodlanders* (1886-87), Hardy even included
a small exchange which could be read as a parody of the Enoch Arden syndrome, and certainly represents a deflation of the traditional
sentiment of the return. A group of rustics, telling tales, come upon
a likely subject:

> "And I knowed a woman, and the husband o' her went away for four-
> and-twenty year," said the barkripper. "And one night he came home
> when she was sitting by the fire, and thereupon he sat down himself on
> the other side of the chimney-corner. 'Well,' says she, 'have ye got any
> news?' 'Don't know as I have,' says he; 'have you?' 'No,' says she, 'ex-
> cept that my daughter by my second husband was married last month,
> which was a year after I was made a widow by him.' 'Oh! Anything
> else?' he says. 'No,' says she. And there they sat, one on each side of that
> chimney-corner, and were found by their neighbors sound asleep in
> their chairs, not having known what to talk about at all." (ch. 48)

But Hardy's most elaborate and subtle exploitation of the return
motif is in his novel, *The Return of the Native* (1878), in which Clym
Yeobright, a bright young man who has been educated far beyond
the level of his rural birthplace, returns to his home town after living
for some time in the most cultivated city in the world, Paris. Ordinarily such a return would be that of a successful young man who
has risen above the rustic limitations of his fellows; instead, Clym
returns as a missionary or prophet. Hardy describes him as "a John
the Baptist who took ennoblement rather than repentance for his

text." (Book 3, ch. 2) Unsatisfied with the sophisticated life of the French capital, Clym has returned to Egdon Heath to serve humble people by becoming a schoolmaster and bringing a richer intellectual life to their rustic world. "He had a conviction that the want of most men was knowledge of a sort which brings wisdom rather than affluence," but he overlooks the fact that "In passing from the bucolic to the intellectual life the intermediate stages are usually two at least, frequently many more; and one of these stages is almost sure to be worldly advance." (Book 3, ch. 2)

Hardy explains that Clym is ahead of his time, and does not recognize certain contradictory impulses in himself, though Hardy freely reveals them to the reader. Clym has been educated and "improved" elsewhere, yet remains intimately connected with the heath. "He was permeated with its scenes, with its substance, and with its odours. He might be said to be its product." And though his purpose in returning to Egdon Heath is to bring cultivation to its inhabitants, he himself is pleased to see that efforts to cultivate the heath have not succeeded; "he could not help indulging in a barbarous satisfaction at observing that, in some of the attempts at reclamation from the waste, tillage, after holding on for a year or two, had receded again in despair, the ferns and furze-tufts stubbornly reasserting themselves." (Book 3, ch. 2) The reluctance of the heath to accept "improvement" is a warning that Clym fails to apprehend.

Ironically, Clym loves Eustacia Vye, whose main desire is to escape the heath she hates. What develops is a tragedy of ironies; for Clym, the sophisticated gentleman, loving the heath, is gradually reduced to the level of a common laborer, while his passionate and wild wife, hating the heath, is driven to Wildeve and finally death. What began as the formulaic return of a fortunate son to the neighborhood of his youth becomes something vastly more important in Hardy's hands; the significance is incorporated in his title. It is not so much the native's return to his old territories, but the return of the native within him that is the crisis of the novel.

Clym is of the heath, but for a time the loves and passions of the heath—representing the fundamental experiences of existence—have been overlaid in him by his adventures in distant, sophisticated places. Upon his return to Egdon Heath, all that is basic in him re-emerges, and finds expression not only in his thinking (which is progressively clouded and obscured), but in his behavior as well (he takes pleasure in his physical occupation as a furze-cutter). What happens to Clym is part of the cycle of human nature itself and is demonstrated in the seasonal festivities of the villagers, representing a revived paganism. It is this that Eustacia wishes to escape. Although she is driven by violent sensuous emotions, she longs for the artificial society that Clym has so willingly abandoned.

The progress of man toward self-knowledge and culture proceeds ineluctably, though it does so neither smoothly, nor by bounds, but in oscillations. Thus, though general British civilization moved forward, the rural hamlets persisted as reminders of another feature of human existence, and "the impulses of all such outlandish hamlets are pagan still." (Book 6, ch. 1) Clym, with all his sophistication, has experienced the return of the native element in himself. His aims have been too ambitious, and his character inadequately proportioned for his task; consequently, in the end, abandoning his earlier plan to become schoolmaster to the rustic community, he adopts, after the manner of Christ, a more modest but also more intimate form of communication. "He left alone creeds and systems of philosophy, finding enough and more than enough to occupy his tongue in the opinions and actions common to all good men." (Book 6, ch. 4)

In a way, Clym's vocation indicates a potential triumph of a religion of humanity over the established religions of Christianity. Perhaps Swinburne's "pale Galilean" had not triumphed after all over the deepest human impulses. Clym is not only a new form of Christ (not yet thirty-three, delivering his own Sermon on the Mount), but has been his own John the Baptist as well. His message is not expressed in doctrine, and "his texts would be taken from all kinds of books." (Book 6, ch. 4) It is a religion drawing upon the native in man, as well as the acquired. Clym's return to Egdon Heath has evoked the return of the heath's spirit in him, and though the collision has ruined much, it has left something of value.

By the latter half of the century, many writers were openly questioning the weary convention. Sir Richard Burton's attack upon the cliché, in *Stone Talk* (1865), was more vicious than many, but not uncharacteristic. When Dr. Polyglot remarks the famous British love of home and happy hearthside, the stone with whom he is conversing replies that this preoccupation shows pride, not delight.

"Your 'happy hearth' is oft a hell
Where Temper, Spite, and Disgust dwell,
And Ennui sheds her baleful gloom,
Making the place a living tomb. . . ."

Britons become sentimental when they talk of home, the stone says;
but their actions belie their words:

"But see, this exile when returned
To all for which his sick heart yearned,
Growls, grumbles, damns, until once more
Escaped from dearest native shore,
Self-banished as he was before. . . ."

Equally disillusioning is Ernest Dowson's pathetic version of the
convention in "The Statute of Limitations" (1893). Michael Garth,
long separated from his fiancée by his need to make a fortune, sets
out on his return from Chili to England. On the journey home, however, he realizes that the homeland and especially the woman to
whom he is returning will have changed. "The notion of the woman,
which now she was, came between him and the girl whom he had
loved, whom he still loved with passion, and separated them." Garth
realizes that his return is merely spatial, whereas the real homeland of his dreams is temporal. For him it is impossible to return, and
he commits suicide before the ship reaches England. Dowson's story
reads almost like a parody of Rider Haggard's novel, *Montezuma's
Daughter*, published in the same year, in which the hero returns to
Renaissance England after a twenty year absence in Spain and Mex-
ico to marry the woman who has faithfully awaited him.

The return convention served also as the medium for social message. In fantasy tales, represented by William Morris' "A Dream of
John Ball," and *News From Nowhere* (1890), characters return to
the present from another time to illuminate their fellow men with a
social philosophy. Later, H. G. Wells' Time Traveller in *The Time
Machine* (1895), would return from distant future times with a far
less hopeful and consoling vision.[9]

DEEPER CONSIDERATIONS

Not all sophistications of the return convention were secular or
melancholy. In many instances, the return is associated with a re-

turn to heaven, as in Adelaide Proctor's "Homeward Bound." An elaborate example of this convention variation occurs in Bulwer-Lytton's *Zanoni* (1842),when the titular hero warns Clarence Glyndon that there are two ways to triumph over the Phantom of the Threshold—to go fearlessly on to the Infinite or turn back to the familiar. Zanoni advises Glyndon to return to the childlike and the commonplace, and not aspire to the Idea. "Return, O wanderer! return. Feel what beauty and holiness dwell in the Customary and the Old." (Bk. 6, ch. 9) Nor was Bulwer-Lytton's sentiment transient and superficial, for, near the end of his life, he wrote about death:

> Still, as nearer and nearer he comes to the sacred precincts, farther and farther fade away his regrets for the things left behind uncompleted. Softer and softer sinks into his soul the tender remembrance that none ever so loved as the father whom he has so often forgotten. It is to a father's judgment that he is to render the account of his wanderings—it is to a father's home that he returns.[10]

In some instances, spirits of the dead return to the world of the living. Thus in Felicia Hemans' "A Spirit's Return," not only does a loved one return, but the spirit indicates to the earth-bound lover that heaven is their final home. The living lover, thereafter, yearns for the release of death, knowing "the day *will* come— / Over the deep the free bird finds its home, / And the stream lingers 'midst the rocks, yet greets / The sea at last!" The notions, as well as the metaphors, are thoroughly commonplace and conventional for Victorian poetry. In Mrs. Oliphant's tales, "Old Lady Mary," (1884) and "Land of Suspense" (1897), spirits return with less effect. However, this direction was less common in literature than the inevitable movement from life to infinity, though there was a substantial tradition of ghost stories in which spirits returned to haunt their former homes. The movement from life to infinity was perhaps most memorably conveyed in Tennyson's *Idylls of the King*, where the convention of the return grandly demonstrates that the real homeland was not a location in England or elsewhere, but a region as yet beyond knowledge. At King Arthur's death, Sir Bedivere recalls the rhyme "From the great deep to the great deep he goes." ("Passing of Arthur") And, from the distance into which Arthur has been borne, he hears "Like the last echo born of a great cry, / Sounds, as if some fair city were one voice / Around a king returning from his wars."[11] This world has been a temporary exile for Arthur and all he represents, and after his passage here, he returns to his true realm. But the process does not end there. When that ideal is needed once more, Arthur will return to the kingdoms of mankind and work his will until he may return once more to his infinite home. The pattern is cyclical and unending and implies that every return is a departure and every parting a return. But this was a philosophy far advanced for its time, though obscured by its conventional trapping.

What distinguishes the use of such conventions by writers like Hardy, or Dowson, or Tennyson, is this extension of their meanings to psychological and intellectual implications. Just as the images of return in Hardy signify complex and subtle attributes of individual human personality and of mankind, and in Dowson suggest subtleties of the imagination, so Tennyson's use of similar images reveals a spiritual conviction in the periodic revival of truth and virtue through the recovery of a belief beyond material proof. Arnold Toynbee declared that many of the great events and great heroes of history were characterized by a pattern of withdrawal and return, but added that this movement was characteristic of life in general, as in the annual procession of the seasons. Still, he noted that in the life of Christ, and particularly in the concept of the Second Coming, "the *motif* of Withdrawal-and-Return attains its deepest spiritual meaning."[12] And it was this spiritual meaning that writers like Tennyson hoped to convey.

There were many manifestations of the desire both to return *to* a place unspoiled by adult disenchantment, and to return *from* such a place, bearing the secret of that lost simplicity. Perhaps the revival of interest in medieval culture could be viewed in these terms. Alice Chandler remarks that in nineteenth-century English culture, "The return to the Middle Ages was conceived of as a homecoming."[13] Certainly, the desire to discover in the medieval past a spiritual, emotional, and esthetic home more suitable than the present played a large part in the Gothic revival in the arts and crafts. Just as surely, George du Maurier's *Peter Ibbetson* (1892) is a stunning example of the craving to escape a tawdry present to live in a world of love and tenderness. If Dowson's Michael Garth died because he could not possess dreams of the past in his present life, in du Maurier's novel, Peter Ibbetson manages to live not metaphorically but actually in his dreams. And, in these dreams, his first desire is to return to the days and scenes of his childhood, which he learns to do with utter freedom. This fantasy was an apotheosis of private nostalgia and an answer to a growing emotional impatience with an increasingly frustrating world. The returns that had been almost exclusively journeys back to regions that could provide surcease, redemption, enlightenment or peace, became, near the century's close, attempted escapes from immediate existence. Whereas the literary convention had earlier described recoveries of the realities of experience after exile, they later became releases from those same realities. The convention of the return, though it retained its traditional functions, had come to represent, as well, an intense desire for release, freedom, and peace. And in this convention, as in many others, we may see reflected the growth of a disenchantment that was incipient in the literature of the early nineteenth century, but became open and elaborate in literature as the Victorian era drew to an end.

THE PRODIGAL SON

One specific use of the return convention was coupled with the familiar figure of the prodigal son, and its persistence indicates a curious fascination on the part of the Victorians for typological figures. Felicia Hemans' "The Voice of Home to the Prodigal" differs little from her "The Return." In the former poem, childhood precincts remind the prodigal of all that he has left, especially the peaceful home and quiet natural surroundings. The scene is set with standard props, and sentiments, and the invitation made, but the prodigal does not actually return.

> Still at thy father's board
>   There is kept a place for thee;
> And, by the smile restored,
>   Joy round the hearth shall be.
>   . . .
> Still, when the prayer is said,
>   For thee kind bosoms yearn,
> For thee fond tears are shed—
>   Oh! when wilt thou return?

The prodigal was traditionally emblematic of wasted life, as illustrations by Bosch and Dürer indicate. In Archbishop Trench's "The

Prodigal," a catechism records the predictable degradation for which the unfortunate individual has traded past joys.

> An exile through the world who bade thee roam?
> None, but I wearied of a happy home.
>
> Why must thou dweller in a desert be?
> A garden seemed not fair enough for me.

Often the prodigal returns too late to offer repentance to his injured family. In a typical example, Paul Tatnall, in Ingraham's *The Gipsy of the Highlands*, returns after a youth devoted to depravity and crime to find a sign "to be let" posted on his mother's house. "Few as the words were, they were significant of the most painful meaning to the prodigal." His mother has died and will not witness his redemption. However, the young woman who has loved him during his long absence does welcome him home, nurses him to health, revives his religious faith, and marries him.

Mary Howitt's "Barbara Fleming's Fidelity" provides a similarly unvarnished example of the convention. Adam Garth of Gordale Hall, after declaring his love for Barbara, decides that he "will not marry! will obey no wife's control!" and leaves Barbara and his home. His father is enraged by this conduct and offers to disown his son and make Barbara his heir. She refuses this offer and other opportunities, remaining confident of her affection. Eventually her patience is rewarded, and Adam returns.

> So, at length by pain grown wiser, all his idols
>   turned to clay.
> All the apples of his promise dust and ashes in
>   his teeth,
> Like the Son in the Evangel, cried he in his soul's
>   dismay—
> "Father, I have sinned! Unworthy of thy love, set
>   me beneath
> Amongst thy servants—son no longer! Only save me,
>   save from death!"[14] (Part 4)

Barbara, sensing that he is coming, goes out to meet Adam, and brings him to her quiet house. There she "Cheered his smitten soul with kindness, gave him wine and choicest meat, / Clasped him like a loving mother, as a servant washed his feet." (Part 4) Adam is reconciled with his father, and both testify to God's goodness and patience before the congregation in the church. Afterward, Adam and Barbara are married according to the original plan.

In chapter ten of Mrs. Gaskell's *Mary Barton*, entitled "Return of the Prodigal," the debauched Esther returns to Manchester to warn John Barton that he must caution his daughter, Mary, against the blandishments of Harry Carson. Barton will not listen to her and casts her off angrily. She is subsequently imprisoned for "disorderly vagrancy," but returns and warns Jem Wilson, who loves Mary, to prevent Carson from taking advantage of her. (ch. 14) Esther, however, can never be fully redeemed, and at the end of the novel she drags herself back to her childhood home "to see the place familiar to her innocence, yet once again before her death," and dies yearning for that lost innocence. (ch. 38)

The convention of the prodigal was popular enough to be used on the stage as well as in novels. Edward Fitzgerald described, in a letter of 27 February 1851, to George Crabbe, the "stupid and gaudy" nature of the play he called the "Prodigal Son" but which was actually an adaptation of Scribe and Auber's *L'enfant prodigue* entitled *Azaël the Prodigal*.[15]

Not all utilizations of the prodigal motif were serious. Most were nothing more than casual allusions. Thus Robin Toodle in *Dombey and Son* who comes to no particular good is described as "The prodigal son." (ch. 22) Captain George in *Bleak House* is a benign version of the type who, though he has not sinned abundantly, is, because of his reduced station in life, ashamed to return to the home and mother he cherishes.[16] And Wopsle in *Great Expectations*, prefigures a subtle theme of the novel in a simple, comic way when he exhorts the company gathered for Christmas dinner at the Gargerys', "Swine were the companions of the prodigal." (ch. 4) The observation has point in this particular scene, since Pip has just stolen a pork pie to feed a genuine prodigal, the convict on the marsh, and has thus allied himself with sinners and outcasts as the prodigal son did. Moreover, his life to come will also be a departure from the values of the home to which he must, like the prodigal, return, having learned the necessary lesson of humility and love.

Often enough, allusions to the prodigal are amusing as when, in

He Knew He Was Right Aunt Jemima Stanbury welcomes the thoroughly good and kind Dorothy Stanbury back to her home with the comment, "You shall have a calf instead, my dear . . . because you are a returned prodigal." (ch. 73) Chapter Two of Book Two in Wilkie Collins' *Hide and Seek* is entitled "The Prodigal's Return," but it describes nothing more remarkable than young Zachary Thorpe's return home at night muddled with drink. Ironically, despite the title, the chapter ends with Zachary's running away from home to seek freedom from his oppressive father. The real returned prodigal in this novel is Matthew Grice, who has returned from America to find the family that he earlier had left so abruptly. His return is beneficial and its effect, though uncomfortable for some, is ultimately good.

The conventional figure of the prodigal son was used in many varied ways, and it usually retained its spiritual significance. One of Hartley Coleridge's sonnets indicates the larger meaning that the emblem of the prodigal could bear, extending its significance from a particular instance to a general condition of mankind.

> Youth, love and mirth, what are they but the portion,
> Wherewith the Prodigal left his Father's home,
> Through foreign lands in search of bliss to roam,
> And find each seeming joy a mere abortion,
> And every smile, an agonised distortion
> Of pale Repentance's face, and barren womb?
> Youth, love, and mirth! too quickly they consume
> Their passive substance, and their small proportion
> Of fleeting life, in memory's backward view,
> Still dwindles to a point, a twinkling star,
> Long gleaming o'er the onward course of Being,
> That tells us whence we came and where we are,
> And tells us too, how swiftly we are fleeing
> From all we were and loved, when life was new.

In Dutton Cook's *A Prodigal Son* (1863), Wilford Hadfield returns to attend his father on his deathbed, and, although the old man plans to forgive his prodigal son, they quarrel and he dies cursing him. Wilford proves to be an amiable man, wins the love of Violet Fuller, and refuses to live with his brother's family on the estate denied to him by his father. The complication of the story arises from an early indiscretion, for Wilford learns that a woman he had married years before is not dead as he supposed, but has returned to claim him. Understandably, this upsets his present domestic arrangements, but all is resolved when it is discovered that the first marriage was not legal. The prodigal motif has served its turn by emphasizing the importance of retribution for early sins. By contrast, Charles Kingsley made more economical use of the convention in *Two Years Ago* (1857) where Tom Thurnall, a good-natured but restless young man, is identified with the prodigal son. Tom has been prodigal not from his earthly father, whom he loves, but from his heavenly Father, to whose care he wishes to return by the end of the novel. Whereas Cook's prodigal taught a practical lesson in morality, Kingsley's conveyed a more spiritual significance.

The most effective use of the convention of the prodigal's return, however, was as irony, revealing how conscious writers were of the emblem's conventional nature. In *The Newcomes* (1853-55), Thackeray used the prodigal convention simply in the character of the reckless Lord Kew, whose mother spends her time "deploring the course upon which her dear young prodigal had entered; and praying with that saintly love, those pure supplications, with which good mothers follow their children, for her boy's repentance and return." (Vol. 1, ch. 37) The motif abounds in the novel, but has its most important manifestation in Colonel Newcome. As a boy, Tommy Newcome had the parable of the prodigal read to him when he had run away from school and returned. (Vol. 1, ch. 2) Later, Hobson and Brian Newcome look upon Thomas as a prodigal, fearing his behavior; yet, when he returns to England from India, it is clear that he comes not in disgrace, but with benevolence. He is a prodigal son, indeed, but his prodigality is that of generosity, not of dissolution. It is a skillful turn upon the convention.

Thackeray presents a similar version of the convention in *The Adventures of Philip* (1861-62), where Philip is accused of playing the part of the prodigal son, thereby bringing about his father's ruin. Actually, Thackeray is describing the common human tendency to think in stereotypes. It is customary to presume that the lively young son is the profligate; in reality Philip's father is the prodigal who ruins his son. (ch. 26) Likewise, in Meredith's *The Adventures of Harry Richmond* (1871), young Harry, suspected of wayward behavior, is instructed to keep the moral lesson of the prodigal son before him.

Yet Harry never requires this caution, for it is his father who behaves like the prodigal and whose escapades endanger the happiness and well-being of the more temperate son.

Robert Louis Stevenson also used the prodigal convention. His "The Story of a Lie" introduces the figure of the prodigal father, but more interesting is his elaboration of the convention in *The Master of Ballantrae* (1888-89). In this novel, the dissolute James Durie returns to a home where his father still values him, and his brother's wife is attracted to him, but where the younger brother himself knows James' true character. James arrogantly refers to himself as the prodigal son, and the father, admitting Henry has played the role of "the elder brother of the parable in the good sense," still fastens his affection upon James. However, James has not returned penitent but to obtain more money to carry on his profligate adventures. James reflects the evil in man and Henry the good, but the evil in man does not of its own accord sue for forgiveness in humility. For Stevenson, the parable of the prodigal was a reminder that man is capable of all the grossness and folly that that figure represented, but he did not pretend that repentance was likely to be the outcome of such devoted folly. In Stevenson's tale, each return of the prodigal is more menacing than the last, each violation of the parable more corruptive of the innocent elder brother, until both meet their end in a distant land. They are as far from all the values that home signifies as they are from that home itself. Stevenson's fable is a grim and sardonic comment on the sentimental emblem of the prodigal.

In the later part of the century, the prodigal was a common subject, though in most cases—as with de Tabley's "The Prodigal" and "The Prodigal (after Albert Durer)," or Arthur Symons' "The Prodigal Son" —the convention is not developed. In some instances, however, a poet might turn the convention to account as Meredith does in "The Empty Purse," subtitled "A Sermon to Our Later Prodigal Son," which is a prolonged denunciation of a society devoted to materialism and therefore incognizant of its relationship to the fundamental principles of nature. After his harangue, the poet exclaims, "Enough, poor prodigal boy!" and apologizes for making "A sermon thy slice of the Scriptural calf!" Then he adds that he hopes men will recognize their folly and recover the lesson of nature. "By my faith, there is feasting to come," he exclaims.

Meredith's poem was a peculiar and highly intellectual modification of the prodigal convention, but even on a rudimentary level, the convention underwent modifications that showed how writers were using it to comment upon moral, social, and even economic issues. In a banal tale, "The Warilows of Welland; or, the Modern Prodigal," which appeared in *Household Words* (1850), Mr. Vandeleur overhears a farmer and his son discussing their economic difficulties.[17] Learning that the farmer is ruined, and even though he is a stranger to them, Vandeleur offers to pay his and his family's passage to America. Touched by this generosity, Farmer Warilow takes the stranger home. There Vandeleur hears the story of a second son who quarrelled with his father and ran off to America because he was jealous of his brother Joseph. No word was ever heard from the son, but the farmer consoled himself for the loss of the boy by reading the parable of the prodigal son. Joseph's wife had said to him one day, "Perhaps, father, he will still come home like the Prodigal Son in the Scripture, and if he does we'll kill the fatted calf for him, and no one will rejoice more truly than Joseph will." Few readers would be surprised to discover that the stranger is really Samuel, the long lost son. Having revealed himself, Samuel is warmly welcomed by all and he subsequently takes the entire family off to America with him, where he is rich and influential. "The Warilows of Welland all bless the Prodigal Son, who, unlike the one of old, came back rich to an indigent father, and made the old man's heart grow young again with joy." No repentance is necessary in this modification of the convention. Moreover, the prodigal here benevolently returns his dependent family to the "exile" that has become his true home, and now theirs as well. The parable has been completely altered and shows, in its hopeful conclusion, a conscious dissatisfaction with the traditional notion that flight from home is necessarily the first step to dissipation.

There is a similar reluctance to accept this cliché in Meredith's *Rhoda Fleming* (1865) when Robert Eccles returns to his stern father, looking like "the prodigal, returned with impudence for his portion instead of repentance." (ch. 17) But Robert is not the typical prodigal. His character is still firm, his feelings generous and worthy. He has, it is true, given himself up to drink in the past, but he returns home mainly cured of his weaknesses.

"Come, father," he said, with a miserable snigger, like a yokel's smile; "here I am at least. I don't say, kill the fatted calf and take a lesson from Scripture, but give me your hand. I've done no man harm but myself—damned if I've done a mean thing anywhere! and there's no shame to you in shaking your son's hand after a long absence." (ch. 17)

As older values were examined with greater scrutiny, the simple patterns of the prodigal's story came in for more critical treatment. A prodigal son like Bertie Stanhope in Trollope's *Barchester Towers* does not return from a dissolute life to find forgiveness, but is, on the contrary, sent away into exile by his Christian family. In Henry Seton Merriman's "The Prodigal's Return" (1896), Stephen Leach, having incurred his father's displeasure by his dissolute and expensive conduct at the university, departs for the New World. He sends no word to his family, though "It was known that he was in Chili, and there was war going on there." Meanwhile, his father dies, and his blind mother, attended by his younger sister, also lies dying. Patiently the mother expects her son's return according to all the conventional models of popular literature. One day a stranger does appear at the door. "Am I too late?" he asks. "No Stephen," Joyce Leach replies. "But mother cannot live much longer. You are just in time." The young man is awkward in his behavior and the narrator remarks that "The return of this prodigal was not a dramatic success." The "prodigal" promises the dying mother that he will go soldiering no more. He watches with Joyce through the lonely night, but his manner remains oddly restrained. As she is expiring, Mrs. Leach thanks God that Stephen has returned and that Joyce will not be alone. "I always knew Stephen would come back," she says. "I found it written everywhere in the Bible." When the dying woman asks what her son looks like, Joyce discovers from her description, that the man who has come back is not her older brother. Nonetheless, she keeps the secret from her mother, and, complying with the old woman's request, kisses the stranger across her mother's bed. After Mrs. Leach's death, the stranger explains that Stephen had been shot as a traitor and that he had come merely bearing that news. He leaves, promising to return in six months, presumably to claim Joyce as his bride. Certainly the irony here is weak, for, despite the title, no real prodigal son does return; instead, the wicked man has met a wicked death, and the mother's Biblical convictions are illusory.

Merriman was clearly playing upon the expectations of an audience accustomed to the prodigal convention.

Two examples, published after the official close of the Victorian period but still in its tradition, must suffice to demonstrate how extremely self-conscious and ironic treatment of the overworked convention had become. In St. John Hankin's play, *The Return of The Prodigal* (1904), the first act ends with the dramatic discovery of Eustace Jackson, the prodigal son of a wealthy textile manufacturer, lying in front of his father's house. It quickly becomes apparent that Eustace is not in a desperate condition, nor is he inclined to repentance. He explains to his brother Henry that he simply got tired of finding jobs and losing them, and, being down on his luck, came up with a splendid solution. "At last I thought of a dramatic *coup*. The Prodigal's Return! The Fatted Calf! A father softened, a mother in tears! The virtuous elder brother scowling in the background! So I came here. Back to the Old Home, you know." (Act 2) All the rest is a careless deception. Eustace's goal is to insure himself an income without having to work. His father threatens to send the young man to a workhouse, but Eustace replies that such a move would spoil Mr. Jackson's parliamentary ambitions. In the end, they come to bargaining. Eustace explains that he hasn't wanted to be a failure, but he is. "Your sensible course," he advises his father, "is to destroy me. But you daren't do that. Social convention won't allow you." (Act 4) They finally agree that Eustace is to receive an allowance of £ 250 a year on the condition that he leave home. Like Bertie Stanhope or James Durie, the prodigal here remains a prodigal and actually profits from his prodigality. More importantly, he is able to do this in Hankin's play because he can exploit the pious hypocrisy and social conventionality of his family—the very sentiments of compassion, forgiveness and love which in their genuine form are the substance of the parable of the prodigal son. But in the England of Victoria or Edward, Hankin seems to be saying, there is no repentance in the prodigal for there is no love in the parent, nor any meaning in the home to which he returns. Only cash is important and only for that does the exile, the wanderer, the prodigal, return.

If Hankin's play was comic and cynical, Hall Caine's novel, *The Prodigal Son*, published in the same year, is wearisomely sentimental. In this story of modern Iceland, two sons, Magnus and Oscar Magnusson, love the same woman. Oscar wins Thora and later betrays her for another woman who brings on his own moral and financial ruin. Living abroad as a self-confessed prodigal, Oscar becomes a composer, while his family in Iceland assume that he is dead. Magnus, who has lost his inheritance as a consequence of his father's bankruptcy brought on by Oscar's folly, does not wish his brother to return. "I don't believe in the return of the prodigal, mother," he asserts, "and I don't believe in the parable either. That may be the way in the other world, but it isn't the way in this one, and it shouldn't be—I say it shouldn't be." (Part 5, ch. 13) Nonetheless, years later, the much altered Oscar returns to Iceland as the famous composer, Christian Christiansson, in a manner he had long dreamed of. "He was going back as the prodigal, yet not, like the prodigal, empty-handed and ashamed, but able to make amends, and to wipe the tears from his eyes." (Part 6, ch. 1) Finding Magnus threatened with eviction from his farm, the disguised Oscar offers to pay the mortgage if Elin, Thora's daughter, will come to study music with him. But Elin will not agree, and Oscar realizes in Magnus' home there is a love that he has lost. Meanwhile, Magnus, having lost his religion and become desperate over the years, goads himself, as he drinks, to plan the murder of the stranger for his money. Once the strong, moral brother, who never wavered from goodness, Magnus now permits himself to contemplate the basest sort of crime. But he is spared the consequence of his temptation, for Oscar departs secretly in the night, leaving a gift of 200,000 crowns for Elin and a disclosure of his identity. Wandering lost among the snowy peaks, Oscar realizes that the meaning of life is duty and the meaning of death is pardon for guilt that the world cannot give. He dies in an avalanche seeing a vision of Thora and hearing a voice that says: "FOR THIS MY SON WAS DEAD AND IS ALIVE AGAIN, WAS LOST AND IS FOUND." (Part 7, ch. 8)

Caine's cloying novel is a summation of many of the notions that had, in the later part of the century, become identified with the convention of the prodigal and the returning exile. The prodigal proves to be more noble than those to whom he returns, and he brings not shame, but, like Samuel Warilow, money and comfort. Moreover, though the prodigal does not find forgiveness and love in the home he abandoned, he finds it in the spiritual home all men must finally seek. Many more examples of this convention exist, but they all reveal the same ironic transformation of a simple to a sophisticated moral model. This modification of the prodigal convention indicates, in its way, an unwillingness to accept a traditional, naive faith in the likelihood of redemption, and a questioning of the values of the home and parental authority. More and more it is the adventuresome young man who breaks away from home that merits approval or respect, while those who stay at home grow stale and mean. In this the prodigal's return is like other uses of the return motif.[18] Finally, the use of the convention of the return in Victorian literature supports other evidence that in the more thoughtful literature of the time, but in a good portion of the popular and trivial writing as well, there was manifest, despite apparent approval of order and social harmony, a growing restlessness to escape existing conditions and an increasing belief that hope rested mainly in those who could so break from the confinement of their oppressive society.

CHAPTER ELEVEN

THE ORPHAN

DICKENS' USE OF THE CONVENTION

In his introduction to the Riverside Edition of *David Copperfield*, George Ford calls attention to the prominent use of orphans in the novel: "What, in particular, does the orphaned person want? In a world where unpredictability seems to reign, he needs warm love and affection to compensate for the mother he has lost; security and wisdom to compensate for the father he has lost."[1] There is more to the use of orphans in Dickens than their stumbling into waiting families. Pip's guardians are not both receptive in *Great Expectations*, for Joe Gargery's warmth is neutralized by his wife's frostiness. The Nickleby children, Nicholas and Kate, are almost grown, but without a father to assist them; and, with a mother who is more of a liability than an asset, they are at the mercy of a society represented by their hard-bitten uncle, Ralph Nickleby. After some time, both children attain a comfortable domestic life, but only after they have labored through difficult times. The "orphans" of Dotheboys Hall in this novel signify that Dickens' moral has to do with social as well as merely parental problems. Tattycoram, in *Little Dorrit*, does find a loving family, but she rebels against the Meagles' generosity, only to undergo a painful education regarding the advantages of orphanhood. David Copperfield and Oliver Twist both spend the greater part of their youths as orphans. George Silverman, too, explains that he was an orphan and had to learn to appreciate parenthood through helping another orphaned child while yet a helpless youngster himself. All of these orphans grow into satisfactory people, but in other cases, evolution is uncertain. The orphans in *The Mystery of Edwin Drood*, for example, cannot be judged as to positive growth, though Helena and Neville Landless—if only by the hint of their surname—are less likely to be accommodated to society than the more conventional Rosa Budd, and Edwin Drood himself. And surely Little Nell and Sissy Jupe are in a separate category, representing not only spiritual but imaginative salvation to a degree that Oliver Twist does not attain.

Unlike some other Victorian writers, Dickens does not seem to have a single defining view of the orphan, but uses it to suit his purpose, realizing its effectiveness for pathos and suspense in his novels. In *The Old Curiosity Shop*, both Little Nell and Dick Swiveller are orphans, but there the resemblance ends. Nell, like Oliver Twist, is the untainted soul exiled in the material world but working its way back to its eternal inheritance. The orphaned Swiveller, on the other hand, is only comic since he is already an adult beyond parental care who serves as foil to Nell's circumstances. Dick appears utterly ludicrous when Quilp offers himself as a fatherly substitute for Swiveller's departed parents. In the end, Dick must himself assume a quasi-parental role toward the Marchioness who is first his student, and then a surrogate nurse and parent herself.

Orphanhood signifies self-reliance for Dickens' characters. Just as the swindle frequently forced characters to draw upon their own moral resources, orphanhood obliged characters to assume an authority that would otherwise not be required of them. The result is a frequent inversion of roles. Lucie Manette, for example, lives the life of an orphan until her father is released from prison, whereat she promptly becomes not a daughter, but a parent. In the same way, Jenny Wren, bereft of her mother, becomes the parent of that wicked child, her drunken father. Walter Gay may be the typical self-reliant orphan, in *Dombey and Son*, but Florence Dombey is, ironically, more orphaned because she *has* a parent who neglects her. Mr. Dombey, in his injured pride, strikes the innocent child, expending rage more appropriately directed toward his rebellious wife. It is an awakening for Florence. "She saw she had no father upon earth, and ran out, orphaned, from his house." (ch. 47) It is possible that Dickens, with his sharp eye for all details of his profession, was consciously exploiting the orphan convention in this novel, as he was to do again in *Bleak House*, where the plot turns upon the highly conventional and interrelated devices of orphanhood, inheritance, and disguise.

What seems clear in Dickens' use of the orphan is that the abandoned state provides a singular opportunity. Partial and genuine orphans may go bad for lack of guidance, but they may also make of their isolated condition a basis for solid growth. They may, like Oliver Twist, and Little Nell, be emblems of the soul outcast from eternity, or, like Sissy Jupe, stand for the preservation of the imaginative faculty in man; or, more realistically, like David Copperfield, Pip, and Florence Dombey, they may be offered the chance to shape their own lives, without the bondage of parental direction, though, it is true, without parental love as well.

VARIATIONS OF THE CONVENTION

Orphanhood was not uncommon in the nineteenth century because of the shorter life expectancy, and especially because of the frequent deaths in childbirth. Queen Victoria was fatherless; Albert was motherless.[2] But while orphans might wander the streets unheeded, or labor long hours in mines and factories without attention, in Victorian literature they were used to evoke sympathetic audience responses, as in Amelia Opie's typical production, "The Orphan Boy's Tale." Two poems by John Clare, written early in the century, provide complementary attitudes toward orphaned children. In "The Workhouse Orphan," an old shepherd tells some children the story of Mary Lee who was born illegitimate and raised in a workhouse. She labored hard, in time was seduced and betrayed, then went mad when left destitute with a bastard of her own. This poem, though basically sentimental in presentation, also describes a realistic prospect for unguided orphans in nineteenth-century society. It is not surprising, with this prospect for orphans and the experience of his own youth that Clare concluded, in "On an Infant's Grave," that the dead child was better off dying before it could be corrupted. "Recall'd to heaven's eternal rest, / Ere it knew how to sin."

Children are appealing because of their innocence and spontaneity, but orphans are more effective because of the added pathos of their condition. It is not surprising, then, that this understandable out-growth of the Romantic exaltation of childhood persevered through-out the nineteenth century. It became a stock-in-trade of the maga-zines and journals. For example, in *Household Words* for June, 1850 appeared the poem, "The Orphan's [sic] Voyage Home," describing the homeward sea voyage of two children who do not know that news of their parents' death awaits them at home. But they never complete the voyage, for they die clasping one another, exposed on deck in the cruel winter weather. Never waking, "They reach'd their *home* this starry night!" The poem concludes with a familiar associ-ation of childhood death and heavenly reward.

But in their deep and freezing sleep
   Clasp'd rigid to each other,
In dreams they cried, "The bright
   morn breaks,
   Home! home! is here, my brother!
The Angel Death has been our friend—
   We come! dear Father! Mother!"

This is the sentimentality that came to be expected in novels about children, until in Florence Montgomery's *Misunderstood* (1869) young Humphrey Duncombe's yearning for reunion with his mother in heaven seems thoroughly credible. For the Victorians, an orphan was already half-engaged to heaven because at least one of his par-ents supposedly dwelt there in constant expectation of his arrival. Late in the century, a widespread interest in the occult led to more overt narrative expressions of this view; Mrs. Oliphant could actually describe her Little Pilgrim's reunion with her parents in heaven.[3]

Orphans often added interesting complications to plot-lines. Thus, Colonel Manners in G. P. R. James' *The Gipsy*, Elinor Clare in Han-nah Maria Jones' *The Gipsey Chief*, and Herbert Walsingham and Elizabeth Wimot in the same author's *The Gipsey Girl*, are orphans. Wherever gypsies and inheritances are involved, real and supposed orphans are likely to abound. Real identities are disclosed in the identification of deceased parents of orphans. Many a fictional or-phan was destined for wealth and high estate in the fiction and mel-odrama of the nineteenth century. But, if Tittlebat Titmouse in Warren's *Ten Thousand A-Year* expressed gladness at being an or-phan—a bad sign in itself—other characters would have been happy to discover lost parents rather than remain lonely and exiled off-spring. There is no humor in the orphaned state of Lucy and Henry Bertram in Scott's *Guy Mannering*, and Edgar Ravenswood, though he is a formidable young man at age twenty, would be more comfortable with parents to advise him in *The Bride of Lammermoor*.

The convention of the orphan was neither well developed nor sophisticated. Although distinction was made between the quasi-orphan and the genuine orphan, it did not come to much unless the real orphan were also raised by unloving guardians. Nor was the orphan, as a type, too far removed from the state of children in general. For those who knew the abuses of the age, children might easily be viewed as pathetic. If those children were orphans, as in *Oliver Twist*, Mrs. Trollope's *Michael Armstrong*, and Charlotte Elizabeth's *Helen Fleetwood*, the pathos was more intense.

To be a female and an orphan as well, was to be doubly disadvantaged in an age that valued family and empowered men. Hence female orphans of all ages come to represent, not surprisingly, a vulnerable and isolated virtue. In Bulwer-Lytton's *The New Timon* (1846), Morvale's heart is moved by his discovery of the young orphan, Lucy. Out of pity, he takes her into his care and gradually comes to love her. Morvale himself is a melancholy, isolated man— an Ishmael by his own description—and Lucy's isolation complements his own. Their growing love is upset, however, when Morvale discovers that Lucy's father is living and is his enemy. Only when Arden has died can Morvale return to Lucy; with his beloved alone once more in orphaned innocence Morvale can unite himself with her.

Writers introduce orphaned girls in their stories when they are already nubile and enticing. In such cases, orphanhood may intensify their pathetic appeal. Some orphans fall, presumably because they lack parental guidance, as in Mrs. Gaskell's *Ruth*. There is something erotic in the emotional helplessness of these attractive orphaned girls, even when they remain virtuous. Mary Corby in Kingsley's *Ravenshoe* is a long-suffering, humble orphan, who must suffer the attentions of unappealing suitors attracted by her beauty, before she accepts her true love, Charles Ravenshoe. Mary Thorne in Trollope's *Dr. Thorne* also demonstrates the appeal of the orphaned young woman. Among the most enticing of these figures is Lucy Desborough in Meredith's *The Ordeal of Richard Feverel*. It is the nature of the orphan to endure more than others. And, in most cases, this suffering is finally rewarded. But Meredith did not employ the conventional pattern. Taken from her Edenic surroundings, Lucy discovers that her orphaned youth was more serene than the supposed haven of her marriage. Most stories trace the orphan's struggles toward the security and happiness of marriage, but Lucy's love leads not to the establishment of a new home to obliterate the orphan's yearnings but to hysteria and death—thereby making her own child an orphan destined to suffer its own peculiar agonies. Meredith consciously twists the reader's expectation of the convention to gain his effect. Later he would do the same with Harry Richmond, who, like Dickens' Steerforth, wishes for a father's guidance. Ironically, it is Harry's father who leads him astray into ways nearly resembling Steerforth's mistakes. Only when he is convincingly orphaned, does Harry correctly guide himself.

The use of orphans is especially clear in novels containing more than one well-developed example. Guy and Philip Morville, in *The Heir of Redclyffe*, represent two different approaches to salvation. Guy overcomes a passionate nature, learning discipline all the harder to attain without parental guidance, while Philip learns to accept the limitations of his similarly self-constructed discipline. In George Eliot's *Adam Bede*, both Dinah Morris and Hetty Sorrel are orphans, yet the one learns to replace parental guidance with self-control, while the other, lacking both forms of discipline, lapses into self-indulgences that bring about her ruin. Frequently writers paired their female orphans to indicate the different ways in which those thrown on their own emotional resources might develop. In Wilkie Collins' *The Woman in White*, both Marian Halcombe and Laura Fairlie are orphans. The one is strong, self-reliant, ready for any occasion, and therefore, admirable; the other is soft, yielding, humble, and pathetically loveable. Again, in *No Name*, Collins used a similar pairing. Magdalene is the aggressive, iron-willed sister, while Norah Vanstone is patient and enduring. Both find appropriate mates; both find the consolations of marriage that cancel the sorrow of a lost home, though their approaches to this final resolution are vastly different.

Owen Meredith employs a similar pairing in *Lucile* (1860), where the orphaned Lucile knows many worldly lessons which help her to survive in a society directed by masculine impulses. She must confront those impulses for her own sake and that of others. On the other hand, Constance, also an orphan, filled with love and trust, brings joy to all she meets. Like Eppie in *Silas Marner*, she is the only force able to revive love in a heart chilled by the world. Here, as elsewhere, the two opposing types, equally outcast, equally self-dependent, conclude by serving one another. Lucile can be an agent of good for Constance, just as Marian Halcombe can aid the weak Laura Fairlie, or as Shirley Keeldar and Caroline Helstone in Charlotte Brontë's *Shirley* (1849), in their similarly contrasting manner, contribute to one another those complementary attributes lost with their parents, for the orphaned girl whose bent is toward self-assertion and exertion of the will incorporates the functions of the missing father, while the more yielding, humble and loving girl, assumes the mother's role. The emotional milieu of the lost family is thus reconstructed in the young orphans without the directing authority which might hinder the free development of their individual spirits.

Familial emotional patterns are also recognized in the coupling of male and female orphans. Hence, in Charlotte Brontë's *The Professor* (1857, published posthumously), both William Crimsworth and Frances Henri are orphans highly conscious of their loss, but both have made the most of their forced independence and therefore bring a richer reward to one another when they finally do marry. Although Crimsworth and Frances Henri are equals, Crimsworth acts as the young woman's guide and counsellor, supplying the expected paternal role. This pattern is evident in Eliot's *Felix Holt, The Radical* (1866), when the fatherless Felix undertakes the motherless Esther Lyon's moral education, but the convention is obscured because Esther, although brought up to believe that Rufus Lyon is her father, is, in fact, a true orphan, her real parents both having died years before. Ironically, Esther can offer Rufus genuine filial love only when she learns that he is not her father. Where there is no dependency, love can be freely given. True parents in Eliot, as in other writers of the period, often merit less love than surrogates. Of course, Eliot's orphans are also capable of showing profound emotion. Hence Tertius Lydgate, Dorothea Brooke, and Will Ladislaw, all orphans in *Middlemarch*, are all capable of a generous bestowal of affection. In each case, as well, there is a form of guidance that is lacking, though it is not just parental authority, since Fred Vincy, who has a father, is less satisfactorily disciplined than the others. In *Daniel Deronda* (1876), Deronda, Gwendolen Harleth, and Mirah Lapidoth are the most noteworthy orphans. Gwendolen, without strong paternal guidance, demonstrates a dangerous willfulness, while Deronda, similarly deprived, has matured as a selfless, generous person. Of course, family relations are often obscured and constitute a major element both of plot and theme in this novel.

Literary orphans, though often shut out from love themselves, are given the capability of feeling great emotion and therefore prompting new sentiments in others. Ruth Hilton in *Ruth* (1853) is one obvious example. Mrs. Gaskell explains that it was one of the faults of Ruth's nature "to be ready to make any sacrifices for those who loved her, and to value affection almost above its price," largely because the impressible years of her youth had been so lonely. (ch. 21) This sensitivity to affection leads Ruth to profound gestures of unselfishness and dedication, which in turn beget thankful love from the community she serves. Pippa, in Browning's *Pippa Passes* (1841), in meditating on love, observes that "Lovers grow cold, men learn to hate their wives, / And only parents' love can last our lives." Pippa feels this conviction all the more because she has no parents and her longing is fully evident in her cry, "If I only knew / What was my mother's face—my father, too!" But the orphan's preoccupation with love leads beyond the personal to a higher purpose and Pippa concludes, "Nay, if you come to that, best love of all is God's."[4] For Pippa, God is the final parent whose love may be assured. It is her faith in this love that makes her a dynamic force toward love for as her life touches other lives, they are transformed for the better.

Charlotte Brontë's famous orphans, Jane Eyre and Lucy Snow, are victims of a society that has little concern for the unprotected. Unloved as they are, they establish their faith in God before they feel the enticement of human love. From deprivation, a stronger character emerges and both heroines prove their worth, not through their material success but through the consolidation of their own characters in a firm religious faith. Character growth is also central to Mrs. Browning's *Aurora Leigh* (1857). Having lost her Florentine mother when only four years old, Aurora thereafter "felt a mother-want about the world" (Book 1): her life lacked maternal tenderness. Aurora grows in mental power but does not permit her tender side to manifest itself. At last, the strength and independence of her highpurposed nature proved, she admits, through the pressure of that love her dying father urged upon her, that she has been mistaken, and has repressed her womanly nature, even as she hungered for the woman-liness of her lost mother. With this admission, Aurora becomes a whole woman again, and the orphanhood that left her alone to fash-ion a durable character while depriving her of a requisite tenderness, is ended at last. As usual, orphanhood ends in marriage, and the emotional circuit is complete once more.

Orphanhood served, then, as a symbol of uncompleted character. Literary orphans frequently embody a pervasive sense of yearning for fulfillment of a vague desire usually stipulated as human love. Their condition emphasizes the nature of the human struggle, as in George Gissing's *Workers in the Dawn* (1880), where the orphaned main character must work his way out of the slums to shape his des-tiny. The orphan's isolation and alienation represented the growing sense of exile many felt in the milieu of the materialistic society of nineteenth-century England. That sense of exile might be merely commercial, as with Gissing's late novel, *Born in Exile* (1892), where the central character, Godwin Peak, because "he shares the tastes and interests of the rich, and has nothing in common with his own im-poverished family," as Jacob Korg explains, "feels that he is in the wrong social class, and that he has been 'born in exile.'"[5] His is an emotional orphanhood just as important as the simpler convention of actual deprivation.

The orphan's sense of exile may be a vague emotional longing, as in Tennyson's *The Lover's Tale*, or suggestive of a sense of disinheri-tance and exclusion from society. Thus the bitter persona of Tenny-son's "Locksley Hall," deciding to seek some useful activity in life, asks, "Mother-Age (for mine I knew not) help me as when life be-gun." The central figure of *Maud* is an amplified version of the same type. His orphanhood is both a consequence of the hostile times he lives in and an emblem of the exile that hostility creates for sensitive spirits. The notion of exile could be even more profound, as the cry of the husband who has survived a suicide attempt in which his wife has died in Tennyson's "Despair" suggests.

"O we poor orphans of nothing—alone
    on that lonely shore—
Born of the brainless Nature who knew
    not that which she bore."

For many writers of the time the image of orphanhood suggested man's spiritual alienation, either from a God who had died or from an indifferent nature.

DEEPER MEANINGS

Early in the century, Carlyle's *Sartor Resartus* (1833-34) provided a monumental transformation of the orphan convention to a spiritual and profound symbolism. If Aurora Leigh felt in the complicated world about her the yearning "mother-want" of the orphan, the mysterious Diogenes Teufelsdröckh, delivered to Andreas and Gretchen Futteral in a basket, had felt a related longing.

> Ever, in my distresses and my loneliness, has Fantasy turned, full of longing (*sehnsuchtsvoll*), to that unknown Father, who perhaps far from me, perhaps near, either way invisible, might have taken me to his paternal bosom, there to lie screened from many a woe. Thou beloved Father, dost thou still, shut out from me only by thin penetrable curtains of earthly Space, wend to and fro among the crowd of the living? Or art thou hidden by those far thicker curtains of the Everlasting Night, or rather of the Everlasting Day, through which my mortal eye and out-stretched arms need not strive to reach? Alas, I know not, and in vain vex myself to know. More than once, heart-deluded, have I taken for thee this and the other noble-looking Stranger; and approached him wistfully, with infinite regard; but he too had to repel me, he too was not thou. (Book 2, ch. 1)

This craving to discover a loving and trustworthy authority to which one might give fully of all his will and love leads on to another question of equal importance—"Who am I; what is this Me?" (Book 1, ch. 9) And this speculation is necessary to prepare man for the work that lies before him. If Teufelsdröckh was stripped of all familial trappings and hence was forced by his craving to identify himself with someone or something higher, so each man might derive an equal energy from a similar intellectual disrobing.

Behind the pathos of the orphan is the Romantic concept of the child as an innocent voyager from a purer realm. Hence to Carlyle and his contemporaries the orphan was a reality, but something more as well; it was the symbol of man's outcast state. As the orphan is left free to seek his own way, create his own identity, suffer and overcome his difficulties, and perhaps after all discover that he is heir to a vast, unsuspected fortune; so man, orphaned from the divine, must work his way through the pilgrimage of the world, fashioning his nature into something worthy of the reward that will be his if he but persevere. Moreover, the orphaned soul is safe if it puts its faith in the spiritual father beyond this vale of tears. At the end of Bulwer-Lytton's *Zanoni* (1842), a priest argues that Zanoni and Viola's infant, left orphaned in a French prison, is in no danger, saying "THE FATHERLESS ARE THE CARE OF GOD." (Book 7, ch. 17) That this expression of hope is not merely an assurance of physical safety is made clear in the description of *Zanoni* appended to the novel explaining the child's allegorical significance: "NEW-BORN INSTINCT, while trained and informed by Idealism, promises a preter-human result by its early, incommunicable vigilance and intelligence, but is compelled, by inevitable orphanhood, and the one-half of the laws of its existence to lapse into ordinary conditions." All men are fatherless, striving to harmonize ideals and instincts in this world, Bulwer-Lytton asserts, and there is hope even in his lonely struggle because a fatherly love and eternal home await each spirit beyond death.

This aspect of the orphan convention had far more mundane applications than those presented by Carlyle or Bulwer-Lytton as seen in the main characters of Miss Mulock's *John Halifax, Gentleman* (1856), the orphaned and pure John and his beloved Ursula. Phineas Fletcher, the narrator, marvels that John, "who had never known his father, should uphold so sternly the duty of filial obedience. I think it ought to act as a solemn warning to those who exact so much from the mere fact and name of parenthood, without having in any way fulfilled its duties, that orphans from birth often revere the ideal of that bond far more than those who have known it in reality." And he adds, as though it would be a very rare curiosity, "Always excepting those children to whose blessed lot it has fallen to have the ideal realized." (ch. 7)

Naturally, not all orphans cherished the values so important to Teufelsdröckh and John Halifax, for, if man was an exile in this world, it remained true for some nineteenth-century thinkers that he was a flawed pilgrim. Carlyle acknowledged as much in providing his character with such an evocative name. Yet Teufelsdröckh labored only for the good. A contrary example occurs in Emily Brontë's

Wuthering Heights (1847), where Heathcliffe, an orphan whose origins are totally unknown, displays from the very first associations that are scarcely divine. Mr. Earnshaw himself remarks to his reluctant wife, " 'you must e'en take it as a gift of God, though it's as dark almost as if it came from the devil.' " (ch. 4) And, thanks to the circumstances of his youth, it is the devilish rather than the divine side of Heathcliffe that matures.

There was room, then, for error. The mysterious orphan might go astray, might receive a fortune only to abuse it, might lust after flesh and goods instead of the ideals described as his proper aim, or mistake the nature of that spiritual aim. Heathcliffe is a gothic variation upon a theme that could be worked at more commonplace levels. Thus Meredith presented in his partially orphaned Harry Richmond almost a parody of the yearning Teufelsdröckh; for Harry, too, yearns to discover his lost, glorious parent. In this case, however, the lost father is no source of salvation, but a mere charlatan. Moreover, it is not from divinity, but from nature that Meredith sees man estranged. Nor is that parent glorious and inevitably redeeming. In truth, no orphanage is possible for Meredith, for we bear our parents within us, as we bear the elements of nature. It was not necessarily social embarrassment alone that led Meredith to cloak his own origins in mystery, but perhaps a desire, reiterated in his novels, to be the creator of his own identity. Ultimately, one's fidelity is to nothing more than the integrity of nature within oneself. Hence, much as Sir Everard Romfrey, in *Beauchamp's Career* (1874-76), might wish to groom his orphaned nephew, Nevil Beauchamp, to inherit his earldom and his opinions, it is clear from the beginning that Nevil's native sentiments will eventually set him against his uncle. What Meredith's orphans and semi-orphans strive toward is an enfranchisement from the mistaken directions put upon them by guardians or society at large. Evan Harrington *is* a gentleman, but he must learn that to be a gentleman is to have qualities, not a social station. Richard Feverel achieves self-knowledge at the expense of all he cherishes, and his life is wasted. Harry Richmond must clear his head of intellectual vapors, come to value his true parentage in nature, and then fashion what he discovers in himself into a worthy character. The same is true for Nevil Beauchamp. It had long been evident in Victorian literature that orphanhood was as much an opportunity as it was a misfortune. For Meredith, the former value far outweighed the latter,

while in Butler's *The Way of All Flesh*, the orphaned characters are
the most fortunate, like Towneley; while Ernest Pontifex, the central character, must overcome the misfortune of having parents.

The orphan, as Carlyle showed clearly, could have broad and suggestive dimensions. Some of these dimensions are implied in Mrs.
Humphry Ward's *Robert Elsmere* (1888). The orphans we meet here
—the Leyburn sisters, Robert Elsmere himself, and even Squire
Wendover—are all fatherless adults when introduced. None of these
semi-orphans suffers want, none expresses the longing for a lost father:
it is spiritual, not familial authority that has somehow been taken
away. The earnest protagonists of the novel are intellectually orphaned because the faith in which they were reared has been called
into serious question. Squire Wendover, who suffered a breakdown
after his father's suicide, is an appropriate representative of one who
has turned from all the abruptly extinguished belief of the past to invest his thoughts in the advanced scepticism of German philosophy.
Edward Langham has grown out of an atmosphere of Calvinism into
a brilliant but indecisive maturity—with no authority to guide him.
Catherine Leyburn, devoted to the memory of her father, has assumed the paternal role in her all-female household, and, appropriately, she clings to the old forms of faith as earnestly as she does to
thoughts of her father, and maintains his religious convictions, described as Evangelical with a dash of Quakerism. The most important figure in this landscape of orphans is Robert Elsmere himself.
He is more flexible in his thoughts and in his character than Catherine, who eventually becomes his wife, and he suffers most acutely
the awareness of his spiritual orphanhood. Exposed to such varying
influences as the genial theistic Grey and the unbelieving Wendover,
both of them willing paternal surrogates, Elsmere is able to construct
from the intellectual chaos around him a new firmness, mainly because, even at the nadir of his strength, when his soul is "stripped of
its old defences," he does not feel himself "utterly forsaken." (ch. 27)
The influence of Henry Grey prevails and Robert's convictions solidify once more. Just as Grey's influence represents Elsmere's acceptance of a terrestrial replacement for his lost father, his rededication
to a workable form of Christianity represents his spiritual rebirth.

Orphaned from divine authority by the time in which he lives,
Elsmere has, through his own exertions, recovered that lost Father.
He has done what is impossible for the physically orphaned. He has

been born again in spirit and has provided himself once more with the divine parent the lack of which threatened to make his life a void. Now, like many another fictional orphan, he can proceed to minister to his brothers, who are equally deluded into feeling that they have been orphaned from God. The romantic convention of the orphan, used by most writers mainly as a convenience or to illustrate a secular moral, here acquires a more exalted purpose. Elsmere has found the Father that Teufelsdröckh so eagerly sought to discover.

REVERSING THE CONVENTION

But not all questing orphans found the consolation of Robert Elsmere. Some did try to recover the domestic happiness of youth. Peter Pasquier (Ibbetson), in *Peter Ibbetson* (1892), orphaned at the age of twelve, later manages to return to his youth to live again in the comforting atmosphere of the family. This, however, was fantasy. Elsmere's solution may have been spiritual, but it was not ethereal. None could hope to go back in reality to a desirable past, and, as the century progressed, there was a growing sentiment that even the imaginative recovery of the past was not viable; the only turning would be a turning within.

Dorian Gray, in Wilde's *The Picture of Dorian Gray* (1890), is the orphaned victim of a conventional romantic tale: a runaway marriage, a contrived duel, a stern parent, a broken-hearted widow. This offspring of what amounts to popular romance and melodrama, matures as a beautiful being with great personal potential. But he falls under the influence of Sir Henry Wotton, whose only values are esthetic and self-indulgent. Under his tutelage, the otherwise unadvised Dorian, gradually succumbs to a life dedicated to the gratification of the senses. He plays the part of a fairy-tale hero, but as Prince Charming he brings desolation in his wake. He is the hero of drawing room fiction, but his adventures sour the lives of others. He becomes the haunted soul of gothic fable, but even the haunting is not sincere. Finally he plays the more genuine role of the murderer in a popular murder tale. In effect, Dorian has recapitulated the roles so familiar to readers of Victorian literature: he comes to represent the gradual debasement of literature, or art, in his own person. It is entirely fitting that, aware of the degraded condition to which he has fallen, he should die into his own violated and putrid art. The necessary guidance and the necessary purpose have been lacking; fathered by romance, but abandoned to a banal society, Dorian ends as a newspaper report and a ghost story.

But, if it is too much to imagine that Wilde meant to present, in Dorian, the history of the decline of English literature of the nineteenth century, it is not assuming too much to say that Dorian surely represents the orphaned spirit of beauty in a gross, unesthetic age. He is the principle of beauty admired by lovely women, by the cynical Henry Wotton, and the zealous Basil Hallward. But there is no one to guide this principle of beauty to any useful end. Dorian remains estranged and isolated. If others were orphans in fact, building characters out of their own inward powers to meet and command unlovely external conditions, or spiritual orphans striving to rediscover a lost divine authority, or mere psychological orphans yearning to recover in dreams the love long lost in the real world, Dorian is orphaned loveliness, doomed in an age interested more in the meretricious than the genuine, to be destroyed by his own boundless and wasted potential.

But, grim as Wilde's conclusion may have been, there was to appear a yet more desolate and definitive image of the orphan. Hardy's *Jude the Obscure* (1895) is definitive in its use of the orphan convention mainly because it self-consciously sums up much of what that convention stood for, and ironically transforms it. Superficially Jude is an orphan like many other Victorian orphans. George H. Ford compares Jude's loneliness to David Copperfield's. In both novels the child is seen completely abandoned. But, Ford sums up, "David can fight to win, whereas 'the predestinate Jude,' as Hardy calls him, is doomed to lose."[6] And Jude does lose. From the beginning he senses that he has been introduced into a world that does not want him. His morose great-aunt informs him that he'd have been better off not to have been born. He feels hated and despised by the world and, in maturity, concludes, "Well—I'm an outsider to the end of my days!" (Part 6, ch. 1) Sue Bridehead, too, "craves to get back to the life of . . . infancy and its freedom," though Hardy gives little indication that her life before being orphaned was any happier than Jude's. What is certain is that she too feels outcast and alone and describes herself as an "Ishmaelite." (Part 3, ch. 2)

Jude does not start out isolated from hope and faith. Indeed, his pilgrimage to Christminster is a secular version of the orphan's progress to happiness in this world or the soul's pilgrimage to heaven, patterns which appeared clearly enough in the novels of Dickens. But Jude's pilgrimage is destined to end in disillusionment and despair. Having worked his way to Christminster, he is rejected by the city. It is as though Christian were to be turned away at the Heavenly City. By the time Jude returns to the city a second time, "hardly a shred of the beliefs with which he had first gone up to Christminster now remain[ed] with him. He was mentally approaching the position which Sue had occupied when he first met her." (Part 5, ch. 7)

If Robert Elsmere had been able to reconstruct a viable faith and rediscover a divine authority, Jude is merely stripped of the old convictions, while no new ones serve to reestablish any authority for him. Jude is almost an ironic parody of Elsmere and his difficult, but fortunate career. Whereas Elsmere begins with advantages of birth and education and never, in his worst moments, feels utterly forsaken, Jude craves education and seeks to advance himself socially but fails and lapses into a feeling of absolute abandonment. Hardy intensifies the dismal character of Jude's spiritual orphanhood by having the initially unbelieving Sue suddenly revert to the very doctrines that Jude has so painfully cast off. Sue's grasping at creeds does not, however, represent a consolation or a return to a divine paternal authority. Instead, it signifies a penance and carries with it only pain, for in turning to old creeds, she turns as well to old Phillotson, her former husband, a man old enough to be her father, for whom she feels a powerful physical aversion.

There is much talk of adultery in the novel, but, in a sense, the real subject is incest. Sue's relations with Jude should have remained platonic, for they are truly two parts of the same whole, representing the union of Christian and pagan, of mind and sense. And in the collapse of their union, Hardy indicates that there cannot be a blending of these dualities in the world of nineteenth-century England, if ever. Moreover, when Sue returns to Phillotson, she forces herself to another form of incest. Her union with Jude was a violation of the self at the highest level. Her marriage with Phillotson is a violation of both her intellectual and physical self; with Phillotson the use of her body is an abomination and accordingly she becomes drawn and wraithlike. The sharing of intellect between Sue and the schoolmaster is mechanical and perfunctory, like the classroom atmosphere that surrounds them. Phillotson is nothing more than her own highest self stultified into the conventional, and by returning to him she commits incest upon her own nature.

If Hardy was unwilling to permit his orphans a rewarding discovery of divine parentage, he was equally unwilling to allow them the glimpse of natural parentage that Meredith permitted his more secular isolatoes. When Jude declares, "I doubt if I have anything more for my present rule of life than following inclinations which do me and nobody else any harm, and actually give pleasure to those I love best" (Part 6, ch. 1), it might appear that Jude has learned to accept himself as a child of nature, and that he is on the way to reintegration through a recognition of that parentage, as is the case with so many of Meredith's characters. But to suppose such a hopeful possibility is to forget the reiterated warning throughout the novel that nature is cruel and merciless and that the "beggarly question of parentage" means nothing at a social or a universal level. (Part 5, ch. 3) Sue recognizes this truth when she discovers her murdered children. We trusted our natural instincts, she says, "And now Fate has given us this stab in the back for being such fools as to take Nature at her word!" (Part 6, ch. 2)

Nothing works. There is no way for these orphans, emblems of man's isolated, disinherited condition, to place themselves in harmony with a higher authority. And that is simply because, for Hardy, if there is a higher force, it too is no authority, but is a random activity. To intensify the orphaned isolation of his central characters, Hardy incorporates a perverse irony. Little Father Time, the child of Jude's marriage with Arabella, despite his having parents and being loved, is every bit as isolated as Jude and Sue—more so, in that he represents a complete nihilism. When Father Time murders the children born of Jude and Sue's love and then kills himself, he has, in effect, orphaned his parents anew. Now the children are more ancient than their parents, and by their deaths make their parents more isolated and outcast than before. They have been cut off from every consolation in their own memories and their own hopes and now the culminating blow is that they are cut off as well from any prospect in the past or in the future. There are no new directions left and so Jude lapses into stagnation and Sue turns back to the hateful marriage she once abandoned with such apparent wisdom. Only one conclusion remains: Jude expresses it as he nears his death: *"Let the day*

*perish wherein I was born, and the night in which it was said, There
is a man child conceived.*" (Part 6, ch. 11)

The convention of the orphan by no means ends with Hardy, but
Hardy's use of it surely signalizes a low point beyond which simple
faith in the trusty convention was no longer possible. And the convention, for the most part, had been, throughout the century, concerned with simple faith. Although there does not seem to be any
clear development of the orphan figure, it does seem apparent that
beyond those writers who used the convention merely to evoke sympathy and pathos, or to provide a complication in the working out of
a plot, there were authors anxious to utilize the figure of the orphan
to point a moral or suggest a religious or philosophical dimension in
their stories.[7] Hardy's use of the convention illustrates how conscious
he and others were of the manner in which it operated. It also illustrates the mounting recognition of how the convention had failed.
His exploitation of it was meant to signify that fact beyond doubt.

CHAPTER TWELVE

INHERITANCE

ASPECTS OF THE CONVENTION

To the reader of nineteenth-century fiction, the subject of inheritance is so familiar as to be almost offensive. By the time Sir Walter Scott came to employ the device in novels such as *Guy Mannering* and *The Antiquary*, it was already an over-worked device. J. T. Christie summarizes the former novel as the familiar story "of the long-lost heir, kidnapped in youth (in this case by smugglers), brought up in ignorance of his identity, and victimized by a rascally attorney whose interest it is to keep him out of his inheritance."[1] Most certainly Scott was utilizing a time-tested plot device to insure a certain degree of attention and suspense. The inheritance is not large; more significant for Harry Bertram is the discovery of his true identity. Scott emphasizes the irony of Bertram's situation, by having him, while still in his identity as Vanbeest Brown, disembark in Scotland on the property that should be his. " 'And the powerful barons who owned this blazonry,' thought Bertram, pursuing the usual train of ideas which flows upon the mind at such scenes,—'do their posterity continue to possess the lands which they had laboured to fortify so strongly? or are they wanderers, ignorant perhaps even of the fame

268

or power of their forefathers, while their hereditary possessions are held by a race of strangers?' " (ch. 41) The outcome of the numerous intrigues and conflicts is that Harry Bertram does recover the Ellangowan estates, and, more important, his identity as a descendent of a noble family.

Inheritance is of greater significance, as the title suggests, in Susan Ferrier's novel, *Inheritance* (1824), where Gertrude St. Clair inherits the wealthy Rossville estate, being supposed the only offspring of Thomas St. Clair, a member of the Rossville clan who was exiled because he had contracted an unsuitable marriage.[2] Influenced by her ambitious mother and an affection for the elegant but undependable Colonel Delmour, Gertrude, who is being corrupted by her wealth and social position, learns that she is not Thomas St. Clair's daughter, and therefore not an heiress. Colonel Delmour promptly deserts her, being committed to the things of this world, while Edward Lyndsay, having a higher interest in Gertrude, stands by her in her adversity and eventually wins her love.

One of the principal conflicts in this novel is between Delmour's material world and Lyndsay's spiritual one. Inheritance of the Rossville estate signals a shift to the material world and threatens spiritual demise for anyone unprepared to subordinate wealth to spiritual concerns. But Gertrude recovers a proper moral perspective, learning once more to value the spiritual. "It, indeed, required no very high sense of religion, at such a time, to feel the utter insignificance of mere worldly greatness—and to acknowledge that its grandeurs are vapours—its pleasures illusions—its promises falsehoods." (Vol. 3, ch. 31) From this point, it is not far to a recognition that man's true inheritance is not a transient earthly one, but permanent and spiritual. Accordingly, Gertrude unites herself with the spokesman of faith and morality, Edward Lyndsay, and the novel closes happily. Replacing the "glare of romantic passion" with "the calm radiance of piety and virtue," Gertrude blesses "the day that had deprived her of her earthly Inheritance," to which she is nonetheless restored "with a mind enlightened as to the true uses and advantages of power and prosperity." (Vol. 3, ch. 35) Thus, in gaining her spiritual inheritance, Gertrude has not really been obliged to yield her earthly dower. Similarly, in *Marriage* (1818), Miss Ferrier provides the virtuous Mary Douglas and her faithful lover, Charles Lennox, with a windfall inheritance from old Sir Sampson, the family enemy. To emphasize the irony of this justice, the news of the inheritance comes to the lovers on their wedding day. Clearly, Ferrier is using the inheritance to reward her model characters for their fidelity and virtue. In the novels of other writers to follow, as in *Inheritance*, loss of material pleasures is only temporary; they are often restored after the chastened hero or heroine comes to appreciate those pleasures for what they really are.

Ordinarily this convention bore little or no spiritual significance and served only to heighten story interest. Following Scott's example in *Guy Mannering*, romancers often associated surprise inheritances with gypsy plotting and intervention. In G. P. R. James' *The Gipsy* (1835), for example, Edward De Vaux's threatened loss of inheritance through his father's crime is merely an additional means of placing the upright young man in an involuted quandary of pain and distress before the inevitable unravelling of difficulties reveals that his father has not murdered his brother and Edward's inheritance is not in jeopardy. The inheritance convention serves mainly to threaten the extreme inconvenience that deprivation of wealth and station would occasion. Beyond this social danger, there is no message.

Inheritance and gypsies are again associated in Hannah Maria Jones' *The Gipsey Girl* (1836-37) and *The Gipsey Chief* (1840), where the one simply provides a needed financial windfall to stimulate the plot and the other allows for complications of identity. In the latter novel, for example, Edward Hatherleigh discovers that he is not, as he supposed, the son of a scoundrel leader of a gypsy band, but Lionel Moreton, the son of a respectable gentleman and heir to that gentleman's fortune. Again, the happy, secure marriage closes all. Gypsies and inheritances are similarly entangled in novels such as William Harrison Ainsworth's *Rookwood* (1834), and, on the other side of the Atlantic, Joseph Holt Ingraham's *The Gipsy of the Highlands* (1843). This coupling of the inheritance with gypsies persisted throughout the century. Mrs. Oliphant's *The Story of Valentine and his Brother* (1875) is a predictable tale of twin brothers separated in infancy by their gypsy mother who later become involved in complications concerning their own and other claims to a rich estate. A later example of this combination is Francis Hindes Groome's *Kriegspiel* (1896), in which Lionel Glenham learns that he is not a gypsy's son, but the legitimate heir of Sir Charles Glenham. Unlike earlier tales of this kind, there is no union of lovers for which the inheritance serves as the social guarantee of success and happiness.

Lionel recovers his true identity and his inheritance too late, for Marjory Avenel, his beloved, has entered a convent and, as Christ's bride, cannot be his. It is a conventional conclusion typically altered by the preoccupations and moods of the nineties.

Typical use of the inheritance convention can be found anywhere in the literature of the nineteenth century. The anticipation of inheritance plays its part, comically, in the case of Dick Swiveller, in *The Old Curiosity Shop*, perfunctorily at the end of *Martin Chuzzlewit*, and more seriously elsewhere, as in *Bleak House* and *Our Mutual Friend*. In Mrs. Oliphant's *Passages in the Life of Mrs. Margaret Maitland of Sunnyside, written by Herself* (1849), Grace Maitland seeks to claim her inheritance from an unscrupulous father. Charles Ravenshoe, in Henry Kingsley's *Ravenshoe* (1861), endures the usual trials of the young man whose identity is uncertain and who must suffer hardships and adventures before he is discovered to be the authentic heir of a large property, and thereafter can marry the woman of his choice. In Ouida's *Under Two Flags* (1867), Bertie Cecil is legally entitled to the rich family estate of Royallieu, but because he has changed his identity and exiled himself from Europe, the estate goes to his unworthy younger brother, for whose crime Bertie has been held guilty. Ultimately Berkeley confesses his guilt and Bertie returns to Royallieu and marries the woman who formerly seemed unattainable. A variation of this pattern occurs in Dutton Cook's *A Prodigal Son* (1863) where Wilford Hadfield is disinherited by his father who passes on the family estates to his younger son. In this case, Stephen wishes to share with Wilford who, however, cannot accept generosity that contradicts his father's intention. There is a slight variation on the inheritance motif in Miss Mulock's *John Halifax, Gentleman* (1856) in that the needed inheritance comes to the virtuous John and his wife Ursula after they are married and at a point when John gravely needs assistance.

Obviously the inheritance may be read as a providential sign of approval, but aside from this moral touch, it is primarily a convenience of plot. This is true of Thackeray's use of the convention. At the end of *The Adventures of Philip* (1861-62), old Lord Ringwood's will is accidentally discovered and Philip Firmin inherits a comfortable sum. It is an easy way for Thackeray to conclude his novel, while indicating some justice for Philip, who has suffered financially and otherwise throughout the novel. In *The Newcomes* (1853-55) there are many examples of the inheritance convention. Rosa Mackenzie's inheritance of James Binnie's money serves one of the grim financial themes of the novel, for the money is invested in the Bundelcund Banking Co., a deceitful speculation. The money that Ethel Newcome receives from Lady Kew seems to carry as well an unpleasant heritage of attitudes. Like Gertrude St. Clair, in Susan Ferrier's *Inheritance*, Ethel's character is endangered through the possession of material wealth. Like Gertrude, Ethel is spared moral collapse by discovering her vanity and its superficiality. Thereafter, she becomes humble and seeks to serve others. Clive Newcome's surprise inheritance from Lady Newcome, his aunt, resembles Philip Firmin's late acquisition of wealth, for, in this case too, the money is long deserved and will clearly be well employed. Again, it is mainly an execution of justice to a favorite character.

The many moral complications and resolutions growing out of the inheritance convention included some interesting variations. In Charlotte Yonge's *The Heir of Redclyffe* (1853) Philip Morville inherits the family estate but does not feel worthy of it and is therefore reluctant to accept it. He suffers from guilt for having been the cause of his cousin Guy Morville's death. Nonetheless, he does accept the inheritance and is therefore enabled to marry Laura Edmonstone. Both have been guilty of injudicious behavior and others have suffered in consequence. Now both are chastened and humbled, and though they do marry and are reasonably content, and Philip goes on to become a respectable Member of Parliament, they can never be truly happy partly because they realize that the inheritance which makes their life possible should never have been theirs. This inheritance brings not happiness and fulfillment, but simple comfort and a persistent sense of duty. But in most cases, the convention was primarily used to further the plot. This is largely the case in *Ralph the Heir* (1870-71), of which Trollope observed, "I have always thought it to be one of the worst novels I have written." (*Autobiography*, ch. 19) In Charles Reade's *Put Yourself In His Place* (1870), there is the usual revelation-of-identity scene in which Henry Little, a young, inventive artisan, is identified as Squire Raby's nephew. The squire offers Henry the position of heir, but for certain reasons of honor and interest, Henry refuses. Instead, with the aid of a Philanthropic Society, he sets up as an independent master of a tool shop, for he is determined to make his own way.[3]

WILKIE COLLINS

Not many Victorian novelists departed from the usual view that an inheritance was welcome when it came. Wilkie Collins based more than one novel on the desire to recover an inheritance falsely or mistakenly assigned. In *The Woman in White* (1859-60), Collins pointed out how important the subject of inheritance was to his tale. "I warn all the readers of these lines," Vincent Gilmore writes, "that Miss Fairlie's inheritance is a very serious part of Miss Fairlie's story." ("Narrative of Vincent Gilmore," part 3) The details of the inheritance are complex, but it is perhaps enough to note that it is because of the inheritance that Sir Percival Glyde and the oily Count Fosco establish their conspiracy to acquire the money by persuading the authorities that Laura Fairlie, by then Lady Glyde, is dead. They do this by making it appear that she, rather than her look-alike, Anne Catherick, the woman in white, has died. Sir Percival's "Secret" also involves a falsely acquired inheritance, for he is actually illegitimate with no title to his property. He has falsified public documents in order to conceal his true legal position, and, appropriately, he meets his death in attempting to destroy the evidence of his misdeeds. With Sir Percival dead, the "heir whose rights he had usurped was the heir who would now have the estate."

The convention of the inheritance in this novel serves almost exclusively as motivation in a complicated, skillfully-drawn plot, although it also had moral overtones. In the best scheme of things, those who deserve high estate inherit it. When that scheme is subverted, complications ensue, but the correct order eventually will be restored. The inheritance enabled Collins to show one way for the just scheme to right itself. The true heir comes to possess the Blackwater estate so evilly usurped by Sir Percival, and Limmeridge House, originally destined for Laura Fairlie's possession, is guaranteed to her and her offspring when she bears her true love, Walter Hartright, a son, who is also called, "Mr. Walter Hartright—*the Heir of Limmeridge.*"

In *No Name* (1862), Collins introduced an interesting variation upon the conventionalities of disinheritance. After a life of domestic, but unsanctioned happiness, Mr. Vanstone is freed by the death of his first wife to marry the mother of his children. Mr. Vanstone dies in a railway accident and the newly legalized Mrs. Vanstone dies soon after from the shock. Ironically, the children of this relationship, Magdalen and Norah, are legally disinherited because their father's will, made before his marriage to their mother and unaltered before his sudden death, is invalidated by that very marriage. The girls are thrown on the mercy of a relative whose callous selfishness prompts Magdalen to devote herself to the recovery of the Combe-Raven property. In the process, she gives herself up to base deceptions and marginally criminal activities. Nonetheless, she fails to regain the inheritance deprived her by chance. Norah, on the other hand, makes no attempt to recover the money, but resigns herself to her changed circumstances. As poetic justice would have it, therefore, it is finally Norah who is instrumental in recovering the heritage. "Openly and honorably, with love on one side and love on the other, Norah had married the man who possessed the way to the event." ("Last Scene," ch. 3)

If, in *No Name*, identity and inheritance are closely entangled, in *Armadale* (1864-65) the inheritance convention serves as an introduction to the greater problem of identity, destiny and self-discovery. The complications and evils of this story grow out of the offenses committed when Allan Wentmore inherits the Armadale estates and takes the Armadale name, thereby driving the disinherited Allan Armadale vengefully to woo and win the lady Wentmore desires. In turn, the new Allan Armadale causes his namesake's death by drowning. The consequences of these crimes are borne by the following generation in the persons of the two Allan Armadales, one of whom is known as Ozias Midwinter. The main function of the inheritance thereafter is as a lure to the scheming and vindictive Miss Gwilt. She fails in her aim to acquire the Thorpe Ambrose estate, and it remains in the hands of Allan Armadale, enabling him to marry faithful Eleanor Milroy.

But, important as the inheritance is in this regard, it serves another function, for the inheritance truly at issue in the novel is the inheritance of evil in man's nature. At one point Collins humorously observes that the "daughters of Eve still inherit their mother's merits and commit their mother's faults. But the sons of Adam, in these latter days, are men who would have handed the famous apple back with a bow, and a "Thanks, no; it might get me into a scrape." (Second Book, ch. 9) And, it is a daughter of Eve, Miss Gwilt, who embodies the crude desires and lust for money that characterized the previous generation in the story. The two Allan Armadales of the subsequent generation demonstrate a kinder and nobler, if not always wiser, behavior; and the love and friendship that they share proves too strong for the evil forces at work in the novel. Miss Gwilt fails in her plot because of her love for Midwinter. At the close of the novel the two young men seal once more the rift in human brotherhood that their unlucky forebears had occasioned. Ozias Midwinter can ask his alter-ego if he is convinced that "I, too, am standing hopefully on the brink of a new life, and that while we live, brother, your love and mine will never be divided again?" (Epilogue) It is a long way from Cain's venom to this cordial address.

THE INHERITANCE AND MORAL WORTH

The convention of the inheritance was, then, though used largely as a technical convenience, also a satisfactory moral barometer. In *Jane Eyre* (1847), for example, Jane inherits wealth from an uncle in Madiera just when her circumstances have reached their nadir. In sharing this wealth with her newly discovered relatives, the Rivers family, she gains more than money; she gains human love and the comforts of home and domestic intimacy. Jane has known how to use her unexpected wealth. Others must learn, more uncomfortably, the meaning of inheritance. In Samuel Warren's *Ten Thousand A-Year* (1841), inheritance is a major issue. The totally undeserving Tittlebat Titmouse—a nasty little fop of slight intelligence and less manners—is awarded the Yatton estate and quickly wastes it, making himself profligate and miserable in the process. Titmouse himself has moments when he acknowledges a sense of imposture. Meanwhile, the dispossessed Aubrey family, the true heirs of Yatton, preserve their high moral tone. Charles Aubrey proves his moral fitness by showing that he can go into the world and marshal financial support. The Aubreys, by their moral strength, deserve to manage the wealth of the land. Aubrey demonstrates abilities independent of the privilege and perquisites associated with the possession of an estate worth £ 10,000 a year. Such proof may have seemed necessary in a time when the landed aristocracy were altogether too frequently given to the abuse rather than the implementation of large fortunes. Contrarily, Titmouse proves, by his wasteful and dissolute behavior, that there is more to social predominance than wealth. Ultimately, the Aubreys return to Yatton and Titmouse is exposed as a false claimant. All of the confusion stems from the ambitious machinations of a scheming lawyer, Gammon. England is, once more, in the hands of those who love it and are worthy to own and govern it. The Gammons and Titmouses, horrible presages of a base and banal future, are ousted in favor of those virtues which made England great.

Earthly and spiritual inheritance are not easily separated in the literature of the Victorian period, as Charles Aubrey's resigned reflection indicates when he consoles himself with the thought that man is on "a long journey . . . he is still journeying on, along a route which he cannot mistake, to the point of his destination, his journey's end—the shores of the vast, immeasurable, boundless ocean of eternity—HIS HOME!" (Vol. 2, ch. 4) Thus, when Lionel Stevenson refers to the "overworked theme of the missing heir" in *Oliver Twist*, he slights the many variations possible in this convention.[4] In *Oliver Twist*, Dickens did much more than retell the story of a lost heir who achieves his proper inheritance. He added great depth to the convention and his story of the unfortunate orphan became, as Steven Marcus has observed, a parable; in this "Parish Boy's Progress," Oliver, like Christian, in *A Pilgrim's Progress*, travels through a world of confusion and sin, to achieve his proper inheritance.[5] It is in its way a parallel to the journey that Charles Aubrey described in *Ten Thousand A-Year*, except that the final destination is not named, but merely implied. Oliver is a figure in a parable, representing the Christian soul seeking to discover its identity and inheritance together. That this discovery should be presented in mundane, commercial terms was not uncharacteristic in a time when wealth and faith were frequently associated.

If a comfortable inheritance was the just due of innocence in *Oliver Twist*, by the time Dickens wrote *Bleak House* (1852-53), his attitude had changed: man's inheritance now was more the suffering and sweat of the brow promised to Adam than the golden streets of heaven offered by a more benign doctrine. The things of this world are slippery temptations, not certain parallels of just reward. The inheritance of *Bleak House* is of this world and earthly, and being earthly, it is corrupt. The expectation of wealth corrupts those who wait in attendance upon it. There is no earthly inheritance that is worth the ignominy necessary to achieve it. Only the spiritual inheritance of love is of value in this stern novel, and only those who can see beyond material concerns are capable of appreciating or inheriting the true treasures.

In *Our Mutual Friend* (1864-65), John Harmon actually refuses a large inheritance because he is more concerned with finding himself than with acquiring wealth. If Oliver Twist's progress was from innocence to innocence through evil, John Harmon's is from innocence to awareness through pain. As John Harmon, he does not want an inheritance that is only dust. In fact, the whole message of the novel is that man's fundamental inheritance is no more than dust—mortality. Much of the story is concerned with origins. Individuals seek to hide or exploit their origins, depending upon their social status, but Dickens makes it abundantly clear that the origin of all men is in the primeval slime. It is for each individual to find his way to something more. Consequently, John Harmon cannot simply inherit the Harmon dust by marrying a woman he does not know. Above all else, he must preserve his integrity. Man's only hope is to strive upward from the slime of predatory feelings and ambitions and to consolidate a personal strength and private heritage. When Rokesmith learns how to transmute the dross of material existence to gold, he is ready to receive the Harmon inheritance and to pass on what he has learned to the fallible, but also perfectible Bella.

In *Our Mutual Friend*, Dickens used the convention of the inheritance psychologically, and even metaphysically, to reveal mankind's illusions and to show how to overcome those illusions. Although Oliver was passive in finally receiving his just inheritance, and the correct inheritance in *Bleak House* came about outside the courts, in *Our Mutual Friend*, no inheritance is of value until love transforms it, and anything that love transforms automatically becomes the inheritance of which man, at his best, is worthy. For the rest, men must console themselves with the knowledge that dust is the inheritance for all those who have not earned a higher reward.

In Meredith's *Evan Harrington* (1860), Evan's actual inheritance is his father's debt which he must repay. Beyond this, however, is a subtle inheritance of deception, for he is heir to a misrepresentation which places him in an unjustified social position. Though more than the equal of the men of rank that he meets, Evan finds himself in social circumstances that do not permit the immediate acknowledgment of his natural nobility. Melchizedek Harrington, his father, could move in the most exalted circles because he was a remarkable man. Evan lives among the upper classes some time before he eventually discovers it is his nature, not his social status, by which he must stand or fall. While his sister Louisa schemes to acquire some portion of the Beckley Court inheritance, Evan, through kindness and gentle good will, inherits what no scheming could win. Because Julianne Bonner loved and admired Evan, despite his low origins, she left the rich bequest to him, and he proves himself worthy of it by returning it once more to those who are most properly its owners. This act, in itself, testifies that Evan is as noble as the Jocelyns. They acknowledge his high nature and accordingly, he is admitted to their ranks.

With Meredith, the concept of inheritance remains at the level of simple justice and social standing. Evan tested, proves that he is worthy of all that material wealth in this novel represents, despite his unimpressive origins as a tailor's son. There is more than poetic justice here, since Evan has earned his inheritance by a long struggle to subdue his more objectionable impulses. The poetic justice in Trollope's *Dr. Thorne* (1858) makes a somewhat similar point. The young lovers, Mary Thorne and Francis Gresham, are prevented from marrying for certain social reasons. It is therefore fitting that Mary who, though illegitimate, has shown that she is not heir to any moral taint, inherits the money that makes her marriage possible. The money that only made the Scatcherd family miserable, now insures the happiness of a virtuous relationship.

In Victorian literature, the poor, by virtue and high-mindedness could prove themselves worthy of the highest award that nineteenth-century England could think to bestow—land, and wealth, and married bliss. In a similar way, the wealthy, by proving that, despite their wealth, they had the moral fiber and the practical ability to live fruitful lives, merited the same award of land and wealth that was their ordinary privilege. Just as Mary Thorne earned her wealth, and Charles Aubrey or Laura Fairlie merited the high position that inheritance in the ordinary course of things allowed them, so John Harmon formed his character to receive the wealth not so nobly won by his forebear. And this is the best function of the convention of inheritance in Victorian literature—to show that all that this earth offers by way of wealth, position and comfort is of little meaning compared to the greater inheritance promised by the Christian faith. As early as Susan Ferrier's *Inheritance* this had been clear, and it remained evident even to those who occupied themselves with far more material concerns. In Mary Elizabeth Braddon's *Charlotte's Inheritance* (1868), the involved legal pursuits and unravellings of family histories lead, after all, to one conclusion—that material wealth, despite what the greater number of Miss Braddon's characters clearly believe, is insignificant in the true scheme of things.

> And after all the groping among dry-as-dust records of a by-gone century, after all the patient following of those faint traces on the sands of time left by the feet of Matthew Haygarth, *this* was Charlotte's Inheritance—a heart whose innocence and affection made home a kind of earthly paradise, and gave to life's commonest things a charm that all the gold ever found in California could not have imparted to them. This was Charlotte's Inheritance—the tender unselfish nature of the Haygarths and the Hallidays; and thus dowered, her husband would not have exchanged her for the wealthiest heiress whose marriage was ever chronicled in *Court Circular* or *Court Journal*. (Book 10, ch. 7)

The inheritance here is warmly human with no suggestion of the eternal home and inheritance that Charles Aubrey envisaged; nonetheless, it indicates that human, not material values are what matter.

Jeremy Taylor, an author familiar for two centuries in English homes, had stated what many another moral guide confirmed, when he remarked that the only inheritance worth considering was one open to all, and not the privileged or lucky, for "married persons, and widows, and virgins, are all servants of God, and coheirs in the inheritance of Jesus, if they live within the restraints and laws of their particular estate chastely, temperately, justly, and religiously."[6] This is the inheritance that any genuine Christian would desire. It is, of course, true that it is not so much the meek, as the staunch and resigned who inherit the earth in Victorian literature, but there is little doubt that the spoils go to the pure of heart. And, what is more, the emblems of that moral inheritance which may be acquired on earth are only a foreshadowing of a more important inheritance elsewhere. Once more, it is Jeremy Taylor who suggests that in heaven, "our passions shall be pure, our charity without fear, our desire without lust, our possessions all our own; and all in the inheritance of Jesus, in the richest soil of God's eternal kingdom."[7]

Nothing could be more reasonable for Edward Bulwer-Lytton, who openly announced in the 1852 Preface to his early novel, *The Disowned* (1828),

At the time this work was written I was deeply engaged in the study of metaphysics and ethics—and out of that study grew the character of Algernon Mordaunt. He is represented as a type of the Heroism of Christian Philosophy—an union of love and knowledge placed in the midst of sorrow, and labouring on through the pilgrimage of life, strong in the fortitude that comes from belief in heaven.[8]

Mordaunt's ultimate reward is spiritual and unearthly, but in his pilgrimage through life he demonstrates his worthiness of that spiritual heritage by treating his material inheritance as befits a Christian. By unscrupulous means, Mordaunt is dispossessed of his rich estates, though he is a worthy aristocrat. He and his family endure a life of poverty and hardship before the selfish usurper, Mr. Vavasour Mordaunt, returns the estate to Algernon, having gained nothing but misery by it. But Algernon does not enjoy his earthly elevation long, being murdered by mistake soon after. The author advises us at the end of his novel not to pity Algernon, for he has his victory—immortality. This victory is foreshadowed before the assassin's attack. Mordaunt and Clarence Linden are walking together in a thoughtful mood:

They looked upon the living and intense stars, and felt palpably at their hearts that spell—wild, but mute—which nothing on or of earth can inspire; that pining of the imprisoned soul, that longing after the immortality on high, which is perhaps no imaginary type of the immortality ourselves are heirs to. (ch. 87)

There can be little doubt of Bulwer-Lytton's moral here; yet he does not stop with one example. If Mordaunt is an emblem of the Christian earning his heavenly inheritance by earthly toil, Clarence Linden represents the struggle of the dispossessed here on earth to prove themselves worthy of the highest earthly station. Mordaunt's was the soul's struggle to achieve immortality; Linden's is the struggle of character to master the circumstances of this world, and in this regard he is a symbol of the power of the human will. The pattern is embodied in a fable: Clarence Linden is disowned by a father who cannot believe him to be his own son. Deprived of his proper inheritance, Clarence sets forth to make his own fortune, and he succeeds. There is a third, less significant, example of an inheritance in the case of King Cole, who, though he has inherited a comfortable income, prefers to live with gypsies, until he discovers the moral de-

generation that such companions encourage, after which he promptly purchases a comfortable house in the country and settles down
with his family to a peaceful and domestic existence. Clearly, Bulwer-Lytton has not thoughtlessly titled his novel, for he does indeed
treat several instances of dispossession, ranging from the most trivial
and banal to the most meaningful, but behind each example is the
great parable of man's temporary exile from a spiritual inheritance,
which must be attained by effort and endurance in this world.

Ordinarily, inheritance in Victorian fiction carried with it suggestions of sudden acquisitions of wealth that enable lost heirs to cease
their wanderings and settle down to happy and useful lives with the
mates of their choice. In addition, there were novelists who wished
to show more realistically what human inheritances were like. Thus
Peter Featherstone's and Mr. Casaubon's wills in *Middlemarch*
(1871-72) reveal the meanness, not the nobility, of men. It is as
though Eliot were consciously correcting the conventional exploitations of inheritance in fiction, whether of banal romance or pious parable. Another aspect of the inheritance convention has already been
adumbrated and requires a slightly more detailed examination. There
is an inheritance that involves duty and obedience in addition to, or
in place of, comfort and wealth. Thus, when Fedalma, in Eliot's *The
Spanish Gypsy* (1868), discovers her gypsy origins, she agrees that
she has an obligation to her race to aid in the building of the new
nation that Zarca, her father, has envisioned. In consenting to join
the gypsies and renounce her lover, she says, "I will bear / The heavy
trust of my inheritance." (Book 3) In *Daniel Deronda* (1876), the disposition of the rich Mallinger and Grandcourt estates is balanced by
the discovery of what Deronda calls his "inheritance," which is the
recognition of his Jewish origins. With this inheritance, Deronda acknowledges a duty to serve his people. It is a more ambitious modern
version of *The Spanish Gypsy's* theme.

Lancelot Smith, in Kingsley's *Yeast* (1848-49), inherits a similar,
though more domestic obligation. When his beloved Argemone dies,
Lancelot inherits her wealth, (ch. 17) and with it a demand to serve
the cause for which she died. On her deathbed, Argemone asks him
to complete the slum clearance that she had hoped to manage her-

self. She asks him to save the poor for whom she feels responsible. (ch. 16) Ultimately, Lancelot chooses to follow the mysterious missionary, Barnakill, to an equally mysterious—and we must assume imaginary—land where man has learned to be at one with his terrestrial dwelling-place, while consecrating himself to the spirit. It is not to Argemone's estates that Lancelot will journey, but beyond to this region "where the body and the spirit, the beautiful and the useful, the human and the divine, are no longer separate, and men have embodied to themselves on earth an image of the 'city not made with hands, eternal in the heavens.'" (ch .17) This ambiguous and mystical conclusion does not necessarily mean that Lancelot would actually undertake a voyage to some Tibetan or Caucasian Shangri-la. It merely signifies that Lancelot has ceased to view the material world as limited to substance; it now becomes an emblem of the final realm that men are heir to. The eternal city has been brought in contact with the earth, and, as at the end of Elizabeth Browning's *Aurora Leigh*, the foundation stones are being laid for that city of Revelation here on earth.

Both *Yeast* and *Aurora Leigh* were concerned with the problem of remedying social evil and of repairing the rent in human nature between the material and the spiritual worlds. It is not remarkable that the convention of inheritance should play a part in such narratives. But there was another feature of this convention which brought it immediately home to the social conditions of the time, as we have already seen implied in works such as *Ten Thousand A-Year* or *The Disowned*. A pronounced example is Disraeli's *Sybil, or the Two Nations* (1845), which describes an England in which the aristocracy, as represented by the House of Marney, aspire to the summit of human authority and influence without considering effort or achievement as necessary preliminary steps. At the top, there is ample supply of comfort and beauty, but as with the countryside near the beautiful Marney estate, so with the country at large, "behind that laughing landscape, penury and disease fed upon the vitals of a miserable population." (Book 2, ch. 3)

It is clear that, for the most part, those who rule do not deserve their place. This situation is embodied in the question of the Mowbray-Gerard inheritance, for, if justice were done, the lands owned by Lord de Mowbray, would pass to Walter Gerard, now forced to live among laborers, a champion of the poor and of the common man. What Disraeli wished and openly asked for was a union not between body and spirit, but between the aristocracy and the working class, between the Monarch and the Multitude. *Sybil* is his parable of how such a union might be effected, and, to embody it in a tale, he employed the dependable convention of inheritance.

Through the assistance of Charles Egremont, who begins as a spoiled aristocrat and ends as a champion of social conscience, the Gerard inheritance is confirmed. When Sybil marries Egremont, she brings to him her inheritance, which is the land of England. Upon the deaths of Gerard and Lord Marney, Charles and Sybil inherit the two massive fortunes described in the novel. In effect, their inheritance represents the assumption of power in a nation destined for better times through their union. The tired convention served Disraeli's purpose well, and acquired a deeper significance in the process.

Not everyone who saw the social problem in England as a matter of inheritance accepted Disraeli's solution. After all, Gerard himself was nobly descended and Sybil's regaining her right was, despite the appearance of elevation, nothing more than a reestablishment of blood rights. There was another way of dealing with this dilemma, and George Eliot chose to develop it in *Felix Holt, The Radical* (1866), which, though scarcely a political novel in the manner of Disraeli's works, is nonetheless, a novel of social problems. Among the problems with which Eliot was concerned was the question of how each class could do its part to improve the lot of the country as a whole. Basically, Eliot favored an acceptance of class distinctions; the sympathetic characters in the novel do not favor extension of the franchise. She wished to demonstrate that personal awareness and the discovery of individual power to do good were the worthwhile inheritance. Esther Lyon is the volatile personality whose conversion one way or another becomes, from this point of view, the central action of the tale. She must be brought to choose between two ways of life—one tending toward wealth and ease, the other toward self-denial and commitment to an ideal. A disputed inheritance plays an important part in Eliot's exposition of this problem. However, as John Morley observed in his early review of the novel, "it is true that in the end the possible possession of the property becomes a hinge in the play of character, but meanwhile it has thrown a considerable artificialness over portions of the story."[9] Manipulations of the plot reveal how Esther happens to be the true heir of the Transome estate, now in the hands of Harold Transome. It is the old story of complicated legal details, secret relatives, undisclosed births and marriages. The disclosures run according to formula, but thereafter Eliot incorporates some interesting modifications. The secrecies in this novel are more believable, if only because they cannot be kept. The secrets of melodrama are never revealed until a sensationally opportune moment. Here, for the most part, secrets ooze into the light from various competing sources. Moreover, when the truth of Esther's claim is made apparent, Harold Transome does not try to burn a will or murder a witness, or the heir herself. Instead, he hopes to reason with Esther. And, when, as conventional literary usage would have it, he decides that marriage to the heir is the best means of securing the inheritance, he does not wheedle or bully her into a contract. In fact, he loses Esther, despite the fact that he genuinely loves her.

Thus far Eliot tampered with the trappings of the convention, but she was prepared to go much further, for Esther finally resigns all claim to the inheritance, having discovered that the world about which she has had so many daydreams is not the world in which she wishes to live and work. In renouncing the Transome estate, Esther accepts the life that Felix has taught her to value. It is a far different inheritance, as Felix indicates midway through the novel. "I have my heritage—an order I belong to," Felix declares. That heritage is to be a leader of the people toward self-awareness and self-fulfillment, not toward the acquisition of wealth and the pursuit of trivial signs of social advancement. "Whatever the hopes for the world may be —whether great or small," Felix says, "I am a man of this generation; I will try to make life less bitter for a few within my reach." (ch. 26)

Felix's inheritance is the inheritance of all true men and women— to work for the betterment of all mankind through self-improvement. But that heritage may not be so simple a matter to carry out, as George Gissing demonstrated with forceful irony in *Demos: A Story of English Socialism* (1886). In this novel, the questions of who is to inherit England, and its corollary, how can an individual best contribute to the future good, are obscured by the nasty realities of individual human limitations. Gissing leaves no doubt that England is destined to fall entirely under the control of Demos—the multitude; and, having acknowledged as much, ruefully examines some of the circumstances associated with the coming transformation. Because old Richard Mutimer's will is presumed lost, young Richard, his nephew, inherits the wealthy estate and coal mine at Wanley, previously the property of the genteel but impoverished Eldon family. Young Richard Mutimer represents the best of the working class. He is handsome, sturdy and intelligent. He wishes to help his class and is willing to suffer inconvenience to accomplish that end. His weakness is that he is not ready. Although he wishes to convert the coal mine at Wanley into a socialist enterprise benefitting the working man, he finds that his operation does not go smoothly. Meanwhile, his acquisition of wealth and influence leads him to crave what never entered his fancy before. He wants his sister to become a lady; he discovers impulses in himself toward delicacies of the palate, toward owning a horse, and toward possessing Adela Waltham, whose manners and elegance attract him. In short, Mutimer is transformed into a simple bourgeois, though he does not recognize the change. Moreover, the transmutation involves ignoble behavior, most prominently Richard's abandonment of Emma Vine, the lower class girl to whom he had engaged himself. Richard has been unaware of his own vanity and desire for personal glory. The acquisition of wealth touches him in that vanity and his inheritance gradually works his moral ruin. But suddenly there is a change. Adela, who has married Mutimer without loving him, discovers the lost will that leaves the Wanley fortune to Hubert Eldon. Mutimer is obliged to abandon his grand socialist scheme, his wealth, and his new way of life. He abruptly returns to life among the poor, where his good purposes begin once more to have effect until they are suddenly terminated by deceit and his death.

Richard Mutimer was Gissing's answer to the proposal that the laboring classes were prepared to govern. For Gissing, as for George Eliot, only those who had reached the necessary stage of self-awareness were entitled to own and direct the resources of the land. A gradual acquisition of manners and understanding would be necessary for the new ruling class. The longed-for inheritance of so many romances proves, as the century draws toward a doubting close, not a blessing but a bane, injuring those who inherit and those dependent upon the inheritors.[10] Richard's younger brother, weak to begin with, is utterly corrupted by his taste of upper-class ease, and his sister loses whatever strength of character she might have had, by seeking to adapt to a manner of life that is beyond her capabilities. That promising world of mystery, dedication, and love, so often viewed just at the horizon of the future, is, in *Demos*, sadly altered. The wise Reverend Wyvern observes, "Progress will have its way, and its path will be a path of bitterness. A pillar of dark cloud leads it by day, and of terrible fire by night. I do not say that the promised land may not lie ahead of its guiding, but woe is me for the desert first to be traversed." (Vol. 3, ch. 6) What is left, then, for those to whom the inheritance, almost as though by default, finally descends? Hubert Eldon, a man of intelligence and refinement, is certain of what he wishes to do. He longs only to reestablish the world of peace and beauty that existed before the interloping Demos stained the hillsides of Wanley. The "ravaged valley" that Adela laments is eventually returned to its original appearance and there, after Mutimer's death, Hubert and Adela can marry.

But what has been the point of it all? Hubert, with his appreciation of the beautiful and his refined sensibilities, is devoted to nothing but the preservation of a way of life that even he admits is doomed. If Mutimer achieved nothing but his own degradation through his inheritance, Eldon achieves little more than the preservation of his integrity. It is a far different world from *Yeast, Aurora Leigh, Sybil* or even *Felix Holt*. The polluted air of nearby Belwick will soon overwhelm picturesque Wanley and London will continue to spread outward, "the familiar streets of pale, damp brick . . . stretching here and there, continuing London, much like the spreading of a disease." (Vol. 2, ch. 4) It is a picture that calls to mind the closing of *Howards End* (1904), a novel equally concerned with the question of who is to inherit England and what that inheritance entails; or of Tony Last's abandonment of Hetton to relatives of a distinctly lower order, who convert the old estate into a silver fox farm in *A Handful of Dust* (1934). Forster's novel is superior to most of those discussed, but its theme of inheritance is related to the convention in which they played an important part, and the difference between the earlier works and *Howards End* requires some comment.

For most Victorians, inheritance meant money and influence, and in their fictions of poetry and prose, they normally accepted the idea that the acquisition of money and influence meant happiness. Thus inheritances tended to be delivered over to lost heirs and the like in sensational scenes at the narrative's end. But there was another dimension to this well-worked convention in which the most worth-while inheritance was not the material one so seductively presented, but the more serious inheritance available only to those who were pre-pared to labor for an eternal reward. In this light, worldly fortunes became either false lures or shadowy emblems of the immortal in-heritance. And, growing out of this higher meaning of a common-place theme, was a more mundane, but no less serious parable of the nature of inherited power and the responsibilities and obligations that such an inheritance involved. If eternal inheritance was to be achieved at last, it was through labor in this world. And this world it-self was a kind of inheritance. "Virtue was the natural state of man, and happiness its environment," Peter Coveney observes, and adds, "For Dickens, as for Rousseau and Blake, man was born of a good father. The evil conditions of society prevented his entering into his kingdom, his inheritance by nature."[11] This attitude was implicit in many writers of the time, but for those who put little faith in any transcendental heritage, there was a temporal fortune that was equal-ly alluring. For one who refused the corrupting material inheritances that this world might provide, there was the greater inward inheri-tance of human growth. The private reward, the discovered treasure within the self became more valuable and more productive than those many fortunes distributed so lavishly upon the heroes of nineteenth-century fiction.

Hence, in Forster's novel, the pattern is a thoroughly familiar one. Those who deserve Howards End ultimately inherit it. Margaret and Helen Schlegel, the defenders of independent thought and the free-dom of the imagination, take control of the threatened but still pure preserve of Howards End. But the property gives neither wealth nor influence. It is a retreat, a salvaged piece of England that is less real estate than it is a homestead of the soul. All claim to actual authority, power, or governance is gone. Now the inheritance is strictly inter-nal, it is itself the achievement and the reward. Ownership is in the heart of the beholder.

Forster's novel represents, in my view, the culmination of the in-heritance convention, for, while avoiding the more wooden details associated with lost wills and laboriously traced genealogies, it makes the grand point that novels such as *Our Mutual Friend*, *Felix Holt*, and others sought to affirm. Beyond the simple convention of the in-heritance is an emblematic meaning of great importance; it is nothing less than the discovery that, in a world too base for beauty to endure, too commercialized for governance to value, the richest inheritance remains, as it was from the first, what is most valuable in the human spirit. It is a recognition that answers in a way A. E. Housman's reminder to his generation, in his introductory lecture as Professor of Latin at University College, London, 1892.

> It may be urged that man stands today in the position of one who has been reared from his cradle as the child of a noble race and the heir to great possessions, and who finds at his coming of age that he has been deceived alike as to his origin and his expectations; that he neither springs of the high lineage he fancied, nor will inherit the vast estate he looked for, but must put off his towering pride, and contract his boundless hopes, and begin the world anew from a lower level.[12]

It was a caution typical of a growing attitude of the time, indicating that the great illusions of the preceding generations were no longer satisfactory. The convention of the inheritance, which had carried with it suggestions of inevitable reward for virtue and fidelity, now required a more realistic assessment of an existence in which any inheritance was doubtful and only the inextinguishable heritage of the individual will and imagination could confirm its possession.

CHAPTER THIRTEEN

DISGUISE

THE DEVICE

Disguise involves the question of identity, one of the major themes in all of literature. In Renaissance literature there is an abundant use of disguise, and it abounds in Restoration drama and the eighteenth-century novel;[1] with the Romantic movement, a renewed fascination with the correspondences of physical and spiritual reality, along with a new attention to the growth of the individual mind, led men to reconsider what may too placidly have been accepted as the Self.[2] In the nineteenth century, identity presented its own new puzzles, many of them occasioned by the conflict men felt between the character that tradition and society required of them and the personality that they felt to be increasingly at odds with that tradition and society.

From the beginning of the century there was an acute awareness of the implications of disguise and false identity, as seen in James Hogg's *Confessions of a Justified Sinner* (1824), and this awareness grew until, in the twentieth century, the theme of identity was to become paramount in writers like Joseph Conrad.[3] But while these new, subjective ramifications of the disguise motif developed, nineteenth-century writers maintained the traditional, moral outlook as well, which is earlier represented in *An Apology for the Life of Mr. Bampfylde-Moore Carew* (1745):

> Think not gentle Reader, these *Deceptions* and *Disguises* incredible; for if thou wilt look into this great Theatre of the World, thou may'st see every Day far greater; thou may'st see bitter *Hatred* wear the cordial Smiles of *Friendship*; lascivious *Wantonness* put on the severe Brow of *Modesty*: *Corruption* the Angel Face of Heaven-born *Innocence*; thou may'st see *Cowardice* concealed under terrible *Looks*; and *Falshood* dress'd in the Robes of *Truth*; *Fraud* borrowing the Looks of her greatest Enemy *Honesty*; and *Oppression* balancing the Scales of *Justice*. (ch. 5)

There was an ample use of the disguise convention in eighteenth-century literature, and certainly Gothic fiction abounds with it, as do the novels of Scott, and this straightforward melodramatic use continued into the Victorian period. In Moore's narrative poem, *Lalla Rookh* (1817), Mokanna is a blatant example of the wicked imposter. And in the popular adventure tales it often seems as though more characters are disguised than are not. In Hannah Maria Jones' *The Gipsey Chief*, most of the main characters are not what they seem, and the same is excessively true in T. P. Prest's *The Gipsy Boy*, where young Rosario is really Eugenia—not a boy, but a girl; Azrah is really Clara—not a man, but a woman; they are not gypsies, as they appear, but the wife and daughter of Sir Laurence Cleveland. Walter Alston and his mother Medala also employ the disguise of gypsies so effectively that Prest himself seems to forget what their true roles are.

Fascination with this sort of disguise was perhaps increased by the popularity of Newgate fiction dealing with highwaymen and other criminals, who were notorious for their use of disguise. Ainsworth's *Jack Sheppard* is one example, while in the same author's *Rookwood*, the elusive Dick Turpin, known as Jack Palmer to most of the characters, convinces people that he is the ghost of the dead Sir Piers Rookwood. And later in the novel, commenting upon the famous disguises of the thief known as the Knight of Malta, Ainsworth says that his history "exemplifies, more strongly than a thousand discourses could do, how prone we are to be governed by appearances, and how easily we may be made dupes of a plausible imposter." (Book 3, ch. 5)

Disguise remained a staple of stage melodrama and comedy, even having a revival of sorts in the character of Hawkshaw, who utilizes disguise beneficently in Tom Taylor's *The Ticket-of-Leave Man* (1863). But, by this time it was considered an overworked device. The *Illustrated London News'* review of Sheridan Knowles' *The Secretary* in 1843 complained of the hackneyed conventions of disguise, changed identity, and so forth. But such reviews had little effect in modifying the use of the convention.

DISGUISE IN THE NINETEENTH CENTURY

Although disguises were frequently used, sometimes improbably, in the literature of the nineteenth century, the device was not always used thoughtlessly. It might serve an allegorical or psychological purpose, but it was true to life as well. Godwin wrote to the famous actor, Charles Mathews, "I am at this moment engaged in writing a work of fiction, a part of the incidents of which will consist of escapes in disguises," and requested an interview with Mathews to benefit from his professional advice. Mathews consented, and convinced Godwin of the feasibility of escape through disguises by demonstrating the types of disguise that would serve.[4] Later in the century, Wilkie Collins found ample evidence from accounts of French court cases by M. Richer and Maurice Méjan of actual crimes in which impersonation and mistaken identity were important, and he did not hesitate to utilize similar instances in his fiction.[5]

Imposture was not uncommon to the nineteenth-century experience as a notorious instance like the Tichborne Claimant case indicates.[6] The Victorians were intrigued by the mystery of birth and family origin in fiction as well as in reality. Yet although mystery and imposture were clearly evident in Victorian society, there were logical reasons why the disguise convention in literature was so acceptable. There simply were not many ways of verifying identification before forms of reproduction such as photography were developed. Written communication was too slow to challenge or forestall forgery and other modes of imposture. And, for most of the century, there was no satisfactory public lighting; hence if a "muffled figure" confronted someone on the street, he might be an intimate acquaintance and yet remain unrecognizable. Eighteenth-century laws had, in fact, made it a capital offense "to be disguised in the Mint" or "to go about at night disguised or with the face blackened."[7] Moreover, with differences between classes so clearly marked by externals, it was possible that someone from the upper classes might conveniently avoid notice by assuming the costume proper to a lower station, as Richard Hare does in *East Lynne,* or Harmon and Headstone do in *Our Mutual Friend.* The reverse, of course, would be less likely.

Charles J. Mathews, a professional entertainer, was an adept at disguises. At the Italian residence of Lord and Lady Blessington, Mathews fooled certain strangers by appearing as a doctor and then returning to mock his previous disguise. But he even deceived Lady Blessington by appearing the next morning disguised as one of her guests, Count Leeven, from the night before, and even a Miss Power, who knew the Count, was taken in.[8] A document from another sphere of society testifies to similar success in disguise. In the slave narrative, "Running A Thousand Miles For Freedom" (1848), the American slaves, Mr. and Mrs. Craft, managed their flight to freedom by means of several disguises. And twelve-year-old Richard Burton and his brother Edward went the death rounds of Naples in disguise, picking up cholera victims. Burton became skillful at disguising himself as a native both in India and later in the Near East. Indeed, he became notorious for being the first white man to penetrate the holy cities of Medina and Mecca, forbidden to Christians, by disguising himself as an Arab. Later, Burton, observing the insignificance of imposture, nonetheless admitted that "it is impossible to ignore the dear delights of fraud and deception, the hourly pleasure taken by some minds in finessing through life, and in playing a part till by habit it becomes a nature."[9]

In addition to the practical credibility of disguise, there was a fascination with disclosure and discovery, and much of nineteenth-century literature is concerned with the uncovering of mysteries. For the audiences brought up on Scott and Byron, personal mystery was not merely a feature of literature, but inextricably bound up with the makers of that literature. If there could be such secrets in the lives of these men, why should there not be comparable secrets in their fictional worlds? Richard Altick has shown how avidly Victorians followed the unravelling of notable crimes.[10] They were equally avid in tracing a scandal.

In the fiction of the nineteenth century, disguise or concealed identity is, to a great extent, merely a convenience of plot, as in Scott
and the Gothic novelists. In Pierce Egan's *Life in London*, Tom and
Jerry visit the slums in disguise. The assumed identities of Mr. Jingle
in *Pickwick Papers* are familiar comic material, and even Peg Woffington's skillful disguises in Charles Reade's *Peg Woffington* (originally entitled *Masks and Faces*) are little more than attempts to lend
appeal to a feeble story. Collins employs a confusion of identities between Anne Catherick and Laura Fairlie in *The Woman in White* to
extend the complexity of the plot. And, in *The Inn Album*, Browning
uses the revelation of the mature woman's identity in a highly contrived and coincidental plot to grease the wheels of his tale.

Some novels are almost totally based on disguise. In Ouida's *Under
Two Flags*, the sustaining force behind Bertie Cecil's agonizing exile
is that he must conceal his identity, especially from the woman he
loves. It is more acute for Bertie since he lives as a lowly legionnaire,
while he is in reality an English aristocrat. Wilkie Collins' *Armadale*
(1864-65) depends not only on the first Allan Armadale's concealing
his identity under the name of Ozias Midwinter, but also of Lydia
Gwilt concealing the facts of her early life, and, by assuming her
maiden name, disguising her marriage and the scandal of her husband's death. There are, as well, minor disguises, as when Miss Gwilt's
servant deceives Mr. Brock into believing she is Miss Gwilt, or when
Dr. Downward is obliged to seek a new and respectable identity as
Dr. Le Doux. *Armadale* could not move without the complications
of disguise. *East Lynne* (1861), by Mrs. Henry Wood, and *Lady Audley's Secret* (1862), by Mary Braddon, are two best-sellers that also
employed disguise as a primary device. In the former, Isabel Vane
returns as the governess, Madame Vine, to the husband and family
she abandoned, while Richard Hare, falsely accused of murder,
makes furtive appearances at his home town in the disguise of a common laborer, false beard and all. Throughout the tale, there is a search
for a Captain Thorn who is suspected of committing an important
murder. It finally transpires that Thorn is the sophisticated seducer,
Francis Levison, in disguise. In *Lady Audley's Secret*, Helen (Mal-
don) Talboys, in order to conceal her identity, assumes the name of

Lucy Graham and begins a new career. It is this disguise that leads Robert Audley on to unravel the mystery of the disappearance of his friend, George Talboys.

DEEPER FUNCTIONS OF DISGUISE

In many of the lesser, and most of the great Victorian novels the convention of disguise, while serving as a convenience of plot, was often of great significance. In *Lady Audley's Secret*, Lady Audley, while reflecting upon her means of avoiding detection, is interrupted by the approach of another person. She quickly seizes a book to appear occupied. The narrator then observes:

> Insignificant as this action was, it spoke very plainly. It spoke very plainly of ever-recurring fears—of fatal necessities for concealment— of a mind that in its silent agonies was ever alive to the importance of outward effect. It told more plainly than anything else could have told how complete an actress my lady had been made by the awful necessity of her life. (ch. 31)

The disguise assumed so casually as a method of achieving some morally questionable end, rapidly becomes a necessity, transforming the deceiver and locking him or her into an identity at first employed merely as a tool. Something similar happens in *East Lynne* when Isabel Vane, having married the upright Archibald Carlyle, runs away with Francis Levison and is soon abandoned by him. Overcome by remorse, she longs to see her husband and children again. After a railway accident in which she is presumed dead and which leaves her disfigured, Isabel returns to her former home at East Lynne as Madame Vine, governess to her own children but in a house where there is a new Mrs. Carlyle. The return becomes a purgatory filled with painful ironies for Isabel. When Isabel was Mrs. Carlyle, young Barbara Hare had peeped enviously into the drawing room where Isabel was singing the song, "Then I'll remember you," to her happy husband. Now it is Isabel who peeps through the same door to see a similar scene in which Barbara sings the same song to Archibald. (Part 3, ch. 4) When Barbara informs Madame Vine that Francis Levison, for whom Isabel sacrificed her home, has been identified as the man long sought for the murder of Mr. Hallijohn, Isabel's grief is intense. "If ever retribution came home to woman, it came home in that hour to Lady Isabel," the novelist declares. (Part 3, ch. 10)

Isabel Vane's physical disfigurement reflects her moral deformity. Her former beauty is gone and she is a grey, wasted shadow of the once virtuous young wife. The love that was her joy becomes her grief, for now she must view the domestic life she misvalued through the glass of her own sin. Ceasing to be Isabel Vane or Mrs. Archibald Carlyle, she has truly become the pinched and veiled Madame Vine. Sin alters identity; and, in some cases, such as Isabel's, creates a mirror image of it. At our most painful hour, we may be obliged to contemplate that image. Isabel Vane has not assumed a disguise, nor merely adopted a new role, she has *become* the new identity.

In *Lady Audley's Secret*, Robert Audley, showing Lady Audley that he knows her true identity, and in trying to forewarn her, says:

> "What do people generally do when they wish to begin a new existence—to start for a second time in the race of life, free from the incumbrances that had fettered their first journey? They change their *names*, Lady Audley." (ch. 29)

In Victorian literature, this is a chief motive leading individuals to assume disguises and new identities, though not always for malign purposes. In Dickens' novels, for example, new identities are assumed by characters who wish to attempt a second life, such as John Harmon in *Our Mutual Friend*, or Nicholas as Mr. Johnson in *Nicholas Nickleby*. In other cases, though no disguise is attempted, new names suggest new stages of a character's career. Thus David Copperfield is also Daisy, Trotwood, Trot and Doady; and Philip Pirrip is Pip or Handel.

Different names may indicate different aspects of personality. There are many examples of this sort of device in nineteenth-century literature, for example, in Bulwer-Lytton's early novel, *The Disowned* (1828). Clarence L'Estrange's father, doubting his son's legitimacy, has cast him off. Clarence assumes the name Linden and in this new identity seeks to create an independent life for himself. He is out, as he says, to seek his fortune. On one level, it is apparent that this false name helps to establish a mystery in the plot and thereby strengthen the tale. At another level, however, the disguise is part of a more elaborate fable. Clarence is nobly born and has a grand inheritance available to him if his origins can be proven. His actions and character indicate the true nobility of his nature, and his search for an identity of his own is not an empty one. He has a real identity to prove or discover. Whose child was he? What future do his origins promise for him? When Clarence discovers that he *is* his father's son, and therefore his inheritance is assured to him, we realize that he has lived into a preestablished identity which he has truly earned. He has not idly accepted the perquisites and advantages of noble birth, but has labored to create the identity for which he was destined. His period of trial proves him worthy and the reward of a just inheritance is his.

Something similar happens with Algernon Mordaunt in the same novel. Mordaunt is noble in all his bearing and behavior. When the grand estate that he has inherited is wrenched from him by a greedy relative, Mordaunt and his new wife are cast into a life of poverty. As a struggling student and writer, Mordaunt assumes the name Glendower; and in their impoverished condition he and his wife suffer not only poverty, but temptation to criminal activity by the arch-villain, Crauford. Like Clarence Linden, but in a more sordid climate and with more intense suffering, Glendower resists all temptation and passes through his period of trial successfully, after which he regains his lost estates, his greedy relative having suffered his own losses—an indication that the inheritance was not rightfully his. In the process of overcoming his sufferings and temptations, however, Mordaunt has lost his beloved wife and resumes his station with melancholy sobriety. More emblematically than with Clarence Linden, Mordaunt embodies the main design of Bulwer-Lytton's novel.[11] It is clear that, despite the superficial changes in his existence, Mordaunt's soul has remained undaunted in its belief in a heavenly home. Although his high identity is questioned and its circumstances altered, it preserves its important qualities. He remains noble in high and low degree. Bulwer-Lytton's story thus provides the interesting, if familiar, narrative of the high-born man temporarily disowned and in disguise, who returns eventually to assume the inheritance that is rightly his. But beyond this simple tale is the grander suggestion that, in a like manner, all men are disguised exiles in this world and must labor to recover their proper inheritance. Underlying the novel of social action and adventure is a fable of eternal meaning.[12]

GOOD AND EVIL IN DISGUISE

In Robert Plumer Ward's novel, *Tremaine, or the Man of Refinement* (1825), the good Dr. Evelyn, in his prolonged conversations with the doubting Tremaine, deals with most of the crucial tests of belief. Near the end of the novel, when he has almost succeeded in persuading Tremaine of the values of the traditional Christian faith, Dr. Evelyn explains the place of evil in God's scheme. Free will, he notes, requires the potential for evil, though he admits that man does not really know who is good and who evil, and therefore cannot know if the misery he endures is a test or a punishment. (ch. 35 [misnumbered 33 in the 1835 edition]) Thus man must accept suffering and trust in Providence. At the same time if man cannot tell the evil from the good, he comes to mistrust all appearances, convinced that only beyond the grave will these mysteries be resolved.

Though he has a respectable position in society, the lawyer, Gammon, in Warren's *Ten Thousand A-Year* (1841), is quickly recognized as a villain by most of the good characters. Placed beside the best of them, Kate Aubrey, Gammon sees his true nature: "he was a fiend beside an angel. What an execrable hypocrite was he! He caught, on that memorable occasion, a sudden glimpse even of his own real inner man—of his infernal SELFISHNESS and HYPOCRISY—and involuntarily shuddered!" (Vol. 2, ch. 12) In *The Disowned*, Richard Crauford is the typical archvillain: "But there are certain vices which require the mask of virtue, and Crauford thought it easier to wear the mask than to school his soul to the reality. So to the villain he added the hypocrite." (ch. 41) Crauford is "a villain upon system," (ch. 40) and does his best to corrupt and exploit Mordaunt, but his illegal schemes collapse, he attempts an escape in disguise, is apprehended, and proves himself a coward in the face of death. Crauford's case, though it ends in justice being served, illustrates that one cannot judge virtue or vice by appearances. Crauford seems eminently virtuous and respectable but is a hypocritical villain, while Mordaunt seems proud and disdainful yet is generous and good. Both the good and the evil wear disguises which confuse and mislead. It is not disguise itself that is reprehensible, but its use. Once discovered, however, the hypocrite reveals himself both at the spiritual and the very material level. Hence Philip Sheldon, in Miss Braddon's *Charlotte's Inheritance* (1868), forced to flee from his collapsing kingdom of fraud, pauses to have a barber shave off his whiskers. The revelation is immediate.

> The sacrifice of these hirsute adornments made an extraordinary change in this man. All the worst characteristics of his countenance came out with a new force, and the face of Mr. Sheldon, undisguised

by the whiskers that had hidden the corners of his mouth, or the wav-
ing locks that had given height and breadth to his forehead, was a face
that no one would be likely to trust. (Book 9, ch. 7)

Generally, Victorian heroes and heroines refuse to dissemble. "The
most ingenuous and upright mind may practise self-control," says Susan Ferrier in *The Inheritance*, "but it is only the artful and the mean
who ever stoop to dissimulate." (Vol. 1, ch. 21) Although evil may
remain hidden for a long time, the noble spirit ordinarily shows
through whatever disguise it may have been obliged to assume. In
ideal characters, this is the case. Miss Mulock, in *John Halifax, Gentleman* (1856), describes her hero's face as

> not one of your impassive faces, whose owners count it pride to harden
> into a mass of stone those lineaments which nature made as the flesh
> and blood representation of the man's soul. True, it had its reticences,
> its sacred disguises, its noble powers of silence and self-control. It was
> a fair-written, open book: only, to read it clearly, you must come from
> its own country, and understand the same language. (ch. 9)

It is appropriate that this remarkable man should find his ideal mate
in Ursula March, who does indeed seem to come from the same
country and understand the same language, for "there was something in her which, piercing all disguises, went at once to the heart
of things. She seemed to hold in her hand the touchstone of truth."
(ch. 14) There are few such touchstones in the literature of the nineteenth century.

Much of the force of the fiction of the period derives from the
small or large mysteries that run through the narratives, and mysteries of identity are prominent among them. Most characters are
incapable of comprehending any disguises, even their own. Early in
the century, James Hogg anonymously published a novel clearly intended to be read as "a religious parable, [written] on purpose to
illustrate something scarcely tangible," which he entitled *The Private Memoirs and Confessions of a Justified Sinner* (1824). The narrative written by the sinner, Robert Wringhim, is contained within a
fictional editorial frame. The editor's opening narrative does not resolve the mystery of the story, but in reporting the case, leaves most
of its puzzling features unresolved. Wringhim's account further complicates it—for Wringhim supposes that Gil-Martin, the young man
who has led him into his crimes of murder, is the devil. Yet he him-

self is so confused that at some points in the narrative he is uncertain of his own identity. He suffers from a delusion that he is two people, neither of which is himself: one is Gil-Martin, the other is his half-brother (or possibly his brother), George. After Wringhim murders George, his demonic second self turns against him. Wringhim now considers the further possibility that he has within himself two souls, one of which is guilty of crimes which he cannot recall committing. Appropriately, when Robert Wringhim flees from the authorities he is provided with a disguise by Gil-Martin. He agrees to commit suicide after torment by fiends.

Additional editorial notes follow this narrative, but they merely indicate that the entire story may be either a fraud or a religious parable. There is no attempt to settle the many mysteries of the story. Since one purpose of the novel was to discredit the vanity of predestinarians, the entire story with its peculiar construction could be seen as a warning that we are surrounded, indeed penetrated, by mystery which we must not presume to interpret, because such presumption leads only to greater confusion. The implication here, as in *Tremaine*, is that God's will is greater than man can know; hence man must not arrogate to himself what resides with God alone. Not only this world, but man's nature is a mystery and there are few like Ursula March capable of piercing it.

This, however, does not mean that we should not seek to understand the world around us. If, by our own individual powers, we are incapable of discriminating good from evil, a multiple view might provide a trustworthy conclusion. To a great extent, this is the point of Browning's *The Ring and the Book* (1868-69). For some, Pompilia is vile and Caponsacchi a sinner, while Guido is the good but abused gentleman. For others, Guido is the sordid villain, while Caponsacchi is a heroic savior and Pompilia clearly a saint. For the lawyers who compose arguments for the contending sides, there is no eagerness to discover the truth or penetrate appearances, for they are concerned in juggling appearances to suit their own purposes. Only the pope attempts to pierce the mystery and arrive at a conclusion regarding the crime placed before him, while resolving the broader questions of good and evil in a world of uncertainties. Much has been said about the way in which patterns of metaphor identify the values Browning placed upon his characters, but after all, these images of serpents, wolves, or saints, merely complicate the problem and must be read within the context of the ambiguous voices of the contending parties.[13] Ultimately, the pope's conclusion must be reached on grounds that transcend competing appearances. Browning's intent is indicated most clearly in that only one character in the story appears twice in different roles. Guido describes himself in at least two incompatible ways: he is abused husband driven by passion to a just act, and he is a clever fellow capable of acting out his revenge. At the last, his jumbled nature, uncertain of its own deepest attributes, veers wildly to some trustworthy source. Finding it, he cries: "Pompilia, will you let them murder me?"

PERVASIVENESS OF DISGUISE

To many, concealment seemed a basic part of man's nature. Owen Meredith's *Lucile* (1860) is founded on the assumption that man has a fundamental, or real nature, but that material existence makes it impossible for him to be open and candid and therefore reveal his better part or outwardly manifest his soul. There is little in the way of outward disguise in this "novel in verse," but the characters continually conceal their feelings from themselves and from one another. Essentially, the poem is an account of Sir Alfred Vargrave's self-discovery through the agency of Lucile de Nevers, who acts out "the mission of woman on earth," by enlightening the minds and generally alleviating the sufferings of men. (Two. VI. xxxix) The instinct to disguise his true emotions is not peculiar to Lord Alfred, but representative of the experience of all men. We are seldom true to our best selves because we are preoccupied with what we might be: "We but catch at the skirts of the thing we would be, / And fall back on the lap of a false destiny." Most men lead false lives. "We are ever behind, or beyond, or beside / Our intrinsic existence. Forever at hide / And seek with our souls." (One. V. i) This notion was elaborated with great skill in Matthew Arnold's writings, where a buried self or a best self implied a deceptive surface requiring penetration in order that man's finest attributes might be set free to improve his general condition.

Beyond the discomfort with and alienation from an inner, better self, is a more fundamental impulse. When man first appeared, "the very first thing / That his naked intelligence taught him to feel / Was the shame of himself; and the wish to conceal / Was the first step of art." And since then, "this art of concealment has greatly increased. / A whole world lies cryptic in each human breast." (One. III. i) What this concealment leads to is "the great masquerade" of civilized existence. (Two. I. ix.) Lord Alfred is inspired by Lucile to struggle with his own nature. "He felt that Lucile penetrated and prized / Whatever was noblest and best, though disguised, / In himself." (One. V. vii.) Alfred, however, cannot appreciate Lucile's true nature, nor can he fully comprehend his own, though his cousin John tells him truly, "you will, I believe / be true, at the last, to what now makes you grieve / For having belied your true nature so long." (Two. IV. vii.) A genuine test of Alfred's character finds him capable. Financial failure becomes a blessing, as we say, in disguise:

> The shock which had suddenly shattered at last
> Alfred Vargrave's fantastical holiday nature,
> Had sharply drawn forth to his full size and
>   stature
> The real man, concealed till that moment beneath
> All he yet had appeared. From the gay broidered
>   sheath
> Which a man in his wrath flings aside, even so
> Leaps the keen trenchant steel summoned forth
>   by a blow.
>
>   (Two. VI. viii.)

The image here is reminiscent of one that Tennyson used years later to describe the young, able, and courageous Gareth's sudden assumption of his first knightly task. The disguise of kitchen vassal no longer necessary, Gareth casts off his dirty cloak and stands revealed in brilliant armor ready for the deed: He "brake bright, and flashed as those / Dull-coated things, that making slide apart / Their dusk wing-cases, all beneath there burns / A jewelled harness, ere they pass and fly." ("Gareth and Lynette")

Lord Alfred's yearning in *Lucile* is for one's best self—the identity that none may know fully in this world. This desire is illustrated when, seeing his wife kneeling in prayer, he prepares to tell her of the misfortune that has befallen them and suddenly observes her in a new light; "she looked to his eyes / Like a young soul escaped from its earthly disguise." (Two. IV. x)

A belief that all earthly being is disguise while spiritual identity is true determines the use of disguise in much of Victorian literature. However, in Lord Alfred Vargrave, as in others, a sense of confusion about and alienation from the "true self" complicates the discovery of one's best self. When a character such as Clarence Linden is obliged to forge a new identity, he begins with a fruitful sense of determination. Ordinarily this discovery is involuntary, as is the case with Charles Ravenshoe in Henry Kingsley's *Ravenshoe* (1861). Discovering that he is not Cuthbert Ravenshoe's brother, Charles sets himself a new life course with different requirements and aims. This new life is less one of conviction than of desperation. What brings on this desperation is a feeling destined to become more familiar to fictional characters in English literature. "I have known," Charles recalls, "what very few men have known, and lived—despair; but perhaps the most terrible agony for a time was the feeling of loss of identity—that I was not myself; that my whole existence from babyhood had been a lie." (ch. 27)

This sense of disorientation was a familiar one. The Prince, in Tennyson's *The Princess* (1847), when afflicted with his weird visions, feels himself "the shadow of a dream," and all of existence a hollow show. These seizures end when he wins the love of Princess Ida, a notable figure of masculine force and authority. To accomplish this object, the Prince and his friends assume female disguises in order that they may penetrate Ida's college for women where men are outlawed and where the women behave, insofar as they can, like men. What is accomplished in this adventure is similar to what Walter Davis sees happening in Sidney's *Arcadia*. The three men have, in entering the female sanctuary, also pierced female identity. By playing the parts of women, they have, in some degree, learned to appreciate the attributes of women. The same is true of the women who have followed Ida. They now can appreciate male identity more fully. But these are only temporary transferals. Women and men are "Distinct in individualities," (vii) and must reverence each other as such. By having penetrated one another's identities, the two sexes learn that there is some maturation yet necessary, of which their experiment is a good beginning, for "in the long years liker must they grow; / The man be more of woman, she of man." (vii) So, recognizing woman's true role, Ida's "falser self slipt from her like a robe, / And left her woman." (vii) Ida, too, has worn a disguise; but now both she and the Prince can discard their masks. By stepping temporarily out of their own identities, they have acquired new insights into themselves and into others.

Throughout Tennyson's *Idylls of the King* this theme of disguised and masked identities persists.[14] Perhaps the most striking instance of illumination through disguise occurs when Lancelot conceals his identity in Arthur's tournament. His concealment hides his duplicity to his king. In his new identity, Lancelot, "lost in fancy," finds himself wandering to the home of Elaine, the one woman, as Arthur observes, who seemed to have been born for him. Elaine immediately falls in love with the unknown knight, loving him not for his name and fame, but for his kind and noble manner. Uncharacteristically wearing a woman's favor to please Elaine and complete his disguise, Lancelot is not recognized at the tournament, yet dominates the field until his own kinsmen, spurred by "A fiery family passion for the name / Of Lancelot," attack him and bear him down. ("Lancelot and Elaine") The Lancelot of Arthur's court is not the real man, but an awesome impostor. In his heart there dwells another self more vulnerable, but also more virtuous. Now, deeply wounded, Lancelot dwindles away from the old superficial self and in his illness grows "Gaunt as it were the skeleton of himself." He is reduced to the rudiments of his nature as well as of his flesh. Elaine tends Lancelot and revives him, hoping to win his love; but Lancelot cannot entirely free himself from his love for the queen. He has learned that his apparent identity was really a mask, and his assumed identity is his true one, but he cannot fully live by the truer self. His identity remains divided, but his ordeal has reminded him of something of great value that will ultimately be his salvation. By inadvertently stepping outside his customary identity, he has been humbled in the flesh, seen what his other life might have been, and realized that the flesh itself is a disguise, a fragment of the Infinite that only temporarily lives estranged from its divine source.

DICKENS

Most writers of this period refrained from such subtle elaborations of the convention. Ordinarily the relationship between spiritual identity and physical disguise was simple and adjunctive. Most writers concerned themselves rather with the complications, not the implications, of human disguises. Dickens, however, used disguise in almost all conceivable ways. There is the incidental assumption of false identity in Nicholas Nickleby's use of the stage name Mr. Johnson; the cruel disguise of a Monks, common to melodrama of the period; or the almost innocent, ebullient disguises of the strolling actor, Mr. Jingle.[15] These uses were common to most writers of fiction, though Dickens was capable of more elaborate exploitations of the theme.

In *Bleak House* (1852-53), Dickens employed several variations of the convention of disguise and altered identity. Like Charles Ravenshoe, Esther Summerson discovers that her parentage is obscure; unlike him, she accepts this obscurity and proceeds to make of her life what she can, not from desperation, but from humility and love. To have no established identity is to be victim of random shaping forces, but it is also to be free. Like orphanhood, an undisclosed identity is as much an opportunity as a misfortune. The mystery of Esther's birth is only one of several mysteries of identity. Captain George hides his identity out of shame, while Captain Hawdon has gone so far as to erase his identity and himself, as his assumed name, Nemo, suggests. But most interesting is the emerging identity of Esther Summerson, who, though born a child of sin, gradually becomes an embodiment of love. She is a true love-child. That Esther resembles her mother, now Lady Dedlock, is a convenient mechanism of the plot to prepare for the discovery of her identity. But it is something more as well. The principal difference between the two women is pride. Conscious of her beauty, Lady Dedlock has used it to gain wealth and position, thereby sacrificing her love. She is constantly referred to as proud, haughty, cold, and indifferent. Secretly, however, her pride has become her cross, for she has never lost the sense of her early romance, of which Esther is the product. Lady Dedlock's name, Honoria, is just another ironic mockery, since the virtuous name disguises a sordid identity. Esther, on the other hand, is all humility and love. She is afflicted not even by the slightest taint of vanity or pride. To make the contrast fully evident, Dickens mars Esther's beauty, by which she has been identified with her sinful mother. This transformation proves that Esther's beauty is spiritual; it is her inner self for which she is beloved, not the mask of physical beauty. Even Guppy comes to realize this fact. Dickens' implication is that man is what he does, not what he claims or appears to be.

If Esther's mother, out of vanity, abandoned the man she loved to marry a man who could provide her with an appropriate setting for her beauty, Esther demonstrates the opposite in her humility, almost abandoning the man she loves to accept John Jarndyce's fatherly proposal. But humility does not doom Esther as vanity had her mother. "I learned in a moment," Esther says of Alan Woodcourt, "that he loved me. I learned in a moment that my scarred face was all unchanged to him. I learned in a moment that what I had thought was pity and compassion, was devoted, generous, faithful love." (ch. 61) With this knowledge, and through the selfless love of John Jarndyce, Esther is able to fulfill her love and marry Alan Woodcourt with her guardian's blessing. She has rectified, in a way, her mother's sin.

Eventually, Lady Dedlock must herself pay the price of her error. The degree of her folly is indicated in another use that Dickens makes of disguise.[16] Lady Dedlock had no "family," but Lord Dedlock married her nonetheless, for love. All that Honoria has to be vain about is her beauty and the social station that it has achieved. Mademoiselle Hortense, her maid, also has no reason to be proud, yet she is extremely so. In this sense, she is her mistress' alter ego. It is thus entirely appropriate that she should murder Tulkinghorn, whose extinction suits her mistress' purpose as well. It is further appropriate that there should be strong similarities between the two women, since, when Lady Dedlock visited the chambers and later the grave of the deceased Captain Nemo, she did so "in the dress of her own maid." Truly either woman might have worn the "loose black mantle with a deep fringe to it," on the night of the murder. (ch. 54) The identities of these two proud and strong-willed women merge in a debasing and downward direction. Lady Dedlock is no grander, no nobler than her haughty servant. Only the superficial distinction of class separates them, but Lady Dedlock has farther to go in her descent to the true level of her nature. In her final flight, Lady Dedlock, in an attempt to deceive anyone following her, changes clothes with Jenny, the brickmaker's wife. It is in this disguise that she makes her way once more to the loathsome graveyard where Hawdon is buried. In assuming this last disguise, Lady Dedlock assumes her true identity. Her beauty masked a series of sins and deceptions; her arrogance hid fear; and her high station was a false position from the start. As her behavior had been of the most common character, so she ends in a vulgar identity. She has descended to the true precincts of her nature in the sordid and disease-ridden neighborhood of the graveyard. Her disguise proves to be her true identity, just as her superficial appearance had been a disguise. Her lower nature is exposed after all.

Predictable disguises of melodrama reappear in *Little Dorrit* (1855-57). Blandois-Rigaud is the shape-shifting villain whose continual reappearance facilitates the plot. Rigaud also hints at the idea of an underlying persistence of evil in a world where the virtuous find it difficult to employ their virtues and the evil assume the guises of benevolence. Mr. Pancks appears to be greedy but is generous and kind, whereas the truly greedy Patriarch, Christopher Casby, convinces everyone of his virtue and benignity merely by his appearance and manner. In the secret places of Mrs. Clennam's house, Jeremiah Flintwinch entertains his accomplice and double, his brother Ephraim. Mr. Dorrit's social prominence after his release from prison is sham. Beneath it all, he remains the Father of the Marshalsea. His position in high society is a deception, which is in keeping with the society he moves in. Mrs. General, the counsellor of good taste, encourages a cultivation of surface, which is, it seems, the chief occupation of society. This superficiality is manifest in Henry Gowan's life as well as in his trivial paintings. Similarly, though Merdle appears extravagantly successful, he hides the secret of imminent financial collapse; and, when he falls, all the airy monetary structure founded on him collapses as surely as Mr. Dorrit's castles in the air. Even Arthur Clennam exhibits the sickness of the age. His harsh upbringing and directionless life have left him without a firm conviction about himself. He suffers a mild case of the malady seen in Clarence Linden, Charles Ravenshoe, and Esther Summerson—he doubts his identity. Convinced that he cannot win Pet Meagles' love, he takes to viewing himself as "Nobody." Still, divided as his nature is, he controls it. But, perhaps because he never does fully step outside himself, he must suffer a different form of self-appraisal, which comes to him through his illness and imprisonment. It is Little Dorrit, neither changing nor doubting herself, who revives and enlivens him. "Nobody" disappears and Arthur Clennam's vague identity is consolidated at last when he becomes Little Dorrit's husband. These devices, illuminating as they may be insofar as Dickens' attitude toward the perception of identity is concerned, are not actually disguises. In the explicit use of the disguise convention, Dickens could be even more inventive.

In *A Tale of Two Cities* (1859), Dickens' skill in the utilization of disguise is evidenced in the use of the double.[17] Darnay-St. Evremonde is first seen reflected in a mirror, and Sydney Carton, his dou-

ble, is among the spectators viewing him. It is convenient to the plot
to have the resemblance clearly noted from the beginning. The later
ironies and reversals of position, when it is Carton as Darnay who
stands before the bar of a peculiar justice in Paris, depend upon this
diagrammatic scene. But there is a good deal more to it than plot
movement.

Doubleness pervades the story, a fact that is perfectly evident in
the novel's structure and title. The complications of the story begin
with the St. Evremonde twin brothers. Both are guilty of offenses
against the French peasantry, and specifically against Doctor Manette. The establishment of look-alikes in an evil compact lends a
sinister atmosphere to any such duplications that might follow.
Charles St. Evremonde-Darnay is the son of the elder marquis, now
dead, and lives under an assumed name in England. Although Darnay is innocent of evil, his disguise has sinister overtones since so
much of the evil of the story relates to concealment. In keeping with
the doubleness of the novel's structure and theme, there are many
other dual identities. John Barsad, who becomes a spy and informer
for the British government, is in reality Solomon Pross, while Jerry
Cruncher is an occasional messenger at Tellson's bank by day and a
"resurrection-man" by night. Dr. Manette himself leads a double life,
his mind dwelling ordinarily in the present of London where he is
safe with his daughter, but, in moments of anxiety, lapsing back to
the horrid conditions of his imprisonment.

Thus the novel's structure is reflected in the divided conscious-
nesses of its characters, and certainly most prominent among these
are Charles Darnay and Sydney Carton. Darnay is clearly two men,
for he has assumed an English identity in England while he retains a
less savory French identity. Carton has only one ostensible identity,
but is, nonetheless, two men. Indeed, the main transformation in Carton is the gradual release and expansion of what is so frequently referred to as his "secret mind." There is much reference throughout the
novel to secrets and secret minds, so that even where there is not actual disguise there is hidden purpose or meaning. This secretiveness is
manifested on a broader scale in the underground plotting of the
French people and the final eruption of that enormous secret into violent action. Beneath all surfaces, then, there are probable secrets. It is
exactly at this point that Dickens plans his most exciting variation
upon this developing theme.

Though Charles Darnay may be an impostor, he is not false. Darnay's apparent falseness is actually authentic. As the heir to the St. Evremonde estates, he sought to establish more egalitarian principles objecting to the absurd perquisites of the French aristocracy. At heart he is not an aristocrat but believes in the equality of all men. Hence it is his identification with the St. Evremonde tradition that is false, and the hard-working, considerate, and middle-class Charles Darnay who is the real man. A similar situation involves Sydney Carton. On the surface, he is an idle wastrel, who has spent his substance foolishly and who cares for nothing. But the superficial man is not the true one, and when he assumes the St. Evremonde identity, he is more truly himself than he was as the feckless Carton. His real nobility manifests itself, and he demonstrates that under the disguise of the indifferent Carton was a noble heart capable of love and self-sacrifice.

It has frequently been observed that the motif of resurrection is prominent throughout *A Tale of Two Cities*. What is being resurrected is not only dead bodies by a grave robber, or an old man from a life of imprisonment, or old crimes of an aristocratic family. In an age of turmoil when the buried secrets are unearthed and exposed, men may draw up from within themselves other hidden secrets, other selves, that are treasures more valuable than anything Jerry Cruncher may turn up on a dark night in the local churchyard. "A wonderful fact to reflect upon," Dickens writes at the opening of chapter three of the First Book of his novel, "that every human creature is constituted to be that profound secret and mystery to every other." Dickens adds that death itself is only "the inexorable consolidation and perpetuation of the secret that was always in that individuality, and which I shall carry in mine to my life's end."

Our Mutual Friend (1864-65) is also concerned with the resurrection and uncovering of identities and is Dickens' most accomplished use of the disguise convention. The novel is characterized by concealment and altered appearances. In "good society" the ascendant Veneerings are, as their name indicates, little more than a surface, a temporary varnish to cover up with cash what has become shameful to admit, the making of money. Lady Tippins represents the falseness of a slightly higher social class, which has for some time depended more upon appearance than merit. "Whereabout in the bonnet and drapery announced by her name, any fragment of the real woman may be concealed, is perhaps known to her maid; but you could easily buy all you see of her, in Bond Street: or you might scalp her, and peel her, and scrape her, and make two Lady Tippinses out of her, and yet not penetrate to the genuine article." (Book 1, ch. 10) This is a society in which people meet and marry only to discover, like Sophronia Akershem and Alfred Lammle, that both are impostors. Neither is what appearance suggested and even those who arranged the marriage know nothing about those with whom they shared this intimate relationship. "Veneering knew as much of me as he knew of you, or as anybody knows of him." (Book 1, ch. 10) Nobody knows much of his associates because it is one purpose of society to keep up appearances and suppress all that might display a genuine self. Even Fascination Fledgeby, who is singularly inept in society, is "sensible of the value of appearances as an investment." (Book 2, ch. 5) And this preoccupation with appearances extends to the lowest degrees of society, for even Silas Wegg "ranged with that very numerous class of impostors, who are quite as determined to keep up appearances to themselves, as to their neighbours." (Book 1, ch. 5)

In a society where authentic qualities must be repressed and all false attributes displayed for admiration, it is no wonder that men like Mortimer Lightwood and Eugene Wrayburn have "hidden with great pains" the human instincts they surely possess. (Book 1, ch. 2) It is no less surprising that any man wishing to understand himself or his fellow men might find it necessary to step outside of his normal identity and play a role among the many roles he sees. Disguise may come to be the only means of revealing the true identities of men and things. It seems one must wear special clothes to seek a treasure in a dunghill.

" 'It's wonderful what's been hid, at one time and another,' said Mr. Boffin, ruminating; 'truly wonderful.' " (Book 3, ch. 6) And primarily what men seek to hide in this novel is their origins. Where did the Veneerings come from? Who were Bradley Headstone's forebears? Even Charley Hexam realizes that he must hide his origins if he is to get ahead. But all men, not only Gaffer Hexam, are "allied to the bottom of the river." (Book 1, ch. 1) Though they live upon the surface, their origins cannot remain hidden. A major image of the novel suggests that the secrets of mankind are constantly being dredged up or washed ashore as so much "moral sewage" from the river of life.

(Book 1, ch. 3) Nor has man progressed far from his ancestral origins. He still dwells in an environment alive with predators of all kinds who, so far as Boffin's situation is concerned, "may be regarded as the Alligators of the Dismal Swamp, and are always lying by to drag the Golden Dustman under." (Book 1, ch. 17) It is entirely appropriate, then, for the objects of such predation to use what defenses they can. In some cases it requires protective coloring, or even the disguise of the enemy. So, to thwart Wegg, Boffin hides himself behind the alligator in Venus' shop—a scene which indicates that Wegg's vicious greed is hardly novel. "The yard or two of smile on the part of the alligator might have been invested with the meaning, 'All about this was quite familiar knowledge down in the depths of the slime, ages ago.'" (Book 3, ch. 14)

Most men find themselves able to ignore this kinship with the slime and to overlook the fact that their feet are still of clay. But Bradley Headstone, though he struggles more than most to command himself, is less capable than others of succeeding. In anger he cries at Eugene Wrayburn, who has been taunting him: "'Do you suppose that a man, in forming himself for the duties I discharge, and in watching and repressing himself daily to discharge them well, dismisses a man's nature?'" (Book 2, ch. 6) Possessed by his desire to end Wrayburn's part in his life, he goads himself toward murder. Though "tied up all day with his disciplined show upon him . . . he broke loose at night like an ill-tamed wild animal." (Book 3, ch. 11) From the first, Headstone is pictured as a man with whom "Suppression of so much to make room for so much, had given him a constrained manner, over and above. Yet there was enough of what was animal, and of what was fiery (though smouldering), still visible in him." (Book 2, ch. 1)

The fact is that Headstone's life is an unconscious disguise. And for him, as for the less stern Dr. Jekyll some years later, an alter ego waits to assist him in yielding to his baser passions. Both Headstone and Rogue Riderhood are at one in their desire to do away with Eugene Wrayburn, and knowing Riderhood brings Headstone closer to the crime—so close, in fact, that his lowest self becomes his ordinary self simply because it becomes the stronger. Riderhood serves as the model that brings it to the surface. Headstone assumes a costume resembling Riderhood's, "And whereas, in his own schoolmaster clothes, he usually looked as if they were the clothes of some other man, he now looked, in the clothes of some other man, or men, as if they were his own." (Book 4, ch. 1) Headstone's disguise is a disclosure, not a concealment. He has never truly been the schoolmaster. Once he appropriates Riderhood's identity, it becomes evident that Headstone is only an ill-tamed Riderhood disguised as a schoolmaster. The disguise is the real identity, and by assuming it, Headstone parts with his former identity forever. After his attempt on Wrayburn's life, Headstone disposes of his disguise and rises, "as it were, out of the ashes of the Bargeman." (Book 4, ch. 15) But this is a specious recovery. The truth is quickly demonstrated when Riderhood confronts Headstone in his classroom. Here, for the first time, he learns Headstone's name and indicates to him that he has the discarded clothing used in the assault upon Wrayburn and that he means to blackmail Headstone. The innocent schoolmaster no longer exists, only the wild animal remains, and, as though to seal this fact, "Bradley, slowly withdrawing his eyes [from Riderhood's], turned his face to the black board and slowly wiped his name out." (Book 4, ch. 15) Headstone has accepted his true identity. He and Riderhood are one. "I am a-going along with you wherever you go," Riderhood tells him, and in truth they end together, drowned "under the ooze and scum" of the lock that Riderhood tended. (Book 4, ch. 15)

The entire world of *Our Mutual Friend* is one of false appearances: the very fable from which Rogue Riderhood's name is drawn depends upon a sinister disguise. And just as wolfishness in that tale cloaked in innocence, so the predators of *Our Mutual Friend* roam their preserves in disguises that mask animal natures. But, whereas Bradley Headstone struggled against the fierce consolidation of his divided self into a destructive single identity, other characters in the novel have an opposite urge, being unable to define themselves satisfactorily. Silas Wegg is the comic version of this dilemma. When he sees prospects ahead for himself, and a chance at "improvement," he remarks that he "Should *not* like—under such circumstances, to be what I may call dispersed, a part of me here, and a part of me there, but should wish to collect myself like a genteel person." (Book 1, ch. 7) But the genteel persons are less collected than Wegg, who only means to recover a missing limb. Eugene Wrayburn goes idly on with his life, not knowing what he means nor understanding what he wants. He has never collected himself. His life is a fraud; he is a species of impostor. Only when he has come near death and been dredged up from the slime is he reborn with a clear knowledge of what he wishes to be.

But this pattern of rebirth along with the discovery of one's true identity is worked out mainly in the character of John Harmon. When reflecting upon the circumstances which almost cost him his life and permitted him to shed his usual identity, Harmon observes, "I came back timid, divided in my mind, afraid of myself and everybody here." (Book 2, ch. 13) This division of himself becomes manifest when he assumes the disguise of John Rokesmith.[18] By so transferring his identity, he is able to view the man that he was objectively. He discovers that John Harmon was loved by the Boffins as a human being, and viewed merely as a material advantage by the woman he was destined to marry. Without his disguise, there may have been no such opportunities to understand himself. Now he can benefit partly from the definitions presented by others. If Bradley Headstone tried to fashion a respectable identity only to discover that it was a disguise, and his true nature was closer to the beasts; John Harmon has the remarkable chance of escaping a false identity by fashioning a true one.

In a society where things were what they seemed, no such detour into a temporary identity would have been necessary for John Harmon. But, as we have seen, the world of *Our Mutual Friend* teems with disguises and deceptions. Like John Harmon, Bella Wilfer possesses a divided, even contradictory nature, which she explains to herself by observing "but my life and fortunes are so contradictory altogether that what can I expect myself to be!" (Book 2, ch. 10) Yet her better nature constantly reveals itself with her father, and her behavior is "very tender and very natural" with the ailing child, Johnny. (Book 3, ch. 9) Characteristically, it is only through a deception that Bella can be made to discover her real self. Boffin must, as an antidote to the opposite tendency around him, mask his better self and play the villain in order to correct Bella. If Harmon found it possible to see his ordinary self as a sort of disguise and thereby established his proper identity, Bella is able to see herself not by her own use of a disguise, but through Boffin's. In the end it serves the same purpose. When E. D. H. Johnson says that "the overworking of the disguise motif makes the Rokesmith-Bella plot of *Our Mutual Friend* . . . implausible,"[19] he is not crediting Dickens' skill in using the entire disguise convention. Bella's life is a disguise. She attempts to mask the better self behind the greedy woman of the world. The closer Bella is to women like Sophronia Lammle, the falser she is, and knows it. She knows as well that she is truer the nearer she draws to Lizzie Hexam in whom "There's no pretending." (Book 2, ch. 1) And at last, when Bella has learned her lesson, she finds it impossible even to conceal the nature of the marriage dinner at Greenwich. "'Disguise is of no use,' said Bella; 'they all find me out; I think it must be, Pa and John dear, because I look so happy!'" (Book 4, ch. 4) And thus happily does Dickens demonstrate the significance of his disguise motif.

In *Our Mutual Friend*, all of existence is mutable, sliding from shape to shape like the river, the mud, or the dust. Unexpected treasures may emerge from any of these substances, just as human identity first emerged from the ancestral slime and better natures draw themselves forth from disfiguring masks. But it is equally possible for treasures to be hidden and lost forever in the slime. Those who recognize the mutable nature of themselves and the world around them can overcome the confusions and fears that cancel useful action. They have seen that all appearances in this world are no more than disguises that cloak a greater and immutable truth. Eventually, they set their sights beyond appearances and no longer have need of masks.

Dickens is concerned not only with the eternal question of the transience of physical existence. He is equally fascinated by the psychological ramifications of disguise. We have seen this interest operating in *Bleak House*, but an additional subtlety appears in Dickens' last and unfinished novel, *The Mystery of Edwin Drood* (1870), where it is clear that John Jasper's nature is divided within itself. Not only does he lead a social life of disguised sensuality and apparent respectability, but within himself his nature seems equally sundered. There is, in John Jasper's condition, a hint of what is to come in later works by Robert Louis Stevenson and Oscar Wilde. It seems likely that Dickens intended to make broad use of doubles and disguises in this novel, and the suggestions of hidden things, as in Durdles' practice of searching out hidden tombs, which fascinates Jasper, indicate that the old themes of concealment and discovery, both in identity and in plot, might have found elaborate manifestation in this last work.

CHARLOTTE BRONTË AND WILKIE COLLINS

Dickens' use of disguise was more accomplished than most of his contemporaries could hope to equal, but others made good use of the convention. In writers such as Charlotte Brontë and Wilkie Collins, disguise indicated both psychological and sociological problems. For Charlotte Brontë the psychological predominated. Given to reserve and even secrecy herself, her fiction was marked as well by the question of concealed identity. Charlotte Brontë, like other Victorians, seemed to entertain a dual interpretation of character. From her frequent references to physiognomy as a signification of character, it is apparent that she believed natures were betrayed from the start by their outward appearances, but at the same time, that character could be concealed.

In her first novel, *The Professor* (1857, published posthumously), Charlotte Brontë's central character, William Crimsworth, is determined not to reveal his character, for to him the better, inward self is a hidden treasure to be salvaged. Yet Crimsworth does not realize that his powerful sense of confinement is largely the consequence of his reserve until he is able to admit his love for Frances Evans Henri and release his inner feelings. Other concealments in the novel include Monsieur Pelet's, or Mademoiselle Zoraïde Reuter's, or even the apparently straightforward Yorke Hunsden's.

Secretiveness and concealment assume greater proportions in *Jane Eyre* (1847). Jane is constantly misunderstood in childhood and thereby learns reserve, though her passions struggle against that reserve. So it is with all strong natures; not merely her own, but Edward Rochester's and St. John Rivers' as well. Both men have secrets which they labor to suppress. Rochester's case is emblematic. The master of Thornfield has hidden in the attic a mad and passionate wife. She is the type of man's "other half" that threatens to overwhelm and ruin him. In the end, some balance must be achieved between passion and control.

There is little actual disguise in *Jane Eyre*. Jane, striving to reorganize her life after her flight from Thornfield, assumes the name Jane Elliott, but this disguise is merely the ordinary device of Victorian novels. A new life may require a new name, as Robert Audley remarked. There is something provocative, however, in Rochester's assuming the guise of an old gipsy woman to tell the fortunes of guests at his home, among them Jane's. In stepping outside his own role, he hopes to achieve what John Harmon does when he becomes John Rokesmith. But Charlotte Brontë was not capable of Dickens' simultaneous simplification and amplification of the disguise. Whereas Harmon discarded one identity to fashion another, Rochester merely disguises his own. The disguise is readily abandoned, since it is only a moment's tool—the business of a commonplace stage melodrama. What is more, Jane is able to penetrate the disguise. Still, rudimentary as this scene may be, there is a hint of subtlety in it, for there is meaning in Rochester's choice of disguise. Prior to Rochester's appearance as a gipsy, he and his guests had been playing at charades, and the roles had more than trifling significance, at least to Jane. When Rochester appears as the gipsy, therefore, it is likely that his role should imply a deeper meaning for gipsies were credited with free and wild natures, and Rochester has been presented as a passionate man. Before the end of the novel, he will also demonstrate a certain uncanniness, often associated with occult powers of gipsies. Rochester's disguise also reinforces suggestions about his character, even hinting of his hidden wife in his attic.

In *Shirley* the theme of disguise is less suggestive than in *Jane Eyre*, but it is in her final completed novel, *Villette* (1853), that Charlotte Brontë brought her ideas and techniques regarding disguise to full maturity. Like the earlier novels, *Villette* creates a pervasive, almost oppressive sense of concealment. To begin with, we know little of Lucy Snowe's origins; more notably, even in her first-person accounts she is reticent about feelings that are obvious to the reader. Lucy dislikes nudity in art and is morally opposed to lying, yet she herself is naked in her emotions and both reticent and deceptive. She is unquestionably appalled by the dissimulations of others, yet she does not want conventional disguises abandoned. Madame Beck is Lucy's principal example of deceit. While masking her own feelings and intentions, the mistress of the girls' school makes every attempt to learn the secrets of those about her. One day Lucy discovers Madame Beck going through her belongings, but she does not accost her, for then "down would have gone conventionalities, away swept disguises, and *I* should have looked in her eyes, and *she* into mine—we should have known that we could work together no more, and parted in this life forever." (ch. 13) Nonetheless, though Lucy does not wish to abandon disguises, she takes a certain pleasure in her capacity to penetrate them, and she boasts finally that Madame Beck's "habitual disguise, her mask and her domino, were to me a mere network reticulated with holes; and I saw underneath a being heartless, self-indulgent, and ignoble." (ch. 38)

But there are appearances that Lucy is not so quick to penetrate. She is slow to discover Paul Emmanuel's genuine character. Content to view him as a friendly but obtrusive eccentric, Lucy changes her view when she learns the secret of his lost love and of his generosity. More important is Lucy's reluctance to admit the multiplicity of her own nature. Some contemporary readers of *Villette* were disturbed by Lucy's being in love with two men at the same time,[20] but it is precisely this ambiguity of emotion with which Lucy must learn to deal. Just as she rushes to a Catholic confessional while despising the church of Rome, so she puts herself in danger of other seductions. In the end she is not seduced by Rome or Paul Emmanuel, but comes to lead an ordered and resigned existence.

Lucy's final resignation comes only when Paul is dead. Throughout the novel, she has lacked a clear vision of herself. She is as much disguised to herself as others are. She is called Madame Minerva Gravity because of her seriousness, and she accepts her role as a serious person. She is surprised by the varied and contradictory attributes ascribed to her by others, and is astonished when she discovers another possible self in her own image in a mirror. When Ginevra Fanshawe asks Lucy who she is, Lucy replies: "Who am I indeed? Perhaps a personage in disguise. Pity I don't look the character." (ch. 27) In her sarcasm, Lucy speaks the truth for she *is* a personage in disguise, though she is unaware of it until the novel's end.

Lucy is herself much given to concealment. In love with Dr. John, she carries his letters into the frightful attic of Madame Beck's house in order to read them privately. There is something in this association of the dingy attic and contained passion that is reminiscent of Bertha Mason raging in her attic chamber. It is worth noting that this attic is also the spectral nun's ingress to the chaste establishment of Madame Beck. Indeed, the figure of the nun may be read as a psychological representation of repressed passion. It is, therefore, ironically fitting that the nun's habiliments should be left on Lucy's virginal bed while Colonel de Hamal, who has used the disguise of the nun to visit Ginevra, elopes with his prize.

If the nun serves as an unconscious projection of a part of Lucy's character, another projection is fully conscious. In an amateur dramatic production, Lucy plays a male part in which she is Dr. John's rival for Ginevra's love. In fact, she uses the part to stand temporarily outside her ordinary self and thereby gain an insight that she had been unwilling, until then, to accept. A similar revelation occurs to her on the evening when, partly drugged and unlike her normal self, she visits the fête in the park and discovers that she is jealous of Paul Emmanuel. Appropriately enough, it is upon her return to her room that evening that she discovers the nun's garments on her loveless bed. Although Lucy is occasionally enabled or obliged to step outside her ordinary self and play roles likely to provide insight into her own nature, she does not generally respect such role-playing. When Dr. John, now revealed to us as the Graham Bretton that Lucy had admired in her childhood, asks Lucy to recall the old days, she resists. "In this matter I was not disposed to gratify Dr. John: not at all. With now welcome force, I realized his entire misapprehension of my character and nature. He wanted always to give me a role not mine. Nature and I opposed him." (ch. 27) Lucy herself is not so certain of what her character and nature may be, but she knows that it is one thing to act out roles that her nature drives her to, and that it is another altogether to pretend at one that she cannot acknowledge.

If Lucy seems uncertain in the regulating of her own nature and the ordering of her confused identity, she is no more alert regarding the men in her life. Lucy quickly understands Ginevra, Polly, and Madame Beck, but she is slow to fathom Paul or Graham Bretton. In the case of Bretton, Lucy's task is complicated because he too is a role-player. He is the romantic lover, Isidore, who interests Ginevra for a time. He is Dr. John, though with characteristic reticence Lucy delays revealing this fact to her readers for a considerable time. Moreover, in Graham Bretton there are two contradictory selves— "the public and private—the out-door and the indoor." The former is earnest and modest; the latter delights in giving and exciting homage. "Both portraits," Lucy remarks, "are correct." (ch. 19)

Robert Moore, in *Shirley*, felt as though he were two men. In *Villette* we learn that men and women may be divided more variously than that, since identity is a matter of perception. Lucy, wondering at the various interpretations of her nature, does not realize that she too discovers different identities in those around her. Life is a sequence of roles and shifting identities so long as we are concerned with the churning emotions that govern men and women. But early in the novel Lucy draws a distinction between the life of thought and the life of reality. Her perception of this duality prepares us for Lucy's eventual resignation. Some people are destined to happy lots; they are, like Graham Bretton and Pauline Home de Bassompierre, "Nature's elect." But others, like Lucy, are given another role to play. They are destined to suffer and endure, and for them all of this life is alien and uncertain. Although Charlotte Brontë expressed this sentiment less forcefully than Tennyson or Dickens, she nonetheless implied that for some, if not for all, this life was shadow and dream and all of its appearances mere disguise worn by a spirit that earnestly longed for its true eternal home.

There is no talk of an eternal home in Wilkie Collins' tales, where concern with disguise was psychological and social. Collins' fictional world is also dominated by secrecy, concealment, and disguise, but these disguises operate on a concrete level and have few spiritual overtones. They reveal, for the most part, the falseness of social appearances and the dangers of pretence. Much of the concealed identity in Collins serves to make unlikely plot movements more serviceable. All of *Hide and Seek* (1854), as the title suggests, turns upon secrets of identity. Matthew Grice, seeking the man responsible for his sister's misfortune, conceals his real name and appears instead as Matthew Marksman. Valentine Blyth correspondingly keeps secret the identity of the deaf and dumb girl known as Madonna, who is, in fact, the illegitimate daughter of Mary Grice. And Mr. Thorpe, through all his years of respectability, has managed to conceal the fact that he is the father of Mary's child. In this novel, little comes of the disguise convention beyond the facilitation of an improbable plot and a suggestion that vice disguised is in its way crueller than open vice.

In *No Name* (1862), Collins made more of this device. Norah and Magdalene Vanstone learn, upon their parents' deaths, that they are illegitimate, their parents having married only recently, due to a series of understandable complications. This marriage inadvertently disinherits the girls, and it becomes Magdalene's purpose to recover that inheritance. Magdalene is an extraordinarily talented amateur actress, and she makes use of her talent for disguise in gaining access to Noel Vanstone, the legal heir, and eventually in deceiving him into marrying her, while cloaking her true identity. Even when Noel has died, Magdalene again resorts to a disguise, this time as a maid, in order to discover what secret trust was included in Noel's will leaving the inheritance to George Bartram, an old family friend. Once more Magdalene's disguise brings no real success. Although she has

begun with the desperate feeling that because she is not really anyone's child she may be anyone she pleases, a better nature in her rebels against her deceptions. In the midst of an early disguise, for example, Magdalene cannot contain her sentiments about the injustice
done to the Vanstone girls. "Once more the inborn nobility of that
perverted nature had risen superior to the deception which it had
stooped to practice."

The title of Collins' novel suggests an identity left to be fulfilled,
but it may be read in another manner as well. No name may designate the virtues of character. Names themselves, as Magdalene
proves, are nothing more than deceptions. Collins makes the same
point that Dickens had presented in the character of Esther Summerson. Only inward qualities are important in judging character,
and, though these qualities, like secret trusts and treasures, may remain long hidden, they will ultimately reveal themselves. "Nothing
in this world is hidden forever," Collins remarks early in the novel,
and though he is speaking of family secrets, it is clear enough by the
novel's end that he has a similar conviction regarding the secrets of
character.

With *Armadale* (1864-65), Collins added another variation in his
use of disguise. In this novel, there are two Allan Armadales, one of
whom has assumed the name of Ozias Midwinter, maintaining the
secret of his real name in order to preserve his alter ego from the
consequences of a vision which he cannot be certain is true or merely
superstitious. The two men are opposites in temperament, Armadale
being thoroughly superficial and thoughtless, Midwinter being meditative, sensitive, and inward. It is Midwinter who appears alien, his
blood being mixed and his manners strange, but Armadale as well is
socially estranged, for his candid behavior is unacceptable to society
at Thorpe Ambrose. In a way, these two men may be viewed as rudimentary doubles, the type and anti-type of a single identity. Eventually Midwinter saves Armadale's life by taking his place, though
he himself survives—a benign version of Carton's sacrifice of himself
for Darnay in Dickens' *A Tale of Two Cities*.[21] This confusion of
identities has implications not evident in earlier novels by Collins
where disguise was primarily concealment for purposes of action, as
with Miss Gwilt in this novel. The implications here are less developed than in *A Tale of Two Cities*, but clearly Collins has seen beyond mere plot requirements. Perhaps Collins learned a great deal

from Dickens about the disguise convention, for in his story, *The New Magdalene* (1873), he uses the same device Dickens used in *Bleak House*, though in reverse. Mercy Merrick has been cast out by society for offenses that society has forced upon her. Although she reforms and accepts her society's standards, the champions of those standards will not accept her. Yet Mercy is a good woman at heart and only longs for an opportunity to prove it. When Grace Roseberry appears to have been killed by a shell burst, Mercy sees her opportunity to take Grace's place. "A new identity, which she might own anywhere! a new name, which was beyond reproach! a new past life, into which all the world might search, and be welcome!" So overwhelming is Mercy's desire for a new life and a new identity, that her "better nature" yields to the deception.

But Grace Roseberry survives her injuries and appears at her rich and highly connected relative, Lady Janet Roy's, to claim the benefits of her kinship. Even considering the upsetting circumstance of discovering an impostor in her place, Grace's behavior is nasty and mean, while Mercy, with so much to lose, struggles to be kind. So obvious is Mercy's finer nature, says Collins, that a stranger, left to guess which was which, would "have picked out Grace as the counterfeit and Mercy as the true woman." Mercy, in assuming the position of respectable woman, has only taken the place she truly deserves. It is the mean-natured Grace Roseberry who is the real impostor and who does not deserve the social station to which her name seems to entitle her. Lady Janet, recognizing this fact, sends Grace away with a suitable compensation, and defends Mercy's elevation to respectability in her marriage to Julian Gray.

Collins' usage here is facile, and not so profound as Dickens'. It is in *The Moonstone* (1868) that he exploited the device more elaborately and more successfully than elsewhere in his writings. William H. Marshall says of this novel that in "the dramatic and ironic manipulation of character, in the exploration of the reality of the self lying beneath the personality, Collins reflected some of the serious intellectual concerns of his age."[22] Collins was always concerned with the ordinarily unexamined layers of character, but here the many levels of character are more explicitly revealed. The stodgy Gabriel Betteredge is disturbed by Franklin Blake's multiple personality with its German, French, Italian, and English sides. Yet it is because of his ability to recognize the multiplicity of personality in himself that

Blake can function as well as he does. It is one of the great ironies of the novel that Blake, with such a varied character, should be ignorant of a critically important region of his personality, the unconscious.

Blake is one of the few characters in the novel to acknowledge his own multiple nature. Cuff can recognize at least a dual personality in the reformed thief, Rosanna Spearman, and Godfrey Ablewhite knows his own duplicity; but awareness of man's potential for mutability or flexibility of character is limited. Instead, characters are forced by a society that requires appearances to be kept up to suppress that part of their character that would most benefit from exposure. It is this easily recognizable form of disguise that signals the shortcomings of English society. Rosanna Spearman, though she has reformed, is obliged to disguise her past, for society would not otherwise accept her. Yet when she dies she reveals that the "imposture" of respectability is her true identity. Her previous identity is now perceivable as the false one. In death she is proven no thief, but a woman willing to sacrifice herself for the man she loves. Rosanna's case is neatly contrasted with that of Godfrey Ablewhite; this spokesman of respectability in reality leads a double life. He is a sensualist, a swindler, and a thief. He too reveals his true identity in death. When the police officer snatches away the false beard from Godfrey's corpse, he discloses the man as a thief whose respectable role was a disguise. At the same time, on a larger scale, in removing Godfrey's disguise, the officer strips the mask from an entire culture that values its Ablewhites and its appearances above the realities of human nature. *The Moonstone* provided England with a means of looking past the many masks it wore, but few were willing to look at the undisguised truth. In his later fiction, Collins concentrated on showing that society its small and large uglinesses without the benefit of disguises.

Collins' sentiments were perfectly clear in a novel such as *The Fallen Leaves* (1878), where one spokesman of proper values remarks that a "selfish and cruel Pretense is set up" in place of Christianity as Christ taught it. (Book 1, ch. 2) When Collins describes the gathering of middle-class citizens at the Farnaby house, all of whom are retailing newspaper opinions as though they were their own, there is no doubt about his judgment. "One enormous Sham, and everybody in a conspiracy to take it for the real thing: that is an accurate description of the state of political feeling among the representative men at Mr. Farnaby's dinner." (Book 2, ch. 1) And Amelius Goldenheart himself decides that insincerity is "one of the established institutions of English Society." (Book 2, ch. 2)[23] For the later Collins, all of English society was a disguise, concealing a falseness of emotion and thought that was, above all else, corruptive of the highest values of humanity. In this opinion he agreed with many of the important writers of his time.

SUBTLE VERSIONS: GEORGE MEREDITH

For the better part of the nineteenth century in Britain disguise was an important literary convention. It could be superficial and mechanical, or symbolic, suggestive and profound. It could hint at the spiritual, or confine itself to psychological and social levels, and was also an accurate indicator of changes in British culture. John A. Lester, Jr. has suggested that Dandyism and a penchant for posing became necessary shields for threatened identities.[24] Early in the century a widespread concern for appearances was resisted by outstanding writers, but by the late nineteenth century more and more writers championed appearance, and in some cases exalted it above the common appreciation. But as this intensifying concern for the trappings of things and identities developed, there also evolved a subtle and reasonable modification of melodramatic versions of disguise. In George Meredith's novels, metaphors of theatricality, role-playing, and mask-wearing abound. In the society that emerges from his writings, intellectual or emotional schemes collapse as they are stripped of their bolstering disguises; impostors of one kind or another are everywhere. Meredith's plots lead his heroes through ordeals that uncover their truest selves and save them from errors of mind and passion.

In Meredith's first novel, *The Shaving of Shagpat* (1855), illusion is a prominent theme, but the disguises that occur throughout the work are set in a fanciful "Arabian Entertainment." Leaving the fanciful structure behind, Meredith maintained a strong interest in the theme of disclosure. In *The Ordeal of Richard Feverel* (1859), almost all of the main characters have secrets to hide. The greatest pretender of all, Sir Austin, is ostensibly the most concerned with truth. Even the narrator advises him to abjure disguises and be himself, but Sir Austin decides that he "must shut his heart and mask his face . . . and it was thus that he set about ruining the work he had done." It is entirely fitting that Mrs. Berry—representative of the authentic and the sincere—should be the servant who "dared to behold the Baronet behind his mask" in the time of his ordeal. (ch. 35) Richard is forced to conceal his marriage to Lucy, Clare conceals her love until death, and other similar concealments and deceits emerge and fade as the novel proceeds. (Chapter headings indicate the prominence of the theme: "The Unmasking of Ripton Thompson," and "A Glimpse Behind the Mask.") Mrs. Mount is among the most facile of all characters, and, while playing the role of "Fair Penitent," brings about Richard's fall from innocence.

For Meredith, men are not deluded by false appearances alone. They are deceived because they have not comprehended their own multiple identities. Is Richard a knight-errant, or is he a dream-beguiled boy? Is Evan Harrington a gentleman or not? It is for Evan to determine within himself just what his identity will be. If the name of gentleman fits that identity, good; otherwise, he must forego it. But it requires the whole of *Evan Harrington* (1860) for the young man to apprehend that fact.

Evan Harrington is a medley of impostures. The Harrington children, not wishing to be known as tailor's offspring, masquerade as gentility. Not all are eager to renounce their actual past, but at the instigation of the most subtle child, Louisa, otherwise the Countess de Saldar, they are persuaded to continue the pretence. Evan does not wish to be known as a tailor or even a tailor's son, but longs to be a gentleman and marry Rose Jocelyn. Unfortunately, "Pride was the one developed faculty of Evan's nature," though in a revealing exchange with a postillion the young man begins to learn certain truths about his false position. "I will not say that the postillion stripped off the mask for him, at that instant completely; but he gave him the first true glimpse of his condition. From the vague sense of being an impostor, Evan awoke to the clear fact that he was likewise a fool." (ch. 6) Evan is moved by this lesson to abjure pretense. He shaves off his moustache to symbolize the decision. The Countess deplores his act, observing with alarm that he could hardly now be distinguished from "the very commonest tradesman," and specifies the value of the moustache. "It's a disguise, Evan—do you know that?" But Evan's response is ready. "'And I've parted with it—that's all,' said Evan. 'No more disguises for me.'" (ch. 9)

Evan struggles to hold to this resolve, but Louisa and circumstances act against him. Even when he publicly admits that he is a tailor's son, his carousing companions refuse to believe him. "Sit down," one of them says, "and don't dare to spoil the fun any more. You a tailor! Who'll believe it? You're a nobleman in disguise. Didn't your friend say so? -ha! ha! Sit down." (ch. 12) What makes Evan's resolve difficult to maintain is the complication of his love for Rose. It is this love that leads him into self-deceptions. "A lover must have his delusions," Meredith notes, "just as a man must have a skin." (ch. 18) Yet he does not condone the young man's error, since delusions are painful when flayed from their anatomy. Just before admitting the lover's need for delusions, Meredith describes Evan's encounter with Polly Wheedle, whose innocent allusion to the tailoring trade ravages the young man's vanity. "Evan," Meredith remarks, "was skinned alive." (ch. 18)

For Meredith, there are no mysterious figures moving in the shadows garbed in great cloaks and wearing false whiskers. The disguises he finds interesting are those which offer the appearance of the man himself, behind which there is either no substance, or the wrong substance. Yet this form of disguise is as dangerous and perhaps more insidious than any other. Evan's beloved sister, Caroline, finding that she herself cannot endure the role-playing that Louisa encourages, begs Evan to admit their family background and endure any suffering that follows. Evan asks her if she can bear the consequences. "Bear it? bear anything rather than perpetual imposture," she replies. (ch. 25) More succinctly, the admirable Rose Jocelyn asserts, "Concealment is never of any service." (ch. 32)

Evan observes what candor can effect in the behavior of Lady Jocelyn, who, though upper class, can value a man for his merits, and who appreciates the suitability of Evan's love for Rose. Lady Jocelyn requires no disguise from Evan. "Unconsciously he felt that she took, and would take, him for what he was, and he rose to his worth in the society she presided over." Moreover, "he felt much less of an impostor now." (ch. 16) Ultimately Evan learns to value himself as a man, and it is in this guise and no other that Rose accepts him, for she will not be fooled by masks, roles, and disguises; "her spirit hurried out of all shows and forms and habits of thought, up to the gates of existence, as it were, where she took him simply as God created him and her, and clave to him." (ch. 29)

Evan is both a natural and a nurtured gentleman. He has had the education of a gentleman, and has known the people that gentlemen know. For him to behave as a gentleman is no imposture, since he also has natural qualities of bravery, integrity and nobility that more highborn men, like Harry Jocelyn, do not possess. The clownish Jack Raikes may declare, "I'm the son of a gentleman!" and behave like a fool, but Evan's appearance is the reality. Only circumstances and the false values of a society dedicated to concealments and deceits can interpret it as a disguise. What the chairman at the table at the Green Dragon says is true. Evan is a nobleman in disguise. But the disguise is only in the eye of the beholder.

Pride may be one reason for acting a part, but sentimentalism is another. In *Emilia in England*, later entitled *Sandra Belloni* (1864), sentimentalism becomes a form of disguise through its inertia toward concealment. The sentimental are also egoists evading a direct view of the actual. In this novel images of acting and masking abound once more and characters move uneasily in their loose-fitting identities. Robert Eccles, in *Rhoda Fleming* (1865), assumes the name of Robert Armstrong from shame. This false self is the product of his intemperate habits and provides an opportunity for resuming his true identity. When Robert recovers his self-respect and devotes himself, through love, to assisting others, he also resumes his proper name.

There are numerous reasons for altering identities, playing roles, masking selves, or assuming actual disguises, but for Meredith it all comes back to man's inability to recognize or accept his own divided nature. True identity is only possible when an equilibrium or proportion is established in the individual—when blood, brain and spirit complement one another and do not wrangle among themselves. In *The Adventures of Harry Richmond* (1871), as elsewhere in Meredith's writings, the protagonist's central problem is controlling both his animal nature and the fantasies of his imagination. Harry's father, Richmond Roy, represents an acute confusion of identity, for he claims to be of royal lineage and publicly puts forward his claim, though he is merely a conniver and an outright impostor.[25] A minor character referred to as the Dauphin is Roy's pathetic foil, for he too makes fanciful claims to royalty, managing only to make himself a foolish spectacle.

Imposture pervades this novel. Even Harry is duped into playing a false part, but so subtly that he scarcely realizes it. In time he does perceive the true case with his father. "Indubitably, then, my father was an impostor: Society proved it." (ch. 41) Squire Beltham is less gentle in his charge against Roy; facing him for the last time, he ends his denunciation by remarking, "the kindest blow to you's to call you impostor." (ch. 52) Harry is threatened with lapsing into a similar form of imposture, and it is the romantic figure of his mysterious father that prepares his way. As a boy he forever expects strangers to emerge as his father "in disguise," and he yearns to seek his father through the world. Reviewing his own development, Harry complains that "At every stage of my growth one or another of my passions was alert to twist me awry, and now I was getting a false self about me and becoming liker to the creature people supposed me to be, despising them for blockheads in my heart, as boys may who preserve a last trace of the ingenuousness denied to seasoned men." (ch. 9) Harry does not at first recognize the false self he begets at the leading edge of tension between his passions of the blood and of the mind, but as he grows in awareness, he comes to recognize this variance within himself. Set against his ideal self, preoccupied with high aims, is his "other eager thirstful self." (ch. 30) One of Harry's gravest disillusions is his realization that, in his love for Ottilia, he has been his father's dupe and has acquiesced in deceptions. Suddenly he sees the baseness of the game in which he is involved and sadly recounts, "So my worthier, or ideal, self fell away from me." (ch. 34)

Harry, like Richard Feverel, Evan Harrington, or Neville Beauchamp—other young idealists—is forced to realize that the disguises of the self are just as likely to be unconscious and insidious accretions as they are conscious maskings and deceits. It is one of the harshest lessons that Meredith's young people endure. Cecilia Halkett, in *Beauchamp's Career* (1875), is of the newly initiated. Attempting to hide her true feelings, she does not realize that they become more evident in the attempt. "She was young in suffering, and thought, as the unseasoned and inexperienced do, that a mask is a concealment." (Ch. 26) If Dickens indicated his characters' true identities by the disguises they employed, Meredith indicates that masks reveal what candor may hide. It is a similar notion translated to a more commonplace manifestation. The roles that we choose to play, the masks we put on to hide our needs, Meredith says throughout his works, give away our deepest hungers more surely than frankness and candor might. This is so, he adds, because in a sophisticated society where deception is the rule and people "Wear masks instead of faces," all masks are penetrable. (*Evan Harrington*, ch. 3) Only honesty can confound habitual dissemblers.

But there is a profound failing, in Meredith's view, that engenders this habitual dissimulation, and that is man's increasing dread of facing natural truths and of acknowledging his bond with nature. It takes a firm, tested character to endure the awareness that Meredith demands. Identity is a hodgepodge of contending instincts and dreams. Men may fabricate identities by refusing to acknowledge the sources of their behavior, but these identities are nothing more than roles assumed by actors on a comic stage. Sir Willoughby, in *The Egoist* (1879), is the pattern of this comic type. He is the consummate actor with many facets to his surface, but this surface is doomed. "The Egoist surely inspires pity. He who would desire to clothe himself at everybody's expense, and is of that desire condemned to strip himself stark naked, he, if pathos ever had a form, might be taken for the actual person." ("Prelude") The image of clothing supports the impression that men are more costume than character. But their tenuous sartorial shells are fragile, as Sir Willoughby discovers after his buffeting experiences with Clara Middleton and Laetitia Dale. "Sir Willoughby's shrunken self-esteem, like a garment hung to the fire after exposure to tempestuous weather, recovered some of the sleekness of its velvet pile in the society of Mrs. Mountstuart Jenkinson." (ch. 17)

Not all performers of this kind are comedians as the title of Meredith's next novel, *The Tragic Comedians* (1880), implies. Alvan is an outstanding example of the man who cannot fully integrate himself. The true nature and cause of his death qualify the over-idealization of him by his followers:

> He was neither fool nor madman, nor man to be adored: his last temptation caught him in the season before he had subdued his blood, and amid the multitudinously simple of this world, stamped him a tragic comedian: that is, a grand pretender, a self-deceiver, one of the lividly ludicrous, whom we cannot laugh at, but must contemplate, to distinguish where their character strikes the note of discord with life; for otherwise in the reflection of their history, life will seem a thing demoniacally inclined by fits to antic and dive into gulfs. (ch. 19)

Only those who accept the springs of their actions and aims are prepared to hammer out what could be called a true identity. Yet even that identity is in constant danger of lapsing into disguise. "O Self! self! self!" Diana Warwick exclaims, in *Diana of the Crossways* (1885), "are we eternally masking in a domino that reveals your hideous old face when we could be most positive we had escaped you? Eternally! the desolating answer knelled." (ch. 4)

The whole of *One of Our Conquerors* (1891), like *Evan Harrington* or *The Adventures of Harry Richmond*, is posited on a grand imposture. Victor Radnor and his presumed wife, Nataly, have never been able to marry; as a consequence, their daughter Nesta is forced into the similar imposture of legitimacy. But whereas illegitimacy of this kind in Collins' *No Name* was largely a stimulant to more disguises and deceits, with Meredith the imposture leads to an important awareness. Nesta faces her nature with greater honesty and courage than either of her parents, for they seek to conceal as shameful an act that honors their love if openly acknowledged. Nesta's danger is that she should become too smug in her frankness. But a conversation with the adultress, Judith Marsett, renders Nesta's intellectual acknowledgments substantial. Now she can admire "the white coat of armour" that the "ignorant-innocent" young women of her society wear, but for herself, despite her knowledge of the world, "It shocked her nevertheless to perceive how much of the world's flayed life and harsh anatomy she had apprehended, and so coldly, previous to Mrs. Marsett's lift of the veil in her story of herself: a skipping revelation, terrible enough to the girl; whose comparison of the previously suspected things with the things now revealed imposed the thought of her having been both a precocious and a callous young woman." (ch. 29)

Gillian Beer observes that "one recurrent image" in Meredith's work "invested with acutely painful emotion, is that of being stripped naked and exposed."[26] There can be no doubt of Meredith's preoccupation with the subject and theme of concealment, but whereas most writers before him were prepared to contrast the spiritual with the phenomenal world and discover the roots of deceit in the inevitable disparity existing there, Meredith, equally moral but more secular, described an opposition between fancy, dreams, and romance, on the one hand, and practical behavior on the other. Tennyson might see all of this world as a disguise of spirit impenetrable to man's paltry senses, but Meredith conceived that whatever man tried to impose upon the natural life around him was in danger of becoming a disguise.

METAPHYSICAL DISGUISE

This literary convention of disguise also reveals some underlying attitudes in nineteenth-century English society. Carlyle, in "Characteristics" (1831), observed that man can understand only surfaces, not the darkness beneath life, and added that "the Perfect, the Great is a mystery to itself, knows not itself." Carlyle thus expressed a widely held view, championing the essential mystery of being. He did not wish to believe, along with the Utilitarians, that that mystery could ever be resolved. Space and time were "illusory Appearances, for hiding Wonder." All of Nature is but God's disguise, and there is no penetrating its appearances. "In vain, while here on Earth, shall you endeavour to strip them off; you can, at best, but rend them asunder for moments, and look through." (*Sartor Resartus*, Book 3, ch. 8) So Tennyson also believed; less certain was Browning. It was enough to see that a divinity had shaped existence; that the design remained a mystery was thereafter of small consequence. This sentiment was in no way new or peculiar to the nineteenth century. Andrew Marvell had written, in "A Dialogue between the Resolved Soul and Created Pleasure," "When the Creator's skill is priz'd / The rest is all but Earth disguis'd." Accompanying the belief that this world was a book in which God's lessons were written was the notion that the text was remarkably difficult to decipher. Like the Ur-text that Tennyson's Merlin inherits from his magical predecessor, the world may be so crabbed a text to interpret that only the commentaries and marginal glosses are ever to be understood. So, too, with God's word. For Augustine, for example, "the Bible became a gigantic puzzle—like a vast inscription in unknown characters. It had all the elemental appeal of the riddle: of that most primitive form of triumph over the unknown which consists in finding the familiar hidden beneath an alien guise."[27]

This familiar desire to believe in an existence and identity beyond the mask of the phenomenal world was common in the nineteenth century. Keats had written of "Nature's universal scroll" in *Hyperion*, and Hawthorne, Poe, and Melville had all suggested the riddle of nature in works such as "Footprints on the Sea-Shore," "Roger Malvin's Burial," *The Narrative of Arthur Gordon Pym*, and *Moby Dick*. Browning, in his "Parleyings with Certain People" has Christopher Smart speculate on the moment when "there fell / Disguise from Nature, so that Truth remained / Naked . . . So that while eye saw, soul to tongue could trust / Thing which struck word out, and once more adjust / Real vision to right language." ("Christopher Smart," sec. vii) Like Robert, Elizabeth Browning felt that it was the poet's task to unite the realms of physical and spiritual experience. In *Aurora Leigh* (1857), she described existence as a "twofold sphere" in which the artist "holds firmly by the natural to reach / The spiritual beyond it" and fixing upon the mortal type, "pierce through / With eyes immortal to the antetype." (Book 7) The service of art, for Mrs. Browning, is to make man aware of life's significance and to emulate the artist who feels "The spiritual significance burn through / The hieroglyphic of material shows," and therefore reverences this world and himself as well. (Book 7) If man could learn the hieroglyphics of phenomenal existence, he would be more prepared to understand the human soul, much in need of rereading:

> Let who says
> "The soul's a clean white paper," rather say,
> A palimpsest, a prophet's holograph,
> Defiled, erased, and covered by a monk's,—
> The apocalypse, by a Longus! poring on
> Which obscene text, we may discern, perhaps,
> Some fair, fine trace of what was written once,
> Some upstroke of an alpha and omega
> Expressing the old scripture. (Book 1)[28]

The disguise of nature was a profoundly spiritual question especially when it was bound up with human identity. In her popular *The Night Side of Nature: Or Ghosts and Ghost Seers* (1848), Catherine Crowe urged her readers to remember "that this earthly body we inhabit is more or less a mask, by means of which we conceal from each other those thoughts which, if constantly exposed, would unfit us for living in community; but when we die, this mask falls away, and the truth shows nakedly. There is no more disguise; we appear as we are, spirits of light or spirits of darkness."[29] Catherine Crowe's view was a common one, but there were more sophisticated and even scientific approaches to the subject. To explain that the truth of nature was spiritual and that it only appeared dead to men, James Hinton declared, "The true being of nature is hidden from our eyes because there is not that within which answers to it."[30] Hinton was, for a time, popular as a philosopher, and it is not hard to understand why his views, with all the appearance of sophisticated thought, and clearly expressing a sincere belief, would be attractive to an age when faith was becoming an emotional and intellectual luxury where it was not a burden. Hinton argued that if phenomenal existence were merely the appearance of an existence we cannot truly perceive, then authentic life had its seat in that which was not phenomenal. Man's higher instincts, therefore, exist for the purpose of enabling and urging him to rise above the physical; and this gradual ascent liberates him; for man is "set free by the knowledge that the physical world with all its laws and forces is but an appearance."[31] For Hinton, if there is what can be called life in nature, it is spiritual life. And, in a mode of argument resembling certain transcendental expositions of the time, Hinton carries his theory to an abstract level. "Interpreted in moral terms," he asks, "is not the law of least resistance this, *Action determined by want; giving, called into operation by need?* Is not this 'appearance,' this disguise of a material law, worthy to present to us a fact of which the verity is love?"[32]

The phenomenal world, for Hinton as much as for Carlyle or Emerson, provided disguised moral lessons for men who could read them; though it was possible to miss those lessons, since philosophy had been for some time obscuring not clarifying the central questions facing man. For James F. Ferrier, even philosophy presented itself in disguise. "Every question in philosophy," he says, "is the mask of another question; and all these masking and masked questions require to be removed and laid aside, until the ultimate but *truly first* question has been reached." Instead, Ferrier complains, men have continued to do the opposite and overlay each old mask with yet another concealing visor. "So that now no question comes before the world which does not present many disguises, both natural and artificial, worn one above another; and these false-faces are continually increasing."[33] This obfuscation has become so persistent, Ferrier asserts, that "it may be affirmed with certainty that no man, for at least two thousand years, has seen the true flesh-and-blood countenance of a single philosophical problem."[34]

THE DESIRE FOR FREEDOM FROM MASKS

The frustration of feeling that a greater truth exists just beyond the threshold of one's capacity to perceive fostered a familiar desire for liberty from the fetters of the flesh. From his early to his late poetry, for example, Tennyson was concerned with the dilemma of mankind desiring to be freed from the prison of matter, yet compelled to work out salvation in it.[35] Edward Fitzgerald gave the sentiment his own tentative rendition in *The Rubáiyát of Omar Khayyám* (1872 version):

> Why, if the Soul can fling the Dust aside,
> And naked on the Air of Heaven ride,
>   Were't not a Shame—were't not a
>   shame for him
> In this clay carcass crippled to abide?
>
>   (stanza 44)

The confinement of the soul is a predominant theme in Mrs. Browning's *Aurora Leigh*. The narrator says, "We are sepulchred alive in this close world, / And want more room," thereby expressing the sensations of an age. (Book 5)[36]

In nineteenth-century British literature the concern for liberation became not only a spiritual yearning, but a more complex psychological desire to outstep the intricacies of an intelligence that creates its own confinements. In the labyrinthine spaces of his novels, Dickens figured human rebellion against the dampening impress both of human circumstances and human carnality. Like Piranesi's prison prints, these involved spaces imply a world from which escape seems impossible. Unlike Piranesi's world, Dickens' is filled with the motion of life, and yet these very movements make the confinement more intense. It is consciousness of the self from which writers of the nineteenth century wished to escape. James Hinton provided a popular moral expression of this desire in *Man and His Dwelling Place* (1857):

> But in his inmost soul [man] cries out to be delivered from himself, to be saved from the fatal spell that is upon him, whereby he must seek his own pleasure, must seek to gratify and to exalt himself; to be saved from passion, from the inward gnawing death that leads him into all evil, itself the greatest of all evils. He wants life, to BE, to act, to be no more a slave.[37]

Dickens' expression of the human yearning for release from one's own consciousness was profound, if not elaborate. Less profound, but more direct was George du Maurier's expression of the desire to escape consciousness in his novel *Peter Ibbetson* (1892). Describing his feeling at passing from sleep to dream life, Peter says, "Then would I stretch my limbs and slip myself free of my outer life, as a new-born butterfly from the durance of its self-spun cocoon, with an unutterable sense of youth and strength and freshness and felicity." (Part 5) It is this felicity, this freedom of the newly freed butterfly, without the moral implications of Thoreau's use of the metaphor in *Walden*, that came to predominate as the nineteenth century drew to a close. Any escape from the confinement of the self seemed desirable. So Dr. Jekyll explains the effect of his newly discovered drug. "The drug had no discriminating action; it was neither diabolical nor divine; it but shook the doors of the prisonhouse of my disposition; and like the captives of Philippi, that which stood within ran forth." The delight of being released from the old restrained self was exhilarating, and the good doctor could exult, "I was the first that could plod in the public eye with a load of genial respectability, and, in a moment, like a schoolboy, strip off these lendings and spring head-long into the sea of liberty."

By this time, however, the liberty has become an enslavement of another kind. The cry to escape the flesh and free the spirit had led that spirit or soul into confrontation with itself. There were varying reactions to this confrontation. One was the Decadent solution of re-treating, by necessity, into the confines of the individual imagination. Pater had set the tone for this form of escape in the "Conclusion" to *The Renaissance* (1873).

> Experience, already reduced to a swarm of impressions, is ringed round for each one of us by that thick wall of personality through which no real voice has ever pierced on its way to us, or from us to that which we can only conjecture to be without. Every one of those impressions is the impression of the individual in his isolation, each mind keeping as a solitary prisoner its own dream of a world.

Lionel Johnson voiced a more despondent view of the same isolation when he referred to "this hollow prison vault of a world, where we fumble and grope in the dark to find the keys."[38] Others, like Wilde, Symons, or Dowson, also conceived of existence as an inevitable confinement of the self within the self.

If one way to deal with the confrontation of the self and other was to plunge back into the flesh to avoid the all-revealing mirror of self-examination, another was this gradual relaxation within the self, contemplating the self. Yet another escape from the flesh was the actual transcendence of matter represented by Peter Ibbetson's living in his dreams instead of in his body, or by the characters in Maria Corelli's *A Romance of Two Worlds*, who actually travel out of their bodies to roam the universe at will, somewhat in the manner of Bulwer-Lytton's earlier adepts in *Zanoni*. Voyages beyond fleshly limits such as these were credited by a number of people, especially when they had supposedly been verified by enthusiasts of Spiritualism.[39]

But most writers accepted imprisonment in the flesh. Arnold even hoped that men might unite their forces by catching glimpses of their buried lives, and Tennyson recommended, in "The Ancient Sage," that men "dive / Into the Temple-cave" of their own selves to "learn the Nameless hath a voice," which if attended can save. This acceptance of the human condition of confinement in the world of matter was defended by the traditional justification that life is a trial to be endured. More important was the example of Christ, the principal model of spirit incarnated. In "Sir John Oldcastle," Tennyson writes, Christ "veiled himself in flesh." The notion of flesh as a disguise grew naturally from the supposition that the true man was hidden. In the "Prelude" (1869) to *Tristram of Lyonesse* (1882), Swinburne provides an equally idealized picture of humanity. "Love," he says, is "The spirit that for temporal veil has on / The souls of all men woven in unison." For Swinburne, individual souls are themselves disguises of the more universal love; man's body holds this soul "prisoner within the fleshy dungeon-dress." ("Sailing of the Swan") And in *Dombey and Son* (1846-48), Dickens is thoroughly traditional when he refers to death as "the fashion that came in with our first garments," meaning the flesh. (ch. 16)

Though men declared the flesh a mere disguise of the soul, they still hoped that some hints of true being might be disclosed in this earthly form. As simple moral disguises became less significant and social and psychological disguises more complex, men were forced to deal with the probability that man had no true nature, or else that that nature wore more disguises than had been supposed. The agony of discovering the possible fragmentations of human nature was met, for the most part, first with stoic resolve, and then with a desire to utilize the changing surface rather than seek the hidden core. Matthew Arnold, in "The Buried Life," had uttered the familiar conviction that man's true self is concealed where men seldom open wide the doors. "Empedocles on Etna" described the fragmentation of human character without offering a solution to the sense of dissociation that inevitably followed. In *Culture and Anarchy* (1869), Arnold urged his fellow men to labor to build a society that would draw forth man's better self, and thereby leaven the ordinary self too much in evidence. The ordinary self was addicted to surfaces, appearances, and artificialities; and therefore the better self was necessary as a guide. Again in *Literature and Dogma* (1873), Arnold asked men to abandon their old selves, implying the release of a new and truer self. Arnold's aspirations were positive, but they were pleadings, not hopeful exclamations. In fact, there seemed little hope for overcoming the rooted division in men's minds between the apparent and the invisible.

Despite many suggestions for a union of the two, the outer and inner lives remain divided in the literature of nineteenth-century England, and the uneasiness arising from the division does not dwindle, but grows. The inner life is a refuge or an agony, or both. Aurora Leigh, like other heroes and heroines of Victorian literature, learns the essential division between the inner and outer life by preserving her true self in a hostile setting. This experience was not unique, though each individual might feel it so. His cousin John tells Alfred Vargrave as much in Owen Meredith's *Lucile*:

> Do you think none have known but yourself all
>   the pain
> Of hopes that retreat, and regrets that remain?
> And all the wide distance fate fixes, no doubt,
> 'Twixt the life that's within, and the life
>   that's without?
>
> (Two. II. i.)

If the self was so complicated and dangerous a thing, one solution was to overcome it. Meredith had his doubts that man could ever thoroughly escape the "Dragon-fowl" of Self, as he called it in "The Woods of Westermain," but he could labor to do so. And Tennyson, though he felt the self a barrier to spiritual knowledge, could not see his way to abandoning all hope for the preservation of individual identity. Others adjured men to escape the self. "To BE is to cast out self," James Hinton said.[40] Gertrude Himmelfarb has written that Victorian believers and unbelievers alike asserted "the abnegation of self" as a basic moral principle.[41] And there were those who declared that the self was a doubtful commodity at any rate, and moved closer to modern psychology in their conclusions. James F. Ferrier, for example, saw the self as "of necessity, absolutely unknowable" by itself, and comprehendable only in relation to "some element contradistinguished from itself."[42]

Though a true inner identity might be hidden from view, men still hoped to find signs of it in external appearances. So phrenologists sought to distinguish overt physical delineations of moral character; and Victorian literature abounds with expressions of faith in physiognomy. George Borrow shows a persistent faith in reading character in human appearances, as in his casual observation of Joanna Correa, his landlady at Tangiers in *The Bible in Spain* (1843). "As I looked upon her countenance, I said within myself, if there be truth in physiognomy, thou art good and gentle, O Joanna; and, indeed, the kindness I experienced from her during the six weeks which I spent beneath her roof would have made me a convert to that science had I doubted before." (ch. 45) By the time he came to write *Lavengro* (1851), Borrow was more cautious in judging by physiognomy, while admitting that he had trusted countenances as a younger man. Charlotte Brontë used phrenological and physiognomic references to define character regularly.[43] Jane Eyre, for example, trusts her initial perception of Rochester, whose brow "showed a solid enough mass of intellectual organs, but an abrupt deficiency where the suave sign of benevolence should have risen." (ch. 14)

Charles Kingsley seemed uncertain of his attitude toward these forms of character interpretation, for in *Yeast*, though he discussed characters in terms of their organs of veneration, or had those characters comment that "the boasted discovery of phrenologists that thought, feeling and passion reside in this material brain and nerve of ours," had been anticipated by the Catholic church's simple faith in scripture, (ch. 5) he could also mock such simple physical interpretations of character. George Eliot's Felix Holt makes fun of "phrenological interpretation of his character," (*Felix Holt, the Radical*, ch. 5) but Eliot herself was not entirely contemptuous of the belief. She was personally acquainted with George Combe, the foremost promoter of phrenology in England, who had given a phrenological reading of her character.[44] She was, nonetheless, skeptical of his teaching. "I never had a higher appreciation than I have now of the services which phrenology has rendered towards the science of man," she wrote in 1855. "But I do not, I think I never shall, consider every man shallow or unconscientious who is unable to embrace all Mr. Combe's views on organology and psychology."[45] Thackeray also used phrenological terms in his fiction, describing George Firmin in *The Adventures of Philip* (1861-62), for example, as "a man with a great development of the back head; when he willed a thing, he willed it so fiercely that he *must* have it, never mind the consequences." (ch. 11) And other writers, to varying degrees, adapted some of the terminology, if not the full concepts of phrenology and physiognomy. The article on physiognomy that appeared in the *Cornhill Magazine* for October, 1861, was only one of many popular explanations of the new "science." As a means of interpreting human character, it was short-lived, yet its popularity revealed an understandable desire to discover some simple, external mode of comprehending character at a time when the identification of the self was becoming more and more dubious.

THE MULTIPLE SELF

Common to both Tennyson and Meredith, as well as to other contemporaries, was a conviction that appearances belie the truths of nature. Browning, in *Fifine at the Fair* (1872), could have his Don Juan make a sophistic plea for the means by which art uncovered the complete identity of beauty in a flawed phenomenal world, but as the century progressed, writers and philosophers expressed the idea that there was no wholeness in human nature comparable to the wholeness of art, and acknowledged the fragmented nature of human personality. Disguise now was not a rare resource of the evil or the shamed or the secretly benevolent; it was the very character of mankind. Recognizing the division of human nature in *Paracelsus*, Browning had tried to suggest that the separate main aspects of human nature, as represented by Paracelsus and Aprile, might be united in one nature. George Eliot's Don Silva, in *The Spanish Gypsy* (1868), discovers the agony of "his many-voiced self, / Whose hungry needs, like petulant multitudes, / Lured from the home that nurtured them to strength, / Made loud insurgence." (Book 4) But whereas Silva cannot accommodate his thronging and multiple selves to "his past-created, unchanged self," characters like Father Isidore demonstrate "resolute undivided souls," because they own one law and obey it. (Book 5) Yet most men are neither so well governed as Father Isidore, nor so conscious of their inner division as Don Silva. Like Tertius Lydgate, in *Middlemarch* (1871-72), they sense a conflict of impulses in themselves but cannot move smoothly from one role to the next. Others find this movement both easy and convenient. Rosamond Vincy "was by nature an actress of parts that entered into her *physique*: she even acted her own character, and so well, that she did not know it to be precisely her own." (Book 1, ch. 12)

Emerson had argued in *Nature* that man was not organized with himself, an idea that pervaded nineteenth-century thought. Laurence Oliphant wrote in his *Episodes in A Life of Adventure, or, Moss from a Rolling Stone* (1887) that he supposed most people to be "more or less conscious of leading a sort of double life," but in his case that consciousness prompted him to spiritual reflection and a search for reality rather than to dismay. (ch. 19) On the other hand, Leslie Stephen never could feel comfortable with a similar knowledge, confessing in a letter to Croom Robertson, "I always suffer from a latent conviction that I am an impostor and that somebody will find me out."[46]

Recognition of the fragmentation in human nature was not reserved to literary men. Sir Henry Holland, surgeon to the queen, recalled in his *Recollections of Past Life* (1872) the case of a man suffering from divided will, who sought protection against himself because one part of him wanted to kill the prominent politician, Canning. We would call the man a schizophrenic, but no matter what he may be called, his behavior, as Holland indicated, gave evidence to men that the human personality was something more elaborate than a soul encased in flesh.

In his *Principles of Psychology* (1890), William James asserted that "*in certain persons*, at least, *the total possible consciousness may be split into parts which coexist but mutually ignore each other*, and share the objects of knowledge between them. More remarkable still, they are complementary."[47] Identity he describes as a loosely constructed general idea perceived by the 'I.' "The identity which the *I* discovers, as it surveys this long procession, can only be a relative identity, that of a slow shifting in which there is always some common ingredient."[48]

Prominent new theories about the nature of the human psyche were propounded at this time by Freud, but in England some equally remarkable notions found expression. In *Unconscious Memory*, Samuel Butler argued that human identity, if it extends from adult to child, by the same analogy extends from the infant to its predecessors. Paraphrasing Professor Hering, Butler explains that personal identity "consists in the uninterruptedness of a sufficient number of vibrations, which have been communicated from molecule to molecule of the nerve fibres, and which go on communicating each one of them its own peculiar characteristic elements to the new matter which we introduce into the body by way of nutrition."[49] In *Life and Habit* (1878), Butler was more specific in describing what men customarily call "we," as "a nebulous and indefinable aggregation of many component parts which war not a little among themselves, our perception of our existence at all being perhaps due to this very clash of warfare."[50]

Frederic W. H. Myers, arguing against traditional notions of a uniform self, asserted that the "conscious self" was a mere selection of a vaster potential awareness. Moreover, human personality was not whole and entire. "Our psychical unity," he said, "is federative and unstable; it has arisen from irregular accretions in the remote past; it consists even now only in the limited collaboration of multiple groups."[51] Myers also said that man possessed a subliminal or unconscious self which operated significantly upon him, and to a great extent this notion of man's personality as a malleable assemblage shaped by unacknowledged forces resembles Samuel Butler's theories of human identity. A last example is from H. G. Wells, who wrote to a friend early in his life: "Disabuse yourself of the illusion of identity,"[52] and near the end of his days referred to the "human machine" as "a multitude of loosely linked series of behavior systems which take control of the body and participate in a common delusion of being one single self."[53]

HYPOCRISY

The nineteenth-century fascination with divided or multiple identity was largely a result of the Romantic movement. Along with the desire to recover an authentic relationship with nature, there existed a corresponding disapproval of established society. In England, it was during the highly artificial Regency period that the most sincere poets made their pleas for a return to nature; and even after the Regency there was no shortage of advocates for a simpler, more natural way of life. Nor was this plea for a more genuine existence addressed only to the ungoverned bucks and Corinthians of the time, but to the fastidious as well. In Robert Plumer Ward's *Tremaine, or the Man of Refinement* (1825), Tremaine is not only converted to a decent religious credo, but is instructed in the need for turning from excessive sophistication and cultivation to natural feelings and thoughts. But despite the clear desire to correct the tendency of cultivation to degenerate into superficiality, this very tendency persisted and even increased in the nineteenth century. In Bulwer-Lytton's *Pelham* (1828), dissimulation is a theme of the novel, but on a larger scale Bulwer-Lytton offers a national summary, observing that the British "offer you an affront, and call it 'plain truth;' they wound your feelings, and tell you it is manly 'to speak their minds;' at the same time, while they have neglected all the graces and charities of artifice, they have adopted all its falsehood and deceit." (ch. 66) Later, Pelham refers to his age as an "age of deceit" and England as a "country of hypocrisy." (ch. 69)[54]

Discussing the moral code and hypocrisy identified with Victorian England, Gertrude Himmelfarb writes that "As scandals, in their very nature, testify to the power of the established code, so cant and hypocrisy also testify to its power. It is a considerable achievement to convert men to the extent that they feel obliged to mask their passions or inclinations."[55] R. L. Stevenson, in comparing Englishmen with Frenchmen, classified them first by the distinction that the former were hypocrites, while the latter were free from hypocrisy.[56] All hypocrisy was not necessarily evil; some was simply banal. John Ruskin found that when "concerned with the energies of man, we find ourselves instantly dealing with a double creature," possessing a true and a false self. His true life "is like that of lower organic beings, the independent force by which he moulds and governs external things," whereas his false life, which is primarily deadening, is the "life of custom and accident." (*Seven Lamps of Architecture*, "The Lamp of Life," ch. 5) In this view, civilized life is inevitably hypocritical; thus an article in *Household Words* in 1852, entitled "Our Doubles," demonstrated how "Everybody . . . can be, and is somebody else." It described the varying contradictory roles men play in their daily lives, and the author of the article admitted, "I am giving another name to the hypocrisy of mankind."

Household Words treated the matter lightly, but others found this sense of doubleness in their lives dismaying. There is a prevailing indictment in the literature of most of the nineteenth century in England of ordinary hypocrisy. I have already suggested that disclosure is one of the most frequently employed narrative devices in Victorian literature, but the subtleties of such disclosures run deeper than the mere unmasking of a Pecksniff; they expose a failing of the age. Diana Paget, in Miss Braddon's *Birds of Prey* (1867), suffering from a sense of loveless desolation, looks back upon her early Bohemian days in the company of her dissolute father and Valentine Hawkeshurst even though "shame and danger lurked at every corner, and poverty, disguised in that tawdry masquerade habit in which the swindler dresses it, accompanied her wherever she went." (Book 3, ch. 4) Here it is hypocrisy of the cheap swindler that is described, but hypocrisy was not confined to the wicked. In *Robert Elsmere*, Rose Leyburn exclaims, "How we all attitudinise to ourselves! The whole of life often seems one long dramatic performance, in which one half of us is ever posing to the other half." (ch. 39) Lord Henry remarks of his countrymen in general, in Wilde's *The Picture of Dorian Gray*, "When they make up their ledger, they balance stupidity by wealth, and vice by hypocrisy." (ch. 17) Later, Mrs. Cheveley, in *An Ideal Husband*, laments the old days when vices were acknowledged and not clumsily disguised by hypocrisy.

Still, hypocrisy was naturally at its worst when it concealed an authentic sinister fact. Wilkie Collins' Count Fosco challenges social conventions unashamedly. "Ah, I am a bad man, Lady Glyde, am I not?" he asks Laura Fairlie. "I say what other people only think; and when all the rest of the world is in a conspiracy to accept the mask for the true face, mine is the rash hand that tears off the plump pasteboard, and shows the bare bones beneath." (*The Woman in White*, "Narrative of Marian Halcombe") The cynical count here assumes that his brand of evil is in fact beneficial to society, that his candid greed is curative of society's secret wickedness. But Count Fosco's mode of hypocrisy—his elegant appearance masking crime—is only the most obvious and evil form of hypocrisy. The good man is not deceived by this or any other attempt to conceal human fallibility as John Halifax's confrontation with Lady Caroline in Dinah Mulock's *John Halifax, Gentleman* (1856) indicates. The unimpeachable John attempts to prevent Lady Caroline from making a highly injudicious

move, and he declares that he will prevent her from breaking the law
if he can. She is puzzled by his declaration.

> "What law?"
> "*Thou shalt not commit adultery.*"
> People do not often utter this plain Bible word. It made Ursula start,
> even when spoken solemnly by her own husband. It tore from the self-
> convicted woman all the sentimental disguises with which the world
> then hid, and still hides—its corruptions. Her sin arose and stared her
> blackly in the face—*as sin.* She cowered before it. (ch. 23)

It is not for the likes of Count Fosco to strip the masks from human
corruptions, but for those who never wear masks and who are untainted by corruption.

This is certainly the most basic Victorian attitude toward hypocrisy, but there is yet another version, for, although good men do not
wish to employ disguises, it is nonetheless true, that if sin nearly always goes in disguise, even good must sometimes wear a mask. The
Golden Dustman must cloak his benevolence to gain a good end,
and, more ironically, the sinful Magwitch must conceal his genuine
benevolence in order that it bear fruit.

If England was particularly notorious for its hypocrisy, other nations did not go unchallenged. With the European uprisings of 1848
in mind, Carlyle declared in his *Latter-Day Pamphlets* (1850) that the
rebellion of the common people "is probably the hugest disclosure of
falsity in human things that was ever at one time made." The rulers
were frauds and the people who believed in them dupes and "*inverse*
cheats." "A universal *Bankruptcy of Imposture*; that may be the
brief definition of it." There were many prominent men willing to
make similar declarations, but perhaps it is equally important to attend to the obscure voices of those who did more than harangue.

In the Victorian period there was a huge demand for accounts of
travel in the Orient, Africa, and the Western world. This literature
demonstrated a desire to escape from the commonplace to the remote
and unfamiliar. Many motives sent Englishmen into odd corners of
the world, but one motive is sharply expressed by Mansfield Parkyns
in his *Life in Abyssinia* (1854). Parkyns went into a wild and alien
country to discover nature and emerged with the conviction that
"Nature is the founder of custom in savage countries" while in civilized parts of the world "custom is the great enemy of nature."[57] He

declares that there is a deep and important attraction in primitive life, for that attraction

> depends on the feeling that what he sees is, and is not merely an appearance,—that his actions will be judged by the motives which actuated them, not by conventionalities,—that his friends will be friends of heart, not of face,—and that his enemies will show their enmity openly before him, not secretly and behind his back. Far be it from me to say that sincerity is unknown or even uncommon in Europe; I only say that there is so much affinity between the tinsel of politeness and the gold of true friendship, that it is difficult for a semi-savage to discriminate between the one and the other.[58]

Nor does Parkyns hesitate to defend the superstitions and practices of the primitive people among whom he lived at the expense of the civilized society from which he fled. No society, he argues, is so free from weaknesses that it can afford to criticize another. The savage's vices and person are exposed to view, but the similar nakedness of the European is cloaked by "civilization," which the savage might "look upon as hypocrisy."[59]

In many ways, for disillusioned writers of the late nineteenth century, that savage nakedness seemed preferable to their own elaborate masks. Not that they believed noble savages were untainted creatures; they felt primitive cultures, in their simplicity, had the virtue of not deceiving. "If our climate were such that we could go about without any clothes on, we probably should," George du Maurier wrote in *Trilby* (1894). We would still commit most of the usual sins, but "much deplorable wickedness of another kind would cease to exist for sheer lack of mystery; and Christianity would be relieved of its hardest task in this sinful world." Venus would have to go begging and our bodies might become classically perfect. But "at all events, there would be no cunning, cruel deceptions, no artful taking in of artless inexperience, no unduly hurried waking-up from Love's young dream, no handing down to posterity of hidden uglinesses and weaknesses, and worse!" (part 2)

FABLES OF THE HIDDEN SELF

The notion that social conventions bred a pernicious hypocrisy was widespread in the Victorian period, but it was toward the end of the century that there appeared tales which examined the nature of this belief. Robert Louis Stevenson suggested that man was a victim of conventional appearances because of his insecurity, while Oscar Wilde insisted that appearances were as important as the perceiver who interpreted them. Stevenson examined the consequences of a divided nature for men who sought to be moral, Oscar Wilde for those who wished to be exquisite. Arthur Symons wrote of Stevenson, "He was never really himself except when he was in some fantastic disguise,"[60] and surely, in his life, Stevenson enjoyed a serious kind of role-playing. It is not unusual therefore that the theme in both obvious and more provocative forms should appear throughout his writings.

The most familiar treatment of the convention is, of course, *The Strange Case of Dr. Jekyll and Mr. Hyde* (1886). In this tale, Dr. Jekyll admits to concealing his pleasures so that his professional life should not suffer. So, more deeply in him than in the majority of men, there developed a trench that severed "those provinces of good and ill which divide and compound man's dual nature." Stevenson, thinking perhaps of his own youth and education in the world, has Jekyll declare that "man is not truly one, but truly two;" moreover, he imagines "that man will be ultimately known for a mere polity of multifarious, incongruous and independent denizens." It is Jekyll's fate to yield too often and too boldly to the pleasures that he has so conveniently suppressed before his remarkable discovery. Jekyll's fate, in a less incorporate manner, haunts all men. We are prepared for the schism from the very beginning of the tale by the description of Mr. Utterson, who "was austere with himself; drank gin when he was alone, to mortify a taste for vintages; and though he enjoyed the theatre, had not crossed the doors of one for twenty years." It is dramatically effective that this man, so capable of self-control, witnesses the disaster of his less controlled friend. With Jekyll-Hyde, Stevenson asserts Meredith's notion that a uniform identity must be forged in the furnace of ordeals that occur when man's will controls his foraging instincts. But, whereas Meredith was content with realistic consequences, Stevenson, following another bent of the later nineteenth century, preferred fabulous results. Like Lady Dedlock, Jekyll's sordid life is in disguise; and just as Lady Dedlock dies in the costume of Jenny, thereby suggesting the base ingredient of her nature, Jekyll *becomes* Hyde. The metaphor is real. The loathsome disguise will not come away. It is Jekyll finally who is the superficial disguise that less and less conceals the true nature of Hyde.[61]

Stevenson was aware of the ideas not only of the concurrent existence of several identities in one man, but also of the implications of sequential multiplicity. The persona of Stevenson's Preface to the first edition of *The Master of Ballantrae* (1888-89) notes some strange effects of his returning to his native city, among them a consciousness of the possibilities of his own nature: "Elsewhere he is content to be his present self; there he is smitten with an equal regret for what he once was and for what he once hoped to be." The novel itself examines obliquely the possible directions individual character may take.

James and Henry Durie, the central characters of the novel, may be seen as two halves of human nature. Henry exclaims of his brother, "He is bound upon my back to all eternity—to all God's eternity. . . . Wherever I am, there will he be." (ch. 6) They die within moments of one another and are buried in the same grave. What is piquing to the imagination is that James, the evil son, is more adventurous, more striking in manner and appearance, a more skillful actor, not at all hindered by principles. Viewing Henry, his wife Alison and James together, Ephraim Mackellar observes, "I seemed to read in their changed faces a *momento mori*; and what affected me still more, it was the wicked man that bore his years the handsomest." (ch. 8) With Mr. Hyde the explanation is clear: he was younger than Dr. Jekyll because he had "lived" a shorter time. On the other hand, he was horrid in appearance to suit his base nature. Perhaps the explanation is that to be good is to spend one's energies in keeping down that other self—a self that, given its sway, would feed on all its base activities. Bulwer-Lytton's Margrave, in *A Strange Story* (1862), was such a being, remaining radiantly beautiful at the cost of losing his soul. The ordinary man suffers from his misdeeds—as Markheim discovers in Stevenson's short story "Markheim"—but the man of evil does not waste his substance on remorse. Within him is no heart or soul, only a vicious hunger. Given up to his base impulses, the individual becomes nothing more than a devouring maw, or a hollow man like Conrad's Kurz. So Mackellar, speculating on James Durie, says: "I had moments when I thought of him as of a man of pasteboard—as though, if one should strike smartly through the buckram of his countenance, there would be found a mere vacuity within." (ch. 9)

In "Markheim," the wicked self is an accretion upon a better self, in a perversion of Arnold's scheme of the ordinary and the best selves. Markheim pleads, "My life is but a travesty and slander on myself. I have lived to belie my nature. All men do; all men are better than this disguise that grows about and stifles them." To behave wickedly is to be wicked; but Markheim is graced with an opportunity to realize that his better self, suppressed so long, has almost disappeared. Contrarily, Dr. Jekyll, having released a hidden Hyde, gradually loses his sway to the evil core of his nature.

Stevenson, utilizing a convention of false identity, added a dimension to that convention when he portrayed the collapse of men for whom it was not possible to believe in a single, secure identity. Charles Ravenshoe had to feel himself a bastard to discover a sensation of lost identity; Dickens' later doubting characters knew themselves to be incomplete or divided but did not doubt the possibility of completion; Meredith saw definable identity as an accomplishment of stoic mastery over what Jekyll called the "polity of multifarious, incongruous and independent denizens;" but Stevenson showed that those independent denizens could live their independent lives, and that, all mastery gone, the features that persevered and the nature that overcame, were perhaps single, but they were bad.

One additional step remained to refine a convention already highly refined. What writers had been castigating throughout the century became admirable: insincerity and false appearance became the mode for the esthetes of the nineties. The moral dilemma of false identities became a titillation. Meredith's persistent metaphor of human behavior as theatrical became a desirable reality. "Role-playing," Masao Miyoshi has correctly observed, "was a matter of dead seriousness with the men of the nineties."[62] But, though role-playing was also serious for Wilde, who himself led a double life, in *The Picture of Dorian Gray* (1890) he was able to summarize with great objectivity a malady that had been maturing throughout the century.[63] Lord Henry explains that appearances are important. "It is only shallow people who do not judge by appearances. The true mystery of the world is the visible, not the invisible." (ch. 2) He defends insincerity as "a method by which we can multiply our personalities." (ch. 11)

Matthew Arnold had wanted poetry to replace religion as an organizing life force; Walter Pater hoped that men could make their lives esthetic entities through the sensitivity of their impressions; but Oscar Wilde, like other esthetes of his time, wanted life to be art. So Lord Henry says to Dorian "You are the type of what the age is searching for, and what it is afraid it has found. . . . Life has been your art." (ch. 19) Dorian is the apotheosis of appearance. He is the exquisite surface that cannot be marred. But, behind the piquant mystery of Dorian's life is the Victorian assumption that evil should be visible. Basil Hallward cannot believe that Dorian is guilty of the sins of which he is accused. "People talk sometimes of secret vices. There are no such things. If a wretched man has a vice, it shows itself in the lines of his mouth, the droop of his eyelids, the moulding of his hands even." (ch. 12) Basil enunciates the Victorian confidence that there could be no permanent disguise for evil—a sentiment frequently expressed by writers such as Dickens or Collins, and indicated in a modified way by Meredith. But Wilde's novel suggests that no such confidence can be placed on superficialities. Within every Dr. Jekyll there is a potential Mr. Hyde, but he need not be ugly. The ugliness may remain hidden in the soul.

Dorian becomes self-conscious not only through Lord Henry, but through Basil as well. He wonders, having met the fascinating Harry, "Why had it been left for a stranger to reveal him to himself?" (ch. 2) But Basil's picture has already played an equal part in Dorian's self-recognition; "it had revealed to him his own body, so it would reveal to him his own soul." (ch. 8) The combination of Basil's art and Lord Henry's opinions has evoked the being within the husk of Dorian Gray. "Out of its secret hiding-place had crept his Soul, and Desire had come to meet it on the way." (ch. 4) The irony of this emergence of Dorian's soul from its secret hiding place is that it breeds disguises which force him to conceal once more the emblem of that very soul. The picture becomes Dorian's "mask of shame" (ch. 8) and must be hidden. But the damage is done. Dorian has become the appearance. The elegant man who lounges in the salons of London is in permanent disguise. He is the embodiment of hypocrisy and deceit. His life has, as Lord Henry notes, become art, but art, like a canvas, is only surface.

Dorian begins his new esthetic life of sensation in what appears to be the innocent disguise of Prince Charming, but ends in frequenting the low-character Inns near the docks "under an assumed name, and in disguise." (ch. 11) He begins by wishing to make all of life as "real" as the theatrical performances of Sybil Vane, and appreciates "How extraordinarily dramatic life is." (ch. 8) But when Sybil prefers love to the "pageant" of the stage, Dorian leaves her; meanwhile the real grief of Sybil's mother and brother appears merely melodramatic. Dorian has his way, and he reconciles himself to Sybil's suicide because it seems to him "like a wonderful ending to a wonderful play." (ch. 8) When Dorian later wishes to reform and spares a young girl from his desires, Lord Henry informs him that he is merely trying out a new role. "A new life! That was what he wanted." (ch. 20) But there are some roles that cannot be played out twice in life. Addicted to disguises and roles, Dorian can no longer recover a single, innocent identity. On the surface he appears unalterable, but within himself, as the picture proves, he is the ever-changing sampler of sensuous experience. His only escape is death.

Earlier maskers and hypocrites had led double lives out of invidious necessity; good men had employed disguises to achieve some noble end; even the unlucky Dr. Jekyll had been prompted in his experiments with his own personality by scientific curiosity. But Dorian is enticed by the desire for sensation alone. Others had endured or even suffered from their divided natures, but Dorian "felt keenly the terrible pleasure of a double life." (ch. 15) All men, Wilde suggests, are in disguise. All men have their secrets which they will not reveal and which convert their everyday appearances into masks at odds with their souls. But this process is arrested in Dorian and he becomes, indeed, the ideal that the late Victorians aspired to—the triumph of surface. The moral seems clear enough, never mind how sincere Wilde may have been.

There is an additional aspect to Dorian's case that gives it a greater psychological depth. The room in which Dorian secretes his guilty picture "had been specially built by the last Lord Kelso, for the use of the little grandson whom, for his strange likeness to his mother, and also for other reasons, he had always hated and desired to keep at a distance." (ch. 10) This room was the principal locale of Dorian's "lonely childhood." Thus it is entirely fitting that the thirsty pursuit of sensation that well might grow out of such a lonely tutelage, should have its incarnation locked away in that same room. It was in this room that Dorian's soul was originally hidden away, and it is to this room that it must return in its mature and infected state. Behind the fantastic fable of a living picture is a sound and mournful truth about the wounded soul and human identity worthy of any modern psychological theory.

A similar psychological truth is implied in Max Beerbohm's parody of *Dorian Gray*, "The Happy Hypocrite," in which the notorious rake, Sir George Hell, falls in love with a beautiful and innocent dancer, Jenny Mere, who will not accept his proposal of marriage because his face reveals the sins of his life. Hell, determined to win Jenny, and consumed by genuine love, purchases the mask of a saint, which he intends to wear for the rest of his life in order to preserve Jenny's love. The mask works; Jenny loves him for his saintly aspect, though she feels some discomfort when she learns that he cannot laugh or smile. However, Hell's old flame, La Gambogi, appears to confront her now married lover, and, in a rage to see his old face again, tears away the saintly mask. Hell, before he married Jenny and changed his name to George Heaven, had satisfied his misgivings about his little deceit by arguing that his mask was "a secret symbol of his true repentance and of his true love." Now he has his reward, for his features duplicate the saintly visage of the mask. Just as Dorian's picture degenerates with his sins, Sir George's real features assume the saintliness of the mask because he has lived according to the saintly role. Surface forms the inner self: conduct is more than three-fourths of life; it informs man's very definition.

Clearly, for writers of the nineties, appearance could be of critical importance. It could also be blatant and complicated. In a society willing, at least in part, to accept a fragmented view of man, a figure such as Baron Corvo was foreseeable. Corvo (Frederick William Rolfe) has the narrator of his quasi-autobiographical romance, *Hadrian VII* (1904), say, "In fact, I split up my personality. As Rose I was a tonsured clerk. As King Clement I wrote and painted and photographed: as Austin White I designed decorations: as Francis Engle I did journalism."[64] But Corvo was the same in his actual life. In his later days "He changed publishers and pseudonyms. He felt thwarted and pursued. He disguised himself with wig and paint, and walked only at night."[65] A contemporary described him as a keenly superficial being with no perception of the inner value of things. Baron Corvo is what one might easily expect to step live from the pages of *The Yellow Book* or *The Savoy*.

LIFE AS ILLUSION

The Victorian attitude of viewing life in terms of roles, masks and disguises arose partly from the Romantic tradition that the material world was illusion and only the spiritual world had reality. Such a belief is behind Tennyson's use of disguise, and much more besides, in *The Idylls of the King*, and was fundamental to James Hinton's philosophy. The images of role-playing and masking became more frequent as the century progressed and all of life began to resolve into a pantomime. The elegant guests at Romney Leigh's unfulfilled wedding are convinced that the whole affair is nothing more than a theatrical display. Aurora Leigh, herself, sees the danger that besets men who tie on "tragic masks" and seek to "play / Heroic parts" to themselves. (Book 4) Robert Browning's Don Juan, in defending "Fifine and all her tribe" of actors, remarks, "We also act, but only they inscribe / Their style and title so, and preface, only they, / Performance with 'A lie is all we do or say.'" (*Fifine at the Fair*, sec. lxxxv) It is the same Don Juan, who, having given a description of his vision of the carnival at Venice with all its maskings of human attributes, concludes, "There went / Conviction to my soul, that what I took of late / For Venice was the world; its Carnival—the state / Of mankind, masquerade in life-long permanence / For all time, and no one particular feast-day." (sec. cviii) Henry Cockton wrote, in his popular novel, *The Life and Adventures of Valentine Vox, The Ventriloquist* (1840), that novelists should not declaim against masquerades, "inasmuch as the world is one grand masquerade, and all who live in it are maskers: from the king to the mendicant, all are masked, and their actions form neither more nor less than one grand social system of mummery. Deception is the primary object of all, and there is nothing they seek to disguise more than that." He concludes, "masquerades are . . . the types of the world. . . ." (ch. 28) Don Silva, in George Eliot's *The Spanish Gypsy*, feels "Life is but poor mockery: / Action, place, power, the visible wide world / Are tattered masquerading of this self, / This pulse of conscious mystery: all change, / Whether to high or low, is change of rags." (Book 4) For Silva, the whole mime of life is a projected phantasmagoria of the self; for Dorothea Casaubon, exposed to Rome and the new life of marriage for the first time, her self resembles "the oppressive masquerade of ages" and becomes "a masque with enigmatical costumes." (*Middle-*

march, Book 2, ch. 20) In Joseph Henry Shorthouse's *John Inglesant* (1880), material life is again presented as a theatrical pantomime. Fascinated by the performance of an Italian masque Inglesant sees its performers as types of humanity: "There seemed to him to be in the world nothing but play within play, scene within scene;" until the most trivial and solemn acts become indistinguishable, all appearing "part of that strange interlude which, between the Dramas of Eternity, is performed continually upon the stage of life." (ch. 31)

Though life may be a series of roles played out in a meaningful drama or pointless farce, it still remains for man to accept and acquiesce in the various roles. If disguises are necessary, men must wear them fittingly and well. One solution was to make personality as multiple and as flexible as possible. So Marius concludes in Pater's *Marius the Epicurean* (1885, modified later) "he too must maintain a harmony with that soul of motion in things, by a constantly renewed mobility of character." (part 2, ch. 8) It was for Oscar Wilde to add his usual ironic touch to this concept and indicate that the roles men played were, after all, imitations of art. If Tennyson had suggested that material existence was only the shadow of Spirit, and Pater had offered a secular enthusiasm for ordering evanescent phenomena, Wilde went so far as to suggest that human identity was a consequence of art. And yet that same art did not necessarily form the identity of the artist, for "Art is always more abstract than we fancy. Form and colour tell us of form and colour—that is all. It often seems to me that art conceals the artist far more completely than it ever reveals him." (*Dorian Gray*, ch. 9)

The increasing sense that existence was a kind of masquerade fortified, perhaps, the traditional sentiment that certain conventional types were appropriate in literature. This feeling could lead in several directions, however, to a more obvious and ironic use of the conventional types, as with Wilde, or to a more realistic, penetrating use, as with Eliot, Gissing, and others. But the artistic sensitivity to disguise and role-playing itself may have been partly affected by the attitudes artists held about their own calling.

ANONYMITY

John Keats, in enunciating his concept of negative capability—the artist's ability to place himself in other identities—voiced a relatively common idea. Given this sensitivity among certain writers, it was not unusual that they might consider the artist as a performer. Economic necessities aside, though they were important, it is worth noticing how much of nineteenth-century literature was published anonymously. "Some novelists of the period indeed were so prolific that they used pseudonyms or published anonymously to avoid flooding the market with their own work."[66] The reasons for this anonymity varied, but there is no ignoring how pervasive a practice it was. Most of the important journals used few signed articles, poems, or tales. And in those instances where a name appeared, it was often a pseudonym, and in this way many a writer could express himself freely and even contradictorily, thereby liberating different sides of his nature. James Hogg derived considerable profit through anonymous publication, while Peacock seems to have amused himself with it. Susan Ferrier's works were published anonymously and her authorship not disclosed until 1851. "Boz" was around for some time before Charles Dickens acknowledged him—perhaps to save him from his many imitators. "Yellowplush" wrote without incriminating Thackeray, and three young Yorkshire women could get their works accepted so long as they presented themselves as the Bell brothers. Coventry Patmore published "The Betrothal" anonymously because he did not wish to be confused with his father, whose notorious memoirs, *My Friends and Acquaintances*, appeared in 1854 as well. Bulwer-Lytton, Charles Kingsley, George Meredith, and Thomas Hardy all published works anonymously, as did numerous other insignificant and major writers. And at the beginning of the century was the most notable masker of them all, the Great Unknown, Sir Walter Scott, who "liked to hide behind masks and disguises and to set traps for the unwary."[67]

There were numerous reasons for such disguises. George Henry Lewes, at one point, was writing his reputable *Comte's Philosophy of the Sciences*, while also doing plain review work under the pen name, Vivian, and writing and adopting plays for Charles Mathews' Lyceum under the pseudonym, Slingsby Lawrence. Lewes' associate, Marian Evans, avoided discrimination by having her novel, *Adam Bede* (1859), appear under a pseudonym. Lewes announced to her publishers: "You may tell it openly to all who care to hear it that the object of anonymity was to get the book judged on its own merits, and not prejudged as the work of a woman, or of a particular woman."[68] Tennyson published *In Memoriam* (1850) anonymously, and it is possible that he did so not merely out of shyness—his excuse for telling no one of his marriage plans at the same time—but because the "different moods of sorrow as in a drama are dramatically given" in the poem, which he asserted, was *"not* an actual biography."[69] Concerned with universal questions, it is not unlikely that Tennyson wished to conceal his own identity and present the views arising from his subject unmasked by his name, though in truth the secret of his authorship was not long kept. It is clear that Anthony Trollope, at the height of his popularity, chose to publish two pieces of fiction anonymously in order to test himself. He found, by the failure of these works, that it was his name that helped to sell his novels,[70] and he promptly resumed the profitable identity.

There are more subtle explanations regarding authorship in which downright anonymity plays no part. Gillian Beer points to the "self-protecting irony with which Meredith has masked his relationship to his work."[71] Carlyle's *Sartor Resartus* is an excellent example of the complicated interweaving of self and guise in a work concerned with guises and selves.[72] And it is possible to see in Dickens a writer who conceived of his work theatrically, and whose characters are primarily manifestations of Dickens' outstanding ventriloquial powers.[73] Dickens is, in fact, a good example of the artist whose fascination with disguise and role-playing blended his life and his art. His theatricality was not limited to amateur productions of plays or popular readings of his works. In his everyday life, Dickens was given to strange eccentricities of dress. "It was Dickens the actor, rather than Dickens the novelist," Ellen Moers says, "who dressed like the Heavy Swell. There had always been something vaguely theatrical about his style of dress."[74] But if Dickens could dress up and attract attention, he could also derive a deep satisfaction from moving amid the low districts of London, like Haroun-al-Raschid in disguise. Robert Louis Stevenson had, for a time at least, a similar penchant. "Louis had occasionally visited working-class groggeries, peered into slum windows, disputed with proletarian doctrinaires. But such explorations by a self-conscious student of human beings could not avoid a touch of young Haroun-al-Raschid exploring the depths of Bagdad."[75] Tennyson, too, enjoyed moving among common people incognito, but mainly to avoid curious fans, and to acquire honest responses to his works and ideas.

This role-playing may have been a manifestation of a deeper need among the Victorian writers. The author of *Vanity Fair* may view himself as "the Manager of the Performance," and Dickens may declare that the techniques he uses in his fiction are "the ways of Providence, of which ways all art is but a little imitation."[76] Or Tennyson may view the matter from another perspective, seeing the purposes of Providence as resembling a work of art. Whatever the case, the moral control exercised by these and other authors of the time suggests that a reason for the prevalence of disguise and role-playing both in the lives and works of writers, was the general suspicion that this world was largely fictitious—despite its canals, machinery, and Manchesters—and that a greater, more important existence lay behind it. Melville's Ahab, plagued by such a belief, but convinced that the unseen forces were malign, sought to "strike through the mask." Tennyson chose to refine the separation until some communication, no matter how transitory, might bridge the gap. Others might see the artist's duty even more sharply. If the artist did not actually imitate the role of Providence in establishing a truth beyond the simple materiality of events, he might serve as a spy for that greater Intelligence, as in Browning's "How It Strikes A Contemporary," or as a liaison, as his wife implied when she asked, in *Aurora Leigh*, "what then, / Unless the artist keep up open roads / Betwixt the seen and unseen . . . to prove what lies beyond / Both speech and imagination." (Book 2)[77]

CLOTHING

If writers found matter for speculation upon disguise in their professional life and in spiritual reflection, they had in every day life such mundane encouragements to reflection as clothing. The fascination with clothing was by no means confined to the nineteenth century, as Overbury's character, "A Fine Gentleman," (1614) which describes the gentleman as a creation of his tailor, demonstrates. Still, there was a marked preoccupation with clothing in the Victorian period. Literary references to clothing are abundant and offer precise indications regarding characters' social identities. Fashion was only one part, but an important one, in a complicated code of distinctions between the classes. "The lady of leisure dressed by a court dressmaker could not be confused with the woman who bought her clothes ready-made; the gentleman in his tall hat and frock-coat was distinct from the man who wore a bowler—and neither of them had anything to do with the cloth-cap wearers belonging to the amorphous mass of the unskilled and the illiterate."[78] The precision of class identification led to what might be considered excesses, as in the Victorian custom of wearing different costumes for different occasions, requiring the man of fashion to change his suit three or four times a day and making it "a matter of grave concern which particular cut of garment or pattern of material or colour could—or could not—be worn at a particular hour for a particular function at a particular season."[79] In George Eliot's *Felix Holt, the Radical,* Felix asserts his humble station with pride, thereby reversing society's values, by declaring "I mean to stick to the class I belong to—people who don't follow the fashions." (ch. 5) But, though his simple directness is admirable, and his dismissal of fashion as folly acceptable, it did not change the habits of society itself, or, for that matter, the expectations of the reading public.

There was in this fascination with clothing an interesting contradiction. Despite the prudery and drabness of much of society, the "*rightness* of the dandy figure remained somehow attractive," suggesting certain leanings toward "anti-bourgeois virtues."[80] Other attitudes toward clothing are equally revealing. "For nearly a century petticoats and prudery combined as a gigantic force . . . a lady's underclothing had become, as it were, an integral part of her personality."[81] Both men and women wore corsets, and women of society wore a variety of bustles and crinolines. There is a teasing insight in the fact that women's undergarments were plain and drab, except where they were exposed to view. The multitudinous petticoats and enormous crinolines were, in their way, fascinations with surface every bit as devoted as the dandy's stays and astonishingly complex cravats. In the seventies the "frank exhibition of underclothing allowed by the later crinoline was no longer thought decent and was replaced by elaborate concealment made as alluring as possible."[82]

In his essay, "On Dress and Deportment," Jerome K. Jerome observed with typical late-century bemusement that "Clothes have more effect upon us than we imagine. Our deportment depends upon our dress."[83] He further asserted that "Clothes alter our very nature,"[84] thereby reversing the Carlylean assumption that men retailor themselves according to their inward moral force, and declaring instead

an amused belief that a new suit of clothes puts in a new man to begin a new endeavor. Jerome carried his conjecture further: "The
world is a grave, middle-aged gentleman in this nineteenth century,
and would be shocked to see itself with a bit of finery on."[85] Modes
did change, though elaborate concealments remained, until, with the
nineties, at least one part of society made an open admission of its
preference, and "The New Dandies of the era, Wilde, Beardsley,
Beerbohm, the Rhymers' Club poets, built a literature around themes
from the dandy tradition: worship of the town and the artificial;
grace, elegance, and the art of the pose; sophistication and the
mask."[86]

COSMETICS

Accompanying this attention to superficial attributes of character,
in its way as much of a science as phrenology, was an increasing concern with concealment. The nineteenth century witnessed a growing fascination with cosmetics, and writers quickly appropriated the
subject for their own purposes. A respectable journal such as the *Cornhill Magazine* could, as late as 1863, announce that "cosmetics are an
imposition,"[87] and recommend exercise for a good complexion while
warning against the use of belladonna or other drugs to produce
bright eyes. The author is piqued into the mildly ascerbic observation that "The succession of fashions seem rather determined by an
ingenious desire of disguising the natural form, and presenting an
image conspicuously unallied to humanity."[88]

Cosmetics and costume had long been subjects for discussion in
English literature. When Pelham is disenchanted by discovering that
the Duchesse de Perpignan's beauty is largely artifact, he reflects as
much an eighteenth-century response as he does a Victorian aversion. But the theme of disguise takes on a notably moral tone in Victorian literature; cosmetics become a symbol for concealment of a
pathetic or even vicious truth. There is no shortage of characters
for whom cosmetics serve this purpose. Most obvious are Dickens'
splendid pictures of Mrs. Skewton, the Cleopatra of *Dombey and
Son*, and Lady Tippens in *Our Mutual Friend*. Other authors also use
the device—for example, G. A. Lawrence, who described the character
Lady Greystroke in *Sans Merci* (1866) as given to obscuring herself
with cosmetics. These are pathetic figures concerned more with their

enamelled surfaces than with their inner natures. Other characters are more suggestive of the pernicious aspect of cosmetology. Miss Mowcher, in *David Copperfield*, makes her living by covering up the flaws in her upper-class clientele. Her business is to make externally attractive the vices as well as the appearances of society. Mrs. Oldershaw in Wilkie Collins' *Armadale* is another cosmetologist who has been primarily concerned with covering up the sins of society that she assists. She ends her career as an evangelist, preaching to "old harridans of the world of fashion whom Mother Oldershaw had enamelled in her time, sitting boldly in the front places, with their cheeks ruddled with paint, in a state of devout enjoyment wonderful to see!" ("Epilogue," ch. 1) Just as she had once used rouge and powder to mask the signs of indulgence, she now uses "faith" and "religion" to smooth over the offenses of society.[89]

"In these days," Trollope wrote in *The Way We Live Now*, "men regard the form and outward lines of a woman's face and figure more than either the colour or the expression, and women fit themselves to men's eyes. With padding and false hair without limit a figure may be constructed of almost any dimension." With a sense of questionable nostalgia, Trollope concludes that "The taste for flesh and blood has for the day given place to an appetite for horsehair and pearl powder." (Vol. 1, ch. 26) Trollope's judgment is obviously condemnatory, but it lacks the ominous note in Thackeray's description of Philip Firmin's naiveté upon being introduced to a cosmetic society in *The Adventures of Philip*. To Philip, women on the stage "looked as lovely as houris. At this time the simple young fellow, surveying the ballet from his stall at the Opera, mistook carmine for blushes, pearl-powder for native snows, and cotton-wool for natural symmetry; and I dare say when he went into the world was not more clear-sighted about its rouged innocence, its padded pretentions, and its painted candour." (ch. 4)

Implications prompted by the image of cosmetology could be even broader, as in Laurence Oliphant's *Piccadilly. A Fragment of Contemporary Biography* (1865, revised 1866), where Frank Vanecourt's meditation has international implications:

> "Wog is right," I mused as I walked home—"*postiche* is everywhere. We certainly do 'make-up' well. I suppose this country never looked more fair and flourishing in the eyes of the world in general than it does at this moment. We have made a great *succès* by means of *postiche*—

there is no denying it. But we shall fall to pieces all of a sudden like old Lady Pimlico; and the wrinkles will appear before long in the national cheeks in spite of the rouge. Ah, the taunts we shall have to endure when the *postiche* is discovered, from the rivals that have always been jealous and are still under the prestige of our former charms! Then the kings of the earth with whom we have lived delicately will turn against us, for they will remember our greed and our pride and our egotism, in the days when we sold our virtue for gold, and our honour for a mess of pottage. Is there no one who will cry aloud in the streets while there is yet time?" (part 5)

Society's need to cover up could only be respectable if it were converted to a virtue, and in 1894, Max Beerbohm sought to do that in his playful essay, "A Defense of Cosmetics." Here Beerbohm declares, "we are ripe for a new epoch of artifice," and adds, "the era of rouge is upon us." Man, Beerbohm says, has distrusted surfaces too much. "The very jargon of the hunting-field connects cunning with a mask. And so perhaps came man's anger at the embellishment of women —that lovely mask of enamel with its shadows of pink and tiny pencilled veins, what must lurk behind it?" But the real problem has been "the tristful confusion man has made of soul and surface. Through trusting so keenly to the detection of the one by keeping watch upon the other, and by force of the thousand errors following, he has come to think of surface even as the reverse of soul." But Beerbohm's forecast is hopeful; with the full renascence of cosmetics, surface will finally be severed from soul and a confusing prejudice will be extinguished. "Too long has the face been degraded from its rank as a thing of beauty to a mere vulgar index of character or emotion." All that moral accumulation will be over, Beerbohm implies, thereby turning the tables on the moralists and implying that the real disguise is moral and not physical.

In this essay, the route comes full circle. The mask becomes acceptable, even desirable; the vulgar desire to seek some meaning in appearance is overcome; and cosmetics, the science of disguising what nature has made, achieves the station for which it has long seemed destined. "It's wonderful what's been hid," Boffin said, but set about discovering all there was that had been hidden, even to the inward nature of the confused Bella Wilfer. No such labor seemed desirable by the end of the century. Other interests had superseded, or other methods of discovery had emerged.[90]

CONCLUSION

Behind the use of disguise in Victorian literature is an assumption about the nature of existence. That assumption was not a universal creed, but, in many different manifestations it influenced the thought of the time. Fundamentally, it was a belief that the phenomenal world was neither fixed nor final. The most obvious expression of this feeling can be found in the moral writings of the time, most of which utilize the traditional duality of spirit and matter to explain the impermanence of this world and the permanence of an unseen and eternal life. But even those who challenged these traditional views used expressions revealing their own suspicions regarding the insubstantiality of forms. In his essay, "The Physical Basis of Life," (1868) Thomas Huxley denied any indestructible or molecular vital force in endless transmutation and asserted that "under whatever disguise it takes refuge, whether fungus or oak, worm or man, the living protoplasm not only ultimately dies and is resolved into its mineral and lifeless constituents, but is always dying, and, strange as the paradox may sound, could not live unless it died."[91] Even in architecture, Victorians sought to correct what they considered to be shams, an interest for which Pugin's works were largely responsible. And yet, the Gothic revival was itself an attempt to disguise a modern industrial society behind a medieval façade.

Just as the German Romantics earlier in the century had stressed the malleability of existence, the transmutation of the visible world by the mind of man, and the multiplicity of human nature, so the English Victorian writers, in a less overt manner, revealed similar beliefs. The frequent use of mystery followed by disclosure in the writings of the time may be considered simply as a popular theme, but it could also indicate a craving, in an age preoccupied with discoveries about the truth of the Bible, and the nature of existence, for the solving of mysteries in a clear and final manner.

The mysteries, however, were not solved, except in novels, dramas, and other forms of narrative. Instead, men were led more and more to recognize that the mystery was as much within themselves as it was a part of the external world. When men began to realize that the phrenologist's bumps, or a high brow, did not necessarily disclose the truths of a man's character; when men were acknowledged to be psychologically complex, writers began to employ consciously what had long been a less skillful device. Disguises were more than plot conveniences or unconscious gratifications; they became indicators of divided natures and revealers of buried selves. Daniel Deronda's career might stand as a representative wish of one element of Victorian culture. Throughout his youth and early manhood Deronda is in ignorance of his true identity, and he hesitates in committing himself to a great task, though he longs for such an occupation. Nonetheless, "That young energy and spirit of adventure which have helped to create the world-wide legends of youthful heroes going to seek the hidden tokens of their birth and its inheritance of tasks, gave him a certain quivering interest in the bare possibility that he was entering on a like track—all the more because the track was one of thought as well as action." (*Daniel Deronda*, ch. 41) Deronda does penetrate his imposed disguise, and learns that he is a Jew and therefore free to devote himself to the great dream of reawakening the Jewish people to a sense of unity with their tradition. Breaking from established monotony to outcast excellence, Deronda embodies a wish implicit in much of the literature of his time. Deronda achieved an extraordinary role and thereby transcended the commonplace most men were doomed to live out. Tess reveals the late-century sentiment in Hardy's *Tess of the d'Urbervilles* when she declares that she does not wish to know that her case is common and that hers is a familiar role:

> Because what's the use of learning that I am one of a long row only —finding out that there is set down in some old book somebody just like me, and to know that I shall only act her part; making me sad, that's all. The best is not to remember that your nature and your past doings have been just like thousands' and thousands', and that your coming life and doings'll be like thousands' and thousands'. (Phase the Third, ch. 19)

At the same time that men saw themselves increasingly as performers in a cosmic farce or tragedy where roles might change abruptly, they also came to see the importance of acknowledging all those indicators outside the self that might aid them in fathoming their own natures. Hence the double became an important convention in the literature of the age. If the ideas of Freud demonstrate the complexity of the self, those of Jung illustrate the need to seek a solution for that complexity in mirroring forces beyond the self. Both of these men explored ideas that bedevilled Victorian thinkers. The discoveries of these two great interpreters of human nature grew out of the traditions and conventions of the nineteenth century. Themes of disguise and multiple selves most certainly did not end with the death of Victoria. Indeed, Conrad's use of the double to examine the disparities between surface and depth in human nature, and Yeats' scheme of a self which required an anti-type by which it could define itself, might be viewed as superb culminations of certain Victorian preoccupations.

Nineteenth-century England had witnessed the maturation of ideas profoundly significant for those who followed. From the simple masked outcast who proved as in a fairy tale to be a prince, to the elegant esthete so enamored of his outward being that he lost his soul, the convention of disguise had revealed a preoccupation abundantly manifest in the literature and culture of the age, a preoccupation which suggests not only a curiosity about human nature and the human condition, but which also reveals a deep discontent with that condition. From its most trivial to its most profound manifestations, the disguise convention in Victorian literature discloses a craving for a different life, perhaps dangerous, but hopefully richer and more true.

CHAPTER FOURTEEN

GYPSIES

Throughout the Victorian period gypsies were a familiar literary convention providing stereotyped furniture for melodramatic literary productions. At the same time, a growing interest in gypsy life produced important scholarly studies as well as an interesting transformation in the literary convention. From mere trappings of romance, gypsies came to represent an idealized alternative to an increasingly dehumanized society.

BACKGROUND

The history of the gypsies in England is not certain, nor are early attitudes toward them clear. It is known that Gypsies lived in England as early as the sixteenth century.[1] Brian Vesey-Fitzgerald writes that the first mention of gypsies in Britain is in Scotland in 1505, but he assumes that they were there before 1449.[2] However, Jean-Paul Clébert notes that there was a public enactment against them as early as 1441.[3] Persecutions were commonplace, and in 1555 there was a public announcement that the "Egyptians" were planning to return to England and resume their wicked practices, and therefore, "anyone importing Gypsies should forfeit forty pounds"; but more stringently, "Any Gypsy so imported who remained in England one month should be deemed a felon and forfeit his life, lands and goods being also deprived of the privileges of a mixed jury, or sanctuary, and of benefit of clergy."[4] George Borrow says that the gypsy race was persecuted throughout the reign of Elizabeth less for their crimes than from the suspicion "that they harboured amidst their companies priests and emissaries of Rome."[5] Whatever the case, Elizabeth ordered the gypsies banished. Nonetheless, in the seventeenth century gypsies were still present in England and had regained their freedom. And, says Clébert, "from then onwards they found a hospitable land in the British Isles."[6] Yet as late as 1819 there were laws in parts of England that stated, "Those who wandered abroad in the habit of Egyptians were punishable by imprisonment and whipping."[7] The interest in gypsies was not peculiar to the nineteenth century in England. The gypsy had long been utilized in Western literature as a figure on the dark periphery of society, from Cervantes to Hugo. Especially in the eighteenth century, gypsy adventures were popular and gypsies figured in life and literature. Adam Smith, the great political economist, was said to have been carried off by gypsies when he was three years old,[8] and exploits of Bampfylde-Moore Carew were well known to all those pretending to an interest in gypsies, as Theodore Watts-Dunton recorded.[9] Even the general Victorian reader may have been expected to recognize Carew's name while reading *Lady Audley's Secret*.

An Apology for the Life of Mr. Bampfylde-Moore Carew, Commonly call'd the King of the Beggars (1749) relates that at about the age of fifteen, Carew ran away from school with some companions and accidentally fell in with a band of gypsies.[10] So great "an Air of Freedom, Mirth, and Pleasure, appeared in the Faces and Gestures of this Society, that our youngsters from that Time conceived a sudden Inclination to enlist in their Company." (ch. 1) Carew was initiated into the gypsies' arts, which seem to have been not so much occult skills as mere confidence tricks, resembling those later described in an official document published in Birmingham in 1841, entitled, *An Exposure of the various Impositions daily practised by Vagrants of every Description*. Carew enjoyed his life with the gypsies, but feeling guilty about the pain he caused his parents, returned home. He could not, however, forget "the uncommon Pleasure he had enjoyed in the Community he had left, the Freedom of their Government, the Simplicity and Sincerity of their Manners, the frequent Change of their Habitation, the perpetual Mirth and good Humour that reigned amongst them." (ch. 2) So he returned to the gypsies and eventually became king among them.

In his article, "Tom Jones and 'His *Egyptian* Majesty': Fielding's Parable of Government," Martin C. Battestin argues that the gypsies used in Fielding's novel were not intended as a faithful representation of the race, but were an imaginative construction to serve a wider purpose, for the organization of their tribe becomes "an ambiguous parable of government," against which the political quarrels of the age might be tested.[11] It is, perhaps, with this concept of social organization in mind, that the author of *An Apology for the Life of Mr. Bampfyld-Moore Carew* describes the government of the gypsies.

> The Laws of these People are few and simple, but most exactly and punctually observed; the Fundamental of which is, that strong Love and mutual Regard for each Member in particular, and for the whole Community in general, which is inculcated into them from their earliest Infancy; so that this whole Community is connected by stronger Bands of Love and Harmony, than oftentimes subsist even in private Families under other Governments: This naturally prevents all Oppressions, Frauds and over-reaching of one another, so common amongst other People, and totally extinguishes that bitter Passion of the Mind (the Source, perhaps, of most other Vices) *Envy*; for it is a great and certain Truth, that *Love worketh no Evil*. (ch. 1)

The gypsies, he continues, use honor and shame, not physical punishment to assure adherence to social rules. They are not preoccupied with money and share willingly with one another. "And this is the Source of their uninterrupted Happiness; for by this Means they have no griping Usurer to grind them, no lordly Possessor to trample on them, nor any Envyings to torment them: They have no settled Habitations, but (like the *Scythians* of old) remove from Place to Place, as often as their Conveniency or Pleasure require it, which renders their Life a perpetual Scene of Variety." (ch. 1)

The picture of gypsy manners here presented seems comparable to later descriptions of Romany life—that gypsies were outcasts, of an idle and thieving nature, and untrustworthy to any but their own kind. But George Borrow dismissed the *Apology* and the earlier *English Rogue, or the Adventures of Merriton Latroon* as useless for serious study, explaining that these works, "though clever and en-

tertaining, and written in the raciest English, are to those who seek
for information respecting Gypsies entirely valueless, the writers having evidently mistaken for Gypsies the Pikers or Abrahamites."[12]

The identification of gypsies with all manner of idle rascals persisted through the eighteenth century. While envied for their freedom
they were scorned for their moral failings. George Crabbe saw the
gypsies as basically a squalid tribe of outcasts. To him they were
wild cheats and thieves, impoverished and vicious, with none of the
family devotion so praised by most scholarly commentators on the
race. Although Crabbe apparently saw the gypsies in this grim light,
he permitted a character in his narrative to take a more sanguine
view. Orlando, in "The Lover's Journey," goes on to admit that gypsies are rogues,

> but merry rogues they be;
> They wander round the land, and be it true,
> They break the laws—then let the laws pursue
> The wanton idlers; for the life they live,
> Acquit I cannot, but I can forgive. (*Tales*, Tale X)

The gypsies were puzzling to the cultivated British of the eighteenth century. William Cowper, comfortably meditating upon the
peculiar race in *The Task* (1784), could enumerate their crudity, skill
in palmistry, and penchant for cheating, and then wonder why a rational creature, "though capable of arts / By which the world might
profit and himself," prefers "Such squalid sloth to honourable toil."
At the same time, he recorded the supposed advantages of the gypsies' wandering way of life.

> Such health and gaiety of heart enjoy
> The houseless rovers of the sylvan world;
> And breathing wholesome air, and wandering much,
> Need other physic none to heal the effects
> Of loathsome diet, penury, and cold. ("The Sofa," Book I)

In *The Pleasures of Memory* (1792), Samuel Rogers presented an
equally conventional picture of a gypsy crone, who lives in a "hazel
copse" tending her brimming "caldron" and a brood of imps fed on
stolen chickens. He recalls visiting this awesome figure to have his
fortune read. Even Wordsworth had a conventional response to the

gypsies in his poem, "Gipsies," (1807) noting that the gypsies he observes near Castle Donnington, have not moved in twelve hours,
while he has journeyed to Derby and back. He says that even the
moon and stars reprove their "torpid life," and then piously concludes: "In scorn I speak not;—they are what their birth / And breed-
ing suffer them to be; / Wild outcasts of society!"

James Crabb was among the first to take a more sober and serious
look at this intriguing race in his *The Gipsies' Advocate* (1832), where
he encouraged better treatment of an unjustly abused people, and
suggested that Christians attempt to draw the gypsies into their fold.
His view of gypsy health is more convincing than Cowper's fanciful
impression. Allowing that "they are not generally subject to the numerous disorders and fevers common in large towns," he points out
that gypsies suffer from scourges of typhus fever, smallpox and mea-
sles.[13] His was a practical, not a typically literary attitude toward the
gypsies. He knew them and had worked among them. And, though
he assigns the usual characteristics to gypsies, he presents them
charitably. Whereas a certain Dr. Walsh could refer to the "unalterable moral qualities" of the gypsies as "an aversion to labour, and a
propensity to petty thefts,"[14] Crabb notes that morals can be altered
and improved through education; he compliments the gypsies on
their family affections and their respect for the dead, but does not
hesitate to admit their foolish love of baubles, their slovenliness, and
their occasional intemperance. He praises their promptness in paying debts, their fidelity in marriage, and general chastity, adding,
"This purity of morals, among a people living as they do, speaks
much in their favor."[15] Still he must admit the common gypsy habits
of petty theft, fortune-telling, and horse-stealing, which he describes
as "one of their principal crimes, and at this they are very dexter-
ous."[16] Crabb pities the gypsies' degraded state, but observes that,
since they have always been suspected and persecuted, they have
had little opportunity to improve. Oppression, he argues, would never reform this people or cure them of their wandering habits, but
only confirm their vagrant propensities.[17] Because Crabb was among
the first in England to make serious efforts to improve their condition, he is therefore to be respected in his judgment that though the
gypsies of his time are of unsettled habits, lacking in religious faith,
and living in a wretched moral state, "They are rational beings, and
have many feelings honourable to human nature."[18]

SCOTT AND THE LITERARY TRADITION OF THE EARLY
NINETEENTH CENTURY

Before Crabb made his appeal for a more humane attitude toward
the gypsies, Sir Walter Scott, in *Guy Mannering* (1815), had already
attempted to indicate the "feelings honourable to human nature" that
gypsies could demonstrate. For the most part, the gypsies in this novel are idle and vicious, but no more so than the smugglers with whom
they are associated. They might have remained more or less sociable,
confining their lawlessness to poaching and petty theft, had they not
been driven from their traditional camping grounds on the Bertram
estate. The gypsies are depicted mainly as outlaws, yet Dandie Din-
mont readily allows that there is good in them also. And, though Dominie Sampson may declare Meg Merrilies a "Harlot, thief, witch and
gypsy," (ch. 3) she proves to be a noble character, for it is through
her that Harry Bertram's true identity is revealed and his inheritance
recovered.

Scott idealized the character of Meg Merrilies; she is as extraordinary in society in general as she is among her own people. This pattern of selecting an exceptional gypsy as a fictional type became commonplace in later fiction. Gypsies as a whole remained a suspicious
crowd, capable of a variety of minor crimes, and demonstrating certain occult powers; but one remarkable gypsy would demonstrate
unlikely virtues beyond the range of normal behavior. These outstanding individuals served as foils, or consciences, to Christian characters.

In creating Meg Merrilies, Scott was not consciously fabricating a
literary type so much as he was creating a vivid character. His sociological views regarding gypsies remained objective, while he shaped
a romantic figure unlike any historical type. In *Guy Mannering*, Scott
wrote that gypsies in Scotland had at an early period been recognized as an independent race who later became equated with thieves.
Despite the severity of the laws, gypsies prospered in Scotland's tur-
bulent times, but by intermarrying with people in the north they lost
the more peaceful character of the gypsy race and became more violent. This account resembles others of the time. Scott himself wrote
a series of articles on Scottish gypsies for *Blackwood's Magazine*.[19]
Thus, while Scott had a clear historical view of the gypsies, he was
willing to alter that view to suit his fictional purposes.

John Clare wrote several poems about gypsies, from "The Gipsy's Song," emphasizing the freedom enjoyed by the wandering tribe, to "Gipsies," giving a plain, realistic picture of gypsy existence, to "Gipsies," depicting the hardships of the Romany hand-to-mouth life, where stolen sticks provide a fire to cook tainted mutton. "Tis thus they live," Clare summarizes, "a picture to the place, / A quiet, pilfering, unprotected race." An early sonnet, "The Gipsies' Evening Blaze" is a commonplace description of gypsies sitting around their fire, but the later "The Gipsy's Camp" is more ominous, recording Clare's growing incredulity about gypsy predictions, which culminate in a gypsy crone's prediction of bad luck and damnation for him. Clare's poems have a certain authenticity, since for a time he lived among the gypsies. He visited constantly at "King Boswell's" camp on Helpston Heath, and, after a romantic disappointment, went to live with his gypsy friends. "He actually carried out this resolve, and enrolled himself as a member of Boswell's crew for a few days; but at the end of this period left them with much internal disgust. The poetry of gypsy life utterly vanished on close examination, giving way to the most disagreeable prose."[20] Nonetheless, Clare remained interested in, and friendly with the gypsies for the remainder of his life. Nor was such commerce with gypsies uncommon among literary men of the time.

Some writers did not permit a real gypsy to be spokesman of the untrammelled life. Adapting the equally familiar convention of the wanderer to the gypsy, a romancer like Bulwer-Lytton could merely have his Ishmaelite join the gypsies, thereby remaining Christian while acquiring all the mystery, freedom and romance associated with the Romany tribe. At the opening of *The Disowned* (1828), Clarence Linden encounters a strange individual calling himself King Cole, who admits, "I am a gipsy by inclination, not birth." (ch. 1) The real gypsies are described as usual; "in all respects of the ordinary race of gipsies; the cunning and flashing eye, the raven locks, the dazzling teeth, the bronzed colour, and the low, slight, active form, were strongly their distinguishing characteristics as the tokens of all their tribe." (ch. 2) Clarence, himself disowned and outcast, feels strongly attracted to the gypsy tribe seeing in the seething pot from which they take their food "an emblem of the mystery, and a promise of the good cheer, which are supposed characteristics of the gipsy race." (ch. 2) Cole's career suggests that this image is false. Joining the gypsies had been an escape for Cole from the "three stuffed birds—how emblematic of domestic life!" that graced his sisters' dull household. (ch. 3) But finally he abandons his free life, having found the pilfering and questionable conduct of the gypsies more than he is willing to accept. He leaves the gypsies to settle down in a pleasant country home, feeling that "there is more happiness in reality than romance." (ch. 65)

For Bulwer-Lytton, the gypsies are essentially part of a romance that exists beyond ordinary society. They are not part of the "real" life.[21] They provide an eccentric frontier beyond the stuffed birds and pleasant country homes, the financial chicanery and political intrigue. They are elements of romance seen from a distance, remaining mysterious, threatening, and still moderately alluring. It is a function of the gypsy convention that will remain serviceable throughout the century. Bulwer-Lytton in his later work, *The New Timon* (1846), again represents the gypsies as attractive wanderers on the perimeter of society. The sombre Morvale sees them as a harsh but preferable alternative to the world he has left.

> Wretched 'tis true, yet less enslaved, their war,
> Than the life's peace with things our souls abhor;
> Convention's lies,—the league with Custom made,
> The crimes of glory, and the frauds of trade.

Attractive as this alternative seems to Morvale at first, it eventually appears that the mystery of the gypsies is only a shadow of a greater mystery; their estrangement from society is emblematic of the spirit's inevitable alienation from the world of matter. Morvale must turn not to fellow outcasts from the society he deplores, but to the Unseen, the spiritual otherness that is more certain than any haven in nature among perennial aliens.[22]

For G. P. R. James, too, the gypsies represent a way of life that contrasts with the shams of ordinary existence. When Colonel Manners, in *The Gipsy* (1835), hopes piously that the gypsies may learn to forego their thievery, his friend, Edward De Vaux, exclaims, "Good God! those gipsies are princes of honesty compared with the great majority of our dear friends and worldly companions." (ch. 1) Like Scott, James acknowledges that the gypsies are "loose and lawless," but unlike his predecessor, does not view them as dangerous.

Moreover, James seems to feel a certain regret for the gypsies' loss of grandeur, viewing them as "the remains of a beautiful nation long passed away from thrones and dignities, and left but as the fragments of a wreck dashed to atoms by the waves of the past." (ch. 1) There is a fatality here that smacks more of romance than of history. In fact, through his fascination with the gypsy heritage, James suggests that the gypsies had preserved certain human values that civilized life was gradually corrupting. It is the independence and integrity of individual freedom, not anonymous racial sins, that they have kept alive through centuries. This notion is condensed in the figure of Pharold, the gypsy leader, who, having been brought up in an aristocratic English home, elects to rejoin his own kind:

> "I quitted a life of sloth, effeminacy, and bondage, for one of ease, freedom, and activity. I left false forms, unnatural restraints, enfeebling habits—ay! and sickness, too, for the customs of my fathers, for man's native mode of life, for a continual existence in the bosom of beautiful nature, and for blessed health. We know no sickness but that which carries us to our grave; we feel no vapours; we know no nerves. Go, ask the multitude of doctors—a curse which man's own luxurious habits have brought upon him—go, ask your doctors, whether a gipsy be not to be envied, for his exemption from the plagues that punish other men's effeminate habits." (ch. 2)

However, only his yearning for freedom and a natural life marks Pharold as a gypsy. In every other aspect he is the familiar Romantic type of the outcast wanderer. Still, by making Pharold a gypsy, James drew upon a growing popular assumption that gypsies were endowed with greater powers of understanding and appreciating nature. Since gypsies were real, not fanciful beings, they could be convincing as a type of acknowledged alienation revealing by contrast the constraint, effeminacy and evil of established society. Pharold has both a physical and moral dislike for the limitations of society and advises his people:

> "Give obedience to their laws, but maintain your own liberties; bend to their power, but preserve the customs of your fathers. Shut them out, too, as far as may be, from amongst you: let them not learn either your history, or your language, or your knowledge; for if they do they will make these the means of softening and enslaving, under the pretence of civilizing and improving you." (ch. 26)

This is as much a warning to any man of integrity as it is a caution to a tribe of outcasts. And despite James' use of the gypsies, his story is really that of an independent spirit seeking to preserve its own integrity. There were few historical examples of gypsies like Pharold, though his breed was becoming more common in fiction. James' gypsies are minor outlaws; it is only one outstanding member who represents the redemptive humanity that other simulacra of the noble savage offer. And yet, what is important about James' Pharold is his moral attractiveness.

Pharold is an exception, however, for the fanciful convention of the gypsy predominated in the early part of the century. Louis James has written that "Gipsies are one of the most persistent elements" in the literature of the early nineteenth century,[23] and suggests that Borrow's writings increased an already active interest in gypsies, who were attractive because of their wandering life.[24] James goes on to describe some of the standard fictional uses of the gypsies. Usually there are curses associated with one or more gypsies; occasionally there is a lost child; and often a gypsy thwarts villainous plans or fulfills some other mysterious destiny. James gives the example of Thomas Peckett Prest's *Ela, The Outcast: Or, The Gipsy of Rosemary Dell* (1838), which used all of these devices and which was a financial success, but does not mention that Prest's novel is a detailed plagiarism of Jones' *The Gipsey Girl, or The Heir of Hazel Dell*, (1836-37). In this novel and *The Gipsey Chief* (1840), Hannah Maria Jones' gypsies are primarily vicious renegades. Both novels are about Christians who live for some time among the gypsies and who are immediately identifiable as nobler types. For example, the virtuous hero of *The Gipsey Chief*, though believing himself to be a gypsy, cannot accept the gypsies' way of life, for, though he admires their affection, fidelity and loyalty among themselves, he still retreats with abhorrence from them, because outside their community, "mankind were to them all lawful prey; and from nothing did they seem to shrink in their attempts to ensnare or to run them down." (ch. 19) In T. P. Prest's *The Gipsy Boy*, the boy is not a boy, nor is she a gypsy. Furthermore, the major gypsy characters who lead the gypsy band are not genuine gypsies but have joined them to achieve revenge. At the same time the supposedly carefree, nature-loving wanderers actually operate as an ominous danger throughout the novel.

Numerous other novels included the gypsy in similar fanciful ways, among them Mrs. Kentish's *The Gipsy Daughter* (1839), Anne Marsh's *Castle Avon* (1852), and later Mrs. Oliphant's *The Story of Valentine and His Brother* (1875). In America, there was J. H. Ingraham's improbable tale, *The Gipsy of the Highlands* (1847), which has nothing to do with Scotland, but is instead the history of two wild young men in upper New York State. The gypsy girl, Catherine Ogilvie, is "in character fearless, something masculine in her amusements, full of the fire of passion and feeling, characteristic of her race, and generous and unsuspecting to a fault." (ch. 3) She is converted to Christianity by Paul Tatnall's dying mother, and later is instrumental in redeeming Paul from a wayward life. She is the flimsiest sort of stage prop.[25]

Of course the stage itself provided a good crop of melodramatic gypsies. In 1842, the reviewer of George Borrow's *The Zincali* observed that on the stage as well as in fiction "the Gypsy hag appears as sorceress and fortune-teller, and the Gypsy girl by her charms weaves the intrigue of the piece, or utters the wild notes, which the musician deems appropriate to her state, or bounds before us as a thing of light in the voluptuous *ballet*."[26] And certainly such plays as John Buckstone's *Flowers of the Forest* (1847) or the American, Lester Wallack's *Rosedale* (1863), based on the English novel, *Lady Lee's Widowhood*, incorporated such conventional figures.[27]

But gypsies were not consigned merely to melodrama and penny novels. Creditable and popular authors used gypsies in the conventional manner as well, though often with a similar lack of understanding. Hence, Ainsworth, in his popular novel *Rookwood* (1834), confuses gypsies with beggars and mumpers, and the jargon that he employs is by no means true Romany. Moreover, Ainsworth's gypsies are got up in stage costumes; the usual gypsy maid dying for love appears in the character of Sybil, while the crone and gypsy queen is depicted in the witch-like old sorceress, Barbara Lovel. Again, the gypsies are vaguely associated with crime and violence.

Ainsworth's friend, Charles Dickens, had an equally conventional view of gypsies. For him, "gipsy" connoted slovenliness and suspicious behavior.[28] John Willet, in *Barnaby Rudge* (1841), describes Hugh as "a dreadful idle vagrant fellow, sir, half a gipsy, as I think." (ch. 10) John's supposition is correct, for Hugh is Mr. Chester's son by a gypsy woman. His gypsy blood, of course, explains Hugh's wildness.

It is this wildness that Dickens assumes as a definite attribute of the gypsies; thus he describes Helena and Neville Landless in *The Mystery of Edwin Drood* (1870), as "almost of the gipsy type; something untamed about them both, a certain air upon them of hunter and huntress." (ch. 6) Although Dickens never made significant use of the gypsy convention he presented gypsies in a favorable light when describing their children. In his description of the race course crowd in *Nicholas Nickleby* (1838-39), Dickens notes that "the sunburnt faces of gipsy children, half naked though they be, suggest a drop of comfort. It is a pleasant thing to see that the sun has been there; to know that the air and light are on them every day; to feel that they *are* children, and lead children's lives." He goes on to contrast their free life in nature with the unnatural circumstances of children raised in the midst of industrial squalor, and then concludes, "God send that old nursery tales were true, and that gipsies stole such children by the score!" (ch. 50) In its modest way, this is an acknowledgment of the growing sentiment connected with the gypsy convention, that those who live outside the ordinary regions of society may be all the better for it, and may even, in their curious way, represent a redemptive power.

It is largely through such incidental references that the conventional image of the gypsy persists outside of the melodramatic literature of the Victorian period. In *Jane Eyre*, for example, Jane associates freedom with living "like gipsies." (ch. 9) There is an amusing utilization of the stereotype when Rochester, later in the novel, disguises himself as a gypsy woman in order to tell the fortunes of his guests. That wild and passionate sojourner in an alien society, Heathcliffe, is described as "a dark skinned gypsy in aspect," (ch. 1) by Lockwood, an impression confirming Mrs. Earnshaw's designation of the orphan child as a "gipsy brat." (ch. 4) The examples are only a few from an overwhelming number of instances of the stereotyped, melodramatic convention of the gypsy. According to this convention, the gypsies are wild and free, ordinarily enjoying greater physical, though corrupt moral life, aside from one or two outstanding individuals, who may turn out to be Christians either in disguise or mistakenly nurtured among the gypsy tribe. Gypsies are clearly outcasts who hint at the occult, the criminal and the mysterious. Seldom is there an attempt to humanise the gypsy figure, aside from notable exceptions like Scott's Meg Merrilies and G. P. R. James' Pharold.

For the most part, the gypsy was an unappealing, though fascinating alien.

GEORGE BORROW

Several historical and sociological studies published in the early nineteenth century promoted a more realistic investigation of the gypsies. Among the most prominent of these was James Crabb's *The Gypsies' Advocate*. But, if Crabb wrote of the real facts about gypsies in the hope of uniting them to society as a whole, the gypsies had, in George Borrow, a champion who wished to prevent that union. For Borrow, the gypsies were symbols of freedom and he wished them to remain free. Borrow is one of the earliest English writers to combine the historical and the fanciful approaches in the investigation of gypsies, and, for many, his accounts of gypsy life became standard texts, though even his close friend, Theodore Watts-Dunton, acknowledged that "Borrow's descriptions of gipsy life are, no doubt, too deeply charged with the rich lights shed from his own personality entirely to satisfy a more matter-of-fact observer."[29] Robert R. Meyers more recently has observed that Borrow's "mystic approach to gypsy life has little appeal for those who favor the straight-facts, no-nonsense approach of modern sociological studies."[30]

With the appearance of Borrow's works, the traditional stereotype of the gypsy received a clear challenge. He was concerned with veritable, not concocted romance; with detail, rather than aura.[31] *The Zincali* (1841) was a fairly straightforward account of the beliefs and mores of the Spanish gypsies. It was also important because of the personal fascination Borrow showed for his subject. Although not entirely impartial, Borrow was more just to his subjects than most. And his willingness to live with them and to speak their language without sharing their moral values, made him an appealing, even exciting intermediary.

Borrow admired the gypsies' system of laws but acknowledged that the rigor of their society had seen a decline, since "the Gypsies are no longer the independent people they were of yore,—dark, mysterious, and dreaded wanderers, living apart in the deserts and heaths with which England at one time abounded." ("The Gypsies") This passage correctly reveals Borrow's romantic attraction for the gypsies as well as his interest in understanding and describing their real life. And even though a reviewer could write of *The Zincali* that "fiction is mingled with sober reality in a manner that throws some discredit on the narrative portions of the work,"[32] he and most readers nevertheless accepted the work as both informative and entertaining. It was, however, not nearly so agreeable to the public as *The Bible in Spain* (1843), where Borrow emphasized his own identification with the gypsies while incorporating them as only one part of a larger narrative. In this work, gypsy characters appear more clearly as individuals, not merely as subjects for study. Antonio, the gypsy who accompanies Borrow across the wild lands between Badajoz and Jaraicejo, is a highly believable figure, and his easy behavior does not entirely cloak his somewhat sinister motives.[33] Antonio, it seems fairly apparent, was one of a number of gypsies who, benefitting from the lawless condition of Spain during its civil disturbances, robbed and murdered travellers freely. Nor does Borrow attempt to disguise the cupidity of the Spanish gypsies he knew. When advised not to trust to "Egyptian faith," Borrow remarks, "I do not intend . . . especially with money." (ch. 17) In another place, Borrow is on his guard when a group of gypsies who are serving as soldiers try to bargain with him for his horse. In general, the gypsies Borrow describes in *The Bible in Spain* are wild and lawless people capable of crimes from murder to simple swindling. They are not sentimentalized, nor are they romanticized any more than other characters or types are in this work. In his private correspondence, Borrow could be more open in his feelings. "Poor people!" he wrote of the gypsies of Spain to his mother, "they are terribly used and hunted like wolves."[34]

Despite the detailed presentation of the gypsy in these works, it is perhaps in the fictional autobiographies *Lavengro* (1851) and *The Romany Rye* (1857) that Borrow made the most telling contribution to the convention of the gypsy in nineteenth-century literature. Borrow claimed that *Lavengro* was "particularly minute with regard to the ways, manners, and speech of the English section of the most extraordinary and mysterious clan or tribe of people to be found in the whole world—the children of Roma," ("Appendix," ch. 1); and, although the descriptions of the conduct and habits of the gypsies is detailed, especially in regard to Borrow's philological preoccupations, the greater popular interest in the book derives from the manner in which the gypsies function as a part of Borrow's own imaginative life.

Actually, gypsies do not figure largely in *Lavengro*. To a great extent, Borrow's interest in them is philological, as he claimed. Like many another curious individual, Borrow was intrigued by the mystery of the gypsy race, but his curiosity took a special turning. Borrow defends Jasper Petulengro against an Armenian merchant's slights. " 'Don't speak contemptuously of Mr. Petulengro,' said I, 'nor of anything belonging to him. He is a dark, mysterious personage; all connected with him is a mystery, especially his language; but I believe that his language is doomed to solve a great philological problem.' " (ch. 47) Borrow does give some pictures of gypsy behavior and customs, showing their superstition, their generosity, their wiliness and their vindictiveness—from which he almost died. But gypsies mean something more than this for Borrow. Lionel Stevenson, arguing that *Lavengro* and *The Romany Rye* do have a unifying structure, observes that "the characters and episodes fall into a symbolic design, with the gypsies representing the hedonistic life of sensation."[35] And surely it is true that what characterizes the gypsies of *Lavengro* is delight in a free and independent life. To the morose Borrow, Jasper Petulengro says, " 'Life is very sweet, brother; who would wish to die?' " When Borrow mildly contests that opinion, Jasper adds, " 'I'll try to make you feel what a sweet thing it is to be alive, brother!' " (ch. 25)

What Borrow admired most about the gypsies was their independence. Late in his life he praised himself for his own "unconquerable love of independence," (*Romany Rye*, ch. 25), and his personal history is a paradigm of the struggle for freedom and self-respect. Frustrated in his high aims, disillusioned with London, the youthful Borrow set out to wander the English roads. The further he progressed with this independent life, the more inclined he was to identify himself with the gypsies whose life he emulated. When the man in black asks him if he is a gypsy, Borrow does not wish to deny it. "What else should I be?" he replies. (*Lavengro*, ch. 90)

It was not in his own time nor has it since then been strange for people to suppose that Borrow himself was a gypsy. The anonymous reviewer of *The Zincali* remarked, "One is tempted to suspect, that he has Gypsy blood in his own veins, for, according to his account, he spoke their language rather better than they did themselves."[36] Borrow, of course, encouraged the identification of himself with the gypsies in his own writings, going so far in his diatribe against his critics at the end of *Romany Rye* as to exclaim triumphantly: "To have your ignorance thus exposed, to be shown up in this manner, and by whom? A gypsy! Ay, a gypsy was the very right person to do it. But is it not galling, after all?" ("Appendix," ch. 9)[37]

Borrow may have boasted that he, as sapengro, had become the honored brother of Jasper Petulengro, the gypsy king, but when he identified himself with the gypsies, he did so knowing that he was in no way truly of that people. He merely wished to show the manner in which his life approximated the mystery, freedom, and virtues of the gypsies. He was aware that the gypsies represented his own idealized aim, and he was not foolish enough to suppose that he could realize it by masquerade. Early in *The Romany Rye* he reflects to himself, "Had I not better become in reality what I had hitherto been merely playing at—a tinker or a gypsy? It was much more agreeable to play the gypsy or the tinker than to become either in reality. I had seen enough of gypsying and tinkering to be convinced of that." (Vol. 1, ch. 12)

In *The Romany Rye*, more than in *Lavengro*, Borrow gave details of real gypsy manners and customs, indicating the weaknesses familiar to gypsies, such as killing pigs, lying, and behaving in a modestly lawless manner. But he also showed the gypsies going to church, and presented Jasper Petulengro denying the familiar charge of gypsy indolence. Jasper humorously remarks that gypsies are not idle: "Never brother; when we are not engaged in our traffic, we are engaged in taking our relaxation: so we have no time to learn." (Vol. 1, ch. 9) Borrow has the gypsy girl, Ursula, dismiss the half-breed gypsies, or "half-and-halfs," as a bad lot, but also, through her discourse, reveals the gypsy virtues of wifely fidelity and extraordinary female chastity. In thus describing gypsy mores, Borrow intended to provide more than simple information. He wished to correct an existing stereotype and explore the imaginative possibilities of this mysterious race.

The reviewer of *The Zincali* in the *North American Review* isolated one of the problems facing Borrow in his books when he remarked that "the remarkable race, concerning whom more can be learned from this work than from any other publication with which we are acquainted, are sufficiently known by name to all readers of modern poetry and romance."[38] It was exactly to correct the stereotypes of poetry and romance that Borrow took pains to describe his gypsies as lavishly as he did. In a conversation with the virtuous but

aggressive Ursula in *The Romany Rye*, Borrow says, "but I suppose
there have been love affairs between gorgios and Romany chies. Why,
novels are stuffed with such matters" (Vol. 1, ch. 9), thereby indicating how common the gypsy was as a literary type and, at the same
time, how little understood. In another place, Borrow elaborates upon this view.

> You are certainly a picturesque people, and in many respects an orna-
> ment both to town and country; painting and lil [book] writing too
> are under great obligations to you. What pretty pictures are made out of
> your campings and groupings, and what pretty books have been writ-
> ten in which gypsies, or at least creatures intended to represent gypsies,
> have been the principal figures. (Vol. 1, ch. 9)

In 1837, the young Queen Victoria was reading Crabb's *The Gipsies'
Advocate* and declaring an encampment of gypsies "the chief orna-
ment of the Portsmouth Road," later sending blankets and soup to
their families while hoping their children might be instructed and presumably harmonized better with the ordinary community.[39] But
Borrow did not wish for the gypsies to be gathered together into
Southampton communities after Crabb's example. Nor did he wish
them to be considered romantic and picturesque figures in the arts.
He wished them to remain free and untrammelled, and his greatest
dread was that the values of the English might corrupt those of his
wild companions. Jasper Petulengro expresses this fear when he says,
"if ever gypsyism breaks up, it will be owing to our chies [women]
having been bitten by that mad puppy they calls gentility." (*Romany
Rye*, vol. 1, ch. 11)

Borrow's scholarly contributions gradually lost credit, and even
his sympathetic biographer, William K. Knapp, could, in 1899, declare that though *The Zincali* created something of a stir when it appeared in 1841, "in so far as its information is concerned about the
race in general, it has long been superseded by the more thorough
works of Jesina, Leland, Miklosich, Paspati, Pott, Simson, Smart and
Crofton, etc."[40] And Francis Hindes Groome, reviewing *Romano
Lavo-Lil* (1874), acknowledged Borrow as an early master of Romany
language and customs, while noting that since his early contributions
he had demonstrated little original matter.[41] Nonetheless, Borrow had
provided a picture of the gypsy that was notably different from prevailing conventional views, and had quite clearly presented an excit-

ing alternative to the previous fanciful picture of the English gypsy. After Borrow, it was possible for the convention of the gypsy in fiction to be more immediate or grand, if not exactly more correct.

THE GYPSY CONVENTION IN LATER VICTORIAN LITERATURE

With the appearance of serious investigations of gypsy life by writers such as Borrow—or Leland and Groome—a less superficial, if not more realistic attitude toward gypsies began to emerge in respectable fiction. Nonetheless, attitudes varied even within a single author's works. George Eliot was capable of describing gypsies in a convincingly realistic way in *The Mill on The Floss* (1860), or of using the reference loosely by calling Will Ladislaw "a sort of gypsy" in *Middlemarch* (Book 5, ch. 46), while also presenting a highly formal and stylized version of gypsydom in her long dramatic poem, *The Spanish Gypsy* (1868). In *The Mill on The Floss*, little Maggie Tulliver, determined to run away from home, settles upon the gypsy encampment as a proper refuge. She soon learns, however, that gypsies are not the romantic figures she supposed. They do not have the "Air of Freedom, Mirth, and Pleasure," that Bampfyld-Moore Carew found so attractive. While Maggie is considering that everything "would be quite charming when she had taught the gypsies to use a washing-basin, and to feel an interest in books," the gypsies are examining her nice clothing and the contents of her pockets, and debating what course of action would bring in the greatest profit from the child. (Book 1, ch. 11)

In *The Spanish Gypsy*, Eliot employs the gypsy convention in a totally different manner, ennobling her gypsies by placing them in the past and in another country according to the customary requirements of heroic romance. Zarca, the noble leader of the gypsies, is motivated by the high purpose of redeeming his race and is successful in persuading his long-estranged daughter (with the almost allegorical name of Fedalma) to join him in this purpose. Fedalma represents the best of flesh and spirit; her "harmoniously bodied soul" gains her the love of the high-minded Duke Silva, while her gypsy passions are revealed when her beautiful body cannot resist dancing to spontaneous music in the public Placa. As she dances, Fedalma sees Zarca and discovers in his eyes "the sorrows unredeemed / Of races outcast, scorned, and wandering." (Part 1)

The gypsy faith that Zarca asserts sounds rather more like liberal nineteenth-century humanitarianism than anything from the sixteenth century. Despite the romantic use of the noble outcast gypsy, or the beautiful enchantress, reminiscent of many an opera gypsy, the gypsiness of characters in this composition is subordinate to Eliot's psychological purpose of showing a young woman forced to make a choice involving a great sacrifice in order to fulfill a great destiny. It seemed to Eliot that the best setting for this dilemma was "that moment in Spanish history when the struggle with the Moors was attaining its climax, and when there was the gypsy race present under such conditions as would enable me to get my heroine and the hereditary claim on her among the gypsies. I required the opposition of race to give the need for renouncing the expectation of marriage."[42] In short, the gypsies were incidental, one of several possible choices. They are confections to garnish a philosophical and psychological treatise.[43]

Just as George Eliot could utilize two views of the gypsy according to her literary needs, so audiences could accept more than one notion of the gypsy. The more conventional view of the gypsy as a free, wild, and mysterious figure, in the nature of Victor Hugo's Esmerelda or Prosper Merimée's Carmen, was the most familiar. Sometimes the gypsy was ideal and virtuous, at other times more realistic and given to minor or more serious breaches of the law. But from the beginning there was the attraction of freedom, mystery and passion in the gypsy. In Henry Kingsley's *Ravenshoe*, gypsies are associated with wild blood. There is a standard view of the romantic gypsy maid who cannot accept the love of a young man who is willing to give up everything, including God, for her, in Philip Bailey's *Festus* (1839, but enlarged later). Sheridan Le Fanu used the gypsy convention in *Bird of Passage* (1870), and R. E. Francillon's *Zelda's Fortune* (1873) included a fairly realistic picture of the gypsy.[44] Although the standard view of the gypsy persisted, new attitudes became more and more obvious. Gradually the gypsy took on a more profound meaning.

When the dark-featured Allan Armadale recounts his early life in Wilkie Collins' *Armadale* (1864-65), he describes the time when a gypsy vagrant took him into his dubious care and kept him with him in his rough, wandering life. Later, thinking back on that life,

Armadale, who has assumed the gypsy's outlandish name of Ozias Midwinter, feels "The life with all its hardships was a life that fitted me and the half-breed gypsy who gave me his name, ruffian as he was, was a ruffian I liked." (Book 1, ch. 2) Armadale-Midwinter is himself a benign version of the half-breed gypsy. He too has mixed blood and is an outcast and a wanderer. His past is cloaked in mystery and he is gifted—or plagued—with a certain occult sense. For Collins, it was enough to use the gypsy suggestion to give a certain depth to his character, but the suggestion was in the direction of the profound.

A certain wistful sorrow begins to attach to the figure of the gypsy, allied to a dissatisfaction with society and a longing for life that is closer to nature and somehow purer and more free. In Matthew Arnold's early poem, "To a Gipsy Child by the Sea-Shore," the infant embodies all the mystery and sorrow of the outcast and wanderer which by this time is closely associated with the gypsy. In "Resignation" the gypsies are again described as endurers of the hard details of existence. "These gypsies," G. Robert Stange notes, "bear none of the connotations of the Scholar Gipsy. They represent a concern with simple survival, the irreducible instinctive life."[45] In "The Scholar-Gipsy" (1853), the image of the gypsy develops further. To the restless scholar, the gypsies are guardians of secret arts and lore which he values, and so he departs to roam the world "with that wild brotherhood." A. Dwight Culler explains that "The gipsies' art represents any kind of divine or natural lore such as cannot be gathered from books but can be gathered intuitively from the world of nature."[46] Arnold's scholar, having acquired those arts, escapes forever from the divided life of modern existence. Essentially, the scholar represents the achieved preservation of innocence impossible to modern man, an achievement made possible through his partaking of the mysterious life of the gypsies. It is important to observe that it is not the gypsies who have acquired immortality, innocence, or ideality, but the half-fabricated figure of Arnold's own imagination. "In Glanvill," Culler points out, "the Scholar-Gipsy was not a wanderer."[47] Only in a post-Romantic mode, where the outcast at home in untamed nature is honored, can the transformed scholar achieve the apotheosis that Arnold describes. Even then, Arnold knows that his dream is only an ideal. Just as he does not really see gypsies as the wards of nature's secret lore, so he does not believe the Scholar-Gipsy has lived and succeeded in his aim. Arnold has merely utilized the conventional figures of escape, mystery, and freedom, to show what men in a harrowing culture do not have.[48]

Arnold had elevated the convention of the gypsy to a philosophical speculation, and in a roughly similar way others altered the gypsy to more favorable positions in their writings. There is little blatant villainy in late gypsy characters. For example, Robert Browning used his gypsies in a highly conventional manner, though he too improved the type. The Pied Piper of Hamelin is not designated as a gypsy, though he is "a wandering fellow / With a gipsy coat of red and yellow," and is credited with two occupations commonly associated with gypsies: rat-catching and child-stealing.[49] This reference, however, is incidental and reveals little except Browning's favorable response to the outcast. In "The Flight of the Duchess" (1845), gypsies betoken the free, wandering life and appear to enjoy a special intimacy with nature, "For the earth—not a use to which they don't turn it." But beyond this naïf closeness to nature, there is a more occult wisdom among the gypsies which is concentrated in an old gypsy hag. The Duchess receives "Life's pure fire" from the old crone who herself appears transformed as she describes the life of freedom and love to the young woman, who promptly abandons her tyrannical husband to follow the gypsies in a life more compatible with the virtues of love. Meanwhile, the servant who has narrated the story explains that he plans eventually to abandon the false social structure that he serves "to get safely out of the turmoil / And arrive one day at the land of the Gipsies" where he hopes to find his Duchess once more. Browning's poem can be read as a parable of the individual's need for freedom from the restrictions imposed by a rigidly stipulative society, such as that of "respectable" Victorian England. And his gypsies, unlike the more realistic though also symbolic figures of Meredith, are really only emblems of escape from the confinements of a life that denies the value of waywardness and liberty. They represent the liberty of a life freely elected, but they are scarcely believable. They are nothing like the real gypsies described by Borrow and others.

Fifine, in "Fifine at the Fair" (1872), is perhaps closer to the reality, and the estimate of the gypsies' attraction there is more succinct. Fifine is "past mistake / The gypsy's foreign self." (xv) She is not above taking a tribute to her beauty from Don Juan, and there is a suggestion that she is willing to earn more of his gold any way she can. Fifine is more credible as a veritable gypsy, but it is clear that she stands for much more, for she "ceases to be a material woman and becomes representative of life itself, with its siren arts, confusing the soul through the dazzling fence of sophistry pointed with truth and beguiling it into disloyalty to its own past."[50] Obviously, Browning was far from original in his use of the convention, though he adapted it to his own philosophies. Don Juan, seeking to understand why rogues like gypsies are tolerated admits that "My heart makes just the same / Passionate stretch, fires up for lawlessness, lays claim / To share the life they lead." (vi) He concludes that since all men feel the need to escape from the confining circumstances of a culture which deprives them of freedom in the name of law and order, the obvious response is toward the freedom denied; that freedom is embodied in the gypsies who preserve a sense of personal integrity and personal liberty. And yet the craving for freedom makes men outcasts.

> Why is it that whene'er a faithful few combine
> To cast allegiance off, play truant, nor repine,
> Agree to bear the worst, forego the best in store
> For us who, left behind, do duty as of yore,—
> Why is it that, disgraced, they seem to relish
>   life the more?
>
> (vii)

The answer is simple: gypsies are content with freedom itself, and their cry is "To the wood then, to the wild: free life, full liberty!" (vii) And yet the gypsies require something from civilization as well. Juan concludes, "They, of the wild, require some touch of us the tame, / Since clothing, meat and drink, mean money all the same," and we, he continues, require a touch of their wildness. (vii) This formula resembles Meredith's scheme for a proportion in human nature, and gypsies here, as in Meredith or Arnold's "The Scholar-Gipsy," are the preservers of the means to that ideal.

For George Meredith, the gypsies' identification with nature's healing forces is prominent. In a poem such as "The Orchard and the Heath" he indicates the basic similarity of Christian and gypsy children despite their different settings; but in his novels, the natural setting of gypsy life suggests a deeper meaning. Gillian Beer says of *The Adventures of Harry Richmond* (1871), "the gypsy sub-plot makes vivid the emotional mingling of freedom and brutality which persist throughout the book."[51] Here, as elsewhere in Meredith, natural life signifies not the highest, but only the most basic aspect of human nature.

When *The Adventures of Harry Richmond* first appeared, reviewers approved of "the exquisite episode of the child's runaway adventure with the gipsy girl Kiomi," and praised the "exquisite sketch of the gipsy Kiomi."[52] The passage is indeed important in the scheme of the novel, for it exposes the principal fault in Harry's nature as well as its cure. Tramping with Kiomi, the romantic young Harry decides that the wandering life appeals to him; "Stars and tramps seemed to go together. Houses imprison us, I thought: a lost father was never to be discovered by remaining in them." (ch. 6) Harry recollects that he "preferred a gipsy life to Riversley," mainly because it was mobile and might lead to his father. Likewise "Kiomi stood for freedom, pointing into the darkness I wished to penetrate that I might find him." (ch. 8) Finally, however, Harry's fantasies must be corrected. He is too much air, and too little earth. Like Kiomi, he has aspired to a station that is beyond him, and just as the gypsy girl may be injured by her aspiration, he too may be maimed by his. Harry realizes that his problem has been simple egoism. No sooner does Harry admit that he has been at odds with his own best nature than he is beset by a gang of gypsies and receives a gruesome battering. The attack is tantamount to a reaction on the part of nature. Although the beating is a mistake, it proves appropriate nonetheless, for Harry has discovered how nature—emblematically represented by the gypsies—whips back upon any who foolishly tamper with it. But if nature can punish, it can also cure; it is the gypsy women who tend Harry in the illness that follows his beating. Meanwhile, Kiomi's career is another verification of the danger men run when they forget the restraints that must accompany either fantasies that take them too far from nature, or the passions which imbed them securely in it.

In *Harry Richmond*, Meredith used the gypsy convention to clarify his point that civilization must establish limits to the natural freedom that gypsies signify. But in *Lord Ormont and his Aminta* (1894), the emphasis is reversed, and Aminta, in breaking free to a truer life than her marriage allows, is identified with gypsies and gypsydom. By this time, gypsy references for Meredith have become a form of shorthand identifying one or another feature of his own beliefs about the values and dangers of natural impulses. He has no thought of providing photographic pictures of gypsy life; he cares only for what they may symbolize.

The gypsy, as a conventional type persisted as a convenient variation on the outcast or wanderer. As Louis James observes, "being both mysterious and actual, 'a singular union of romance and reality,' the gypsies provided a natural bridge between the Gothic and the domestic novel."[53] But they were more than that, as the literature of the latter part of the century demonstrates. From vagrants and tramps, or wild supernumeraries of romance, the gypsies had become wards of human integrity. Still undomesticated, they now came to represent the human values that excessive domestication seemed inclined to compromise.

LATER NINETEENTH-CENTURY INVESTIGATORS

While this change was taking place in the literary gypsy, serious students of Romany life continued their investigations. Two of the most authoritative and popular scholars of gypsy lore in England were Charles G. Leland and Francis Hindes Groome, who approached their subject with a personal enthusiasm that reinforced the increasingly sympathetic attitude toward the gypsies. The more humane nature of Romany studies in England might be attributable to Borrow's popularization of the subject. Leland admitted that his curiosity about Romany matters was prompted by reading Borrow, and his own study, *The English Gipsies And Their Language* (1874), is typical of the interest in the later part of the century. Much of Leland's book deals with gypsy manners, language, and beliefs, but it is clear throughout that Leland is a partisan, for he delights in contrasting gypsy and civilized societies to the detriment of the latter. Leland overlooks the petty thievery and swindling often associated with gypsy life and concentrates instead upon the "curious *inner life* and freemasonry of secret intelligence, ties of blood and information, useful to a class who have much in common with one another, and very little in common with the settled tradesman or worthy citizen."[54] Leland makes scarcely any mention of hunger, disease, dirt and squalor, concluding that they are petty fees of a greater freedom, because a man who is able to eat anything and sleep anywhere without being conscious of any shame, "is independent to a degree which of itself confers a character which is not easy to understand."[55]

But Leland's real attraction to the gypsies is less that of a scholar than that of a poet. For him, "there is a strange goblinesque charm in Gipsydom—something of nature, and green leaves, and silent nights —but it is ever strangely commingled with the forbidden."[56] He admires the gypsy's "scouting, slippery night-life," his use of a secret language, his superstitions, and "habit of concealing everything from everybody."[57] Despite his realistic description of gypsy ways, Leland clung to the romantic image and therefore, in a scholarly way, reinforced the mysterious association of gypsies with nature that Arnold, Meredith, Browning and others had suggested. The popular attitude was therefore given intellectual credence through the works of authentic scholars.

Sir Richard Francis Burton, a mysterious and compelling figure, was not a romantic, but he studied the gypsies carefully and was himself identified with the race. He seems to have felt "a special affinity" for the gypsies,[58] a favorable sentiment which may have been initiated during his university days, when he became acquainted with a gypsy girl named Selina whom he visited in Bagley Wood.[59] There was speculation about Burton's connections, some considering that his notorious restlessness, peculiarly piercing eyes, and horror of the circumstances surrounding death, along with the fact "that 'Burton' is one of the half-dozen distinctively Romany names," justified the supposition that he had gypsy blood in him.[60] Lady Burton said that although there was no evidence of Burton having gypsy blood, there was "no question that he showed many of their peculiarities in appearance, disposition, and speech—speaking Romany like themselves. Nor did we ever enter a Gypsy camp without their claiming him: 'What are you doing with a black coat on?' they would say; 'why don't you join us and be our King?' "[61]

When she was still Isabel Arundell, Lady Burton had been told by a gypsy woman named Hagar Burton, that she would marry a man named Burton.[62] Some time later, the young Miss Arundell had a reminder of the prediction when the gypsy woman asked her, " 'Are you Daisy Burton yet?' "

"Would to God I were," she answered fervently.

"Patience," the gypsy answered, her grave eyes alight, "it is just coming."

"I never saw her again," Isabel wrote, "but I was engaged to Richard two months later."[63]

It is not remarkable to anyone who has seen photographs of Burton that he should be described as resembling a gypsy. But it is an indication of the changing attitudes that this aspect of his nature could be emphasized without its appearing vulgar. On the contrary, it enhanced his reputation considerably, just as a similar identification added a romantic luster to Tennyson's character. Mrs. Carlyle found the "something of the gipsy in his appearance" perfectly charming.[64]

Theodore Watts-Dunton did Burton the honor of declaring that he, Borrow, and Tom Taylor were the only men of letters he knew, before meeting Groome, that understood gypsies.[65] But Burton's own work, published posthumously, is primarily concerned with the tracing of gypsy origins to the Indian Jats. He spends a good deal of his time quarrelling with M. Paul Bataillard's work and makes some general remarks about gypsies of Asia, Africa, Europe, and the New World. He offers observations on language and on incidental details —such as his noticing the outstanding beauty of Spanish gypsy women—but on the whole, his essay is not an important contribution. Nonetheless, he did understand the gypsies and would have easily appreciated the growing tendency of the age to present their way of life as at least a symbolic alternative to England's, which he considered to be practically moribund.

Burton combined a personal and a scholarly fascination with gypsies. Leland's work, like Borrow's, combines personal, scholarly, and literary interests, and indicates the manner in which the gypsy convention operated upon the imagination even of a disciplined investigator. Leland managed to combine the two modes in one work, but in the writings of Francis Hindes Groome the different ways of viewing the gypsies are separated. Groome had written the entry on gypsies in the *Encyclopaedia Britannica*; and later contributed an essay, "The Gypsies," to a series of addresses entitled *National Life and Thought of the various nations throughout the world* (1891), which, by including gypsies, demonstrated how far Romany studies had progressed. He also attempted a novel in which gypsies played an important part. In "The Gypsies," Groome summarized the familiar charges of child-stealing, cannibalism, thievery and fortune-telling often made against gypsies, while emphasizing their many contributions, concluding that "Gypsies have possibly been greater benefactors to the Gentiles than even was Watt or Stevenson. I have shown, too, that the Gentiles rewarded them—as benefactors often are rewarded—with persecution. For surely any wrong-doings of the Gypsies fade into insignificance by the side of the wrongs that were done them."[66] As for Borrow and Leland, the gypsy life had a romantic appeal for Groome that was strong enough to intrude itself into his formal address. "To step out of one's tent right into the star-lit night," he rhapsodizes, "to fall asleep to the murmur of a brook, all one's life long to lie in nature's bosom—that life, with few cares about Heaven, is Heaven already."[67]

Much of the matter of this essay on gypsies and more of the mood had already appeared in Groome's casual account of gypsy life called *In Gipsy Tents* (1880), which consists largely of anecdotes about gypsy life and folktales told by gypsies. The gypsies described by Groome, who was praised by Theodore Watts-Dunton for his photographic accuracy,[68] are notably benign and almost childlike. We hear the by now familiar assertions that gypsy men are sober and their women chaste, that gypsies are generally honest and healthy, that accounts of kidnapping and other major crimes are false or inflated. But Groome also describes gypsy burial customs, and argues that gypsies are capable of religious belief and have a touching "unquestioning faith in the incredible."[69] Nothing of the former stereotype of the intemperate, crafty renegade persists in Groome's picture. In fact, Groome actively disputes George Smith's charges that the gypsies are vile thieves and beggars living in squalid and filthy conditions and abusing their children who would benefit from being removed and placed under the protection of the Education Board. All in all, *In Gipsy Tents* is a defense of the gypsies as innocent outsiders, more at peace with themselves and nature than are their enemies, who denigrate them, while boasting of their own civilized state.[70]

Despite the romantic scholarship of men like Leland and Groome, in fact the gypsies, as George Smith's denunciations indicated, remained the subjects of great political and social scorn. In reality, they were still distrusted and even feared. Only among a small band of partisans and in literature were they acceptable as proponents of a better way of life.

OTHER LITERATURE OF THE LATE NINETEENTH CENTURY

In some cases the distinction between fiction and fact was by no means clear. In *No. 747. Being the Autobiography of a Gipsy* (1891),

Dr. Francis Wylde Carew claimed to have recorded the conversations of a gypsy convict in Moorport Prison between the years 1860-70. The gypsy Samson Loveridge's history is quite as romantic as many of the popular tales of the time. Loveridge himself refers to the gypsy's "naturally predatory instincts"[71] and records some commonplace methods of gypsy cheating and thievery. At the same time, he tells of good gypsy characters who live untainted and close to nature. Loveridge's tale includes the romantic attachment of a well-born English gentleman for the gypsy's handsome mother, as well as an account of a disputed inheritance. Loveridge is temporarily associated with unscrupulous horse-dealers and smugglers, and later lives in a nobleman's house as a domestic servant. He has romantic adventures in the United States, and is acquainted with gypsy boxing champions, and so on. In short, the story smacks a good deal of Borrow and the improbable, yet it is put forth as fact. Loveridge even records his contempt for the conventional image of the gypsy as found in popular romances.

> In *The Romany's Curse: or the Moaning Mountain Maniac*, the romantic gipsy in his traditional costume of slouched sombrero, scarlet sash, and long mysterious mantle, avenged with ready *churi* [knife] the insults offered by the licentious nobleman to his dark-eyed *pirreni* [sweetheart], the while the wrinkled beldame snatched the youthful heir from his nurse's arms, devoting the hated race to perdition, and uttering the most blood-curdling maledictions in that strange mixture of thieves' Latin and mumpers' talk which has so often done duty for genuine Romnimus.[72]

There was most certainly a continuing output of this sort of gypsy romance. In addition to those we have already noted, there appeared such works as Daniel Copsey's *The Gypsy's Warning* (c. 1838), Richard Howitt's *The Gipsy King, and other poems* (1840), William Bance's *Ralph; a legend of the Gipsies in four cantos* (1845), Lydia Huntley Sigourney's *The Gipsy Mother* (a poem) (1858), and George Searle Phillips' *The Gypsies of the Danes' Dike. A Story of hedge-side life in England, in the year 1855* (1864). But from the 1870s on, a revived interest in the gypsy stimulated a new crop of tales, of which the following are a mere sampling: R. E. Francillon's *Zelda's Fortune* (1873), B.L.A.'s *Ketura, the Gypsy Queen* (c. 1875), and *Gypsy. A Tale* (1879), Henry Woodcock's *Zana, the Gypsy, or, Heiress of Clair Hall* (c. 1877), L. Neville's *A Romany Queen* (c. 1880),

Hugh de Normand's *The Gipsy Queen* (1882), Charles Stuart's *David Blythe, the Gipsy King* (1883), Emma Leslie's *The Gipsy Queen* (1885), Nelli Hellis' *Gypsy Jan. A Tale* (c. 1886), Mary Bennett's *The Gipsey Queen; or, The changed bridegrooms* (c. 1890), Robert Leighton's *Gipsy Kit, or the man with the tatooed face* (1893), and Charlotte Grace O'Brien's *Gipsy Marion: a story of the New Forest* (1895). Aside from romances of this sort devoted to the subject of the gypsy, other stories employed gypsies incidentally in the conventional manner. Thus the typical view of the gypsy as a wild wanderer and outcast persisted in Bram Stoker's *Dracula* (1897) where Jonathan Harker, visiting Count Dracula's castle in Transylvania, describes a band of Szgany, or gipsies, as "fearless and without religion, save superstition, and they talk only their own varieties of the Romany tongue." (ch. 4) They are, in this instance, unscrupulous cohorts of the thoroughly evil Count Dracula. The mysterious and occult Natalie, in Robert Cromie's *The Crack of Doom* (1895) is all the more mysterious for being described as gypsylike in appearance.

Despite this continuing flow of popular romances, there were, as we have seen, attempts in fiction, as with Meredith's Kiomi, to present a more accurate image of the gypsy. Francis Hindes Groome himself did not stop at scholarly depiction of the gypsies, but in *Kriegspiel* (1896) introduced them as romantic characters in an improbable romance. It would be difficult to explain the plot of this deplorable novel, but it is enough to state that the hero, Lionel Glenham, who is part gypsy, is led to believe that he is full-blooded gypsy and technically illegitimate.[73] The evil machinations involving Lionel are the work of a mysterious Dr. Watson, whose motives are never entirely clear. Aside from Perun Stanley, Watson's gypsy assistant—who, in a drunken state, mistakenly buries his chief instead of Lionel, and who concludes his adventures in a madhouse in Brooklyn—most of the gypsies in the novel are not objectionable or are admirable. The focus, however, is on the gypsy girl, Sagul, for whom George Meredith professed great admiration, describing her as a "memorable gypsy heroine."[74] Sagul, like so many of her sisters in fiction, is a dauntless woman of great courage and great passion. It is she who helps Lionel thwart Dr. Watson's schemes, and she who proves that he is the legitimate son of Sir Charles Glenham. However, because Lionel cannot love her, Sagul is doomed to the fate of the truly passionate, dying of unrequited love. Despite his obvious qualifications—he had lived with the gypsies and married a gypsy wife—Groome was no writer of romances. Watts-Dunton praised the authenticity of Groome's Romany allusions but could not praise the book. He was disappointed that such an excellent scholar of gypsy-dom had failed to produce the great gypsy novel of the age, for *Krieg-spiel* deservedly failed with the public.

Watts-Dunton had hesitated to publish his own gypsy romances because he had had great hopes for Groome's work, but once it was clear that Groome had failed, he decided to make his own writings public. In Watts-Dunton's sequence poem, *The Coming of Love: Rhona Boswell's Story* (1897), Percy Aylwin falls in love with the beautiful gypsy girl, Rhona Boswell. Their love is tempestuous, but ends in marriage. Rhona, however, has murdered a gypsy in self-defense, and the curse for her act manifests itself in what appears to be a mystic sign. She leaves Percy, fearing her doom, and never returns. From Rhona, Percy had learned that "through the unsophisticated movements of the female heart, Natura Benigna can express herself." (I. v.) Persuaded of his beloved's death by the vision of a Golden Hand and Rhona's face in a misty sunrise, Percy sets forth on his wanderings in despair, until, at the end of the poem, another mystic sign convinces him of the benevolence of nature.

The Coming of Love is vague and suggestive, being more concerned with poetical moments than sustained narrative. But in his highly successful novel, *Aylwin* (1898), Watts-Dunton was more precise in his use of the gypsy convention.[75] The hero of this story, Henry Aylwin, has gypsy blood in his veins. In attempting to locate his lost love, Winifred Wynne, Henry joins a band of gypsies travelling through Wales. There he encounters the remarkable gypsy girl, Sinfi Lovell, who helps him to recover Winifred with the help of what appear to be supernatural powers. Meredith admired Sinfi more than he had Groome's Sagul and with good reason, for she is an interesting and attractive character. Like Sagul, Sinfi falls in love with her gorgio friend, Henry, but unlike the former heroine, she is able to overcome her "Dukkeripen," or fate, and in the end she parts amicably from the reunited lovers.

The gypsies in this novel are as fanciful in their way as those of earlier romances of the century. Moreover, there is a great deal of the supernatural that, though it might have appeared improbable to many at mid-century, was more acceptable to a society that had demonstrated a renewed interest in the occult.[76] Sophia Morgan, for example, a prominent defender of Spiritualist activity, expressed her faith in the "natural" ability of gypsies to see the future and interpret the past.[77]

Of course, gypsies had long been credited with fortune-telling abilities and other occult powers.[78] Such an attribution in *Aylwin* would not therefore seem unusual. In any case, authorities on the subject declared that Watts-Dunton's pictures of gypsies, as well as those of Bohemians, East Enders and Aristocrats, were true and vivid.[79] Watts-Dunton had been careful to show a range of attitudes toward gypsies in his novel. Henry Aylwin's mother, for example, "associated the word 'Gypsy' with everything that is wild, passionate, and lawless;" an unfair, but traditional attitude. (Book 1, ch. 6) At the same time, the lower element of gypsydom appears in Herne, the gypsy "Scollard."

> A very different kind of Romany was the Scollard—so different, indeed, that it was hard to think that he was of the same race: Romany guile incarnate was the Scollard. He suggested even in his personal appearance the typical Gypsy of the novel and the stage, rather than the true Gypsy as he lives and moves. (Book 4, ch. 4)

Watts-Dunton was less concerned in *Aylwin* with the faithful depiction of gypsy life than he was with indicating that gypsies represented a free and natural life which conferred upon them both natural and supernatural powers of appreciation. Gypsies, unlike the British, the narrator remarks, feel that nature is free and unowned. Here, as elsewhere in the literature of the age, gypsy life is the key to authentic existence, to real life. So Henry Aylwin comes to feel:

> I had been trying to educate myself in the new and wonderful cosmogony of growth which was first enunciated in the sixties, and was going to be, as I firmly believed, the basis of a new philosophy, a new system of ethics, a new poetry, a new everything. But in knowledge of nature as a sublime consciousness, in knowledge of the human heart, Sinfi was far more learned than I. And believing as I did that education will in the twentieth century consist of unlearning, of unlading the mind of the trash previously called knowledge, I could not help feeling that Sinfi was far more advanced, far more in harmony than I could hope to be with the new morning of Life of which we are just beginning to see the streaks of dawn. (Book 7, ch. 3)

Watts-Dunton had been interested in gypsies since his childhood when his father introduced him to a friendly tribe who travelled the East Anglian countryside. He never became a Romany scholar, but he remained curious about the outcast race throughout his life.[80] However, he did not write *Aylwin* as a simple adventure involving gypsies, for he intended his novel as an illustration of his belief in what he called "The Renascence of Wonder."[81]

In *Aylwin* gypsies signify the possibility of freedom from a depressing and etiolated civilization. Watts-Dunton had written that in the "bastard civilization [of the West] life becomes poorer and poorer, paltrier and paltrier, till at last life goes out of fashion altogether, and is supplanted by work. True freedom is more remote from us than ever. For modern Freedom is thus defined: the exchange of the slavery of feudality for the slavery of opinion."[82] Gypsies, he asserted, remain uncontaminated by this state of mind, for, "notwithstanding certain undeniable obliquities in matters of morals and cuisine, [they] are the only people left in the island [England] who are still free from British vulgarity."[83] Watts-Dunton felt that "the basis of the Romany character is a joyous frankness."[84] It was this joy, naturalness and spontaneity that he wished to stimulate.

By the end of the century it was this image of the gypsy that established itself in the better grade of literature. In "To Ocean Hazard: Gipsy," Lionel Johnson said "Closer they, than other men, / To the heart of earth have come." And this was the belief of many writers discontented with a life too much departed from nature. William Sharp identified himself strongly with the gypsies. Once, as a restless young man, he had run off with them. "During the summer of 1874, when he was eighteen, he 'took,' as he says, 'to the heather,' joining a troupe of gypsies, and wandering all over the countryside with them for three months.[85] Seeing himself as a wandering outcast, uncomfortable in the society he was forced to endure, Sharp sympathized with the gypsies as an outcast but free race. Like them, he "at all times hated the restrictions and limitations of conventional life."[86] His story, "The Gipsy Christ" (1895), although not specifically autobiographical, reveals some of Sharp's own discontents, projected in the circumstances of the central character of the tale, half-English and half-gypsy, who is driven to serve his gypsy blood.

Arthur Symons had been awakened to "a sort of Gypsy element in literature" by reading R. L. Stevenson.[87] Through reading *Lavengro* he discovered that there was a way to escape conventional and commonplace life. "Humanity began to exist for me," he says.[88] As a young man he became romantically attached to a gypsy ballet dancer but had been interested in gypsies since his adolescence, had learned Romany, and was a member of the Gypsy Lore Society. He wrote poems about gypsies such as "Gipsy Mother's Song," "The Gypsy's Song," "The Old Gypsy," and translated a Baudelaire poem "Gypsies on the Road." In "Gipsy Love" Symons strikes the note of escape characteristically associated with gypsies when the persona sings "And it's O to be off and away from the town / With a gipsy for my dear!"

Describing his own vagabond nature and his restless desire to wander, Symons claimed that they freed him from prejudices, and insisted that "It was the wandering wise, outcast sons of Pharaoh, the dark roofless ones, the Gypsies, who taught me their wisdom."[89] It was most certainly freedom and natural wisdom that Symons attributed to the gypsies. In an essay, "In Praise of Gypsies," published in the *Journal of the Gypsy Lore Society* (April, 1908) and reprinted in *Eleonora Duse*, Symons set the gypsy off as a symbol of redemption, in contrast to a civilization degenerated by merchants. His affirmation of what he believed gypsies to represent is a summary of what many other writers had been saying.

> They are the symbol of our aspirations, and we do not know it; they stand for the will for freedom, for friendship with nature, for the open air, for change and the sight of many lands; for all in us that is a protest against progress. Progress is a heavy wheel, turned backward upon us. The Gypsy represents nature before civilisation. He is the wanderer whom all of us who are poets, or love the wind, are summed up in. He does what we dream. He is the last romance left in the world. His is the only free race, and the tyranny of law and progress would suppress his liberty. That is the curse of all civilisation, it is a tyranny, it is the force of repression. To try to repress the Gypsies is to fight against instinct, to try to cut out of humanity its rarest impulse.[90]

In a world threatened by mechanical control, industrial pollution, and bureaucratic confinement, the gypsy represented a source of freedom. He was a spokesman from nature. "To the natural man, the freedom of the Gypsy is like a lesson against civilisation," for it shows him he can still do as he likes, thrive and be healthy and preserve his soul untainted.

Symons' image of the gypsy as symbol of freedom was in keeping with the revised convention of the gypsy, but the convention was not always in keeping with reality. In the successful evangelist preacher, Gipsy Smith's, account of his life and work, published in 1906, the gypsy emerges as essentially benign, but he is scarcely the wild hero of Symons' pages. Smith credits the gypsies with the usual knowledge of horses and goes over some familiar customs, such as marriage, which is celebrated, he admits, without ceremony. Smith claims that Christians have forced the disgraceful profession of fortune-telling on the gypsies, who do not believe in it, but who "are not averse to making a profit out of the folly and superstition of the 'gorgios.' "[91] More improbably, Smith claims that "the poor gipsies believe in God, and believe that he is good and merciful."[92] Not even the most favorable commentators on gypsies credit any more than a few with religious sentiment of any kind. Smith's estimate of his race was definitely affected by his own acculturation. His eldest sister was the wife of Councillor Ball of Hanley, the first gypsy in the history of England to occupy a seat in a town council. There were other gypsies as well who were choosing to accept the gorgio's way of life and establish themselves within that commonplace society of which Symons had sought to make them the symbolic antithesis.

It is a long way from the gypsy handkerchief of Othello, or Bampfylde-Moore Carew's mendicants and the impoverished gypsy types of Crabbe and Cowper, or the numerous stage figures of English romance, to Sagul, Rhona Boswell and Sinfi Lovell. Watts-Dunton could declare that "Scott's idea of the Scottish gipsy woman was conventional—a fancy portrait in which are depicted some of the loftiest characteristics of the Highland woman rather than of the Scottish gipsy."[93] Still, his own gypsies were conventional in their own right.

The romantic gypsies of late Victorian literature, possessed of untrammelled spirits and gifted with natural and supernatural acuity were as far from the reality of the abused, distrusted, unkempt people wandering the English countryside in fewer and fewer numbers than had been the dark outcasts at the century's outset. Nonetheless, it became customary in the latter part of the nineteenth century to dismiss earlier pictures of gypsies in literature as thoroughly unreal. Leland declared, "with the exception of Lavengro and the Rommany [sic] Rye, I cannot recall a single novel, in our language, in which the writer has shown familiarity with the *real* life, habits, or language of the vast majority of that very large class, the itinerants of the road."[94] Watts-Dunton pronounced the popular notion of the gypsy girl taken mainly from stage tradition as "fantastically wrong," and added that "with regard to the stage, no characters in the least like gipsies ever appeared on the boards, save the characters in Tom Taylor's 'Sir Roger de Coverley.' "[95] Tom Taylor himself had written in 1851: "It is curious, indeed, considering how many Gipsies there are still in England, and how much the race has been worked by painters, dramatists, and novelists, to find how untruthfully they have, as a rule, been represented by all these artists"; and went on to assert, "I cannot remember a single genuine Gipsy in a novel, though both Bulwer and Disraeli have tried their hands at the class. And among stage plays, the only one in which I have ever seen the Gipsy introduced, with evidence of a real life-like knowledge of the race, is in a version of Sir Roger de Coverly [sic], played at the Olympic Theatre during the present year."[96]

There is little doubt that early utilizations of gypsies in nineteenth-century English literature were highly conventional and based upon little or no direct experience of Romany life. Nonetheless, the gypsy served as a convenient emblem of outcast, lawless and passionate life. Gypsies were evil as frequently as they were grand or good; ordinarily one gypsy hero or heroine exhibited noble qualities distinctly uncharacteristic of the race as a whole, and an attractive version of the gypsy convention was to present a Christian character as a temporary member of the gypsy race. But while this conventional type continued through the century, a new emblematic function grew with it; the notion of gypsyism became more attractive and less frightening. As genuine gypsies decreased in numbers, the abstract notion of gypsy character became more appealing. Hence it was something of a compliment to be described as having a gypsy appearance, and notable literary figures, such as Tennyson and Sir Richard Burton, both romantically handsome men, were all the more attractive for being gypsy-like in feature. Still, the gypsy was honored more as an adjective than as a neighbor.

The conventional figure of the gypsy, while maintaining its romantic cast, came also to signify a more profound sentiment. Particularly in the writings of a certain group of literary men, it signified freedom from a life of sham and emptiness, as well as the promise of a reawakened life of both senses and spirit. However, though this figure appeared in its most developed form in only a few works late in the century, it was the outgrowth of a consistent symbolic convention utilized by numerous writers, both famous and insignificant. Nor did the image die easily. Browning, who knew little of gypsy life, could see them as symbols of free and spontaneous life, and so could D. H. Lawrence in *The Virgin and the Gipsy* (1930, written 1925-26). In that story, Yvette Saywell finds gypsies attractive largely because they represent the opposite of her stifled way of life at her father's rectory. She "lay and wished she were a gipsy. To live in a camp, in a caravan, and never set foot in a house, not know the existence of a parish, never look at a church. Her heart was hard with repugnance against the rectory." (ch. 4) The vitalizing force of the gypsy symbol is clear in Yvette's response to the mere thought of gypsy life. "The thought of the gipsy had released the life of her limbs, and crystallized in her heart the hate of the rectory: so that now she felt potent, instead of impotent." (ch. 4) Lawrence continued the tradition of the gypsy as a redemptive outcast, and merely emphasized his own preoccupation with a mysterious life force to that traditional type.[97]

The study of gypsy life did not end with the nineteenth century, but has persisted strongly into our own time. Histories and other scholarly studies continue to appear, though their tone has gradually changed. Konrad Bercovici, in *The Story of the Gypsies* (1928), a national account of gypsies, reviewed the usual customs and attributes of the Romany race and defended them as representatives of freedom as Symons had done. He too saw them as gift-bringers scorned. In England, "where the poor have always worked so hard for so little, the Gypsies who turned their backs on factories and smirched cities were hated by the very people for whom they should have served as models."[98] The gypsies are, Bercovici explained, conscientious objectors to "all the soul-killing inventions of a haphazard civilization."[99] They may be given to thievery and cheating, but "Their petty swindles are more amusing than the wholesale swindles of great financiers," and their fortune-telling less harmful than psychoanalysis.[100] Bercovici admires the gypsy spirit finally because it is free and because the gypsies are convinced that "they are a superior race of cleaner and better blood."[101] Brian Vesey-Fitzgerald, writing as late as 1944, sounded a note of wistful and envious nostalgia in his otherwise sociological account of gypsy life.

> They are no better and no worse than other men anywhere. But there is danger in knowing them. Do you remember Mathew [sic] Arnold's Scholar Gypsy? He did not come back. And there are many more who have joined the travelling folk and have not come back. There is an overwhelming fascination about them and their mode of life. It is the fascination of freedom. We think that we are free: indeed we boast that we are. But of our civilisation we have made a tyrant. We are the slaves of money, of convention, of time-tables, of forms. We are the cogs in the gigantic machine of bureaucracy. The Gypsy, despite the unremitting attentions of the police, is still free. You know real freedom, real liberty, the moment you put foot on the road with the men and women who live on the road, the moment you sit, legs a-dangle, on the foot-board of a waggon, a good horse in front of you and fortune-knows-what around the corner.[102]

Imitators of George Borrow have travelled among the gypsies in the twentieth century, as G. E. C. Webb's *Gypsies: The Secret People* (1960) and Walter Starkie's *Don Gypsy* (1937) and *In Sara's Tents* (1953) indicate. Famous artists such as Vaughan Williams and Augustus John have identified themselves with the gypsies and gained from them artistically, as Sven Berlin, in a recent account of life among gypsies, *Dromengro: Man of the Road* (1971), points out. Berlin's picture of the gypsies is realistic in the sense that it describes a people oppressed and suffering from hunger and hardship. Still, the gypsies seemed to be "a token in some way of a dream which still lives on in men's hearts in spite of the claims of office and of existence: one of freedom."[103] The gypsy arranges his life as he pleases, says Berlin, and pays the price. Berlin was attracted to the gypsies and for the most part lived comfortably with them; yet he saw that there had been a noticeable decline in the character of the Forest gypsies.

Berlin's book is one of many indicating a revived interest in the gypsy, perhaps from a sense of nostalgia for the free life they represent. Donald Kenrich and Grattan Puxon's *The Destiny of Europe's Gypsies* (1972) discusses the gypsies' European background and their circumstances during the Nazi period. Thomas Münster's *Zigeuner-Saga: Von Geigern, Gauklern und Galgenvögeln* (1969), indicates that the interest is not only alive in England. Nonetheless, English interest in gypsies is particularly active as Jeremy Sandford's record of interviews with English gypsies, entitled *Gypsies* (1973), suggests. Some books, like C. H. Ward-Jackson and Denis E. Harvey's *The English Gypsy Caravan: Its Origins, Builders, Technology, and Conservation* (1972) are concerned with details of gypsy life while others, such as Dorothy Strange's *Born on the Straw: A Romany Biography* (1968), largely an account of the love of a gypsy man and a gorgio woman, takes a personal approach to the subject.

In some cases, recent books on gypsies have come from the gypsies themselves, as in Silvester Boswell's *The Book of Boswell* (1970) or Manfri Frederick Wood's *In The Life Of A Romany Gypsy* (1973), by no means the first gypsy autobiographies. Such matter-of-fact accounts indicate how ordinary, if colorful, gypsy life really is, how practical and even banal, how preoccupied not with the supernatural, but with the immediate. When the gypsies themselves found a voice, literary artists lost a volatile symbol.

This, then, has been the outcome of the Victorian transformation of the conventional emblem of the gypsy. Nothing remains of the vicious bandit, the child-stealer, the occult magus. And only in the cinema—that last retreat of Victorian romance—have gypsies maintained their later, more sympathetic associations. In films such as *The Wolf Man* (1941) and its successors, gypsies preserve their occult wisdom, while in pictures such as *The Great Moment* (1921), *Golden Earrings* (1947), or the urbanized *Hot Blood* (1956), gypsy girls exert a characteristic passional attraction. Q. D. Leavis, quoting from the Readers' Library Film Edition promotional material for an early film, shows to what extent the gypsy figure had degenerated toward the operetta type.

> "The Rogue Song," based on the popular romantic music comedy "Gipsy Love," is one of the most colourful achievements of the talking screen. The story makes a gripping novel, and Mr. Val Lewton's style has captured all the melody and romance of the film, which has for its star Lawrence Tibbett, America's greatest baritone. . . . This heart-throbbing romance of a gypsy bandit's love for a beautiful princess forms one of the most delightful film novels we have yet published.[104]

Victorian scholars and romancers had taken the melodramatic convention of the gypsy and transformed it from something frightening and strange, to something rich and awesome. But the enticing image could persevere only so long. As the civilization that writers like

Watts-Dunton, Borrow, and others deplored reached further and further into the quiet reclusive parts of the British Isles, it became all too evident that gypsies were subject to the monotonizing forces that many a novelist and poet had hoped they might help to overcome. The gypsy convention of Victorian literature was one of the last emblems of hope for a regeneration through spiritual and natural forces that a mechanistic culture persistently destroyed. The gypsy represented a longed-for freedom, an opportunity to escape from conditions rapidly becoming intolerable for those who wished to preserve human "naturalness" and sensitivity. For a time the convention served its purpose and was understood by nineteenth-century readers as a moral hieroglyph; but outside of literature that sentiment dissolved and eventually the image, along with the moral framework of which it had been a part, became no more than a diverting antique.

CHAPTER FIFTEEN

MEMORY

MEMORY: AN OVERVIEW

Memory, a persistent mystery of man's nature, has been a perennial subject in literature. During the nineteenth century, when questions of human identity and man's relationship to a greater existence were changing, memory developed as an important literary convention. Memory has always fascinated men because human nature itself depends largely upon how memory is defined and what place it has in the larger structure of man's intelligence. Theories of memory may be reduced to two basic types. The representative theory argues that we establish from the experience of remembering that what we remember did happen, but that what we are aware of, when we remember, are images of past things produced in our minds.[1] According to the realist theory, however, in remembering, the mind is aware of past things themselves.[2]

These are simple distinctions and do not suggest the complex attitudes toward memory expressed in ancient to modern thought. One important concern with memory, for example, was the desire to achieve technical skill. The study of this skill, called mnemonics, supposedly originated in the fifth century B.C. with Simonides. During classical and medieval times the technique was mainly topical. The anonymous *Ad Herennium* is a major source of information on this method. The topical mode persisted into the Renaissance with variations by different scholars such as the Dutch writer, De Krypse, and the Englishmen Thomas Watson and John Willis. Peter Ramus dismissed the old art of memory, substituting his own system, which was logical rather than image related. Although his techniques established themselves, they did not entirely supplant other forms, and to this day a wide variety of mnemonic techniques are proposed for improving memory; in fact, as I. M. L. Hunter remarks in *Memory*, "there are as many different mnemonic systems as there are people who employ them."[3] Harry Caplan's "Memoria: Treasure-House of Eloquence" provides an excellent summary of early theories of memory especially as they related to rhetoric, while indicating as well the metaphysical significance of the subject.[4]

If memory was associated with the divine in pagan thought, it was equally important in Christian belief. Saint Augustine, in Book Ten of the *Confessions*, marvels at the wonderful variety of human memory and asserts his conviction that God, and therefore Truth, dwells everywhere in the memory. He says to God, "you have deigned to be present in my memory ever since I first learned of you. . . . Truly you do dwell in it, because I remember you ever since I first came to learn of you, and it is there that I find you when I am reminded of you." (sec. 25) For Augustine, memory acts as a form of conscience in that it keeps the presence of God and Truth ever before the attention of the individual.

During the Renaissance, while the rhetorical tradition of memory with its various theories persisted, there was no shortage of profounder minds who argued, as Ficino did, that through the mystical use of memory, man could establish contact with the divine. Frances Yates has ably demonstrated in *The Art of Memory*, that memory became a central feature of hermetic or occult art. The Christian Hermeticists transformed the philosophy and psychology of memory from a scholastic to a Neoplatonic and occult study. Camillo's memory theater was designed to harness the power of the world harmony, and Giordano Bruno created a similar scheme, borrowed, as Professor Yates observes, from Metrodorus, though modified to Bruno's peculiar interests.[5]

THE IDEA OF MEMORY IN THE NINETEENTH CENTURY

Although the more esoteric and occult attitudes toward memory lost ground and the more practical and objective notions predominated for more than a century in England a new awareness of the significance and mystery of memory began with the Romantic movement. Nostalgia was a prominent feature of Romantic writing. For many, memory meant personal memory of childhood representing an inviolable sanctuary. For others, consciousness of the mystery of memory led to more expansive speculations. A. W. Schlegel noted that "As a sentient being man is set as it were in time, however as a spontaneous being he carries time within him, and this means that he can live in the past and dwell in the spirit wherever he pleases."[6] Explaining the melancholy character of Northern poetry, Schlegel observed that "the poetry of the ancients was that of possession; ours is that of yearning. The former stands rooted in the present; the latter sways between memory and presentiment."[7] Memory here is not concerned with mere human happiness, but with the imagined ideal world from which the soul has been estranged into the earthly world of shadows. In E. T. A. Hoffmann's *Der Goldene Topf*, the salamander, Lindhorst, retains a "remembrance of his first state," while exiled from his divine existence into terrestrial life. Although the tale is a fable, Hoffmann's point is that man possesses in the power of his imagination a divine quality transcending the mere association of ideas—a theory already accepted as the scientific explanation of memory's mechanism. Goethe's *Faust* reasserts the importance of memory, both personal and cultural, in the creative fashioning of a world view. Even those who acknowledged the correctness of David Hartley's theories found more in memory than mere interconnected ideas governed by a law of association. Coleridge, if he did not revere memory as a means of communication with an ineffable divinity, surely recognized its importance as a communication with one's own deepest self.

> Men are ungrateful to others only when they have ceased to look back on their former selves with joy and tenderness. They exist in fragments, annihilated as to the Past, they are dead to the future, or seek for the proofs of it everywhere, only not (where alone they can be found) in themselves.[8]

The anonymous reviewer of William Forbes' *Life of Dr. Beattie* in the *Edinburgh Review* for July, 1807, presents the argument between "sceptics" and "orthodox philosophers" of his time. The former group suggests that memories are present sensations and may provide only an illusion of an actual past, while the latter group contends that man's instinctive faith in memory "is complete and satisfactory proof of its accuracy." The reviewer's conclusion is a commonsensical response to a subtle dispute. "The truth is," he says, "that all men have a practical and irresistible belief both in the existence of matter, and in the accuracy of memory," and that sceptical writers do not really seek to destroy this belief, but only to demonstrate their own ingenuity. Such a response to the complex philosophic notion of memory was as common at the outset of the nineteenth century as it would be today. When Isaac Taylor remarked that "considered as a function of the brain, the memory retains what it retains, and reproduces what it reproduces, according to the law of an arbitrary, and often accidental connexion of ideas,"[9] he expressed a common view. There were, however, other forces at work which were to revive a nobler function for memory.

Memory can be both personal and cultural, and the nineteenth-century mind was equally concerned with both areas of recollection. In *A Dream of Order*, Alice Chandler provides a serious investigation of the Victorian interest in the medieval. Examining the various social, political and esthetic aspects of the theme, Professor Chandler indicates the manner in which Tory and Whig historians distorted historical facts in order to emphasize their own political biases related to medieval thought, and illustrates the way in which English thinkers, such as Carlyle, were influenced by the German Romantic fascination with the art and culture of the Middle Ages. William Cobbett compared the society of his own time unfavorably with that of the Middle Ages, and later Thomas Love Peacock began work on a novel, *Calidore* "in which the naive comments of a visitor from Arthur's court to modern England serve as a bitter commentary on the times."[10]

Interest in medievalism waxed throughout the century, despite the opposition of such figures as Mill and Macaulay. The yearning for the past that was a central feature of Romanticism was reflected in medievalism where a craving for the ideal and a "nostalgia for the ordinary" could combine.[11] The medieval and the Gothic were identified with the natural and the free, representing admirable qualities of life felt to be waning in the mechanical society of the nineteenth century. "The association of such ideas as nature, harmony, creativity, and joy with medievalism points up the other major aspects of the medieval revival, its attempt to create a coherent world view."[12] Both Scott and Carlyle, in their different ways, identified medievalism with ordered society and an ordered universe. As Kenneth Clark has shown, the Gothic revival in architecture involved not only the desire to resurrect a form of art, but to recover as well a form of sanctity. Pugin, for example, felt that "the life of the Middle Ages was not strange or impossible, but the only good life."[13] And he contrasted the men of those times with his own "faithless contemporaries."[14] Pugin himself had written that true Gothic architecture could be restored only "by a restoration of the ancient feeling and sentiments that characterized the Middle Ages."[15]

The concern for memory, then, was not merely personal and mechanical, but historical and in a sense racial in nineteenth-century England. Victorians looked back from the cultural maturity of their own time to the happy racial memory of the nation's youth. This act of popular nostalgia was largely moral. Scott idealized feudalism—his own version of the historic past—because it represented a moral order. Ruskin had gone so far as to declare that it was "as the centralisation and protectress" of the sacred influence of memory that Architecture was "to be regarded by us with the most serious thought," for Architecture and Poetry were the only "two strong conquerors of the forgetfulness of man." (*Seven Lamps of Architecture*, "Lamp of Memory") Memory was important as a personal and cultural preserver of valuable experience. An entire age which had been forgotten was now considered worth recalling. Certainly the desire to recall a racial infancy was as strong among nineteenth-century artists and thinkers as was the fascination with personal memories of childhood. Still, Schiller had pointed out that "historical awareness ought to prevent an excessive admiration for the past and to check our desire for returning to a projected 'state of innocence and bliss.' "[16]

In *The Triumph of Time*, Jerome Hamilton Buckley remarks that the nineteenth century was "the great age of English autobiography,"[17] and indicates the fascination of men with their own histories and the history of their times. Wordsworth idealized his personal past. He vivified childhood memories because they had not played

him false; "they stood in his mind as a living reality. They were for
him the source of joy, freedom, and intimations of immortality."[18]
The autobiographical impulse, Professor Buckley shows, exerted
itself in the creative writing of the time in works such as Meredith's
Modern Love, Dickens' *David Copperfield*, or Rossetti's *The House
of Life*. He concludes, after touching upon several major literary
works, that for the Victorians, "the meaning of the past remembered
lay in its power to enhance the quality of life in the all-demanding
present."[19] But, in several ways, this assertion is misleading. Bound
up with the fascination for the personal and historical past was a
moral concern that projected the interests of memory into aspirations
for the future. Victorian thought was often preoccupied with what
was to be, rather than with what had been or was. Carlyle declared
that "most of us, looking back on young years, may remember seasons of a light aërial translucency and elasticity and perfect freedom," before the soul was entirely imprisoned by the body. "The
memory of that first state of Freedom and paradisiac Unconscious-
ness had faded away into an ideal poetic dream," ("Characteristics")
but that dream could lead to some proper future action. In acknowledging the need for change in times that he considered bleak, Carlyle
averred that "if Memory have its force and worth, so also has Hope."
    Lytton Strachey described Newman as "a child of the Romantic
Revival, a creature of emotion and memory," and in so doing indicated clearly two concepts of Romantic thought that affected the
nineteenth century profoundly.[20] Whereas memory had been conceived mainly as a mental warehouse in the eighteenth century, with
the Romantic movement, the new exaltation of strong emotion coupled with an increased interest in personal memory placed greater
emphasis upon the subjective, the individual ego. Samuel Rogers'
successful poem, *The Pleasures of Memory* (1792) is an interesting
transitional poem and summarizes many standard responses to memory, both historical and personal, from the mundane to the spiritual.
In the first part of the poem, the poet's return to a childhood home
prompts a sequence of memories:

> Indulgent MEMORY wakes, and lo, they live!
> Clothed with far softer hues than Light can give.
> Thou first, best friend that Heaven assigns below,
> To sooth and sweeten all the cares we know.

(Part One)

To Rogers, memory is based upon an incomprehensible association of ideas: "Lulled in the countless chambers of the brain, / Our thoughts are linked by many a hidden chain." (Part One) Places and events are clothed with feeling through the power of memory. All the actions of memory seem benevolent. In the second part of his poem, Rogers shows how science, art, and other disciplines of thought are dependent upon memory. Both Hope and Fancy, he says, are subject to Memory's laws, and there follows a sequence showing various operations of memory. All of these are commonplace circumstances, presented sentimentally. Rogers then asserts the exalted memory of souls beyond the grave and concludes his poem: "Hail, MEMORY, hail! in thy exhaustless mine / From age to age unnumbered treasures shine!" (Part Two)

Rogers' is clearly not a profound poem, but the views presented in his work remained commonplace for much of the poetry that followed. An obscure poet, Frances Brown, in "The Bright Hours of Memory," presented similar positive and traditional attitudes toward memory as the repository of joyful and consoling experiences; a nostalgic treasury. Looking back along the path of life, says the poet, one may always find spots of greenness beyond the "desert of years." Perhaps these memories of triumphs, loves, and childhood delights have been obscured, but they have left "their bright track" in the soul, and they remain a source of pleasure and consolation, a faithful resource for the weary spirit. They are, in fact, man's least perishable heritage:

> Bright, bright shines the beacon of hope from afar!—
> And strong is the faith of our youth to pursue
> The path of its promise, till dim grows the star,
> And faint grow our steps in the wilderness too;—
> But ne'er of her treasures can memory be reft—
> And dark must the days of his pilgrimage be
> Who finds not one hour in his retrospect left
> Like a full ark of joy on the desolate sea.

There is nothing here of the remorseful aspect of memory in the works of writers such as Byron or Coleridge. Instead, memory is associated with the notion of youthful innocence and truth. It is identified primarily with consolation and reserves of faith and spiritual strength.

Fascination with memory could be unwise as well, as Felicia Hemans suggested in her poem, "The Boon of Memory," where the persona's maudlin desire that some memory of himself remain in the place of his childhood receives a stern answer from Memory, Love, Song, and even Death, all of whom state that no such memory can last. Finally, Nature declares, "Earth has *no* heart, fond dreamer! with a tone / To send thee back the spirit of thine own—Seek it in heaven." The desire for physical memory is foolish, since the true answer to the human craving for permanence or for the recovery of innocence is a heavenly one.

TENNYSON'S USE OF MEMORY

Among Victorian writers, Tennyson provides one of the most complex and wide-ranging examinations of memory. For him personal and cultural past were related. It is a cliché to say that Tennyson was deeply fascinated by the past.[21] From his earliest poems, the subject of past civilizations, individuals, and states of mind intrigued him. Most frequently, the world of the present appeared to varying degrees degenerate compared to the past. Although it can well be argued that *The Idylls of the King* bears directly upon Victorian times, it is also apparent that behind the conception of the poem is a nostalgia for another, perhaps simpler and more innocent, age. A similar sentiment is more directly evident in *The Princess*.

But if Tennyson was thus intrigued by the preservation of the cultural past, he was equally concerned about personal memory. In "Memory (Memory, dear enchanter)," (1827), the persona laments his power of memory because it recalls to his mind "Days of youth, now shaded / By twilight of long years," when his heart was filled with futile false hopes: "All those dear hopes are dead, / Remembrance wakes them only." Just as cultural memory may recall a fallen Jerusalem, Persia, or Camelot, so personal memory recalls the innocence of youth now lost. In both cases, memory is painful, though potentially useful, as the unpublished poem, "Sense and Conscience" indicates. In this allegorical poem, Conscience, "the boldest of the warriors of Time, / Prime mover of those wars of Spirit and Sense, / The wisest of the councillors of Time," has been put to sleep by Sense. Memory comes at last "with stern / Sad eyes and temples wan cinctured with yew" and recalls Conscience to full awareness of his lapse. This poem is a fragment and ends with Conscience in pain. But in "Memory (Ay me!)," a poem of the same period, memory is again "A conscience dropping tears of fire," and although the persona remembers "that Hope is born of Memory / Nightly in the house of dreams," he does not go beyond anxiety and despair in his waking life.

Memory is not merely a moral prod for Tennyson; it can also be artistically useful. In "Ode to Memory," published in 1830, the persona apostrophizes memory, requesting that it come benignly, bringing recollections of happy youth and its pleasant landscapes. When memory satisfies his desire, the speaker admiringly refers to the success of the "great artist Memory," who "Artist-like" gazes "On the prime labour of thine early days." Memory imitates art in its power to organize past experience and thereby becomes the source for the individual's willed recollection, so that in later life, "We may hold converse with all forms / Of the many-sided mind, / And those whom passion hath not blinded, / Subtle-thoughted, myriad-minded."

If memory can recall innocence, it may also preserve love. This is, of course, the substance of *In Memoriam* (1850) which enshrines Tennyson's love for his dead friend, Arthur Henry Hallam. In an earlier poem, *The Lover's Tale*, Julian, recounting his unsuccessful love, declares that for him, "The Present is the vassal of the Past;" he is hopeless and in all his senses weakened, "save in that, / Which long ago they had gleaned and garnered up / Into the granaries of memory." He then compares his memory to the camel who, though driven through wildernesses far from the oases where he began, "yet in him keeps / A draught of that sweet fountain that he loves, / To stay his feet from falling and his spirit / From bitterness of death." Memory provides nourishment from the past for a tasteless present. Though memory may be related to hope, as in "On a Mourner," where they are described as "spouse and bride," in *The Lover's Tale* they are divorced, for, as Tennyson's interpolated allegory indicates, memory has supplanted hope by default.

> They said that Love would die when Hope was gone,
> And Love mourned long, and sorrowed after Hope;
> At last she sought out Memory, and they trod
> The same old paths where Love had walked with Hope,
> And Memory fed the soul of Love with tears.[22]

Although Tennyson distrusted the fair picture that memory might paint, wondering if "the past will always win / A glory from its being far; / And orb into the perfect star / We saw not, when we moved therein" (*In Memoriam*, xxiv), he also realized that it was memory that consolidated man's human identity (xlv), and provided him with hopes perhaps more important than Julian's romantic longing in *The Lover's Tale*. In "A Dream of Fair Women," the persona tells how, in a familiar setting, "The smell of violets, hidden in the green, / Poured back into my empty soul and frame / The times when I remember to have been / Joyful and free from blame." Soon after begin his encounters with extraordinary women, notable in the history of mankind. From his personal memories, the speaker has glided into the early memories of humankind. When the dream is past, he is unable to recover it, and he laments "As when a soul laments, which hath been blest, / Desiring what is mingled with past years." Tennyson may here have been suggesting the power of the individual human mind to recover racial memories, as the popular poet Martin Tupper did in his poem, "Memory," where he speculated on whether memory had "some grand globe, some common hall of intellect, / Some spacious market-place for thought, where all do bring their wares, / And gladly rescued from the littleness, the narrow closet of a self, / The privileged soul hath large access, coming in the livery of learning." Both Tupper and Tennyson were thinking more of the imaginative recapture of racial memories than their actual recovery. Both poets are suggesting that this recovery of the past was available to great minds through the exercise of the imagination, and Tennyson made such an attempt at recovery in *The Idylls of the King*, at the same time fashioning an artistic work into a memory for mankind. Swinburne, as we shall see, was equally eager to retain for mankind the memory of its youth in *Tristram of Lyonnesse*.

Beyond the recollection of a nobler time in man's past, Tennyson conceived of a yet more intriguing possibility in human memory, the recollection of prenatal experience. Arguing, in "The Two Voices," that memory, being bound up with matter could not easily provide recollections of a life before earthly existence, the persona expresses his sense that some fragmentary recollection remains. These "mystic gleams, / Like glimpses of forgotten dreams," suggest memories from a prior existence, but they are so vague that they resolve themselves into simple intimations of faith. This sentiment is related to Wordsworth's in his "Intimations of Immortality," and was not uncommon in the early nineteenth century, as the anonymous poem *The Mystery of Time* (1849) suggests.

But if,—if there are, buried in the shrine
Of thy most secret soul experiences,
Memories, thoughts, convictions forced on thee
In memory's soberest hours, which stir the heart
With more than a suspicion, more than fear—
With a deep sense most irresistible
And most mysterious—that there is a God,
And that he rules,—say, is it not this to have
The proof of facts within thee of the being
And rule of God?

Tennyson was concerned with memory as something more than the commonplace storehouse of impressions, and went beyond this speculation concerning prenatal memories, touched upon again in *In Memoriam* (xliv), to a consideration of whether or not man preserved "the eternal landscape of the past" after death. (xlvi) For him the foundation of human personality, memory, was potentially a unifying force between the historical and personal present and past, it was a moral goad either through individual or racial conscience, or a private retreat from an unattractive present, and it was a source of hope for continued consciousness beyond death. Moreover, poetry itself was a means of preserving what was worthy of preservation in human experience. Tennyson thus had a complex and profound sense of the function of memory, and he elaborated the convention beyond the commonplace.

THE ATTRACTIVE PAST: MEMORY AND HOPE

In one regard Tennyson anticipated a major concern of the Victorians in his attitude toward memory. His Lotos-Eaters were one early manifestation of a potential antagonism toward the aggressiveness of the age. Displaced, and incapable of the many labors they would face if they could return home, Ulysses' seduced crew accept the very minimum of existence. They live in bare sensation; yet in their half-slumbering state they delight "To muse and brood and live again in memory," the real origins of which are long destroyed and lost. Pleasurable sensation is equated for them largely with inactivity and the impressions of memory. Moreover, though their desires yearn backward in their dream of peace, the Lotos-Eaters feel a more revealing

lust to live "like gods together, careless of mankind," in a sort of pleasurable overseeing of man's painful existence. By converting their
life into a dream—a mixture of memory and desire—the Lotos-Eaters
achieve the illusion of escaping life's suffering.

In blending personal memories with aspirations toward a transcendent state partly engendered by an awareness of the futility of all
that is personal, the Lotos-Eaters anticipate the poetic fascinations
with the past as escape that gradually intensified during the nineteenth century. Wistful backward glances to a golden classical age,
like those of Gissing's character Henry Ryecroft, were not simply
the result of classical education. D. G. James declared that, for Matthew Arnold, "the classical becomes only a symbol for the inviolable
thing, the other, the unattainable, the transcendent."[23] William A.
Madden, more specifically, describes Arnold's conversion of nostalgia for an unrecoverable past into a hope for an unattainable future,
in which "the proposed England of the future is a projection into the
future of the image of this idealized moment from the past [Peri-
clean Athens]."[24] The seductiveness of medievalism as we have seen
was also associated with similar wistful reflections. Out of the contrast
between the lovely, lost past, and the crude, unlovely present, there
developed a friction which, while it may have been aberrant or affected, could also be grandiose and genuine. As we shall see, the so-
called Decadents, while oppressed by nostalgia for a vanished age,
were aware of the idealization of their nostalgic fable. Pain, therefore,
was manifold, arising not only from the contrast of an esthetically
uniform past and a discordant present, but as well from the knowledge that the paradigm against which the grim present was contrasted was itself a poetic fabrication. Were this the sum of discontent that self-conscious poets of the late nineteenth century felt, it
would not be a profound subject for analysis, but when we recall that
these men were, as well, craftsmen of language, another and more
interesting dimension appears.

In "Pictures at Oxford and Blenheim" (1824), Hazlitt expressed
characteristic yearnings after a past time, as well as lofty aspirations
for the future. This combination was not unusual. But between the
idealized past and the glorified future: the inescapable present remained, where the pressures of recollected charm and foreseeable joy
produced only pain. Swinburne, while acknowledging that pain and
suffering were as much a part of the historical past as of the indi-

vidual present, argued that there is an element of the past that lives beautifully in remembrance, and that, as he indicates in "The Interpreters," is its articulation. Nature, Swinburne allows, would still have offered its music whether or not Homer, Hugo, or Sappho sang, yet the great poets have achieved another kind of music by giving mere matter "sense and soul by song, and dwelling in thought," where "their being endures." Poets, through their power of expression have kept the past, and the sense of the past, alive, and, in so doing, have themselves become deathlessly united with natural powers. Like Thallasius, each poet, achieving his power, is "no more a singer, but a song." ("Thallasius")

> But thought and faith are mightier things than time
>   Can wrong,
> Made splendid once with speech, or made sublime
>   By song.
> Remembrance, though the tide of change that rolls
>   Wax hoary,
> Gives earth and heaven, for song's sake and the soul's,
>   Their glory.
>
> ("The Interpreters")

The poet, by recording his "interpretation" of existence, becomes one with it, merging himself and his art with the force that includes both. Moreover, in so doing, the poet not only creates, but becomes a part of a cultural memory, for it is through *his* private experience that *we* acquire remembrance of times past. And it is through the preserved beauty of a memorialized past that we of the present fabricate hopes for our future. In this way, the individual poet, through his private exposition, participates in a cultural life that is vast, mysterious, and ultimately transcendent.

In "Prelude: Tristram and Iseult," Swinburne explains that he has taken the story of these ancient lives because

> Some yet are good, if aught be good, to save
> Some while from washing wreck and wrecking wave.
> Was such not theirs, the twain I take, and give
> Out of my life to make their dead life live
> Some days of mine, and blow my living breath
> Between dead lips forgotten even of death?

The most intriguing feature of this passage is its dignified irony; for the poet, as he composes, well knows that he too will become only a memory. However, just as he revives the living poem—the existing music that was the fable of Tristram and Iseult—and just as he converts their lives into art through his language, so he, in this creation becomes no more a singer but a song echoing in the cultural memory of man. Art is both hope and memory in the face of phenomenal uncertainty, and Tristram, himself the emblem of life as esthetic event, recognizes as much. Facing "only certitude of death and change," Tristram's senses are troubled by manifold impressions, "Or memory mixed with forecasts fain to rise / And fancies faint as ghostliest prophecies." His mood ascends and plummets; he is aspirant, but uncertain and fearful. Still, he

> Lost heart not wholly, lacked not wholly light,
> Seeing over life and death one star in sight
> Where evening's gates as fair as morning's ope,
> Whose name was memory, but whose flame was hope.
> (*Tristram of Lyonesse*, "The Last Pilgrimage")

As the rest of *Tristram of Lyonesse* reveals, this passage is far subtler than it seems, for the evening and dawn mentioned here are not merely actual, nor historical, they are psychological as well. The dying away of memory may be as superb as the dawning of that same memory reborn in a new guise of hope. A memory of simplicity located in classical or medieval time may be reborn in a simplified future just as an old tale may be reborn for the future in present activity of the poet. It matters little to the poet, whose memories are fashioned as much by desire as by what is past, that the simple glory of the past is a fiction of his own devising.

Few poets of his time were so hopeful as Swinburne in this regard. The attitude expressed in Swinburne's poem is related to Arthur O'Shaughnessy's Shelleyan assertion that poets, in the broad sense, "are the dreamers of dreams," and "the movers and shakers / Of the world forever." O'Shaughnessy declares that "each age is a dream that is dying, / Or one that is coming to birth," and it is the music and vision of the poet that originates either dream. ("Ode") But Swinburne's view is less naive; his poets are not inventors nor "movers and shakers," they are interpreters who consolidated experience through utterance. The actual movers and shakers are the heroes, undeniably appreciated by Swinburne. But the means of fixing heroes, deeds, "dead shapes and shadows," in the cultural memory, is the utterance of the poet. Swinburne's perception unites the half-historical attitude of O'Shaughnessy's "Ode" with the apparently contrary import of a characteristically ninetyish poem such as Arthur Symons' "The Loom of Dreams," and surpasses both.[25]

I am suggesting that there is a connection between the fashioned nostalgia for the past, the wistful hope for an altered future, and the esthetic self-consciousness of the writers of the late nineteenth century in England. Furthermore, I am suggesting that the frequent references to memory and to hopeful dreams uncover a fundamental attribute of the esthetic presuppositions of these writers, rising out of the conventional use of themes in earlier literature. Elizabeth Barrett Browning had been thoroughly conventional when, in "Memory and Hope," she pictured Memory in a mournful state after man's exclusion from Eden, while Hope goes joyfully tripping on. Eventually Memory overtakes and almost kills Joy, but Christ intervenes and tells Hope to live, promising that she will dwell beside Him after all, implying that man's only hope is for another life beyond this one, and that Memory is essentially related to conscience and the consciousness of sin. Tennyson had sought to transcend this simple notion, setting up models of memory's function which implied an interrelatedness of memory and hope. If Arthur's realm had once achieved harmony and order, a new realm of virtue might do the same. If one man could achieve a sense of faith through enshrining the memory of a lost friend, then mankind might find a similar strength. In an age when models of conduct and emblems of moral value were important, each memorable act became an aid to behavior and a historical and personal guide, as R. H. Horne indicated in his poem, *Orion* (1843).

In every age an emblem and a type,
Premature, single, ending with itself,
Of loftier being in an after-time,
May germinate, develope, radiate,
And, like a star go out, and leave no mark
Save a high memory.

(Book 3, canto 1)

It is just this kind of high memory that poets such as Tennyson and Swinburne sought to preserve. But while they wrote, new attitudes toward memory were developing.

In 1854, the Reverend Henry Calderwood, in his *The Philosophy of the Infinite*, assumed the function of memory as permitting "consciousness of *continued personal existence*," thereby defining personal identity.[26] At the same time, Calderwood asserted that, although the elusive present is the only actual time, men may command the past by representing past events to consciousness through memory and imagination, while the future could be mastered through the imagination alone.[27] Calderwood was not examining human psychology, but attempting to show that although man cannot prove the existence of a First Cause, he can, by examining his own capabilities, come to a limited knowledge of what the Infinite One must be. Man's capacity for memory, as a feature of his comprehension of an existence conceivable only in terms of duration and therefore of successive mental states, was of great importance, and Calderwood accepted the validity of memory without question, as would most of his fellow philosophers.

William B. Carpenter approached the subject of memory with a scientific purpose in his important work, *Principles of Mental Physiology* (1874). He described the "Physiological basis of Memory" as the "singular power of recording ideational changes,"[28] and defined memory itself as the *"reproduction of past states of consciousness . . .* supplemented by the *recognition* of them as having been formerly experienced."[29] Like most of his contemporaries, Carpenter assumed memory as "the basis of our feeling of *personal identity*."[30] He recognized that memory could be faulty, and he explained its lapses as often traceable to lowering of circulation, physical weariness, and so forth. Carpenter also proposed that the mind's recording processes "seem to be dependent upon nutritive changes in the brain."[31] For him, memory was clearly a physical event, a property of the mind as matter.

But Carpenter, in dealing with mental physiology, was by no means presenting a materialist scientific theory. Quite the contrary, as he pointed out in his preface to the fourth edition of *Principles of*

Mental Physiology, where he took issue with genuine materialists such as Professors Huxley and Clifford. Carpenter's purpose was to support the principles of Christianity by drawing science and theology together. He wished to demonstrate that the universe was ordered according to a fixed purpose and predetermined plan; "of the existence of such a plan," he wrote, "the Revelations of Science furnish Theology with its best evidence."[32] He used memory, as he had the other attributes of man, to show both a physical state and a religious hope. In so doing, he assumed the validity of memory. Not all of his contemporaries were willing to concede that point.

In *Illusions: A Psychological Study* (1881), James Sully explained that memory was not, as had at one time been supposed, a drawing of images out of the dark vaults of the unconscious mind into consciousness. "On the purely psychical side," he said, "Memory is nothing but an occasional reappearance of a past mental experience. And the sole mental conditions of this reappearance are to be found in the circumstances of the moment of the original experience and in those of the moment of the reappearance."[33] Sully's purpose was to indicate the untrustworthiness of memory, suggesting that, although memory may bind up our consciousness of personal identity, it also restores "only fragments of our past life."[34] Moreover, we tend to project present modes of experience into the past. In a time when fascination with the distant personal and historical past was fashionable, Sully's caution about the backward psychic glance had meaning.

> In this way, through the corruption of our memory, a kind of sham self gets mixed up with the real self, so that we cannot, strictly speaking, be sure that when we project a mnemonic image into the remote past we are not really running away from our true personality.[35]

Sully's quiet, scientific observation would have been worth noting by many of the poets and novelists of the late nineteenth century who very consciously sought to discover their true personality in that region which was for Sully so dangerously illusional.

By the time William James published his *Principles of Psychology* (1890), the prevailing scientific attitude toward memory had become mechanistic and clinical. For James, memory refers only to conscious phenomena; his definition of memory is broad enough to be acceptable to most. It is "the knowledge of a former state of mind after it has already once dropped from consciousness; or rather *it is the knowl-*

edge of an event, or fact, of which meantime we have not been thinking, *with the additional consciousness that we have thought or experienced it before.*"[36] Equally traditional is his explanation that "*the
cause both of retention and of recollection is the law of habit in the
nervous system, working as it does in the 'association of ideas.' *"[37] The
remainder of his concern with memory is empirical, having to do with
the qualities of retentiveness in individuals, and the measuring of
memory.

There were other notions about the nature of memory, however,
which, if not professionally acknowledged in their time, were nonetheless intriguing and provocative. One such theory was put forward
by Samuel Butler in *Life and Habit* (1878) and later in *Unconscious
Memory* (1880). Butler defined life as "that property of matter where-
by it can remember," adding that "Matter which can remember is
living; matter which cannot remember is dead," and concluding un-
ambiguously, "*Life, then, is memory.*"[38] The great difference in Butler's view of memory is that he emphasizes its unconscious character.
He identifies memory with heredity. Butler described four main principles in *Life and Habit:*

> the oneness of personality between parents and offspring; memory on the
> part of offspring of certain actions which it did when in the persons of
> its forefathers; the latency of that memory until it is rekindled by a re-
> currence of the associated ideas; and the unconsciousness with which
> habitual actions come to be performed.[39]

Any experience that impresses itself upon the organism becomes a
memory; when that memory is so frequently reenacted that it becomes an unconscious habit, the memory is, in effect, an inherited
characteristic. Therefore, when Butler speaks of the impregnate
ovum as having "a potential recollection of all that has happened to
each one of its ancestors prior to the period at which any such ancestor has issued from the bodies of its progenitors—provided, that is to
say, a sufficiently deep, or sufficiently often-repeated, impression has
been made to admit of its being remembered at all," he is describing
the process now referred to as genetic coding.[40] "This memory of the
most striking events of varied lifetimes," Butler asserts elsewhere, is
"the differentiating cause, which, accumulated in countless generations, has led up from the amoeba to man."[41]

At the same time that Butler asserts the continuous identity of the old man with the infant, the infant with the fetus, the fetus with its parents, and so on in endless backward extension, he also contends that all men are part of a larger creature that he calls Life and speculates that "this huge compound creature, LIFE, probably thinks itself but one single animal whose component cells, as it may imagine, grow, and it may be waste and repair, but do not die."[42] Later, Butler was to identify this creature as God, adding that the being was very likely only a part of a vaster and more complex being, and so on beyond that.[43]

Butler's concept of memory is in many ways reminiscent of Schopenhauer's much earlier theories. In Schopenhauer's philosophy, true memory distinguished men from animals; it was based on the association of ideas, was viewed as a faculty, not a receptacle. Unlike Butler, Schopenhauer saw memory as conscious, being primarily related to the activity of reasoning rather than intuitive knowledge, and operating as a function of the will.[44] But in Schopenhauer's pessimistic philosophy, very much in fashion in England at the end of the nineteenth century, memory ultimately could be overcome.[45] For "what sleep is for the individual," he wrote, "death is for the will as thing-in-itself. It could not bear to continue throughout endless time the same actions and sufferings without true gain, if memory and individuality were left to it. It throws them off; this is Lethe; and through this sleep of death it reappears as a new being, refreshed and equipped with another intellect; 'A new day beckons to a newer shore!' "[46]

Butler was not so grim. He agreed that "Man's conscious memory comes to an end at death, but the unconscious memory of Nature is true and ineradicable."[47] Butler's version of Schopenhauer's conclusion is more benign.

Death is deducible; life is not deducible. Death is a change of memories; it is not the destruction of all memory. It is as the liquidation of one company, each member of which will presently join a new one, and retain a trifle even of the old cancelled memory, by way of greater aptitude for working in concert with other molecules.[48]

Ultimately, Butler offered a modest but certain hope of immortality for men, since, as parts of the Spirit of Life, they would live so long as life continued. They would know no resurrection nor continue as distinct identities, but they would live in God in the sense that they had produced an effect, or left a memory, upon the universal Life.[49]

Truly, neither Butler's nor James' theory of memory would satisfy most readers entirely. Materialists would mock Butler and gingerly accept James. It is not clear who, at that time, would have taken Butler seriously.[50] But the problem remained unresolved and seemed critical enough to demand the attention of the prominent French philosopher, Henri Bergson, who declared in the preface to *Matter and Memory* (1896), "this book affirms the reality of spirit and the reality of matter, and tries to determine the relation of the one to the other by the study of a definite example, that of memory."[51] For Bergson, memory is the spirit operating upon matter. It is the one area of experience where the two realms meet and interact in a measurable way. Bergson distinguishes between unconscious memory (such as bodily habit) and voluntary recollection, and proposes that memory is "in no degree an emanation of matter"; on the contrary, "matter as grasped in concrete perception which always occupies a certain duration, is in great part the work of memory."[52] For Bergson, spirit is what binds together the successive moments in the duration of things, thereby coming in contact with matter. Memory, of course, is the agent of that union, for "Every perception fills a certain depth of duration, prolongs the past into the present, and thereby partakes of memory. So that if we take perception in its concrete form, as a synthesis of pure memory and pure perception, that is to say of mind and matter, we compress within its narrow limits the problem of the union of soul and body."[53]

MEMORY AS LITERARY CONVENTION

It is against the background of such speculations that we must view the appearance of the convention of memory in Victorian literature. Surely, as James Sully had suggested, the yearning for a personal or historical past could be dangerously delusive, an attempt to recover memories never experienced. A yearning for a Gothic, classical or other idealized past was but a version of a romantic longing for an Unattainable Ideal, and was, in Sully's view, a pernicious self-deception. Attitudes toward memory continued to become complex. George Eliot had felt sufficient trust in memory to make it one of the two angels guiding man on his path. Memory, or Tradition, is the companion of Reason.

> Memory yields,
> Yet clings with loving check, and shines anew
> Reflecting all the rays of that bright lamp
> Our angel Reason holds. We had not walked
> But for Tradition; we walk evermore
> To higher paths, by brightening Reason's lamp.
> Still we are purblind, tottering. (*The Spanish Gypsy*, Book 2)

These sentiments were conventional, but not everyone displayed such confidence. Tennyson, for example, conceived of memory both as a delight and as a function of conscience. In this regard memory might be identified with Eliot's tradition. But aside from such moral associations, memory could have other lugubrious effects. "To remember that we did know once," said Amiel in a characteristic mood, "is not a sign of possession, but a sign of loss."[54] And, at the end of the century, as at the beginning, what was often lost was not only the thing known, but the thing forsaken. Thus Oscar Wilde's Dorian Gray could remorsefully recall what he had not preserved. "He was prisoned in thought. Memory, like a horrible malady, was eating his soul away." (*The Picture of Dorian Gray*, ch. 16) Still, the self-conscious awareness of memory's importance in personal and social history did not lead only to moroseness and sorrow. George Meredith might lament lost youth and the desire of the aged to recover it in memory yet arrive at an optimistic conclusion in "Youth in Memory"; and Henry Aylwin, in Theodore Watts-Dunton's *Aylwin*, discovers that memory may be both consolation and agony, but concludes, upon reading his father's mystic book, that memory plays an important part in what he calls the Renascence of Wonder.

Poets continued to write conventional addresses to lost sweethearts, as in Arthur Symons' "Memory," or "The Last Memory," or yearn after the manner of the old hermetic philosophers to employ memory in grander schemes, as did W. B. Yeats. But more and more, writers sought to discover a greater meaning in this commonplace of thought and convention of literature. In "A Ballad of Past Meridian," George Meredith has Life say, "As thou hast carved me, such am I," but memory and "sightless hope" counterbalance the bleak view of life by joining "notes of Death and Life till night's decline," and the poet adds: "Of Death, of Life, those inwound notes are mine." It was in these inwound notes of memory and hope that others sought a positive answer to the misgivings that characterized their time.

In 1894, Richard Le Gallienne, in "A Conspiracy of Silence," asked the surprising, but characteristically decadent question, "Why do we go on talking?" We talk, he said, "Mainly about our business, our food, or our diseases," and our conversation is submerged in a flood of facts, until the glorious, but imprecise conversation of friends, lovers, or "holiest converse of all, the mystic prattle of mother and babe," is lost in the rushing demand for matter to stock "pigeon-holes of memory."[55] Le Gallienne considered this modernized memory a degradation, because, for him, "memory was once a honeycomb, a hive of all the wonderful words of poets, of all the marvellous moods of lovers." Now it had become a "phonograph catching every word that [fell] from the mouths of the board of guardians." From classical times, memory had been associated with poetry. Mnemosyne was the muse of poetry. But to writers late in the nineteenth century, the banal commercial world had suborned memory to its own tedious purposes. Le Gallienne and others like him longed for an imaginative medium that would identify cultural past and present with individual past and present. Art required articulation, but memory did not. Memory was a realm neither unreal nor true—ideally malleable to the imaginative idealist. Its charm was in its evocations, and its evocations were consequent upon silence. Memory seemed the last magic in a world increasingly intent upon replacing charms with appliances; and its highest sorcery was silence.

One remedy for sensitive spirits confronted with a discordant present was withdrawal. Le Gallienne, like many of his contemporaries, found the past alluring. As we have seen, a pleasant confusion of utterance and time permitted the agreeable illusion of a vanished age of mystery and charm. More specifically, for the learned, the classical age, represented by its art, became emblematic of that which abides. An esthetically "recollected" past promised attractive refuge because through its speechless art it provided sensations subject to the reflective will. A quiet volitional confinement within the greater penitentiary of loud modern existence might facilitate the incorporation of the cultural past into the private memories of the individual. In his apostrophe to the "Happy Monks of La Trappe," for example, Le Gallienne envied a life converted to a private reflective museum shut off from the insensitive clamor of the modern world.

But thus to make the world's past one's own memory for brooding upon in silence was not the only solution. Another alternative was in turning outward, looking to the material world and to the future. Le Gallienne voiced an attitude shared by more notable contemporaries when he hopefully anticipated "an imminent Return to Simplicity—Socialism the unwise it call." Yet if the conversion of the past into a private memory was intellectual legerdemain, the placing of recovered simplicity in the future could often be mere private dreaming. The discontented poetic soul might anticipate a fiat that would, with one grand social revolution, convert a cacophonous, bustling urban civilization into a peaceful pastoral community, as William Morris did in "The Day is Coming" and other poems (though Morris did not stop there).

Le Gallienne called this a *return* to simplicity, as though there really was a time, within memory, that enjoyed an ideal simpleness. Modern hopes for the future would then be only a conversion of that memory into a new reality. But not all of the hopeful writers of the late nineteenth century were so easily persuaded. Oscar Wilde, in "The Soul of Man Under Socialism," was prepared to admit that past eras, Hellenic or Renaissance, approached the simplicity of true individuality without achieving it. Yet, even for Wilde "The new Individualism is the new Hellenism," a conversion of a cultural memory into an improved future. The circular pattern remains the same.

In his essay, "Of Memory," Jerome K. Jerome had cautioned against the folly of wishing for the old days. "There is no returning on the way of life," he commented, and the cliché had greater meaning at his time. Jerome acknowledged that earlier times must have been sweeter and fresher than the present, but added in a tone characteristic of the later part of the century when men were uneasily beginning to recognize the massive changes that surrounded them, "Those days are past now. The quiet childhood of Humanity, spent in the far-off forest glades, and by the murmuring rivers, is gone for ever; and human life is deepening down to manhood amidst tumult, doubt, and hope." Jerome urged his readers to have done with vain longings and regret. "A new life begins for us with every second. Let us go forward joyously to meet it. We must press on, whether we will or no, and we shall walk better with our eyes before us than with them ever cast behind."

Jerome, in trying to correct certain attitudes of his time, inadvertently supported them, for in encouraging his contemporaries to look to the present rather than the past, he at the same time accepted the doubtful picture of a childhood of Humanity that was somehow fresher and sweeter. And it was this very illusion that attracted those sensitive spirits trapped in an ugly industrial society to turn wistfully to the past for consolation. Jerome accepted this stereotype easily despite his own observation that memory is basically untrustworthy and gives us back the brightnesses and not the darkness of the past. It is all too evident that Jerome's struggle with memory and the past was an extension of his own personal craving. Light as the tone of his essay may be, it reveals a genuine nostalgia within him; and his admonition to be up and active in the present is a caution more to himself than to his imagined reader. Nonetheless, he indulges in a sentimental conversation with his own youthful self, making the journey with that self through early experiences and up to the point of his first real romance, after which the young self disappears into the identity of the mature narrator. His own life is identical to that of humanity's—"deepening down to manhood amidst tumult, doubt, and hope." Obviously Jerome's reflections were contradictory and not well-reasoned, yet they incorporated sentiments common to his day.

In much of the writing of this period dealing with the past and the future, the true fascination remained private and reflexive, not social and historical. Admirations for the past and hopes for the future were frequently by-products of the persistent concern of late nineteenth-century writers with the fashioning of the self. Socialism to Wilde meant the assurance of individualism for all men, the achievement of a utopia in which the state provided the useful, while men produced the beautiful. Like Le Gallienne, Wilde saw socialism as a simplifying force, purifying man's nature to the "true note of the perfect personality"—peace. "It will be a marvellous thing—the true personality of man—when we see it," Wilde said. "It will grow naturally and simply flowerlike, or as a tree grows. It will not be a discord. It will never argue or dispute." ("Soul of Man Under Socialism") William Hale White, from a slightly different perspective, also complained, "We cannot bring ourselves into a unity. The time is yet to come when we shall live by a faith which is a harmony of all our faculties."[56] These writers, and others like them, saw the resolution of man's fragmented nature set in a future when all of man's cultural past had been assimilated into a unified present.

Like William Morris, Wilde saw mankind passing through a barren, painful period in order to achieve its peaceful utopia where pleasure would reign, "For it is through joy that the Individualism of the future will develop itself." "Pain," Wilde later emphasizes, "is not the ultimate mode of perfection," though Christ, the ultimate individualist and principal object of Christian art, is typically the paradigm of joy through pain. An unstated parallel between Christ and mankind exists in Wilde's essay. As Christ was the embattled spokesman of joy who necessarily died to bring men the promise of everlasting life, so mankind, preserving always the joy and beauty of life in its heart, endures the anguish of conflict with an ugly, nonindividuating existence, to achieve at some future time its true aim. "For what man has sought for is, indeed, neither pain nor pleasure, but simply life." ("Soul of Man Under Socialism")

Through the emblematic use of Christ, Wilde converts the history of man into a vast personality. Emotions such as joy and pain fashion that personality; events are of no consequence. The new Hellenism that Wilde described was no more than mankind's remembered youth reborn as a dream of the future. Mankind's dream in its highest form was art. The salvation of society projected by Wilde is in achieving individualism and recapturing that undesperate peace and communality from which man is temporarily barred; and, for Wilde, "Art is the most intense mood of Individualism that the world has known." If the artist, as spokesman of joy—a species of esthetic Christ —suffers pain at the hands of an unbeautiful world, an apt solution is to convert all men into artists. With all men artists, life becomes a beautiful creation; in the community of the future, life itself will be art. Such speculations may produce a realm as inviting as any dream world, or land of sleep, or island of peace that other poets of the late nineteenth century might envision, but that realm remains, like the others, a solution in arranged language, a triumph of articulation— the one locus where, for the poet, memory, hope, and action surely meet. James Sully had cautioned against the fragmentary nature of memory, and against man's tendency to fabricate a personal past, while Samuel Butler was not the only one to associate personal and cultural memory. Bergson, meanwhile, identified memory with the spiritual capacity of mankind. These ideas, in vague and unformulated ways, found their way into many of the writings at the end of the nineteenth century. But, in the most interesting cases, they included as well the notion that the artist's mind exploits memory and is not merely a vehicle for random recollection. They import the notion of will governing the nature of what is recollected. It was well enough for philosophers and artists to describe the *picture* created by memory, but for the subtle mind of a Wilde, or others like him, the metaphor was insufficient. Only *in* art does life assume the aspect of art. One problem facing writers of this period was the reconciliation of their personal memories and hopeful dreams with history and with art.[57] When such reconciliation was not forthcoming in art or in act, only Le Gallienne's conspiracy of silence remained.

LIONEL JOHNSON

Lionel Johnson may perhaps be considered a typical representative of the Decadents, and in his poems we can examine the involved program of memory, dream, magical past, and esthetic desire that I have been describing. "The Age of a Dream" is a characteristic lament for an age gone by; an age of courtesy, saints, and love; a time of "Lights on earth more fair, than shone from Plato's page." "Vanished those high conceits! Desolate and forlorn, / We hunger against hope for that lost heritage." With "the carven work," "the golden shrine," "the glorious organs" gone, all that is left for the solemn bell that still tolls is to "mourn the death of beauty and of grace."

In "Magic," Johnson contrasts the artist's world of esthetic labor with the modern atmosphere of science and logic, as well as with the blatantly sensuous modern outlook, only to discover that this elevated "world is done: / For all the witchery of the world is fled, / And lost all wanton wisdom long since won." So powerful is the poet's desire to identify himself with the vast cultural memory of poetic achievement, that his individual failure signifies for him the failure of all future esthetic aspiration. Ernest Dowson, too, longed to escape the world's noise and turmoil in his art, desiring, like Johnson, a sacred, silent austerity which, in "Carthusians," he hoped would surely prevail; but for him, as well, it failed. Oscar Wilde had already lamented that by attempting to convert his life into a work of art, he robbed his art of its working life. Rejecting the simplicity of the past, the poet, by transforming his life into an esthetic design without the medium of art, has ruined the very design he craved, for it is his art not his life that creates the order.

> Methinks my life is a twice-written scroll
> Scrawled over on some boyish holiday
> With idle songs for pipe and virelay
> Which do but mar the secret of the whole. ("Helás")

Now, the moment seemingly lost, the poet can only lament, "And must I lose my soul's inheritance?"

Swinburne's Thallasius had become not a singer, but a song; he had lost himself in the greater moment of his art, knowing that the order of his life derived therefrom. But Wilde's lament pictures the poet as "a stringed lute on which all winds can play," the mere mechanism for those songs that the true singer must *become*. If all winds can raise a tune upon this instrument, then, when the winds pass, all memory of the tune dies as well and the soul has lost its inheritance, which was to be a part of the dream binding past and future.

The psychological event in these two poems is better illustrated in Lionel Johnson's "Upon a Drawing," where the historical subject, a young man in a drawing, is located beyond the classical ages Johnson so admired. "Of dreamland only he is a citizen." Mysterious and intriguing as a Grecian urn, the young man gradually draws closer to the speaker as the poem proceeds until the poet's personality defines the figure according to its own inclinations. "Thou'rt fallen in love with thine own mystery!" At the end of the poem, the reader feels that he is overhearing an innocent Dorian Gray address his own unaltered portrait.

> What wondrous land within the unvoyaged sea
> Haunts then thy thoughts, thy memories, thy dreams?
> Nay! be my friend; and share with me thy past:
> If haply I may catch enchaunting gleams,
> Catch marvellous music, while our friendship last:
> Tell me thy visions: though their true home be
> Some land, that was a legend in old Troy.

The "wondrous land" is a timeless legend known only in "visions," of a timeless past from which the poet eagerly hopes to extract en-

chantment. But this past is known only as a part of memory and
dream, of what the mind chooses to believe it has already known and
which it aspires to meet once more. Personal memory has no part in
the poet's aspiration. Even the memory here is a fabrication, an amplification of a work of art. An imagined memory is evoked to create a
sense of an ideal past, but both memory and idealized past are illusions of the poet's mind.

REACTION TO ILLUSION

This stroking of the imagination could become abrasive as in Rossetti's "The Burden of Nineveh." The poet, emerging from a museum
where the gathered art of the past has given him intense pleasure,
finds himself amid the "London dirt and din." Although the contrast
of modern tumult and ancient peace is conventional, this poem does
not permit the usual self-indulgent lament for a superior and elegant
bygone age; instead, the poet realizes, through his reflections upon a
"wingéd beast from Nineveh," that the past, precisely like the present, was unlovely and brutal. Shocked from his reveries, the poet
recognizes a vision of all times confused in similarities that do not at
all resemble the charmingly muddled memories and desires pictured
in Lionel Johnson's poems.

In a poem of the following century, which in many ways constitutes a formal farewell to the sentiments of the *fin de siècle*, T. S.
Eliot expressed the harsh truth about that moment when past and future mingle in the imagination.

> April is the cruellest month, breeding
> Lilacs out of the dead land, mixing
> Memory and desire, stirring
> Dull roots with spring rain.
>
> ("The Waste Land")

In part, what "The Waste Land" says is that there is no future for
those who, without engagement, desire that their fabricated memories be realized. The mingling of memory and desire should be no
soft withdrawal, but a painful awakening, as Swinburne and Wilde
had long acknowledged.

Eliot's poem reveals an awareness of the false sentiment involved
in the late nineteenth-century convention of an esthetic cultural

memory appropriated in the present by a poetic, but inactive soul. William Morris sought to deal with that contradiction in his own work. In "The Aims of Art," he pictured himself as dominated by two moods. In the mood of idleness, memory amuses him, while in the mood of energy, hope cheers him. "I must," he said, "either be making something or making believe to make it." For Morris, undeceived by "elegant poetic regret" for a vanished time, sustaining fragments from the past was not enough. No matter how much a Rossetti might delight in old objects of art, ultimately he must return to the London dirt and din and find some shocking reminder that present and past are alike not in their elegant art, but in their brutal greed. Morris, equally interested in the past, but convinced of the importance of timely art, warned that

> Soon there will be nothing left except the lying dreams of history, the miserable wreckage of our museums and picture-galleries, and the carefully guarded interiors of our aesthetic drawing-rooms, unreal and foolish. ("The Aims of Art")

Dowson, Johnson, Wilde, Rossetti, and others were aware that their elegant poetic regrets for an ideal past were, in reality, "lying dreams of history." But so confused were their personal cravings to blend the elegance of the past—for them embodied largely in art, and often specifically in verbal art—with their own aspirations and dreams of an ideal future, that they failed to project any solution; failed, in fact, to command what was really no more than an exquisite metaphor enchanting their imaginations, a subdued longing for the ultimate austere yet exquisite style. They wished to live in and by memory and to transform their arranged memories into hope but few succeeded in converting past into future in anything but a verbal manner. Nonetheless, there were some, besides Swinburne, who realized that the verbal manner itself might be the agency through which the evening gates of memory might open as fair as morning's with the flame of hope.

To Walter Pater, for whom the Dionysian and Apollonian relationship was both privately and culturally memorable, a resolution was in the deaths of his fictional heroes. "Only by dying does he [the hero] reveal, in a single supreme moment of tragic joy, that greater Apollonian light within himself and call forth the permanent flower of art."[58] So, too, the artist might die into art, as Swinburne's poet is transformed from singer to song, without abandoning the "inheritance" and the future that Wilde seemed convinced he had lost by considering life's sensations more important than art. So might each individual, or mankind, emulate Christ and Pater's heroes, cancelled in the present between the forces of past pain and anticipated joy in order that the permanent and timeless esthetic work of art might live. There is a curious combination in these writings of Christian allusions and the pagan assumptions of Schopenhauer or Butler that human history and memory were contained in racial rather than personal terms. William Sharp asserted "the persistence of racial or animal memory throughout the evolutionary process—a subliminal knowledge of generic past experience in each individual creature at her particular level of developed consciousness." In her biography of Sharp, Flavia Alaya suggests that several other writers shared to varying degrees his belief in physical or psychical heredity expressed in a poem such as "Motherhood."[59] For some, then, this cultural memory was a physical fact; for others, such as those I have been discussing here, it was esthetic. Renunciation of the self might insure the preservation of a transcendent memory, not, as in Butler, Sharp, or Lafcadio Hearn, through actual racial memory, but through the more certain cultural memory of embodied art.

HOPE AND MEMORY

The hope that Pater offers is ambiguously personal and historical. His highly successful *Studies in the History of the Renaissance* (1873) later became *The Renaissance: Studies in Art and Poetry*, adding another dimension to the title. Other commentators, such as W. G. Blaikie Murdoch wrote about the "Renaissance of the Nineties" without offering a rebirth themselves; but Pater, writing about the past, presented a workable esthetic for the future. This rebirth of a cultural and historical esthetic responsiveness was found in the individual imagination where time and matter maintain an atomized, eternally revisable character. "Every one of those impressions is the impression of the individual in his isolation, each mind keeping as a solitary prisoner its own dream of a world." Symons was later to declare, "the only world is the world of my dreams," but such a declaration would reduce Pater's esthetic experience to a Lotos-Eater's doctrine. What Pater really did was to present the designing power of

memory as Le Gallienne's "impressionist of divine moments," a force
blending the elegance of the past with the dream of the future
through the medium of imagination. Preserving its nearly sacred isolation, each mind can become gem-like, achieving its own silently
exquisite style through the fashioning from memory and desire "its
own dream of a world," thereby making more valuable the experiences of the moment. Personal and cultural memories merge in an
esthetic triumph of the imagination. History is enclosed within the
willed design of the self. The Victorian desire to control material
existence here moves inward to a subjective world equally in need of
domination. The multiple external world now becomes the multiple
self requiring an esthetic governance. It is the dominion of the self
as envisioned by Tennyson in the *Idylls of the King*, where a moral
authority, embodied in Arthur, draws an unruly realm under his control. The established order may fail, but the images of action and
force with which the governed self is depicted, indicate the general
need that some Victorian writers felt for applying the principles of
imperial control to the kingdom of the imagination.

Some writers sought to influence both inward and outer worlds.
William Morris hoped to extend his "dream of a world" beyond the
frontiers of his imagination to the world at large, whereas Pater intended mainly to transfer his own gem-like flame to other individuals
in isolation. Morris made no attempt to present figures of the past in
the manner of private memories or "impressions" retold, but insisted
that to memory must be added hope, and through hope, energy. For
him, "the true secret of happiness" lay *"in the taking a genuine interest in all the details of daily life."* ("The Aims of Art") And if men were
to "try to realize the aims of art without much troubling [themselves]
what the aspect of art itself shall be, we shall find we shall have what
we want at last: whether it is to be called art or not, it will at least
be life; and, after all, that is what we want." Like Pater and Wilde,
Morris wished to unite art and life. But, less inclined to convert life
into art, he hoped to adapt art to living. He resisted the decadent impulse to fashion a world of memory within the imagination, and
sought instead to draw the racial memory back from the self to be
applied to the world of the present at large.

Lionel Johnson's attempt to recover the thoughts, memories, and
desires of a pictured figure from a vague and prelegendary time
ended only in the vain request to hear the figure's "visions," but Mor-

ris was not content with the titillation of untold memories and dreams; he made both explicit. In *A Dream of John Ball* (1888), the narrator returns to a past time. By becoming, at least in dream, a part of that time, he is able to return to the present with the cultural past transformed to a private memory. At the same time, what was the future throughout the tale suddenly becomes the present in which thoughts, dreams, and desires are all united by a vision—a dream of a world. In parting with the narrator of the tale, John Ball had said: "Thou has been a dream to me as I to thee, and sorry and glad have we made each other, as tales of old time and the longing of times to come shall ever make men be."

Later Morris was to embody both of these sentiments in a fable effectively utilizing the metaphor that so entrapped and intrigued his contemporaries, for in *News From Nowhere* (1890), the narrator succeeds in converting the future, itself possessed of ideal elements from the historical past, into a genuine memory. The entire work is an example of "the effort of our past to transform itself into our future." No longer does the narrator make only the past a memory, while himself bearing the full burden of hope which remains undesignated, as in *John Ball*; now the future itself becomes memory and brings hope through the guarantee of its fulfillment. Memory and desire are no longer frustratingly mixed, but are fused with the energy of hope. And the narrator, with his dream still in his mind, exclaims: "Yes, surely! and if others can see it as I have seen it, then it may be called a vision rather than a dream."

The late nineteenth century, we all realize, was represented not only by effete and melancholy dreamers. Identical cultural preoccupations could occasion multiple and contradictory resolutions or irresolutions. The enchanting if dispirited dreams that trapped men in their own metaphorical despair could also be the visions of those who were determinedly abandoning the land of Cokayne and Lotos-Eaters. Though many writers of the period demonstrated similar attitudes toward the idealizing power of memory and the value of hopeful visions, not all utilized this pervasive fascination in the same manner. Some looked backward toward Romantic attitudes, for example, while others looked forward to equally complex utilizations of cultural and private memories and desires in the works of writers such as Yeats, Eliot, and Pound.

Not all writers at the end of the nineteenth century in England would have been content to join Le Gallienne's conspiracy of silence.

It is true that some, like Dowson and Johnson, were equally repelled by the modern din and the reduction of an impressionistic memory —personal yet vast—to "pigeon-holes" containing barren facts, and thereby came with equal amorousness to value silence and dreams. But there were also those who denied that the magic of memory had died. Pater, though he spoke in a low, modulated, and seductive tone, offered not silent withdrawal, but elegantly whispered participation. Like the great artists of the past who had, according to Swinburne, "interpreted" existence, Pater now offered his own "interpretations" or "impressions" of existence through the medium of earlier interpreters who were already a part of the cultural memory that he strove to enrich. And Morris, convinced of what Le Gallienne described as the "imminent Return to Simplicity," chose not to envy Trappist monks their silence and austerity, nor to yearn for a perfect style of articulation. Instead, he adapted the frustrating metaphors of his contemporaries to his own hopeful mythology, combining in a casual style mingled memories and dreams of the past with hopes and dreams of the future, so that in his present there might be no melancholy silence, but the heartful cheering of men at work.

Morris' hopeful mingling of memory and anticipatory dream was not the only positive expression of these entwined themes. In the late part of the century, while memory, dream and hope fascinated the so-called Decadents, other writers carried on and extended surprisingly what had been a prominent Victorian literary convention. In Mrs. Oliphant's *A Little Pilgrim in the Unseen* (1882), the pure spirit of a humble spinster finds itself in the hereafter and discovers, among many other things, that her cherished memories were not futile, but are real. Having seen Christ and met God, the Little Pilgrim encounters her own parents who are beautiful and loving. "And thus she learned that though the new may take the place of the old, and many things may blossom out of it like flowers, yet that the old is never done away."

Mrs. Oliphant's hopeful suggestion that memories will actually be recovered in a world after death must have appealed to many people, since her book sold very well. Equally attractive to a large number of readers were the fanciful notions put forward by George du Maurier in his successful novel, *Peter Ibbetson* (1891). This remarkable story combines yearnings for the past, hopes for an eternal future, fascination with the supernatural and the desire to withdraw into a world of dream—all sentiments highly conventionalized by the time du

Maurier provided his version of them.[60] The central narrative of Peter Ibbetson begins with the narrator's memories of his happy childhood. These are presented lovingly and in great detail. They end abruptly with the death of Peter Pasquier's mother and father, at which time he goes to live with the harsh and immoral Colonel Ibbetson, taking his name at the same time. Young Peter is given to dreaming, living much in the realm of his own imagination. Meanwhile he quarrels with his selfish relative and runs away to fashion his own life. Preoccupied with memories of the past, Peter makes a visit to Paris, the scene of his happy childhood, and is profoundly disillusioned by all that has changed. His disappointment moves him to a woeful lamentation over the past that is lost forever.

> Oh, surely, surely, I cried to myself, we ought to find some means of possessing the past more fully and completely than we do. Life is not worth living for many of us if a want so desperate and yet so natural can never be satisfied. Memory is but a poor, rudimentary thing that we had better be without, if it can only lead us to the verge of consummation like this, and madden us with a desire it cannot slake. The touch of a vanished hand, the sound of a voice that is still, the tender grace of a day that is dead, should be ours forever, at our beck and call, by some exquisite and quite conceivable illusion of the senses. (ch. 3)

Peter meets and falls in love with the Duchess of Towers, who visits him in a dream and leads him back to his own lost past, gratifying his desire to be able to possess the past again. She teaches him how to exploit and control his dream world. When he was a child, his young friend Mimsey Seraskier and he had phantom friends. Now he realizes that in revisiting his own past in dreams he is one of those phantoms known as Prince Charming. With practice, Peter even learns to enter into his childhood self. He quickly becomes a master at "dreaming true," and realizes that the brain recovers everything, that nothing is lost. Indeed, he soon concludes that true dreams are far preferable to daily life.

Meeting the Duchess of Towers again in the real world, Peter discovers that she is his childhood friend, Mimsey, or Mary, Seraskier. She says that they must not dream one another again, for she is married, though unhappily. Soon after, Peter kills his uncle in a quarrel over the latter's slanders. Committed to prison for what is to be a quarter of a century of confinement for apparent madness, Peter struggles to recover his capacity to achieve true dreams. When Mary is separated from her husband, she and Peter begin to enjoy a fabulous life together in their dream world where either can furnish that unlimited existence with anything that either has ever experienced. Not only are the dreamers able to live in exquisite physical circumstances, but they can move at will into the past, even to recover "ante-natal memories." (ch. 6) Peter and Mary discover that they are descended from the same great-great-grandmother and realize that they are capable of becoming any of their ancestors whenever they please. Moreover they can bring ancestors to the present in their own identities. Among many other remarkable experiences, the dreamers travel into the deep past, even to the age of Mammoths. They are capable, in short, of actually recovering all of the memories of their own private existence, as well as those available to their ancestors. Private and racial memories lie fully open to their minds. They verify Samuel Butler's theory of racially communicated memories in a way he surely had not foreseen.

These ideal circumstances end with Mary's death in the real world. After a fit of madness, Peter returns again to his dream world and eventually meets there an old woman who turns out to be his beloved Mary. For the first time in their dream they are old, since they had always before maintained an ideal youthfulness. Mary has managed with great difficulty to return in order to inform Peter that all will be well after death. In a series of visits she provides him with a description of the life to come, echoing what Peter had earlier remarked about human memory. After death, she assures him, "Nothing is lost—nothing!" (ch. 6) When Peter joins her, Mary says, they will melt into the One. The story ends with the comments of those who retain the dead Peter Ibbetson's incredible manuscript. In this way, du Maurier leaves the fictional possibility that Peter's account of his dream experiences is nothing more than madness. But whatever the case, the story itself is a stunning manifestation of the yearning to recover a personal and racial past and to carry the whole of that plenary experience on to the world after death where nothing will be lost.

Du Maurier's novel may be seen as the last forceful statement of this profound yearning. More common in the literature of the late nineteenth century was the growing sense that not only the past, but the future as well was lost. If some poets strove in their art to preserve the past while projecting a hopeful future, others desired only to create a memory or the illusion of a memory into which they could retreat from offensive realities. Certain writers brutally and directly indicated the futility of any hope either to recover the past or to project the best of that past into a promising future.

In George Gissing's *Demos* (1886), Henry Mutimer's socialist dream of a prosperous future for all men is defeated by the realities of human nature, while the nostalgic backward glances of Hubert Eldon suggest the determination of an effete upper class to cling to a doomed way of life. Eldon comes into possession of the lands Mutimer had mistakenly inherited, and when Adela Waltham pleads with Hubert to retain the New Wanley works, designed by Mutimer to benefit the working man, he abruptly refuses, being determined at any cost to return the entire neighborhood to its former appearance. "I was born here," he says, "and every dearest memory of my life connects itself with the valley as it used to be." (Vol. 3, ch. 2) Concerned only with his own esthetic feelings and his private memories, he cares nothing for all those who will be dispossessed by his action. Gissing's is a grimmer view of socialism and the elite than Morris would have cared to allow.

A more general, but perhaps more gruesome, view of the human desire to retain the past and enrich the future occurs in Thomas Hardy's *Jude the Obscure* (1895). Jude, of course, wishes to make himself a part of the long tradition of learning represented by the ancient educational center called Christminster. His feelings about Christminster echo Hazlitt's in "Pictures at Oxford and Blenheim," combining a love of the past and aspirations for the future. In effect Jude wishes to draw upon the cultural memory of that society, though his personal memories are also thoroughly interwoven with the nation's memorable past as represented by Christminster. Jude's desire to become a part of an intellectual community carrying on a living tradition is reflected in his craft. He becomes a restorer of Gothic structures, themselves symbolic—as our brief discussion of the Gothic revival has indicated—of a time when society was harmonious, rich and whole. Jude's hopes, however, are doomed to fail, not only because of his own failings, but because the tradition represented by Christminster is not a living tradition at all; it is a stagnant pool with no outflowing toward the future. Similarly, there is no future for Jude's profession, which consists of little more than patching up what is outmoded and rapidly deteriorating.

Hardy might have left his dismal message thus embodied in his narrative, but he preferred to make it abundantly manifest in the character of the child, Father Time.

> He was Age masquerading as Juvenility, and doing it so badly that his real self showed through crevices. A ground swell from ancient years of night seemed now and then to lift the child in this his morning-life, when his face took a back view over some great Atlantic of Time, and appeared not to care about what it saw. (Part 5, sec. 3)

Here then is Hardy's perversion of the convention. Instead of recovering a memory of the past as a fruitful aid to the present and a promise of the future, the reborn past carries into the present instead a blighting negation. Little Father Time represents the perversion of the hopeful dream of the future as well. Tennyson may have viewed his lost friend Arthur Hallam as a type of the nobler race to come, but a doctor, commenting on the dead child who has murdered his siblings, says that there are many boys like Father Time, "a sort unknown in the last generation—the outcome of new views of life. They seem to see all its terrors before they are old enough to have staying power to resist them." He sees Father Time as a manifestation "of the coming universal wish not to live." (Part 6, sec. 2)

If Hardy's bleak ironies constituted a general attempt to refute hopeful formulations of the convention of memory, H. G. Wells' *The Time Machine* (1895) was a more precise negation of earlier aims. Whereas Morris' voyager into the future found a utopian culture that had preserved the best from its long tradition, and especially its simple earlier times, Wells' voyager into the future finds a society that has reduced its long tradition to a rudimentary and doomed existence of mere play and predation. And while Morris' time traveller returns with a hopeful memory of the future, Wells' Time Traveller returns to the present bearing not only his memories of the Eloi and Morlocks, but recollections of the eventual end of the failing earth. His future, like Morris', has become a memory, but unlike Morris' it is a memory of cosmic sorrow. The narrator of Wells' tale, in speculating on the fate of the Time Traveller, who had set off once more and never returned, imagines that he may have travelled fatally into the past or into the nearer future, the hopeful "manhood of the race," as he calls it, echoing the optimistic formulations of preceding decades.

The narrator himself feels that such a joyful time is coming, but he adds that the Time Traveller "thought but cheerlessly of the Advancement of Mankind, and saw in the growing pile of civilization only a foolish heaping that must inevitably fall back upon and destroy its makers in the end." ("Epilogue")[61]

SUMMARY

Thus did the convention of memory, so comforting and so rich throughout the nineteenth century, come to an end as the century ended. The convention had been reborn with the Romantic movement, and with its rebirth was born a craving for the ideal, for the unknown, for something complete and timeless. And while the ordinary convention of memory as comforter of human suffering, or as goad to the conscience persisted, another function of memory became prominent and engrossed the literary imagination. Memory became associated with identity in a manner which made the craving for the past more than a mere desire to achieve comfort in the bitter present. Applied to political or supernatural purposes it went so far as to picture a means of recovering the past and even of creating of the future a memory to be employed in bringing about that very memory. Miguel de Unamuno, who came to maturity at the end of the nineteenth century and who was familiar with many of the influential writings of the period from Carlyle, to Schopenhauer, to Senancour, accurately estimated the tendencies of his contemporaries and predecessors when he observed, "We live in memory and by memory, and our spiritual life is at bottom simply the effort of our memory to persist, to transform itself into hope, the effort of our past to transform itself into our future."[62] For most writers at the end of the century the wonders of memory became only lovely fancies, and despite a strong desire to see such wonders made real, the increasingly pessimistic spirit of the time determined that the hopeful convention should encounter its grim mirror image. Even in Yeats' gigantic scheme, so reminiscent of the designs of Giordano Bruno in its hermetic and occult detail, holding past and future in the memory could not forestall the fated alternation of contrasting periods of good and evil. The triumphant aspiration toward a recovered golden age was to become at best a doubtful cosmic supposition, for there were few who believed any longer that the golden past or the golden future existed anywhere but in the imagination of men, or in works of art that were their own memory.

CHAPTER SIXTEEN

THE OCCULT

VICTORIAN ATTITUDE

In the preface to his novel, *A Strange Story* (1862), Bulwer-Lytton declared that he had availed himself of "the marvellous agencies which have ever been at the legitimate command of the fabulist." He added that prose romance, like drama and the epic, had always utilized the marvellous, for humanity always is interested in the more than human. "Now, to my mind," Bulwer-Lytton continued, "the true reason why a supernatural agency is indispensable to the conception of the Epic, is that the Epic is the highest and the completest form in which Art can express either Man or Nature, and that without some gleams of the supernatural, Man is not man, nor Nature, nature." He strengthens this argument with a quotation from Sir William Hamilton who asked, "Is it unreasonable to confess that we believe in God, not by reason of Nature which conceals Him, but by reason of the supernatural in Man which alone reveals and proves Him to exist?"[1]

Bulwer-Lytton asserted the legitimate place of the supernatural and the occult in literature by tracing their histories to the earliest times. The supernatural had reasserted itself near the end of the eighteenth century in the Gothic novel; Dorothy Scarborough remarked in *The Supernatural in Modern English Fiction,* that "the Ghost is the real hero or heroine of the Gothic novel,"[2] and indeed spectral forms abound in these fictions; as many as two thousand at a time in William Beckford's *Vathek.* Portents and dreams are also significant in these romances, and sometimes dreams are the very source of a tale, most notably Walpole's *Castle of Otranto* (1764). The Gothic fashion faded, thanks partly to such adept satires as Jane Austen's *Northanger Abbey* and Eaton Stannard Barnett's *The Heroine, or The Adventures of Cherubina*; thereafter fiction tended more toward elements of ordinary experience though "supernatural machinery had become so well established in prose fiction that even realists were moved by it."[3]

At the same time that Gothic fiction prospered in England, and elsewhere, particularly Germany, serious investigations of the unknown were under way in Europe. The late eighteenth-century interest in science actually encouraged an interest in the occult, for scientific experiments had revealed to men that they were surrounded by wonderful and invisible forces. The public, unable to distinguish between the real and the imaginary, accepted any ostensibly scientific explanation of wonders they saw around them. "In the eighteenth century," writes Robert Darnton in his study of Anton Mesmer, "the view of literate Frenchmen opened upon a splendid, baroque universe, where their gaze rode on waves of invisible fluid into realms of infinite speculation."[4] Mesmer's theory, referred to as animal magnetism, argued that a magnetic fluid pervaded the universe, including the human body, and that this fluid could be controlled and communicated to improve health and achieve "harmony." Mesmer was remarkably successful in promoting his views in Paris in the years just preceding the Revolution. In England, a Dr. Mainaduc, a pupil of Mesmer and D'Eslon, established himself successfully in Bristol in 1788 and a painter, Mr. Loutherbourg and his wife set up an equally successful Hygeian Society.

The Romantic movement began in an atmosphere of the unusual. Not only mesmerism, but somnambulism, clairvoyance, and similar phenomena occasioned great public interest. Even alchemy continued to fascinate many with its symbolic language and trust in the occult. Secret societies such as the Rosicrucians flourished, and Charles Mackay credited them with having "spiritualised and refined" the study of alchemy.[5] Occult phenomena played a significant part in literature of the Romantic movement. E. T. A. Hoffmann's *Der Magnetiseur* and *Der unheimliche Gast* are only two examples from Germany. Coleridge's "The Rhyme of the Ancient Mariner" and "Christabel" exploit the supernatural, and Sir Walter Scott did not hesitate to make use of the uncanny in his works. *Guy Mannering* opens with a bizarre astrological prediction, and mysterious fates and witchcraft are referred to with respect.[6] In *The Bride of Lammermoor* premonitions, prophecies, at least one spectre, and a fateful legend are used, but these are mainly trappings to color the tale. They are of the same stamp as the supernatural summons to Ranulph in Ainsworth's *Rookwood*, or the scene in the same novel where Lady Rookwood is led to her death by the spectre of her dead husband.

As manifested by Scott and Ainsworth, supernaturalism derived from Gothic fiction was primarily a sensational narrative device. Other writers exhibited a more serious use of the supernatural. Mary Douglas, in Susan Ferrier's *Marriage*, stands midway between the Gothic *frisson* of supernatural references, and a more spiritual Victorian attitude. Visiting the bloodstained chamber in Edinburgh associated with Queen Mary, Mary acknowledges a certain thrilling sensation: "I own I love to believe in things supernatural," she says, "it seems to connect us more with another world than when everything is seen to proceed in the more ordinary course of nature, as it is called. I cannot bear to imagine a dreary chasm betwixt the inhabitants of this world and beings of a higher sphere; I love to fancy myself surrounded by. . . ." (Vol. 1, ch. 33) At this point she breaks off abruptly. Mrs. Gaskell was less reticent in her supernatural speculations, suggesting that God might permit "the forms of those who were dearest when living, to hover round the bed of the dying." (*Mary Barton*, ch. 25) And the popular proverbial versifier, Martin Tupper, allowed in "Spiritual Presences" that, in a few instances, spirits might return from beyond the grave. About ministering angels he felt more secure, asserting that "doubtless, these be sent." Glanville, in Bulwer-Lytton's *Pelham*, admits to some belief in the occult, by which he means that he has a faith in the return of spirits from the dead. (ch. 28) Sir Walter Scott's *Letters on Demonology and Witchcraft* (1830) clearly indicates, however, that for anyone who believed in traditional Christian faith, a belief in the survival of the human spirit beyond death was customary, and that it was scarcely a great step from that belief to a conviction that contact could be established between the spirit of the living and the spirit of the dead.

Bulwer-Lytton believed that man maintained a relationship with forces beyond human understanding. Further, he credited certain individuals with supernatural powers.[7] Both views were compatible with traditional Christian thought; but in Bulwer-Lytton's writing these ideas are manifested as Gothic extravagances, not religious beliefs. As early as 1835 he was seriously investigating medieval astrology and other occult studies.[8] His interest was manifested in his early "occult" novel, *Zanoni* (1842).

Bulwer-Lytton said that *Zanoni* was not an allegory, but in a note to a later edition of the novel, acknowledged that a "typical" or emblematic reading of the work was possible.[9] In fact, the novel is a highly schematic rendering of man's craving for the ideal. Zanoni, a mysterious stranger, is in reality one of the two remaining representatives of an occult order possessing the secret of eternal life.[10] Whereas Zanoni stands for the abiding influence of Poetry, his compeer, Mejnour, represents Science. For Zanoni, human emotions, values, and individual worth are important, while Mejnour cares only for knowledge. Mejnour's ambition includes an imperialism that would dwarf the mere political and economic version cherished by Englishmen later in the century. His grand hope is "to form a mighty and numerous race with a force and power sufficient to permit them to acknowledge to mankind" their dominion over the earth and conquest of other planets, as well as of invisible spiritual tribes; a race that may proceed by stages to rank as the highest ministrants "gathered round the Throne of Thrones." (Book 3, ch. 16) What Zanoni discovers through his love for Viola Pisani, a gifted singer with a pure, spiritual nature, is that human love is more important than the knowledge he values so highly. Granting that "to know nature is to know there must be a God," Zanoni asserts that "a pure mind, however ignorant and childlike" better reveals "the August and Immaterial One." (Book 4, ch. 10) Once he had sought to live forever, and urged Viola to pursue this false goal with him, but Viola senses the truth. Of Viola's joy in her love for Zanoni, the narrator observes, "In a moment, there often dwells the sense of eternity; for when profoundly happy, we know that it is impossible to die. Whenever the soul *feels itself*, it feels everlasting life!" (Book 4, ch. 10) Zanoni himself admits to Mejnour his conviction that "to live for ever upon this earth, is to live in nothing diviner than ourselves." (Book 6, ch. 3)

Accordingly, Zanoni forsakes earthly immortality and sacrifices his own life to spare Viola. Upon his execution, his Image rises up to the accompaniment of a vast choral welcome, while spiritual hosts of Beauty congregate around him. Enraptured, he exclaims, "*this* it is to die!" (Book 6, ch. 14) Not here on earth, but in the world hereafter is the true value of everlasting existence. It is this that Bulwer-Lytton wishes to teach us.

Bulwer-Lytton had much to say about the Ideal in art and human knowledge, but his main emphasis was clear: the importance of love, and the value of earthly existence as preliminary to a greater mystery. In the 1853 Preface to his novel, Bulwer-Lytton ranked *Zanoni* highest of his prose fictions, classing it with his favorite composition, the epic poem, *King Arthur*. Both works were designed to demonstrate similar truths.

> As man has two lives—that of action and that of thought—so I conceive that work to be the truest representation of Humanity which faithfully delineates both, and opens some elevating glimpse into the sublimest mysteries of our being, by establishing the inevitable union that exists between the plain things of the day, in which our earthly bodies perform their allotted part, and the latent, often uncultivated, often invisible, affinities of the soul with all the powers that externally breathe and move throughout the Universe of Spirit.

Much of Bulwer-Lytton's writing attempts to show the manner in which the known material world and the unknown supernatural world are dependent upon one another.

There are touches of supernaturalism throughout Bulwer-Lytton's writings, but uncanny circumstances are central in "The Haunters and the Haunted, or The House and The Brain" (1859) and *A Strange Story* (1862).[11] "The Haunters" is a peculiar account of a house cursed by an evil brain by means of an occult apparatus. *A Strange Story* does not openly assume the existence of occult forces, but allows for possible material and psychological explanations of the unusual events described by the narrator, Dr. Allan Fenwick.[12] Fenwick begins as a determined materialist, a "disciple of Condillac," as he describes himself. (ch. 1) Early in his career, he denounces a rival physician for his belief in mesmerism and the advice of clairvoyantes. Later, the dying rival prophecies suffering for Fenwick.

Fenwick falls in love with Lilian Ashleigh, a young lady much given to spiritual fantasies, which the doctor considers unhealthy. At the same time, he also meets Margrave, a young man with great physical attractions and powers, who represents soulless animal force— just as Lilian represents mankind's spiritual capacity. Margrave is man's animal nature, Lilian his soul, and Fenwick his intellect. Margrave proceeds to establish authority over Lilian by supernatural means because he wishes to utilize her spiritual gifts. Fenwick, in his attempts to protect Lilian and himself from the strange youth's powers, must reevaluate his materialist convictions. The sceptical doctor cannot dismiss the wonders he beholds. Margrave, for example, is capable of influencing the wills of others and of projecting his shade, or Scin-Laeca, to great distances. He has only one driving purpose— to maintain earthly existence. Lacking belief in a subsequent life, he cares nothing for human beings except insofar as they aid his purpose.[13]

In an effort to save Lilian's life, Fenwick abandons his scepticism to assist the rapidly decaying Margrave in concocting an elixir of life, necessary to sustain the ancient villain's appearance of youth. The novel's final pages are largely taken up with the description of lurid preparations for condensing a secret ingredient into the precious elixir. A boiling cauldron, a fairy circle incorporating the occult pentacle, strange chants, hostile invisible creatures, as well as a giant foot emerging from a cloud play a part in this outrageous finale. But Bulwer-Lytton's main purpose is to indicate that the materialist, Fenwick, has had recourse to a superstitious occultism far less appealing than the simple Christian beliefs he has so long rejected. Margrave dies and Fenwick, science and occultism having failed him, returns to a faith in the soul and in God who placed the instinct toward immortality in man. He prays, and within moments learns that Lilian has recovered from her malady.

When Fenwick marries Lilian, he quarrels with the worldly Mrs. Poyntz who says she prefers Intellect over Nature, a view resembling Fenwick's former attitude. Now Fenwick willingly rejects this materialism, realizing that as the book of Esdras declares, man may understand the phenomenal world, but not those things above the earth and his intellect alike, and he asks himself, "Is it love which must tell me that man has a soul, and that in soul will be found the solution of problems, never to be solved in body or mind alone?" (ch. 69) The answer to his question is affirmative as seen in his love for Lilian and his rejection of Margrave and Mrs. Poyntz.

When Lilian revives from her illness at the end of the novel, she realizes that she has attached too little significance to the material world, just as Fenwick has valued it too greatly. She has cherished the imagination, he the interpretive intellect. Though both were wrong, Lilian was closer to the proper course, since imagination imitates the creative activity of God and provides the surest means of interpreting His purpose. Mrs. Poyntz may prefer Intellect to Nature, but in so doing she abandons all hope of discovering any divine truth. Margrave, by submerging himself in physical nature, equally disqualifies himself.

> In Lilian, the sympathy with Nature was not, as in Margrave, from the joyous sense of Nature's lavish vitality; it was refined into exquisite perception of the diviner spirit by which that vitality is informed. Thus, like the artist, from outward forms of beauty she drew forth the covert types, lending to things the most familiar exquisite meanings unconceived before. (ch. 61)

Here, as elsewhere, Bulwer-Lytton explains that, like art, the supernatural indicated a higher existence available to man. If that existence was not, in fact, one where invisible beings waited to torment audacious humans, it was at least a realm in which ideals might become manifest through faith. If Bulwer-Lytton did not believe in the more startling and Gothic supernaturalisms that appeared in his narratives, he certainly believed in a life higher and greater than what most men knew and which was implicitly revealed to men through the powers not of their intellects but of their imaginations as manifested in works of art.

THE OCCULT IN OTHER LITERATURE

Meaningful use of the convention of the occult was often subtle. Too frequently the conventional devices enhance a tale with sensational touches. Or, as with the Brontës, supernatural details suggested vague profundities in external or human nature. The preternatural call that Jane Eyre hears summoning her to the maimed Rochester is of a piece with mad Bertha burning in an attic, but not with the simple Christianity of dutiful Jane. The forecast of Jessy Yorke's death in the otherwise matter-of-fact *Shirley* seems out of place. Heathcliffe's overwhelming desire for supernatural communication gives to *Wuthering Heights* a sensational atmosphere but does

not directly indicate any genuine suprahuman e'
poem "The Haunted House. A Romance" ('
devoted chiefly to descriptions of settings tha.
ness.[14] Owen Meredith used the vampire theme i.
long poem, *The Wanderer* (1857) for sensational effec.
had been common in Romantic productions such as Southe,
aba the Destroyer (1801), Byron's *The Giaour* (1813), John Do..
The Vampire Bride (1821), and Dr. Polidori's *The Vampyre* (1819).
Dickens seldom used the uncanny except in an atmospheric way;
according to Peter Penzoldt, he "used the supernatural as an embellishment to his stories, not as their main theme."[15] Even so serious a
writer as George Eliot was not above concocting the fantastic story,
"The Lifted Veil," (1859) in which the narrator, Latimer, describes
his misery resulting from his gift for mind reading and of foreseeing
future events. Eliot seems to have composed this ill-constructed tale
to illustrate her thesis that men require mystery to sustain hope and
would only suffer from knowing the future. She thought little of the
story, calling it a mere *jeu de melancolie*.[16]

In 1862, the year of Bulwer-Lytton's *A Strange Story*, Thackeray
published a satirical piece on the occult in one of his Roundabout
Papers entitled, "The Notch on the Axe. A Story à la Mode." The narrator of the story describes his encounter with a peculiar individual
calling himself Mr. Pinto, who seems capable of reading minds and
casting them into trances, and who claims memories from the reign
of Elizabeth I, indicating personal recollections of Swift, Sir Joshua
Reynolds, and others. He tells stories of his early experiences, including a love story of the French revolution, and concludes by summoning a ghostly hand to sign a check which the bank later honors! Imi-
tating the tone not only of Bulwer-Lytton but other writers of similar
tales, the narrator pauses to exclaim: "Is life a dream? Are dreams
facts? Is sleeping being really awake?" and to note that he has read
The Woman in White, *The Strange Story*, and other books on the
occult. He then declares that he has "had messages from the dead;
and not only from the dead, but from people who never existed at
all." (Book 1) Thackeray concludes his tale with the typical device
of having his narrator awake to find that he has dreamed the entire
adventure, and to observe a sensation novel beside him on the table.
He ends lamely by threatening that "if the fashion for sensation novels
goes on, I tell you I will write one in fifty volumes." (Part 3)

We have already seen that sensation novels were by no means a fashion only of the sixties. Occult conventions had been common for some time in the Gothic novel and after. Bulwer-Lytton may have generated a renewed interest in the convention with his supernatural tales, but English literature had not lacked for supernatural manifestations.

DREAMS

Among the most common of supernatural literary conventions is the prophetic dream. Dreams act as a stylized method of conveying theme as in Tennyson's "Balin and Balan," or "The Coming of Arthur,"[17] or, more directly in "Sea Dreams." Prophetic dreams were commonly used in literature largely because they were not considered uncommon to life. Richard Altick, in his account of the Red Barn murder of 1827, for example, tells how the murdered Maria Marten's mother dreamed that her daughter had been murdered and buried in the red barn. Her dream proved true, Maria's body was discovered, and her murderer was caught and executed.[18] Isabel Arundell, inclined to a belief in the supernatural claimed to have dreamed that her lover, Richard Burton, would leave her; and though her brother scoffed at the idea, it proved true. Moreover, Isabel even claimed to have foreseen in her dreams the letter that Burton left for her the following day.[19] There are other examples of prophetic dreams too numerous to mention.

The most popular layman's study of supernatural phenomena during the Victorian period was Catherine Crowe's *The Night Side of Nature: or, Ghosts & Ghost Seers* (1848).[20] Mrs. Crowe believed that the phenomena she described were ultimately not unearthly, but were open to proofs of science, though the means for such proof were not yet available to men. "All people and all ages," she argued, "have believed, more or less, in prophetic dreams, presentiments, and apparitions, and all histories have furnished examples of them." (ch. 2) This in itself was a powerful argument, to her mind, that there must be substance in the belief. Mrs. Crowe's personal conviction was that dreams represented the liberated faculty of spiritual seeing. Her book contains numerous instances of prophetic dreams, some of them traditional, others gathered at first hand from personal acquaintances. To Mrs. Crowe the issue was not whether prophetic dreams occurred but what permitted men to experience them. Late in the century, James Sully sought to explain the operation of dreaming and remarked that although dreams had always been associated with the supernatural they were in reality only forms of sense illusion.[21] Yet despite his and other explanations, men remained slow to relinquish the mystery of dreams to science.

Dreams have always been associated with artistic creation—from the dream visions of medieval literature to the structural uses in Tennyson, or even to the dream that opens William Styron's *Nat Turner*. Gothic novels supposedly had their inception in weird dreams, Romantic poems were declared to have been composed in dreams, and dreams provided mastering images of both literary and pictorial art.[22] Bulwer-Lytton, somewhat later, declared that both *Zanoni* and *A Strange Story* originated in dreams.[23]

Dreams, then, were both properties and realities of literature during the nineteenth century. In Germany at this time, they held a prominent place in fiction and poetry. At times it is difficult to say if the prophetic dream is merely a convention, is believed literally, or is a symbol not of the supernatural, but of the accessible human imagination. The ambiguity of men's attitudes toward premonitory dreams is well-illustrated by George Borrow's account of an incident in Spain. Returning to that country after a long absence, Borrow discovered awaiting him at the posada in Madrid, his old servant, Antonio, who had not been notified of his return, but dreamed that he would arrive that day. "I do not pretend to offer an opinion concerning this narrative," Borrow says, but adds that "only two individuals in Madrid were aware of my arrival in Spain." (*Bible in Spain*, ch. 45)

Whether the premonitory dreams that appeared in the literature of the time were credible or not, they appeared regularly, and often as extraordinary circumstances not to be ignored. For example, Charles Aubrey, in Warren's *Ten Thousand A-Year*, though wishing to appear rational, cannot deny that he has had a dream in which he has heard a warning from an old woman. (Vol. 1, ch. 8)[24] The symbolic dream in Brontë's *The Professor* is not very convincing, though Jane Eyre's symbolically prophetic dreams in *Jane Eyre* are far more persuasive and integrated into a novel that borrows much besides dreams from the Gothic tradition.[25] Lockwood's dream in *Wuthering Heights* is presented less as a believable incident than as a clever means of presenting the themes of the story that is to come.

Thomas Hood indicated the ambiguous nature of dreams in "The Haunted House":

> Some dreams we have are nothing else but dreams,
> Unnatural, and full of contradictions;
> Yet others of our most romantic schemes
> Are something more than fictions.

Although it is not always possible to distinguish what degree of credibility authors assume in their use of dreams, it is clear enough that dreams generally contribute a sensational note to a novel or poem. Wilkie Collins used the presaging dream in his short story, "The Dream Woman," but his later novel, *Armadale* (1864-65), is actually structured to a great extent upon Allan Armadale's dream, which occurs on the very ship where Armadale's father was murdered many years before, and which contains some hints regarding that event. More importantly, the dream portends Armadale's involvement with Midwinter and Lydia Gwilt. Gradually the details of Armadale's dream are fulfilled; he falls under the influence of the baleful Miss Gwilt, he parts from Midwinter, and so forth. This gradual disclosure of the accuracy of the dream provides the main driving force of the story. In the end, Armadale's dream proves to be not the horrible nemesis that Midwinter has feared, but a providential guide.

Collins employed prophetic dreams elsewhere in his fiction as in the most typical of sensational novels, *The Woman in White*, where Marian Halcombe dreams that the far distant Walter Hartright will survive a series of dangers to return home safely. Her dream is later confirmed in detail by Hartright's account of his adventures. Earlier in the novel, Anne Catherick, claiming to have dreamed of the misery in store for Laura Fairlie if she marries Sir Percival Glyde, urges her to believe in dreams. "See what Scripture says about dreams and their fulfillment (Genesis xl. 8, xli. 25; Daniel iv. 18-25)," she adds, to strengthen her assertion, "and take the warning I send you before it is too late." ("Narrative of Walter Hartright") Mrs. Farnaby's premonitory dream in *The Fallen Leaves*, in which she sees Amelius Goldenheart return her lost daughter to her, is too patently a device for evoking an atmosphere of mystery to serve its purpose. The dream, not surprisingly, in this highly contrived novel, comes true.

Prophetic dreams were part of the regular equipment of sensational novels, which shunned most uncanny devices; thus, in generally matter-of-fact stories by Miss Braddon and Charles Reade, prophetic dreams play a part. Robert Audley, in *Lady Audley's Secret* (1862), has a dream which sets him investigating the disappearance of his friend George Talboys; while Valentine Hawkehurst, in *Birds of Prey* (1867), has a dream which accurately forecasts events in the novel. Mrs. Dodd, in Reade's *Hard Cash* (1863), not only experiences inexplicable intimations of trouble, but has a dream about her absent husband which corresponds to the actual circumstances.

The prophetic dream as a convention was a constant ingredient in the literature of the nineteenth century in England, though it did not have there the same profound associations that German Romantic writers conferred upon it. Ordinarily it did not rise above the function of emphasizing a sensational point; and after a time, writers came to treat the convention less seriously. Unlike other Victorian writers, Charles Reade violated conventional expectations of dreams almost playfully. Thus, in his novel, *Put Yourself in His Place* (1870), Henry Little dreams that his beloved Grace Carden goes to heaven among angels where he may love her. He also dreams of a knight springing out of a grave in the old church where he works. In fact, neither of his dreams comes true and Reade's description of them merely highlights features of Henry's character, in particular his follies, while offering no confirmation of the subject matter of the dreams. Similarly, in Robert Louis Stevenson's *The Master of Ballantrae* (1888-89), a novel which freely employs the weird and outlandish, old Ephraim Mackellar relates how, sleeping or waking, he felt a grim premonition of approaching ruin pursuing him and standing before him "with the colors of a true illusion." Yet having built up our expectations, Mackellar goes on perversely to explain that the illusion was neither the result of lunacy nor divine warning, "for all manner of calamities befell, not that calamity—and I saw many pitiful sights, but never that one." (ch. 9)

Long after the convention of prophetic dreams ceased to be literally acceptable to most readers, it remained a convention of literature. Holly's prescient dream in Rider Haggard's *She* (1886-87), is related to Job's true presentiment of death in the same novel, but their dangerous circumstances sufficiently explain these psychological manifestations of anxiety and require no supernatural source. Perhaps the convention persisted because dreams long remained an intriguing mystery. Readers at the end of the nineteenth century might well have responded as old Matthew Dunn, in Lever's *Davenport Dunn* (1859), does to his son, who tells him that dreams mean nothing and are only interpreted by superstition.

> How do you know that more than me? Who told you they were miserable superstitions? I call them warnings—warnings that come out of our own hearts; and they come to us in our sleep just because that's the time our minds is not full of cares and troubles, but is just taking up whatever chances to cross them. (Vol. 2, ch. 63)

Indeed, it is just this sort of caution that many writers who used the convention of the dream wished to convey.

VICTORIAN STUDIES OF THE OCCULT

It is often assumed that Victorian culture in England was given over almost exclusively to materialism, and that metaphysical concerns were a peculiarity of the late part of the century. Samuel Hynes, in *The Edwardian Turn of Mind*, suggests that "one strong intellectual line through the late Victorian and Edwardian years [was] made up of reactions to Victorian materialism," and he includes psychical research as one such reaction.[26] Hynes points to the fascination with the supernatural and fantastic in the literature of this period and concludes that "After the social realism of the Victorians, from Dickens to George Moore, Edwardian novelists (some of them, at any rate) turned toward the mysterious and the unseen, just as the psychic researchers turned from the natural sciences to spiritualism."[27] Hynes' summary is misleading. I have already suggested that there was a continuing interest in the supernatural throughout the century. There was, in fact, a continuing series of studies designed to investigate objectively the nature of occult phenomena.

Early in the century Sir Walter Scott had examined uncanny subjects in *Letters on Demonology and Witchcraft* (1830). Isaac Taylor's *Physical Theory of Another Life* (1836) provided elaborate and closely argued theories regarding the probability of an existence beyond the common material existence most men regard as reality. Although writers sought to cure men of what Charles Mackay called "delusions," others argued for the existence of such forces. In *Extraordinary Popular Delusions and the Madness of Crowds* (1841), Mackay contended that ghosts were frauds and considered fortune-telling an imposition, founded on the vanity of men. The belief that man was of signal importance in the scale of creation was the basis for Catherine Crowe's popular works, in particular *The Night Side of Nature*, a book greatly indebted to the German scholar, G. H. Schubert. Mrs. Crowe examined such phenomena as dreams, presentiments, trances, wraiths, apparitions, and haunted houses, while presenting a Swedenborgian theory concerning the nature of the life hereafter. "What a man has made himself, he will be," she asserts; "his state is the result of his past life, and his heaven or hell are in himself. At death, we enter upon a new course of life; and what that life shall be, depends upon ourselves." (ch. 18) Mrs. Crowe's conclusion resembles many similar conclusions arrived at by equally sincere, though less successful writers. After all, she says, "we are the subjects, and so is everything around us, of all manner of subtle and inexplicable influences; and if our ancestors attached too much importance to these ill-understood arcana of the Night Side of nature, we have attached too little." It is necessary, she argues, to view the various inexplicable phenomena with the same objectivity and absence of prejudice that we bring to other matters of science, and she is convinced that ultimately explanations will be forthcoming. "For I take it, that as there is no such thing as chance, but all would be certainty if we knew the whole of the conditions, so no phenomena are really capricious and uncertain; they only appear so to our ignorance and short-sightedness." (ch. 18) William and Mary Howitt also were persuaded of the value of spiritualism as early as the 1850s. They believed that they had communicated with their dead son, Claude, and later with their son Charlton. Although he abandoned the more overt aspects of spiritualism, William continued to believe in it, hoping for reunion after death with those he loved. Mary ultimately dismissed it, saying that "spiritualism was one of the greatest misfortunes that ever visited us; it was false, all false and full of lies. Revelations seemed to come, and they were nothing but the suggestions of devils."[28] Nevertheless, for the years that they defended the spiritualists, the Howitts lent their respected names to a creed that influenced many besides fools and dupes.

In 1860, the American, Robert Dale Owen, published *Footfalls on the Boundary of Another World*, in which he provided instances of mysterious phenomena, and in 1872, he followed that study with *The Debatable Land Between This World and The Next*, in which he argued for the reality of these phenomena.[29] Owens witnessed the evocation of apparitions by mediums and had been convinced by his experiences. In his books he presented examples of occult experiences, dealing with hauntings, spirit rappings, spirit writing, spirit touches, and so forth. His enthusiasm in discovering, to his satisfaction, that these phenomena were scientifically verifiable followed from his eagerness to defend rudimentary religious faith, for it was his conviction that modern spiritualism would lead men from dogma back to primitive Christianity and the teachings of Christ, and provide evidence to support belief in immortality.[30]

Mrs. Sophia Morgan announced in *From Matter to Spirit. The Result of Ten Years' Experience in Spirit Manifestations*, published anonymously in 1863, that "one thing is certain; if these phenomena are *not* the result of imposture and delusion, the study of them involves questions worthy the deepest consideration of the theologian and the man of science."[31] She goes on to present examples of various types of mediumship, including mesmeric trances, guided writing, and aural communications from spirits and explains that men can become receptive of "the streams of influx from higher beings" by harmonizing their pulmonary and spiritual breathing.[32] She relates the process of death and the formation of the spiritual body, provides a description of the home of spirits after death, and gives accounts of spirits who had appeared after death. Clearly, Mrs. Morgan was convinced of the possibility of spirit communication, which she equated with electrical force and magnetic influence, after the theories of Anton Mesmer. Reputable medical men, such as the converts to magnetism, Dr. James Braid, Dr. John Elliotson, or Dr. James Esdaile, were not so much champions of the occult as they were scientific investigators of the mysteries of human nature. Nonetheless, the experiments described in a study such as Braid's *Neurypnology* (1843) offered grist for the spiritualist mill. American promoters of the new "sciences" of phrenology and animal magnetism were less disciplined in their investigations, but more visible.[33]

There were numerous disciplined and undisciplined studies putting forth manifold claims regarding supernatural experiences, appearing throughout the century. Animal magnetism, mesmerism, Swedenborgianism, even Galvani's experiments with electricity, or von Reichenbach's supposed discovery of the Odic or Odylic Force, had contributed to an increasing secular interest in the mysteries of the spirit. But spiritualism rapidly emerged as the dominant occult study. Modern spiritualism began with the Fox family of Hydesville, New York, in 1848.[34] From that place and time it spread rapidly, dying out in America only around 1870, but persisting much longer in England. It arrived in England in 1852 when Mr. Stone, a lecturer on animal magnetism, brought the medium Mrs. Hayden across the Atlantic from America.[35] Thereafter, several remarkable mediums came into prominence, most notable among them being Daniel Dunglas Home. Spiritualism was popular in other countries as well, and the chief of the early French spiritualists, Allan Kardec, who wrote *Le Livre des Esprits* (1857), was quite influential and succeeded in popularizing his brand of spiritualism.

Before long, spiritualists sought to establish separate societies, and many local organizations came into being, though attempts at a national organization from 1865 on were frustrated by internal bickering. The most successful of all organizations concerned with spiritual phenomena was the Society for Psychical Research, founded in 1882. Alan Gauld, in *The Founders of Psychical Research*, has given a thorough account of the men and events associated with the development of the Society, especially Henry Sidgwick, its first president, and Edmund Gurney and Frederic Myers, two of its most enthusiastic researchers.[36] Mainly, the Society hoped to prove that there was, in one form or another, survival after death. Researches made by members of the Society were as controlled and unbiased as circumstances allowed and in most cases the putative phenomena were declared fraudulent or unconvincing. Certain of the members most thoroughly engaged in these investigations, such as Myers and Richard Hodgson, arrived at a full belief in survival.[37] Myers became convinced that the everyday world is interpenetrated and acted upon by another order of things, a spiritual world of which we are already in a sense participants.[38]

When the Society was founded, Gladstone declared psychical research "the most important work, which is being done in the world. By far the most important."[39] And the Society was both successful and fashionable from the beginning. Members and associates in its first year included Arthur Balfour, Leslie Stephen, John Ruskin, John Addington Symonds, A. R. Wallace, and the Rev. C. L. Dodgson. Later, Gladstone and Tennyson accepted honorary memberships and William James and Samuel Clemens demonstrated their interest.[40] Inter-

est in the Society was symptomatic of a yearning which had remained
unexpressed or was channelled through traditional forms of religion.
Now it found a more agreeable form of expression:

> Spiritualism was comforting, cosy, humane. Compared at any rate with
> the fiercer Christian sects it had a great deal to offer plain men: ora-
> tory quite as colourful as any the nonconformists could provide, but
> without the disquieting undertones; word not of a Day of Judgment,
> but of reunion with those we love; talk not of man's sinfulness, but of
> the eternity of moral progress which awaits him; above all miracles not
> distant and dubious, but worked here and now by ordinary people.[41]

Arthur Symons followed the proceedings of the Society, having been
for some time interested in spiritualism and the science of the occult,
partly through the influence of his friend, W. B. Yeats. Like many
others, he sought for consolation in spiritualism. But not only artists
and men committed to fancy demonstrated an interest in spiritualism. If Harriet Beecher Stowe was converted to spiritualism, Abraham Lincoln and Wild Bill Hickok also showed an interest in it.
Oliver Lodge, a prominent British scientist, expended considerable
energy demonstrating the manner in which the material and the spiritual world were related, as the matter-of-fact Robert Dale Owen had
before him. Lodge wished to prove the oneness of the universe, and,
while arguing that life after was similar to life before death, he "envisioned a psychic realm consisting of ether and mind. Central to his
vision was the ethereal body which co-exists with the material
body."[42] Lodge was by no means the only scientist interested in psychic research. William Crookes, J. J. Thomson, John Strutts and
others also sought explanations beyond ordinary experience. But perhaps the most notable exposition of the idea that science and religion
were compatible was *The Unseen Universe*, published anonymously
in 1875 by Balfour Steward and P. G. Tait. In 1874, the reputable
scientist, Alfred Russell Wallace, published *Miracles and Modern
Spiritualism*, in which he argued for spiritualism as "an experimental science." He himself had been an absolute materialist, but the facts
of spiritualism, he admitted, had won him. For Wallace modern spiritualism's claims were no more unnatural nor remarkable than such
phenomena as electricity and other discoveries would have been to
earlier times. He argued that spiritualism was a strong moral force
and accepted its teaching that "The new state of existence [after

death] is a natural continuation of the old one," (ch. 8) and that the surviving spirit undergoes an endless progression continued in proportion to the mental and moral faculties exhibited in this life. Testimony of this kind indicates that psychical research was not viewed superstitiously, but with the greatest seriousness by impressive minds. Nor were attempts to reconcile science and religion confined to England and America. Stanislas de Guaïta's *Au Seuil du Mystère* (1886) and Papu's [Dr. Encausse] *Traité elementaire de science occulte* (1888) similarly aimed to extend the scientific horizon to include more than material existence.[43]

These assertions were not unchallenged by other scientists. W. B. Carpenter had contested Wallace's views, and Frederic Harrison, in an article entitled "The Soul and Future Life," which appeared in *The Nineteenth Century* in June of 1877, defended materialists against charges by supernaturalists, and explained that they distinguished moral from biologic fact but were nonetheless fully convinced of "the supreme importance of spiritual life." Materialists, he explained, see the soul not as an "indescribable entity," but as the idea emerging from the whole operation of the individual, and "the combined activity of the human powers organized around the highest of them," they called the Soul. Harrison's article was an answer to all of the intuitionists and supernaturalist schools of thought, but it is important to note that such a response was considered necessary. Psychical studies were not a laughing matter, though they were frequently mocked; they were viewed with gravity by serious minds.

When the Society for Psychical Research began its investigations of apparitions, hundreds of people came forth voluntarily to present evidence about their psychical experience. Apparently there was a lively contemporary interest in the subject.[44] What Edmund Gurney investigated in *Phantasms of the Living* (1886) were such various phenomena as thought transference and spontaneous telepathy; communication with the physically dead; apparitions, hauntings, and hallucinations; prophecies and veridical dreams; mediumship; hypnotism; astral projection; and automatic writing. And what the work claimed to show was "(1) that experimental telepathy exists, and (2) that apparitions at death, &c., are a result of something beyond chance; whence it follows (3) that these experimental and these spontaneous cases of the action of mind on mind are in some way allied."[45] Frederic Myers, who wrote the Introduction for *Phantasms of the Living,* named Carlyle, Emerson, Mazzini, Renan, Tennyson, Matthew Arnold and Ruskin as "discoursers on things spiritual who have been most listened to in our day," and pointed out that their beliefs and aspirations went beyond dogma and external influence, resembling rather "the awakening into fuller consciousness of some inherited and instinctive need."[46] In a similar way, Myers argued, men are not emotionally at home with the dogma or materialism of the age. Thus, he concluded, the time was ripe "for some such extension of scientific knowledge as we claim that we are offering here—an extension which, in my view, lifts us above the materialistic standpoint altogether, and which gives at least a possible reality to those subtle inter-communications between spirit and spirit, and even between visible and invisible things, of which Art and Literature are still as full as in any 'Age of Faith' which preceded us."[47]

In his own ample study, *Human Personality and its Survival of Bodily Death* (1903), Myers stated his belief in man's ability to communicate with a spiritual state and to advance gradually in it after death. His argument, supported by instances of supposed spiritual communications, and buttressed by acute speculations on human nature, comes to a conclusion not unlike those arrived at by other less dependable individuals and their associations. MacGregor Mathers' Order of the Golden Dawn, which fascinated Yeats, was subject to serious challenge. Madame Blavatsky was actually accused of fraud. Nonetheless, esoteric Buddhism continued to maintain a following and found other spokesmen, such as A. P. Sinnett, who even went so far as to claim Tennyson as an occultist, just as Myers had claimed him as the greatest poet to reveal cosmic law and to describe the "interpenetration of the spiritual and material worlds."[48]

Psychical research was clearly not peculiar to the late Victorian period. From the beginning of the century, the supernatural was a constant subject of serious intellectual speculation. There was a lively exchange of opinion on the topic ranging from Isaac Taylor's metaphysical optimism, to Scott's critical history, to such works as John Alderson's *An Essay on Apparitions, in which their Appearance is Accounted for by Causes wholly Independent of Preternatural Agency* (1811), John Ferriar's *An Essay Toward a Theory of Apparitions* (1813), or Dr. Samuel Hibbert's *Sketches of the Philosophy of Apparitions: or, an Attempt to Trace such Illusions to their Physical Causes* (1824).[49] This interest in the uncanny and the occult was emotional as well as scientific or theological. Yet Catherine Crowe, dedicated as she was to belief in ghosts and spiritual influences, considered herself open to other explanations for the various supernatural phenomena she described. Moreover, in the introduction to her first study of the occult, *The Night Side of Nature*, she explained that "in undertaking to treat of the phenomena in question, I do not propose to consider them as supernatural; on the contrary, I am persuaded that the time will come, when they will be reduced strictly within the bounds of science." (ch. 1) And a respectable popular philosopher such as James Hinton felt that all dreams and illusions, because they were transient to the self, were open to investigation, and might prove aids to a true perception of reality.[50]

Most certainly interest in the uncanny was more fashionable and prominent at the close of the century, but it was neither an abrupt nor an unexpected development. Romanticism had exploited the theme of the supernatural. "The world view of the romantic movement," John Senior writes, "is occultism."[51] German Romantics were among the first to incorporate this material into their writings, but it found a prominent place in French literature as well. Balzac exploited supernaturalism and the occult in his fiction, while Gautier and Gerard de Nerval were also influenced by the occult. The latter had read widely in occult literature. Victor Hugo, in the later part of his career, demonstrated a profound interest in occultism, and his trilogy *La Légende des siècles*, *La Fin de Satan*, and *Dieu*, show the effects of this interest. The symbolist writers of France were closely associated with occultism not only in sentiment, but also in particular theories and by personal contact with spiritual occultists such as the Abbe Alphonse Constant, called Eliphas Levi.[52] Interest in the occult, then, was international and renewed exploitation of supernatural effects in later Victorian literature may be seen as an outgrowth of persistent concerns of the preceding decades throughout Europe and America.

THE OCCULT IN LATER VICTORIAN LITERATURE

In addition to utilizing uncanny subject matter in their writings, many Victorian authors were familiar with mesmerism, spiritualism, and other versions of occult study. The Tennyson family is an example. Mary Tennyson was devoted to spiritualism through most of her life. At the time of Arthur Hallam's death she claimed to have seen an apparition that she took to be that of her brother's friend. Frederick Tennyson began to entertain spiritualist beliefs from the 1840s and eventually became a convinced advocate.[53] Alfred himself was curious about, if never convinced by spiritualist thought. His poetry continually reveals a lively interest in the supernatural. *In Memoriam* records his speculations on survival after death and the relationship of the living to the dead as he speaks of "spiritual presentiments" wishing for Hallam's spirit to return to earth. Later, in "Aylmer's Field," the character Leolin wakes from sleep to respond, without understanding his act, to a preternatural call from his beloved Edith, and the poet wonders, "Star to star vibrates light: may soul to soul / Strike through a finer element of her own? / So, from afar, touch us at once?" "Demeter and Persephone" contains a simile comparing Persephone's manner of appearing before her mother to the likeness of a dying man's appearance to a far-off friend. And "The Ring" concerns the actual interference of a spirit in the lives of its relations. A. P. Sinnett listed many other poems of Tennyson's as occult works, considering himself most suited to interpret them. "I am the better able to accomplish this," Sinnett wrote in 1920, "because I have had several recent opportunities of discussing the subject with the great poet himself, now, of course, in life on a higher plane of existence."[54] Tennyson may not have been an occultist, nor the latest reincarnation of a spirit who had led earlier lives as Virgil, Omar Khayyam, Dante and Spenser, as Sinnett claimed, but he did understand a good deal about occult thought and did not hesitate to make use of it in his poetry. Moreover, if he was not a spiritualist, he clearly had not given up belief in the possibility of a spiritual existence beyond the grave.

Robert Browning, too, maintained a faith in the reality of the spirit, though he remained unconvinced of spiritualism. His wife, however, was for a long time persuaded of its validity particularly because of the medium, Daniel Dunglas Home. "She was more and more convinced that the world was on the verge of a great revelation; that the widespread aliveness to the supernatural was a reaction from the materialism of the age."[55] She was disillusioned, though, by the fraudulent impositions of Mrs. Sophia Eckley, in whom she had believed. The circle in Florence, with whom the Brownings were friendly, also exhibited varying degrees of interest in spiritualism, Hiram Powers, James Jackson Jarves and Seymour Stocker Kirkup being enthusiastic, while Robert Lytton and Thomas Adolphus Trollope remained somewhat skeptical.[56]

William Bell Scott claimed to be familiar with the "shop filled with alchymical [sic] and astrological books and other related works, described by Bulwer in the introduction to" *Zanoni*, and he saw it and the club attended by some of his artistic friends and devoted to what he called "scientific superstition"—some of the members were engaged in a search for the *elixir vitae*—as signs of an interest in the occult in the first half of the nineteenth century.[57] Scott himself did not credit spiritualism, but he asserted that Rossetti had, and he told a story of Holman Hunt's encounter with what he supposed was the devil to illustrate the belief, among intelligent men, in the supernatural.[58] Richard Burton was very superstitious and maintained an interest in alchemy and spiritualism. Like Tennyson and Dickens, he was a capable hypnotist at a time when hypnotism was associated with the concept of animal magnetism formulated by Mesmer and later Count Puysegur. Burton's wife believed in gypsy horoscope predictions of future events and credited telepathic communication and hypnotism over long distances.[59] Laurence Oliphant offered a mystical substitute for traditional religion in its dogmatic form in the peculiar conclusion to *Piccadilly* (1866), and later, in his autobiographical *Episodes in a Life of Adventure, or, Moss from a Rolling Stone* (1887), he explained what moved him to withdraw from a life of politics and public events and devote himself to researches into "the more hidden laws which govern human action and control events."

> I had long been interested in a class of psychic phenomena which, under the names of magnetism, hypnotism, and spiritualism, have since been forcing themselves upon public attention, and had even been conscious of these phenomena in my own experiences, and of the existence of forces in my own organism which science was utterly unable to account for, and therefore turned its back upon, and relegated to the domain of the unknowable.[60]

Naturally there was a good deal of debate in the periodical literature of the time about spiritualism, dreams and the supernatural. Although Dickens published articles critical of, and even mocking spiritualist pretentions in *Household Words* and *All The Year Round*, he also published stories based upon the supernatural in the latter journal, including his own tale, "The Haunted House." If *Black-wood's Edinburgh Magazine* considered spiritualism as anti-Christian in "Spiritual Manifestations," the *Cornhill Magazine* printed Robert Bell's favorable account of spiritualism, "Stranger Than Fiction," which Thackeray defended.[61] The subject was clearly of interest to the general public and among literary people. That interest manifested itself as a literary convention in the later nineteenth century in England.

Nineteenth-century British literature demonstrated a Gothic fascination for supernatural events, either in quasi-mystical works such as Maturin's *Melmoth, The Wanderer* (1820), or in shockers, such as the vampire novels from Polidori's *The Vampyre* (1819), through T. P. Prest's *Varney the Vampyre, or the Feast of Blood* (1847) and Sheridan Le Fanu's *Carmilla* (1871-72), to Bram Stoker's *Dracula* (1897). Most popular fiction exploited conventional forms of premonition, prevision, and other occult warnings and communications. Finally, there were poems such as Adelaide Proctor's "Unseen," which reminded their readers of the mysterious forces surrounding them and sometimes touching their experience; "though a veil of shadow hangs between / That hidden life and what we see and hear, / Let us revere the power of the Unseen, / And know a world of mystery is near." Most references to the occult and supernatural were made in a Christian context. Major poets employed the convention of the supernatural without necessarily admitting a faith in occult experience. Thus Browning alludes to the occult in *Paracelsus* and describes a gypsy's mysterious power in "The Flight of the Duchess"; Rossetti employs occult elements in "Rose Mary";[62] and Tennyson utilized traditional occult devices in several poems, for example, in the prevenient sign that Annie misinterprets, and the aural sign Enoch experiences in the very popular *Enoch Arden*.

From the sixties on, the occult played a prominent part in literature, reflecting the growing interest in spiritualism and the supernatural. Popular interest in spiritualism coincided with a renewed fascination for sensational novels and marvellous romances, but the two interests should not be confused. Many writers of romance wished to be associated with neither development, and many who had comfortably employed the conventions of the occult in their work, mocked the new attitudes. Browning, for example, wrote "Mr. Sludge, The Medium," designed to cut figures such as D. D. Home down to size, as well as the more obscure poem, "Mesmerism," which reads like a parody of circumstances in certain sensational novels of the time. Joseph Sheridan Le Fanu, for one, fashioned his career upon tales of the uncanny, and though he was familiar with the writings of Swedenborg and other occultists, he never accepted spiritualism.[63] George MacDonald was writing stories pertaining to the marvellous as early as *The Phantastes* (1858) and in the preface to *The Portent: A Story of the Inner Vision of the Highlanders, Commonly Called The Second Sight* (published periodically in 1860, in book form in 1864), he specifically designated his story as a romance, explaining that although it was "founded in the marvellous" it was "true to human nature and to itself." He clearly asserted that his story was not to be classed "with what are commonly called *sensation novels.*"

The Portent describes the special sensibilities of three persons: Duncan Campbell who can hear a warning of impending trouble; Lady Alice, who has the same ability; and Margaret, Duncan's old nurse, who is able to project her soul according to her will. Lady Alice's soul is also given to drifting away from her body; the greater part of her early life has consisted of a tranced existence by day modified by a nocturnal spiritual life. After Duncan and Lady Alice have discovered their mutual spiritual attraction (they may even, it is hinted, be reincarnated lovers), and have been separated by a clumsy plot device, to be rejoined later through old Margaret's powers, they marry and assume a normal existence. Only at this point is the traditional moral presented: "love was the gate to an unseen world infinitely beyond that region of the psychological in which we had hitherto moved; for this love was teaching us to love all men, and live for all men." (ch. 26)

MacDonald continued to employ what may be called occult and even mystical elements in later novels such as *David Elginbrod* (1863), where mesmerism plays an important part, and *Lilith* (1895), in which a world on the other side of a mirror contains Adam and his first wife, Lilith, a vampire-like creature who fascinates the main character, Mr. Vane. Other writers were also eager to offer sophisticated, not to say learned, amplifications of the occult convention. In Joseph Henry Shorthouse's *John Inglesant* (1880), an historical romance, set largely in Renaissance England and Italy, there is frequent reference to such subjects as mystical Platonism or Rosicrucianism. There are instances of true prevision, and in one experience

Inglesant actually sees the future in a crystal ball. These, however, are little more than trappings, for the novel's real concern was with spiritual maturation.

The interest in spiritualism was as active in America as it was in England. Prominent authors such as Hawthorne, Lowell, Howells, James and Twain, wrote of spiritualism, though they were largely hostile to the belief itself.[64] In England, there was more of the traditionally supernatural, as MacDonald's works indicate.

Even Thomas Hardy used conventional occult devices, as in *Tess of the d'Urbervilles*, where the sound of an evil ghostly coach is perceivable only to true d'Urbervilles. Rudyard Kipling's tales of the uncanny, such as "The Phantom Rickshaw" and "The Mark of the Beast," are, despite Kipling's interest in spiritualism, largely conventional, while "My Own True Ghost Story" is a takeoff on ghost stories. But conventions of this sort gradually yielded to more sophisticated spiritualist approaches in fiction. Ephemeral works such as the American, Elizabeth Stuart Phelps' *The Gates Ajar* (1869) or Mrs. Adeline Whitney's *Hitherto* (1869), prepared the way for more accomplished writers like Mrs. Oliphant.

Underlying all of Mrs. Oliphant's stories of the Seen and Unseen was the desire to affirm the existence of a transcendental, Christian creator and the immortality of the soul against the increasing materialism and estheticism of her time. In 1880, Mrs. Oliphant published *A Beleaguered City, Being a Narrative of Certain Events in the City of Semur, in the Department of the Haute Bourgogne. A Story of the Seen and the Unseen.* In this graceful fable, the city of Semur is occupied by a ghostly, oppressive darkness. Unseen visitants force the city's inhabitants to leave. When the mayor, Martin Dupin, and the local priest venture into the city, they encounter the visionary Paul Lecamus, who alone has been permitted to remain conscious among the occupying spirits. Lecamus records his experiences, explaining that the visitants identified themselves as spirits of the city's dead who have returned out of love to teach its populace. Lecamus had always been interested in the mysterious and the unseen, but particularly since losing the wife he loved deeply. Here, as in other works of the time, love interrupted by death leads to a conviction of the reality of another life. It is yearning toward the life hereafter that enables Lecamus to believe in, and to experience spiritual existence.

When the spirits depart from Semur, Lecamus' spirit goes with them and he dies.

The reason for the return of the spirits of the dead is purposely left ambiguous, but their general motive may be assumed both from Dupin's acknowledgment that "the thirst for money and for pleasure has increased among us to an extent which I cannot but consider alarming," (ch. 1) and from the ghostly "Sommation" placarded on the cathedral door, declaring "Go! leave this place to us who know the true signification of life." (ch. 2) Although this ghostly experience draws the community together and revives its religious faith, the agnostic Dupin, himself much moved by the mysterious events, sadly reports that the effects have not been lasting and the "wonderful manifestation which interrupted our existence has passed absolutely as if it had never been." (ch. 10) Mrs. Oliphant expressed both hope and dismay regarding human faith and the influence of the unseen. In *A Beleaguered City*, she was not merely exploiting a public taste for the marvellous and uncanny, for she felt a serious desire to revitalize religious emotion. There is a marked difference between this kind of uncanny tale and earlier Gothic novels. Though less intellectual, and less adept, Mrs. Oliphant's tale is in the tradition of Bulwer-Lytton's supernatural stories, rather than those of Le Fanu.

If *A Beleaguered City* is an account of a supposedly real though extraordinary event, Mrs. Oliphant's *A Little Pilgrim in the Unseen* (1883) takes us into the next world—a bright and airy place where Christ strolls casually among the spirits of the dead.[65] The Little Pilgrim, a sweet-natured spinster, having passed easily from earthly to spiritual life, learns that spirits do not communicate with the living for fear of weighing down their minds, although she is told that upon rare occasion, contact is possible in order to help those on the other side. Christ gives the Little Pilgrim a commission to greet those entering the spiritual world, but her duties are interrupted by a visit to a beautiful city where she has an interview with the Father and where she learns that there are various classes of spirits in this world, and that there is a Land of Darkness where unprepared spirits must go to be purified. Ultimately, having met her own mother and father, the Little Pilgrim returns to her assignment at the boundary between the world of spirit and of earth and her voice is heard echoing through the universe as she welcomes newcomers. It cheered, we are told, "the anxious faces of some great lords and princes far more great than she, who were of a nobler race than man; for it was said among the stars that when such a little sound could reach so far, it was a token that the Lord had chosen aright, and that His method must be the best."

Obviously, such a thoroughly fanciful tale was not meant to persuade doubting minds of the reality of another world, but the sale of *A Little Pilgrim of the Unseen*—it was Mrs. Oliphant's most popular book—indicates that it gratified a large part of the populace. The acceptance of other novels about the next world, such as Anita Silvani's *The Strange Story of Ahrinziman* (1906), and the outrageous popularity of Marie Corelli's *A Romance of Two Worlds* (1886), indicate more than a voguish fascination with a literary curiosity, though, of course, some writers exploited this interest. Robert Buchanan's *The Moment After: A Tale of The Unseen* (1890), describing a murderer's experience in the hereafter during a temporary "death" during his hanging, which fails to kill him, is an obvious attempt to capitalize on a favorable market.

In 1886, two novels appeared that are representative of the directions that the occult convention took late in the century. H. Rider Haggard's *She* appeared serially in *The Graphic*. He had written the novel during February and March of 1886 in a little over six weeks and the book was a smashing best-seller from the start.[66] Haggard himself was interested in the supernatural and the tale came easily. He considered himself attuned to the spiritual, read Oliver Lodge's books on psychic research, studied Eastern religions, corresponded with individuals who believed in mystical experience and followed the activities of the Psychical Research Society. Haggard came to believe in reincarnation, finding it a sufficient explanation of the mystery of life and death. The rejuvenation theme itself was not unusual in English literature, and given Haggard's interests, it is not surprising that he used it in *She*; also, in keeping with conventional use, he associated true love with the eternal spirit.[67] Haggard continued to employ similar occult material in later novels, including the sequels to *She* and the late novel, *Love Eternal* (1918), but *She* remained the classic. The basic plot of the novel is simple. Leo Vincey is a reincarnation of Kallikrates, an ancient Egyptian. With his guardian, Ludwig Horace Holly, Leo goes to seek a strange land in Africa where his ancestor died at the hands of a mysteriously powerful white woman. At the ancient city of Kôr they encounter the irresistible, but

cruel and violent Ayesha who has waited thousands of years for Kallikrates' return and now wishes to make his present physical embodiment as enduring as her own, but in the attempt she herself is reduced
to dust. Both Leo and Holly become wanderers haunted by Ayesha's beauty.

One of Haggard's favorite novelists was Bulwer-Lytton, and much
of *She* bears resemblance to both *Zanoni* and *A Strange Story*. In
Zanoni simple faith was favorably contrasted to a lust for knowledge;
similarly, Haggard writes that "Truth is veiled, because we could no
more look upon her glory than we can upon the sun. It would destroy
us. Full knowledge is not for man as man is here, for his capacities,
which he is apt to think so great, are indeed but small." (ch. 10) Just
as Zanoni discovers that physical immortality is not preferable to
death, so Holly tells She that her offer of long life is nothing compared to what he anticipates; "the immortality to which I look, and
which my faith doth promise to me," he says, "shall be free from the
bonds that here must tie my spirit down." (ch. 22) Ayesha says that
the next life differs little, morally, from this one (a view presented
as early as Swedenborg and echoed in such writers as Catherine
Crowe and Mrs. Oliphant). Ayesha considers religions generally inclined to error because of their confidence in dogma. "Ah!" she exclaims, "if man would but see that hope is from within, and not from
without—that he himself must work out his salvation! He is there,
and within him is the breath of life and a knowledge of good and
evil, as good and evil are to him." (ch. 17) Despite her intelligence,
Ayesha is not wise enough for humility. Her name is borrowed from
A Strange Story, where Ayesha is the loving companion of the radiantly handsome Margrave, whose attempt to achieve immortality is
rebuked by spirits in the air. Haggard's She also fails in her desire for
prolonged existence. As the moral Holly observes, "she opposed herself to the eternal law, and, strong though she was, by it was swept
back into nothingness—swept back with shame and hideous mockery!" (ch. 26) Haggard made full use of supernatural and uncanny
conventions, incorporating them in a confusedly affirmative view of
traditional morality. Though *She* may be viewed as a thriller, it is also
a serious expression of opinion regarding the unseen and the unknown.

The second highly successful novel dealing with the marvellous
appearing in 1886 was Marie Corelli's *A Romance of Two Worlds*.
If Haggard had been willing to consider features of spiritualism as

proof of Christianity, Marie Corelli quite clearly distinguished her beliefs from anything related to what she called the craze for occult-ism or spiritualism. In her preface to a new edition of the novel, she asserted that her faith was based solely on Christ, and her answer to the yearning for a spiritual progress was love for God. Yet any reader of Corelli's novel might have been forgiven his confusion, since, al-though in the Prologue to the tale the narrator explains that her ex-periences offer evidence of the real existence of the supernatural around us—evidence she expects will be disbelieved in this age of materialistic skepticism—actually her supernaturalism sounds more hermetic and occult than strictly Christian.

The nameless narrator is a young *improvatrice* suffering from a pe-culiar physical malaise. From a friend she receives an elixir that re-veals to her that her malady is spiritual. She is directed to the sage Heliobas, who undertakes not only to cure her, but to educate her as well. Heliobas promotes an Electric Creed of Christianity, based on the notion, later verified by the narrator's spiritual journey, that di-vinity is a sphere within a ring of light from which electricity extends throughout the universe. That electricity is of two kinds—external, bound by universal law, and internal.

> Internally it is the germ of a soul or spirit, and is placed there to be either cultivated or neglected as suits the will of man. It is indestructi-ble; yet, if neglected, it remains always a germ; and, at the death of the body it inhabits, goes elsewhere to seek another chance of develop-ment. If, on the contrary, its growth is fostered by a persevering, reso-lute WILL, it becomes a spiritual creature, glorious and supremely powerful, for which a new, brilliant, and endless existence commences when its clay chrysalis perishes. (ch. 7)

When, through Heliobas' power, the narrator journeys to the spiri-tual realm, she learns what Heliobas later relates more prosaically: God's likeness in man is an electric flame which may be fostered or neglected; Christ came to earth not as a sacrifice, but to establish an electric communication (compared to a telegraph cable) between men and the central sphere; the soul may progress or regress after physical death; and also, "this world is *the only spot in the Universe* where His existence is actually questioned and doubted." (ch. 14)

The narrator also learns, through her acquaintance with Casimir Heliobas and his lovely sister, Zara, that each soul has a twin soul either embodied in flesh or not. Heliobas' spiritual mate is Azúl, who watches over him. Zara's unearthly lover comes to possess her finally in a bolt of lightning, freeing her from the restrictive flesh. With this knowledge to fortify her, and increasing electrical powers to both disturb and console her, the narrator goes on to lead a satisfying earthly life, concluding her tale with a plea to her readers to think seriously about their own lives, to consider what Progress really means, and not to lightly deny God. It is, she asserts, a universe powered by love in which our wills are free.

Corelli referred to the uncanny and the life beyond death in later works such as *The Soul of Lilith* (1892) and *The Sorrows of Satan* (1895). The latter novel tells of Goeffrey Tempest's temptation by the devil in the form of one Rimanez. After a prolonged struggle, Tempest frees himself from the devil by choosing God instead. This novel was praised by defenders of Christianity. Eileen Bigland, in her biography of Corelli, quotes from a certain Father Ignatius' sermon delivered at Portman Rooms in Baker Street, who thanked God for the book and declared "*The Sorrows of Satan* is flung down into the midst of English society, as it is constituted at present, as an heroic challenge to that society and to the Church."[68] Corelli's supernatural novels were almost evangelical in their spirit and did constitute challenges, as Father Ignatius asserted. But other writers could be equally positive, yet less aggressive, and more sentimental in their use of the occult convention.

In *Peter Ibbetson* (1892), George du Maurier relates the history of a man who comes to live a real life in dreams with the woman he loves. In the disembodied world of dreams, their spirits meet, controlling time and space. The lovers marvel at their shared gift, "penetrated to the very heart's core by a dim sense of some vast, mysterious power, latent in the subconsciousness of man—unheard of, undreamed of as yet, but linking him with the Infinite and the Eternal." (ch. 5) When Peter's beloved dies, the dream world changes; whereas they had enjoyed perennial youth, now Peter is left old and alone. But Mimsey is able to return to him from beyond death to tell Peter they will unite with the One when he joins her in the next life. She tells him that the foundation of the next life is earthly existence and that earth is the most favored planet. "Like many who lived before me," she admits, "I cannot prove—I can only affirm." (ch. 6) But what she affirms is that "Nothing is lost—nothing," of human experience, though the cause of all being remains inscrutable. There is continual advance without end, she assures Peter and leaves him with the promise *"that all will be well for us all, and of such a kind that all who do not sigh for the moon will be well content."* (ch. 6)

George du Maurier also wrote *The Martian* (1897) as well as the amazingly popular *Trilby* (1894), which exploited another aspect of occult interest, mesmerism. In *Trilby*, the hypnotist, Svengali, controls young Trilby's nature to such an extent that she unknowingly leads two distinct and contradictory lives. When Svengali dies and his power fades, Trilby also expires. This relationship recalls George MacDonald's earlier novel, *David Elginbrod* (1863), where the character, Euphra, is mesmerized by an evil figure named Funkelstein, supposedly drawn partly from a Pole named Zamoyski who was lecturing on "electrobiology" in England at the time MacDonald wrote his story.[69] But hypnotism had long been a familiar part of the occult convention, as seen in E. T. A. Hoffmann's tale *Der Magnetiseur*, published in 1814.

Spiritualist or not, the convention of the occult was used largely as a defense of religious belief among late-Victorian writers. Early in the century, supernatural visitations and portents abounded, but they served more often to arouse thrills than to support a larger scheme of faith.[70] As the century proceeded, several notable utilizations of the occult convention in fiction indicated a change in literary approaches. Just as philosophical, religious and "psychological" tracts were more ambitiously examining the possibilities of the verification of the supernatural, literary artists were learning to utilize old conventions in new or more serious ways.

This force of serious conviction altered what might otherwise have been mere sensational writing. In Bram Stoker's *Dracula* (1897), the characters are appalled at the prospect of a deathless being gradually accumulating knowledge and power, a dread that had troubled Holly soon after experiencing Ayesha's power, when he considered "what may not be possible to a being who, unconstrained by human law, is also absolutely unshackled by a moral sense of right and wrong." (*She*, ch. 18) Bulwer-Lytton and Haggard wrote to scold an age that refused to believe in mysteries which it could not explain; so in part, did Stoker. His open-minded Professor Von Helsing, Count Dracula's true antagonist, is obliged to instruct his brilliant, but materialistic friend, Dr. John Seward, that there are things outside everyday life that cannot be accounted for. "Do you not think," he asks, "that there are things which you cannot understand, and yet which are; that some people see thing that others cannot?" He then criticizes science for Seward's attitude because "if it explain not, then it says there is nothing to explain." (ch. 14) Von Helsing concludes his argument abruptly. "My thesis is this: I want you to believe." "To believe what?" the puzzled Seward replies, and the doctor responds: "To believe in things that you cannot." (ch. 14) *Dracula* implicitly denounces its "sceptical and selfish" age; and the threat of "a spreading army of soulless Un-Dead" is, to some extent, a warning about a world peopled by materialistic, and therefore soulless men, unable to value life. Appropriately, Stoker has Dracula defeated by his own selfish purpose, for it is through his own volitional powers that his enemies are able to pursue and destroy him. Stoker continued to exploit supernaturalism in novels such as *The Mystery of the Sea* (1902), *The Jewel of Seven Stars* (1904) and *The Lair of the White Worm* (1911), but never approached the power of *Dracula* again.

The use of the occult by writers of romance provided an opportunity for yet another, similar utilization of the convention, as in Theodore Watts-Dunton's *Aylwin* (1898). For Watts-Dunton, as for many spiritualists, the spiritual was less divine than earthly. *Aylwin* is filled with secular superstitions, especially related to gypsies, who were customarily identified with the occult; it utilizes the ancient convention of a curse, but makes it plausible psychologically. Even Winifred Wynne's astonishing cure by magnetism Watts-Dunton defended as scientifically possible. But essentially the novel describes Henry Aylwin's progress from stern determinism to a new, open-minded and open-hearted acceptance of wonder and mystery in existence. His friend, D'Arcy, writes to him when his greatest ordeal is ended: "As Job's faith was tried by Heaven, so has your love been tried by the power which you call 'circumstance' and which Wilderspin calls 'the spiritual world.' All that death has to teach the mind and the heart of man you have learnt to the very full." (ch. 16)

What Henry learns is the spiritual power of love. The death of a beloved is the greatest human tragedy and leads a man to supernaturalism in the desperate hope not to be separated forever.[71] Henry might have learned from his own father's history. Philip Aylwin had seen his first wife die and thereafter, prompted by desperate longing, became a mystic in a sect founded by Lavater, putting his convictions down in a book entitled *The Veiled Queen,* and believing himself in communication with his dead wife. But Henry despises superstition, and struggles to forge a way of life to contend with all-powerful Circumstance. His ordeal, as we have noted, brings him finally to a belief in mysteries beyond the ken of materialist philosophies.

SUMMARY

Seeming to alter considerably, the occult convention had changed only slightly, though significantly, in the nineteenth century. It still was used to suggest the existence of another world affecting our own, but as the nineteenth century progressed, it came to have a more serious function in English literature. Oscar Wilde's delightful tale, "The Canterville Ghost" (1891), in which a respectably ancient ghost is driven to despair by an American family who purchase the estate he haunts and who refuse to be terrified by him, is a fine satire upon the kinds of sensational and popular ghost stories. But while many writers continued to employ the convention superficially, others based their fables upon the probable reality of the Unseen. Moreover, if earlier supernatural phenomena in literature were random and mainly ominous, by the end of the century such occurrences were largely benign and hopeful. With or without religious belief, many literary people exhibited some degree of faith in spiritualist revelations, and one of the greatest, W. B. Yeats, not only became a student of the occult and fashioned his own occult scheme, he married a medium, Georgie Hyde Lees, in 1917 and benefitted thereafter from her skill.

This developing interest in the uncanny and the modifications it occasioned in a traditional literary convention, indicates a powerful desire during the nineteenth century for some means of escape from a depressingly materialistic existence. Amice Lee, describing William Howitt's reaction against the spirit of his time, writes that "Howitt believed with all the vehemence of his nature that spiritualism militated against the fierce materialism of the age. Nothing seemed to matter except to get on and make money—money, that was all men cared for now. In the London streets, he said, the very air you breathed hummed with voices discussing 'Shares.' "[72] Time and again rationalist heroes, such as Bulwer-Lytton's Dr. Fenwick, Stoker's Dr. Seward, or Watts-Dunton's Henry Aylwin, when faced with inexplicable events, are obliged to recognize that there are powers beyond man's ability to comprehend or control. If the sense of such ominous powers had once been primarily associated with demonic forces which made acceptance of a secure social existence valuable and desirable, by the end of the century the Unknown had become an attractive intellectual magnet, promising an experience beyond the dull confinement of modern life, promising, in fact, a release from an existence which seemed drained of meaning and feeling. In novels such as *Zanoni* and *A Romance of Two Worlds*, the possibility of liberation from the flesh itself fulfilled the fantasy of absolute freedom of the mind. But perhaps du Maurier's Peter Ibbetson is the archetypal hero of this mode. Bound in the triple prison of an actual institution, meaningless modern life, and the flesh, he escapes by apparent madness, life in dreams, and the promise of an eternity of love. If the convention of the occult and uncanny continued, then, with its ghosts and marvels, it acquired a higher purpose as well, for it came to represent release from confinements which appeared, to many, more and more intolerable. The uncanny was an antidote to relentless materialism, it was a promise of love and fullness of feeling beyond the unfeeling mechanization of modern society. In this sense it was a form of social protest. At the same time it represented a metaphysical craving for the liberation of the mind from the statistical and measurable habits of the late nineteenth century. In this modification of a perennial literary convention, it is possible to see how subtle if not always skillful an artistic accommodation had taken place; and also how responsive to its society, and therefore revelatory of that society, such conventions can be.

CHAPTER SEVENTEEN

CONCLUSION

In examining Victorian literary conventions, I have tried to show that stylizations of character types, social situations, and, for lack of a better designation, what I may call emotional predilections, participate in a broad moral scheme, definable in some cases as a fairly precise design that involves a necessary humbling and a form of real or symbolic redemption. Although I have, in my first chapter, emphasized one particularly common design, I certainly do not mean to suggest that there were not other designs, nor would I assert that all of Victorian literature employs one or another of these patterns. I do hope to have demonstrated that a large number of literary works employed such conventions and schemes, some with premeditation, others unconsciously. If we may assume that these conventions did function in the manner I have described, then I believe a further speculation is justified, that many underlying fears, beliefs, and aspirations of Victorian society may be deduced from the use of literary conventions.

REVIEW OF LITERARY CONVENTIONS

The idealization of a type of woman who is saintly, yielding, forgiving and faithful openly accents the prevailing Victorian view of men as makers and doers, with women serving as their moral consciences. But placing the ideal, obedient woman beyond the sordid realities of sexuality and substituting an eager delight in infants and drawing rooms creates a need for some manifestation of the sensual elements of human life. These socially disapproved features of behavior are mainly displaced to the passionate, willful and violent figure of the rebellious or seductive woman, who, like Judith, Jael or Salome, is prepared to contend with men, but who, unlike those Scriptural models, does so out of frustrated passion or pride, and thereby brings about her own sorrow. The opposition of these two basic types is resolved in yet another prominent conventional figure, the Magdalene, especially the repentant Magdalene. For those who might have considered their society's attitudes toward human relationships in general, and sexual relations in particular, unsatisfactory or hypocritical, the Magdalene offered a desirable alternative. As a fallen woman, she was outcast from respectable society and therefore experienced an important sense of alienation which more often than not opened her eyes to the sham that surrounded her. At first this type is merely pitied, as in Dickens, Hood, and other popular writers, but gradually a certain degree of respect attaches to her, as in Mrs. Gaskell's *Ruth* or Henry Kingsley's *Ravenshoe*, and finally she becomes a preferred partner in novels by Wilkie Collins or George Meredith, though this sentimental extreme is mocked by several writers, among them Samuel Butler. Guilt is transferred from the offending woman to the society that caused her suffering. Thus Mrs. Browning's *Aurora Leigh* and Collins' *The New Magdalen* elevate the Magdalen above normal society. Now respectable women begin to appear unprepossessing and unexciting. They have not ventured. Even for those who have not been forced into sin, voluntarily succumbing to sin may only indicate a greater capacity for love and trust in the offender than in her chillier but more respectable sisters. The sexual offender now unites the passion, independence and clear vision of the Judith figure, with the capacity for faithful and sustained love of the Griselda. She is more appealing than either, and more enticing precisely because she stands out against a restrictive and largely hypocritical society.

In this and other conventional types there often appears an implicit, and sometimes overt, criticism of respectable society. The faithful Jacob-like lover is, presumably, no ordinary man. He aspires to the love of a woman who embodies his ideal, and although he may never possess her, his emotion ennobles him; and, by not possessing her, he achieves a purer and more exalted existence than the lover who consummates his desire. Sometimes Jacob is rewarded, but too often, as G. A. Lawrence suggested, he either lost his Rachel altogether or gave in to the values of his culture and married Leah for her dower. If the highest value of love seemed to be confined to those who did not physically fulfill it, the highest form of charity and compassion, signified by the conventional type of the Good Samaritan, was all too often reduced to crude financial terms. Even those writers who encouraged the finest sentiments did not offer a Samaritanism that went far beyond cash gifts, and when it came to institutionalized charity, they could only lament the manner in which the Samaritan himself had turned thief or Pharisee. The figure of the poor scholar likewise implies the poverty of one alternative to worldliness. Characteristically, the poor scholar is either foolish in his learning, as with Bulwer-Lytton's Clutterbuck, or dignified but ineffective, as with Eliot's Mordecai. The type could represent noble withdrawal from the world or foolish waste of high faculties. And yet, when the scholar attempts to offer his wisdom to the world, to participate in its doings, the world will not accept him. The reality, as expressed most bitterly in Gissing's novels, is that respectable society does not desire the true scholar's knowledge. In the end, such men are driven back to dreams of the past and images of an unreal existence. There is no liberation through learning, as Hardy's Jude savagely discovers. This too is a sham of respectable society.

The discontent becomes yet more evident in the multiple convention of marriage; for there is much comment, especially on the part of unquestionably fine writers, about the abuses of the institution. Forced marriages and marriages of convenience are constantly attacked, and yet true marriages are hard to define and even more difficult to describe.[1] Thus marriage ends a tale more often than it begins one. Though Dickens and Thackeray might describe unsuccessful marriages successfully, most stories were overwhelmingly concerned with the vicissitudes of lovers preceding the accomplishment of their desires. It is, in fact, surprising to discover how very much of nineteenth-century English literature, despite its praise of home and family, really depicts broken homes and contentious families; how often young people in the narratives of the time find themselves in a world hostile to their noblest instincts, a world governed by their implacable parents and infiltrated by seditious siblings.

If ordinary social institutions were not so comfortable as they seemed, on a metaphysical level old certainties also appeared doubtful. The coincidences that once were attributed to a governing providence became evidences instead of ungoverned chance or a deterministic fate. Once men could resign themselves to the apparent loss of their free will by accepting a benign, overall design for existence; but when that benignity was gone, there were few excuses left for the apparent inability of man to control a random or destined life.

Some literary conventions reflected a desire to retain or recover a romantic activity. Thus, while duelling disappeared as a social reality, it remained a popular but increasingly empty commonplace of romantic adventure tales, as well as of some more respectable forms of literature. But, it was evident that the heroism of the late nineteenth century would be confined mainly to romance and financial derring-do, not to displays of chivalry and valor. Nor could even the most sacred moments retain their significance. The ultimate moment of truth on the deathbed ceased to convey the necessary awe and virtue. Instead, the moving deathbed scenes of early and mid-century literature became either mawkishly sentimental or savagely realistic. Jude, dying alone, neglected, and despairing, seemed a more accurate representation of men's feelings than the sweetly fading Constance Brandon in *Guy Livingstone* or the visionary mortal moments of Paul Dombey or little Humphrey in *Misunderstood*.

What seemed to be secure, if hope in the next world was not, was greed in this world. Financial grappling, rapine, and deceit were regularly attributed to the commercialized society of Victorian England. Writers persistently deplored and attacked the debasement of values to a cash level. From the fiery Carlyle, to an indignant Dickens, or a milder Trollope, accusations of cupidity accompanied lamentations on the sad degradation of moral values until, in these writers and others, swindling became not merely a realistic ingredient of their narratives, but a symbol of a moral bankruptcy as well.

In a world where the highest values appeared to be mocked and the basest cherished, madness—which society at large was coming to view more humanely—seemed less an aberration cutting the individual off from normal human intercourse than an enviable escape to less corrupted realms of existence. Dowson's bedlamite was a pathetic figure, it is true, but not so sad as he who could witness a cruel and tawdry reality and not achieve the comforting illusions of madness. In a related manner, whereas the return home, especially by the repentant prodigal, had always constituted a reassuring conclusion to a tale of moral or material waywardness, in the later nineteenth century, it was the wanderer who returned home bearing gifts, the outcast who returned to aid those whom he had left long ago. The prodigal returns to demonstrate that those at home are morally akin to himself. He returns to bestow, not receive gifts. Those who stay at home, snugly consolidating what appears to be a more and more banal and hypocritical existence, are the ones who require forgiveness or redemption.

Similarly, orphans, while they represent, as in Mary Shelley's writings, a craving for lost affection, which becomes, in Mrs. Browning's *Aurora Leigh* representative of a metaphysical *Sehnsucht*, also imply a conviction that self-help, from the very beginning, is preferable to an existence conditioned by strict social conventions. Literary orphans, for the most part, are better off for being alone, despite perfunctory sorrowing at their condition. In orphanhood is a freedom not available to the products of a definite, respectable position, as Butler's *The Way of All Flesh* seems to emphasize.

If orphans ceased to prefer discovered parents and sought instead a self-created identity, the inheritance so often associated with orphans and long-lost offspring also altered its function. It had represented a simple material reward in the form of estates and identities, as well as a spiritual reward in heaven or in this world, but it gradually came to signify as well an awareness of the heritage of all men in individual qualities; the integrity of the self became the true inheritance for which each man might wisely labor.

But integrity of the self was the most difficult achievement. What began as a mere convention of adventure matured as a device for examining the hidden characteristics of human nature. Disguises, whether in the form of false beards and costumes, or deceptive modes of behavior, led in many narratives of the century to discoveries of the multiplicity of the self. Man's doubleness, or worse, was a natural discovery for men who acknowledged their nation as the homeland of hypocrisy. Jekyll always bore in him a Hyde, Dorian Gray must always have a hidden picture. No man is what he seems. And yet, for many, consciously wearing masks or playing roles seemed preferable to the pretence of a secure and identifiable self. At the same time, the preponderance of assumed identities in the literature of the age, while it shows an ordinary interest in tales of detection, mystery and adventure, also implies a covert, and sometimes obvious desire to achieve an identity other than that imposed by circumstance.

A similar longing to escape a respectable, conventional and stifling identity is evident in the literary glorification of the gypsy. While, in reality, these outcasts of society were distrusted and abused by a society supposedly concerned with order and respectability, in literature gypsies became spokesmen of the free life and occult knowledge; they were even hailed as preservers of man's most valuable sentiments.

If none of these modes of escape was practicable, neither was that other perennial ambition of escaping the present through a return to the past or a visit to the future. Memory has always been viewed as both a blessing and a bane, for while it preserves valued experiences, it retains as well the plagues of sorrow and guilt. So Tennyson and other writers of the time conceived of memory. But it also became a conventional device for implying discontent with an immediate reality and a device for indicating values either lost, or, in the case of futuristic visitations, not yet attained. But from the beginning, memory was a desperate alternative, for it was more and more evident to men that retreats into the self, into personal memory, or cultural recollection, could scarcely cure present ills. Nor could the past be revived in the present, as some, like William Morris, might wish. Still, later ambitious schemes, such as those described by Yeats and Jung, implied in their way, as Freud's did in his, that memory was a tool for dealing with an antagonistic present reality. It was not escape, but accommodation.

Only through the occult, so long as it could be believed, was there a genuine hope for escape. In various forms of occultism, from simple superstition to the pseudo-sciences growing out of mesmerism, to the esotericism of Madame Blavatsky, to the spiritualism that had such a credible vogue in the late nineteenth century, there was a latent promise of escape from an unappealing present earthly existence to a realm free from material cares. Bulwer-Lytton's *Zanoni* was not the first narrative suggesting regions beyond the everyday where man could voyage bodiless and free, or live beyond the normal term, or view past and future with equal clarity.[2] But the dreams of spiritual communication and liberation faded in time. The last escape out of this world was closed. Before long a grim reality of the everyday world would call men back to the task of the present and convince them that work in this world was the only escape. The conventions of Victorian literature did not disappear altogether after the Great War, but those that survived were for the most part markedly altered.

NINETEENTH-CENTURY MODE OF STYLIZATION

The conventions of eighteenth-century fiction were not much removed from those of the century to follow. Long-lost heirs, orphans, shocking madnesses, and so forth occur in many narratives of Smollett, Fielding and others, and become even more prominent in Gothic fiction, where madness, disguise, memory, and deathbeds take on a lurid cast.[3] But in the Victorian period a different sort of moral scheme informs many of these traditional conventions, though they lived on as well in their most superficial form—as some Hogarth House Gem Pocket Library titles suggest[4]—and survived Victoria's death in tales like William de Morgan's *An Affair of Dishonour* (1909), that suffers an abundance of the creaky conventions, including duels, altered identities, witchcraft and the like.

But Victorians had a characteristic manner of conceiving their narratives. "Ah! yes;" Thackeray exclaimed in *The Newcomes*, "all stories are old," and went on to describe the Biblical prototypes repeated among the crowds gathered at Baden. (Vol. 1, ch. 28) Biblical patterns proliferate in his fiction and even serve as the bases for narrative structures. *The Adventures of Philip* is a modern version of the Good Samaritan parable, and William H. Marshall suggests that the frontispiece in old Osborne's family Bible, representing Abraham sacrificing Isaac, "becomes a kind of emblem for Vanity Fair, where, one after another, sons are sacrificed and an alien world remains."[5] Moreover, in a traditional manner, revived for the nineteenth century largely through the influence of Wordsworth's writings, poets and novelists sought in everyday experience and natural objects, emblems of moral import. The characters in Coventry Patmore's poem, "Tamerton Church-Towers," gazing at a picturesque scene and noting the weather, self-consciously perceive in themselves the impulse to elicit from their observations "Some sentimental homily / On Duty, Death, or Man."

Moralizing was accepted because such secular homilies implied a spiritual purpose in being. Moralizing of this kind was, in fact, a habit largely derived from exposure to numerous sermons of the time. Some of the best sermons in nineteenth-century England were composed and delivered by Frederick W. Robertson, who addressed himself to the theme of the orphan in "The Orphanage of Moses," which, while emphasizing a Biblical prototype, brought the subject home to an immediate condition. Having described the infant Moses' danger when abandoned to the river, Robertson says, "Such is the state of orphanage. Because it is unprotected, it is therefore exposed to terrible evils. There are worse evils than the Nile, the crocodile, or starvation."[6] For, in Victorian England, "it is true that to say that a girl is unprotected, fatherless, and poor, is almost equivalent to saying that she will fall into sin."[7] The model is ancient, traditional and hallowed, but the application is current and imperative. Robertson preached this sermon as a plea for his audience to support a Female Orphan Asylum in need of funds to continue its charitable work.

Robertson dealt with another type familiar to readers of this book in his sermon on "The Prodigal and His Brother," where, in the most conventional manner he drew a three-fold lesson from the story. This parable, he said, exhibits the alienation of man's heart from God, indicates the unsatisfying nature of worldly happiness, and shows that a life of irreligion is a degradation. The man who returns to his spiritual home comes back to servitude at first, not freedom. The sinful man who has been the victim of his ungovernable propensities is "an object of compassion rather than of condemnation."[8] It was to this sorrow of human existence that Christ was drawn. "That which was melancholy, and marred, and miserable in this world, was more congenial to the heart of Christ than that which is proudly happy."[9] The true and faithful Christian, signified in the Elder Brother of the parable, must therefore accept God's mysterious way and manifest a generous thankfulness for the redemption of the sinner, not a selfish jealousy. It is not difficult to see how a sermon of this nature fell in with the nineteenth-century fascination with suffering and marred grandeur and prepared the way for the acceptance and even exaltation of the redeemed sinner above the smug and workaday saint. Nor is it difficult to see how closely related such sermons were in spirit to the Victorian narrative mode, which assumed both a moral scheme and employed emblematic devices.

NINETEENTH-CENTURY RESTLESSNESS

Moralizing of this nature, whether clerical or secular, was part of a broader movement described by Cazamian as the "Idealistic Reaction."[10] In fact, this impulse was simply the Romantic yearning for transcendence. The idealization of the Ideal, if I may so phrase it was an ultimately frustrating act, for it bred a serious discontent with the real. Discontent with immediate reality begot, in turn, a desire to fly from conventional existence. Associated with the nineteenth-century urge to escape the ordinary was a definite rebelliousness against conventional existence. Devendra P. Varma has described the way in which Gothic fiction represented a revolutionary spirit and embodied a definite form of social protest.[11] Kenneth Clark remarks that "the Gothic novelists screamed—screamed in complete reaction to everything stuffy and probable."[12] In this reaction was their one resemblance to the spirit of Gothic in the architectural revival of the time.

Both in literature and in life, Romantic writers displayed symptoms of rebellion. Chateaubriand's René fled from society and civilization, and Chateaubriand did the same. "The quest of the highly sophisticated scion of an old European aristocracy for the savage way of life, his 'emigration from the world,' to use his own descriptive phrase," is characteristic.[13] But the Romantic restlessness was equally evident in Byron's career, and the theme of the Wanderer—a commonplace of literature—became a favorite with nineteenth-century authors, especially after the violent revival of the theme in Gothic fiction, particularly such novels as Godwin's *St. Leon* and Maturin's *Melmoth the Wanderer*.[14] The wandering urge was as strong in the Victorian years as it was earlier, manifesting itself in numerous accounts of travellers—of adventurous missionaries such as Mungo Park or David Livingstone; adventurers and explorers like Sir Richard Burton or Samuel Baker; and interested travellers such as Sir Basil Hall or Anthony Trollope. In poetry, wanderers were not so wild as Melmoth; Owen Meredith's *The Wanderer* is patterned more upon Byron's *Childe Harold*, duly toned down to a melancholy acceptable to Victorian audiences. The urge was still evident in writers of the later part of the century. William Sharp and Arthur Symons, for example, both testified to an impulsive restlessness, though for the most part this wanderlust was frustrated in them. With Richard Le Gallienne, the wandering urge had dwindled to a form of nostalgia, as in a way it did with Wilde, who dramatized his late, outcast years under the assumed name of Sebastian Melmoth. In "The Wandering Home," Le Gallienne explains that "For the average, or, if you prefer, the normal temperament, the world seems insecure unless it has assured for itself, by irrefragable legal holdfasts, a lifelong anchorage in the treacherous stream of existence."[15] For others, he says, such fixedness implies mortality, and to his view the best life avoids as much as possible contemplation of its end. Meanwhile, "Life is, and must be, made up of the same things. But the art of life is to make ourselves forget that they are the same things—the art and the problem."[16]

Le Gallienne's essay reveals a diminution of the Paterian creed. Though each moment must be valued and all of life converted to an art, Le Gallienne would achieve this aim by external movement—an induced action to break the monotonous inertia of the ordinary, whereas Pater sought to achieve proportion and harmony by having the self put itself into the flow and change of experience in general. In the latter case, the excitement and delight arises from an internal authority over impressions; in the former instance, external impressions bombard a jaded sensibility to keep it alert. The yearning for movement and escape from the humdrum in Le Gallienne is banal— a mere matter of changing scene. It contrasts with the impulsive travels of a Richard Burton, who seemed to devour new experiences and digest them, not merely look, nod approval, and pass on.

Arthur Symons, closer to Pater's philosophy, had his own version of it. "We shall not find ourselves in drawing-rooms or in museums," he says, echoing William Morris. "A man who goes through a day without some fine emotion has wasted his day, whatever he has gained in it. And it is easy to go through day after day, busily and agreeably, without ever really living for a single instant. Art begins when a man wishes to immortalize the most vivid moment he has ever lived. Life has already, to one not an artist, become art in that moment. And the making of one's life into art is after all the first duty and privilege of every man."[17] Nonetheless, for Symons that art required the stimulation of movement as he indicates in his poem, "Wanderers," in which he describes those continually amove while "life, a long white road, / Winds ever from the dark into the dark, / And they, as days, return not." Still, they have the freedom and freshness of movement toward something new, abandoning the past.

Wanderers, you have the sunrise and the stars;
And we, beneath our comfortable roofs,

Lamplight, and daily fire upon the hearth,
And four walls of a prison, and sure food.
But God has given you freedom, wanderers!

It was this nostalgia for a freedom and sense of unconstrainedness that led many writers and members of their audience to imagine in the figure of the gypsy a type of liberty, and a boundless possibility for mystery, adventure, and the exertion of the individual will. Similarly, many writers throughout the century, from Coleridge, Cobbett and Carlyle, to Ruskin and Morris, appreciated the feudalistic medieval past above the ugliness of the modern world. "Bad as feudal times were," Southey wrote, "they were less injurious than these commercial ones to the kindly and generous feelings of human nature."[18] But less hopeful voices saw in this backward glancing a futile parody of art. To Amiel, *le grande monde*, with its elegance and fastidiousness was an unconscious means of exchanging associations of reality for associations of imagination.

> So understood, society is a form of poetry; the cultivated classes deliberately recompose the idyll of the past, and the buried world of Astraea. Paradox or not, I believe that these fugitive attempts to reconstruct a dream, whose only end is beauty, represent confused reminiscences of an age of gold haunting the human heart; or rather, aspirations towards a harmony of things which everyday reality denies to us, and of which art alone gives us a glimpse.[19]

As we have already seen, some men looked back not to the cultural or racial past, but to an individual past preceding human awareness. Coventry Patmore, in his poem, "The Yewberry," wrote specifically of glimpses of ante-natal experience.

At times, some gap in sequence frees the spirit,
    and, anon,

We remember of states of living ended ere we
    left the womb,
And see a vague aurora flashing to us from the
    tomb,
The dreamy light of new states, dashed tremendously
    with gloom.

> We tremble for an instant, and a single instant
>   more
> Brings absolute oblivion, and we pass on as before!

But James Sully warned that memory was capricious and its very illusions indicated that "our consciousness of personal identity is by no means the simple and exact process which it is commonly supposed to be."[20] Moreover, error in perception was not the rare event, but the common fact. "Our luminous circle of rational perception is surrounded by a misty penumbra of illusion."[21] In elaborating this view, Sully was merely expressing a long evident sense of his times; writers had, for some time, concerned themselves on many levels with the infiltration of "rational perception" by illusions. This sense might become manifest in illusions of identity, where the convention of disguise became prominent. Some writers, like William Sharp, fostered in themselves the sense of imposture and fantasized about their origins, while others, like Max Beerbohm, extolled the virtues of appearances over realities. But there were more commonplace reasons for distrusting the illusion of coherence, not the least of which involved the commercial events of the age. When, for example, the firm of Messrs. Harman and Co. failed in the crisis of 1847, no one had suspected how very rotten it was beneath its outward prosperity. As Dickens announced soon after in *Dombey and Son*, financial bankruptcy was only one form of failure arising from only one form of fraud.

SOCIAL DISSATISFACTION AND DESIRE FOR ESCAPE

It was disgust with England's "commercial mire," as Tennyson called it, that led many to wish for some form of escape.[22] The central character of *Maud* deplores the mammonry of his time but realizes that his inner world is no better organized than the commercial jungle around him. The narrator of "Locksley Hall" also wishes to escape from the stifling social atmosphere of England. Many writers, who, like Tennyson, never really did flee from the society they claimed was oppressive, continued to abuse that society. There is more bite, though, in jibes by those who had fled, returned, and fled again. Thus Sir Richard Burton's contemptuous treatment of British customs, attitudes and practices, especially in *Stone Talk*, offers a sharp example of informed discontent. Milder, but no less critical, was Owen Meredith's satire, *King Poppy*.

But with better writers such as Dickens, Collins, Reade, Trollope, Hardy and Gissing all offering sterner and sterner criticisms of their society's failures, there is no need to turn to less prominent writers for evidence, except to indicate how widespread and various these sentiments were. Gissing, for example, viewed the evils of society as part of "a cosmic necessity too powerful for human resources to resist."[23] Marie Corelli was equally appalled at what human society was doing to itself—particularly, its young. Childhood, Heliobas says, in *A Romance of Two Worlds*, "is being gradually stamped out under the cruel iron heel of the Period—a period not of wisdom, health, or beauty, but one of drunken delirium, in which the world rushes feverishly along, its eyes fixed on one hard glittering, stony-featured idol —Gold." (ch. 15) But Corelli ends her novel with her narrator's appeal to her readers to think about their lives and not to deny God lightly. Consider, she says, where our progress may lead, for our wills are free and we live in a universe powered by love. (ch. 17)

OPTIMISM AND PESSIMISM

To a certain extent, Victorian thinking was divided into optimistic and pessimistic channels.[24] There is no need for me to go over ground so ably examined and presented already in Part One of Walter E. Houghton's *The Victorian Frame of Mind*. A few examples should serve. The basic optimistic view of the Victorian age was that of material progress and with it the more exalted concept of spiritual evolution. Robert Browning had his vision of man's progress toward perfection in *Paracelsus*, his wife hers at the end of *Aurora Leigh*; William Whewell described mankind's movement toward angelic status in *The Plurality of Worlds*;[25] Tennyson hinted at an ultimate scheme in *In Memoriam*, and one of Owen Meredith's characters in *Lucile* describes his vision of "the whole / Vast design of the ages," of "infinite art, / In infinite power proving infinite love," explaining "The divine Whence and Wither of life!" (Book 1, canto 4, sec. 21)

Some felt that this progress was not confined to external events or to perceptions of a vast providential scheme but arose from within man himself. R. H. Horne wrote, early in the century, "each soul may to itself . . . Become both Time and Nature . . . And in the Universal Movement join." (*Orion*, Book 3, canto 3) Frederic Myers conceded that the times he and his contemporaries lived in were bad, but said they were so because men were divided in their attitudes and lacked belief. Man's true aim, he urged in *Human Personality*, was spiritual evolution. William Carpenter specified how this spiritual evolution might be accelerated through the improvement of each individual. "In the higher grades of Mental development," he wrote, "there is a continual looking-upwards, not (as in the lower) towards a more elevated Human standard, but at once to something *beyond* and *above* Man and material nature." And if our incentive to intellectual efforts is the love of truth, goodness and beauty we are "not only elevating *ourselves* towards our Ideal, but contributing to the elevation of our race."[26]

The late nineteenth century saw many Utopian schemes based upon notions of this kind. William Morris' *News from Nowhere* and Richard Jeffries' *After London: or, Wild England*, are examples of a recovery of a future that may repeat the best elements of the agrestic past. One discursive work that caught the imagination of late-century readers was William Winwood Reade's *The Martyrdom of Man* (1872), which presented a thoroughly secular, Darwinian progress of man toward an ideal society. Reade surveyed human culture, describing a gradual advance through the stages of War, Religion, and Liberty toward that of Intellect. In a passage resembling ideas in Swinburne and Samuel Butler, he says: "As drops in the ocean of water, as atoms in the ocean of air, as sparks in the ocean of fire within the earth, our minds do their appointed work and serve to build up the strength and beauty of the one great Human Mind which grows from century to century, from age to age, and is perhaps itself a mere molecule within some higher mind."[27] Reade asserts that man must abandon illusions of a hereafter, since it is through science alone that man's destiny will be fulfilled. Mastering the forces of nature, man will become perfect, "he will then be a creator; he will therefore be what the vulgar worship as a God."[28] After a season of mental anguish, Reade felt, man would attain a "heavenly Commune," and would labor together in "the Sacred Cause—the extinction of disease, the extinction of sin, the perfection of genius, the perfection of love, the invention of immortality, the exploration of the infinite, the conquest of creation."[29]

Equally scientific in its pretentions and likewise popular with the reading public, was the Canadian, Richard Maurice Bucke's *Cosmic Consciousness: A Study in the Evolution of the Human Mind* (1901), which charted the gradual advance not of man's physical progress, but of his mental stages from simple physical perception to a Cosmic Consciousness opening his mind to the oneness of existence and the rule of love that orders the universe. These ideas had been adumbrated in other earlier writers. Bucke's ideal is a state of being recommended also by Theodore Watts-Dunton in his popular novel, *Aylwin*, and elsewhere, and termed by him the Renascence of Wonder.

Sir Charles Tennyson remarked that *The Martyrdom of Man* "had a powerful effect" upon Tennyson, but that leaves us to wonder if the effect was cheering or depressing.[30] After all, it can easily be argued that hopeful projections like Reade's, or Morris', were just as concerned with escape from present reality as other speculations involving escape into the self or into art. J. O. Bailey's *Pilgrims Through Space and Time: Trends and Patterns in Scientific and Utopian Fiction*, reveals how much of nineteenth-century thought was concerned with the possibility of removal to an alien sphere of existence, especially in fancy or by fanciful means. Utopianism itself could be a form of escapism, like madness or spiritualism. Other conventions represented similar disguised retreats from immediate realities. Peter Coveney explains how the nostalgic cult of the child in the late nineteenth century represented a failure of adjustment. Such cultists "indulged nostalgia because they refused or failed to come to sensitive terms with the cultural realities of the time. Regret for childhood takes on the same obsessive emotional quality as the exile's nostalgia for home. Certain artists at the end of the century were clearly very much abroad in an alien world."[31]

In his study of H. G. Wells, Bernard Bergonzi gave a broad definition of the *fin de siècle* as "the expression of a prevalent mood: a feeling that the nineteenth century—which had contained more events, more history than any other—had gone on too long, and that sensitive souls were growing weary of it."[32] James Sully had his own contemporary view of the growing pessimism of his age.

> Now this temper of the European mind seems to be accounted for partly as a form of intellectual cynicism, called forth by religious scepticism, and a sense of the hollowness of the last century optimism, partly as the depressing reaction after a period of extraordinary emotional tension, and of exalted confidence in ideal aims. In its earlier manifes-

tations it was the apparent failure of a social and political ideal which brought about this state of despondency. In more recent years, the collapse of the extravagant aspirations and endeavours of certain aesthetic schools, has probably perpetuated, if it has not deepened, the pessimistic mood.[33]

It seems that the profound *Weltschmerz* of the Romantic movement, after some decades of partial latency, had emerged again in sharp conflict with hopeful views. During the greater part of the nineteenth century, a sense of hope and positive anticipation for the future prevailed, but as the century neared its end, a growing discontent and distrust challenged what became more shrill defenses of the world to come. This despondency might be attributed to any number of causes—a failing belief in a benevolent universal design, an anxiety about material circumstances, a doubt about the nature of human personality. Whatever the cause, the result was clear: the design no longer attributed to divinity was now to be preserved in literature. The divided modern self, itself related to, if not derived from, Hegelian dichotomies, disintegrated into a fascination with masks and hidden, darker, unconscious attributes of the psyche. The Victorian conviction that striving was good, though it led to suffering (which was also beneficial), produced a code exalting the capacity for renunciation from Goethe to Carlyle to Eliot; but this very acknowledgment of the ubiquity of human misery, without a divine purpose to redeem it, transformed the formerly noble renunciation into Schopenhauer's fierce denial of the will to live and Dowson's mild refusal to persist. The opposition of a residual optimism and a waxing pessimism begot an ironic attention to conventionalities. Representatives of the *fin de siècle* had in common "a contempt for traditional views of custom and morality," and for conventions of art and thought as well.[34] Oscar Wilde loved to affront both literary and social conventions not by denying them, but by stylizing them in the extreme. George Meredith subtly elaborated some of the most cherished conventions in a manner resembling Thackeray's, while writers such as Thomas Hardy and George Gissing imitated Dickens' directness, though not his incredible intricacy. Hardy's alertness to the effect of reversing conventions is revealed in *The Hand of Ethelberta* where Mrs. Doncastle exclaims with ill-concealed dismay, "The times have taken a strange turn when the angry parent of the comedy, who goes post-haste to prevent the undutiful daughter's rash marriage, is a gentleman from below stairs, and the unworthy lover a peer of the realm!" (ch. 42)

CONCLUSION

Neil D. Isaacs, in an essay on Old English poetry, explained that what counts in literary conventions is the differing, not the adhering.[35] I have tried to concentrate on the various shades of difference, hoping thereby that the less exciting common elements of the conventions would thereby become apparent. While dealing with these conventions I have kept in mind Louis James' wise caution. "Even with literature consistently chosen by a mass audience for casual reading," he says, "while the results will show mental attitudes, it is important not to take the implications of these too far, for ideals accepted in reading are not necessarily those accepted in real life."[36] Still, I have also accepted Northrop Frye's assumption that "At any given period of literature the conventions of literature are enclosed within a total mythological structure, which may not be explicitly known to anyone, but is nevertheless present as a shaping principle."[37] The Victorian "mythology" was basically the Christian faith and, even when Victorian authors departed from actual religious tenets, as, for example, George Eliot did, they yet retained the moral schemes that were a part of that creed. And, just as German Romantic writers converted the stale conventions of the preceding century into profound emblems, so writers of the nineteenth century in England revealed, either consciously or unconsciously, significances beyond the level of mere surface events.[38]

James Wright observed that "It is characteristic of Dickens throughout his career that he was able to use a variety of literary conventions for the fulfillment of some deeper imaginative intention."[39] Believing Dickens to be an outstanding performer in this regard, I have had frequent reference to his novels to demonstrate the uses certain conventions could be put to. Thus I have written at some length about his use of disguise in works such as *Bleak House* and *Our Mutual Friend*, or about his treatment of female types, of the swindle convention, and so on. I might have used Thackeray to a greater extent than I have, because he is so playful, though obvious, in his toying with literary conventions. But I have chosen to forego some major works and authors in order to examine a good deal of insignificant literature because I believe that it is in that subworld of literary history that the truths about great literature must be tested and proven.

Stylization in literature is a way of consolidating and preserving the state of the times. By understanding the forms that stylization takes, one may discover anxieties and hopes of the audiences who accept such conventions. Insofar as writers alter, attack, or ironically reverse stylizations or conventions, these conventions become indicators of new modes of perception, and often of some form of discontent as well. Ordinarily, the preoccupations of an age would seem to be represented best in its intellectual and reflective literature, but it might equally be argued that popular literature is as good an indicator of cultural sentiments. Mrs. Margaret Oliphant, discussing the subject of success in literature, admires the "fine workmanship" of Henry James, but adds that his "inconclusive renderings of a life too full of motive . . . naturally gives the fascinated yet unsatisfied reader an appetite for the downright effects of Mr. Rider Haggard." Haggard's brand of fiction represents a return to clarity, simplicity, and action. "This," Mrs. Oliphant says, "is quite enough to account for the sudden surging up of the ancient legend of adventure and movement, amidst a society which has had its fill of philosophy, of domesticity, of criticism, and all the analytical processes."[40] Thus, although Hardy's novels ironically bludgeoned the old conventions and commandeered them to present a new message, a novel like She, through its exaggerations, consolidated what Hardy sought to uproot. Ayesha is the Judith figure exalted to near divine proportions. She is as well a Magdalene potentially (though not probably) open to the redemptive power of love. She lives a centuries-long life, feeding on Memory and Hope, which, in the return of Leo Vincy, becomes reality in the present. In a similar fashion, Bram Stoker's Dracula and The Lair of The White Worm, through the use of the occult, employ the convention of disguise not to mask a thief or wicked seducer, but to cloak a monster of immeasurable evil in Count Dracula, or an ancient evil power in Lady Arabella March.

These brief examples merely indicate some simple reasons why all forms of literature are important while investigating literary conventions. We have already seen, for example, how H. G. Wells' popular tales embody a world view that would not be immediately evident to the everyday reader, but which becomes obvious to a subsequent generation. Robert Cromie's *Crack of Doom* (1895) is a good instance of this fact. Underlying this science fiction tale of a warped genius who plans to destroy the world and thereby return the universe to a state of rest, is a sense, characteristic of the century's close, that beneath ordinary appearances, evil, not good, is the force that makes for vital movement. Immortality, if not an illusion, is treated as a tedious prospect; science becomes a menace rather than a boon; and love is put forth as the sole redemptive power available to man. Hence, a popular science fiction novel embodies, in simplified and exaggerated form, the same concepts and assumptions that prompt more thoughtful and more skillful literary productions.

I have tried to show the way in which literary conventions, in a variety of modes, operate as technical devices and means of gaining insight about a historical period. I have as well tried to indicate that many views that we hold concerning the Victorian period must be qualified by attitudes revealed in the conventions of its literature. Unquestionably, I have only touched the surface of a vast ocean of material; but I hope that in my ambitious desire to project a large scheme illustrating some form of development not only chronologically, but from simple to complex forms of expression, I have not blundered too egregiously and that these beginnings may prove useful to the more precise investigations that they invite.

NOTES

PREFACE

1. This is by no means a recent convention. In the nineteenth century it is represented by Mary Shelley's *The Last Man* and other works mentioned by Elizabeth Nitchie in *Mary Shelley: Author of "Frankenstein"* (New Brunswick, New Jersey, 1953), p. 152.

2. Louis James, "The Rational Amusement: 'Minor' Fiction and Victorian Studies," *Victorian Studies* 14, no. 2, (1970): 193-99. Review of Myron F. Brightfield's *Victorian England in its Novels 1840-70.*

3. Richard D. Altick, "Victorian Readers and the Sense of the Present," *Midway* 10, no. 4 (1970): 95-96.

CHAPTER ONE: INTRODUCTION

1. W. L. Burn, *The Age of Equipoise: A Study of the Mid-Victorian Generation* (London, 1964), p. 246.

2. Studies demonstrating the emblematic or iconographic qualities in various periods of English literature include D. W. Robertson, *A Preface to Chaucer: Studies in Medieval Perspectives* (Princeton, 1962); Rosamund Tuve, *Allegorical Imagery: Some Medieval Books and Their Posterity* (Princeton, 1966); J. Paul Hunter, *The Reluctant Pilgrim: Defoe's Emblematic Method and Quest for Form in Robinson Crusoe* (Baltimore, 1966); Alexander Welsh, "'The Allegory of Truth in English Fiction," *Victorian Studies*, 9, 7-28; Gillian Beer, "Charles Kingsley and the Literary Image of the Countryside," *Victorian Studies*, 8, 243-54.

3. Anthony Trollope, *Thackeray* (London, 1887), p. 185.

4. Ibid., p. 196.

5. Robert Louis Stevenson, "A Note on Realism," *Essays in the Art of Writing* (London, 1910), p. 102. In "The Morality of the Profession of Letters," Stevenson listed the first and second duties of a writer as being "intellectual" and "moral," (pp. 64-65) and the two important classes of facts as "those which are coloured, picturesque, human, and rooted in morality," and those "which are clear, indisputable, and a part of science." (pp. 60-61)

6. There is, for example, a well-argued defense of physiognomy as distinguished from phrenology, in the *Cornhill Magazine*, October, 1861. Also, see my later chapter on disguise, where some references to physiognomy and phrenology occur.

7. Victorians could readily credit both attitudes at the same time:
It [the novel] may be true to its object of giving us the external aspects of human life, of setting forth those moral and social phenomena we have spoken of; may delight us with characters so painted that fiction becomes reality; and may yet attune our minds to the music of the spheres. . . . Writing as one who aims always at discerning and being true to the deeper, underlying truth of things, [the novelist] will show you the meaning of those phenomena; he will reflect not only the thought of the age, but will prepare our minds for the thought of the future." ("The Novels of George Meredith," *British Quarterly Review*, 69 (1879), pp. 411-13, quoted by Graham, *English Criticism of the Novel, 1865-1900*, p. 8.)
In *Anthony Trollope and His Contemporaries* (New York, 1972) David Skilton emphasizes the same capacity of audiences to entertain moral and material considerations simultaneously.

8. F. D. Maurice, "Preface" to Charles Kingsley's *The Saint's Tragedy* in *Poems* (London, 1891), pp. 6-7.

9. Leslie Stephen, "Art and Morality," *The Cornhill Magazine* 32 (1875), p. 101.

10. Lionel Stevenson, *The English Novel. A Panorama* (Boston, 1960), p. 291. Of course one must always keep in mind that the pretense and the practice of morality might not always have been at one. For example, panderers of "true-murder literature" during the nineteenth century also boasted of their moral nature. See Richard Altick's, *Victorian Studies in Scarlet: Murders and Manners in the Age of Victoria* (New York, 1970), p. 66.

11. Anne's stern position is echoed by Charlotte when she replies to her editors, "*You* both of you dwell too much on what you regard as the *artistic* treatment of a subject. Say what you will, gentlemen, say it as ably as you will—truth is better than art." (Letter to Mr. Williams, 2, April 1849, quoted by Winifred Gérin in *Charlotte Brontë: The Evolution of a Genius* [Oxford, 1967], p. 393).

12. John R. Reed, *Perception and Design in Tennyson's Idylls of the King* (Athens, Ohio, 1969).

13. Critics such as Jerome H. Buckley in *The Victorian Temper: A Study in Literary Culture* (New York, 1964), p. 92, and Dwight Culler in *Imaginative Reason: The Poetry of Matthew Arnold* (New Haven, 1966), pp. 4-5, among others, have noted this pattern.

14. Margaret Dalziel makes this point more than once in *Popular Fiction 100 Years Ago: an Unexplored Tract of Literary History* (London, 1957).

15. H. G. Schenk has written that "In marked opposition to the optimism of the Enlightenment, the Romantics can be said to have rediscovered human suffering" (*The Mind of the European Romantics* [Garden City, 1969], p. 100). But it can be argued that the Victorians, equally aware of the reality of human suffering, found it an earnest of eventual reward.

16. S. M. Ellis points out that the "hero of the virile novel" of the forties and fifties was a commonplace when Lawrence took up the type (*Wilkie Collins, Le Fanu, and Others* [London, 1951], p. 198).

17. R. H. Horne, "Commentary," *Orion. An Epic Poem* (London, 1872), p. v.

18. Similar uses of musical performances which contribute to their novels' structures occur in *Martin Chuzzlewit* with Tom Pinch's organ playing, and E. M. Forster's *Howards End* at the performance of Beethoven's Fifth Symphony.

19. Samuel Warren, "Intriguing and Madness," *Passages from the Diary of a Late Physician*, (Edinburgh, 1838), p. 147.

20. Aurelia Brooks Harlan says, in *Owen Meredith: A Critical Biography of Robert, First Earl of Lytton* (New York, 1946), that the circumstances of this poem are largely autobiographical.

21. See U. C. Knoepflmacher, *Laughter & Despair: Readings in Ten Novels of the Victorian Era* (Berkeley, 1971), pp. 231ff.

22. The next chapter, chapter 30, is entitled "The Expiation."

23. Thomas Mann, "The Making of *The Magic Mountain*," in *The Magic Mountain*, Trans. H. T. Lowe-Porter (New York, n.d.), pp. 724-25.

24. Suffering could also have its secular rewards. Many Victorian heroines, like Gertrude St. Clair, in Ferrier's *Marriage*, or Ethel Newcome in *The Newcomes*, are only more interesting and attractive, if less beautiful, for having suffered.

25. F. D. Maurice, *The Doctrine of Sacrifice, Deduced from Scriptures: Sermons* (Cambridge, 1854), p. 66.

26. See such recent works as: J. Paul Hunter's *The Reluctant Pilgrim* (Baltimore, 1966); Paul J. Korshin's "Swift and Typological Narrative in *A Tale of a Tub*" in *The Interpretation of Narrative: Theory and Practice*, ed. Morton W. Bloomfield (Cambridge, Mass., 1970), pp. 67-91; John M. Steadman's "Falstaff as Actaeon: A Dramatic Emblem," *Shakespeare Quarterly* (1965), pp. 231-36; and James Hoyle's "Some Emblems in Shakespeare's Henry IV Plays," *ELH* 38, no. 4 (1971), pp. 512-27.

27. One must not forget the graphic parallel in this case, since Dickens might easily have intended an echo of Hogarth's "Progress" illustrations. See John Harvey, *Victorian Novelists and Their Illustrators* (New York, 1971).

28. See Chapter Two, in which some pictorial associations and representations are discussed as they relate to female types in Victorian literature.

29. See John Harvey, *Victorian Novelists and Their Illustrators*, passim. Michael Steig examines the subject in "The Iconography of *David Copperfield*," *Hartford Studies in Literature* 2, no. 1 (1970), pp. 1-18.

30. Allusive and overt references to Renaissance emblem books in Victorian fiction indicate how present to the mind emblematic figures remained, as in George Eliot's description of the world as an udder for fools to suck, in *Middlemarch*, Book 2, ch. 21.

31. In Book Four of *The Prelude*, Wordsworth sees a brook as emblematic of life, and in Book Fourteen a mountain view becomes emblematic of the sublime poetic mind. In a sense the whole poem concerns itself with emblematic perception, since it deals with the poet's ability to recognize emblems of moral states in natural scenes and objects.

32. See Gillian Avery, *Nineteenth Century Children: Heroes and Heroines in English Children's Stories, 1780-1900* (London, 1965) for a description of how allegorical and stylized children's stories could be.

33. W. J. Linton quoted by Louis James in *Fiction for the Working Man 1830-1850* (London, 1963), p. 65. John Killham approves of the word "emblem" to describe the kinds of symbols Dickens uses often in his fiction ("Pickwick: Dickens and the Art of Fiction," *Dickens and the Twentieth Century*, eds. John Gross and Gabriel Pearson [Toronto, 1962], p. 38), and Lionel Trilling employs the term in his introduction to the New Oxford edition of *Little Dorrit*.

34. A poem, "Emblems," which appeared in the March, 1850, issue of *The Germ*, and which is attributed to Thomas Woolner by Robert Stahr Hosmon in *The Germ:*

A Pre-Raphaelite Little Magazine (Coral Gables, Florida, 1970), simply lists a series of observations by the poet who converts, or interprets, each description emblematically.

35. See Walter C. Phillips, *Dickens, Reade and Collins* (New York, 1919), p. 127. Collins spoke precisely to this point in "A Petition to the Novelist" in *My Miscellanies*.

36. Quoted in Harlan, *Owen Meredith*, p. 126.

37. George Eliot humorously suggests that *Middlemarch*, and especially Fred Vincy's story (Book 4, ch. 36), might be read as a parable.

38. See also *Culture and Anarchy*, ch. 2.

39. Quoted by Walter Kaufmann in *Nietzsche: Philosopher, Psychologist, Antichrist* (New York, 1956), p. 219.

40. I am not implying that Arnold was the model for Grey, since it is well known that that office was supplied by T. H. Green.

41. See Chapter Two of this study for additional commentary on this subject.

42. Arnold himself recommended that poetry replace formal religion, thereby indicating that he approved the replacement of an exclusively moral organization of experience by an esthetic one.

43. K. M. Briggs, *The Fairies in English Tradition and Literature* (Chicago, 1967), p. 182. See also Avery, *English Children's Stories 1780-1900*, chapters 2 and 6 especially. There was a good deal of interest in nursery rhymes and fairy tales at this time. An article entitled "A Witch in the Nursery," *Household Words* (20 September, 1851), calls attention, for example, to the dreadful, even murderous, nature of many nursery rhymes.

44. See for example, Harry Stone's "Fire, Hand, and Gate: Dickens' *Great Expectations*," *Kenyon Review* 24, no. 4 (1962), pp. 662-91; "Dickens' Artistry and *The Haunted Man*," *South Atlantic Quarterly*, 61 (1962), pp. 492-505; and "The Novel as Fairy Tale: Dickens' *Dombey and Son*," *English Studies* 47 (1966), pp. 1-27. A recent study is devoted to the subject: Michael Kotzin, *Dickens and the Fairy Tale* (Bowling Green, Ohio, 1972).

45. Harvey, *Victorian Illustrators*, p. 69.

46. Thackeray used fairy-tale elements elsewhere in his fiction. In *The Adventures of Philip*, for example, the Cinderella motif recurs regularly.

47. These stories, by Anne Thackeray Ritchie, who collected her more traditional fairy tales in *Bluebeard's Keys and Other Stories* (1875), appeared as follows: "Sleeping Beauty" (May, 1866); "Cinderella" (June, 1866); "Beauty and the Beast" (June, 1867); "Red Riding Hood" (October, 1867); and "Jack the Giant-Killer" (November and December, 1867, and January, 1868).

48. Ritchie, "Cinderella," p. 74.

49. In the twentieth century, it seems as though more patterns for narratives begin to come from the classical sources, as in Joyce's *Ulysses*, or from preceding national classics, as with Thomas Mann's novels.

CHAPTER TWO: WOMEN

1. Katharine M. Rogers, *The Troublesome Helpmate: A History of Misogyny in Literature* (Seattle, 1966), p. 180.

2. The argument was carried on by figures such as J. S. Mill, H. Taylor, and H. Spencer.

3. Hazel Mews, *Frail Vessels: Woman's Role in Women's Novels from Fanny Burney to George Eliot* (London, 1969), p. 19.

4. Quoted by Aina Rubenius in *The Woman Question in Mrs. Gaskell's Life and Works* (Upsala, 1950), pp. 2-3.

5. Rogers, *Troublesome Helpmate*, p. 190.

6. Mews, *Frail Vessels*, p. 10.

7. Rogers, *Troublesome Helpmate*, p. 190.

8. Samuel Hynes, *The Edwardian Turn of Mind* (Princeton, 1968), p. 179.

9. As its title suggests, Lawrence's later novel, *Sans Merci* (1866), is concerned with women who are destructive toward men. They range from the low-born, but statuesque, Bessie Standen to the true Judith type, Flora Dorrillon, who at one point is likened to the "syren" in Noel Paton's painting of the figure leading men to destruction.

10. Rogers, *Troublesome Helpmate*, p. 193.

11. Cruikshank's use of "The History of Chaste Susannah" as a background detail in his illustration, "the name on the beam," for Ainsworth's *Jack Sheppard*, indicates how commonplace the association of threatened chastity and the Susannah story was for the ordinary reader. See John Harvey's explanation of this illustration in *Victorian Novelists and Their Illustrators* (New York, 1971), p. 46.

12. "The novels lack any supernatural or metaphysical framework; George Eliot is concerned solely with man's moral struggle in this world" (W. J. Harvey, *The Art of George Eliot* [London, 1961], p. 47).

13. Kenneth Graham is perhaps unfair to Eliot when he says that her novels "in their use of convention and the devices of melodrama," do not fulfill her declarations about realism, since he assumes that her realistic view could not contain convention and melodrama. There is no reason to suppose that these "inconsistencies" were not quite harmonious in a nineteenth-century view of the "real" world (*English Criticism of the Novel, 1865-1900* [Oxford, 1965], pp. 20-21.)

14. Both Rose and Agnes Leyburn refer to their sister as a Saint Elizabeth. When Robert Elsmere becomes acquainted with Catherine, we are told that "He, too, mentally compared her to Saint Elizabeth." (*Robert Elsmere*, ch. 3) Among other things, such a consistency of identification seems to assume a common knowledge of the saint.

15. J. P. Eggers remarks that "Some reviewers tried to find a respectable prototype for the Geraint idylls in Boccaccio's Griselda story" (*King Arthur's Laureate: A Study of Tennyson's Idylls of the King* (New York, 1971), pp. 85-86).

16. Edward Fitzgerald, *Letters & Literary Remains of Edward Fitzgerald*, 7 vols. (New York, 1966), 1, p. 102.

17. Adelaide Summers suffers the same kind of invalidism, more seriously, in Henry Kingsley's *Ravenshoe* (1861).

18. The German dramatist, Christian Friedrich Hebbel (1813-63), in his first drama, *Judith* (1840), while employing the traditional Biblical figure of Judith, enriched her character with a private psychological motivation while preserving her symbolic significance. In a letter to Madame Stich of 3 April 1840, Hebbel wrote: "Judith und Holofernes sind, obgleich, wenn ich meine Aufgabe löste, wahre Individualitäten, dennoch zugleich die Repräsentanten ihrer Völker. . . . Judentum und Heidentum aber sind wiederum nur Repräsentanten der von Anbeginn in einem unlösbaren Dualismus gespaltenen Menschheit; und so hat der Kampf, in dem die Elemente meiner Tragödie sich gegenseitig aneinander zerreiben, die höchste symbolische Bedeutung, obwohl er von der Leidenschaft entzündet und durch die Wallungen des Bluts und die Verirrungen der Sinne zu Ende gebracht wird" (quoted in *Hebbels Werke*, Zweiter Teil, herausgegeben von Theodor Poppe [Berlin, n.d.], p. 15). Interestingly enough, Hebbel seems to have gotten his idea for his drama from a painting of Judith in the Munich Gallery. The pictorial association is continually an intriguing aspect of the Judith emblem. Hebbel's interest in the emblematic types that fascinated Victorian writers was persistent, for he described another man-destroyer, Rhodope, in *Gyges*

und sein Ring (1856), again adding a dark psychological dimension; reanimated a medieval legend in *Genoveva* (1843); and composed an ironic tragedy upon the modern type of the traditional sinner in *Maria Magdalena* (1844). For a discussion of the comment upon the modern failure of Christianity in the play, see Jerry H. Glenn, "The Title of Hebbel's Maria Magdalena," *Papers on Language and Literature* (1967), pp. 122-23. Heinrich von Treitschke wrote in *Politics* (1897), "To modern poets Judith is a tragic figure, but to her contemporaries she appeared only as a heroine worthy of all fame." (*Politics*, trans. Blanche Dugdale and Turben de Bille [New York: Macmillan, 1916], vol. 1, p. 81.)

19.   Helen Osterman Borowitz, in "Visions of Salome," (*Criticism* [1972], pp. 12-21) describes some of the pictorial approaches to the Salome e. She describes the type's attractiveness to the decadents, especially in France, and aracterizes the figure as struggling with the "conflict between her virginal frigidity and her growing passion." (p. 15)

20.   In *A Pair of Blue Eyes* (1873), Thomas Hardy describes the manner in which the affected senses make of their object a mnemonic icon. Ironically enough, in this case it is a saintly figure, but the point is clearly made nonetheless. Just as a beloved is recollected with special iconographic attributes, so the emblematically bad tend to reappear with the attributes and accessories of their prototypes: Judiths, Jaels, Salomes or Circes.

> As the patron Saint has her attitude and accessories in medieval illumination, so the sweetheart may be said to have hers upon the tablet of her true Love's fancy, without which she is rarely introduced there except by effort; and this though she may, on further acquaintance, have been observed in many other phases which one would imagine to be far more appropriate to Love's young dream. (ch. 3)

The irony is greater yet, since Elfride hardly turns out to be a very useful patron Saint, though she is, in a remote sense, a martyr. This could be read as a comment upon the attempt to conceive of Victorian women as secular saints rather than as ordinary women.

21.   Quoted by Richard Altick in *Victorian Studies in Scarlet: Murders and Manners in the Age of Victoria* (New York, 1970), pp. 293-94.

22.   See Norman Holland, Jr.'s " 'Jude the Obscure': Hardy's Symbolic Indictment of Christianity," *Nineteenth-Century Fiction* 9, no. 1 (1954), pp. 50-60.

23.   However, as Mario Praz has indicated in chapter 4 of *The Romantic Agony*, the figure of the fateful woman persisted in the literature of the nineteenth century. G. H. Ford, in fact, points to its survival, with Salome references and all, in Lawrence's early novel, *The White Peacock* (1911). (*Double Measure: A Study of the Novels and Stories of D. H. Lawrence* [New York, 1965], pp. 52-55).

24.   Many of O'Shaughnessy's poems have a strong misogynist bias. He converts Cleopatra, for example, into a calculating woman, surely not dying for love, and the penultimate stanza of his poem, "Creation," gives some idea of his views regarding women.

> He [God] feasted her [woman] with ease and idle food
>   Of gods, and taught her lusts to fill the whole
> Of life; withal He gave her nothing good,
>   And left her as He made her—without soul.

25.   V. A. G. R. Lytton, *The Life of Edward Bulwer, First Lord Lytton*, (London, 1913), p. 360. Wilson had been a high-class prostitute, not a common street variety.

26.   Margaret Dalziel lists "the seduction of an innocent girl by a designing aristocrat" as a standard motif of the "penny dreadfuls" (*Popular Fiction 100 Years Ago: An Unexplored Tract of Literary History* [London, 1957], p. 16). But sometimes the convention had a turn that made it more legitimate, if no more acceptable. In T. P. Prest's *Vice and Victim; or, Phoebe, the Peasant's Daughter*, the heroine elopes with a profligate lord, but later returns to a faithful lover. It turns out that Phoebe's marriage

was actually legal, thereby making her honest, and when her husband dies she is free to marry her patient admirer.

27. G. M. Trevelyan, *English Social History: A Survey of Six Centuries: Chaucer to Queen Victoria* (London, 1943), p. 491.

28. The seamstress in Caroline Norton's poem, "The Child of the Islands" (1845) is also a ruined country girl, the victim of social inequities. The ruined country girl was a standard form of the convention.

29. See notes in *Selected Poems of Thomas Hood*, ed., and intro. by, John Clubbe (Cambridge, Mass., 1970), p. 392. A dissertation takes its title from one of Hood's lines from this po Bruce Alder Billingsley's " 'Take her up tenderly' a study of the fallen woman in th ineteenth century English novel" (Ph.D. diss., University of Texas, 1962).

30. See also William Bell Scott's "Rosabell."

31. See Helene E. Roberts' "Marriage, Redundancy or Sin: The Painter's View of Women in the First Twenty-Five Years of Victoria's Reign" in *Suffer and Be Still: Women in the Victorian Age* (Bloomington, 1973), for artists' versions of the fallen woman and other themes.

32. Rubenius observes that all of the points that caused outcry against *Ruth* had already been made in journalistic accounts, especially in the *Westminster Review* of April-June, 1850 (Rubenius, *The Woman Question in Mrs. Gaskell's Life and Works* p. 204).

33. Mrs. Margaret Oliphant, "Sensation Novels," *Blackwood's Magazine* 91, no. 69, 1892), p. 567.

34. From *The Saturday Review* no. 520 (14 October 1865); reprinted in *George Meredith: Some Early Appreciations*, selected by Maurice Buxton Forman (London, 1909), p. 121.

35. From *The Morning Post*, 18 October 1865, p. 658; reprinted in Forman, *George Meredith*, p. 130.

36. Ibid., p. 122.

37. It turns out, as we later learn, that Mercy's fall was no more voluntary or responsible than Marian Erle's in *Aurora Leigh*, for Mercy too was introduced to a life of sin by being drugged and ravished.

38. See Dalziel, *Popular Fiction*, chapter 14.

39. "Four of his novels, *The Emancipated, The Odd Women, In the Year of Jubilee*, and *The Whirlpool*, form a searching examination of such aspects of the problem as courtship, marriage, sexual mores, and the fate of single women" (Jacob Korg, *George Gissing: A Critical Biography* [Seattle, 1963], p. 185).

40. Ibid., p. 12.

41. Having given an account of the wealthy but wild William Frederick Windham's marriage to a high-class whore, Cyril Pearl remarks that "the frequency and casualness with which these middle- or upper-class Englishmen married strumpets is one of the curiosities of the times" (*The Girl with the Swansdown Seat* [London, 1955], p. 124).

42. Mrs. Margaret Oliphant's review in *Blackwood's Magazine*, 151 (March, 1892), reprinted in *Thomas Hardy: The Critical Heritage*, ed. R. G. Cox (New York, 1970), p. 204.

43. R. H. Hutton declared that Tess "was pure enough in her instincts, considering the circumstances and the class in which she was born. But she had no deep sense of fidelity to those instincts" (Review in *The Spectator* [23 Jan. 1892], reprinted in Cox, *Thomas Hardy*, p. 193.)

44. See ibid., pp. 186-87.

45. Another "pretty horsebreaker," or high-class prostitute in *Under Two Flags*

is ZuZu, a vivacious, but coarse woman, supposedly patterned upon one of the most famous nineteenth-century harlots, Catherine Walters, known as Skittles.

46.   Raymond S. Nelson describes the social conditions out of which Shaw's play developed in *"Mrs. Warren's Profession* and English Prostitution," 2, no. 3, *Journal of Modern Literature*, pp. 357-66.

47.   Hynes, *Edwardian Turn of Mind*, p. 182.

48.   A year later, William H. White published his novel, *Clara Hopgood*, in which Madge Hopgood decides not to marry the man who is responsible for her child because she discovers she does not really love or admire him; but such a decision was old-hat by this time, drawing upon the earlier examples of Mrs. Gaskell's Ruth or George Meredith's Dahlia Fleming. Allen's rendering of the situation was genuinely new and shocking, since it involved a determinedly voluntary fall. It was a direct assault upon social convention.

49.   Hynes, *Edwardian Turn of Mind*, p. 194.

CHAPTER THREE: MALE TYPES

1.   Dowson conveyed his own peculiar version of the faithful and patient lover in other stories, such as "The Diary of a Successful Man," where Lorimer waits for the one moment he will be able to see his beloved Delphine who has joined a strict religious order: the moment when she is borne dead from the church. In "Countess Marie of the Angels," Colonel Sebastian Mallory is obliged to renounce the woman he has so faithfully loved at her own sad and tender request.

2.   John Harvey, *Victorian Novelists and Their Illustrators* (New York, 1971), pp. 99-100. Harvey writes that "The Good Samaritan was a common subject in illustrations" and lists textual and pictorial uses of the figures in Charles Lever's *The Knight of Gwynne* and Ainsworth's *The Miser's Daughter*. "Cruikshank also hung a Good Samaritan in a plate for *Oliver Twist*, with obvious relevance to Mr. Brownlow's kindness." (p. 100)

3.   "Metropolitan Sanitary Association," Feb. 6, 1850, in *The Speeches of Charles Dickens*, ed. by K. J. Fielding (Oxford, 1960), p. 108.

4.   Mordecai was supposedly based upon Emanuel Deutsch. See Gordon S. Haight, *George Eliot: A Biography* (New York, 1968), p. 471.

5.   Gissing considered his characteristic contribution to fiction to have been the type of the young man, "well-educated, fairly bred, *but without money."* (Jacob Korg, *George Gissing: A Critical Biography* [Seattle, 1963], p. 66) This is not the poor scholar convention, but it reveals Gissing's awareness of the separation of learning and money in a society where values were not generally scholastic.

CHAPTER FOUR: MARRIAGE

1.   Janet Dunbar, *The Early Victorian Woman: Some Aspects of Her Life (1837-57)* (London, 1953), p. 17.

2.   Quoted in Walter E. Houghton's *The Victorian Frame of Mind 1830-1870* (New Haven, 1964), p. 381. Bulwer-Lytton asserts in *England and the English* (1833) that the English are given to marketing their unmarried women quite openly, but that few marriages are made for love and those generally with the assurance of a good settlement. (Book 2, ch. 1)

3.   Quoted in Patricia Thomson's *The Victorian Heroine: A Changing Ideal 1837-1873* (London, 1956), p. 87.

4. W. L. Burn, *The Age of Equipoise: A Study of the Mid-Victorian Generation* (New York, 1965), p. 251. In actual fact, however, marriage settlements much modified the operations of the law, as an article in the *Cornhill Magazine* for December, 1863, demonstrates. The author explains that the wedding or marriage settlement "is as much a part of the business as the wedding breakfast, or anything else connected with the transaction." In effect, the marriage settlement was designed to protect the woman's rights, which the law denied.

5. One thinks immediately of Rachel Wardle in *Pickwick Papers*. Though she is certainly no young lady, she is the victim of that rascally adventurer, Mr. Jingle.

6. Duncan Crow records that in the early 1830s, Lady Charlotte Neville-Grenville told her niece:

> Women are not like men, they cannot chuse, nor it is creditable or lady-like to be what is called in love; I believe that few, very few, well-regulated minds ever have been and that romantic attachment is confined to novels and novel-readers, ye silly and numerous class of young persons ill-educated at home or brought up in boarding-schools. (*The Victorian Woman* [London, 1971], pp. 38-39)

7. V. A. G. R. Lytton, *The Life of Edward Bulwer, First Lord Lytton*, (London, 1913), 1, p. 65.

8. See Ralph Wilson Rader's *Tennyson's Maud: The Biographical Genesis* (Berkeley, 1963) for a thorough account of the affair.

9. See John Harvey's *Victorian Novelists and Their Illustrators* (New York, 1971), pp. 95-98, for a discussion of the parallel.

10. Mrs. Merdle in Dickens' *Little Dorrit* "knew what Society's mothers were, and what Society's daughters were, and what Society's matrimonial market was, and how prices ruled in it, and what scheming and counter-scheming took place for the high buyers and what bargaining and huckstering went on." (Book 1, ch. 33) The slave trade and the commercial exchange were the analogies that came most readily to the minds of those who objected to Victorian marriage customs.

11. George Bullock, *Marie Corelli: The Life and Death of a Best-Seller* (London, 1940), pp. 126-27. The analogy of the Turkish slave-market persisted into the twentieth century, as in one of a series of articles by Rita entitled "The Sin and Scandal of the Smart Set" which appeared in *The Gentlewoman* in 1904. (Amy Cruse, *After the Victorians* [London, 1938], p. 208).

12. Margaret Dalziel, *Popular Fiction 100 Years Ago: An Unexplored Tract of Literary History* (London, 1957), p. 110.

13. "King Cophetua and the Beggar-Maid," Thomas Percy, *Reliques of Ancient English Poetry* (London, 1857), pp. 93-96. Percy is perhaps the earliest revival of this legend.

14. F. M. L. Thompson discusses this subject from more than one angle in *English Landed Society In The Nineteenth Century* (London, 1963).

15. Bullock, *Marie Corelli*, p. 119.

16. Lionel Stevenson, *The English Novel. A Panorama* (Boston, 1960), p. 403.

17. Other writers asked the same general question, but with more seriousness. Kingsley wondered, in *Yeast*, why the death of one lover was not a satisfactory denouement, when their marriage would have been accepted as such. "As if the history of love always ended at the altar! Oftener it only begins there; and all before it is but a mere longing to love." ("Epilogue")

18. U. C. Knoepflmacher writes that *Middlemarch* is "often mislabeled as a novel 'about marriage,'" though he affirms that the novel "does nonetheless invite us to assess the marriages that take place at the outset and to scale them, at the end, against the delayed union of Mary and Fred" (*Laughter & Despair: Readings in Ten Novels of the Victorian Era* [Berkeley, 1971], p. 196).

19.   Vineta and Robert A. Colby, *The Equivocal Virtue: Mrs. Oliphant and the Victorian Literary Market Place* (New York, 1966), p. 128.

20.   In his story, "The Dame of Athelhall," Hardy tells of a wife returning from an elopement to find her husband glad to think that she is gone and prepared, himself, to marry again.

CHAPTER FIVE: COINCIDENCE

1.   Lionel Stevenson, *The English Novel. A Panorama* (Boston, 1960), p. 298.

2.   Edgar Johnson, *Charles Dickens, His Tragedy and Triumph* (New York, 1952), 1, p. 102.

3.   E. D. H. Johnson, *Charles Dickens: An Introduction To His Novels* (New York, 1969), p. 101.

4.   Edgar Johnson, *Charles Dickens*, p. 101.

5.   Wilkie Collins expressed a similar fascination with the inter-relatedness of human careers, as in the opening of his novel, *The Fallen Leaves* (1878). "The resistless influences which are one day to reign supreme over our poor hearts, and to shape the sad short course of our lives, are sometimes of mysteriously remote origin, and find their devious ways to us through the hearts and the lives of strangers." ("Prologue," sec. 1)

6.   Steven Marcus, *Dickens: From Pickwick to Dombey* (New York, 1965), pp. 78-79.

7.   Quoted by Monroe Engel in *The Maturity of Dickens* (Cambridge, Mass., 1959) from a letter of 6 October 1859 to Wilkie Collins.

8.   See David Goldknopf, "Coincidence in the Victorian Novel: The Trajectory of a Narrative-Device," *College English* 31, no. 1 (October, 1969), on coincidence in Charlotte Brontë's works, especially, pp. 41-42. W. A. Craik also discusses concidence in *The Brontë Novels* (London, 1968), p. 166.

9.   Richard Altick, *Victorian Studies in Scarlet: Murders and Manners in the Age of Victoria* (New York, 1970), pp. 201-2.

10.   R. T. Jones, *George Eliot* (Cambridge, 1970), pp. 46-47.

11.   Goldknopf, "Coincidence," p. 41.

12.   "In the 'sensation novels' of Wilkie Collins and Miss Braddon, the author's ingenious manipulation of circumstances was to be imagined as the work of Providence—a force that punished villains and rewarded heroes with lovely brides and substantial property" (Max K. Sutton, "The Affront to Victorian Dignity in the Satire of the Eighteen-Seventies," *The Nineteenth-Century Writer and his Audience: Selected Problems in Theory, Form, and Content*, ed. Harold Orel and George J. Worth [Lawrence, Kansas, 1969], p. 105).

13.   Goldknopf, "Coincidence," p. 44.

14.   For example, the coincidence of Lady Stratton's death at the wrong moment, preventing useful money from going to the Aubreys is referred to as "an inscrutable and awful Providence," but is not to be contested or questioned. (Vol. 3, ch. 5) In "The Spirit's Trial," J. A. Froude describes one purpose of providence. "Providence has many spare cables, with which she holds her sons at their moorings, when wilfulness, or the waves of circumstances have broke them from their own." (ch. 4) This function is exhibited in the character, Edward Fowler, for a "profound belief in God and God's providence, lay at the very core of his soul," even when all else seemed uncertain and disordered. (ch. 9)

15.   In *The Adventures of Harry Richmond*, Meredith makes an equally severe at-

tack upon the selfish individual appropriation of Providence. Like the Countess de Saldar, Richmond Roy's dependence upon providential assistance proves ill-conceived. An article entitled "Coincidences and Superstitions," which appeared in the *Cornhill Magazine* for November, 1972, cautioned that the fact that coincidences were improbable and therefore striking when they occurred, did not justify superstitious conclusions nor a belief in providential intervention.

16. Goldknopf, "Coincidence," p. 45.

17. In E. T. A. Hoffmann's "The Sand-Man," Nathanael believes that he is bound by an iron destiny, while Clara, a representative of reason and common sense tries to persuade him that so long as he believes in external hostile forces and a relentless destiny, he makes them real. Man's nature begets its own fateful courses, Hoffmann suggests.

18. Frank Chapman, "Hardy the Novelist," *Scrutiny* (June, 1934), reprinted and excerpted in *The Return of the Native*, ed. James Gindin (New York, 1969), Norton Critical edition, p. 432.

19. Stevenson, *English Novel*, p. 389.

20. Bert G. Hornback, *The Metaphor of Chance: Vision and Technique in the Works of Thomas Hardy* (Athens, Ohio, 1971), p. 4.

21. Ibid., p. 147.

22. Goldknopf, "Coincidence," p. 47.

23. James Hinton, *Man and his Dwelling Place. An Essay Toward the Interpretation of Nature* (New York, 1872), p. 135.

24. In *A Room With A View*, E. M. Forster's Mr. Beebe is deeply interested in the subject of Coincidence, while young Emerson, who reads Nietzsche and Schopenhauer, believes in Fate. Young Emerson has not learned to will to live, instead of willing to die. It is part of his necessary education and the answer to his ever-present question: "Why?"

CHAPTER SIX: DUELLING

1. W. L. Burn, *The Age of Equipoise: A Study of the Mid-Victorian Generation* (New York, 1965), p. 258.

2. *Encyclopaedia Britannica*, 11th ed., S.V. "Duelling." Robert Baldick's *The Duel: A History of Duelling* (London, 1970) provides accounts of duels in nineteenth-century England, among others.

3. William Hunter, *An Essay on Duelling. Written with a view to discountenance this barbarous and disgraceful practice* (London, 1792), second edition, p. 36.

4. Abraham Bosquett, *The Young Man of Honour's Vade-Mecum, Being A Salutary Treatise on Duelling, Together with the Annals of Chivalry, the Ordeal Trial, and Judicial Combat, from the Earliest Times* (London, 1817), p. 1.

5. Ibid., p. 27.

6. Ibid., p. 90.

7. Ibid., pp. 23-24.

8. Charles Hay Cameron, "On Duelling," as a printed pamphlet not for publication; but the article originally appeared in the seventh number of the *Westminster Review*.

9. Ibid., p. 72.

10. Ibid., pp. 78-79.

11. Burn, *Age of Equipoise*, p. 258.

12. Accounts of the Campbell and the Fawcett duels appear in Baldick's *The Duel*, pp. 98-101 and p. 113. Elie Halévy notes an early attempt to suppress duelling in the Navy in *England in 1815* (New York, 1961), p. 453.

13. Burn, *Age of Equipoise*, p. 258.

14. Lorenzo Sabine, *Notes on Duels and Duelling, alphabetically arranged, with a Preliminary Historical Essay* (Boston, 1856), p. 43.

15. *Britannica*, p. 642. See also, Baldick, *The Duel*, pp. 113-14.

16. Justin McCarthy, *A Short History of Our Own Times: From the Accession of Queen Victoria to the General Election of 1880* (New York, 1884), p. 42.

17. Charles Mackay, *Extraordinary Popular Delusions and the Madness of Crowds* (Boston, 1932), p. 688.

18. Ibid., p. 694.

19. Burn, *Age of Equipoise*, p. 257.

20. *Britannica*, p. 642.

21. Elizabeth Longford, *Queen Victoria: Born to Succeed* (New York, 1966), p. 355.

22. Burn, *Age of Equipoise*, p. 259.

23. Byron Farwell, *Burton: A Biography of Sir Richard Francis Burton* (London, 1963), p. 7.

24. Andrew Steinmetz, *The Romance of Duelling in All Times and Countries*, 2 vols (London, 1868), vol. 2, p. 255. Mr. Scott was editor of the London Magazine and Mr. Christie was a barrister.

25. Derek Patmore, *The Life and Times of Coventry Patmore* (London, 1949), pp. 28-31.

26. Charles James Mathews, *The Life of Charles James Mathews. Chiefly Autobiographical with Selections From His Correspondence and Speeches*, ed. Charles Dickens, 2 vols (London, 1879), pp. 111ff.

27. Sabine, in *Notes on Duels and Duelling*, admires the duelling scene in *The Monastery*, agreeing that in many actual incidents the principals behaved as they do in Scott's novel, feeling immediate remorse for a rash act. (pp. iv-v)

28. Mortimer R. Proctor, *The English University Novel* (Berkeley, 1957), p. 63.

29. Bulwer-Lytton continued to use the duel in his novels, normally associating it with violent men, as in the case of Louis Grayle in *A Strange Story*. Bulwer-Lytton himself was involved in a duel as a second. (See V. A. G. R. Lytton, *The Life of Edward Bulwer, First Lord Lytton* [London, 1913], vol. 1, pp. 130-32.)

30. Sabine quotes, in an appendix to his book, a story entitled "Duelling: A Tale of Woe," which first appeared in *Bentley's Miscellany*, vol. 30. It is a story of a duel provoked by jealousy and unfairly executed, which begets an equally violent vengeance on the murderer. The jealous woman ends her life in an institution for the insane.

31. Unsigned review from *Saturday Review*, 78 (7 July 1894), on *Lord Ormont and His Aminta*, in *Meredith: The Critical Heritage*, ed. Ioan Williams (New York, 1971), p. 385.

CHAPTER SEVEN: DEATHBEDS

1. E. M. Forster, *Marianne Thornton (1797-1887): A Domestic Biography* (London, 1956), see chapter four entitled "The Death Beds."

2. Elizabeth Longford, *Queen Victoria: Born to Succeed* (New York, 1966), p. 310.

3. See Sir James Fitzjames Stephen on *A Tale of Two Cities* in *Saturday Review*,

17 Dec. 1859; reprinted in *The Dickens Critics*, eds. George H. Ford and Lauriat Lane, Jr. (Ithaca, New York, 1961), pp. 38-46.

4. Janet Dunbar, *The Early Victorian Woman: Some Aspects of Her Life (1837-57)* (London, 1953), p. 60. John Morley's *Death, Heaven and the Victorians* (Pittsburgh, 1971), describes in detail the Victorian preoccupation with death and burial, and the numerous moral, social, and economic implications that influenced mourning customs of the time.

5. Coventry Patmore's wife, Emily, considered Taylor's *Holy Living and Holy Dying* her favorite book (Derek Patmore, *The Life and Times of Coventry Patmore* [London, 1949], p. 107). Since she died in 1863, it may be assumed that Taylor's work was still well known and respected. John Morley notes that Taylor was often quoted on matters concerning death and the rites of burial. (p. 21)

6. Hallam Tennyson, *Alfred Lord Tennyson: A Memoir by His Son*, 2 vols. (New York, 1905), 2, pp. 428-29. Thomas Hardy supposedly asked to have stanza 81 of Fitzgerald's *Rubaiyat* read to him on his deathbed. Not all poets died grandly, though reports might make it seem so. B. R. Jerman has an interesting study, "The Death of Robert Browning" in the *University of Toronto Quarterly* 35, no. 1 (1965), pp. 47-74. In *The Brothers Karamazov*, Father Zossima's corpse causes a scandal, because his fellow monks have not expected such a saintly man's remains to stink of corruption. (Part 3, Book 7, ch. 1)

7. Edward Fitzgerald, *Letters & Literary Remains of Edward Fitzgerald*, 7 vols. (New York, 1966: reprint), 2, p. 4; dated, 1852.

8. An earlier reference to Colonel Newcome's "Adsum," shows that Braddon was fully conscious of Thackeray's earlier and more memorable employment of the convention.

9. The crusty old character, Bernard Haldane, in George Alfred Lawrence's *Barren Honour. A Tale* (1868), does not die a calm and reconciled death, but remains bitter toward the woman who broke his heart.

10. Dunbar, *Victorian Women*, p. 122.

11. Gillian Avery, *Nineteenth Century Children: Heroes and Heroines in English Children's Stories 1780-1900* (London, 1965), p. 212.

12. Ibid., p. 220.

13. Peter Coveney, *The Image of Childhood: The Individual and Society: A Study of the Theme in English Literature* (Baltimore, 1967), p. 188.

14. Avery, *Nineteenth Century Children*, p. 174.

15. Ibid., p. 175.

16. Coveney, *Image of Childhood*, p. 179.

17. Ibid., p. 193. However, the negation of life in the child is intended to lead to positive results in the way that evil was, through the inscrutable ways of providence, meant to perpetrate a greater good. An example of this is in a tale published in the March, 1865 issue of the *Cornhill Magazine*, entitled "Willie Baird: a Winter Idyll," in which a little scholar dies, and his saddened teacher lives on with the boy's dog, who had tried to lead the teacher into the storm to save the dying boy. The teacher had not understood, and the boy had died. But the death has a moral effect upon the teacher. "I read my Bible more and Euclid less," he says.

18. U. C. Knoepflmacher writes of *Vanity Fair* that "The novel's many death scenes are not due to a mawkish Victorian fascination with such situations, but rather stem from Thackeray's desire to remind the reader that death, the end of life, is the only true vanquisher of vanity" (*Laughter & Despair: Readings in Ten Novels of the Victorian Era* [Berkeley, 1971], p. 82).

19. Patricia Thomson, *The Victorian Heroine: A Changing Ideal 1837-1873* (London, 1956), p. 158.

20. Walter E. Houghton, *The Victorian Frame of Mind 1830-1870* (New Haven, 1964), p. 277.

21. As one might expect, deathbed scenes retained an interest for spiritualists. Sophia Morgan wrote, in *From Matter to Spirit* (London, 1863): "The apparent recognition by the dying of those who have gone before, is a common and notorious fact." (p. 176) She gives several instances in chapter ten of deathbed recognitions of dead beings.

CHAPTER EIGHT: SWINDLES

1. G. M. Young, *Victorian England: Portrait of an Age* (London, 1960), p. 7.

2. Asa Briggs, *The Age of Improvement 1783-1867* (London, 1964), p. 211.

3. Elie Halévy, *The Liberal Awakening 1815-1830*, trans. E. K. Watkin (New York, 1961), p. 234.

4. E. L. Woodward, *The Age of Reform 1815-1870* (Oxford, 1958), p. 584. D. Morier Evans attributed panic only partly to speculation, but indicated that it usually preceded a crash. For example, the panic of 1826 "arose from excessive speculations in foreign mines, in cotton and other products" and other causes. "The panic of 1847 was caused by a bad harvest and great speculations in corn and railways," and the panic of 1857 followed largely from improvident advances made by managers of several large joint-stock banks in the North of England (*The History of the Commercial Crisis, 1857-58, and the Stock Exchange Panic of 1859* [New York, 1969], p. 13).

5. D. Morier Evans, *The Commercial Crisis 1847-1848; being facts and figures illustrative of the events of that important period, considered in relation to the three epochs of the railway mania, the food and money panic, and the french revolution. To which is added; an appendix, containing an alphabetical list of the English and foreign mercantile failures, with the balance sheets and statements, of the most important houses* (London, 1848), pp. 48-49.

6. Woodward, *Age of Reform*, p. 584.

7. Briggs, *Age of Improvement*, pp. 339-40.

8. Michael Robbins, *The Railway Age in Britain and Its Impact on the World* (Baltimore, 1962), p. 91.

9. Ibid., p. 34.

10. Richard S. Lambert, *The Railway King 1800-1871: A Study of George Hudson and the Business Morals of his Time* (London, 1964), p. 18.

11. Evans, *Crisis 1847-1848*, p. 45.

12. Lambert, *Railway King*, pp. 166-67.

13. Evans, *Crisis 1847-1848*, p. 5.

14. Charles James Mathews, *The Life of Charles James Mathews. Chiefly Autobiographical with Selections From His Correspondence and Speeches*, ed. Charles Dickens, 2 vols (London, 1879), 1, p. 170.

15. Milbank in Geraldine Jewsbury's *Marian Withers* (1851) also absconds to America with joint-stock company funds.

16. Ivan Melada, *The Captain of Industry in English Fiction, 1821-1871* (Albuquerque, 1970), p. 40.

17. In another poem, "Sea Dreams," Tennyson presented the character of a speculator whose ambitions bring about financial difficulty for a clerk and his wife. Tennyson himself had good reason to understand the bitterness that unsuccessful speculation could bring, since he had lost a considerable sum in that way.

18. In Ouida's late novel, *The Massarenes* (1897), William Massarene is partly based upon George Hudson.

19. Woodward, *Age of Reform*, p. 342.

20. Grahame Smith, *Dickens, Money, and Society* (Berkeley, 1968), p. 221.

21. Merdle was supposedly based on such figures as John Sadlier and Leopold Redpath, notable thieves of their time (K. J. Fielding, *Charles Dickens: A Critical Introduction* [Boston, 1964], p. 180).

22. D. Morier Evans, *Speculative Notes and Notes on Speculation, Ideal and Real* (New York, 1968: reprint), p. 52.

23. Ibid., p. 79.

24. William Ashworth, *An Economic History of England 1870-1939* (London, 1960), p. 20. But see also, chapter seven.

25. Ibid., p. 179.

26. Evans, *Commercial Crisis, 1857-58*, p. 37.

27. Ibid., p. 37.

28. Ibid., p. 38.

29. Max K. Sutton, "The Affront to Victorian Dignity in the Satire of the Eighteen-Seventies," *The Nineteenth-Century Writer and his Audience: Selected Problems in Theory, Form, and Content*, eds. Harold Orel and George J. Worth (Lawrence, Kansas, 1969), p. 101.

30. Wells showed his concern over uncontrolled speculation elsewhere in his writings, as in *Anticipations* (1901), where he argued for its abolition, and in his science fiction novel, *When The Sleeper Wakes* (1899), where, in the world of the future, speculation has gone amok and revealed itself for the outright gambling that Wells believed it to be.

CHAPTER NINE: MADNESS

1. Michel Foucault, *Madness and Civilization: A History of Insanity in the Age of Reason*, trans. Richard Howard (New York, 1967), p. 161.

2. Ibid., p. 93.

3. Kathleen Jones, *Lunacy, Law, and Conscience 1744-1845* (London, 1955), p. 7.

4. See W. B. C. Watkins' discussion of this subject in *Perilous Balance: The Tragic Genius of Swift, Johnson, & Sterne* (Cambridge, 1960), pp. 90ff.

5. Nigel Walker, *Crime and Insanity in England: Volume One: The Historical Perspective* (Edinburgh, 1968), p. 43.

6. Ibid., p. 70. This subject is also treated in William Ll. Parry-Jones' *The Trade in Lunacy. A Study of Private Madhouses in the Eighteenth and Nineteenth Centuries* (London, 1972).

7. Walker, *Crime and Insanity*, p. 71.

8. Jones, *Lunacy, Law*, p. 32.

9. Ibid., p. 26.

10. Ibid., p. 66. William Ll. Parry-Jones discusses the growth and function of the private lunatic asylums thoroughly.

11. In *The Mind of the European Romantic* (Garden City, 1969), H. G. Schenk has written that the explosion of irrational or subconscious behavior associated with the French Revolution "was the signal for the Romantic battle against Reason." (p. 3) Mental aberration may also, he argues, be attributed to the stress of a philosophy of "nihilistic subjectivism," and he points out that artists such as Nikolaus Lenau, Gerard

de Nerval, and Caspar David Friedrich died mad. (p. 52) E. T. A. Hoffmann maintained that "some measure of madness, or folly, is so deeply rooted in human nature that one cannot come to know human nature better than through a careful study of the insane and the mentally deficient" (Quoted in Harvey W. Hewett-Thayer's *Hoffmann: Author of the Tales* [New York, 1971], p. 185).

12.　Quoted in George Rosen's *Madness in Society: Chapters in the Historical Sociology of Mental Illness* (Chicago, 1968), p. 183.

13.　Quoted in ibid.

14.　Parry-Jones insists more than once in his book that there was actually very little evidence presented to justify charges of false incarceration in mental institutions being a practice in any way common.

15.　Jones, *Lunacy, Law*, p. 183. In an article entitled "Commissions of Lunacy," which appeared in the *Cornhill Magazine* for February, 1862, madness is defined as "an insensibility to the general principles of human nature caused by disease." The article asserts that madness is not merely advanced eccentricity, and occupies itself with the legal aspects of insanity. The article was prompted by the famous Windham Case.

16.　Lorenzo Sabine, *Notes on Duels and Duelling* (Boston, 1856), 2, p. 15. In fiction, Jack Sheppard's mother, in William Harrison Ainsworth's *Jack Sheppard*, is driven insane by her son's crimes and confined to Bedlam.

17.　This novel was based upon Mrs. Opie's play, *Father and Daughter* (1802). See Louis James, *Fiction for the Working Man 1830-1850* (London, 1963), p. 100.

18.　Bulwer-Lytton was driven at one point in his quarrels with his wife to have her certified insane and detained with medical attention. The same doctor, however, conveniently certified her as fit to travel with her son, whom she abused mercilessly. This illustrates not only Bulwer-Lytton's familiarity with aberrant behavior later in his career, but also the ease with which individuals could be confined and classified as lunatics (V. A. G. R. Lytton, *The Life of Edward Bulwer, First Lord Lytton* [London, 1913], 2, pp. 273-74).

19.　Kathleen Jones, *Mental Health and Social Policy 1845-1959* (London, 1960), p. 21. In the *Cornhill Magazine* for July, 1900, Andrew Lang suggested that the hidden mad wife in Jane Eyre was borrowed from Mrs. Radcliffe's *A Sicilian Romance*.

20.　See George H. Ford, *Dickens and His Readers: Aspects of Novel-Criticism Since 1836* (New York, 1965), p. 18.

21.　Kathleen Tillotson, "Introduction," *Barnaby Rudge: A Tale of the Riots of 'Eighty* (London, 1954), New Oxford Illustrated Edition, p. xii.

22.　The Medical Registration Act of 1858 prescribed examinations for medical men to treat the insane. Kathleen Jones concludes that, in the early part of the century, there were many cases of illegal detention, in which patients' names were changed and they were forbidden to communicate with the outside world. Often such patients were victims of greedy relatives. The madhouse keeper, meanwhile, "had a vested interest in the continuation of the "illness," since he was able to charge a high fee for his doubtful "care"; it was scarcely in his interest to discharge a patient while the relatives were willing to pay for his confinement" (*Mental Health*, p. 11). But Parry-Jones contends that, whatever abuses may have occurred early on, by the mid-nineteenth century there was little evidence of false confinement (*Trade in Lunacy*, pp. 26, 222, etc.).

23.　Jones, *Mental Health*, p. 20.

24.　Jack Lindsay discusses the motif of the fall in *George Meredith: His Life and Works* (London, 1956), pp. 284ff.

25.　William B. Carpenter, *Principles of Mental Physiology, with their applications to the training and discipline of the mind, and the study of its morbid conditions* (New York, 1896), p. 671.

26. Winifred's madness is cured by being transferred to the healthier Sinfi Lovell by magnetic means, a practice that Watts-Dunton defended as medically performable.

27. Julius and Augustus Hare, *Guesses at Truth by Two Brothers* (London, 1889), p. 159.

28. In his memoir, *Episodes in A Life of Adventure, or, Moss from a Rolling Stone* (1887), Oliphant said that "The world, with its bloody wars, its political intrigues, its social evils, its religious cant, its financial frauds, and its glaring anomalies, assumed in my eyes more and more the aspect of a gigantic lunatic asylum. And the question occurred to me whether there might not be latent forces in nature, by the application of which this profound moral malady might be reached." (p. 342) See Robert Lee Wolff's *Strange Stories: And Other Explorations in Victorian Fiction* (New York, 1972) for an interesting account of Oliphant and his religious views.

29. John Charles Bucknill, M.D., review of *Maud and Other Poems* in *The Asylum Journal of Mental Science*, no. 15 (Oct., 1855), p. 96.

30. Ibid., p. 103.

31. See *The Poems of Tennyson*, ed. Christopher Ricks (London, 1969), p. 1038, for notes on similarities of plot and so forth.

32. Hallam Tennyson, *Alfred Lord Tennyson: A Memoir by His Son*, 2 vols. (New York, 1905) 1, p. 396.

33. Carpenter, *Mental Physiology*, p. 673.

34. John A. Lester, Jr., *Journey Through Despair: 1880-1914. Transformations in British Literary Culture* (Princeton, 1968), p. 59.

35. Jones, *Mental Health*, p. 26.

CHAPTER TEN: THE RETURN

1. Critics such as Kenneth Allott, in *The Poems of Matthew Arnold* (London, 1965), Dwight Culler in *Imaginative Reason* (New Haven, 1966), and Alan Roper in *Arnold's Poetic Landscapes* (Baltimore, 1969), have treated this relationship.

2. The poem appears in Harris' collection, *Lays from The Mine, The Moor, and The Mountain* (London, 1853).

3. The return of a character from Australia was common in Victorian literature, since so many convicts had been transported there and because it had a reputation as a source of easy wealth. Hence, in George Gissing's *The Nether World* (1889), Michael Snowdon returns from Australia where he has acquired wealth that he keeps secret. He now regrets his misspent youth and wishes to use his money philanthropically.

4. See *The Poems of Tennyson*, ed. Christopher Ricks (London, 1869), p. 1129, and P. G. Scott, *Tennyson's Enoch Arden: A Victorian Best-Seller* (Lincoln, 1970), pp. 5-6.

5. Scott, *Enoch Arden*, p. 6.

6. Ibid., p. 13.

7. Ibid., p. 15.

8. Peter J. Casagrande, "The Shifted 'Centre of Altruism' in *The Woodlanders*: Thomas Hardy's Third '"Return of a Native",'" 38 No. 1 *ELH* (March 1971), p. 124. In addition to discussing *The Woodlanders*, this article treats *Under the Greenwood Tree* and *The Return of the Native*.

9. For more on this theme, see my later chapter on memory.

10. V. A. G. R. Lytton, *The Life of Edward Bulwer, First Lord Lytton*, 2 vols. (London, 1913), 2, p. 488.

11. Heaven as man's fatherland was a familiar theme of German Romantic litera-

ture, for example, appearing as a dominant theme in the first of the *Geistliche Lieder* and in Novalis' *Hymnen an die Nacht* (H. G. Schenk, *The Mind of the European Romantics* [Garden City, 1969], p. 92).

12. Arnold J. Toynbee, *A Study of History* (London, 1935), 3, p. 263.

13. Alice Chandler, *A Dream of Order: The Medieval Ideal in 19th-Century English Literature* (Lincoln, Nebraska, 1970), p. 8. See my later chapter on memory for more on this subject.

14. The poem appeared in the *Cornhill Magazine* for October, 1861.

15. Edward Fitzgerald, *Letters & Literary Remains of Edward Fitzgerald*, 7 vols. (New York, 1966: reprint), 2, p. 313. Forty years later, George Meredith wrote to Miss Louisa Lawrence, describing a play entitled the *Enfant Prodigue*. A play without words, *L'enfant prodigue* was arranged by Michel Carré with music by Andre Wormser (*The Letters of George Meredith*, ed. C. L. Cline [Oxford, 1970], 3, pp. 1035-36).

16. See George H. Ford's "Self-Help and the Helpless in *Bleak House*," in *From Jane Austen to Joseph Conrad*, eds. Robert C. Rathburn and Martin Steinmann, Jr. (Minneapolis, 1958), p. 96.

17. "The Warilows of Welland; or, The Modern Prodigal," *Household Words* 2, no. 27 (28 Sept. 1850), pp. 12-19.

18. The theme of the prodigal remained of interest on the Continent, as well. Gide wrote *Retour de l'enfant prodigue* (1907), and Rilke gave the convention an ironic twist by having the prodigal desire to escape love at the end of *Die Aufzeichnungen des Malte Laurids Brigge* (1910).

CHAPTER ELEVEN: THE ORPHAN

1. George H. Ford, "Introduction," *David Copperfield* (Boston, 1958), p. vii.

2. Elizabeth Longford, *Queen Victoria: Born to Succeed* (New York, 1966), p. 130.

3. The Little Pilgrim was different from the usual pattern in that she died as an adult. In our own time, a similar convention is the much-employed search for the father.

4. Claude Amelius Goldenheart is another example of the generous orphan capable of love beyond the ordinary in Collins' *The Fallen Leaves* (1878). He is a sort of ungoverned Deronda. Regina Mildmay, in the same novel, is the meek version of the orphan—apparently, to Collins' taste, too meek.

5. Jacob Korg, *George Gissing: A Critical Biography* (Seattle, 1963), p. 169.

6. Ford, "Introduction," p. ix.

7. Morse Peckham writes of nineteenth-century literature, that the "orphan, the illegitimate child, the foundling, are literary figures used again and again to symbolize social alienation when the author is after the uniqueness of the self and its opposition to the social role." (*Beyond The Tragic Vision* [New York, 1962], p. 108)

CHAPTER TWELVE: INHERITANCE

1. J. T. Christie, "Introduction," *Guy Mannering* (London, 1955), p. 11. E. S. Turner describes the basic plot of the nineteenth century, derived from the Gothic thriller, as "the young and rightful heir deprived of his birthright by evil-scheming relatives or guardians" (*Boys Will Be Boys* [London, 1957: rev. ed.], p. 18).

2. Frequent references in Ferrier's novel to Scott's *Mannering* suggest her awareness of the employment of the inheritance convention in the novel. Scott praised Ferrier as one of the few rising Scottish novelists.

3. Reade wrote a novel entitled *The Wandering Heir* (1872), during a time when the most famous of nineteenth-century "heirs," the Tichborne Claimant, had his case very much in the public eye.

4. Lionel Stevenson, *The English Novel. A Panorama* (Boston, 1960), p. 244.

5. Steven Marcus, *Dickens: From Pickwick to Dombey* (New York, 1965), ch. 2, passim.

6. Jeremy Taylor, *The Rule and Exercises of Holy Living* (London, 1930), p. 63.

7. Jeremy Taylor, *The Rule and Exercises of Holy Dying* (London, 1929), p. 76.

8. Bulwer-Lytton could be more obvious and superficial with the inheritance convention as in his dramatic production, *The Sea Captain; or the Birthright* (1840). Later this play was entitled *The Rightful Heir* (1868).

9. John Morley, review of *Felix Holt, The Radical* in *Saturday Review* (16 June 1866) reprinted in *A Century of George Eliot Criticism*, ed. Gordon S. Haight (Boston, 1965), pp. 35-36.

10. In a later novel, *The Nether World*, Gissing showed the extent of misconceived evaluations of this kind. There he describes Michael Snowdon's desire that his fortune should be used in the service of the poor, designating Jane Snowdon to administer this philanthropy. But Jane lacks the character and inclination to carry out old Snowdon's wishes and thereby loses not only the inheritance, but her lover and happiness as well. H. G. Wells' *When The Sleeper Wakes* (1899) is a marvellous parody and exaggeration of the Inheritance convention, for when the central character of this novel, Graham, awakens two hundred and fifty years after he has fallen into a trance, he discovers that his fortune has been accumulating during that time and that he is now virtually owner of the entire world. Grave responsibilities accompany this inheritance of the New World of the future, and, having struggled against conditions he finds existing then, Graham bequeathes all of his property to the people of the world.

11. Peter Coveney, *The Image of Childhood: The Individual and Society: A Study of the Theme in English Literature* (Baltimore, 1967), p. 124.

12. Quoted in David Daiches' *Some Late Victorian Attitudes* (New York, 1969), p. 13.

CHAPTER THIRTEEN: DISGUISE

1. See, for example, Walter R. Davis' *Idea and Act in Elizabethan Fiction* (Princeton, 1969) and Norman H. Holland's *The First Modern Comedies: The Significance of Etherege, Wycherley, and Congreve* (Cambridge, Mass., 1959).

2. This was a principal concern of German literature of the nineteenth century. Oscar Walzel writes that "the protean mobility of the romantic spirit is based upon the consciousness of being able at all times to rise above itself (*German Romanticism*, trans. Alma Elise Lussky [New York, 1966], p. 24). E. T. A. Hoffmann wrote: "I fancy [seeing] myself through a multiplying glass—all forms that move around about me are myselfs [ichs], and I am vexed at what they do and leave undone" (Quoted in Harvey W. Hewett-Thayer's *Hoffmann: Author of the Tales* [New York, 1971], p. 373). William Marshall, in *The World of the Victorian Novel* (London, 1967), describes the way in which the new concepts of self are revealed in Victorian fiction. See also Morse Peckham's broadly inclusive study, *Beyond The Tragic Vision: The Quest for Identity in the Nineteenth Century* (New York, 1962).

3. There have been a number of studies in recent years on the subject of the

double, or the divided self, in literature. Otto Rank's *Der Doppelgänger* was an early venture into the field. Others include Ralph Tymms' *Doubles in Literary Psychology* (Cambridge, 1949), Masao Miyoshi's *The Divided Self* (New York, 1969), Robert Rogers' *The Double in Literature* (Detroit, 1970), and C. F. Keppler's *The Literature of the Second Self* (Tucson, Arizona, 1972).

4. From "Mathews the Comedian," *Blackwood's Edinburgh Magazine* 9, no. 6 (Dec. 1839) p. 793. The article is a review of Mathews' wife's biography of him.

5. See Nuel Pharr Davis, *The Life of Wilkie Collins* (Urbana, 1956), p. 213, and elsewhere.

6. Douglas Woodruff's thorough and interesting investigation of the case in *The Tichborne Claimant: A Victorian Mystery* (New York, 1957), shows just how confusing and mystifying some impostures could be. It also implies that some genuine identities might easily be made to appear as impostures.

7. Keith Hollingsworth, *The Newgate Novel 1830-1847: Bulwer, Ainsworth, Dickens, & Thackeray* (Detroit, 1963), p. 20.

8. Charles James Mathews, *The Life of Charles James Mathews. Chiefly Autobiographical with Selections From His Correspondence and Speeches*, ed. Charles Dickens, 2 vols. (London, 1879), 1, p. 141, from a letter of 13 Feb. 1824.

9. Fawn M. Brodie, *The Devil Drives: A Life of Sir Richard Burton* (New York, 1967), p. 89. Brodie says that Burton's fascination with disguise "suggests a savage dissatisfaction with himself," and points out that, though he was always in control of the roles he assumed, they were "always accompanied by danger." (p. 89) It is interesting that Burton, so intrigued by imposture, seems to have believed in the Tichborne Claimant's identity when he became familiar with him in South America. (See Woodruff, pp. 128-30, and Byron Farwell, *Burton: A Biography of Sir Richard Francis Burton* [London, 1963], pp. 292-93.)

10. Richard Altick, *Victorian Studies in Scarlet: Murders and Manners in the Age of Victoria* (New York, 1970).

11. See the discussion of this subject in the chapter on inheritance.

12. Bulwer-Lytton could use the device in a more melodramatic way as well, as he did in *The Lady of Lyons; or, Love and Pride* (1838), where Melnotte returns in disguise to claim his bride.

13. See Richard D. Altick and James F. Loucks II, *Browning's Roman Murder Story: A Reading of The Ring and the Book* (Chicago, 1968).

14. John R. Reed, *Perception and Design in Tennyson's Idylls of the King* (Athens, Ohio, 1970), pp. 184-98.

15. Of *Pickwick* Monroe Engel observes that its main plots are "romantic, and all involve, in one way or another, problems of disguise or false appearance" (*The Maturity of Dickens* [Cambridge, Mass., 1959], p. 80). Other varieties of disguise include Hugh's suppressed identity in *Barnaby Rudge*, or the several disguises in *Martin Chuzzlewit*, where the greater theme of hypocrisy and concealed truths establishes a broader concept of disguise. See also Lauriat Lane's "Dickens and the Double," no. 55 *Dickensian* (1959) p. 49 concerning Jonas Chuzzlewit's disguise in the murder of his relative.

16. See E. D. H. Johnson, *Charles Dickens: An Introduction To His Novels* (New York, 1969), pp. 134ff on disguise and the double.

17. See John Gross on *A Tale of Two Cities*, in *Dickens and the Twentieth Century*, eds. John Gross and Gabriel Pearson (Toronto, 1962), pp. 187-197.

18. Harmon has several disguises, since he is also the man who wishes to see the drowned man's corpse, and he visits the riverfront in disguise when he is searching out information later.

19. E. D. H. Johnson, *Charles Dickens*, p. 110.

20. See Winifred Gérin, *Charlotte Brontë: The Evolution of Genius* (Oxford, 1967), p. 522, on objections of Thackeray and Harriet Martineau.

21. Dickens and Collins worked together on a play, *The Frozen North*. Dickens later said that the idea of *Cities* occurred to him while working on that play. (See J. K. Fielding, *Charles Dickens. A Critical Introduction* [Boston, 1964] pp. 201-2.)

22. William H. Marshall, *Wilkie Collins* (New York, 1970), p. 82.

23. See also references to the sham character of society, as seen by Amelius, in the chapter on swindles.

24. John A. Lester, Jr., *Journey Through Despair: 1880-1914. Transformation in British Literary Culture* (Princeton, 1968), p. 141.

25. Roy's claim is reminiscent of the Tichborne Claimant case, which was very much before public notice at the time that Meredith wrote his novel.

26. Gillian Beer, *Meredith: A Change of Masks. A Study of the Novels* (London, 1970), p. 8.

27. Quoted in Christopher Butler's *Number Symbolism* (New York, 1970), p. 25.

28. Robert Browning was less doubtful of fathoming the individual soul, but more skeptical of the achievement of his art. He draws near his ending to *The Ring and the Book* (1868-69) with this familiar apostrophe:

So, British Public, who may like me yet,
(Marry and amen!) learn one lesson hence
Of many which whatever lives should teach:
This lesson, that our human speech is naught,
Our human testimony false, our fame
And human estimation words and wind.
Why take the artistic way to prove so much?
Because, it is the glory and good of Art,
That Art remains the one way possible
Of speaking truth, to mouths like mine at least. (Book 12)

29. Catherine Crowe's interest in having truths displayed nakedly took a rather shocking turn when she walked through the public streets naked and had to be confined, later in her life.

30. James Hinton, *Man and his Dwelling Place. An Essay Toward the Interpretation of Nature* (New York, 1872), p. 9.

31. James Hinton, *Life in Nature* (London, 1862), p. 161.

32 Ibid., p. 166.

33. James F. Ferrier, *Institutes of Metaphysic: The Theory of Knowing and Being* (Edinburgh, 1854), pp. 8-9.

34. Ibid., p. 9.

35. Reed, *Perception and Design*, pp. 205-15.

36. This sentiment was common particularly among the Decadents. See Barbara Charlesworth, *Dark Passages: The Decadent Consciousness in Victorian Literature* (Madison, 1965).

37. Hinton, *Man and His Dwelling Place*, p. 92.

38. Quoted in Charlesworth, *Dark Passages*, p. 92.

39. See the chapter on the occult.

40. Hinton, *Man and His Dwelling Place*, "Dialogue IV," p. 272.

41. Gertrude Himmelfarb, *Victorian Minds: A Study of Intellectuals in Crisis and of Ideologies in Transition* (New York, 1970), p. 309.

42. Ferrier, *Institutes*, p. 235.

43. See Andrew D. Hook, "Charlotte Brontë, The Imagination, and *Villette*," *The*

Brontës: A Collection of Critical Essays, ed. Ian Gregor (Englewood Cliffs, 1970), p. 149.

44. Gordon S. Haight, *George Eliot: A Biography* (New York, 1968), p. 51. Henry Cockton mocked phrenology as early as 1840 in his popular novel, *Valentine Vox, the Ventriloquist*. (ch. 23)

45. Haight, *George Eliot*, p. 188.

46. Letter of 31 July 1892, quoted in Frederic William Maitland, *The Life and Letters of Leslie Stephen* (New York, 1906), p. 413.

47. William James, *The Principles of Psychology*, 2 vols. (New York, 1918), 1, p. 206.

48. Ibid., p. 372.

49. Samuel Butler, *Unconscious Memory* (New York, 1924), p. 60.

50. Samuel Butler, *Life and Habit* (New York, 1923), p. 64.

51. Frederic W. H. Myers, *Human Personality and its Survival of Bodily Death* 2 vols. (London, 1954), 1, p. 16. Alan Gauld explains that Myers used the word self in many ways; it could be part of the Self, which might include several coexisting selves: even a "soul" or unifying principle (*The Founders of Psychical Research* [London, 1968], p. 281).

52. Geoffrey West, *H. G. Wells* (New York, 1930), p. 84.

53. H. G. Wells, "Appendix (1)," *'42 to '44: A Contemporary Memoir* (London, 1944), p. 169.

54. Bulwer-Lytton published a few years later a study of the national attributes, including love of appearances in *England and the English* (1833).

55. Himmelfarb, *Victorian Minds*, p. 278. See chapter fourteen on hypocrisy in Walter E. Houghton's *The Victorian Frame of Mind 1830-1870* (New Haven, 1964).

56. J. C. Furnas, *Voyage to Windward: The Life of Robert Louis Stevenson* (New York, 1951), p. 112.

57. Mansfield Parkyns, *Life in Abyssinia: Being Notes Collected During Three Years' Residence and Travels In That Country*, 2 vols (New York, 1854), 1, p. 22.

58. Ibid., pp. 225-26.

59. Ibid., 2, p. 152. Dutton Cook advises his readers in *A Prodigal Son* (1863), "Wear a mask. . . . Shams are now and then abused, but they are dearly loved for all that; and they are indispensable to civilization." (Vol. 1, ch, 11)

60. Arthur Symons, "Robert Louis Stevenson," *Studies in Prose and Verse* (New York, 1922), p. 79.

61. Masao Miyoshi, *The Divided Self: A Perspective on the Literature of the Victorians* (New York, 1969), p. 290; pp. 296-301. Although I do not agree with all of what Miyoshi has to say, there is no doubt that his is a useful reading.

62. Miyoshi, *Divided Self*, p. 320.

63. See Charlesworth on the theme of the multiple self.

64. Donald Weeks examines the many self-portraits and private personal allusions Corvo made to himself in his works (*Corvo* [London, 1971]).

65. Shane Leslie, Introduction to *In His Own Image* by Frederick Baron Corvo (London, 1924), p. xix.

66. Vineta and Robert A. Colby, *The Equivocal Virtue: Mrs. Oliphant and the Victorian Literary Market Place* (New York, 1966) p. 3.

67. Review in *Times Literary Supplement* 8 January 1971, p. 40.

68. Haight, p. 290.

69. Hallam Tennyson, *Alfred Lord Tennyson: A Memoir by His Son*, 2 vols. (New York, 1905), 1, p. 304.

70. Trollope was prompted to his experiment by his observation that established artists were accepted with too much favor at the expense of newer aspiring authors. "In order to test this, I determined to be such an aspirant myself, and to begin a course of novels anonymously, in order that I might see whether I could obtain a second identity—whether as I had made one mark by such literary ability as I possessed, I might succeed in doing so again" (*Autobiography*, ch. 11). In *A Book of Recollections*, 2 vols. (London, 1894), John Cordy Jeaffreson tells of how his friends felt free to alter their names as they saw fit, for professional or trivial reasons, without troubling themselves about legal obligations. (vol. 2, p. 87) He also cited some dangers associated with the practice of anonymous reviewing.

71. Beer, *Meredith*, p. 15.

72. See G. B. Tennyson, *Sartor Called Resartus* (Princeton, 1965).

73. See Robert Garis, *The Dickens Theatre: A Reassessment of the Novels* (Oxford, 1965), which offers an interesting perspective on this aspect of Dickens' talent.

74. Ellen Moers, *The Dandy: Brummell to Beerbohm* (New York, 1960), pp. 222 and 227.

75. Furnas, *Voyage*, p. 156. D. G. Rossetti appears as D'Arcy, nicknamed "Haroun-al-Raschid the Painter," in Theodore Watts-Dunton's *Aylwin*. Charles Augustus Howell had actually given Rossetti the name because the poet would disguise himself as a poor person when out buying antiques from the Hebrews in Wardour Street (Thomas Hake and Arthur Compton-Rickett, *The Life and Letters of Theodore Watts-Dunton* [London, 1916], p. 189). The Haroun-al-Raschid syndrome is obvious in much of the literature of the time. Enoch Arden, for example, is a benevolent figure in disguise. More appropriate, however, would be a character such as the aristocratic Charles Egremont in Disraeli's *Sybil*, who presents himself to the Gerards as Mr. Franklin because he would otherwise be associated with those who unjustly hold the Gerard property and therefore would be prevented from doing good.

76. Quoted in Monroe Engel. *The Maturity of Dickens* (Cambridge, Mass., 1959), p. 19.

77. The notion of the poet being the mouthpiece for divinity was an important feature of symbolist poetry according to John Senior in *The Way Down and Out: The Occult in Symbolist Literature* (Ithaca, New York, 1959).

78. Stella Margetson, *Leisure and Pleasure in the Nineteenth Century* (New York, 1969), p. 176. "As the task of identifying oneself with a class grew in difficulty, the attempts that many made to accomplish it increased in intensity, and clothes became a fully developed social symbol" (Marshall, *The World of the Victorian Novel*, p. 95). Marshall discusses the subject of clothing and identity with particular reference to Dickens.

79. C. Willett and Phillis Cunnington, *Handbook of English Costume in the Nineteenth Century* (London, 1966), p. 26.

80. Moers, *The Dandy*, p. 14.

81. C. Willett and Phillis Cunnington, *The History of Underclothes* (London, 1951), p. 121.

82. Ibid., p. 170. Cyril Pearl reports that false bellies made of gutta-percha were sold to women in order to provide them with the necessary tightness in the dresses of the day. See chapter five of *The Girl With The Swansdown Seat* (London, 1955), for a discussion of Victorian clothing.

83. Jerome K. Jerome, "On Dress and Deportment," *The Idle Thoughts of an Idle Fellow: A Book for an Idle Holiday* (New York, 1890), p. 177.

84. Ibid., p. 178.

85. Ibid., p. 179.

86. Moers, *The Dandy*, p. 288.

87. "Aids to Beauty, Real and Artificial," *Cornhill Magazine* 7 (March, 1863), pp. 391-400. Some of the author's recommendations are not so good, however. He is interesting on his objections to age disguising as youth. Another article, "Paint, Powder, Patches," *Cornhill Magazine* 7 (June, 1863), pp. 706-19, is mainly historical, and also warns against excesses.

88. "Aids to Beauty," p. 398.

89. Collins may have had the celebrated London whore of the fifties, Laura Bell, in mind, for, by the sixties, following an unhappy marriage to a man of higher station, "she had emerged as a fervent and eloquent preacher—'A sinner saved by grace through faith in the Lamb of God,' she signed herself" (Pearl, *Swansdown Seat*, p. 143).

90. Cosmetics play a large part in late nineteenth- and early twentieth-century literature outside of England as well. Wylie Sypher writes that "Baudelaire specified the faculty of the modern poet as *le sentiment de l'artificiel*, a fascination with *maquillage* (make-up), which is the technology of Beauty" (*Literature and Technology: The Alien Vision* [New York, 1968], p. 62). In the writings of Thomas Mann, as *Death in Venice, Buddenbrooks*, or *Felix Krull* demonstrate, the motif persisted and was elaborated in a formidable way.

91. Thomas H. Huxley, "On The Physical Basis of Life," *Methods and Results: Essays* (London: Macmillan, 1893), p. 145.

CHAPTER FOURTEEN: GYPSIES

1. See H. T. Crofton, "Early Annals of the Gypsies in England," *Journal of the Gypsy Lore Society*, (July, 1888), 1, pp. 5-24.

2. Brian Vesey-Fitzgerald, *Gypsies of Britain: An Introduction to Their History* (London, 1944), p. 20.

3. Jean-Paul Clébert, *The Gypsies*, trans. Charles Duff (Baltimore, 1967), p. 111.

4. Crofton, "Early Annals," p. 13.

5. George Borrow, "The English Gypsies," *Romano Lavo-Lil: Word-Book of the Romany or English Language with specimens of gypsy poetry, and an account of certain gypsyries or places inhabited by them, and of various things relating to gypsy life in England*, Norwich Edition (London, 1923), p. 168.

6. Clébert, *The Gypsies*, p. 111.

7. *Encyclopaedia Britannica*, 11th ed., s.v. "Gypsy." The Eleventh Edition of the *Britannica* was a thorough history and an excellent bibliography to that time. Thereafter, the *Journal of the Gypsy Lore Society* is the best source.

8. Francis Hindes Groome mentions the story as a standard one in *In Gipsy Tents* (Edinburgh, 1880), p. 244, and "The Gypsies," *National Life and Thought of the various nations throughout the world: A Series of Addresses* (New York, 1891), p. 384. R. B. Haldane, however, refers to the supposed kidnappers as tinkers rather than gypsies (*Life of Adam Smith* [London, 1887], p. 16). C. R. Fay, more generously declared his belief that young Smith had merely wandered off and was lost for a few hours, and that he was found, not stolen by gypsies (*Adam Smith and the Scotland of His Day* [Cambridge, 1956], p. 17).

9. Theodore Watts-Dunton, *Old Familiar Faces* (New York, 1916), p. 46.

10. *An Apology for the Life of Mr. Bampfylde-Moore Carew, Commonly call'd the King of the Beggars*, 7th ed. (London, 1763), p. 7. An earlier version, "The Life and adventures of Bampfylde Moore Carew, the noted Devonshire Stroller," (1745) has been attributed to Thomas Price.

11. Martin C. Battestin, "Tom Jones and 'His *Egyptian* Majesty': Fielding's Parable of Government," 82, no. 1 PMLA (1967), p. 68.

12. Borrow had already explained that the difference was important, for "the Gypsies are a people of Oriental origin, whilst the Abrahamites are the scurf of the English body corporate," and while the one had a real language, the other merely employed a crude jargon (*Romano Lavo-Lil*, p. 169).

13. James Crabb, *The Gipsies' Advocate; or Observations on the Origins, Character, Manners, and Habits, of the English Gipsies: to which are added many interesting anecdotes on the success that has attended the plans of several benevolent individuals who anxiously desire their conversion to God*, 3d ed. (London, 1832), p. 31. John Hoyland printed an earlier study, *A Historical Survey of the Customs, Habits and Present State of the Gypsies; designed to develope the Origin of this Singular People, and to promote the Amelioration of their Condition* (York, 1816).

14. Crabb, *Gypsies' Advocates*, p. 11.

15. Ibid., p. 33.

16. Ibid., p. 51.

17. Ibid., pp. 59-60.

18. Ibid., p. 64.

19. He used gypsies as well in his historical novel, *Quentin Durward*, and the series in *Blackwood's Magazine*, entitled "Notices Concerning the Scottish Gypsies," ran as follows: April, 1817, vol. 1, no. 1, pp. 43-58; May, 1817, no. 2, pp. 154-61; September, 1817, no. 6, pp. 615-20.

20. Frederick Martin, *The Life of John Clare*, intro. and notes by Eric Robinson and Geoffrey Summerfield (London, 1964), p. 50.

21. Bulwer-Lytton had been acquainted with gypsies himself. A handsome gypsy girl had accurately read his past and future. He wished to stay among her gypsy band, and she felt a strong attraction to him, but warned him to leave his money with her grandmother. He was forced to leave the gypsy company when the young men became jealous. He never saw her again and later said, "How, even if we met again, should I ever recognize her? Gypsy beauty fades so soon—fades like all illusion and all romance" (V. A. G. R. Lytton, *The Life of Edward Bulwer, First Lord Lytton*, 2 vols. [London, 1913], 1, p. 115).

22. The gypsy as provider of refuge for social outcasts was not a new or remarkable figure. Götz von Berlichingen, in Goethe's play of the same name, found refuge with a band of gypsies when he was at odds with the powers of his country.

23. Louis James, *Fiction for the Working Man 1830-1850* (London, 1963), pp. 104-5.

24. Ibid., p. 26.

25. There are studies of gypsies in American life and literature too. One example is Irving Brown's *Gypsy Fires in America: A Narrative of Life Among the Romanies of the United States and Canada* (New York, 1924).

26. Review of *The Zincali* in the *North American Review* 55, no. 116 (July, 1842), p. 75.

27. A glance at Nicoll's bibliography of Victorian drama shows how many of the plays of the time included some reference to gypsies. I have, however, chosen not to discuss too many of the popular treatments of gypsies, hoping that a few representative works might suffice.

28. Gypsies are regularly associated with race courses and card sharping, as in *The Old Curiosity Shop*. There are brief allusions to gypsy qualities in *Dombey and Son* and *Our Mutual Friend*.

29. Watts-Dunton, *Familiar Faces*, p. 28.

30. Robert R. Meyers, *George Borrow* (New York, 1966), p. 7. The brief passage on Borrow in the English translation of Jean-Paul Clébert's *The Gypsies* is scarcely trustworthy, but is perhaps most nearly correct in asserting that "Borrow's work is

important, not merely because of the passion with which it was received in England, but also because of the impetus which it gave to the gypsiology dawning at that time." (p. 126)

31.   Borrow, of course, did not disguise the moral obliquities of the gypsies. In fact, he zestfully described their various swindles and tricks. He was willing to allow that child-stealing for the slave trade may have been practiced at one time by the gypsies of southern Spain, but contrarily, he defended the gypsies against other charges. "Whatever crimes they may commit," he said, "their vices are few, for the men are not drunkards nor are the women harlots; there are no two characters which they hold in so much abhorrence, nor do any words when applied by them convey so much execration as these two" (*The Zincali: An Account of the Gypsies of Spain with an original collection of their songs and poetry*, Norwich Edition [London, 1963], p. 16).

32.   *North American Review*, p. 73.

33.   William I. Knapp verifies this trip (*Life, Writings and Correspondence of George Borrow (1803-1881)*, 2 vols. [New York, 1899], pp. 224ff).

34.   Letter of 24 February 1836, quoted by ibid., 2, pp. 272.

35.   Lionel Stevenson, *The English Novel. A Panorama* (Boston, 1960), p. 293.

36.   *North American Review*, p. 83.

37.   In a passage borrowed from Watts-Dunton's *Old Familiar Faces* without acknowledgment, Robert R. Meyers states that Borrow's contemporaries sometimes viewed him as a gypsy, and that Borrow was most at home and least self-conscious among them. (p. 61) Meyers implies that Isopel Berners was a gypsy, which she definitely was not.

38.   *North American Review*, p. 74.

39.   Elizabeth Longford, *Queen Victoria: Born to Succeed* (New York, 1966), p. 44, where Crabb is spelled Crabbe.

40.   Knapp, *George Borrow*, 1, p. 351.

41.   Ibid., 2, p. 227. Even so, Borrow presented some information about Romany language, as well as interesting descriptions of metropolitan gypseries in England in this late collection.

42.   Gordon S. Haight, *George Eliot: A Biography* (New York, 1968), p. 376.

43.   Surprisingly enough the poem was well received (see ibid., p. 404). There were, however, dissenting views, among them, Henry James'. He flatly declared, "Fedalma is not a real Gypsy maiden"; instead, he said, she and Zarca were "ideal figures" (*North American Review* 107 [October, 1868], reprinted in *A Century of George Eliot Criticism*, ed. Gordon S. Haight [Boston, 1965], p. 58).

44.   See ch. 38 of *Ravenshoe*, Book 10 of *Festus*; Le Fanu's tale appeared first in *Temple Bar*; and *Zelda's Fortune* appeared in the *Cornhill Magazine*.

45.   G. Robert Stange, *Matthew Arnold: The Poet as Humanist* (Princeton, 1967), p. 61.

46.   A. Dwight Culler, *Imaginative Reason: The Poetry of Matthew Arnold* (New Haven, 1966), p. 183.

47.   Ibid., p. 182.

48.   To show how little Arnold's variation of the convention was appreciated, it is only necessary to refer to Theodore Watts-Dunton's account of a discussion of Arnold's poem with George Borrow. Borrow asserted that "whatever the merits of Matthew Arnold's poem might be, from any supposed artistic point of view, it showed that Arnold had no conception of the Romany temper, and that no gipsy could sympathise with it, or even understand its motive in the least degree" (James Douglas, *Theodore Watts-Dunton: Poet, Novelist, Critic* [New York, n.d.], p. 108).

49.   Charles G. Leland, *The English Gipsies and Their Language* (London, 1874), pp. 43-44.

50. William O. Raymond, *The Infinite Moment and Other Essays in Robert Browning* (Toronto, 1965), p. 121.

51. Gillian Beer, *Meredith: A Change of Masks. A Study of the Novels* (London, 1970), p. 50.

52. See R. H. Hutton in *The Spectator* 20 Jan. 1872, p. 167, and an anonymous review in *The Daily News* 6 Nov. 1871, p. 156, both reprinted in Maurice Buxton Forman's *George Meredith: Some Early Appreciations* (London, 1970). Kiomi's "original was a gypsy model who sat for Sandys for a numbers of his paintings and was well known to the frequenters of his studio" (Stevenson, *Panorama*, p. 184). Watts-Dunton praised the character of Kiomi (*Old Familiar Faces*, p. 287) and used the name for an incidental gypsy character of his own in *Aylwin* (ch. 5).

53. Louis James, *Working Man*, p. 105.

54. Leland, *English Gipsies*, p. 3.

55. Ibid., pp. 9-10.

56. Ibid., p. 143.

57. Ibid., p. 152.

58. Fawn M. Brodie, *The Devil Drives: A Life of Sir Richard Burton* (New York, 1967), p. 273.

59. Byron Farwell, *Burton: A Biography of Sir Richard Francis Burton* (London, 1963), p. 22.

60. Quoted in "Preface" to Sir Richard F. Burton's *The Jew, The Gypsy and El Islam*, ed. W. H. Wilkins (London, 1898), pp. xii-xiii. The passage about the eyes is attributed to Lady Burton by Brodie *Devil Drives*, p. 81.

61. "Preface" to *The Jew, The Gypsy and El Islam*, quoting Lady Burton's *Life of Her Husband*, vol. 1, p. 252 (pp. xiii-xiv).

62. Brodie, *Devil Drives*, p. 81.

63. Ibid., p. 134.

64. Arthur Waugh, *Alfred Lord Tennyson. A Study of His Life and Work* (New York, 1892), p. 92.

65. Watts-Dunton, *Old Familiar Faces*, pp. 286-87.

66. Groome, "The Gypsies," p. 391.

67. Ibid., p. 394.

68. Watts-Dunton, *Old Familiar Faces*, pp. 28 and 60.

69. Groome, *In Gipsy Tents*, p. 12.

70. James Simson, in a fugitive pamphlet entitled "John Bunyan and the gypsies" (New York, 1886), is concerned mainly with praising his own edition of Walter Simson's *History of the Gipsies*, but he also declared that Borrow, Groome and Leland "spoil" the study of gypsies because they do not introduce the philosophy of the subject into their work.

71. Francis Wylde Carew (editor), *No. 747, Being the Autobiography of a Gipsy* (London, 1891), p. 15.

72. Ibid., p. 161.

73. Theodore Watts-Dunton said of his reading the manuscript of Groome's novel: "I found, as I expected to find, that the gipsy chapters were simply perfect, and that it was altogether an extremely clever romance; but I felt also that Groome had given no attention whatever to the structure of a story" (*Old Familiar Faces*, p. 282).

74. Letter #2057 to Watts-Dunton in 1902 in *The Letters of George Meredith*, ed. C. L. Cline, 3 vols. (Oxford, 1970), 3, p. 1423.

75. See Thomas Hake and Arthur Compton-Rickett, *The Life and Letters of Theodore Watts-Dunton* (London, 1916), vol. 1, on the success of the novel (p. 319).

Meredith wrote to Watts-Dunton on Dec. 19, 1898: "I must thank you for the full pleasure I have had in *Aylwin*—and only these later days, for I have been at work and dared not let a magician interpose. I am in love with Sinfi. Nowhere can fiction give us one to match her, not even the *Kriegspiel* heroine, who touched me to the deeps" (#1866, *Letters*, 3, p. 1318).

76. See the chapter on the occult.

77. Mrs. Sophia Morgan, *From Matter to Spirit* (London, 1863), pp. 294-95.

78. In E. T. A. Hoffmann's *Kater Murr* (1820-21), the gypsy girl, Chiara, has extraordinary psychic powers which are exploited by the magician Severino.

79. Douglas, *Theodore Watts-Dunton*, pp. 351-52.

80. Watts-Dunton explained to Francis Hindes Groome that he did not consider himself a Romany scholar but was sympathetic toward the gypsies because they had so long suffered ill-usage, because of the mystery connected with their history, and because they led an open-air life that he envied (Hake and Rickett, *Watts-Dunton*, 2, p. 81).

81. "The phrase, the Renascence of Wonder, merely indicates that there are two great impulses governing man, and probably not man only, but the entire world of conscious life: the impulse of acceptance—the impulse to take unchallenged and for granted all the phenomena of the outer world as they are—and the impulse to confront these phenomena with eyes of inquiry and wonder" ("Author's Preface," *Aylwin: The Renascence of Wonder*, The World's Classic Series [London, 1934], p. xii).

82. Quoted in Douglas, *Watts-Dunton*, p. 70.

83. Watts-Dunton, *Old Familiar Faces*, p. 28.

84. Ibid., p. 55.

85. Flavia Alaya, *William Sharp—"Fiona Macleod" 1855-1905* (Cambridge, Mass., 1970), p. 20.

86. Quoting Sharp's wife in Ibid., p. 22.

87. Arthur Symons, "A Prelude to Life," *Spiritual Adventures* (London, 1928), p. 34.

88. Ibid., p. 35.

89. Arthur Symons, *Eleanora Duse* (London, 1926), p. 90.

90. Arthur Symons, "In Praise of Gypsies," *Journal of the Gypsy Lore Society*, n. s. 1, no. 4 (April, 1908), p. 296.

91. Gipsy (Rodney) Smith, *Gipsy Smith: His Life and Work, by Himself*, intro. by G. Campbell Morgan and Alexander McLaren, (New York, 1906), p. 25.

92. Ibid., p. 29.

93. Watts-Dunton, *Old Familiar Faces*, pp. 294-95.

94. Leland goes on to describe the typical product that fostered the false image of the gypsy:

One novel which I once read, is so full of "the dark blood," that it might almost be called a gipsy novel. The hero is a gipsy; he lives among his kind—the book is full of them; and yet, with all due respect to its author, who is one of the most gifted and best-informed romance writers of the century, I must declare that, from beginning to end, there is not in the novel the slightest indication of any real and familiar knowledge of gipsies. (*The English Gipsies*, p. 6.)

95. Watts-Dunton, *Old Familiar Faces*, p. 302. Watts-Dunton objected that Prosper Merimee's Carmen was "the greatest of all caricatures of the gipsy girl." (p. 302) He found little fiction that qualified. He gave G. P. R. James' *The Gipsy* and Sheridan Le Fanu's *Bird of Passage* credit for some sense of authenticity, but felt the gypsy passages here and elsewhere were "the merest daubs compared with the Kiomi of George Meredith's story 'Harry Richmond.'" (p. 302)

96. Quoted by Groome in *Tents*, from *The Illustrated London News*, 29 Nov., 13 Dec., and 27 Dec., 1851, p. 323.

97. George Orwell, in *A Clergyman's Daughter* (1935) ch. 3, was more accurate and realistic in describing the gypsies as hop-pickers, a low form of migratory labor.

98. Konrad Bercovici, *The Story of the Gypsies* (New York, 1928), p. 218.

99. Ibid., p. 237.

100. Ibid., p. 236.

101. Ibid., p. 294.

102. Vesey-Fitzgerald, *Gypsies of Britain*, p. xvi.

103. Sven Berlin, *Dromengro: Man of the Road* (London, 1971), p. 155.

104. Q. D. Leavis, *Fiction and the Reading Public* (London, 1939), p. 16.

CHAPTER FIFTEEN: MEMORY

1. Don Locke, *Memory* (Garden City, New York, 1971), p. 17.

2. Ibid., p. 24.

3. I. M. L. Hunter, *Memory* (Baltimore, 1964), p. 294.

4. Harry Caplan, "Memoria: Treasure-House of Eloquence," *Of Eloquence: Studies in Ancient and Medieval Rhetoric*, ed. and intro. Anne King and Helen North (Ithaca, 1970), p. 197.

5. Frances A. Yates, *The Art of Memory* (London, 1966), p. 217.

6. Quoted by H. G. Schenk in *The Mind of the European Romantics* (Garden City, New York, 1969), p. 34.

7. Quoted in Oskar Walzel, *German Romanticism*, trans. Alma Elise Lussky (New York, 1966), p. 110.

8. Quoted in Peter Coveney, *The Image of Childhood* (Baltimore, 1967), p. 84.

9. Isaac Taylor [published anonymously], *Physical Theory of Another Life* (New York, 1836), p. 66.

10. Alice Chandler, *A Dream of Order: The Medieval Ideal in 19th-Century English Literature* (Lincoln, Nebraska, 1970), p. 117.

11. Ibid., p. 52.

12. Ibid., p. 7.

13. Kenneth Clark, *The Gothic Revival* (London, 1964), p. 129.

14. Ibid., p. 15.

15. Quoted by Clark, p. 122.

16. Horst S. Daemmrich, "Classicism," *The Challenge of German Literature*, eds. Horst S. Daemmrich and Diether H. Haenicke (Detroit, 1971), p. 150.

17. Jerome Hamilton Buckley, *The Triumph of Time: A Study of the Victorian Concepts of Time, History, Progress, and Decadence* (Cambridge, Mass., 1966), p. 97.

18. Solomon F. Gingerich, *Wordsworth, Tennyson, and Browning: A Study in Human Freedom* (Ann Arbor, 1911), p. 62.

19. Buckley, *Triumph*, p. 115.

20. Lytton Strachey, "Cardinal Manning," *Eminent Victorians*, Modern Library Edition (New York, n.d.), p. 16.

21. Several scholars have treated the subject of Tennyson's fascination with the past, among them are Arthur J. Carr, "Tennyson as a Modern Poet," *University of Toronto Quarterly* 19 (1950), pp. 361-82; Jerome Hamilton Buckley, *Tennyson: The*

Growth of a Poet (Cambridge, Mass., 1960); Gerhard Joseph, *Tennysonian Love: The Strange Diagonal* (Minneapolis, 1969); and James Kissane, *Alfred Tennyson* (New York, 1970).

22. See Byron's "Lines Written Beneath a Picture," where the poet laments that only his beloved's picture is left to reconcile him with despair.

'Tis said with Sorrow Time can cope;
    But this I feel can ne'er be true:
For by the death-blow of my Hope
    My Memory immortal grew.

23. D. G. James, *Matthew Arnold and the Decline of English Romanticism* (Oxford, 1961), p. 65.

24. William A. Madden, *Matthew Arnold: A Study of the Aesthetic Temperament in Victorian England* (Bloomington, 1967), p. 136.

25. A familiar decadent attitude is expressed in the well-known lines from this poem, "And the only world is the world of my dreams, / And my weaving the only happiness; / For what is the world but what it seems?"

26. The Rev. Henry Calderwood, *Philosophy of the Infinite. A Treatise on Man's Knowledge of the Infinite Being, in answer to Sir William Hamilton and Dr. Mansel* (London, 1861), p. 305.

27. Ibid., pp. 312-13.

28. William B. Carpenter, *Principles of Mental Physiology, with their applications to the training and discipline of the mind, and the study of its morbid conditions* (New York, 1896), p. 221.

29. Ibid., p. 429. Herbert Spencer had argued, in *The Principles of Psychology* (1855), that memory "pertains to that class of psychical states which are in the process of being organized," and can be viewed as "a kind of incipient instinct," since once the psychical state becomes habitual it no longer requires conscious recollection and it ceases to be part of memory. (ch. 6)

30. Ibid., p. 455.

31. Ibid., p. 448.

32. Ibid., p. 704.

33. James Sully, *Illusions: A Psychological Study* (New York, 1881), p. 236.

34. Ibid., p. 262.

35. Ibid., p. 284.

36. William James, *The Principles of Psychology*, 2 vols. (New York, 1918), 1, p. 648.

37. Ibid., p. 653.

38. Samuel Butler, *Life and Habit* (New York, 1923), p. 244.

39. Samuel Butler, *Unconscious Memory* (New York, 1924), p. 21. This is Butler's own summary of his earlier work.

40. Butler, *Life and Habit*, p. 242.

41. Butler, *Unconscious Memory*, 192.

42. Butler, *Life and Habit*, p. 104.

43. Samuel Butler, "God the Known and God the Unknown," *Collected Essays*, (New York, 1925), 1, p. 46. Butler felt that Giordano Bruno was prophetic when he "maintained the world of sense to be 'a vast animal having the Deity for its living soul.'" (p. 17)

44. Arthur Schopenhauer, *The World as Will and Representation*, trans. E. F. J. Payne 2 vols. (New York, 1966), 2, p. 222.

45. Most histories of the late nineteenth-century cultural situation mention the

popularity of Schopenhauer's philosophy in England at the time. There was, of course, a good deal written in contradiction of his philosophy; an obvious example is James Sully's *Pessimism: A History and A Criticism* (London, 1877).

46.   Schopenhauer, 2, p. 501; the quote is from *Faust.*

47.   Butler, *Unconscious Memory,* p. 94.

48.   Ibid., p. 197.

49.   Butler, "God the Known," p. 43.

50.   Flavia Alaya says that William Sharp accepted Butler's views on this subject. (*William Sharp—"Fiona Macleod" 1855-1905* [Cambridge, Mass., 1970], p. 37.

51.   Henri Bergson, *Matter and Memory,* trans. Nancy Margaret Paul and W. Scott Palmer (New York, 1912), p. vii. In chapter twenty-five of Farrar's *Julian Home* (1859), entitled "Memory the Book of God," the characters, by debating whether memory is sheerly material or if it has a spiritual quality, demonstrate that the subject was before the minds of mid-Victorians in these terms.

52.   Bergson, *Matter and Memory,* p. 237.

53.   Ibid., p. 325.

54.   Henri-Frédéric Amiel, *Amiel's Journal: The Journal Intime of Henri-Frédéric Amiel,* trans. Mrs. Humphry Ward (London, 1889), p. 275; entry for 8 July 1880.

55.   James Sully had already announced that "modern psychology recognizes no such pigeon-hole apparatus in unconscious mind. . . . On the purely psychical side, memory is nothing but an occasional reappearance of a past mental experience" (Sully, *Illusions,* p. 236).

56.   William Hale White [published anonymously], *John Bunyan* (London, 1905), pp. 249-50.

57.   Barbara Charlesworth discusses Pater's emphasis upon the importance of memory, especially in that art is the fixing of individual memories in esthetic form (*Dark Passages: The Decadent Consciousness in Victorian Literature* [Madison, 1965], pp. 42ff).

58.   Gerald Cornelius Monsman, *Pater's Portraits: Mythic Pattern in the Fiction of Walter Pater* (Baltimore, 1967), p. 204.

59.   Alaya, *William Sharp,* pp. 37-38.

60.   The view of memory in du Maurier's novel resembles that presented by Swedenborg. For a brief description of Swedenborg's attitude, see Slater Brown's *The Heyday of Spiritualism* (New York, 1972), p. 57.

61.   See Robert M. Philmus, *Into the Unknown: The Evolution of Science Fiction from Francis Godwin to H. G. Wells* (Berkeley, 1970), for an explanation of H. G. Wells' obvious desire to contradict the golden ideas of progress so rampant in the decades preceding. (pp. 71-72) Norman and Jeanne MacKenzie offer a more elaborate examination of Wells' complicated attitudes toward the ideas of progress and decadence in *H. G. Wells: A Biography* (New York, 1973).

62.   Miguel de Unamuno, *The Tragic Sense of Life in Men and in Peoples,* intro. Salvador de Madariaga, trans. J. E. Crawford Flitch (London, 1921), p. 9.

CHAPTER SIXTEEN: THE OCCULT

1.   Dorothy Scarborough writes that the "continuing presence of the weird in literature shows the popular demand for it and must have some basis in human psychosis. . . . Man loves the frozen touch of fear, and realizes pure terror only when touched by the unmortal." She goes on to speculate that "Man loves the supernatural elements in literature perhaps because they dignify him by giving his existence a feeling of in-

finity otherwise denied" (*The Supernatural in Modern English Fiction* [New York, 1967], p. 2).

2. See Devendra P. Varma's *The Gothic Flame. Being a History of the Gothic Novel in England: Its Origins, Efflorescence, Disintegration, and Residuary Influences* (New York, 1966) for an examination of the history and nature of gothic fiction.

3. Scarborough, *Supernatural*, pp. 54-55.

4. Robert Darnton, *Mesmerism and the End of the Enlightenment in France* (New York, 1970), p. 44.

5. Charles Mackay, *Extraordinary Popular Delusions and the Madness of Crowds* (Boston, 1932), p. 189. Mackay assured his readers that in his own time (1841) alchemy had been exploded in Europe, though it remained reputable in the East. Robert Lee Wolff's *Strange Stories and other Explorations in Victorian Fiction* (Boston, 1971) gives an excellent account of Rosicrucianism in his discussion of Bulwer-Lytton's occult novels.

6. Scott wrote an extended study of witchcraft, *Letters on Demonology and Witchcraft* (1830), and published an article, "On The Supernatural in Fictitious Composition," in the *Quarterly Review* (July, 1826). See Coleman O. Parsons, *Witchcraft and Demonology in Scott's Fiction. With chapters on the Supernatural in Scottish Literature* (Edinburgh, 1964).

7. At one time he was apparently fascinated by Eliphas Levi and "actually invited him to conjure up none less than Apollonius of Tyana in the flesh." See Wolff's *Strange Stories* for a thorough study of Bulwer-Lytton and the occult. See also John Senior, *The Way Down and Out: The Occult in Symbolist Literature* (Ithaca, 1959), p. 51.

8. V. A. G. R. Lytton, *The Life of Edward Bulwer, First Lord Lytton*, 2 vols. (London, 1913), 2, p. 35; 40.

9. Ibid., 2, p. 38, J. C. Bailey, in *Pilgrims Through Space and Time: Trends and Patterns in Scientific and Utopian Fiction* (New York, 1947), describes *Zanoni* as "an allegory attacking the mechanistic interpretation of life," (p. 30) and says that *A Strange Story* was also an attack upon orthodox science. In both cases, Bailey says, Bulwer-Lytton "was attempting to defend wisdom beyond that of science, and yet to use the knowledge of science to support this defense." (p. 31)

10. *Zanoni* was supposedly modelled on Saint-Martin (Senior, *Way Down*, p. 51), But see Wolff's chapters on Zanoni in *Strange Stories*.

11. Dorothy Scarborough suggests that Bulwer-Lytton got the idea of this novel from Balzac's "The Elixir of Life," but Balzac's story of Don Juan's attempt to maintain his own earthly life by means of an elixir that he has refused to use for that purpose on his own father, is in no particular like Bulwer-Lytton's, except for the notion of the elixir itself—a notion that went back at least as far as Godwin's *St. Leon.* Balzac credited Hoffmann as the most likely source for the idea of the elixir.

12. Bulwer-Lytton had written of *A Strange Story* to his son Robert on 14 September 1861, "I fancy it deals with mysteries within and without us wholly untouched as yet by poets" (*Life*, 2, p. 345).

13. Different characters in the novel advance the theory that an electrical force accounts for occult activities. This theory is akin to Mesmer's animal magnetism and was a common explanation of the uncanny.

14. The poem was possibly prompted by the idea of David Rizzio's blood on the wall in Edinburgh Castle.

15. Peter Penzoldt, *The Supernatural in Fiction* (London, 1952), p. 96.

16. Gordon S. Haight, *George Eliot: A Biography* (New York, 1968), pp. 295-96.

17. See J. M. Gray's "A Study of Idyl: Tennyson's 'The Coming of Arthur,' *Renaissance and Modern Studies* 14 (1970), pp. 135-37.

18. Richard Altick, *Victorian Studies in Scarlet: Murders and Manners in the Age of Victoria* (New York, 1970), pp. 30-31.

19. Fawn M. Brodie, *The Devil Drives: A Life of Sir Richard Burton* (New York, 1967), p. 139.

20. In addition to some fiction, Catherine Crowe also wrote other studies in the occult: *Light and Darkness: or Mysteries of Life* (1850) and *Spiritualism and The Age We Live In* (1859).

21. James Sully, *Illusions: A Psychological Study* (New York, 1881), chapter seven, for a discussion of dreams. The author of an essay, "Dreams," which appeared in the *Cornhill Magazine* for January, 1874, asserted that it was his opinion that "even the most extraordinary dreams are capable of rational explanation." (p. 720) He gives examples of dreams that can be explained by influence upon the dreamers' minds, but he then comes to premonitory and retrospective dreams which he feels do present faithful pictures of events. His conclusion is worth quoting in full, for it conveys the curious blend of scientific belief and occult inclination that characterized much thinking at the time.

It requires but a small stretch of imagination to conceive that the particles thrown off by human beings bear the impress of their thoughts, feelings, hopes, fears, and expectations—as they exist at the moment of separation. We may conceive, too, that there exist in us senses acute enough to distinguish, under favourable circumstances, all the peculiarities of these particles when they are brought in contact with us. As to that contact, it is not so very unreasonable to suppose, in these days of electric wonders, that the fixed affection of persons may give a fixed direction to such emanations, and thus originate and maintain, through all chances and changes, those delicate chains of intercommunication between friends and foes, to which, rather than to supernatural agency, we prefer to ascribe our startling, truthful dreams and premonitions. (p. 726)

22. Walpole, Coleridge, Mary Shelley, Fuseli and others claimed to have been inspired by dreams.

23. Lytton, *Life*, 2, p. 340.

24. Warren also describes a dream of Titmouse's that is both a powerful and a psychologically credible dream. (vol. 1, ch. 4)

25. See Robert B. Heilman's "Charlotte Brontë's 'New' Gothic," *From Austen to Conrad*, eds. R. C. Rathburn and M. Steinmann (Minneapolis, 1958), for an examination of Brontë's exploitation of Gothic suggestions in her fiction.

26. Samuel Hynes, *The Edwardian Turn of Mind* (Princeton, 1968), p. 134.

27. Ibid., p. 147.

28. Quoted in Amice Lee's *Laurels and Rosemary: The Life of William and Mary Howitt* (London, 1955), p. 333.

29. Owen's biographer, Richard William Leopold, writes that "In the history of American spiritualism *Footfalls on the Boundary of Another World* deserves a prominent place. It was exceptional in that it was the first book of its kind to be brought out by a nationally known, non-spiritualist publisher" (*Robert Dale Owen. A Biography* [Cambridge, Mass., 1940], p. 334). Nonetheless, he later observes that "*The Debatable Land between This World and the Next* represented ten years of more or less constant psychical research and should properly be regarded as the outstanding writing of Owen's late years." (p. 386)

30. Robert Dale Owen, *The Debatable Land Between this world and the next with illustrative narrations* (New York, 1872), p. ix. Owen's reputation as an effective spokesman for spiritualism was destroyed by the Katie King affair, which Howard Kerr describes in *Mediums and Spirit-Rappers and Roaring Radicals: Spiritualism in American Literature 1850-1900* (Urbana, 1972), pp. 112ff. Although he admitted his mistake about Katie King, Owen still felt certain about the truth of spiritualism. In

1875 Owen was admitted to the Indiana Hospital for the Insane, and was released shortly after, but the fact of his being admitted at all also eroded his credibility.

31. Mrs. Sophia Elizabeth Morgan [published pseudonymously], *From Matter to Spirit. The Result of Ten Years' Experience in Spirit Manifestations. Intended as a guide to enquirers* (London, 1863), p. 2.

32. Ibid., p. 91.

33. See Slater Brown's *The Heyday of Spiritualism* (New York, 1972), for an account of these investigators.

34. See Frank Podmore, *Modern Spiritualism: A History and a Criticism*, 2 vols. (London, 1902), and Kerr, Brown, and Alan Gauld's *The Founders of Psychical Research* (London, 1968), which mentions the location as Rochester, incorrectly.

35. Geoffrey K. Nelson, *Spiritualism and Society* (New York, 1969), p. 89.

36. See also Alan Willard Brown, *The Metaphysical Society: Victorian Minds in Crisis 1869-1880* (New York, 1947), pp. 238ff.

37. Gauld, *Founders*, p. 275.

38. Ibid., p. 306.

39. Quoted in ibid., p. 140.

40. Hynes, *Edwardian Mind*, p. 140.

41. Gauld, p. 76.

42. David B. Wilson, "The Thought of Late Victorian Physicists: Oliver Lodge's Ethereal Body," *Victorian Studies* 15, no. 1 (1971), p. 33.

43. Gwendolyn Bays, *The Orphic Vision: Seer Poets from Novalis to Rimbaud* (Lincoln, Nebraska, 1964), p. 34. In England, Arthur James Balfour argued in his essay "Psychical Research" (1894) that scientists who have previously avoided this form of research would, because of the concrete evidence being put forward, be obliged to study it with scientific caution.

44. See introduction to *Phantasms of the Living*, 2 vols. (Gainesville, 1970) by Edmund Gurney, Frederic W. H. Myers, and Frank Podmore, p. xi.

45. Ibid., p. xii.

46. Ibid., p. liv.

47. Ibid., lv.

48. A. P. Sinnett, *Tennyson An Occultist as His Writings Prove* (London, 1920). See also F. W. H. Myers' "Modern Poets and the Meaning of Life," *The Nineteenth Century* 33, no. 191 (1893), p. 106.

49. See Parsons, p. 5.

50. See Dialogue III in James Hinton's *Man and his Dwelling Place. An Essay Toward the Interpretation of Nature* (New York, 1872).

51. Senior, *Way Down*, p. 50.

52. See a full study of this subject in ibid.

53. See Sir Charles Tennyson's, "The Somersby Tennysons," *Victorian Studies Christmas Supplement* (December, 1963).

54. Sinnett, *Tennyson*, pp. 6-7.

55. Katherine H. Porter, *Through a Glass Darkly. Spiritualism in the Browning Circle* (Lawrence, 1958), p. 46.

56. See Porter and also Aurelia Brooks Harlan's *Owen Meredith: A Critical Biography of Robert, First Earl of Lytton* (New York, 1946).

57. William Bell Scott, *Autobiographical Notes of the Life of William Bell Scott And Notices of his Artistic and Poetic Circle of Friends 1830 and 1882*, ed. W. Minto, 2 vols. (New York, 1892), 1, p. 118.

58. Ibid., 2, p. 66; 231.

59. Brodie, *Devil Drives*, p. 136.

60. Laurence Oliphant, *Episodes in A Life of Adventure, or, Moss from a Rolling Stone* (New York, 1887), pp. 342-43.

61. See vol. 73 of *Blackwood's*, pp. 629-46 and *Cornhill* for 1860, but also an article "Spiritualism," in the same journal for June, 1863.

62. See Clyde K. Hyder's "Rossetti's *Rose Mary*: A Study in the Occult," *Victorian Poetry* 1 (1963), pp. 197ff.

63. See S. M. Ellis, *Wilkie Collins, Le Fanu and Others* (London, 1931), p. 176.

64. See Kerr for a full treatment of the literary manifestations of spiritualism in nineteenth-century America.

65. Vineta and Robert A. Colby, *The Equivocal Virtue: Mrs. Oliphant and the Victorian Literary Market Place* (New York, 1966), p. 88. "These superterrestrial travels evoke not so much the poems of Dante as the hymns of Adelaide Procter and the stained glass of the Gothic Revival." (p. 103)

66. Morton Cohen, *Rider Haggard: His life and works* (London, 1960), p. 97.

67. Ibid., p. 111.

68. Eileen Bigland, *Marie Corelli: The Woman and the Legend. A Biography.* (London, 1953), p. 163.

69. See Robert Lee Wolff, *The Golden Key: A Study of the Fiction of George MacDonald* (New Haven, 1961), p. 401 n.18.

70. Devendra P. Varma mentions more than once in *The Gothic Flame*, that Gothic fiction often treated tales in which poetic justice exhibited itself and moral virtue triumphed. This is not entirely the same sort of scheme of faith that I am referring to. See Chapter One of the present study for a development of this point.

71. Novalis' religious susceptibilities, and concern for a life hereafter, were heightened by the loss of his fiancée, Sophie von Kühn. Tennyson's mind dwelt upon similar subjects after the death of Arthur Henry Hallam. This sense of loss appears as an important feature of Bulwer-Lytton's *A Strange Story*, and other fiction. Both Frederic Myers and Oliver Lodge were moved to investigations of the possibilities of life after death by their bereavements.

72. Lee, *Laurels and Rosemary*, p. 224.

CHAPTER SEVENTEEN: CONCLUSION

1. Bulwer-Lytton, in his survey of his nation and its people, *England and the English*, examined some causes of English customs, among them marriage, in Book 2, chapter 1.

2. The tradition was revived for the nineteenth century by works such as Godwin's *St. Leon*. In earlier literature of the Romantic revival, aspirations to this condition were viewed as presumptuous and accordingly punished.

3. Frank Rahill points out how common the conventions of orphans, disguise, exile and return, and so forth were in the drama of the late eighteenth century (*The World of Melodrama* [University Park, 1967], pp. 104-5).

4. Nicolas Bentley reproduces the covers of some of the Hogarth House *Gem Pocket Library* books. Some of the titles include, "Mistaken Identity," "The Forged Will," "Done to Death, or the Millionaires Heiress," and an obvious attempt to cash in on a popular success, "A Difficult Case, or Lady Dudley's Secret" (*The Victorian Scene: A Picture Book of the Period 1837-1901* [London, 1968], p. 48).

5. William H. Marshall, *The World of the Victorian Novel* (London, 1967), p. 259.

6. Frederick W. Robertson, "The Orphanage of Moses," *Sermons on Bible Subjects* (London, 1906), p. 58. The sermon was delivered on 16 February 1851.

7. Ibid., p. 59.

8. Frederick W. Robertson, "The Prodigal and His Brother," *Sermons*, p. 271. The sermon was delivered on 21 February 1853.

9. Ibid., p. 272.

10. Emile Legouis, Louis Cazamian, and Raymond Los Vergnas, *A History of English Literature*, rev. ed. (London, 1964); see Part 2, Book 6, ch. 3, pp. 1122ff.

11. Devendra P. Varma, *The Gothic Flame. Being a History of the Gothic Novel in England: Its Origins, Efflorescence, Disintegration, and Residuary Influences* (New York, 1966), p. 216.

12. Kenneth Clark, *The Gothic Revival* (London, 1964), pp. 32-33.

13. H. G. Schenk, *The Mind of the European Romantics* (Garden City, 1969), p. 130.

14. See George K. Anderson's *The Legend of the Wandering Jew* (Providence, 1965), for a thorough study of this aspect of the wanderer motif in literature.

15. Richard Le Gallienne, "The Wandering Home," *Painted Shadows* (Freeport, New York, 1969), p. 97.

16. Ibid., p. 101.

17. Arthur Symons, "The Choice," *Studies in Prose and Verse* (New York, 1922), p. 290.

18. Quoted by Raymond Williams in *Culture and Society 1780-1950* (New York, 1958), p. 24.

19. Arnold quotes this passage in his essay on Amiel.

20. James Sully, *Illusions: A Psychological Study* (New York, 1881), p. 284.

21. Ibid., p. 3.

22. See Tennyson's pseudonymous poem, "Suggested by Reading an Article in a Newspaper," published in *The Examiner*, 14 February 1852.

23. Jacob Korg, *George Gissing: A Critical Biography* (Seattle, 1963), p. 115.

24. James Sully felt that the idea of progress was "the one vital type of optimism of our age," and added that it was confronted by a pessimistic theory of life denying the possibility of happiness (*Pessimism: A History and A Criticism* [London, 1877], p. 73).

25. See especially chapter thirteen of Whewell's anonymously published *The Plurality of Worlds* (Boston, 1855), where he sees man improving not only to a possibly higher physical being, but to a more direct relationship with the divine, even perhaps to a second divine interposition.

26. William B. Carpenter, *Principles of Mental Physiology* (New York, 1896), p. 108.

27. William Winwood Reade, *The Martyrdom of Man* (New York, n.d.), pp. 243-44.

28. Ibid., p. 514.

29. This sounds a good deal like what Mejnour foresaw in Bulwer-Lytton's *Zanoni*.

30. Charles Tennyson, *Alfred Tennyson* (New York, 1949), p. 361.

31. Peter Coveney, *The Image of Childhood* (Baltimore, 1967), p. 241. Gillian Avery writes that one class of children's authors provided their audience "with an escape from the dreariness of industrialized Victorian England into some idealized realm of the imagination" (*Nineteenth Century Children: Heroes and Heroines in English Children's Stories 1780-1900* [London, 1965], p. 134). In this regard, they merely imitated adult literature.

32. Bernard Bergonzi, *The Early H. G. Wells: A Study of the Scientific Romances* (Toronto, 1961), p. 3.

33. Sully, *Pessimism*, p. 449.

34. Bergonzi, *H. G. Wells*, p. 6.

35. See Neil D. Isaacs' "The Convention of Personification in *Beowulf*," *Old English Poetry: Fifteen Essays*, ed. Robert P. Creed (Providence, 1967), pp. 215-48.

36. Louis James, *Fiction for the Working Man 1830-1850* (London, 1963), p. 46.

37. Northrop Frye, *A Study of English Romanticism* (New York, 1968), p. 5.

38. "In the marvellous and surprising coincidences, the revelations of concealed identities, the magic talismans and other devices contributing to the suspense of eighteenth-century popular fiction Novalis saw clues to the kind of mystic interpretation of phenomenal experience which he practised himself" (Raymond Immerwahr's "Romanticism," in *The Challenge of German Literature*, eds. Horst S. Daemmrich and Diether H. Haenicke [Detroit, 1971], p. 211).

39. James Wright, "Afterword," to *The Mystery of Edwin Drood* (New York, 1961), p. 276.

40. Mrs. Margaret Oliphant, "Success in Fiction," *The Forum* 7 (May, 1889), p. 315.

BIBLIOGRAPHICAL ESSAY

It is pointless to list the many primary sources that are referred to in this study. Many more than appear here had to be eliminated in an effort to keep an already large book within reasonable limits. Thus, I shall mention only those secondary sources which I found particularly useful in one way or another, though I consulted many others, some of which appear in footnotes to the text.

Certain general works were broadly useful throughout my study, such as H. G. Schenk's *The Mind of the European Romantics* (Garden City, 1969) for patterns of European thought in the nineteenth century. Such standard works as Walter E. Houghton's *The Victorian Frame of Mind 1830-1870* (New Haven, 1964) and W. L. Burn's *The Age of Equipoise: A Study of the Mid-Victorian Generation* (New York, 1965) provided reliable sources for assumptions of the Victorians, while Lionel Stevenson's *The English Novel. A Panorama* (Boston, 1960) gave a broad outline of the English novel. More specialized studies such as Margaret Dalziel's *Popular Fiction 100 Years Ago: An unexplored tract of literary history* (London, 1957), Louis James' *Fiction for the Working Man 1830-1850* (London, 1963) and Patricia Thomson's *The Victorian Heroine: A Changing Ideal 1837-1873*

(London, 1965) were useful both generally and for particular chapters. John A. Lester, Jr.'s *Journey Through Despair: 1880-1914: Transformations in British Literary Culture* (Princeton, 1968) discusses predominant themes of the late nineteenth century, while Max K. Sutton's "The Affront to Victorian Dignity in the Satire of the Eighteen-Seventies" in *The Nineteenth-Century Writer and his Audience* (Lawrence, Kansas, 1969) I found variously interesting and helpful. Because it treats of fiction in relationship to illustration and touches upon some conventional themes, John Harvey's *Victorian Novelists and Their Illustrators* (New York, 1971) was a welcome special study. Finally, two excellent articles reassured me in pursuing the form of research represented by this book. Both Richard D. Altick's "Victorian Readers and the Sense of the Present" in *Midway* (Spring, 1970) and Louis James' "The Rational Amusement: 'Minor' Fiction and Victorian Studies" in *Victorian Studies* (December, 1970) show the value of examining general ideas through the full range of Victorian literature, not restricting research to the major writers.

General studies of women in the nineteenth century that I found helpful include Duncan Crow's *The Victorian Woman* (London, 1971), Janet Dunbar's *The Early Victorian Woman: Some Aspects of Her Life (1837-57)* (London, 1953) and Katharine M. Rogers' *The Troublesome Helpmate: A History of Misogyny in Literature* (Seattle, 1966), while Hazel Mews' *Frail Vessels: Woman's Role in Women's Novels from Fanny Burney to George Eliot* (London, 1969) and Patricia Thomson's *The Victorian Heroine*, mentioned above, were concerned with women in literature. Brian Harrison's "Underneath the Victorians," in *Victorian Studies* (March, 1967), Cyril Pearl's *The Girl with the Swansdown Seat* (London, 1955), and to a lesser extent, Martin Seymour-Smith's *Fallen Women: A sceptical enquiry into the treatment of prostitutes, their clients and their pimps, in literature* (London, 1969) were good sources for information on the question of women and illicit sexuality. I was not able to make much use of a collection of essays, *Suffer and Be Still: Women in the Victorian Age*, edited by Martha Vicinus (Bloomington, 1972), only because so much of my work was complete when the book became available to me.

Although other sources were helpful, I found only one study, David Goldknopf's "Coincidence in the Victorian Novel: The Trajectory of a Narrative-Device" in *College English* (October, 1969), that was substantial in its treatment of coincidence in Victorian literature, and there were few recent books to help me with the chapter on duelling. Robert Baldick's *The Duel: A History of Duelling* (London, 1970) is a good recent study of the subject, but I found Lorenzo Sabine's *Notes on Duels and Duelling, alphabetically arranged, with a Preliminary Historical Essay* (Boston, 1856) and Andrew Steinmetz' *The Romance of Duelling in All Times and Countries* (London, 1868) most useful. John Morley's *Death, Heaven and the Victorians* (Pittsburgh, 1971) provided necessary background for my chapter on Deathbed scenes, while Gillian Avery's *Nineteenth Century Children: Heroes and Heroines in English Children's Stories 1780-1900* (London, 1965) and Peter Coveney's *The Image of Childhood: The Individual and Society: A study of the Theme in English Literature,* rev. ed. (Baltimore, 1967) were useful insofar as children's deaths were concerned. The latter was also valuable for my chapter on the orphan.

I required a number of secondary sources to aid me in presenting the facts and generalizations in the chapter on swindles. David Morier Evans' contemporary reports, including *The Commercial Crisis 1847-1848* (London, 1848), *The History of the Commercial Crisis, 1857-58, and the Stock Exchange Panic of 1859* (New York, 1969, reprint) and *Speculative Notes and Notes on Speculation, Ideal and Real* (New York, 1968, reprint) were fundamental, while William Ashworth's *An Economic History of England 1870-1939* (London, 1960), Asa Briggs' *The Age of Improvement 1783-1867* (London, 1964) and E. L. Woodward's *The Age of Reform 1815-1870* (Oxford, 1958) provided general economic history for the age. Ivan Melada's *The Captain of Industry in English Fiction, 1821-1871* (Albuquerque, 1970) was not so useful as I had hoped, but is the only full-length study I know of that deals with the figure of the businessman in Victorian Literature. The two books most helpful to me in dealing with railway speculations were Richard S. Lambert's *The Railway King 1800-1871: A Study of George Hudson and The Business Morals of His Time* (London, 1964) and the general, but clear, *The Railway Age in Britain and Its Impact on The World* (Baltimore, 1962) by Michael Robbins. Aylmer Vallance's *Very Private Enterprise: An Anatomy of Fraud and High Finance* (London, 1955) is a survey of frauds concentrating on the later nineteenth and early twentieth centuries.

Michel Foucault's *Madness and Civilization: A History of Insanity in the Age of Reason* (New York, 1967; trans. Richard Howard), though it does not deal with the nineteenth century, was among the most provocative and exciting books I encountered on the subject of madness. More particular works dealing with madness in Victorian England include Kathleen Jones' *Lunacy, Law, and Conscience 1744-1845* (London, 1955) and *Mental Health and Social Policy 1845-1959* (London, 1960), William Ll. Parry-Jones' *The Trade in Lunacy. A Study of Private Madhouses in the Eighteenth and Nineteenth Centuries* (London, 1972) and Nigel Walker's *Crime and Insanity in England* (Edinburgh, 1968).

On the subject of the Return, P. G. Scott's *Tennyson's Enoch Arden: A Victorian Best-Seller* (Lincoln, 1970), Peter J. Casagrande's "The Shifted 'Centre of Altruism' in *The Woodlanders*: Thomas Hardy's Third 'Return of a Native'," in ELH (March, 1971) and Alice Chandler's *A Dream of Order: The Medieval Ideal in 19th-Century English Literature* (Lincoln, Nebraska, 1970) were all helpful in their special ways. Any number of works might be included as having helped me with my ideas on the convention of Disguise, but I shall mention only a few. Masao Miyoshi's *The Divided Self: A Perspective on the Literature of the Victorians* (New York, 1969) discusses the subject of identity throughout the nineteenth century, William H. Marshall's *The World of the Victorian Novel* (London, 1967) shows the importance of disguise in Dickens, and Barbara Charlesworth's *Dark Passages: The Decadent Consciousness in Victorian Literature* (Madison, 1965) examines some late nineteenth-century attitudes concerning identity. The two most useful general studies on the gypsy were Brian Vesey-Fitzgerald's *Gypsies of Britain: An Introduction to Their History* (London, 1946) and Jean-Paul Clébert's *The Gypsies* (Baltimore, 1967), though I noted some errors in the latter. If there was more than I care to list on the theme of disguise, concerning memory I found very little of broad use, though there are some good partial examinations of the subject. However, Don Locke's *Memory* (Garden City, 1971) is a simple, helpful summary of modern ideas on memory and Harry Caplan's "Memoria:

Treasure-House of Eloquence" in *Of Eloquence: Studies in Ancient and Medieval Rhetoric* (Ithaca, 1970) is a sound survey of ancient attitudes. Though I made little specific use of Frances A. Yates' *The Art of Memory* (London, 1966), it helped me to view the larger subject with a sharper eye.

There seems to be no end to studies on the occult, many of which have appeared since I completed my manuscript and put it in the hands of the press, but these studies vary widely in quality. Works that I found dependable and helpful are sober histories for the most part. Robert Darnton's *Mesmerism and the End of the Enlightenment in France* (New York, 1970) is an entertaining and exciting view of certain occult practices and their relationship to science prior to the French Revolution. Slater Brown's *The Heyday of Spiritualism* (New York, 1972), Geoffrey K. Nelson's *Spiritualism and Society* (New York, 1969), and Alan Gauld's *The Founders of Psychical Research* (London, 1968) provide histories of the many-headed movement known as Spiritualism, while Alan Willard Brown examines a related area of inquiry in his *The Metaphysical Society: Victorian Minds in Crisis 1869-1880* (New York, 1947). Dorothy Scarborough's *The Supernatural in Modern English Fiction* (New York, 1967, reprint), Peter Penzoldt's *The Supernatural in Fiction* (London, 1952) and Howard Kerr's *Mediums, and Spirit-Rappers, and Roaring Radicals: Spiritualism in American Literature, 1850-1900* (Urbana, 1972) are broad studies of the occult in literature. Coleman O. Parsons' *Witchcraft and Demonology in Scott's Fiction. With chapters on the Supernatural in Scottish Literature* (Edinburgh, 1946) is an example of a more concentrated approach of the same sort, and Katherine H. Porter's *Through a Glass Darkly. Spiritualism in the Browning Circle* (Lawrence, 1958) investigates the subject as it manifested itself in a specific group of individuals. Colin Wilson's *The Occult* (New York, 1973) is an ambitious and wide-ranging study which includes a chapter on the nineteenth century.

As I said at the outset of this bibliographical essay, it would be possible to go on indefinitely listing works that I found useful in one way or another during my research. Many additional works are cited in the notes, others that I consulted are not mentioned at all. The works that I have noted here are not necessarily the best studies in their fields, but they are studies that have been useful for my own special interests.

INDEX

NOTE: Names, titles and subjects are all entered separately in this index, but listings after authors' names include pages where their works are mentioned, and authors' names appear in parentheses after titles whenever those names are known. Certain titles I have entered in their familiar form (i.e., *Oliver Twist*), while with less familiar works I have used more complete titles (i.e., *The Life and Adventures of Valentine Vox*). In some cases it has been necessary to give shortened forms of titles (i.e., *The Gipsies' Advocate*).